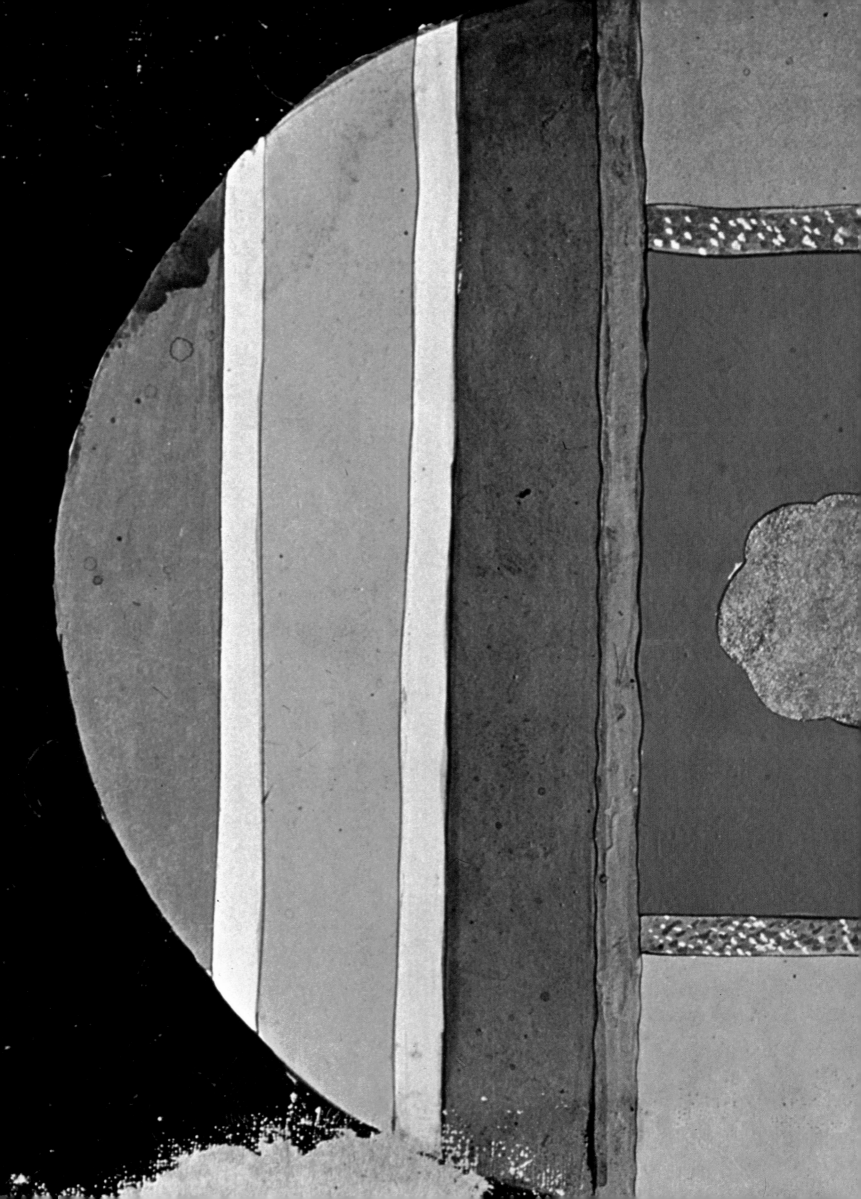

In many mythic cosmogonies the first meaningful form to emerge from the primal ocean of chaos was the egg. Designed as a Tantric aid to meditation, the magnificent painting reproduced overleaf, from Rajasthan in India, shows the cosmic or *lingam* (phallic) egg at the dawn of creation. At its center is a still unformed core of light, a gleam of gold representing the hub of the unfolding forces.

Alexander Eliot

With contributions by:

Mircea Eliade

Professor of History of Religions and Sewell L. Avery Distinguished Service Professor, University of Chicago

Joseph Campbell

Professor Emeritus, Sarah Lawrence College, Bronxville, New York

Captions and graphic essays by:

Detlef-I. Lauf

Professor of Comparative Religions, California Institute of Asian Studies, San Francisco, and C. G. Jung Institute, Zürich

Creative design and selection of graphics by:

Emil Bührer

Myths

McGraw-Hill Book Company

NEW YORK   ST. LOUIS   SAN FRANCISCO

MONTREAL   NEW DELHI   SÃO PAULO

SINGAPORE   TORONTO

A McGraw-Hill Co-Publication

"Myths and Mythical Thought" by Mircea
Eliade, "Myths from West to East" by
Joseph Campbell, graphic essays and
captions by Detlef-I. Lauf, illustration
compilation by McGraw-Hill Book Co.
(UK) Limited, Maidenhead, England,

Library of Congress Cataloging in Publication Data
Main entry under title:
Myths.

  Bibliography: p.
  Includes index.
  1. Mythology – Addresses, essays, lectures.
  2. Myth – Addresses, essays, lectures.
  I. Eliot, Alexander.

BL315.M95   291.1'3   76-20186

ISBN 0-07-019193-X

FLOYD YEAROUT, Editor

FRANCINE PEETERS, Graphics Coordinator

FRANZ GISLER, Production Manager

VIOLA SPERKA, Copy Editor

JANINE PARSON, Editorial Supervisor

DARYL SHARP, Copy Editor and Proofreader

FRANZ CORAY, Artist

BILL BUTLER, Editorial Consultant

ROLF THEILER, Graphics Assistant

LILIANE FIELD, Picture Researcher

JAMES UNDERWOOD, Translator of Dr. Lauf's German text

DELIGHT ANSLEY, Indexer

Printed and bound by
ARNOLDO MONDADORI
in Verona, Italy.

Composition by
NATIONAL-ZEITUNG AG,
Basel, Switzerland.

Photolithography by
FOTO-LITHO HEGO AG,
Littau, Switzerland.

TABLE OF CONTENTS

*The world of myth is seen through
the stories people have told and the
iconography they have created to
answer the recurring questions of
existence. The tapestry of myths
here retold by Alexander Eliot is divided into basic themes that have re-
curred throughout our time and in
all parts of the world. In addition,
specific themes, as indicated under
each chapter heading, are depicted
graphically in layouts by Emil Bührer and described in brief essays and
captions by Detlef Lauf.*

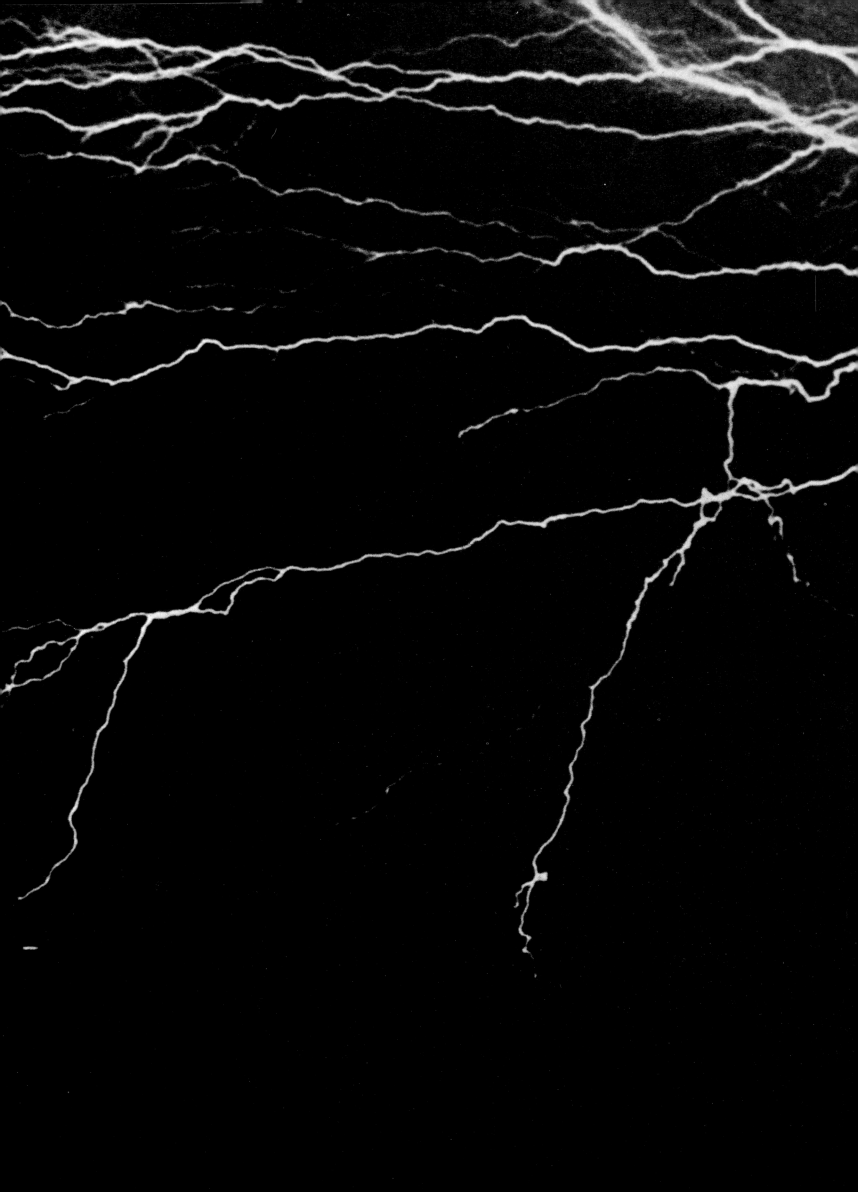

The first function of a mythology
– myths and mythic rituals,
sacred songs
and ceremonial dances –
is to waken in the individual
a sense of awe,
wonder, and participation
in the inscrutable mystery of being.

Joseph Campbell

Not even a total eclipse of the sun can obscure the omnipresence of the light that quickens all life.

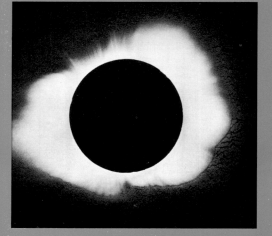

For the soul
is the
beginning
of all things;
it is the soul
that lends
all things
movement.

PLOTINUS

MYThS AND MYThICAL ThOUGHT

MIRCEA ELIADE

The alternation of day and night – the cycle of light and darkness – is often depicted by man symbolically. In this Buddhist wheel of life man is shown moving through light (knowledge) and darkness (ignorance). The animals in the center symbolize the desire for rebirth, which may be into either the path of knowledge or of ignorance.

The Christian view of "God the Father" – framed in the sign of the Cross – shows him as axis of the world rising above the whirling confusion of the cosmos. The four corner spirals, united by the great central spiral, all spring from the Creator's tree (the Cross). Together they provide the way to God.

INTERPRETATIONS OF MYTH: FROM THE GREEKS TO ASTRAL MYTHOLOGY

For nineteenth-century men, "myth" was anything that was opposed to "reality." Thus, the creation of Adam and the notion of the invisible man were "myths" no less than Polynesian legends or the *Theogony* of Hesiod. Like so many other positivist clichés, this view was of Christian, and ultimately of Greek, origin. The word *mythos* in Greek meant "fable," "tale," "talk," or simply "speech," but it came to be used in contrast with *logos* and *historia*, thus coming to denote "that which cannot really exist." Even the earliest Greek philosophers criticized and rejected the Homeric myths as fictions. Xenophanes (sixth-fifth century B.C.) refused to accept that God moves about from place to place as Homer told. He rejected the immorality of the gods described by Homer and Hesiod, and especially criticized their anthropomorphism: "But if cattle and horses or lions had hands, or were able to draw with their hands and do the works that man can do, horses would draw the forms of gods like horses, and cattle like cattle, and they would make their bodies such as they each had themselves." Criticism of mythic traditions took on a special character among the scholars of Alexandria in the Hellenistic age, but the myths of Homer and Hesiod continued to interest the elite throughout their world. The myths were no longer taken literally, however, and men now sought their "hidden meanings." Theagenes of Rhegium (flourished ca. 525 B.C.) had already suggested that the names of the gods in Homer represented either the human faculties or the natural elements. But the Stoics more than any other group developed the allegorical interpretation of Homer and of all religious traditions. For example, the myth in which Zeus binds Hera was taken to mean that the ether is the limit of the air, and so on.

About the beginning of the third century B.C., Euhemerus published a romance in the form of a philosophical voyage, entitled *Sacred Writings,* which enjoyed an enormous and immediate success. Euhemerus felt that he had discovered the origin of all the gods: they were ancient kings who had been deified. This, of course, was another "rational" way to preserve Homer's gods, who now took on a historical (or, more precisely, prehistorical) brand of "reality." The myths merely represented the confused memory or imaginative transfiguration of the exploits of the great primitive kings. These two forms of interpretation, allegorical and euhemerist, had wide repercussions. Thanks to these methods, the Greek gods and heroes did not sink into oblivion after the long process of "demythicization," or even after the triumph of Christianity.

The scientific study of myth, however, did not begin until Karl Ottfried Müller's *Prolegomena zu einer wissenschaftlichen Mythologie* (*Introduction to a Scientific Mythology*) was published in 1825. Later, through the numerous and frequently brilliant works of Friedrich Max Müller in the latter half of the nineteenth century, the study of myth took on a more general popularity. According to Max Müller, myth is the result of what he called "disease of language." The fact that one object can have many names (polyonymy) and conversely that one name can be applied to several objects (homonymy) gave rise to a confusion of names whereby several gods might be combined into one figure, and one might be broken up into many. What was at first merely a name, *nomen*, became a deity, *numen*; thus Max Müller's famous formula, *nomina = numina*. Moreover, in his view, the use of endings denoting grammatical gender led to the personification of abstract ideas as gods and goddesses, with the pantheon being constructed around the sun, the dawn, and the sky. Thus, the myth of Cronus swallowing and later disgorging his children was only the "mythopoeic" expression of a meteorological phenomenon, namely, the sky devouring and later releasing the clouds. So too, the tales of a golden boat sinking in the sea and of an apple falling from a tree tell of the setting sun. In his old age, Max Müller witnessed the collapse of his theory of solar mythology. His main critic was Andrew Lang, who utilized the data collected by the new science of anthropology, especially drawing from E. B. Tylor's *Primitive Culture* (1871). Tylor observed that primitive tribes of his day were still living in the mythmaking stage of the mind. Mythical thought, for him, was specific "to the human intellect in its *early childlike* state," and the study of myth must then begin "at the beginning," among the less civilized peoples who are the nearest representatives of primeval culture. (This, of course, was an attack on Müller's exaggerated emphasis on the archaism of Indian culture.) Tylor argued that the chief cause of the transfiguration of daily experience into myth was the general belief of primitives that nature is *animated* and thus is susceptible to *personification*. Tylor thus held that *animism,* the belief in spiritual beings (but not yet gods), was the first stage of religion, followed by polytheism and finally by monotheism.

For more than twenty years, Andrew Lang attacked Max Müller's doctrine, mainly inspired by Tylor's anthropological interpretation of mythology and religion. He pointed out that myths reflect actions, ideas, and institutions which actually existed at some time in the past. For instance, in his opinion the myth of Cronus dated from an epoch in which cannibalism was practiced, and in the mythology of Zeus we can decipher a primitive medicine man. But after reading some reports on the High Beings of the Australians and other archaic peoples, Lang rejected Tylor's theory of animism as the first stage of religion. For, according to Tylor, the idea of God emerged from belief in nature spirits and the cult of ancestors, but among the Australians and the Andaman Islanders, Lang found neither ancestor worship nor nature cults, but rather the belief in an exalted and remote deity.

The discovery of the priority of such High Beings marks the beginning of a long controversy over the origins of religion and of "primeval monotheism," in which Lang's evaluation of myth plays an important role. Here, the later Lang saw mythical creativity as a sign of degeneration, for he felt myth to be irrational, and thus associated it to animistic beliefs. In contrast to this, the belief in High Beings, which is the real substance of religion and chronologically prior to animism, is rational. Thus, Lang saw a radical difference between myth and religion, and his theories were largely taken over, corrected, and systematized by Wilhelm Schmidt in his massive twelve-volume work, *Der Ursprung der Gottesidee (The Origin of the Idea of God,* 1912-1955.)

At the beginning of this century, the so-called Astral Mythological or Pan-Babylonian school became popular in Germany. According to the founder and leader of this new school of thought, E. Siecke, myths must be understood literally because their contents always refer to some specific celestial phenomena, namely, the forms and movements of the planets, stars, and moon. Siecke and his collaborators emphasized the role of the moon so strongly that their doctrines could be called "pan-lunarism." E. Stucken, one of the most prolific of the group, tried to prove the direct or indirect Mesopotamian origin of all the mythologies of the world. Despite their learning and productivity, though, very little of these scholars' work has retained any lasting significance.

MYTHS AND RITUALS

W. Robertson Smith, the great Orientalist

These squares on Irish megaliths are regarded as primitive depictions of time. Points on the triangles give the sun's course from morning through evening to the new day.

Cronus *(above)* the father of time and earthly fertility, every year devoured the children borne by his wife Rhea. However, she cunningly substituted a stone in place of their son Zeus, who later forced Cronus to disgorge the children from his stomach alive.

Myth images begin to reveal their secret only when interpreted in the light of primitive symbolism. This page shows symbolic forms expressive of time, which through graphic depiction of the progress of the heavenly bodies emerges as a cosmic phenomenon. Sun and moon are experienced by mythic man as, respectively, the bringer of light and the cause of the cool, moist, procreative power of "mother" night. Moon and stars represent female forces responsible for

Apis, the Egyptian bull of heavenly birth, symbolizes virility and fertility through the cycle of sun (on its head) and moon (as procreation; on its flanks).

procreation and fertility, as in the Australian aborigine depiction of the Great Mother being impregnated by the light of the morning star *(right)*. And when the ancient-Egyptian barge of the sun disappears behind the western mountain *(below left)*, in myth this represents the nocturnal path of the sun towards the east and the return of day. The arrival of the reborn light is depicted in the ascension of the Greek sun god Helios *(below right)*. Helios, the sun, rides up in his horsedrawn chariot as the stars, represented by gamboling children, sink under the waves.

A coin from *magna graecia (above)* shows the sun symbol in the tidal rotation of its rising (birth), zenith (life), and setting (death) — the eternal round of light and life.

and theologian, already at the end of the nineteenth century, took myth to be the explanation of ritual, and as such altogether secondary. In his most important work, *Lectures on the Religion of the Semites* (1888), Smith elaborated the theory that, since myth is the interpretation of a specific ritual, in many cases it would not have arisen until the original meaning of that rite had been forgotten. Over the course of the next half century, similar ideas were expressed by specialists in a great many fields. One may distinguish three important groups, however: classicists, anthropologists, and Old Testament specialists. The most articulate of the classicists was Jane Ellen Harrison, who argued that *mythos* was, for the ancient Greeks, primarily "just a thing spoken, uttered by the *mouth*." Its corollary is "the thing done, enacted, the *ergon* or work" (*Themis*, 1912, p. 328). A number of outstanding classicists from Cambridge applied her "ritualist" model to other Greek creations. F. M. Cornford traced the ritual origins of Attic comedy and of some philosophical ideas, and Gilbert Murray reconstructed the ritual pattern of Greek tragedy.

The British anthropologists A. M. Hocart and Lord Raglan generalized the ritualist approach and proclaimed the priority of ritual as the most important element in understanding human culture. Hocart claimed that myth is only the verbal explanation and justification of ritual: the actors impersonate the supposed inventors of the rite, and this impersonation must be expressed verbally; it is their speech in this impersonation which we come to know as myth. Thus, for Hocart, *all* myths *must* have a ritual origin. To prove this principle, he derived the myths of flying through the air from some climbing rituals, neglecting the fact that myths of flying are archaic and universally distributed, whereas climbing rites are rare and limited to certain very specific areas.

Many famous Old Testament scholars — H. Gunkel, H. Gressmann, S. Mowinckel, and others — explicated the cultic background of the Psalms, and insisted on the religious role of the king. Following their lead, a group of English Orientalists and Biblical experts launched a movement known as the Myth and Ritual school, or Patternism, in the thirties. A few years later, the Swedish scholars Ivan Engnell and Geo Widengren developed their ideas in greater detail, though at times overstating the main thesis of the British school. The Myth and Ritual position has been strongly criticized by Henri Frankfort in his Frazer Lecture of 1951, *The Problem of Similarity in Ancient*

15

Near Eastern Religions, and the impassioned debate still goes on.

There is something in common for all those authors who take myth to be nothing more than a verbalization or interpretation of ritual. All of them take for granted that the fundamental element of religion and of human culture is the act *done by man,* not the *story of divine activity.* Freud accepted this presupposition and tended to push it even further, identifying the one primordial *act* which established the human condition and opened the way to mythic and religious creation. This act was the primordial parricide, in which he supposed that a band of brothers killed their father, ate him, and appropriated his women for themselves. By devouring him, the sons accomplished their identification with the father, and each of them acquired a portion of his strength. "The totem meal, which is perhaps mankind's earliest festival, would thus be a repetition and a commemoration of this memorable and criminal deed, which was the beginning of so many things – of social organization, of moral restrictions, and of religion" (Freud, *Totem and Taboo,* 1946, pp. 141 f.).

We shall not discuss this interpretation of the origins of religion, culture, and society, since it has been rejected by most anthropologists. Suffice it to add that Freud interpreted myths as substantive gratifications via fantasy, and as such comparable to dreams and other means of wish-fulfillment fantasy. For him, myths were the reveries of the race, the imaginary realization of repressed desire, that is, of the Oedipal impulse. In sum, myth was for Freud a *fantasy repetition* of a *real act,* the original parricide.

Another attempt at a psychological understanding of myth is that of C. G. Jung, whose theory of myth is interdependent on his theory of the collective unconscious. Indeed, it was mainly the striking similarities between myths, dreams, and symbols of widely separated peoples and civilizations which led Jung to postulate the existence of a collective unconscious. He noticed that the images and structures of this collective unconscious manifest themselves in regularly repeating forms, which he called "archetypes." Like Freud, Jung considered myth, dream, and fantasy to be the indifferent products of the unconscious. But in marked contrast to Freud, he did not consider the unconscious mind to be a reservoir of repressed personal libido. Consequently, fantasy images and mythical forms are not for him a sort of "wish fulfillment" of the repressed libido, as they never were conscious and thus could never have been repressed. These mythical images are structures of the collective unconscious and are an impersonal possession. They are present in all peoples, though resting in a state of potentiality, and may become activated in myth or dream at any given moment. "The primitive mentality," writes Jung, "does not *invent* myths, it *experiences* them" (Jung and Kerényi, *Essays on a Science of Mythology,* 1949, p. 101). In other words, myths precede any type of culture, even the most primitive, though, of course, their verbal expressions are molded according to different cultural styles. In contrast to Freud's insistence on the primary position of the *deed* (the first parricide), myths are for Jung the expressions of *a primordial psychic process that may even precede the advent of the human race.* Together with symbols, myths are the most archaic structures of the psychic life. They did not need rituals, "things done," to emerge from the deep layers of the collective unconscious.

THE STRUCTURAL INTERPRETATION OF MYTH

In the last thirty years, the investigation of mythical thought has attracted a number of philosophers. We may cite E. Cassirer, Suzanne Langer, G. Gusdorf, G. Bachelard, Paul Ricoeur, Gilbert Durand, and others. The majority of these authors approached the problem of myth in a larger perspective: that of the study of language or of symbol, or that of the analysis of imagination. On the other hand, a number of anthropologists and folklorists have considered myths as a special form of the folktale, that is, as a traditional dramatic oral narrative. The investigations have followed two main orientations: *historical* (e.g., Franz Boas, W. E. Peuckert, C. W. von Sydow), and *morphological* (Vladimir Propp) or *structural* (Claude Lévi-Strauss).

By far the most important contribution to the structuralist interpretation of myth is that of Lévi-Strauss. In linguistics and ethnology, a structure is taken to be a combinatory game independent of consciousness. Consequently, Lévi-Strauss does not look for the "meaning" of myth on the level of consciousness. Myth, being an expression *par excellence* of primitive thought, has as its purpose "to provide a logical model capable of overcoming a contradiction." For Lévi-Strauss, "the kind of logic which is used in mythical thought is as rigorous as that of modern science, and the difference lies not in the quality of the intellectual process, but in the nature of the things to which it is applied." Indeed, "man has always been thinking equally well" (*Structural Anthropology,* 1963, p. 179).

Trees inhabited by spirits occur in many myths. An example is the tree goddess of the sacred sycamore in ancient Egypt *(above).* As the soul of the departed bows before the tree in the form of a spirit bird, the relatives offer sacrifices to the goddess on behalf of the dead man and receive her blessing from the ewer of the water of life.

The terrible Palden Lhamo *(right)* rides with an escort of demons over a sea of blood – the blood of the enemies she has slain. She appears in a visionary circle of flame and is the tutelary goddess of Lhasa in Tibet. She represents the negative, demonic aspect of the Great Mother Devi.

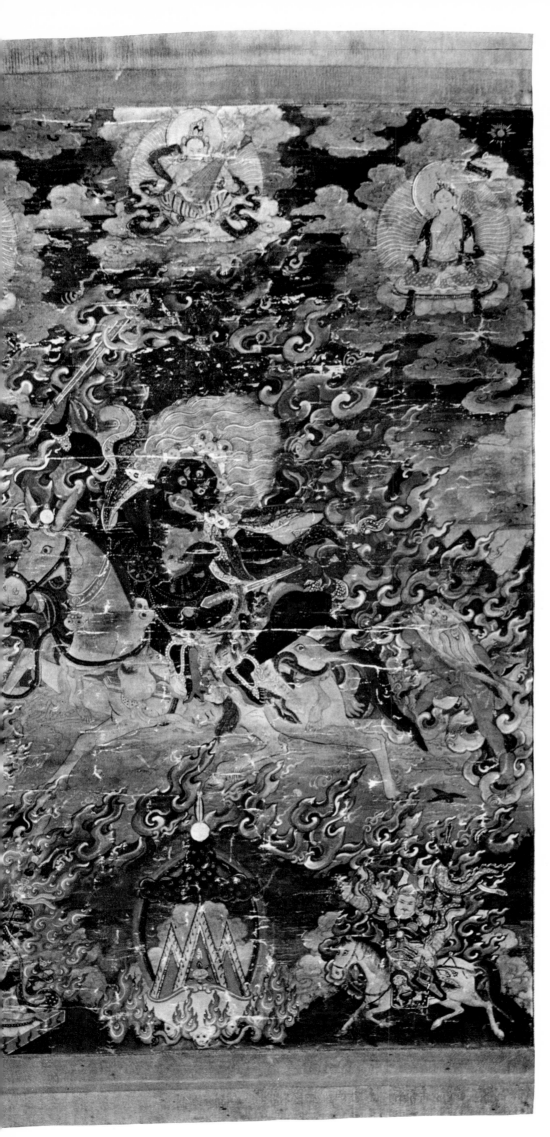

In his book *The Savage Mind* (Engl. trans., 1966), Lévi-Strauss asserts that mythical thought and modern scientific thought simply represent "two strategic levels at which nature is accessible to scientific enquiries" (p. 15). The basic characteristic of mythical thought consists in its concreteness: it works with *signs* which have the peculiar character of lying *between* images and concepts. That is, signs resemble images in that they are concrete, as concepts are not; however, their power of reference also likens them to concepts. Mythical thought is a kind of intellectual *bricolage* ("tinkering") in the sense that it works with all sorts of heterogeneous material which happens to be available.

Lévi-Strauss returns to this problem in his four-volume series on South and North American Indian myths, *Mythologiques* (1964-1971). This considerable work is difficult reading owing to the technicalities and intricate analysis of a great number of myths, but at the same time it represents a new and more personal evaluation of mythical thought. Here, Lévi-Strauss goes beyond the linguistic model and recognizes that the structure of myths is closer to music than to language. Lévi-Strauss's method and interpretation have made a notable impact on the cultivated public in Europe and America. Nevertheless, the majority of anthropologists, in spite of their admiration for his brilliance, maintain a more or less polite reserve with regard to his theories.

THE MEANING OF MYTH IN THE HISTORY OF RELIGIONS

For the historian of religions, the understanding of myth is of considerable importance, and the best opportunity for grasping the structure of mythical thought is the study of cultures where myth is still a "living thing," where it constitutes the very ground of social, religious, and cultural life. My own interpretation of myth is based primarily on the study of such cultures. Briefly stated, it is my opinion that for members of archaic and traditional societies, myth narrates a sacred history, telling of events that took place in primordial time, the fabulous time of the "beginnings." Myth is thus always an account of a "creation" of one sort or another, as it tells of how something came into being. The actors are supernatural beings, and myths disclose their creative activity and reveal the sacredness (or simply the "supernaturalness") of their work. Thus, the history of this activity is considered to be absolutely *true* (because it is concerned with realities) and *sacred* (be-

17

cause it is the work of supernatural beings). The cosmogonic myth is "true" because the existence of the world is there to prove it; the myth of the origin of death is equally true because man's mortality proves it, and so on.

Since myth is always related to a "creation" (the world, man, a specific institution, etc.), it constitutes the paradigm for all significant human acts. By knowing it, one knows the "origin" of things, and hence can control and manipulate them at will. This is a knowledge that one "experiences" ritually, either by ceremonially recounting the myth or by performing the ritual for which it serves as both a model and a justification. In traditional societies, one "lives" the myth in the sense that one is seized by the sacred, exalting power of the events recollected or reenacted.

To cite one well-known example, Australian totemic myths usually consist of a rather monotonous story of the wanderings of mythic ancestors or totem animals. They tell how in the ancient "dreamtime" *(alcheringa)* – that is, in mythical time – these supernatural beings made their appearance on earth, and how they set out on long journeys, stopping now and again to change the landscape or to produce certain animals and plants, and finally vanishing underground when their work was done. Knowledge of these tedious myths in all their details is essential for the life of the Australians, for the myths teach them how to repeat the creative acts of the supernatural beings and thus how to ensure the continued existence of the various species of animals and plants.

These myths are told to young men during their initiation; or rather, they are performed or reenacted. The "story" told in the myth is thus a sort of "knowledge," an esoteric knowledge that is secret, handed down during initiatory rites, and is accompanied by magico-religious power.

According to the Cuna Indians of Panama, the lucky hunter is he who knows the origin of the game. Further, certain animals can be tamed, but only because the magicians know the secret of their creation. Similarly, one can hold red-hot iron or grasp a poisonous snake if only one knows their origin. This is an extremely widespread belief, unconnected with any particular type of culture. In Timor, for example, when a rice field sprouts, someone who knows the mythical traditions concerning rice goes to the spot. He spends the night there in the plantation hut, reciting the legends that explain how man came to possess rice. The recitation of this origin myth compels the rice to come up as fine and thick and vigor-

ous as it was when it first appeared at the beginning of time. He who recites or performs the origin myth is thereby steeped in the sacred, creative atmosphere in which these miraculous events took place. The mythical time of origins is a "strong" time because it was transfigured by the active, creative presence of the supernatural beings. By reciting the myths, one re-creates that fabulous time and becomes contemporary with the events described, coming into the presence of the gods or heroes. By "living" the myths, one emerges from profane, chronologically ordered time and enters a time that is of a different quality – a "sacred" time, at once primordial and infinitely recoverable.

MYTHS AND FOLKTALES

In societies where myth is still alive, the people carefully distinguish myths, that is, "true stories," from fables or tales, which they call "false stories." Many North American Indians differentiate between sacred myths such as the cosmogony, creation of the stars, origin of death, exploits of a culture hero, etc., and profane stories, which tell the adventures of the trickster (Coyote) or explain certain anatomical peculiarities of animals. This same distinction is found in Africa and Oceania. Myths cannot be related without regard to circumstances. Among many tribes they are not recited before women and children, both of whom are uninitiated. Usually the old teachers communicate the myths to the neophytes during their isolation in the bush, and this forms a crucial part of their initiation. Whereas "false stories" can be told anywhere or at any time, myths may not be recited except during a sacred period.

Myths narrate not only the origin of the world and all the things in it, but also the primordial events which shaped man into what he is today – mortal, differentiated by sex, organized into a society, forced to work in order to live, and obliged to work in accordance with certain rules. All these are the consequence of events in the primordial times. Man is mortal because something happened in the mythic era, and if that thing had not happened, he would not be mortal but might have gone on existing indefinitely, like rocks, or changing his skin every so often, like snakes, and continuing to live thus renewed. But the myth of the origin of death tells what happened at the beginning of time, and in relating that incident, it establishes why man is mortal.

Similarly, certain tribes live by fishing, because in the mythic times a supernatural

For the Aztecs of Mexico, the androgynous god Ometecuhtli was responsible for creation. His primal, bisexual potency made him master of the fate of the emergent world.

Adam and Eve's original sin gave rise to the separation of paradise from the terrestrial world of birth-and-death suffering. Below, God

divides the ideal first state of pure creation and allocates the couple a new, mortal cosmos.

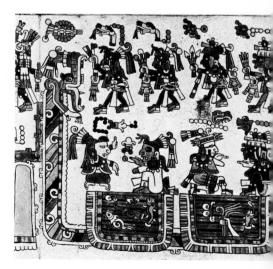

18

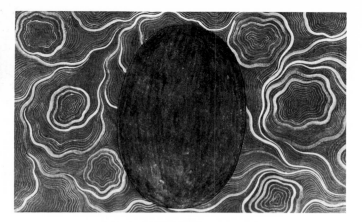

In the beginning of the Indian mythical cosmogony, chaos and darkness rule the primal waters and Brahma's golden egg appears as the first seed of the process of dividing up creation.

An important motif in myths of creation is the battle of the powers of day and light against the primeval demon of the sea. In this Babylonian relief (right) Marduk attacks the sea-serpent Tiamat.

One of the most beautiful creation images (below) is from ancient Egypt. Geb, who is the earth and earth god in one, lies on the ground while his consort Nut, the goddess of the sky, forms a vault

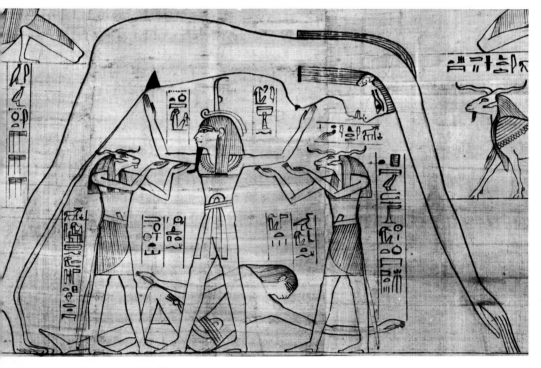

over him. Holding up Nut is Shu, the air god, to ensure that earth and sky remain forever divided.

A pre-Columbian manuscript from Mexico shows the creation of the Mixtecs (left) within the great circle of the gods and the serpent of heaven.

When the ancient-Indian god Brahma commences the creation of the world he appears as an all-seeing being (right) whose eye penetrates to the four corners of heaven and earth, while his look shapes and orders them.

being taught their ancestors to catch and cook fish. The myth tells of the first fishery, and in so doing it simultaneously reveals a superhuman act, teaches men how to perform it, and explains why they procure their food in this way. Thus, for archaic man, myth is a matter of primary importance, while tales and fables, however amusing they may be, are not. Myth teaches him the primordial events which have made him what he is; everything thus connected with his existence and his legitimate mode of existence in the cosmos concerns him directly. What is more, everything that happened *ab origine* can be repeated by the power of rites.

MYTHS OF CREATION: COSMOGONY AS AN EXEMPLARY MODEL

There is a great variety of cosmogonic myths. They can be generally classified as follows: (1) Creation *ex nihilo,* whereby a High Being creates the world by thought, by word, by heating himself in a steam hut, and so forth. Among the most famous examples are the Egyptian god Ptah, the Polynesian Io, Yahweh, and the Earthmaker of the Winnebago Indians. (2) The Earth Diver motif, in which a god sends aquatic birds or amphibious animals, or himself dives to the bottom of the primordial ocean and brings up a particle of earth, from which the whole world grows. This myth is particularly popular in central and northern Asia, North America, pre-Aryan India, and also in the folklore of eastern Europe and Russia. (3) Creation by the division of a primordial unity. Here, one can distinguish three variants: the separation of heaven and earth (often seen as world parents), an archaic and widely diffused myth – from Old Egyptian, Mesopotamian, and Greek mythologies to East Asia and Polynesia; separation of an original amorphous mass, chaos, as seen in the Japanese and Orphic cosmogonies; cutting in two of a cosmogonic egg, a motif encountered in Polynesia, Indonesia, India, Iran, Greece, Phoenicia, Finland, Central America, and the west coast of South America. (4) Creation by dismemberment of a primordial being, either a voluntary anthropomorphic victim (Ymir of Norse mythology, the Vedic Indian Purusha, the Chinese Pan-Ku) or an aquatic monster conquered after a terrific battle (the Mesopotamian Tiamat).

Every mythic account of the origin of anything – a tool, a custom, a disease – presupposes and continues the cosmogony. From a structural point of view, origin myths (or etiological myths) can be grouped together

19

with the cosmogonic myth. The creation of the world is the preeminent instance of creation, and the cosmogony is thus the exemplary model for all creative activity. This does not mean that an origin myth of necessity imitates or copies the cosmogonic model, for no concerted or systematic reflection need be involved. But every new appearance – an animal, a plant, an institution – implies the existence of a world. Each origin myth narrates and justifies a new situation – new in the sense that it came into being only as a result of certain actions of long ago. Origin myths thus continue and complete the cosmogonic myth; they tell how the world was changed, enhanced, or impoverished.

This is why some origin myths begin with a cosmogony. Thus, the history of the great families and dynasties of Tibet opens with the birth of the cosmos from an egg. The Polynesian genealogical chants begin in the same way. Such ritual genealogies are composed by bards when a princess becomes pregnant, and they are given to the hula dancers, who learn them by heart. These dancers, men and women alike, dance and recite the chant continuously, until the child is born, as if assisting in the embryological development of the future chief by their recapitulation of the cosmogony, the history of the world, and the history of the tribe. The gestation of a chief is the occasion for a symbolic recreation of the world. The performance is both a remembrance and a ritual reactualization via song and dance of the essential mythical events which have occurred since the creation.

The close connection between the cosmogonic myth, the myth of the origin of sickness and cure, and the ritual of magical healing is clearly seen in the ancient Near East and in Tibet. Often a solemn recitation of the cosmogony is enough to cure an illness. The ideology is not difficult to perceive: as the cosmogony is an exemplary model for all creation, its recitation helps the patient to make a new beginning of his life. The return to origins gives the means for a rebirth. All this is clear in the numerous ritual applications of the Polynesian cosmogonic myth. According to this myth, only waters and darkness existed in the beginning, and Io (the supreme being) separated the waters by the power of his thought and words, and then created the sky and earth. He said, "Let the waters be separated, let the heavens be formed, let the earth be!" These words of Io's, through which the world came to be, are creative words, charged with sacred power. Whenever there is something in need of creating,

THE FLOOD

The all-destroying flood of Noah's time and the Maya's serpent of the universal flood *(right)* depict the end of the world, while Vishnu in the primal egg of the cosmic ocean looks forward to a new creation. In Indian myth it is usually Vishnu who is represented as Creator. Here we see him reclining on the back of the world serpent, the *naga* Ananta, symbol of cosmic energy, who offers him the shelter of his thousand heads. The god is resting on the day before the new creation, and with him is Lakshmi, the incarnation of Mother Nature.

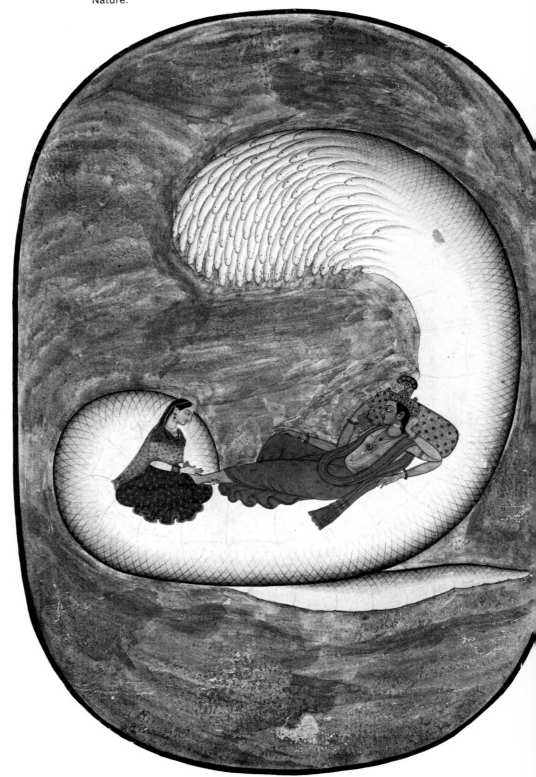

Noah, having preserved life in the ark as the old world sank beneath the Flood *(above left),* is prompted by a new dawn of creation to make sacrifice to the Lord *(above right).*

End - of - the - world flood legends are known as far afield as Alaska, where the Indians erected this great totem pole *(left)* near Sitka as a warning reminder.

Whether, following the revelation to Saint John, fire and water did fall from heaven *(below),* or whether the last path does lead *(bottom)* to the fiery jaws of hell, myth is full of such apocalyptic visions.

men can utter them and appropriate their sacred force. They are repeated during the rite for making a sterile womb fecund, or for curing body and mind, and also on the occasion of death, of war, and when genealogies are recited.

Much the same thing is seen in a custom of the Osage Indians. When a child is born, they summon "a man who has talked with the gods," and when he reaches the mother's house, he recites the creation of the universe and the terrestrial animals to the newborn baby. Not until this has been done is the child given the breast. Later, when it wants to drink water, the same man is called in again. Again he recites the creation, ending this time with the creation of water. When the child is old enough to take solid food, this "man who has talked with the gods" comes again and recites the creation, this time ending with the origin of grains and other foods. It would be hard to find a more eloquent example of the belief that each new birth represents a symbolic reca-

pitulation of the cosmogony and the tribe's mythic history. The object of this recapitulation is to introduce the newborn child by means of ritual into the sacramental reality of the world, and to validate its new existence by announcing that it conforms with the mythical paradigms.

In many cultures, the cosmogony was annually or periodically reenacted. The implicit idea is that the world is regularly threatened with ruin, and that it must be ritually re-created lest it perish. Mythico-ritual scenarios of periodic renovation are found among many Californian tribes (e.g., Hupa, Yurok, the Hill and Plains Maidu, the Eastern Pomo) and in Melanesia. Such scenarios played an important role in the religions of the ancient Near East as well. The Egyptians, the Mesopotamians, the Israelites, and others all felt the need to renew the world periodically. This renewal consisted in a cultic festival, the chief rite of which symbolized or reiterated the cosmogonic myth. In Mesopotamia, the creation of the world was ritually repeated during the New Year festival, as a series of rites reenacted the fight between Marduk and Tiamat (the dragon of the primordial ocean), the victory of Marduk, and his cosmogonic labors. The Hymn of Creation (Enuma elish) was recited in the temple, recounting all these events and thus making their power real once again.

MYTHS OF THE END OF THE WORLD

Myths of cosmic cataclysms are extremely widespread among primitives, telling of how the world was destroyed with the exception of a small number of survivors (often a single couple). Myths of the flood are the most numerous and are known practically everywhere, though rather rare in Africa. Other myths tell of man's destruction by earthquake, conflagration, falling mountains, epidemic, and so forth. Clearly, this end of the world was not final but was just the end of one human race or one period in history, followed by the appearance of another. But the total submergence of the earth under the waters, or its complete destruction by fire, symbolizes the return to chaos and is always followed by a new cosmogony with the appearance of a virgin earth.

In many myths, the flood is connected with a ritual fault that aroused the wrath of the supreme being. Sometimes it is just the result of his wish to put an end to humanity. But if we examine the various myths of the flood, we find that among its chief causes are the sins of mankind and the decrepitude of the world. The flood opened the way to both re-creation of the exhausted world and a regeneration of the fallen humanity.

Most American Indian myths of the end imply either a cyclic theory (as among the Aztecs), or the belief that the catastrophe will be followed by a new creation, or the belief in a universal regeneration without a cataclysm at all, in which only sinners will

perish. But the belief that the catastrophe is the inevitable consequence of the "old age" or decrepitude of the world does appear to be common. All in all, these myths express the same archaic idea of the progressive degradation of the cosmos, ultimately necessitating its destruction and re-creation. These myths of a final catastrophe have often been the basis for prophetic and millenarian movements, for the catastrophe is also the sign which announces the imminent re-creation of the world.

In all probability, the doctrine of the destruction of the world (pralaya) was already known in Vedic times (see Atharva Veda 10.8.39-40), and the universal conflagration (Ragnarok or Götterdämmerung) followed by a new creation is an element in Germanic mythology. These facts seem to show that the Indo-Europeans were not unacquainted with the end-of-the-world myth. But beginning with the Brahmanas, and especially in the Puranas, the Indians focused their attention on the doctrine of the four yugas, the four ages of the world. The essence of this theory is the cyclical creation and destruction of the world and the belief in the "perfection of the beginnings." As the Buddhists and Jains hold the same views, the doctrine of the eternal creation and destruction of the universe is evidently a pan-Indian idea. The complete cycle is ended with a dissolution, a pralaya, which is repeated more intensely at the end of the thousandth cycle. According to the Mahabharata and the Puranas, the horizon will burst into flame, seven or twelve suns will appear in the heavens, drying up the seas and scorching the earth. The Samvartaka, or cosmic conflagration, will destroy the entire universe. Then rain will fall in floods for twelve years, and the earth will be submerged and mankind destroyed (Vishnu Purana 24, 25). Sitting on the cosmic snake Shesha on the surface of the ocean, Vishnu is sunk in yogic sleep (Vishnu Purana 6.4.1-11), and then all begins again. And so on, ad infinitum.

The Indian doctrine of the world ages is to some extent similar to the primitive concepts of the annual renewal of the world, but there are important differences. In India, man plays no part at all in the periodic re-creation. Moreover, basically man does not want this re-creation and yearns only to escape from the cosmic cycle. Here there is no final end, only periods of varying lengths between the annihilation of one universe and the appearance of the next. The "end" has no meaning in a cosmic sense but applies only to the human condition, for man cannot halt the process of transmigration in which he is blindly carried along.

Even the iconography of the great living religions retains overt or hidden references to the symbols and patterns of myth. In fact such references do a great deal to bring out and enhance the significance of a picture's religious content. Here we see the Tibetan reformer Tsong-khapa at the top of a genealogical tree tracing the spiritual lineage of the Buddha, bodhisattvas, lamas, goddesses, and tutelary deities of the Yellow Church of the Dalai Lamas of Tibet. The whole picture is based on highly primitive modes of representation. The family tree is shown as the center of the world and the tree of the gods, growing out of the ocean of consciousness as a cosmic vision. At the bottom, to the left of the trunk, we have the Indian model of the world mountain (Mount Meru). The world tree reaches up to heaven in four directions, where the gurus and saints of Buddhism are found. The seven bodhisattvas (in a line running down from the top center) show the spiritual descent of the divine emanation as far as Tsong-khapa.

In Greece there are two different but connected traditions: the theory of the ages of the world and the cyclic doctrine. Hesiod is the first to describe the progressive degeneration of humanity during the five ages (*Works and Days* 109-201). The first, the Age of Gold under the reign of Cronus, was a sort of paradise: men lived for a long time without aging, and their life was like that of the gods, but this happy state did not continue, and gradually man's life became ever harder. The cyclic theory makes its appearance with Heraclitus, who greatly influenced the Stoic doctrine of the eternal return, in which everything that has happened will happen again. The two mythical themes – the ages of the world and the continuous cycle of creation and destruction – are already associated in Empedocles. There is no need to discuss the different forms that these theories took in Greece, often as the result of Oriental influence. Suffice it to say that the Stoics took over from Heraclitus the idea of the end of the world by fire *(ekpyrosis)* and that Plato knew of the end by flood (*Timaeus* 22, C). These two cataclysms determined the rhythm of the Great Year, and according to a lost work of Aristotle *(Protrepticus)*, the two catastrophes occurred at the solstices – fire in summer and flood in winter.

Some of these apocalyptic images of the end of the world recur in Judeo-Christian eschatology. But here there is an innovation of the greatest import: the end will come only once, just as creation occurred only once. The cosmos which will appear after the cataclysm is the same cosmos God created at the beginning, but purified, regenerated, restored to its original glory. This earthly paradise will not be destroyed again, and it will have no end. Time here is not the circular time of the eternal return; it has become a linear and irreversible time. Nor is this all: the eschatology shows the triumph of a sacred valuation of history, for the end of the world will reveal the religious value of human acts and men will be judged by these. This is not the cosmic regeneration of a collective group or the whole human race, but rather a judgment, a selection, a separation of righteous from unrighteous. The chosen will be saved by their loyalty to a sacred history; faced by the powers and temptations of this world, they will have remained true to the kingdom of heaven.

Another point which distinguishes Judeo-Christian eschatology from that of the cosmic religions is that the end of the world is seen as part of the messianic mystery. For the Jews, the coming of the Messiah will announce the end of the world and the restoration of paradise. For Christians, the end will proceed from the second coming of Christ and the Last Judgment. But for both, the triumph of sacred history – manifested by the end of the world – in some measure implies the restoration of paradise. The prophets proclaim that the cosmos will be renewed: there will be a new heaven and a new earth. There will be an abundance of all things, as in the Garden of Eden (Amos 9:13 ff., Isaiah 30:33 ff., etc.). For the Christians, too, the total renewal of the cosmos and the restoration of paradise are essential characteristics of the end-time. In Revelation (21:1-5) we read: "Then I saw a new heaven and a new earth; for the first heaven and the first earth had passed away . . . and I heard a great voice from the throne saying . . . 'and death shall be no more, neither shall there be mourning nor crying nor pain any more . . . . Behold, I make all things new.' "

But this new creation will rise on the ruins of the first. The syndrome of the final catastrophe resembles Indian descriptions of the destruction of the universe. There will be drought and famine, and the days will grow short. The period immediately preceding the end will be dominated by the Antichrist, but Christ will come and purify the world by fire. As Saint Ephraem Syrus expressed it: "The sea shall roar and be dried up . . . the heaven and earth shall be dissolved, and darkness and smoke shall prevail. Against the earth shall the Lord send fire, which lasting forty days shall cleanse it from wickedness and the stains of sins."

The reign of the Antichrist is in some sense equivalent to a return into chaos. On the one hand, the Antichrist is presented in the form of a dragon or demon, and this is reminiscent of the old myth of the fight between God and the dragon; the fight took place in the beginning, before the creation of the world, and it will take place again at the end. On the other hand, when the Antichrist comes to be regarded as the false Messiah, his reign will represent the total overthrow of social, moral, and religious values – that is, the return to chaos.

MYTHS OF HIGH GODS;
THE SUN AND THE MOON

The types of myth discussed thus far are all directly or indirectly dependent on the cosmogonic myth. Thus, myths of origins complete and prolong the creation story, and the myths of the end with their intimation of the periodic regeneration of the universe are all structurally related to the cosmogony. These types of myth have been

stressed because of the important role they play in the religious life of primitive and traditional societies. But there are other types of myth, which might be classified as follows: (1) myths of the gods and of other divine beings; (2) myths of the creation of man; (3) myths which tell of subsequent modifications of the world and the human condition; (4) myths associated with celestial bodies and the life of nature; (5) myths of heroes.

Common to all these is the fact that they relate events occurring after the creation of the world. Some may be considered myths of origins, as, for instance, the anthropogenic myth telling of the creation of man, or the myths of the origin of death. Moreover, many of those myths which tell of radical modifications in the nature of the world are also myths of origins, as those myths which tell of the earth's transformation by a demiurge, a culture hero, or a trickster.

All the events related in myths belong to the fabulous past. But it is possible to distinguish between a primordial epoch corresponding to the very beginnings and the subsequent changes of that initial situation. Thus there are (1) myths narrating the creation of the world and of man, and describing that primeval epoch which lasted until the first change in the structure of the cosmos or in man's essential mode of being; (2) myths relating the countless dramatic modifications of the world and of man which took place from that moment until the end of the mythical time. A third group of myths is concerned with the adventures of gods, supernatural beings, and heroes; it is not necessarily related directly to this time structure.

Among the most primitive societies (i.e., those of hunters and food-gatherers), myths of the high gods are simple. The supreme being is believed to have created the world and man, but he soon abandoned his creations and withdrew into the sky. Sometimes he did not even complete his work of creation, and another divine being took over the task. In some cases, his withdrawal was responsible for a breach in communications between heaven and earth, or for a great increase in the distance between them. In some myths, the original proximity of the sky and the presence of God on earth constitute a paradisal state. The place of this more or less forgotten *deus otiosus* was taken by various divinities, all of whom are closer to man and help or persecute him in a more direct and active way than the remote sky.

The celestial supreme being and creator recovers his religious activity only in certain pastoral cultures such as the Turko-Mon-

Change and succession among the gods are oft-recurring themes in classical myth. Vasari's painting *(above)* depicts the castration of the Titan god Uranus by his son Cronus. The old gods turn away as Cronus, father of time, wields the scythe. But his days too are numbered; his son Zeus, shown beside Cronus's throne *(top)*, will grow in strength and soon oust him and banish him forever.

24

Good Ishtar, one and only Ishtar,
whose gift is the growth of plants;
Great Ishtar,
girded with power in battle . . .
a storm in battle, devastating
heaven and earth;
Sublime Ishtar, governess of lands,
creatrix of mankind,
shepherdess of the lands of the universe,
without you no river is let flow,
no river dammed, that furthers life.

BABYLONIAN HYMN

Looked at in this way the gods of myth are not just graphic emanations of the numinous and holy in religion; they are fundamental images of the origin, existence, and decline of man's world, transformed by time and history.

The metamorphosis of the gods is particularly clear in the rich mythology of India. Varuna *(far left)* is probably the most ancient creator of heaven and earth; later, in the Vedas, he became the god of night and the firmament, and today he is a god of water. Next to him is a statue of Indra, once god of the sky, creating lightning, thunder, and rain. Then Vishnu appeared as lord of light, mover of the waters, and preserver of creation in his ten incarnations. Finally Bhairava *(left)* represents the destructive side of the god Shiva before the regeneration of the universe.

With Apollo *(above)* there emerged in Greece the classical god of order and of the salvation of the good and beautiful in nature and man. As god of the arts and muses he became the ideal of antiquity.

EL, an age-old root for "god" known from Akkadia and Babylon through to the Semitic civilization of the Phoenicians, is here personified as El, creator and father of the world and the supreme deity of the Canaanites and Phoenicians *(far left)*. Later, Baal *(left)*, was known to the Phoenicians as creator and as god of war.

The three gods on the left again exemplify the tidal rhythm of death and rebirth that is central to nature. The Egyptian god Osiris *(far left)*, as ruler of the land of the dead, leads the departed into the realm of eternal life. For the Greeks, Adonis *(center)* stood for the death and resurrection of nature. The fertility goddess Ishtar of Babylon *(left)* likewise represented the dying and begetting power of the created world.

25

gols, in Yahwism, in the reform of Zoroaster, and in Islam. In other cases, even when his name is remembered – as with An (Anu) of the Mesopotamians, El of the Canaanites, Dyaus of the Vedic Indians, Uranus of the Greeks – the supreme celestial being no longer plays any important role in religious life and is almost ignored in mythology. The "passivity" of Uranus as *deus otiosus* is plastically expressed by his castration: he has become impotent, unable to take part in the affairs of the world, drained of creative power. In Vedic India Varuna supplanted Dyaus, and he in turn gave way to the warrior god Indra, who then yielded to Vishnu and Shiva. El yielded primacy to Baal, as An did to Marduk. With the exception of Marduk, these supreme gods are no longer "creative" in the active sense. They did not create the world, but only organized it and assumed responsibility for its maintenance. They are primarily fecundators like Zeus or Baal, who by their union with earth goddesses ensure the fertility of the fields and the abundance of harvests. Marduk himself is only the creator of *this* world, that is, the universe as it exists *today*. Another "world" – almost unthinkable for us, because it existed only as fluid, the restless infinite ocean – existed before this one: it was ruled by Tiamat and her spouse, in which three generations of gods lived.

The polytheistic religions are generally characterized by rich, variegated, and dramatic mythologies. In addition to sky gods and storm gods, important roles are played by deities of vegetation and chthonic fertility. Special mention must be made of the tragic myths of the young gods who die (often by murder) and sometimes come back to life, such as Osiris, Tammuz, Attis, and Adonis, or the goddess who descends to the underworld (Ishtar, Inanna) or is forced to dwell there (Persephone). These "deaths" are all creative in the sense that they bear a consistent relation to vegetation, the period of "death" or the stay in the nether regions being related to the winter season. Around these myths of violent death or descent to hell, many of the mystery religions later developed.

Rich and varied mythologies have also grown up around the two great luminaries, sun and moon. In many cultures these celestial bodies are considered as the eyes of a supreme being. Even more frequent is the process of "solarization" of the supreme being, that is, his transformation into a sun god. Myths of man's descent from the sun are know among some North American tribes (Blackfoot, Arapaho) and are especially prevalent in Indonesia and Melane-

sia. The sun is also conceived as a hero and is symbolized by an eagle or a falcon. Dynasties and military aristocracies have often traced their origins to solar heroes (Egypt, Melanesia, etc.), and the well-known motif of two antagonistic brothers may well be related to the mythic conflict of sun and moon. Many myths of this type have survived in folklore, and together with myths of the animal world (Master of Animals, theriomorphic guardian spirits, etc.) they have provided most of the world's folklore themes. Certain solar myths, for example, have survived in secularized form as folk-

tales or sagas long after being emptied of their religious content.

Lunar mythologies are often even more dramatic. For while the sun always remains the same, the moon waxes and wanes – disappearing, only to come to life again after three moonless nights. In the religion of many primitive peoples, the moon is considered to be the first man who died. But for the religious man, death is not an extinction but only a change, a new kind of life. A number of myths are related to the phases of the moon, its death and resurrection, including myths of the land of the dead, of the adventures of the first ancestor, of the mysteries of fertility and birth, of initiation, magic, etc. Most of these myths have sur-

Many myths tell how mankind was created by the shaping hand of a god, demiurge, or primal man. A mythical being is celebrated as sculptor of the human race on earth. Below we see the creation of the Nugu by Ipila (Melanesia). He carves him from a tree trunk and gives him life by rubbing his face with sago milk, a symbol of the quickening of life.

In myth the creation of man is often at the same time an initiation into life that men undergo in order to re-emerge as pure creatures. For the Toltecs of Mexico the first step was a ritual purification with hot water; then came the way through the seven hells of the divine language before the word of the gods entitled him on whom it was bestowed to embark on a new life.

vived, though degraded and transformed, preserved in the world's folklore.

MYTHS OF THE CREATION OF MAN AND THE ORIGIN OF DEATH

The myths of the creation of man represent in some respects a continuation of the cosmogony. In a great number of myths, man is created from some material substance. Thus, for example, the Yoruba of Nigeria believe the primordial couple to have been fashioned from mud by the god Obatala; Indonesian and Melanesian myths tell how the first man was created from a stone. In Oceania, a god created man from earth or from a figure drawn upon the ground which he then sprinkled with his blood. In some mythologies (e.g., Southeast Asia, Iran) man is believed to have been created from an animal or plant. Other myths tell of an original androgynous state of the first human. Here, either the creator separates the two sexes from the androgyne, or he draws the woman forth from the body of the man. In some cases, the god creates the first man *ex nihilo* by power of his thought. Thus the Californian Wiyot say that Gudatrigakwitl, the high god, used neither sand nor earth to fashion man; he simply thought, and man came into being.

Far and away the most complex and dramatic category of myths, however, are those which tell of radical transformations in the structure of the world and of man's mode of being. One group of such myths tells of cosmic changes which occurred in the primordial past: when heaven became remote, mountains flattened, or the tree or liana connecting earth and heaven suddenly was cut. As a result of changes like this rupture between heaven and earth, the paradisiacal age ended, and men and gods no longer mingled easily. Man then became mortal, sexed, and obliged to work for his living.

Other myths of a similar sort tell of the origin of death. The most common African motif is what has been called "the message that failed," in which, for instance, God sent the chameleon to the mythic ancestors with the message that they would be immortal, and he sent the lizard with the message that they would die. When the lizard arrived first, man's fate was sealed. Another African motif is that of "death in a bundle": God allowed the first men to choose between two bundles, one of which contained life, the other, death. According to a third motif, mortality is the result of man's transgressing a divine commandment.

Among the myths recounting changes in man's condition, perhaps the most pathetic are those of the *dema* type. *Dema* is the name given to the primordial beings by the Marind-Anim of New Guinea, and their central myth tells of the slaying of a *dema* deity by the *dema* men. Its general outlines are as follows. A lovely maiden named Hainuwele grew miraculously from a coconut palm and was blessed with the power to produce rich gifts from her body. During a great festival, Hainuwele stood in the middle of the dance ground distributing gifts to the dancers. But near the end of the festival, the men killed Hainuwele and buried her. The next morning, one of the men dug up the body, however, and cut it into pieces, which he buried in various places, except for the arms. These pieces gave birth to plants previously unknown, especially tubers, which since then have been the chief food of men. He then took her arms to another *dema* deity, Satene. From Hainuwele's arms she made a door, and then summoned the men who had killed her. "Since you have killed," she said, "I will no longer live here. I shall leave this very day. Now you will have to come to me through this door." Those who were able to pass through the door remained human beings, while those who were not became animals and spirits. Satene announced that from that time forth, men would meet her only after death, and then she vanished from the earth.

A. E. Jensen has shown the great importance of this myth for an understanding of the religion and world image of the ancient planters. The murder of a *dema* divinity by the *dema* ancestors ended an epoch and opened that in which we live today. The *dema* became men, that is, sexually differentiated and mortal beings. As for the murdered *dema* divinity, she survives in her creations (food, plants, animals, etc.) and in the house of the dead. In another sense, she can be said to survive in the "mode of being of death," which she established through her own death. The violent demise of the *dema* divinity is not only a creative death; it is also a way of being continually present in the life of men, and even in their death. For by feeding on the plants and animals that sprang from her body, men feed on the very substance of the *dema* divinity.

Another class of widespread myths are those of the king's son who is abandoned after birth because of a prophecy threatening danger to the king. Consigned to the waters, the child is saved by animals or shepherds, and is suckled by a female animal or a humble woman. When fully grown, he embarks on extraordinary adventures

MYTH TODAY

We have our myths and cultivate our deities today, just as mankind has always done. Examples are Superman *(above)*, the Phantom, Tarzan – and of course the ever-recurring mother figure, seen opposite in the eroticized form of the "goddess" Marilyn Monroe, as she was deified in the film *Tommy*. The modern bard, too, as artist forging new life truths from old yearnings, is a mythological figure of magus-like appearance.

Through the power and fascination of technology, one can still court a victorious, heroic death. Modern man identifies with his car, for instance, in a positively magical way; the automobile has become an almost sacred symbol of status and power. Battles of heroes before a marveling public now take place on the speedway.

(monster slaying, etc.). Later he finds his parents and takes revenge, finally being recognized and winning rank and honor. In most of these myths, the dangers and trials of the hero (encounters with monsters and demons, descents into hell, being swallowed by an aquatic monster, etc.) have an initiatory meaning. By overcoming all these ordeals, the young man proves that he has surpassed the human condition and henceforth he belongs to a class of semidivine beings. Many epic legends and folktales utilize and readapt the highly dramatic scenarios of a hero's initiation (e.g., Siegfried, Arthur, Robin Hood, etc.).

The folklore of all nations contains a large number of myths and mythical motifs emptied of their religious values and functions, but preserved for their epic or fantastic qualities. Moreover, the heroic poetry of the world's oral tradition, as well as the beginnings of drama and comedy, is directly dependent upon the mythical traditions of the world. Some forms of "mythical behavior" still survive in our own day; one can speak of "myths of the modern world," as, for instance, the eschatological and millenarian structures of Marxist communism, the mythic structures of the images and behavior imposed on collectivities by the power of the mass media, and so forth. The characters in comic strips present the modern version of mythological folklore heroes. Superman has become extremely popular, owing particularly to his dual identity: though he comes from a planet destroyed by a catastrophe, and though he possesses prodigious powers, Superman lives in the modest guise of a timid, unassertive journalist, bullied and dominated by his colleagues. This humiliating camouflage of the hero follows the well-known mythic theme of the abandoned hero we have discussed above.

The mythicization of public figures through the mass media, the transformation of a personality into an exemplary image, is also a frequent phenomenon in today's most developed societies. Mythological behavior can be recognized likewise in the obsession with "success" that expresses an obscure wish to transcend the limits of the human condition; in the exodus to suburbia, in which we can detect the nostalgia for "primordial perfection"; in the paraphernalia and emotional intensity that characterize what has been called the "cult of the sacred automobile," and so on. The mythic imagination can hardly be said to have disappeared; it is still very much with us, having only adapted its workings to the material now at hand.

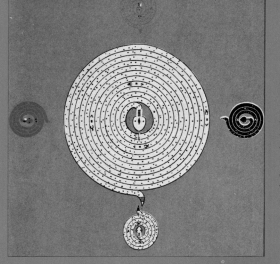

The snake motif is virtually ubiquitous in the world of myth, although its meaning is not always the same, and wherever it appears it is in the local form and coloring. The two small illustrations on this page come from widely separate parts of the world: on the left is a sand painting by the Navaho of Arizona depicting the "Great Serpent without End"; the snake god couple below is from India.

Myths from West to East

JOSEPH CAMPBELL

The photograph on the right was taken in the Djema el Fna, the main square of Marrakesh, immediately adjacent to the *suks* or bazaars. Every day, amid its bustle of activity, groups of people gather round to listen to the professional storytellers. In passing on to a new generation the treasury of myths, legends, and fairy tales – much of which does not exist in written form – these men continue the oral tradition to which we owe a great part of our knowledge of the myths of the world.

The retelling of age-old tales for the sheer delight of their "once-upon-a-time" is an art little practiced in our day, at least in the Western world; and yet, when such a colorful sampling of the art as that of the present collection is brought to us, the enchantment works and we are carried in imagination to a Never-Never-Land that we, somehow, have long known. The reading is a little like a visit to a bazaar, say in Istanbul or Old Delhi. We stroll about, at first casually, just looking, but then enter one or another of the shops and become caught there in the fascination of gems in unforeseen settings, curious images of unheard-of gods, bolts of incredible gold brocade, and all in a setting of incense. The shopkeeper begins telling us of the lands from which his wares have been brought, and something of the ways of life in those regions begins appearing to us through the settings of the gems, the figures woven in the gold brocades, and the attitudes of the gods. Their fascination is of ways of life fundamentally different from our own, which yet speak, somehow, to some part of us to which, perhaps, we have not been paying attention: the part of fantasy and dream, which may lead to vision and from vision on to a revelation of some kind – if not about the universe, then at least about ourselves.

For in the past, and today throughout the primitive world that is so fast disappearing even from the hidden corners of the earth, people lived largely out of the visions, either of great teachers, such as the Buddha, Moses, Zarathustra, Jesus, and Muhammad, or, in less developed lands, of their own village seers and shamans. The fabrics and art works of their hands, consequently, were shaped by the visions that had shaped their lives, and these speak subliminally to our own possibilities of vision, telling of qualities of life either lost to us or waiting to be realized. And if this be true of the fascinations of bazaars, how much more so of mythologies – or rather, of such fragments of mythologies as the myths of the present collection. For we live today in the midst of a terminal moraine of mythologies no longer serving to support and inform great civilizations. Their fragments, radiant and lovely, or sometimes merely grotesque, are scattered everywhere about. We enter from the street, for example, a cathedral, a temple, or a shrine, which stands like the vestige of an earlier age in a city of different architecture; and yet – unless we are merely tourists – it will be there that we shall seek most seriously to evaluate our living and to find direction.

The tales retold here by Alexander Eliot are so arranged that the commonality of many of their themes should be apparent even to the most casual reader. Professor Eliade in his Introduction has already alluded to the "striking similarities between myths, dreams, and symbols of widely separated peoples and civilizations," and in his discussion of origin myths and myths of the end of the world, myths of high gods and of the creation of man and origin of death, a great number of widely shared themes and motifs do indeed appear. How so? "Whence do all these so widely shared themes and motifs derive?" we might ask. "Where do dragons come from? Where, for example, on the map, might I draw a circle to mark the homeland of the species *dragon?* Or is that place not to be found, perhaps, in any part of the map at all?" If questions of this kind occur to us and we take them seriously enough to begin to look for answers, the quest may take us not only into every part of the world and century of the past, into oriental temples, painted paleolithic caves, and the deepest jungle sanctuaries, but also, in some way or other, inward, upward, and downward, following shamans on their visionary journeys and witches to their sabbaths.

Adolf Bastian (1826–1905) was one of the first great scholars of this subject to take such questions seriously enough to make them his central concern. He was not only one of the major anthropologists of the last century and a profound student of mythologies but also a medical man and world traveler; and he coined the term *Elementargedanken*, "elementary ideas," to characterize the recurrent themes and motifs that he was everywhere encountering. He also recognized, however, that wherever and whenever they appeared it would be in costumes local to the region. They could never be pinned down, experienced, and defined, in anything like a primary, uncommitted shape or form, but, like the Greek sea god Proteus, were forever shifting shape and slipping away. The Fire Bringer, for example, known to classical mythology in the figure of Prometheus, appears in three of the tales of the present collection – from Peru, Australia, and Mexico – as a hummingbird. Among the Indians of the American Northwest Coast he was Raven; among the Plains tribes, Coyote; while on the Andaman Islands, in the Bay of Bengal, he is a kingfisher. Bastian called such local transformations "ethnic ideas," *Völkergedanken*, and recognized that, whereas the enigma of the elementary forms leads inevitably to psychological considerations, studies of the ethnic turn us, rather, toward history and sociology. And these, in fact, are the two faces or departments of our

subject: on one hand, the psychological or general, having to do with the common ground and laws of all human thinking, dreaming, and fantasizing whatsoever, and on the other hand, what might perhaps best be called the environmental, or provincial, conditions – geographical, historical, and sociological, which show great local differences in various parts of the world – out of which not only the images but also the local motivations for any specific peoples' thinking, dreaming, and fantasizing have always been and still are being derived.

For example, no one would expect to find among Alaskan Eskimos a legend of the origin of coconuts, or on a South Pacific island legends of the origin of seals. Yet a comparison of the tale on page 138 of this collection, from the South Pacific Mangeia Islands, of the decapitated eel whose buried head gave rise to the first coconut tree, with that on page 172, from the Eskimos of Alaska, of the woman whose chopped-off fingers became seals, reveals in the two the same essential theme: namely, that to which Professor Eliade has already introduced us in his discussion of the legend from New Guinea of the sacrificed maiden Hainuwele, the pieces of whose chopped-up body, when buried, gave rise to the food plants which since that mythological time have supported human life on that island. Another example of the same elementary idea in this collection will be found in the tale on page 138, from Peru, of Pachacamac and the child-sacrifice out of which the food plants of pre-Columbian South America were derived.

This, in fact, is a fundamental legend, found in local transformations throughout the tropical, equatorial zone, wherever gardening and agriculture provide the mainstays of human life. It is not typical of hunting tribes. A real question, therefore, which has been variously argued, has to do with the surprise of its appearance among the Eskimo in the figure of their Seal Mother Sedna, or Takánakapsâluk. Have we an example here of independent, parallel development? Or can it be shown that the Eskimo, whose cultural equipment resembles that of Late Paleolithic hunting cultures, were significantly touched by influences stemming either from the tropics or from Early Neolithic developments in Siberia?

Origin legends tend to be diffused along with the arts to which they are attached. However, the Eskimo are not planters and their version of the legend has to do with the origin, not of food plants, but of seals. Moreover, there is the no less interesting question of why the Hainuwele theme ap-

pears at all in the Americas, as it does in New Guinea, Borneo, and the Celebes (see the tales on pages 88 and 100), as well as across the Pacific, in Peru (page 138). Tantalizing questions of this kind turn up on every side as we peer ever more deeply into the very deep well of the past out of which the myths and legends of our world have come, and which Thomas Mann, in the opening sentence of his four-volume mythological novel, *Joseph and His Brothers*, suggests may be bottomless: as bottomless, deep and dark, that is to say, as the human psyche itself.

Bottomless, in any case, is the view of the origins of our race that is even now opening to our sciences, where, for the past forty years or so, the focus has been closing in on Africa as our motherland: South and East Africa and, most recently, the Kenya-Tanzania highlands, from the Olduvai Gorge to Lake Rudolf. The antiquity of the genus *Homo* in that area goes back, it now appears, some four or more million years; and from there, apparently, by slow diffusion, the race spread northward and eastward, until by the middle of the second interglacial age, about 500,000 B.C., a zone of human habitation had been established

The earliest evidence of religious rites and the myths relating to them is provided by the rock and cave paintings that have come down to us from between thirty and ten thousand years ago – a period from which no verbal traditions have survived. Rock paintings and engravings occur in almost every part of the world.

through all of southern Asia, with two northward extensions: into Europe in the West, as far as England, and into China in the East, to about the latitude of Peking. However, in no part of this immense domain do we find, through all those hundreds of thousands of years, any sign of anything like a religious rite or of mythological thinking, until, toward the coming of the last of the ice ages, about 150,000 B.C., Neanderthal Man *(Homo sapiens neanderthalensis)* had evolved and appeared in Europe and Southwest Asia. We now begin to find burials, and at one important site, at Shanidar in northern Iraq, there has been recently dis-

The row of stags shown at the top is from the Lascaux cave in southern France which was evidently devoted to the performance of hunting rites. The center picture shows a group of prehistoric rock paintings in Wyoming, U.S.A., and on the left is a hunting scene from M'toko Cave in Rhodesia.

covered a cave containing a number of burials, in one of which the body had been laid to rest on a bier of evergreen boughs overspread with flowers, the pollens of which could still be traced, and all of which have turned out to be plants with hallucinogenic properties. Some sort of belief in a life beyond death is here indicated, inspired perhaps by visions. Dating also from this period of earliest evidences are a number of small cave sanctuaries high among the Alpine peaks of Switzerland and Silesia, wherein collections of cave-bear skulls have been found, some stored in stone-slab cabinets, one in the midst of a circle of

33

stones, one with the long bones of a bear thrust through its eye sockets, and another with such a long bone crosswise under its mouth. The indication here seems to be of some sort of worship of the bear.

Our first extensive body of evidence of developed religious rites and associated myths, however, comes to view only in the great painted caves of southern France and northern Spain – Lascaux, Altamira, and the rest – which date from about 30,000 to about 10,000 B.C., when the glaciers of the last ice age were retreating. That was a world of magnificent hunting, reaching all the way from the plains of western Europe, eastward across Siberia and the Bering Strait, into North and then South America. We even have evidence from the southernmost point of an arrival of hunters and gatherers at the Strait of Magellan as early as about 6500 B.C. That was the period of the classic Stone Age "great hunt," when the food supply of the peoples of the bountiful animal plains was procured and provided chiefly by the males of the tribes. The

From western Europe to the Far East we find symbols of the worship of the Great Mother and her power of eternal renewal. This graceful figurine is of Egyptian origin.

Another universal mythic concept is that of the voyage of the dead to the Beyond. Often it is a ship that ferries the souls of the departed; for the Tsimshian Indians of British Columbia it is a sea monster (below).

Bear worship seems to have been the earliest of man's religions and also one of the most widely distributed, ranging from western Europe right across Siberia to the North American continent. It is still practiced by the Ainu of Japan, among many others. A bear-worship ceremony decorates this Etruscan bronze urn (below).

The concept of a world center or world axis around which everything revolves perhaps arose out ot early man's observations of the night sky. It has found expression in many mythic symbols: the great tentpole of the Lapps, the world tree of the Icelandic *Ed-das*, the holy mountain (e.g., Olympus), the Mesopotamian ziggurat, and temple architecture from India to Japan. This picture *(above)* represents such a world center: it is a modern water color by Standing Bear of his friend, the Sioux medicine man Black Elk, sitting on his horse on the summit of Harney Peak, which for him was the midpoint of the world.

bow and arrow had not yet been invented; their weapons were javelins, spears, and rocks. And many of the beasts were prodigious, mammoths, rhinos, and the like, with the human species a minute minority in a world of great ranging herds.

Clearly, the conditions of life for the shaping of the ethnic ideas of the peoples inhabiting such an environment would be radically different from those of tropical jungle tribes. We are dwelling and moving about upon broadly spreading animal plains, among herds of reindeer, woolly ponies, cattle of various kinds, and here and there a mammoth or two or surly rhinoceros. The horizon is cleanly and well defined – a perfect circle, all about, for 360 degrees. And there is the great blue dome of heaven above, with the mysterious sun crossing it daily, alone, from east to west, and at night the moon, waning and waxing, among stars. A very different world from the green hell of a jungle with no horizon anywhere, only forest in all directions; above, a ceiling of leaves inhabited by screeching feathery tribes, and below, a treacherous flooring under which scorpions lurk with serpents and the like. Legends of the Hainuwele type are typical of peoples dwelling in such plant-dominated environments, and they are generally accompanied by horrific rites of human and animal sacrifice. Apparently the observation that from dead and rotting vegetation green shoots arise led to the conclusion that from death comes life, and accordingly, that the way to increase life is to increase death. An almost incredible history of human sacrifice is amply documented for the whole equatorial belt, from West Africa, through India, Southeast Asia, and Oceania, to the New World, where it came to a sort of pathological climax in the Aztec system of Mexico. The head-hunting cults of Brazil and Indonesia are local expressions of this elementary idea, and from Africa we have in the present collection the Wahungwe legend from Southern Rhodesia of the maiden sacrificed to bring rain (page 294).

The northern peoples of the great hunting plains were inspired by a totally different set of observations. They were killing and slaughtering beasts every day, wearing the skins of beasts as clothing, enjoying their flesh, and dwelling in huts or tents made of their skins. Moreover, since primitive peoples do not set mankind, as we do, above and apart from the beasts, killing animals, like killing men, is for them a serious affair. There is a problem of guilt and of fear of revenge to be dealt with, and rites of atonement, propitiation, and magical banning are consequently of the utmost importance.

Those Neanderthal cave-bear sanctuaries can well have been devoted to rituals of this kind. The great caves of the later postglacial periods almost certainly were. They were sanctuaries of the men's hunting rites and of the initiation of boys both into manhood and into the ritual lore by which the good will of the beasts on whose lives the human community depended was to be maintained. The underlying myth – at least as we find it among hunting peoples to this day – is of a covenant between the human tribe and the animals, according to which the lifeblood of the beasts is to be returned ritually to the Great Mother Earth for rebirth, and the animal herds, then, will be released by the Animal Master to come back as willing victims again next season. For there is no such thing as death. There is only a passing back and forth, as it were, through a veil.

Essentially, then, the informing observation supporting these two widely flung mythologies is the same. It is that life lives on life, and that without this continuing sacrifice there would be no life whatsoever on this earth. The other part of the realization is that there is a renewing principle everywhere operative that is of the nature of the earth and of the mystery of the womb, which receives seed and returns it as renewed life. The function of the myth is to bring this truth to mind, and of the ritual, to turn it into action. The individual is thereby united with the way of nature, centered not in self-preservation but in accord with the wonder of the whole. "Oh, wonderful! Oh, wonderful! Oh, wonderful!" we read in the Indian Taittiriya Upanishad. "I am food! I am food! I am food! I am a food eater! I am a food eater! I am a food eater! I am a fame maker! I am a fame maker! I am a fame maker! I am the first-born of the world-order, earlier than the gods, in the navel of immortality! Who gives me away, he indeed has aided me! I, who am food, eat the eater of food! I have overcome the whole world! – He who knows this," the text concludes, "has a brilliantly shining light" (Taittiriya Upanishad 3.10).

The "I" with which the celebrant of this poem has identified himself is not, of course, either the "I" that eats or the "I" that is eaten, but the "I" that both eats and is eaten, transcendent and yet immanent in all – all processes and all things – which in India is called *brahman* and was to the Algonquin known as Manitou, as Wakonda to the Sioux, and to the Iroquois as Orenda, is called Mana in Melanesia, and among the Bantu tribes of Africa is Bwanga. It may be symbolized in myths and rites as the pivotal center of the universe, around which all revolves, for example, the Sky Nail of the Buryat and Lappish shamans, of which we read on page 112. Or it is the axial pole of the world, symbolized in the central pole of

Masks as cult objects occur in bewildering profusion among all peoples. They are as varied in appearance, significance, and use as the lives of the men and women who create them. Illustrated here are a ritual

mask from Gabon (left), a mask image of a fearsome demon from Sri Lanka (center), and the face of the Aztec god Xiuhtecuhtli (right).

the tent up which the shaman ascends to heaven. The Icelandic *Eddas* describe it as Yggdrasil, in Greece it is Olympus, and in India, Mount Meru. It is what was symbolized in the ziggurats of Sumer, Akkad, and Babylonia. Muhammad, in the Koran, calls such a centering point the *qibla,* the place to which to turn and bow in submission: Mecca for his own followers, Jerusalem for others, Benares, Rome, or (until 1959) the Potala, the residence of the Dalai Lama in the sacred city of Lhasa. In all religions and mythologies it is thus symbolically denoted. That is the ethnic inflection of the elementary idea, which in itself, however, is without location – as all sages know, but devotees and fanatics apparently do not. This unfortunate misunderstanding then throws them seriously off center, so that while imagining themselves to be grounded in the ultimate ground of all being, what they are actually grounded in is no more than the ground of their own symbolic system. One of the great dangers to be avoided in the interpretation of *all* symbolic systems is that of mistaking the symbol for its reference – which, curiously, seems to be a mistake more likely to be made by teachers and students of our own symbolic heritage than even by illiterate hunters.

For example, in that beautiful little book by John G. Neihardt, *Black Elk Speaks* (1961), the old Oglala Sioux medicine man, Black Elk, who at the time of this telling of his story was some eighty-odd years old, speaks of the vision he once had of himself, mounted on his horse, at the center of the world. "I was standing on the highest mountain of them all," he said, "and round about beneath me was the whole hoop of the world." The mountain that he was standing on was Harney Peak in the Black

Hills, he said. "But anywhere," he then added, "is the center of the world."

Here we have it, perfectly stated, from an old Indian veteran of Wounded Knee and of General Custer's Last Stand: a survivor into our own day of an era that dawned and made its first great statement some 30,000 years ago, in the art of the painted caves of

western Europe. In the present collection (page 59), we have a creation legend of his people. And from a twelfth-century Latin translation of a late Hellenistic hermetic scripture, *The Book of the Twenty-four Philosophers,* there comes a statement very much like his, which has been quoted, through the centuries, by a number of significant Western thinkers – Alan of Lille, Nicholas Cusanus, Rabelais, and Giordano Bruno, Pascal, and Voltaire – and which is a wonderfully apt epitomization of the mys-

tery that speaks to us everywhere through mythic vehicles: "God is an intelligible sphere, whose center is everywhere and circumference nowhere."

That is the ultimate elementary idea, and the function of all ethnic ideas is to link, as by a flexible tethering, all the acts, thoughts, and experiences of our daily lives – individual and social – to this realization. Mythology, that is to say, resides along the interface of timelessness and time, exactly between the nowhere-nowhen that ever was, and is, and shall be, and is to be recognized in all things, and on the other hand, the passing world of these things in which we all, for a brief time, reside.

Now it was in the period of the great painted caves – which are deep and dark, chilly, frightening, just the place for initiations – that those little naked female figurines were fashioned (see pages 184 and 185) that have become known as "Paleolithic Venuses," the famous statuettes of Willendorf, Menton, Lespugue, and many others, scattered eastward, as far as Siberian Lake Baikal, along the whole range of the Old Stone Age mammoth hunt. They were not made for use in the caves, the men's initiation temples, but have been found chiefly in dwelling sites. Without feet, they were made to be set up in little household shrines, for veneration in some sort of household cult. And whereas the male shamans that appear in the paintings on the walls of the caves, among the animals of the old hunting covenant, are clothed and costumed as in the practice of their art, conjuring forth the magnificent herds, or as initiators and mystagogues, the female statuettes are, with but one or two exceptions, nude, representing thus the power of the female, whose magic is of nature and the transform-

ing miracle of the womb and of the earth. The virtue of the male, on the other hand, is in his power of performance, whether as shamanizing miracle man or as hunter.

One of the most famous of the female figures – sculptured large in bas-relief on the wall of a rock shelter in Laussel, France – holds aloft, in her right hand, a bison horn. From about 23,000 B.C. or so, standing in silence thus before us, what is she saying? The answer, apparently, has been given from South Africa in the two tales related in this volume of the magical life-creating power of something called the *ngona* horn (pages 88 and 264). These tales were recorded by Leo Frobenius in the years 1928 to 1930, from the people of an area not far from the great stone temple site of Zimbabwe, the dating of which has been roughly placed, by various authorities, between the twelfth and seventeenth centu-

ries. Likewise from that area, and from some part of the same period, comes the magnificent rock painting, also discovered by Frobenius on that expedition and here reproduced on page 55, of a reclining, animal-masked male, holding high in his right hand an unidentified object that may well be a *ngona* horn. Frobenius himself, in a tentative way, has suggested that there may have been a connection between the figure here represented and the legend of Mwuetsi the moon man (page 89) – who, in turn, he would associate with that ancient Bronze Age custom of ritual regicide which Sir James G. Frazer has so amply documented in his volumes of *The Golden Bough*.

But again, we have here broken into an area of the deepest mystery. The same collector, on an earlier expedition made into North Africa, discovered there, engraved on a rock wall of the Sahara Atlas Mountains,

The eight maps on the next sixteen pages represent an approach to a geography of myth. The numerals in italic type refer the reader to the text pages where he will find narrated one or more myths from that particular part of the world.

The numerals printed in ordinary type and set in boxes relate to the pages on which illustrations from that part of the world appear, enabling the reader to form, in conjunction with the brief essays and captions, an overall picture of the mythologies of the world.

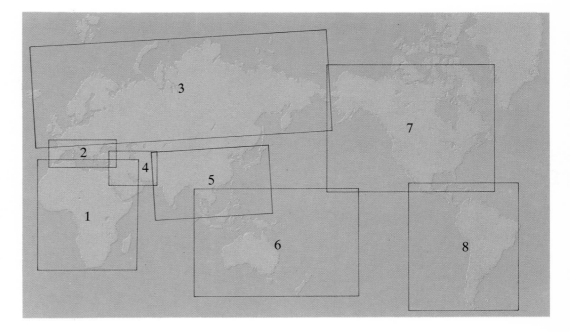

The illustrations accompanying the maps show the principal type of pictorial expression occurring among a particular people. They provide a concise but representative glimpse of the rich treasury of art to which mythic and religious forms of belief and worship have given rise.

AFRICA

In North Africa, from the Atlas massif to the Nile, the ram played an essential part in man's mythical representations. Shown above is the "sun ram" mentioned in the Kabyle myth on page 162.

The names appearing on the map indicate the approximate locations of tribes or myth-producing cultures represented in the graphics and myths included in this book.

The numbers refer to the pages on which illustrations .(boxed numbers) and myths (italic numbers) from these cultures appear.

The areas indicated by rust-colored shading are territories in which rock paintings are found. Those indicated by yellow are the main areas of stone, wood, and bronze sculpture.

Further south in the Atlas region, one finds an amazing number of drawings representing the frontal-faced lion.

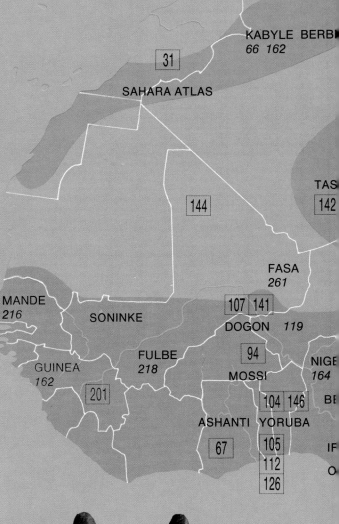

KABYLE BERB
66 162

31

SAHARA ATLAS

TAS

144   142

FASA
261

MANDE
216   107 141
SONINKE   DOGON 119

FULBE   94
218

GUINEA   NIGE
162   164
MOSSI

201   104 146
ASHANTI YORUBA   B

67   105   IF
112   O
126

Ritual baton; Yoruba.

Female figure used in
early birth rituals; centra
Congo.

Hunting scene (rock painting); Abrak (Nubian desert).

Female idol; Ashanti (Ghana).

Detail of a carved temple door; Yoruba.

Detail of a female statuette; West Sudan.

Ritual statuettes: Dogon *(right);* Congo *(above).*

Dance mask; Ogoni.

King's bronze portrait
Ife (South Nigeria).

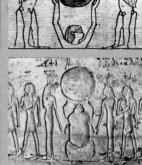

EGYPTIAN

15	16	19	25	63	65	90	92	93	94
96	97	101	111	112	116	120	123	125	127
129	136	137	141	145	156	157	160	163	166
173	175	178	203	204	205	239	261	276	279
281	286	290	297	300					

EGYPT
62 64 122 202 258 284

FEZZAN

LAKE CHAD

NUER *166*

SONINKE
188 248

!UPE
92

279

8

ABAR *192*

LAKE RUDOLF

36

LAKE VICTORIA

OLDUVAI

WAHUNGWE MAKONI
88 264 294

MADAGASCAR

ZIMBABWE

33	55	141

KALAHARI BUSHMEN
174

NATAL

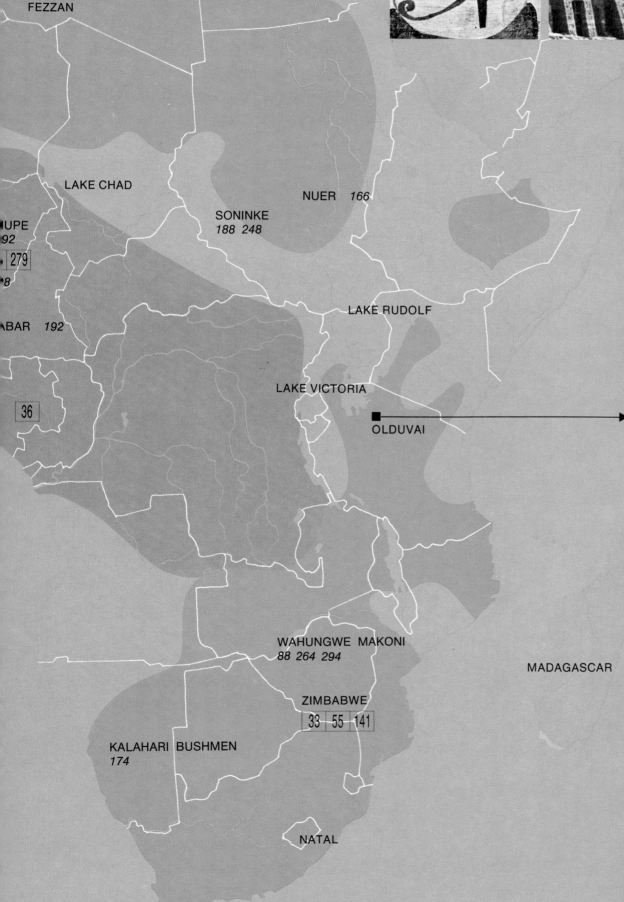

Top row: The weighing of souls, from an Egyptian funeral papyrus; the king god Osiris; the symbolic representation of sunrise and sunset.
Bottom row: The eye of Horus, symbolic of sacrifice; façade of the temple of Queen Nefertiti, at Abu Simbel; the scarab.

The iconography from Egypt reproduced in this book has inevitably grown to a rather large collection. This is because it reflects a high culture, such as is found in only a few places of the world, and certainly nowhere else in Africa.

Lake Rudolf and Olduvai Gorge: The earliest traces of man found to date have come from the Highlands of East Africa. This is about one thousand miles south of the lower Nile valley, where the most important Egyptian civilization grew and developed.

Mossi shamans; West Central Sudan.

Shaman rock painting from the Cinyati Cave in Natal, South Africa.

THE MEDITERRANEAN

The numbers refer to the pages for illustrations (boxed numbers) and myths (italic numbers) from the respective cultures.

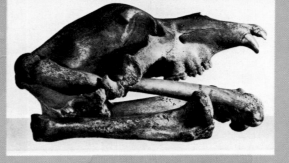

The earliest-known religion, practiced by Neanderthal man, was bear worship. One of the earliest pieces of evidence for this primitive cult *(above)*, was found in the Drachenloch, a cave in the Swiss Alps.

Neanderthal, a valley in Germany, gave its name to the primitive species of man first found there, *Homo neanderthalensis*. He was the first man to bury his dead and believe in a life after death.

■ NEANDERTH.

At Heidelberg the first remains were found of a human species that may have made the immense journey from southern Africa. The finds date from the Günz-Mindel Interglacial Age.

HEIDELBERG ■

WILDKIRCHLI ■
DRACHENLOCH

The earliest traces of Neanderthal man's bear cult were found in these two caves in the Alps of eastern Switzerland.

- Extent of Celtic settlement.
- The country of the Etruscans.
- Areas of Greek colonization.

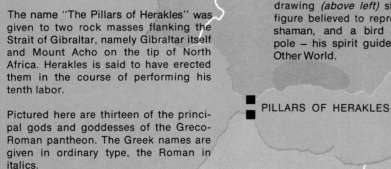

Dis Pater *(left)* is believed to be identical with the supreme god of the Celts in the period before the Roman conquest. After the conquest the Celts adopted Roman rites and the Roman pantheon.

LASCAUX ■
LAUSSEL ■

- The country of the Illyrians.
- Areas where Stone Age cave and rock paintings occur.
- Northern frontier of the Roman empire under Emperor Augustus.
- The wanderings of Odysseus.
- The voyage of the Argonauts.

The cave paintings of southwest France, the Pyrenees, Altamira, and southern Spain, which date back some thirty thousand years, represent more than man's earliest ventures in art. The caves in which they appear were cult sites of Cro-Magnon man, and among other elements the paintings contain clear indications of shamanism, which over the millennia seems to have spread from southwest Europe through the entire world. The Lascaux cave drawing *(above left)* shows a figure believed to represent a shaman, and a bird atop a pole – his spirit guide to the Other World.

MENTON ■

CELTS AND GAULS

131	153	161	165	180	237
244	253	254	270	274	

CAVES IN FRANCE	
	33
	133
	158
110	184
	185

ROMAN

15	25	58	76	95	98
111	122	123	127	128	129
135	136	137	138	143	147
152	153	154	158	159	160
161	173	175	182	183	186
187	188	190	191	193	198
199	201	202	205	208	209
216	218	219	229	236	237
238	240	241	244	249	264
277	278	279	282	295	297

Here Ody us' ships destroyed cannibals

The name "The Pillars of Herakles" was given to two rock masses flanking the Strait of Gibraltar, namely Gibraltar itself and Mount Acho on the tip of North Africa. Herakles is said to have erected them in the course of performing his tenth labor.

Pictured here are thirteen of the principal gods and goddesses of the Greco-Roman pantheon. The Greek names are given in ordinary type, the Roman in italics.

■
■ PILLARS OF HERAKLES

ZEUS ▶
JUPITER
Father of the gods
and supreme deity

HERA ▶▶
JUNO
Wife of Zeus/*Jupiter*

POSEIDON
NEPTUNE
God of the sea

PERSEPHONE
PROSERPINA
Goddess of
the underworld

HADES
PLUTO
Lord of
the underworld

ATHENE
MINERVA
Goddess of wisdom
and of war

ARES/MARS
God of war

DIONYSUS/*BACCHUS*

God of viticulture
and agriculture

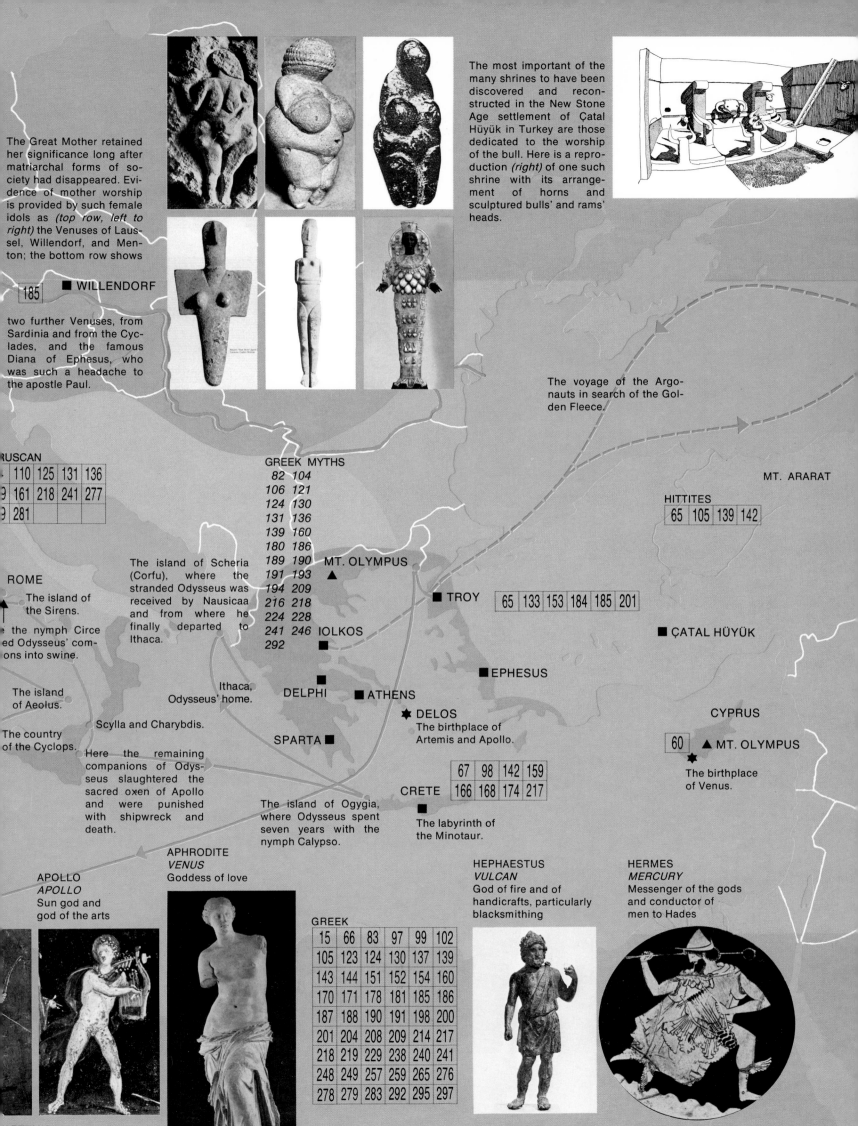

The Great Mother retained her significance long after matriarchal forms of society had disappeared. Evidence of mother worship is provided by such female idols as *(top row, left to right)* the Venuses of Laussel, Willendorf, and Menton; the bottom row shows

| 185 | ■ WILLENDORF |

two further Venuses, from Sardinia and from the Cyclades, and the famous Diana of Ephesus, who was such a headache to the apostle Paul.

The most important of the many shrines to have been discovered and reconstructed in the New Stone Age settlement of Çatal Hüyük in Turkey are those dedicated to the worship of the bull. Here is a reproduction *(right)* of one such shrine with its arrangement of horns and sculptured bulls' and rams' heads.

The voyage of the Argonauts in search of the Golden Fleece.

MT. ARARAT

HITTITES

| 65 | 105 | 139 | 142 |

...RUSCAN

	110	125	131	136
9	161	218	241	277
9	281			

GREEK MYTHS

82	104
106	121
124	130
131	136
139	160
180	186
189	190
191	193
194	209
216	218
224	228
241	246
292	

ROME

The island of the Sirens.

the nymph Circe ...ed Odysseus' com...ons into swine.

The island of Aeolus.

The country of the Cyclops.

The island of Scheria (Corfu), where the stranded Odysseus was received by Nausicaa and from where he finally departed to Ithaca.

MT. OLYMPUS ▲

■ TROY

| 65 | 133 | 153 | 184 | 185 | 201 |

■ ÇATAL HÜYÜK

IOLKOS ■

Ithaca, Odysseus' home.

■ EPHESUS

DELPHI ■   ■ ATHENS

★ DELOS
The birthplace of Artemis and Apollo.

CYPRUS

| 60 | ▲ MT. OLYMPUS

Scylla and Charybdis.

SPARTA ■

Here the remaining companions of Odysseus slaughtered the sacred oxen of Apollo and were punished with shipwreck and death.

| 67 | 98 | 142 | 159 |
| 166 | 168 | 174 | 217 |

CRETE
■

The labyrinth of the Minotaur.

The island of Ogygia, where Odysseus spent seven years with the nymph Calypso.

★ The birthplace of Venus.

APHRODITE
VENUS
Goddess of love

HEPHAESTUS
VULCAN
God of fire and of handicrafts, particularly blacksmithing

HERMES
MERCURY
Messenger of the gods and conductor of men to Hades

APOLLO
APOLLO
Sun god and god of the arts

GREEK

15	66	83	97	99	102
105	123	124	130	137	139
143	144	151	152	154	160
170	171	178	181	185	186
187	188	190	191	198	200
201	204	208	209	214	217
218	219	229	238	240	241
248	249	257	259	265	276
278	279	283	292	295	297

ARTEMIS
DIANA
Goddess of hunting

41

THE FAR NORTH

The numbers on the map refer to the page locations for illustrations (boxed numbers) and myths (italic numbers) from the respective cultures.

Megalith shrines occur all over the world, but perhaps the most famous is the circular arrangement at Stonehenge in southern England. This was not only a place of worship dedicated to the sky and sun god; it was also a source of precise information about the calendar and the stars.

A cultic bear figure from Resen Mose in Denmark. Archaeological finds have traced the spread of the bear cult from western Europe via Siberia to Japan and America.

CELTIC GODS: Esus, the Gallic god of war and vegetation *(above),* often appears in the form of a woodcutter.

The White Horse of Uffington in southern England dates from the Celtic period. Three hundred and seventy feet in length and carved out of the turf of a hillside, it can only be appreciated fully from the air. This suggests that it was created to appeal to a deity who lived in the sky.

Pictured on the right are four representations of the Nordic tree of life or world axis. The idea that the world turned on an axis occurred to man very early on and had a profound effect on his religious thought, particularly in the North. Whereas in the Mediterranean region the tree tends to represent simply the tree of life, in the North it has the double significance of an axis and a path to the world above, a path used by the shaman to reach the realm of the gods and spirits.

ICELAND *171*

77	104

ISLAND CELTS

IRISH
106

101	154	201
233	239	250

WELSH
233

14	97	135	152
189	254	255	264

CELTIC
186

131	153	161	165
180	237	244	253
254	270	274	

NORSE
80 84 124 221 230 294

97	102	108/109	111
126	133	147	154	159
160	171	200	201	224
225	230	231	233	247
251	261	269		

LAPPS

111	133	202

CONTINENTAL CELTS

81	160	170
172	233	

GERMANIC
225 228 233

135	153	163	165	204
245	247	264	288	

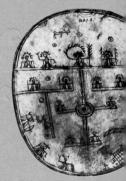

Above:
A typical form of Germanic and Nordic pictorial expression was the carved menhir. This picture stone from Gotland shows scenes from the warlike life of the Nordic gods and heroes. To the Nordic warrior death in battle was the highest honor, guaranteeing entry into Valhalla *(top).* The scene below illustrates the Nordic custom of putting the bodies of the fallen in a boat to sail toward the setting sun.

LAKE ONEGA

133

TATARS
262

RUSSIA

111	152	160

OSTYAKS SAMOYED
128

One of the earliest Celtic representations of a deity is this two-faced, horned figure from Holzgerlingen in southern Germany, believed to be a moon goddess.

BESSARABIA
296

TURKO-TATAR
100

The attributes of the Gallic Mercury *(above left)* show the merging of Roman and Celtic influences. Epona *(above right)*, was the Celtic goddess of horses.

NORDIC GODS *(left to right):* Odin, supreme deity and lord of Asgard, the Nordic heaven; Thor, god of war and thunder; Freyr, god of fertility; and Odin's brother Loki, a schemer and sower of discord.

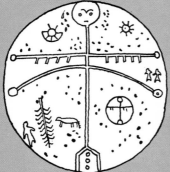

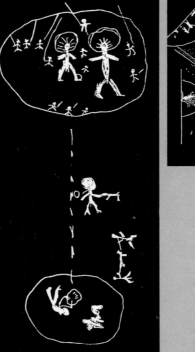

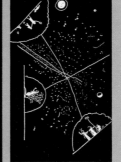

Left, from left to right: The world ash Yggdrasil of Germanic myth is both tree of life and world axis (page 108). The next drawing shows the world tree/axis rising through the world of men and animals to the vault of heaven and the realm of the Great Spirit. In the Koryak drawing the world axis (the dotted line) is the path by which the shaman travels to visit the great gods. Finally, a Chukchi drawing shows four heavenly directions and three worlds.

As the human race spread over the globe in a gradual, lengthy process starting in western Europe between forty and thirty thousand years ago, its forms of worship also spread. The white line represents a much-simplified version of the route along which this process carried the bear cult of Neanderthal man and the shamanism of Cro-Magnon man across northern Europe and Asia. It was toward the end of the last Ice Age that men crossed the strip of land joining Siberia and Alaska to bring these cults and forms of belief to the American continent.

A drum from Lapland *(above left)* shows the three cosmic zones of underworld, earth, and heaven. Above is a Finno-Ugric drawing of a shaman, and the white drawing *(right)* is an "x-ray" of a Yakut shaman from northern Siberia. Such schematic views reflect the widespread belief that the shaman's soul is located in his skeleton. (Note the remarkable similarity between the drawing above and the photograph below.)

Both shamanism and magic achieved great importance in the North. Possibly the most important of the shaman's cult objects — by means of which he made contact with the gods and spirits — was his drum, and the drawings found on shaman drums provide us with valuable information about these people.

CHUKCHI
133

YAKUTS
100 122 124

KORYAK
112

133

SIBERIA *106*

111 113 133 287 293

Shamanism is still a living religion in certain parts of the world. The photograph here shows a shaman of the Siberian Karagasy standing in front of his tent.

SAKHALIN GILYAK
122

ALTAI *94*

BURYATS *122 159 202*

THE MIDDLE EAST

The white lines trace the movements of the different peoples who occupied the Mesopotamian region and there developed their civilizations.

Abraham's route from Ur to the Promised Land.

The path taken by the Children of Israel through the desert.

The area in which ziggurats occur.

Area of Sumerian cultivation

This relief fragment *(left)* from Huttusa in Turkey shows a Hittite god of war.

The Garden of Eden was said to be watered by four rivers (Gen. 2: 10–14). Two are the Euphrates and the Tigris (called Hiddekel in Genesis); of the other two it has been suggested that "Pishon" represents the Nile and "Gihon" the Persian Gulf.

The numbers on the map refer to the page locations for illustrations (boxed numbers) and myths (italic numbers) from the respective cultures.

HITTITES

■ HARAN

■ NINEVEH

■ ALEPPO

■ UGARIT

ASSUR ■

| 95 | 96 | 105 | 111 | 25 |

MESOPOTAMIAN
65 158 246

PHOENICIAN *62*

| 24 | 128 | 204 | 217 | 239 |

BABYL

| 19 | 96 | 122 | 216 | 236 | 250 | 251 |

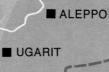

HEBREWS
116 122

JERICHO

| 200 |

■ JERUSALEM

BETHLEHEM
BIRTHPLACE OF CHRIST

■ RAMESES

The Middle East was the birthplace of three of the great bringers of religion *(left to right):* Jesus Christ was born in Bethlehem, the prophet Zarathustra (or Zoroaster) in what is now Iran, and Muhammad in Mecca.

The red line *(right)* traces the Children of Israel's route from Egypt to Canaan, a journey marked by various manifestations of the power of Israel's God. The first was the miraculous "division" of the waters of the Red Sea to let the Israelites across

Marah, where the bitter water was miraculously made sweet.

Here God fed the Children of Israel with quails and manna.

Mount Sinai or Horeb, where God gave Israel the Ten Commandments *(below).*

SEMITES

and the subsequent destruction of the Egyptian army in the returning flood *(above).*

Lilithu *(above left)* of Babylon and Sumer was a demonic goddess; the Babylonian sun god Nergal *(above right)* was also judge of the dead and king of the underworld.

Mecca, birthplace of the prophet Muhammad, became the holy city of Islam. Every Muslim tries to make the pilgrimage to Mecca at least once in his life to walk round the Kaaba, the sacred shrine and center of the Islamic universe.

The earliest of the three great bringers of religion to this area was the prophet Zarathustra (ca. 628–551 B.C.) or Zoroaster as the Greeks came to call him. The supreme deity in Zarathustra's teaching is the androgynous Zervan (right). From the body of Zervan sprang the twins Ahura Mazda (good) and Ariman (evil).

■ The possible birthplace of Zarathustra.

This clay Great Mother figure (below) from ancient Persia stresses the fertility aspect.

ARMENIAN
'96

Shanidar in Iraq is the site of the earliest-known burials. Dating from the period of Neanderthal man, the grave objects found there indicate that belief in a life after death was already current at that time.

ARYANS

■ SHANIDAR

MITANNI
MEDES
MEDES

The ziggurats, terraced temple towers, were erected in honor of the sky and sun god and to demonstrate the might of the Assyro-Babylonian city-states. The Tower of Babel (below left) was a ziggurat.

PERSIANS

67	99	107	152	160
197	199	237	250	251
264	265	268	291	

NIPPUR

SUMER 246

| 101 | 135 |

■ SUSA

PERSEPOLIS ■

RUK ■ LARSA

■ UR

ERIDU 81

142 181 197 200

SEMITES

Anahita (below), one of the "honorable servants" of Ahura Mazda, was the goddess of water, fertility, and procreation. She was widely worshiped in the Achaemenid empire. The Sassanids, like their

predecessors the Achaemenids, also derived their kingly status from God. The stone relief (above right) shows the first king of the Sassanid dynasty receiving the royal diadem from Ahura Mazda, whose horse is in the act of trampling the evil spirit Ariman.

This Assyrian winged figure (below) was a benevolent spirit.

This ancient-Persian terracotta figurine of a sacrificial bull dates from the third millennium B.C.

A clay statue of the Great Mother and fertility goddess Ishtar (below), who was deeply revered by most of the peoples of the Middle East. The stone relief (below right) shows a Babylonian priest walking toward the altar.

The large illustration (left) shows Baal (meaning "lord"), the supreme deity of the ancient-Semitic peoples. As the embodiment of procreative power he was the god of fertility, thunder and rain.

An old seal impression (above) shows the Assyrian supreme deity Ashur in the form of the winged sun disk. Below the sun disk a kneeling female figure is attended by two winged gods.

The Babylonian version of the Flood is told in the Gilgamesh Epic on stone tablets in Akkadian cuneiform (left).

45

THE FAR EAST

The numbers on the map refer to the page locations for illustrations (boxed numbers) and myths (italic numbers) from the respective cultures.

The myths, religions, and major civilizations of southern Asia and the Far East have given rise to many great symbols. Some of the more important are pictured here. As well as being typical of a particular area, these symbols often made major migrations along the great trade routes, thereby spreading whole cultures and different ways of thinking.

The image of the four-headed Buddha is a key symbol of the Hindu religion. It spread from Elephanta in India all the way to Thailand and Cambodia, as this sculpture from Battambang shows (left).

Lamaism, the type of Buddhism practiced in Tibet, produced magnificent cosmographic mandalas, such as the one below.

BAMIAN
The largest Buddhist shrine in Afghanistan, with a Buddha statue 175 feet high. ■

TIBET
108 126

TIBET

12	17	23
56	80	102
104	106	107
122	123	161
202	210	212
257	274	275
287	291	301

INDIA
62 84 104 108 122 125
139 166 179 195 196 207
234 242 243 286

MT. KAILASA
The mythic dwelling of Shiva. Also called Mt. Meru. ▲

MOHENJO-DARO ■
Cult site of Mother Goddess and bull worship.

NEPAL

25	79	137
170	212	257

LHASA ■
The holy city of Lamaism.

MATHURA ■
The center of Krishna worship.

MT. ABU ▲
Sacred world center of the Jain religion.

LUMBINI ■
Birthplace of the Buddha.

KATMANDU ■
Site of the Bodhnath *stupa*, a Buddhist world center.

KUSINAGARA
The Buddha's Nirvana. ■

BODH-GAYA ■
Here the Buddha achieved Enlightenment.

BENGAL

200	225

ELEPHANTA ■
Shrine of Shiva Trimurti, the three-faced creator god.

The miraculous births (above) of Shiva (left) and the Buddha (right) were both accompanied by supernatural manifestations. Shiva and the Buddha are deities of the two great religions of India.

The starting-point of many Indian creation myths: Vishnu as creator of the world on the back of the cosmic serpent (right).

Shiva Nataraja (below) symbolizes the cosmic dance of creation and the overcoming of the demonic forces of destruction.

1/2	19	20	24	25	30	34	61
67	81	95	96	97	99	116	125
137	139	152	159	160	165	174	176
177	189	194	197	199	202	203	205
206	207	212	213	216	217	233	235
237	239	242	243	247	266	277	298

Originating in India, the architectural form of the *stupa* eventually spread throughout southern Asia. *Stupas* represent the sacred world center or world mountain of Buddhist teaching. These two examples are the Brihadisvara temple at Tanjore, South India (below left), and a tower of the Bayon temple at Angkor Thom, Cambodia (below).

MADURAI ■
Shiva shrine.

| 36 |

ANURADHAPURA ■
Buddhist world center.

The young god Krishna (left) conquered the serpent demon Kaliya. This cult spread throughout the Indian subcontinent.

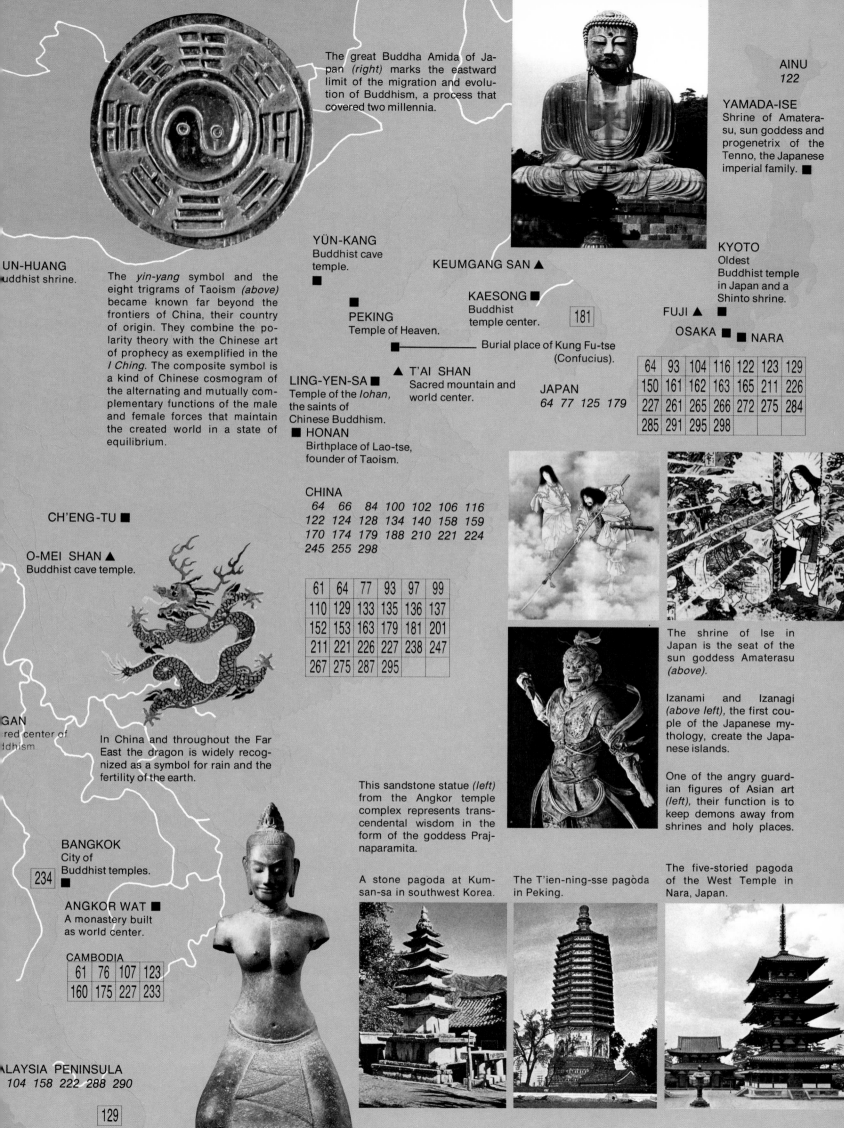

The *yin-yang* symbol and the eight trigrams of Taoism *(above)* became known far beyond the frontiers of China, their country of origin. They combine the polarity theory with the Chinese art of prophecy as exemplified in the *I Ching*. The composite symbol is a kind of Chinese cosmogram of the alternating and mutually complementary functions of the male and female forces that maintain the created world in a state of equilibrium.

The great Buddha Amida of Japan *(right)* marks the eastward limit of the migration and evolution of Buddhism, a process that covered two millennia.

AINU
122

YAMADA-ISE
Shrine of Amaterasu, sun goddess and progenetrix of the Tenno, the Japanese imperial family. ■

UN-HUANG
uddhist shrine.

YÜN-KANG
Buddhist cave temple.
■

KEUMGANG SAN ▲

PEKING
Temple of Heaven.

KAESONG ■
Buddhist temple center.

181

Burial place of Kung Fu-tse (Confucius).

▲ T'AI SHAN
Sacred mountain and world center.

JAPAN
64 77 125 179

KYOTO
Oldest Buddhist temple in Japan and a Shinto shrine.

FUJI ▲ ■

OSAKA ■ ■ NARA

64	93	104	116	122	123	129
150	161	162	163	165	211	226
227	261	265	266	272	275	284
285	291	295	298			

LING-YEN-SA ■
Temple of the *lohan*, the saints of Chinese Buddhism.
■ HONAN
Birthplace of Lao-tse, founder of Taoism.

CHINA
64 66 84 100 102 106 116
122 124 128 134 140 158 159
170 174 179 188 210 221 224
245 255 298

61	64	77	93	97	99
110	129	133	135	136	137
152	153	163	179	181	201
211	221	226	227	238	247
267	275	287	295		

CH'ENG-TU ■

O-MEI SHAN ▲
Buddhist cave temple.

In China and throughout the Far East the dragon is widely recognized as a symbol for rain and the fertility of the earth.

GAN
red center of
dhism

The shrine of Ise in Japan is the seat of the sun goddess Amaterasu *(above)*.

Izanami and Izanagi *(above left)*, the first couple of the Japanese mythology, create the Japanese islands.

One of the angry guardian figures of Asian art *(left)*, their function is to keep demons away from shrines and holy places.

This sandstone statue *(left)* from the Angkor temple complex represents transcendental wisdom in the form of the goddess Prajnaparamita.

BANGKOK
City of Buddhist temples.

234 ■

ANGKOR WAT ■
A monastery built as world center.

CAMBODIA
61	76	107	123
160	175	227	233

ALAYSIA PENINSULA
104 158 222 288 290

129

A stone pagoda at Kumsan-sa in southwest Korea.

The T'ien-ning-sse pagoda in Peking.

The five-storied pagoda of the West Temple in Nara, Japan.

OCEANIA

Among the islands of the South Pacific, in the part of the world known as Oceania, mythic ideas and practices are still very much a part of everyday life. The medicine man, for example, is both healer of men and the interme-

CHINA

The numbers on the map refer to the page locations for illustrations (boxed numbers) and myths (italic numbers) from the respective cultures.

Many mythologies tell of a voyage to a land of the dead lying in the west. Egyptians, Greeks, and Teutons all knew of a ship that plied between the two worlds. The two "ships of the dead" above are from Sumatra *(left)* and western New Guinea *(right).*

PHILIPPINES
134 284

CAROLINES

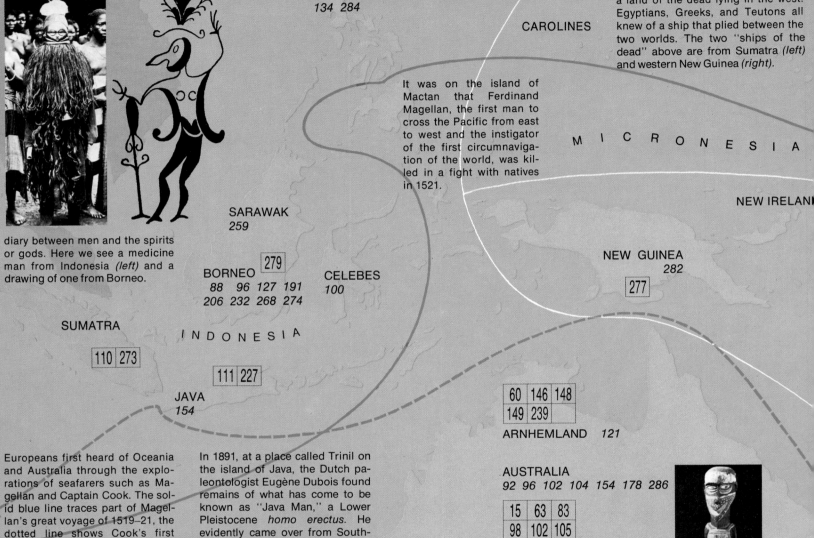

diary between men and the spirits or gods. Here we see a medicine man from Indonesia *(left)* and a drawing of one from Borneo.

It was on the island of Mactan that Ferdinand Magellan, the first man to cross the Pacific from east to west and the instigator of the first circumnavigation of the world, was killed in a fight with natives in 1521.

M I C R O N E S I A

NEW IRELAND

SARAWAK
259

BORNEO $\boxed{279}$
88 96 127 191
206 232 268 274

CELEBES
100

NEW GUINEA
282
$\boxed{277}$

SUMATRA

I N D O N E S I A

$\boxed{110}$ $\boxed{273}$

$\boxed{111}$ $\boxed{227}$

JAVA
154

| 60 | 146 | 148 |
| 149 | 239 | |

ARNHEMLAND *121*

Europeans first heard of Oceania and Australia through the explorations of seafarers such as Magellan and Captain Cook. The solid blue line traces part of Magellan's great voyage of 1519–21, the dotted line shows Cook's first voyage of 1768–71. In a total of four voyages Cook explored the entire Pacific Ocean, from the Arctic to the Antarctic.

In 1891, at a place called Trinil on the island of Java, the Dutch paleontologist Eugène Dubois found remains of what has come to be known as "Java Man," a Lower Pleistocene *homo erectus.* He evidently came over from Southeast Asia when Java, Sumatra, and Borneo were still connected with what is now the mainland.

AUSTRALIA
92 96 102 104 154 178 286

15	63	83
98	102	105
202	277	

Certain aboriginal tribes worship Banaitja as their creator god.

KIMBERLEY
$\boxed{85}$

The aboriginal population of Australia developed an unmistakable style of its own in the conception and expression of mythic material. On the left we see *(from left to right)* the kangaroo woman who makes the rain; the creation story of the two primal sisters who bore the human race; a group of *mimis,* the spirit folk who hide in clefts in the rock; two aborigines performing a ritual dance; and Timara, the spectral fisherman whom no one has ever set eyes on.

HAWAII
106 164 252

| 60 | 125 |

Ku, the Hawaiian creator and protector of the world, is also the god of war.

The five mythic figures pictured above are *(from left to right)* Nomoi, the benevolent spirit of Micronesia who has the power to ward off the typhoon; a rainmaker from New Caledonia; a fetish with a terrifying face that the inhabitants of New Ireland use to drive off evil spirits; an idol from Nukuoro in the central Carolines; and lastly Maui, the great Polynesian god, folk hero, and teacher of mankind.

GILBERTS

POLYNESIA
89 98 144 146 148 250 268 276

| 84 |

| 107 |

OLOMON ISLANDS

M E L A N E S I A

P O L Y N E S I A

| 26 |

NEW HEBRIDES
162 262

SAMOA
164

FIJI

SOUTH PACIFIC ISLANDS
91 136 138 172 184

The Polynesians believe that man, the animals and all living things were created by the sea god Tangaroa.

Belan is a Melanesian deity. His function is to cleanse sick souls.

COOK ISLANDS

| 10/11 | 63 | 107 |

EASTER ISLAND

We can still only guess at the significance of the gigantic sculptures of volcanic stone that stand on Easter Island.

New Zealand's Maoris worship Tiki as the first god and creator of mankind.

NEW ZEALAND

MAORI
138 192 232 236 292

| 60 | 102 | 107 |
| 145 | 147 | |

49

NORTH AMERICA

SIBERIA

The white line indicates the general path of earliest human migration from Siberia across the Bering Strait and the dispersion into the Americas.

The Tlingit shaman's charm in the shape of a spirit canoe *(above)* and the Hopi *kachina* bear *(above right)* indicate a possible carry-over from northern Asia of two early forms of religion: shamanism and the bear cult. But whatever form the mythologies took, the common denominator was animals; as creators, totems (clan or ancestral symbols), tricksters, and deities.

ALASKA
21

33

TLINGIT   *136 158*

The Great Hare (Manibozho) of the Algonquins was sun god and trickster.

The Thunderbird *(above left* and *above)* was the supreme deity of the Eskimos and other Indians of the Northwest.

NORTH WEST COAST
105
165

BLACKFOOT *138*

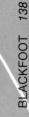

Spider Grandmother, Earth Mother for the Hopi Indians of the Southwest, helped them discover the link between earth and heaven.

The colorful and dramatic art of carving totem poles was practiced along the Pacific coast from northern Alaska to southern Canada. The poles were erected to honor a family's noble animal ancestors.

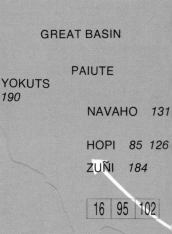

PLATEAU

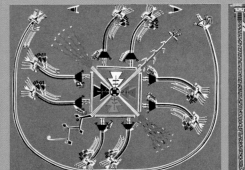

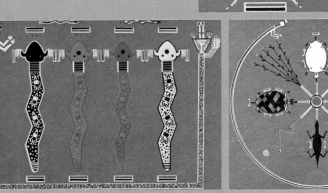

GREAT BASIN

PAIUTE

YOKUTS
190

NAVAHO   *131*

HOPI   *85 126*

ZUÑI   *184*

16 95 102

Navaho Indians conducted elaborate myth-telling ceremonies. Sand paintings (five examples are shown here) were created during a ceremony to illustrate the essential characters or subjects of the myths, which were told through chant or dance.

GREENLAND

The numbers on the map refer to the page locations for illustrations (boxed numbers) and myths (italic numbers) from the respective cultures.

ARCTIC

For the Eskimos of North America, the sea was an essential source of life-support. Fish, seals, and whales provided not only food but clothing, building materials, tools, and fuel. No wonder, then, that they ascribed spiritual power to the creatures of the sea, as in this fish with a woman's head.

ESKIMO *172*

| 107 | 144 | 146 |

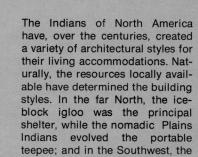

The Indians of North America have, over the centuries, created a variety of architectural styles for their living accommodations. Naturally, the resources locally available have determined the building styles. In the far North, the ice-block igloo was the principal shelter, while the nomadic Plains Indians evolved the portable teepee; and in the Southwest, the

SUBARCTIC

CANADA

| 34 | 63 | 133 |

ALGONQUIN *108*

HURON *60 286*

adobe honeycomb village replaced the ancient fortresses carved in the canyon walls *(above)*.

GLALA (SIOUX)

| 35 | 97 |

OJIBWA

IROQUOIS

OMAHA *59*

EASTERN WOODLAND

PLAINS

KENTUCKY

| 82 | 101 | 102 |
| 141 | 142 | |

| 247 |

| 63 |

The Plains Indians imbued nature with spirit power and called upon those spirits for health, protection, success, and knowledge. They called their spirits *kachinas* and personified them in drawings and doll-like objects. Below are depictions of two bee *kachinas* and Tawa, the Sun Spirit.

The sun dance was a religious rite performed by many Plains Indian tribes. A mass tribal ceremony, it involved self-torture, chants, and dances.

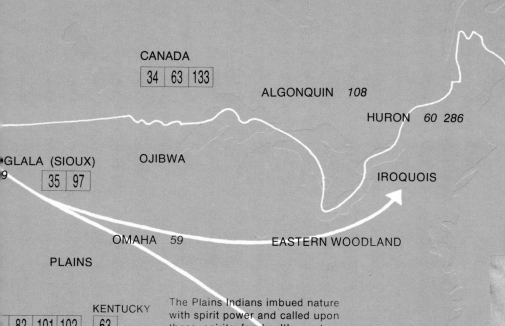

CUBA

MEXICO

51

MEXICO, CENTRAL AND SOUTH AMERICA

The numbers on the map refer to the page locations for illustrations (boxed numbers) and myths (italic numbers) from the respective cultures.

The white line, which can be traced on the preceding map as far as the Bering Strait and on the map on page 42 (The Far North) to western Europe, shows one of the paths along which the human race spread over the surface of the earth. Men reached northern Mexico about twenty thousand years ago.

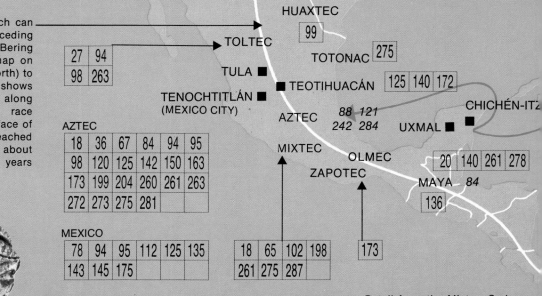

HUAXTEC
| 99 |

TOLTEC

TOTONAC | 275 |

| 27 | 94 |
| 98 | 263 |

TULA ■

■ TEOTIHUACÁN | 125 | 140 | 172 |

TENOCHTITLÁN ■
(MEXICO CITY)

CHICHÉN-ITZ

AZTEC   *88 121*
         242 284   UXMAL ■ ■

MIXTEC

OLMEC
ZAPOTEC

MAYA *84*

| 20 | 140 | 261 | 278 |

| 136 |

AZTEC

18	36	67	84	94	95
98	120	125	142	150	163
173	199	204	260	261	263
272	273	275	281		

MEXICO

| 78 | 94 | 95 | 112 | 125 | 135 |
| 143 | 145 | 175 | | | |

| 18 | 65 | 102 | 198 |
| 261 | 275 | 287 | |

| 173 |

Gigantic Olmec stone head.

Ancient-Olmec clay figurine *(above)*. Aztec goddess of war *(right)*.

Quetzalcoatl, the Aztec plumed serpent *(below)*.

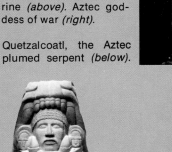

Detail from the Mixtec *Codex Laud (left)* showing a sacrifice to the sun god.

The earliest traces of pottery or of works of art yet discovered in the Americas were found in Ecuador (indicated by this arrow). The pieces of pottery and figurines date from ca. 3000 B.C. and have characteristics resembling those on similar objects produced during the same period in Southeast Asia and Japan. Such indications have caused a good deal of speculation regarding trans-Pacific migration even at this early date.

Mayan version of the feathered serpent, Quetzalcoatl.

Coyote, divine dog of the Aztecs.

Pre-Columbian Central America was the seat of four major civilizations rich in culture. The earliest, lasting from about 1700 B.C. to A.D. 400, was that of the Olmecs. The Maya civilization ran from the beginning of our era until the Spanish conquest at the end of the fifteenth century. The Toltecs flourished from about 900 to 1200, and the Aztecs from about 1300 until they were conquered by the Spanish in the sixteenth century. Pictured on these two pages are some of the typical forms of mythic iconography created by these civilizations.

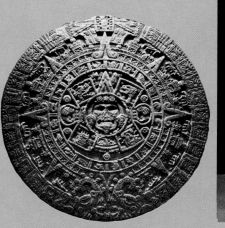

Great pyramid of the sun in Teotihuacán.

Toltec column *(right)* from atop the pyramid of Tula.

Aztec calendar stone from 1502 *(above)* found in Tenochtitlán.

Mayan pyramid of Huracan in Chichén Itzá.

SAN SALVADOR Columbus, 1492; first landing by Europeans in the Americas.

Cortez, 1519; route of the conquest of Mexico.

BA

The conquest of the Americas by Europeans destroyed the religions, mythologies, and native cultures that had developed over the centuries. Columbus (left) was first to make the journey to the west and was followed by Cortez, conqueror of Mexico, and Pizarro, victor over the Incas.

zarro invasion routes, 24–1527.

JIVARO 121

OASTAL INDIANS
8

| 63 | 120 | 122 |

PERU | 165 | 272 |

BRAZIL INDIANS
92 282 284

INCA 298

CHE ■ | 154 |

Machu Picchu, an Inca mountain fortress, (below), was a center for sun worship.

CHACAMAC ■   ■ MACHU PICCHU
CUZCO ■

■ TIAHUANACO

The Inca civilization of South America achieved its greatest extension of conquest and rule in the relatively short period of thirty years from 1463 to 1493. Its capital was Cuzco, but it ranged for 2500 miles along the west coast and into the high Andes. Roads of stone, traced on the map, tied the empire together and indicate a high level of cultural development. The gate below shows typical Inca construction methods using interlocking stone blocks. Worship of the sun was common to most cultures of this area, and the king, who was sun god, was all-powerful.

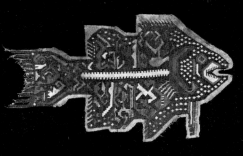

The white line tracing the spread of the human race ends here. The first tribes appeared in this area around 6500 B.C.

Prior to the Inca conquest, there existed numerous independent cultures, such as the Mochicas represented by the pottery corn goddess (top). The two embroidered figures above come from the Pachacamac (left) and Tiahuanaco cultures.

the representation of two gigantic animal-masked hunters hauling off a slain rhinoceros, and one of these is holding aloft what appears to be a bison horn. The date of this engraving would be about halfway between the Venus of Laussel and the rock painting from Rhodesia, say about 10,000 B.C. A postglacial period of abundant rain had by then turned the whole Sahara into a grazing plain, where herds of antelopes and gazelles, giraffes, elephants, and rhinos ranged. The rock paintings of Tassili have left us a record of that period to about 2500 B.C., when desert conditions returned and the hunting tribes moved south. It is thought by some that the Bushmen of the Kalahari Desert may be late survivors of that movement. They once were a dominant people over a large part of southern Africa, where their characteristic rock paintings attest to the extent of their domain before black Bantu tribes, around A.D. 500, began spreading southward from the Congo basin.

Can it be that such a motif as the cornucopia, the horn of plenty of classical mythology, is to be recognized prefigured in the uplifted hand of the Venus of Laussel? And would this then be the same horn, ten thousand or so years later, in the hand of the giant masked hunter of the Sahara? Surely no gem in the bazaars of Istanbul or Old Delhi could carry a more interesting legend in its background than that of this wondrous horn, which again appears, apparently, in the legend of Mwuetsi the moon man. For the horns of the newborn crescent moon are in no end of mythologies interpreted as symbolic of the ever recurrent renewal of life. There is even a Blackfoot Indian legend of the woman who married a buffalo, through whose power to restore the dead to life the covenant was established of the willing offering of the animals to the people's arrows; and she appears in one critical episode of this legend with a buffalo horn in her hand (Joseph Campbell, *The Masks of God*, 1959). In Greek mythology the cornucopia is a vessel of the nourishing nymphs fostering the motherless infant Dionysus. It is a possession, also, of Pluto, lord of the treasures of the earth. And if the recumbent figure in the great Rhodesian pietà is indeed, as Frobenius suspects, the ritually sacrificed moon man, then surely the horn held high in his hand is that of the legend. Admittedly we do not know how far we can let our imagination go in the reconstruction of this history, but where everything points so consistently to a theme of death and renewal in association with a horn held aloft, it does seem possible, even probable, that we have here another elementary idea

that has held its own for infinite years. A problem of the greatest interest, both to anthropologists and to archaeologists and historians, is of the origins in space and time of the arts of plant and animal domestication. Three primary centers are now recognized, but the question is still being argued as to the possibility of shared influences versus strictly independent origins. The critical matrices are (1) *the Near East*, from about 9000 B.C., when sickles of flint begin to appear among late hunting-culture remains, together with evidences, here and there, of the domestication of goats, also possibly of swine, sheep, and, a little later, cattle; (2) *the fertile riverlands of Southeast Asia*, Burma, Thailand, Cambodia and South Vietnam, where a number of plants reproduced from clones and cuttings – taro and yams, bananas, turmeric, and the sago palm, for example; coconuts, bamboo, and bottle gourds – were cultivated, some as early as 12,000 B.C. at the latest; the basic animals here were the dog, the pig, and barnyard fowl; and then, finally, the youngest center, (3) *Middle and South America*, from the south of Mexico to Peru, where maize, manioc, various beans, tomatoes, squash, and potatoes, sweet potatoes, avocados, rubber, tobacco, and some sixty other plant domesticates were cultivated; the animals here were turkeys, the guinea pig, llamas, alpacas, again the dog, and (according to some authorities) chickens; the dating, as already remarked, was late: 3000 B.C. or so, plus or minus three or four centuries.

Now although the Southeast Asian center has not yet been sufficiently investigated, recent archaeological researches in northern Thailand have made it all but certain that this area is by a considerable margin the earliest of the primary three. Moreover, there is a type of cord-marked ceramic ware, characteristic of this area, for which we have datings from Japan as early as 10,000 B.C., which is a good four thousand years earlier than anything for ceramic wares of any kind in the Near East. An astonishing deposit of sherds of this Japanese cord-marked ware, together with a sampling of ceramic female figurines, was unearthed on the coast of Ecuador by a team of archaeologists in December 1960, the confirmed date of the material found being about 3000 B.C., which is the earliest both for pottery and for figurines in the New World. Add to this the fact that the inventory of Middle American animal and plant domesticates shares with that of Southeast Asia – besides the dog and (possibly) chickens – cotton, the true gourd, coconuts, plantains, amaranth, jackbeans,

and the sweet potato (which is called "cumara" both in Peru and in Oceania). The appearance of the Hainuwele motif in the Peruvian Pachacamac legend, as well as in the Algonquin of the origin of maize, should perhaps be taken as additional evidence for a significant influence from the oldest primary center to the youngest, across the Pacific Ocean. However, the whole question is still in debate.

Characteristic of both areas, and distinguishing them from the Near Eastern, is the lack of signs of any substantial town or city growth during their early stages. The plant and animal domesticates and the pottery as well, were merely contributory to what long continued to be an essentially hunting and fishing, seminomadic order of life; whereas in the nuclear Near East, and in nearby southeastern Europe, there were already in existence by 7000 B.C. a number of established villages and towns – among others, Çatal Hüyük in southern Turkey and Jericho in Palestine. Moreover, it was in this part of the world that the earliest cities and city-states appeared in the Tigris-Euphrates and Nile valleys, toward the close of the fourth millenium B.C. The presence of the dog and of domesticated swine suggests early Southeast Asian influences, as do certain features of the mythologies; but the development as a whole was unique and marked the beginning of what is generally thought of today as world history.

The mythic tales of Sumer and of Egypt represent, in this collection, the lore of this epochal moment. They have been selected from the earliest recorded mythologies known, for the art of writing had just then been invented, as had mathematical numeration, both decimal and sexagesimal. Exact astronomical observation had opened a new vista into the wonder of the universe with the realization that the seven visible spheres – Sun, Moon, Mercury, Venus, Mars, Jupiter, and Saturn – move in mathematically ordered courses through the fields of the fixed constellations. The idea of an ever-cycling cosmic order thereupon became the controlling idea of all religious thought; monumental temples arose in recognition of the mystery; and whereas formerly animal and plant mythologies had sufficed to inspire the lives and works of nonliterate hunters and villagers, the whole focus now was on the great wonder of the seven revolving spheres; priestly kings and their courts imitated in hieratic

The famous moon king and his people, a Rhodesian cave painting discussed on page 37.

rites their motions; elaborate festival calendars linked the whole life of the city to the mystic round; and the final government of each little city-state was founded in the worship of its chosen celestial god.

This new order of human thought and life can be recognized as having arrived in Crete about 2300 B.C.; India, in the Indus Valley, a century or two later; China, with the Shang dynasty, about 1500 B.C.; and across the Pacific, in southern Mexico, with the abrupt appearance there of monumental ceremonial centers, about 1100 B.C. The last three of these new high-culture matrices – those of India, China, and Mexico – remained, as a glance at any map will show, comparatively isolated, hence conservative. Their mythologies carry intact into the modern period, consequently, mythic and ritual forms from the period of their establishment. The early centers, on the other hand, of the Near East and of Europe, were vulnerable to massive attacks from both north and south: Indo-European cattle herders from the north, who in the course of the fourth millennium B.C. had not only mastered the horse but also learned to make weapons of bronze; while from the Syro-Arabian desert in the south, successive waves of Semitic, sheep-herding Bedouins finally made nearly all of the Near East their own. The principal Semitic peoples represented in our text are the Akkadians of about 2350–2150 B.C.; the Babylonians, about 1728–1530 B.C.; the Assyrians of about 1500–606 B.C.; the Phoenicians, about 1200–146 B.C.; and the Hebrews. The Indo-Europeans are represented in the Greek and Roman selections, the Norse, Irish, and Welsh, and, in India, the Rig Vedic and Aitareya Brahmanic pieces. The other Indian materials, from the *Mahabharata,* Markandeya Purana, Brihadaranyaka Upanishad, and Buddhist *Jatakas,* or "Birth Tales of the Buddha," are from very much later periods, when the impact of the early Indo-European invasions of about 1250 B.C. had lost its force, and the gods and magic of the chariot fighters and their magician-priests had been absorbed and assimilated into the older Indus valley mythologies of the cosmic round.

Two more great tribal groups of warrior-nomads are to be mentioned: the Berbers, namely, of the northwest African deserts, and the Turks, Tatars, and Mongols of the rugged central Asian wastes. Of the former we have two Kabyle legends: one telling of the origin of the first people, emergent from below ground (page 66), and the other of a primal sun ram, found represented in a rock engraving high on a peak of the Saharan

Atlas Mountains, south of Algiers (page 162). As their collector, Leo Frobenius, points out in *African Genesis* (1931), the particular interest of these two Kabyle legends lies in their carriage of motifs derived both from the late Paleolithic Age of the North African rock engravings and from the immediately following period of the earliest agriculturalists of the region.

The other African tales of our collection are of equal historical interest. The Sudanese legend of Dogon, the first blacksmith (page 119), for example, points to an important moment for Africa, namely the introduction of iron, about 500 B.C., after which that flowering of Iron Age native states occurred, continuing through many centuries, of which the brilliant Fasa, Fulbe, Nupe, and Soninke tales here presented carry the elegant style and flavor – telling of times and traditions of heroic bardic epics and romances, noble and sophisticated, not a little like those of our own high Middle Ages. The legends from the Guinea coast and Congo basin, on the other hand, are rather of tropical planters, as are also those of the Bantu tribes that began spreading, around A.D. 500, southward from the Congo basin, given new strength both by their own recently acquired knowledge of iron and by a number of new agricultural products lately introduced from Indonesia by seafaring Malayo-Polynesians. The charming Bushman legends of little Cagn, a praying mantis (page 174), signal the end of the long hunting history of a late Stone Age folk, pressed southward by the expanding Bantu planters, and locked now in what can only be their ultimate retreat, the Kalahari Desert. They may have come in their beginning, in fact, from the same North African hunting lands now occupied by the Kabyle Berbers. And then, finally, again from southern Africa, we have those mysterious legends of the Wahungwe of Rhodesia: of Mwuetsi, the moon man, and of the maiden sacrificed to bring rain. There is surely a late echo, here, of that grim tradition, studied by Frazer in *The Golden Bough*, of ritual regicide.

But to return, now, to our nomads: one of the broadest, most important, and least well investigated culture areas of the planet is that of the great central Asian steppes, where, from the end of the ice ages, late Paleolithic tribes ranging in race from Caucasoid Finnish and Turkish types to pure Mongolians in the East, hunted, fought, and intermarried. The whole region is the classic area of shamanism. It is also the area from which the American Indian migrations must have taken their start. Throughout the northernmost, circumpolar parts

are simple hunting and fishing tribes. From the central steppes, on the other hand, the Huns of the fifth century and Mongols of the Golden Horde – Genghis Khan, Ogotai, Hulagu, and Tammerlane, dread names of about A.D. 1200 to 1400 – took their rise. A goodly number of tales from these areas will be found in our collection: tales of the

One of the most fascinating phenomena in the field of mythology is the similarity between widespread religious and mystical experiences. Such similarities extend not only to modes of thinking and believing but also to modes of pictorial represen-

tation. A startling comparison is offered by the two illustrations on this page: a Buddhist mandala *(above)* embodying the teaching of the Guhyasamâja Tantra, and a Navaho sand painting *(right)* entitled "People of the Myth."

Altai and Siberian shamans; of the Lapps, Finns, Estonians; of the Samoyeds, Ostyaks, Buryats, Yakuts; and of the Gilyaks, Kalmyks, Kirghiz, Bashkir, and various Tatars. Finally, also, the Caucasoid Ainu of northern Japan should be reckoned in this company, and, remotely, the Japanese themselves, who are of Uralo-Altai provenance, and came into their island home by way of Korea about 300 B.C. The American Indian tribes that appear to share most closely both physical and mythical features related to those of these regions are the Algonquins and Athapascans, which latter include, in southern extension, the Navaho and Apache. Indian tales of the flood and of

Also yet to be well explored is the infinitely difficult Southeast Asian-Oceanic quarter of the world, where the continent of Australia rests apart, as an especial enigma in itself. It has been inhabited, apparently, since about 25,000 B.C. by tribes that have continued to be hunters, even though in closely neighboring New Guinea, to the

find many origin legends – a number of the Hainuwele type – reflecting this order of life, from Borneo and the Celebes, Solomons, and Torres Strait. One of the most fascinating features of the area is the great variety of its sailing craft: all sorts of catamarans, outriggers, and canoes have apparently plied its waters for millenniums. We have a date for the Mariannas, in Micronesia, from about 1500 B.C.; and from around A.D. 500, Malayo-Polynesian seamen had spanned the entire waterway from Madagascar, off the coast of Africa, to Easter Island. Maui the trickster, of whose popular feats we have examples on pages 146–49, was known and loved from New Zealand to the Tuamotus and Hawaii, over thousands of miles of sheer water. Hindu and Buddhist communities and dynasties had meanwhile been established throughout Southeast Asia, and in Sumatra, Java, and Bali; also in parts of Borneo. Indian Bharata Natya dancers can carry on hand conversations with Hawaiian hula mistresses. And perhaps the most remarkable interlocking of all is that which the reader will discover between the New Zealand version of the separation of Sky and Earth, Rangi and Papa, by Tanemahuta (page 89), and the classical deed of Cronus's separation of Uranus and Gaea (page 82).

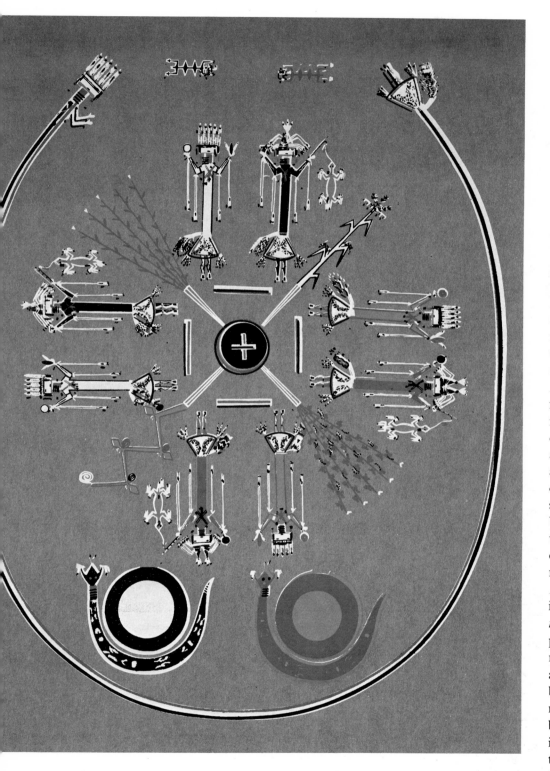

And so these are the mythological gems we find set forth in this treasury. They are indeed from every part of the world and century of the past, and we can readily date and place them all. But no one has yet dated and placed the region from which their common themes are derived, and if we should follow the lead of these, we should be carried on a very different journey from that of any geographical mapping. The Hindus, like Adolf Bastian, have noticed and named the distinction between *Völker-* and *Elementargedanken*, ethnic and elementary ideas. Their terms for the same are *dési* and *màrga*. *Dési* means "that which is local, provincial," and refers to those forms of myth and ritual that we recognize as culturally shaped, and whose areas of origin can be mapped. *Màrga,* on the other hand, means "path or track, trail of an animal, to be followed," and this is precisely what is implied by C.G. Jung's term, "the archetypes of the unconscious" (see Professor Eliade's explication, above). Following their lead, disengaged from the local tasks and ideas to which their socially functioning ethnic inflections had formerly bound us, we are led – if we can follow – beyond maps, according to the Indian view, to that seat from which all the gods have sprung, which is the revelation of the deepest source and being of ourselves.

the earth-diver who brings up mud from the bottom to be magically made into a new earth, are perfectly matched by legends from Siberia, while the sand paintings of the Navaho remarkably suggest those of the Tantric colleges of Tibet. But the whole problem of these cross-continental relationships has yet to be well explored.

north, primitive gardening has been practiced since about 3000 B.C. In the Philippines, Malaya, and in the Andamans, in the Bay of Bengal, black pygmy tribes (Negritos) likewise continue to exist in the most primitive hunting and fishing styles. More generally, however, throughout this area, gardening is practiced, and the reader will

CREATORS OF NATURE AND MANKIND

Night,
it is you
I hymn,
mother
of gods
and men.
The ground
of all being
is night.

ORPHIC

And God made

the two great lights,

the greater light to rule the day,

and the lesser light to rule the night;

he made the stars also.

GENESIS 1: 16

This depiction of God creating the heavenly bodies is from the Monreale Cathedral in Sicily, where the entire Biblical account of Creation is shown.

The same themes recur in myths all over the world. They form a manifold pattern or palimpsest which can reveal something of how human imagination works collectively and creatively to illuminate great questions. Whence came the ocean with its storms? What does thunder speak out of the night? What signifies the bright calligraphy of lightning? Such questions as these loomed very large during the long childhood of the human race. Myth, together with its sometimes light-hearted derivatives in legend and folktale, was made to answer them. Questions concerning the creation of the

moved on to the moon, but it proved too cold for their home. Finally they descended to the place where we are now, but at that time it was submerged under water. Disconsolate, the thoughts of all creatures floated north, south, east, and west upon the flood. They remained sorrowful wraiths for a long time. But one day an immense boulder rose to break the surface of the deep. The boulder burst open with a terrible roar and flamed out heavenward. The waters steamed, swirled, and retreated as puffs of cloud. Dry land appeared. Then it was that the spirits of vegetation descended

For by far the greater span of human history, the night sky has been a mystery of light, an inconceivable miracle of creation that mythic man pictured to himself as the seat of the gods. Modern astronomy has enormously broadened our horizon, but the mystery of cosmic creation remains.

cosmos and of mankind in particular receive hundreds of answers in mythology, an astonishing number of which seem interrelated. Many mythic accounts accord in some degree with, for example, the Book of Genesis, while others seem to foreshadow the conclusions of modern science. For instance, the astro-physicists' theory that the universe began with a "big bang" — an explosion of cosmic dimensions — some billions of years ago, finds corroboration of a dreamlike sort in the following myth of North America's Omaha Indians.

All creatures, including man, the Omaha maintained, were once mere thoughts swimming bodiless in space. They were searching for a place where they could come into actual existence. They tried the sun, to begin with, but it was too hot. They

to make their home on the earth. The spirits of animals followed, and they too achieved bodily form. Finally, mankind also made the transition to solidity.

WAKANTAKA, GREAT SPIRIT OF THE SIOUX

Sioux Indian mythology centers upon four colors: red for the sun, blue for the sky, green for the earth, and yellow for the rock. As colors are united in the rainbow, said the Sioux, so all things are united in a single Great Spirit, Wakantaka.

The following catechism was inparted by an Oglala Sioux medicine man named Sword. "Who is the oldest? Rock is the oldest, the grandfather. Who is the next oldest? Earth is the next oldest, the grandmother. Who is the next oldest? Sky is the next oldest, giver of life and motion. Who is the next oldest? Sun is the next oldest, above us."

The Sioux believed that once upon a time, the first elk appeared on the top of the primeval rock and bayed loudly. In answer, the first dawn arose out of the dark abyss which confronted the rock. But naturally the elk, the rock, the dawn, and the abyss, were all really Wakantaka.

The Polynesian creator of the Maori people is the god Tiki *(left)*, who made the first man out of clay. Lunar traditions of the origin of species trace man back to the Great Mother Goddess, generatrix of life, represented by this clay figure from Cyprus *(right)*.

A volcano emerging from the sea *(left)* offers a striking image of creation from chaos, the phenomenon that myth sets out to describe. Michelangelo's fresco depicts God in the clouds calling creation into being by his word alone *(right)*.

HURON CREATION MYTH

In contrast to the Sioux, the Huron Indians of North America's Great Lakes region used to tell about a goddess named Ataentsic. Some nameless being, like an exhalation from the underworld, seduced and impregnated her. Immediately, she found herself cast out from heaven, falling and falling, gently spinning, cartwheeling through space. Twins were rapidly growing in Ataentsic's womb, but there was no place for her lying-in.

She fell into a watery waste, with no land in sight. Turtle, however, arose from the depths to give her shelter on its back. It was there that she brought forth the spiritual beings who created day and night. Muskrat, meanwhile, fetched up solid ground from the ocean's depths, and this became the earth we know.

The dilemma of the falling Red Indian goddess recalls that of the Greek Titaness Leto, who had such trouble giving birth to the twin Greek deities of the sun and moon: Apollo and Artemis. The land and sea alike had sworn to allow Leto no resting-place; yet finally the Aegean island of Delos arose out of the depths to shelter her and to be the twins' cradle.

Primal gods, creators, and upholders of the world are common to the myths of all peoples. The war god Ku of Hawaii *(above left)* is his people's protector; the creator Banaitja *(above right)* is sacred to certain aboriginal tribes of Australia.

CREATOR GODS

Pictured here are just a few of the deities myth has associated with creation. The Memphis civilization of ancient Egypt worshiped the god Ptah *(left)* as molder of images, creator of the world, father of the gods, and as the god of the beginning of all things; his symbol is the scepter of power. Creator gods appear in a variety of roles – author of the cosmos, lord of heaven, creator of mankind – and a corresponding variety of guises in different civilizations. Creation may be the work of a god, a cosmic spirit, heaven itself, or creator gods acting as emissaries of heaven. The primal god may call into being a demiurge, giant, or first man (Purusha in Vedic myth, Ymir in Norse myth, Pan-Ku in Chinese Taoism), who is then sacrificed and dismembered to form the world and mankind. Alternatively, creation may stem from a primal couple or an androgynous deity. In lunar civilizations the generative force is a Mother Goddess, whereas in solar traditions the hierarchy of gods and men has its origin in the sun and the sun god. Another mythic concept sees the origin of the creative process in the hierogamy or sacred marriage between the sky as father of all things and the earth as mother.

The Indian Vedas contain a wealth of quite different accounts of creation featuring the first spirit or god as principle of the world, and his various emanations as the creators of the cyclic ages. The best-known creator figure, however, is Brahma (myth, page 62), represented here *(above)* with four heads looking in the four directions.

Right: One Chinese creation myth (page 66) tells how Pan-Ku came forth from chaos, which was in the form of an egg. He divided the world into *yin* (earth) and *yang* (heaven). Parts of his body gave rise to the creatures and elements of the cosmos.

By Word and Deed

"In the beginning was the Word." So states the Gospel of John. The Hindu Markandeya Purana agrees. In the beginning, it relates, Brahma existed independently of space-time. Letters exist in the same way, Hindu commentators explain. That is to say, letters possess existence in the realm of ideas whether or not they are pronounced or written down.

Akshara-Brahma, Brahma in the formless realm of pure ideas, first showed himself as a golden embryo of sound. He was a vowel, vibrating outward through nothingness. The sound re-echoed back upon itself; its waves crisscrossed and became water and wind. The interplay of wind and water then began weaving the misty womb of the world.

A different Hindu myth, however, credits the double-sexed deity Purusha with creating life on earth. Purusha began by splitting in half and embracing himself-herself. From that union swarmed the first of all living things, namely, humanity.

The female half of Purusha felt pain and shame. She made an effort to vanish but could not. Instead, she found herself transformed into a cow. Her male half immediately mated with her once again, this time in the shape of a primordial bull. Thus cattle were produced. The male half of Purusha went on to pursue his female counterpart through every form of life, down to the ants.

The Churning of the Ocean

Yet another Hindu myth concerns Mount Meru which stood hip-deep in an ocean of milk. That ocean was home to a race of serpents, each many thousands of miles long. Vasuki, the monarch of the serpents, used to loop and sidle up out of the sea and coil himself about Meru. He slept that way, with his head resting on the snowy summit of the mountain.

One day the gods, in a spirit of play, seized hold of Vasuki and pulled at him with all their might. The demons, equally playful, grabbed and pulled him in the opposite direction. Mount Meru spun back and forth in the snake's tightened coils. Between them, gods and demons made the mountain behave like a rotary churn, rocked right and left in turn. The sea of milk seethed round and round the whirling base of the mountain. It curdled up, gradually, like cheese in a churn.

Seven precious things, Hindu myth goes on to say, arose from the curdled milk and venom which poor Vasuki vomited. Among

them were the mother stone of all gems whatsoever, a heavenly tree, and Lakshmi, the goddess of beauty.

A Phoenician Account of Creation

Our generation upon the earth is by no means the first, nor will it be the last, to yearn for knowledge of the world's beginning and end. A thousand years before the time of Christ, in a Phoenician city on the eastern shore of the Mediterranean Sea, there lived a mythographer called Sanchuniathon. His account of creation, preserved

by Philo of Byblos, reads rather like a lesson in natural history.

In the beginning, there was nothing but a dark and windy weltering. The blind winds twisted themselves up to make a sort of love knot whose nature was desire. During aeons of time, Desire precipitated a watery slime called Mot. That slime bred living things, simple creatures without consciousness. From them, in turn, more complex and conscious beings arose. Those proved to be contemplators of the heavens. They saw that "Mot was egg-shaped and shining, and there were Sun, Moon, Stars, and Planets."

Egyptian Creation Myths

According to their own account, as reported by Herodotus, the priests of Egypt possessed the most ancient and reliable mythic tradition in the world. One brief but

Animals too may take an active part in the creation of the world, as well as play an auxiliary role in the evolution of life. The illustration shown on the left is a major creation symbol: a serpent coiled round the World Egg (myth, page 82). Myth often seems to classify animals according to their symbolic relationship to either sun

or moon. Lion, bull, ram, eagle, falcon, and phoenix belong to solar mythologies; wolf, dog, snake, hare, and frog occur more frequently in lunar traditions. The usual functions of animals in myth have to do with fertility, procreation, magic, and the communication of messages and of light, though animals also occur as guides of the soul and of the dead.

Above: The frog (left) is seen as procreative Mother Goddess of the element water by Indians of the southern states of America. The heroic figure of the Great Hare (center) belongs to the mythology of many North American Indians. In the ancient-Egyptian sun mythology of Amon-Ra, the creator as sun takes the form of a ram (right) and is protector of the pharaohs.

This pre-Columbian drinking vessel (above) depicts the dog which the Indians of Peru associated with the creation of the world.

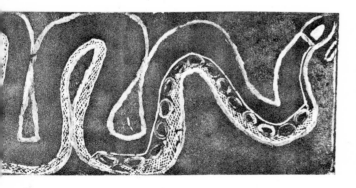

The two birdlike creatures on this stone from Easter Island (above), having brought the first men to earth, are here seen protecting them with their wings. Some Australian aborigines believe that the cosmos was produced by the world serpent (left) out of its own body. For the ancient Egyptians the ibis god Thoth (right) was the creator; he was also the bringer of wisdom and the art of writing.

In myth, as in reality, the creation and formation of the world often involves a division into opposites. From the polarity of these opposites springs the power that shapes the cosmos. In Chinese myth the cosmic symbol of the interchangeable polarity of opposites is the *yin-yang* figure *(right)*. The eight trigrams around it symbolize the cyclic change from the female force *(yin)* to the male *(yang)*. *Yin,* the moist, dark, earth element, is black; *yang,* firm and bright, representing heaven, is white. Each is germinally present inside the other; each contains its opposite. The crouching tiger in the form of the primal egg *(right below)* is another *yin-yang* symbol. Although this is the female, *yin* tiger of soft, lithe, devouring ways, its great strength derives from *yang.* Both Chinese and Japanese myth take as their starting point the indivisible unity of such opposites. In the Chinese first couple we have the polarity of mind and knowledge, as personified by Fu Hsi, and life and nature, as personified by his wife Nu Kua. The beautiful but terrifying story of Izanagi and Izanami (page 77), a mythic account of the creation of Japan, again suggests the *yin-yang* polarity. Egyptian myth (page 65) tells of various primal couples, including Isis and Osiris, who contribute to a continuing process of evolution.

The Japanese creation myth (page 77) describes how Izanagi and Izanami summoned the first land mass from the misty sea by churning it with a spear.

This Han-dynasty stone rubbing shows the Chinese first couple, Fu Hsi *(left)* and Nu Kua *(right).* Their union is the mythic hierogamy underlying the creation of the world. Fu Hsi is author of the eight trigrams of knowledge; Nu Kua is creator of mankind (myth, page 66).

Above: There is an archaic compactness about this early-Hittite clay figure of the divine first couple emerging from the circle of the cosmos.

The beginnings of differentiation are visible in this ancient-Egyptian stele *(above left)* depicting the union of the gods Shu and Tefnut. The small double idol *(right),* also of Hittite origin, again represents a divine creator couple.

In this pre-Columbian depiction, the two people sitting on the back of the great serpent apparently represent a Mixtec first couple.

pregnant piece of evidence for this is to be found in the collection of the British Museum in London. It consists of a rock slab which appears to have served for centuries as a millstone and yet bears hieroglyphic inscriptions. The stone came into the museum's collection in 1805. After a century had passed, the American Egyptologist James Henry Breasted undertook to decipher it. He found that Stela 797, as it was known, has this to say: "Every divine word came into existence by the thought of the heart and the commandment of the tongue. When the eyes see, the ears hear, and the nose breathes, they report to the heart. It is the heart that brings forth every issue, and the tongue that repeats the thought of the heart. Thus were fashioned all the gods, from Atum on."

This curiously metaphysical passage was inscribed during the reign of Pharaoh Sabakos in the eighth century B.C. But, as Professor Adolf Erman was first to demonstrate, it repeats an infinitely older text, dating to about the year 2850 B.C. and long since lost. Thus one of the most ancient paragraphs in the present possession of mankind likens the Creator of all things to the creative heart of man himself. It says, too, that the act of creation was originally a sort of speech and "commandment of the tongue," which repeats the heart's thought.

Somewhat later in origin are two inscriptions from the tombs of Saqqara near ancient Memphis, which have been dated between 2350 and 2175 B.C. They agree that Atum, the first deity, stood alone. One says that he spat his twin children, Shu and Tefnut, from his mouth. The second text maintains that he produced them by means of masturbation. However that may have been, Shu and Tefnut made love in the usual way and so produced a second pair of twins, whose names were Nut and Geb. Twins often appear very near the beginning of things in mythology and have important roles to play for human imagination.

In this particular myth the twin Geb was the earth, whom the Egyptians pictured as a giant stretched at ease upon his back. His sister Nut showed herself in the Milky Way, bending down like an arched bridge across Geb's body.

The love of Earth and Sky in turn engendered further sets of twins, namely, Osiris and Isis, Set and Nephthys. The first pair were suffering and sorrowing deities, intensely sympathetic to the human condition. The second pair, Set and Nephthys, gave play to dark, destructive forces, without whose cleansing powers life would soon degenerate into mere brilliance, fruitfulness, and glut.

MESOPOTAMIAN CREATION MYTHS

Not much more than a century ago, an adventurous archaeologist named George Smith uncovered masses of clay tablets in what had been the palace of the Assyrian king Ashurbanipal. The cuneiform writing on those tablets showed them to be fragments of the world's oldest surviving library. Among the king's "books" were some which explained the beginning of the world. The story was Babylonian in origin. It centered on an epic struggle between two deities. The first of these, Tiamat, is difficult to picture with any precision, but she seems to have been female, vast, fruitful, dragonlike, and spontaneous in nature. Her divine opponent, Marduk, god of the sun and of the city of Babylon, was male, dynamic, energetic, fierce, proud, and essentially a shaping deity.

Marduk set forth in his chariot. The mere sight of his coming caused Tiamat's eleven allies to flee for their lives. Tiamat lay waiting alone. The sun god caught her in a net of light. He flung the hurricane between her watery jaws and shot her through and through with his arrows. Finally, he sliced Tiamat in two like a flatfish. He set her spotted top half on high, to be earth's heaven. Her bottom half became the earth itself, with all its seas and oceans.

Like Jehovah in the Old Testament, Marduk then proceeded to shape and arrange nature as we know it. In the process he created mankind. "Blood will I take," Marduk informed his fellow deities, "and bone will I fashion. I will invent humanity, to inhabit the earth and be our slaves."

Scattered Sumerian fragments have been shown to foreshadow the account of creation found among the ruins of Ashurbanipal's palace. In particular, they lend support to the sobering crunch on which that story ends, namely, the idea that the gods created mankind to be their slaves. This concept has a certain rough logic. Here myth veers, early on, in the direction of philosophy. The Sumerians, and afterward the Babylonians, appear to have been anxious to find a reason for the unfree, bodybound, mortal condition of mankind. Then the question arose: Since we are nothing but slaves to the gods, why did they not make us more healthy, whole, and useful?

Texts painstakingly collated by the Sumerologist Samuel Noah Kramer provide answers to such difficulties. As restored by Professor Kramer, exceedingly ancient Sumerian myth relates that once upon a time, the gods themselves had no choice but to till the earth and earn their own bread by the sweat of their brows. The cleverest among them, the god of fresh water, deliberately dozed through that period.

The fresh water god, whose name was Enki, finally found himself shaken into wakefulness by his mother Nammu, Goddess of the Watery Abyss. Nammu complained about the hard toil of the gods. Enki at once suggested creating a marionettelike race to do the necessary work in their place. The first requirement, he said, would be a handful of mud from the middle region between earth itself and the watery abyss beneath. This mud was to be severed from the physical existence of Nammu as one cuts an infant's umbilical cord. From it, the heart of humanity was to be made. Eight deities, whose names do not appear in the much-defaced text which has come down to us, were to assist in the shaping and animating of human beings.

When people had been successfully produced, Enki held a feast of celebration. Quantities of beer were consumed. Enki's wife, the Earth Mother, whose name is given in the text as Ninmah, became especially light-headed. She called over to Enki, "How good or bad is a human body? I could reshape it at my own pleasure." Enki accepted the challenge in a spirit of fun. "Do that," he suggested, "and I promise to find a place for any kind of human that you may invent."

Thereupon Ninmah shaped a eunuch, a barren woman, and four more deprived or crippled beings. Enki assigned positions in human society to each one of them. The eunuch he made a civil servant. The barren woman he made a concubine. Then he challenged Ninmah to a continuation of the game. He would do the shaping, and she the placing, of freakish people. Ninmah agreed. Enki's first effort was a man "whose birthday was remote," the first aged human being. This creature stood before Ninmah. She offered him a piece of bread, but the toothless and suffering old man was too feeble to reach out and take it. Ninmah could find no use for this unfortunate. Enki followed up his victory, drunkenly driving his divine bride to the wall, by producing five more men and women who were heavily burdened with deformities and calamities. Ninmah could find no work for them. The party dispersed in uproar.

UNANSWERED QUESTIONS

Not all peoples choose to answer the questions of creation; some mythologies, in fact, seemingly veil what caused what. The Kabyle Berbers of the Djurdjura Mountains east of Algiers say simply that the first

human beings were an ageless pair who fought over a water hole and found themselves copulating outside of time, as it were, deep underneath the earth. Their fifty daughters and fifty sons climbed and climbed to reach the earth's surface.

The fifty maidens emerged first. They saw the plants and asked, "Who made you?" The plants replied, "Earth did." Turning and bending down, the maidens asked the earth, "Who made you?" Earth rumbled and explained, "I was always here."

Night came on, and then for the first time the maidens saw the moon and stars glittering overhead. They cried, "Who made you, moon and stars, to stand so high above us and above the trees? Are you perhaps the ones who have created everything else around us?" The maidens kept on calling and crying questions like these, but the moon and stars were too high to hear them or to reply.

FROM THE BODY OF A GOD

The god Pan-Ku appears in Chinese art as a dwarfish fellow, scantily attired in leaves or a bearskin cape. Like Moses, he has young horns sprouting from his brow. He holds a hammer and a chisel, for Pan-Ku is the world's sculptor. He is surrounded by his helpers: the unicorn, the phoenix, the tortoise, and the dragon.

Aided by his four friends, this amiable demiurge carved out all nature as we see it now. When he began the work, he was an infinitesimal being, hardly more than a speck of dust. Each day he grew larger, for no less than 18,000 years. During all that time he carved upon the only material available, his own body, and in the end he died so that nature might live.

Pan-Ku's hair became the whirling constellations of the night sky. His eyes turned inward, as the sun and moon. Now his breath is earth's atmosphere. His body is the earth itself, and his blood the oceans.

Pan-Ku became nature, but Nu Kua, later on, made mankind. The Chinese recognize five basic elements: earth, air, fire, water, and, finally, wood. Nu Kua was the reptilian sovereign of that rather surprising fifth element. She appears to have recognized Fire as a somehow superior authority. When Water rebelled in the early days, Nu Kua went to war for Fire's sake.

Water retreated to a height called Imperfect Mountain. The other elements laid siege to him. Finding the position hopeless, Water despairingly struck his icy brow against the mountainside. Imperfect Mountain split in half, a deluge poured forth, the

You alone can grant us forgiveness,
great mother, Brahma-high,
you we salute,
whose mercy lies all about us
like a blaze of light.
Enthroned on high,
higher than the Most-High,
you too contemn the cosmic laws:
oneness of mind and being, you are yet
duality in your union of the sexes.
Eternal creations eternally
roll into being at your mighty summons;
beauty and love rejoice therein,
ebbing and exulting
on the shores of everlasting joy.
You open your eye and in a whirl of color

patterns of creation go dancing by,
a dance through eternity,
going and coming in countless ranks,
o mother, o mildness.
Your game of creation calls worlds
into being, dashes them back
into nothingness and ruin —
we laud you, all-powerful mistress.

FROM THE SAKTIGITA (INDIA)

THE GREAT MOTHER

The mythologies and religions of the world have handed down to us an endless wealth of images of the Great Mother, that is to say of the manifestations of those aspects of the female having to do with procreation, preservation, and destruction. Typical of these images is a certain ambivalence of form, as can be seen from the selection illustrated here. The Great Mother is the creatrix of life, the bearer of being, the origin of the gods

Pillars of Heaven tottered, and the foundations of earth gave way. Thereupon the war ended in common distress. Nu Kua undertook to repair the damage as best she could. Somehow she succeeded in damming up the flood with ashes of burned reeds. With melted stones of five colors, she carefully repaired heaven's pillars. To set earth steady once again, she planted the feet of a giant tortoise at its northern, southern, eastern, and western extremes. Last but not quite least, according to some accounts, Nu Kua molded little people out of yellow earth and set them on the ground as earth's inhabitants.

1 This voluptuous image of Gaea, the Great Mother of Greek myth (page 82), radiates a half-human, half-divine erotic power.
2 A Khond bronze from India shows the Great Mother serenely nursing and caring for children.

4 An enormous variety of Mother Goddesses is found in India. This clay figure, for example, is from the second millennium B.C. In her later manifestations as Yakshi, Deva, Radha, Maya, Kali, and Durga she came to represent all aspects of creation – birth, life, death, and supreme wisdom.

6 Another well-developed pantheon is that of the Ashanti of Ghana, who produced this clay Earth Mother holding an oil lamp.

3 The ancient-Minoan civilization on Crete produced this painted clay Mother Goddess figure, which was found in the "Shrine of the Double Ax" in the palace at Knossos.

5 Early Middle Eastern cultures, particularly in the Mesopotamian region, also left a great many clay figures of Great Mothers. This Iranian statue symbolizes her fertility aspect. Later figures were Ishtar, Inanna, Samas-Belil, and Tiamat, the demonic Mother of Chaos in Babylonian myth (page 65).

7 A powerful image of fertility and the yearly renewal of life is the Aztec Divine Mother Tlazolteotl giving birth to the maize god Centeotl. The delivery was performed ritually by a priest at the harvest festival each year as a prayer for the following year's crop.

themselves; she gives birth to heroes, fosters the growth of life, and destroys life's enemies. As Mother Earth she takes back dying life in order to transform it. Both numinous and profane, she brings the world into being and is the knowledge that sustains it.

8 The ambivalence of the Great Mother figure comes out clearly in this Aztec statue of Coatlicue. It shows her in her negative, dreadful aspect as the mistress of opposites, the woman in the skirt of snakes. For the Aztecs she symbolized the dynamism arising out of the polarity of procreation and annihilation in death. In her, genesis and decay were one.

67

THE GREEK GODS FROM CHAOS TO ZEUS

CHAOS

A formless emergence, akin to the "Deep" which preceded the Biblical Creation, Chaos was endowed with at least one of the mortal attributes common to the later gods: he is pictured as being made quite uncomfortable by the thunderbolts promiscuously tossed about in the gigantic conflict known as the War of the Titans. But having served his purpose as the logical first of a complex family tree, the role assigned to him ultimately became as vaguely defined as the essence of his being. Recorded mythology gives him a very minor place in that wonderful series of deified dynasties which the early Greeks established as a foundation for many of the classical stories enjoyed by all later civilized peoples.

GAEA

Gaea, our "broad-bosomed Mother Earth," was conceived as a flat disk encircled by the great river Oceanus, whose unbounded waters were said to "backward flow," because the stream flowed into itself. Gaea was quite naturally revered as the fruitful power sustaining universal life, and was recognized as the common ancestress of practically all the gods and demigods in the Greek theogony. Although other and more personalized deities of subsequent generations assumed many of the functions originally hers alone, yet the old Earth Goddess was never wholly supplanted in the thoughts of men – for it was she who first was called "Mother."

EROS

Eros was the powerful personification of love, conceived as the irresistible influence responsible for reducing the conflicting elements of Chaos to the harmony and order necessary for the world's completion. He should not be confused with the later Eros, known to the Romans as Cupid, that mischievous little son of Aphrodite who was in the habit of directing his love arrows to whatever objects his volatile fancy suggested. The original Eros was a serious and fundamental cause in the scheme of creation, and persisted as the force which ruled the councils of both gods and men for the ultimate and common good of all. This philosophic conception was so far above the level of personal amours and sensual love that only Eros, of all the primeval deities, had no offspring to become actors in the fascinating theogony which was both history and religion to the ancient Greeks.

TARTARUS

Primeval Tartarus was the complete underworld, the permanent abode of all perished souls, good or bad. Its distance below Gaea's surface was equal to that covered by nine days' fall of a brazen anvil. Upon arriving in Tartarus, one found it surrounded by a fence of bronze, triply reinforced with circles of darkest night. After the gates were passed, the floor of Tartarus was not reached until a full year had run its course, because for that long period each newly arrived spirit was cruelly tossed about by the dark and loathsome wind which constantly churned the entire region. In order to bring forth the monster Typhon, Gaea mated with Tartarus; this made him the ancestor of a series of fearful beings.

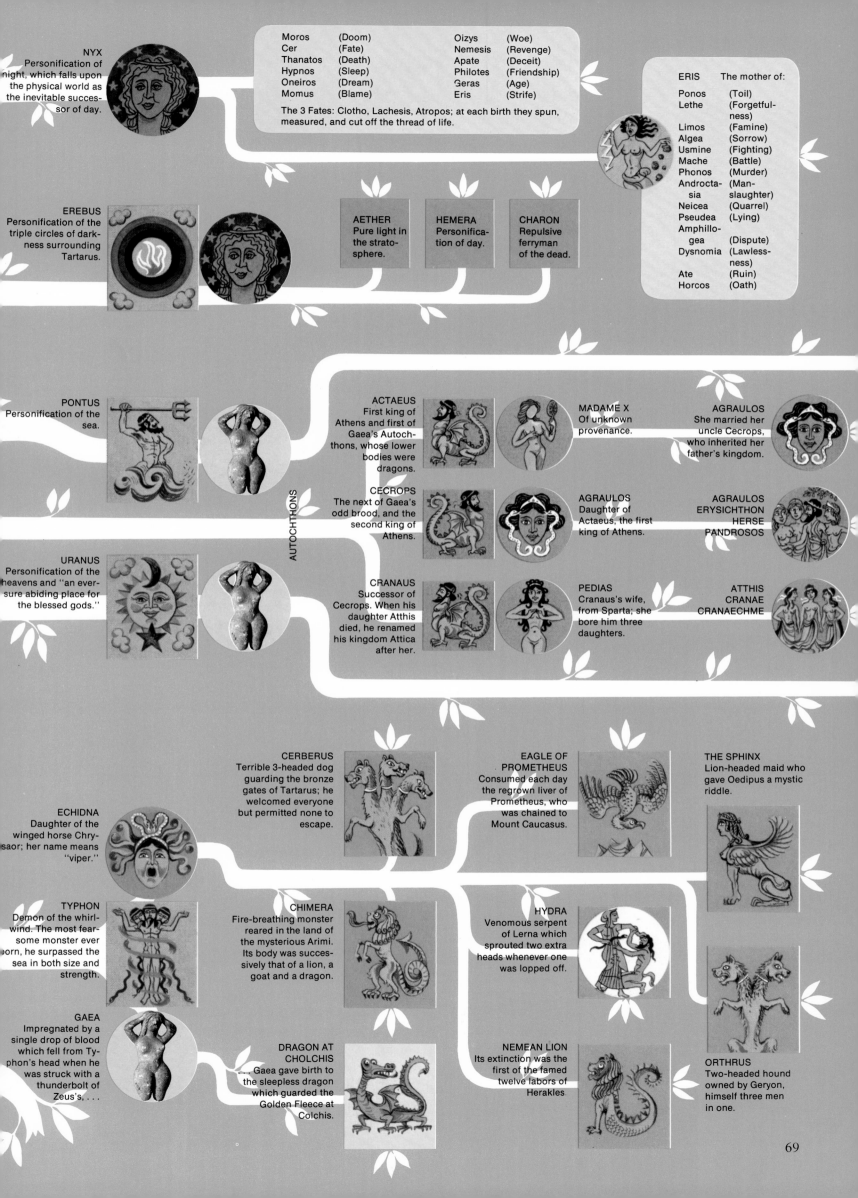

NYX
Personification of night, which falls upon the physical world as the inevitable successor of day.

Moros (Doom)
Cer (Fate)
Thanatos (Death)
Hypnos (Sleep)
Oneiros (Dream)
Momus (Blame)
Oizys (Woe)
Nemesis (Revenge)
Apate (Deceit)
Philotes (Friendship)
Geras (Age)
Eris (Strife)

The 3 Fates: Clotho, Lachesis, Atropos; at each birth they spun, measured, and cut off the thread of life.

ERIS The mother of:
Ponos (Toil)
Lethe (Forgetfulness)
Limos (Famine)
Algea (Sorrow)
Usmine (Fighting)
Mache (Battle)
Phonos (Murder)
Androctasia (Manslaughter)
Neicea (Quarrel)
Pseudea (Lying)
Amphillogea (Dispute)
Dysnomia (Lawlessness)
Ate (Ruin)
Horcos (Oath)

EREBUS
Personification of the triple circles of darkness surrounding Tartarus.

AETHER
Pure light in the stratosphere.

HEMERA
Personification of day.

CHARON
Repulsive ferryman of the dead.

PONTUS
Personification of the sea.

ACTAEUS
First king of Athens and first of Gaea's Autochthons, whose lower bodies were dragons.

MADAME X
Of unknown provenance.

AGRAULOS
She married her uncle Cecrops, who inherited her father's kingdom.

CECROPS
The next of Gaea's odd brood, and the second king of Athens.

AGRAULOS
Daughter of Actaeus, the first king of Athens.

AGRAULOS ERYSICHTHON HERSE PANDROSOS

AUTOCHTHONS

URANUS
Personification of the heavens and "an ever-sure abiding place for the blessed gods."

CRANAUS
Successor of Cecrops. When his daughter Atthis died, he renamed his kingdom Attica after her.

PEDIAS
Cranaus's wife, from Sparta; she bore him three daughters.

ATTHIS CRANAE CRANAECHME

CERBERUS
Terrible 3-headed dog guarding the bronze gates of Tartarus; he welcomed everyone but permitted none to escape.

EAGLE OF PROMETHEUS
Consumed each day the regrown liver of Prometheus, who was chained to Mount Caucasus.

THE SPHINX
Lion-headed maid who gave Oedipus a mystic riddle.

ECHIDNA
Daughter of the winged horse Chrysaor; her name means "viper."

TYPHON
Demon of the whirlwind. The most fearsome monster ever born, he surpassed the sea in both size and strength.

CHIMERA
Fire-breathing monster reared in the land of the mysterious Arimi. Its body was successively that of a lion, a goat and a dragon.

HYDRA
Venomous serpent of Lerna which sprouted two extra heads whenever one was lopped off.

GAEA
Impregnated by a single drop of blood which fell from Typhon's head when he was struck with a thunderbolt of Zeus's, . . .

DRAGON AT CHOLCHIS
Gaea gave birth to the sleepless dragon which guarded the Golden Fleece at Colchis.

NEMEAN LION
Its extinction was the first of the famed twelve labors of Herakles

ORTHRUS
Two-headed hound owned by Geryon, himself three men in one.

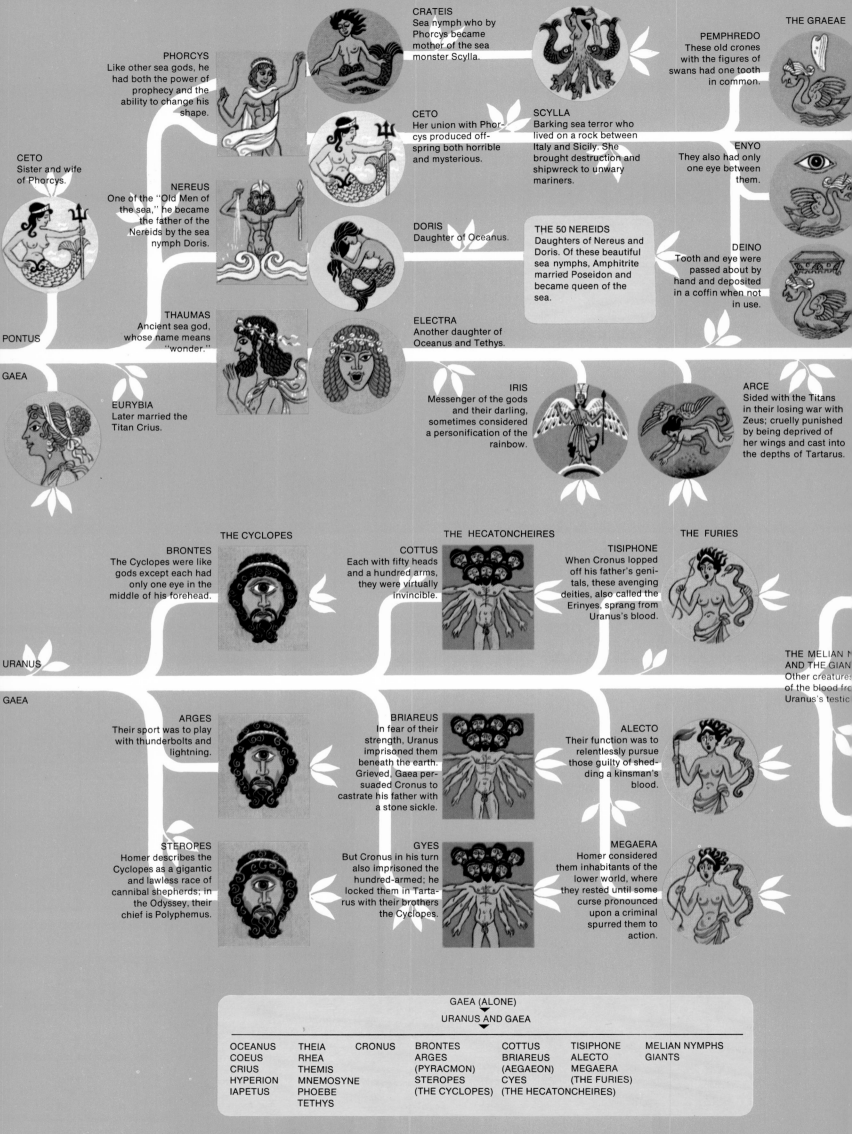

CRATEIS
Sea nymph who by Phorcys became mother of the sea monster Scylla.

PHORCYS
Like other sea gods, he had both the power of prophecy and the ability to change his shape.

CETO
Her union with Phorcys produced offspring both horrible and mysterious.

SCYLLA
Barking sea terror who lived on a rock between Italy and Sicily. She brought destruction and shipwreck to unwary mariners.

PEMPHREDO
These old crones with the figures of swans had one tooth in common.

THE GRAEAE

CETO
Sister and wife of Phorcys.

NEREUS
One of the "Old Men of the sea," he became the father of the Nereids by the sea nymph Doris.

DORIS
Daughter of Oceanus.

ENYO
They also had only one eye between them.

THE 50 NEREIDS
Daughters of Nereus and Doris. Of these beautiful sea nymphs, Amphitrite married Poseidon and became queen of the sea.

PONTUS

THAUMAS
Ancient sea god, whose name means "wonder."

ELECTRA
Another daughter of Oceanus and Tethys.

DEINO
Tooth and eye were passed about by hand and deposited in a coffin when not in use.

GAEA

EURYBIA
Later married the Titan Crius.

IRIS
Messenger of the gods and their darling, sometimes considered a personification of the rainbow.

ARCE
Sided with the Titans in their losing war with Zeus; cruelly punished by being deprived of her wings and cast into the depths of Tartarus.

THE CYCLOPES

BRONTES
The Cyclopes were like gods except each had only one eye in the middle of his forehead.

THE HECATONCHEIRES

COTTUS
Each with fifty heads and a hundred arms, they were virtually invincible.

THE FURIES

TISIPHONE
When Cronus lopped off his father's genitals, these avenging deities, also called the Erinyes, sprang from Uranus's blood.

URANUS

GAEA

ARGES
Their sport was to play with thunderbolts and lightning.

BRIAREUS
In fear of their strength, Uranus imprisoned them beneath the earth. Grieved, Gaea persuaded Cronus to castrate his father with a stone sickle.

ALECTO
Their function was to relentlessly pursue those guilty of shedding a kinsman's blood.

THE MELIAN NYMPHS AND THE GIANTS
Other creatures of the blood from Uranus's testicles.

STEROPES
Homer describes the Cyclopes as a gigantic and lawless race of cannibal shepherds; in the Odyssey, their chief is Polyphemus.

GYES
But Cronus in his turn also imprisoned the hundred-armed; he locked them in Tartarus with their brothers the Cyclopes.

MEGAERA
Homer considered them inhabitants of the lower world, where they rested until some curse pronounced upon a criminal spurred them to action.

GAEA (ALONE)						
URANUS AND GAEA						
OCEANUS	THEIA	CRONUS	BRONTES	COTTUS	TISIPHONE	MELIAN NYMPHS
COEUS	RHEA		ARGES	BRIAREUS	ALECTO	GIANTS
CRIUS	THEMIS		(PYRACMON)	(AEGAEON)	MEGAERA	
HYPERION	MNEMOSYNE		STEROPES	CYES	(THE FURIES)	
IAPETUS	PHOEBE		(THE CYCLOPES)	(THE HECATONCHEIRES)		
	TETHYS					

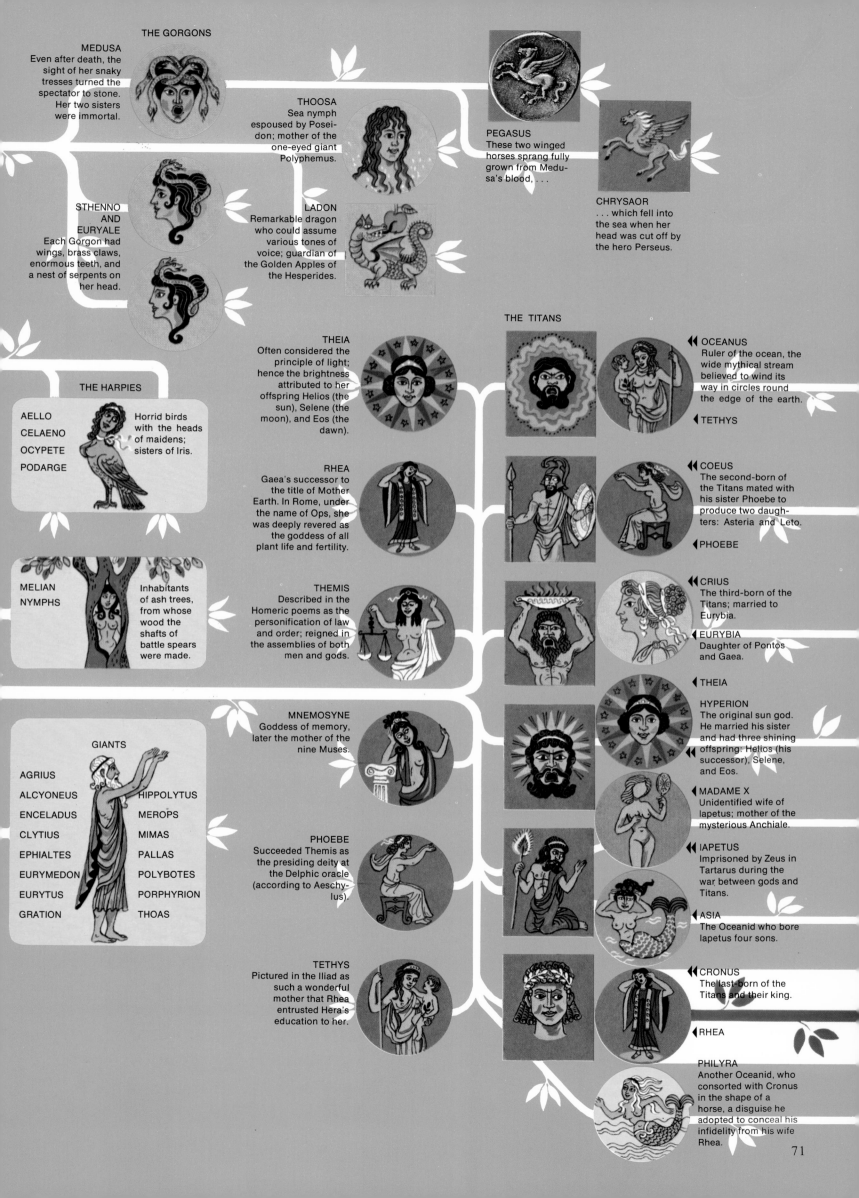

THE GORGONS

MEDUSA
Even after death, the sight of her snaky tresses turned the spectator to stone. Her two sisters were immortal.

STHENNO AND EURYALE
Each Gorgon had wings, brass claws, enormous teeth, and a nest of serpents on her head.

THOOSA
Sea nymph espoused by Poseidon; mother of the one-eyed giant Polyphemus.

LADON
Remarkable dragon who could assume various tones of voice; guardian of the Golden Apples of the Hesperides.

PEGASUS
These two winged horses sprang fully grown from Medusa's blood, . . .

CHRYSAOR
. . . which fell into the sea when her head was cut off by the hero Perseus.

THE HARPIES

AELLO

CELAENO

OCYPETE

PODARGE

Horrid birds with the heads of maidens; sisters of Iris.

MELIAN NYMPHS
Inhabitants of ash trees, from whose wood the shafts of battle spears were made.

GIANTS

AGRIUS

ALCYONEUS

ENCELADUS

CLYTIUS

EPHIALTES

EURYMEDON

EURYTUS

GRATION

HIPPOLYTUS

MEROPS

MIMAS

PALLAS

POLYBOTES

PORPHYRION

THOAS

THE TITANS

THEIA
Often considered the principle of light; hence the brightness attributed to her offspring Helios (the sun), Selene (the moon), and Eos (the dawn).

RHEA
Gaea's successor to the title of Mother Earth. In Rome, under the name of Ops, she was deeply revered as the goddess of all plant life and fertility.

THEMIS
Described in the Homeric poems as the personification of law and order; reigned in the assemblies of both men and gods.

MNEMOSYNE
Goddess of memory, later the mother of the nine Muses.

PHOEBE
Succeeded Themis as the presiding deity at the Delphic oracle (according to Aeschylus).

TETHYS
Pictured in the Iliad as such a wonderful mother that Rhea entrusted Hera's education to her.

OCEANUS
Ruler of the ocean, the wide mythical stream believed to wind its way in circles round the edge of the earth.

TETHYS

COEUS
The second-born of the Titans mated with his sister Phoebe to produce two daughters: Asteria and Leto.

PHOEBE

CRIUS
The third-born of the Titans; married to Eurybia.

EURYBIA
Daughter of Pontos and Gaea.

THEIA

HYPERION
The original sun god. He married his sister and had three shining offspring: Helios (his successor), Selene, and Eos.

MADAME X
Unidentified wife of Iapetus; mother of the mysterious Anchiale.

IAPETUS
Imprisoned by Zeus in Tartarus during the war between gods and Titans.

ASIA
The Oceanid who bore Iapetus four sons.

CRONUS
The last-born of the Titans and their king.

RHEA

PHILYRA
Another Oceanid, who consorted with Cronus in the shape of a horse, a disguise he adopted to conceal his infidelity from his wife Rhea.

71

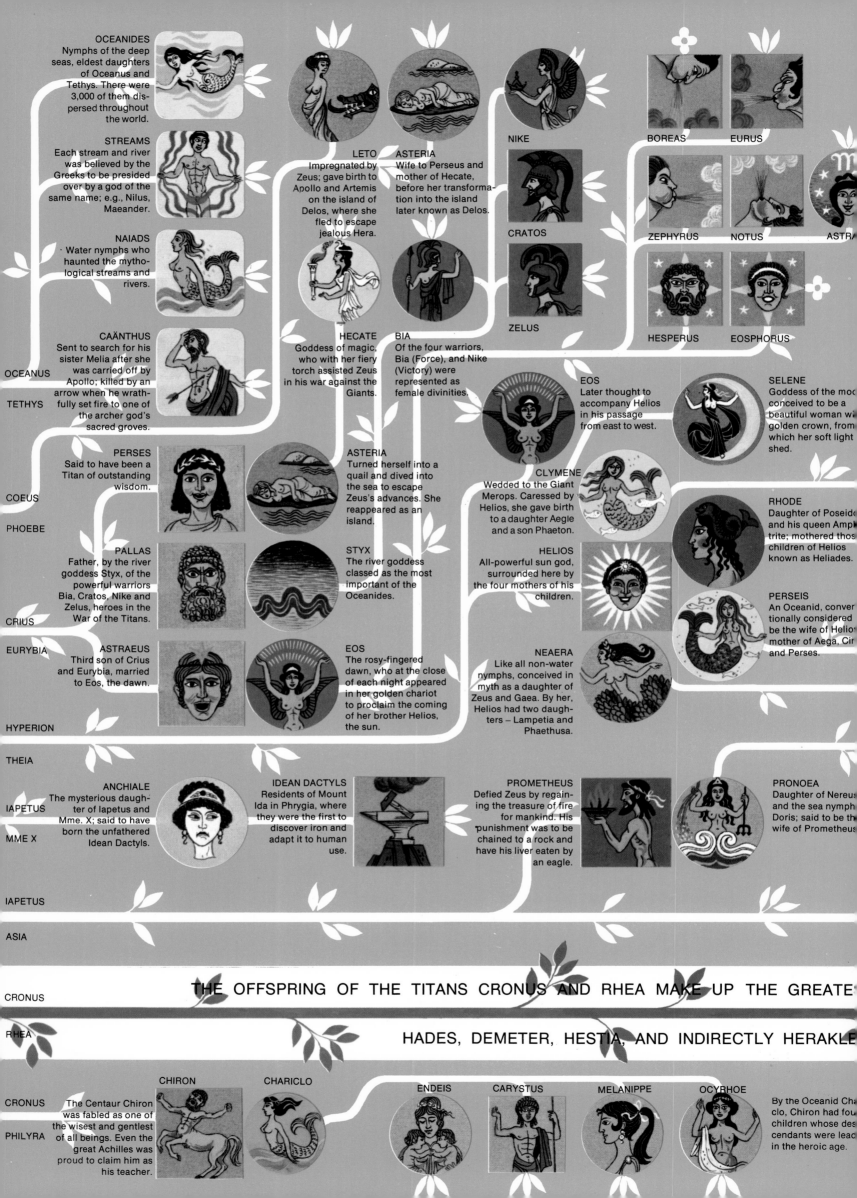

OCEANIDES
Nymphs of the deep seas, eldest daughters of Oceanus and Tethys. There were 3,000 of them dispersed throughout the world.

STREAMS
Each stream and river was believed by the Greeks to be presided over by a god of the same name; e.g., Nilus, Maeander.

NAIADS
Water nymphs who haunted the mythological streams and rivers.

CAÄNTHUS
Sent to search for his sister Melia after she was carried off by Apollo; killed by an arrow when he wrathfully set fire to one of the archer god's sacred groves.

OCEANUS

TETHYS

PERSES
Said to have been a Titan of outstanding wisdom.

COEUS

PHOEBE

PALLAS
Father, by the river goddess Styx, of the powerful warriors Bia, Cratos, Nike and Zelus, heroes in the War of the Titans.

CRIUS

EURYBIA

ASTRAEUS
Third son of Crius and Eurybia, married to Eos, the dawn.

HYPERION

THEIA

ANCHIALE
The mysterious daughter of Iapetus and Mme. X; said to have born the unfathered Idean Dactyls.

IAPETUS

MME X

IAPETUS

ASIA

LETO
Impregnated by Zeus; gave birth to Apollo and Artemis on the island of Delos, where she fled to escape jealous Hera.

ASTERIA
Wife to Perseus and mother of Hecate, before her transformation into the island later known as Delos.

HECATE
Goddess of magic, who with her fiery torch assisted Zeus in his war against the Giants.

BIA
Of the four warriors, Bia (Force), and Nike (Victory) were represented as female divinities.

ASTERIA
Turned herself into a quail and dived into the sea to escape Zeus's advances. She reappeared as an island.

STYX
The river goddess classed as the most important of the Oceanides.

EOS
The rosy-fingered dawn, who at the close of each night appeared in her golden chariot to proclaim the coming of her brother Helios, the sun.

IDEAN DACTYLS
Residents of Mount Ida in Phrygia, where they were the first to discover iron and adapt it to human use.

NIKE

CRATOS

ZELUS

EOS
Later thought to accompany Helios in his passage from east to west.

CLYMENE
Wedded to the Giant Merops. Caressed by Helios, she gave birth to a daughter Aegle and a son Phaeton.

HELIOS
All-powerful sun god, surrounded here by the four mothers of his children.

NEAERA
Like all non-water nymphs, conceived in myth as a daughter of Zeus and Gaea. By her, Helios had two daughters – Lampetia and Phaethusa.

PROMETHEUS
Defied Zeus by regaining the treasure of fire for mankind. His punishment was to be chained to a rock and have his liver eaten by an eagle.

BOREAS

EURUS

ZEPHYRUS

NOTUS

ASTR

HESPERUS

EOSPHORUS

SELENE
Goddess of the moon, conceived to be a beautiful woman with golden crown, from which her soft light shed.

RHODE
Daughter of Poseidon and his queen Amphitrite; mothered those children of Helios known as Heliades.

PERSEIS
An Oceanid, conventionally considered be the wife of Helios, mother of Aega, Circe and Perses.

PRONOEA
Daughter of Nereus and the sea nymph Doris; said to be the wife of Prometheus.

THE OFFSPRING OF THE TITANS CRONUS AND RHEA MAKE UP THE GREATE

CRONUS

RHEA

HADES, DEMETER, HESTIA, AND INDIRECTLY HERAKLE

CRONUS

PHILYRA

CHIRON
The Centaur Chiron was fabled as one of the wisest and gentlest of all beings. Even the great Achilles was proud to claim him as his teacher.

CHARICLO

ENDEIS

CARYSTUS

MELANIPPE

OCYRHOE

By the Oceanid Chariclo, Chiron had four children whose descendants were leading in the heroic age.

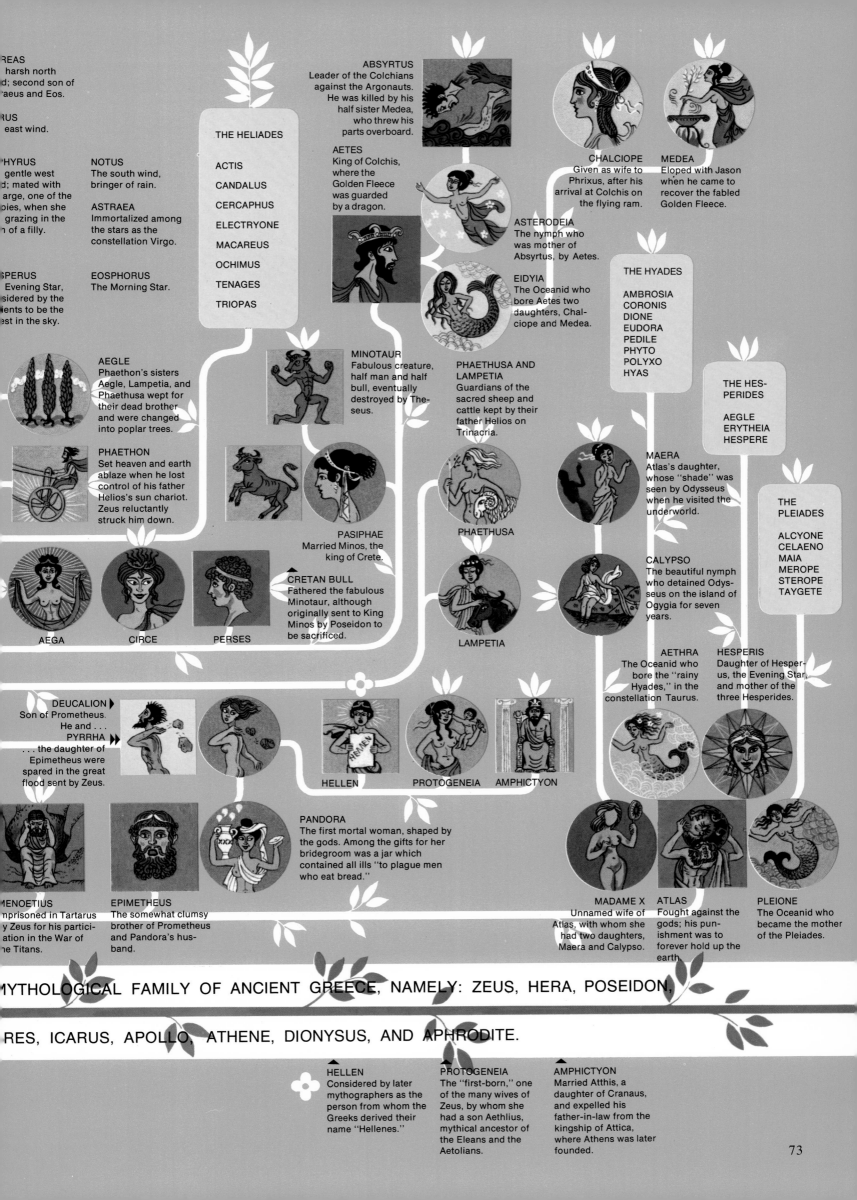

REAS
...harsh north
...d; second son of
...raeus and Eos.

...RUS
...east wind.

...HYRUS
...gentle west
...d; mated with
...arge, one of the
...pies, when she
...grazing in the
...of a filly.

...SPERUS
...Evening Star,
...sidered by the
...ients to be the
...est in the sky.

NOTUS
The south wind, bringer of rain.

ASTRAEA
Immortalized among the stars as the constellation Virgo.

EOSPHORUS
The Morning Star.

THE HELIADES
ACTIS
CANDALUS
CERCAPHUS
ELECTRYONE
MACAREUS
OCHIMUS
TENAGES
TRIOPAS

ABSYRTUS
Leader of the Colchians against the Argonauts. He was killed by his half sister Medea, who threw his parts overboard.

AETES
King of Colchis, where the Golden Fleece was guarded by a dragon.

CHALCIOPE
Given as wife to Phrixus, after his arrival at Colchis on the flying ram.

MEDEA
Eloped with Jason when he came to recover the fabled Golden Fleece.

ASTERODEIA
The nymph who was mother of Absyrtus, by Aetes.

EIDYIA
The Oceanid who bore Aetes two daughters, Chalciope and Medea.

THE HYADES
AMBROSIA
CORONIS
DIONE
EUDORA
PEDILE
PHYTO
POLYXO
HYAS

THE HESPERIDES
AEGLE
ERYTHEIA
HESPERE

AEGLE
Phaethon's sisters Aegle, Lampetia, and Phaethusa wept for their dead brother and were changed into poplar trees.

PHAETHON
Set heaven and earth ablaze when he lost control of his father Helios's sun chariot. Zeus reluctantly struck him down.

MINOTAUR
Fabulous creature, half man and half bull, eventually destroyed by Theseus.

PHAETHUSA AND LAMPETIA
Guardians of the sacred sheep and cattle kept by their father Helios on Trinacria.

MAERA
Atlas's daughter, whose "shade" was seen by Odysseus when he visited the underworld.

THE PLEIADES
ALCYONE
CELAENO
MAIA
MEROPE
STEROPE
TAYGETE

AEGA   **CIRCE**   **PERSES**

PASIPHAE
Married Minos, the king of Crete.

CRETAN BULL
Fathered the fabulous Minotaur, although originally sent to King Minos by Poseidon to be sacrificed.

PHAETHUSA

LAMPETIA

CALYPSO
The beautiful nymph who detained Odysseus on the island of Ogygia for seven years.

AETHRA
The Oceanid who bore the "rainy Hyades," in the constellation Taurus.

HESPERIS
Daughter of Hesperus, the Evening Star, and mother of the three Hesperides.

DEUCALION
Son of Prometheus. He and . . .

PYRRHA
. . . the daughter of Epimetheus were spared in the great flood sent by Zeus.

HELLEN   **PROTOGENEIA**   **AMPHICTYON**

PANDORA
The first mortal woman, shaped by the gods. Among the gifts for her bridegroom was a jar which contained all ills "to plague men who eat bread."

...MENOETIUS
...imprisoned in Tartarus
...y Zeus for his partici-
...ation in the War of
...ne Titans.

EPIMETHEUS
The somewhat clumsy brother of Prometheus and Pandora's husband.

MADAME X
Unnamed wife of Atlas, with whom she had two daughters, Maera and Calypso.

ATLAS
Fought against the gods; his punishment was to forever hold up the earth.

PLEIONE
The Oceanid who became the mother of the Pleiades.

MYTHOLOGICAL FAMILY OF ANCIENT GREECE, NAMELY: ZEUS, HERA, POSEIDON,

RES, ICARUS, APOLLO, ATHENE, DIONYSUS, AND APHRODITE.

HELLEN
Considered by later mythographers as the person from whom the Greeks derived their name "Hellenes."

PROTOGENEIA
The "first-born," one of the many wives of Zeus, by whom she had a son Aethlius, mythical ancestor of the Eleans and the Aetolians.

AMPHICTYON
Married Atthis, a daughter of Cranaus, and expelled his father-in-law from the kingship of Attica, where Athens was later founded.

73

IASION
The goddess Demeter's lover, whose presumption in mating with an immortal so angered Zeus that he struck him dead.

ELECTRA
A Pleiad daughter of Atlas. She had two sons by Zeus: Dardanus and Iasion, the former being the founder of Dardania (Illium – ancient Troy).

The Nereid Amphitrite was conventionally acknowledged as Poseidon's wife, but he had a host of other inamoratas, whose names are:

AMPHITRITE	EURYTE
ALCYONE	GAEA
ALOPE	HELLE
AMYMONE	HIPPOTHOE
APHRODITE	HISTORIS
ARNE	IPHIMEDEIA
ASTYPALAEA	LIBYA
CALCHINIA	MEDUSA
CALYCE	MELIA
CANACE	PEIRENE
CELAENO	PERIBOEA
CHIONE	PITANE
CHRYSOGENEIA	SALAMIS
CORCYRA	SYLEA
DEMETER	THEOPHANE
EUROPA	THOOSA
EURYCYDA	TYRO

ATHENE
Goddess of both wisdom and war, miraculously born from the forehead of her father Zeus after he had swallowed the pregnant Metis.

METIS
Titaness of Wisdom, the first love and wife of Zeus. She assisted him in the scheme to make his father Cronus vomit up Zeus's brothers and sisters.

PANDIA
Selene "conceived and bore a daughter Pandia, exceedingly lovely amongst the deathless gods."

SELENE
In the "Homeric Hymn to Selene," it is related that Zeus was "joined with the moon goddess Selene in love."

THE NYMPHS

DRYADS
The immortal woodland nymphs.

HAMADRYADS
Associated with a single tree and perished with it.

OREADS
Mountain nymphs associated with individual mountains.

GAEA
Zeus and Gaea were considered to be the parents of the nymphs, except those associated with the watery elements.

POSEIDON
Zeus's brother, to whom was given the rulership of the seas; often called "the earthshaker" because of his power to raise storms.

Poseidon had 34 wives. Their names are given in the chart above.

THE MUSES

CLIO (History)	MELPOMENE (Tragedy)	POLYMNIA (Hymnals)
EUTERPE (Lyric Poetry)	TERPSICHORE (Song and Dance)	URANIA (Astronomy)
THALEIA (Comedy)	ERATO (Love Poetry)	CALLIOPE (Epic Poetry)

MNEMOSYNE
Goddess of Memory, daughter of Uranus and Gaea. She became the mother of the nine Muses.

HADES
Ruler of the lower world, the eldest son of Cronus and Rhea. When he was in his infernal realm, only the oaths and curses of men reached his ears.

THE 3 GRACES
Aglaea, Euphrosyne, and Thaleia were the personifications of brilliance, joy, and bloom.

EURYNOME
By Zeus became the mother of the three Graces (or Charites).

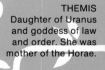

HESTIA
Goddess of the hearth. Although both Poseidon and Apollo sued for her hand, she swore by the head of Zeus to remain a maid forever.

THE HORAE
Known as the Hours and the Seasons, Eunomia, Dike, and Eirene were considered the goddesses of order, justice, and peace, respectively.

THEMIS
Daughter of Uranus and goddess of law and order. She was mother of the Horae.

DEMETER
Goddess of the harvest, second child of Cronus and Rhea. Those who were favored by her were blessed with bountiful crops.

PERSEPHONE
Became queen of the lower worlds and wife to Hades after she was betrothed to him by his brother Zeus, without Demeter's knowledge.

DEMETER
Zeus's sister and wife, and the mother of Persephone.

HERA
Wife of Zeus and, properly speaking, the only married goddess among the Olympians. Hera was recognized as divinity of marriage and childbirth.

APHRODITE
Sometimes called "foam-born," due to the legend that she was born in the sea of a drop of blood from the severed testicles of Uranus.

DIONE
The Oceanid usually regarded as the mother, by Zeus, of Aphrodite, goddess of love and beauty.

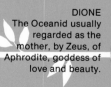

ZEUS — Zeus was conceived by the Greeks as the presiding deity of the universe, the god who controlled the forces of nature as well as the daily existence of men and the immortals. By shaking his fearful aegis (his shield), he could produce storms and darkness; at his command the sun and the moon paused in their courses. By his direction, the change of the seasons was brought about, and day followed night in regular succession. He settled disputes in heaven, assisted earthly princes in the just government of their peoples, and watched with paternal interest over the actions of all mortals.

HERA
Zeus fathered only three children by his wife Hera: Ares, the war god; Hebe, the personification of eternal youth; and Eileithyia, the goddess who had the power of easing the birth labors of women.

ELARA
Daughter of Minyas and Tritogeneia. She was debauched by Zeus, who hid her in a cave beneath the island of Euboea to keep the affair from Hera.

NIOBE
Daughter of Phoroneus and grand-daughter of the river god Inachus. In spite of her descent, it is said that she was the first mortal woman with whom Zeus consorted.

DANAË
Daughter of Acrisius, king of Argos, who imprisoned her in a tower. Zeus came down through a skylight in the roof, in the form of a shower of gold, thus conceiving the hero Perseus.

CALLISTO
Although she had vowed a life of chastity, Zeus persuaded her to submit to his advances. In order to conceal this illicit affair from Hera, he changed Callisto into a she-bear.

EURYMEDUSA
Daughter of Cleitus, who bore a son to Zeus called Myrmidon, because the god had seduced her in the form of an ant ("myrmex" in Greek).

SEMELE
Zeus, in the form of an eagle, spied Semele as she lay naked on the bank of a river. When he revealed his divine identity she willingly accepted his embraces.

LEDA
She became the mother of the Dioscuri Castor and Polydeuces, and some say of Helen of Troy as well, when Zeus consorted with her in the form of a swan.

PROTOGENEIA (Daughter of Deucalion)
The Eleans and Aetolians claimed that their common ancestor was Aethlius, a son born to Zeus by Protogeneia, whose parents – Deucalion and Pyrrha – were the only survivers of the great deluge.

AEGINA
Zeus carried off Aegina from the Peloponnesus to the nearby island of Oenone, where she gave birth to a son, Aeacus. The island was thereafter called Aegina in her honor.

EURYODIA
Ancestor of the hero Odysseus, through her son Arceisius and his wife Chalcomedusa.

PLOUTO
By the Oceanid Plouto, Zeus had a son named Tantalus who became re-nowned as a wealthy king of Lydia. He was celebrated in ancient legend because of the severe punishment inflicted on him in the lower world.

TAYGETE
By Taygete, one of the Pleiades, Zeus had a son named Lacedaemon who married Sparta, King Euratas's daughter. When his father-in-law died, he succeeded to the kingdom and called it Lacedaemonia.

LETO
Daughter of the Titan Coeus on the island of Delos. Apollo and his twin sister Artemis were children of Zeus borne by Leto.

IO
Another of Zeus's conquests. When Hera approached, he sought to hide his unfaithful act by changing the maid into a white cow.

ALCMENE
Seduced by Zeus when he assumed the likeness of Amphitryon, her hus-band. Thus she conceived the fabled hero Herakles, whose mortal twin brother Iphikles was said to be father-ed by Amphitryon.

EUROPA
In the form of a white bull, Zeus ab-ducted King Agenor's daughter Eu-ropa from Phoenicia to the island of Crete where his lovely burden bore him three sons who were named Mi-nos, Rhadamanthys, and Sarpedon.

ANTIOPE
A king's daughter in Thebes, ac-counted among the most beautiful of mortal women. Zeus himself was at-tracted by the lovely maiden and lay with her in the form of a satyr.

PERSEPHONE
According to the Orphic theogony, Persephone bore to her own father Zeus a horned child named Zagreus, who was predestined, if he should reach maturity, to succeed his father.

LAODAMEIA
When Isander and Hippolochus were disputing about the kingdom of Lycia, it was proposed to shoot arrows through a ring fixed on a child's breast. When Laodameia, their sister, offered her son for the purpose, his uncles solved their quarrel by appoint-ing him king.

PROTOGENEIA (Mother of Opus)
Since Protogeneia, the daughter of Deucalion, had already been appro-priated by the Eleans and Aetolians, the Locrians invented a second Proto-geneia, fathered by Zeus, in order to enhance their ancestry.

MAIA
Eldest of the seven Pleiades, daugh-ters of Atlas and Pleione. She became the mother of Hermes, the messenger and herald of the gods, protector of cattle and herds, patron of thieves, and deity of gain.

AEGA
Daughter of the ancient sun god Hel-ios, so dazzling herself that the Titans prevailed upon Gaea to place her in a Cretan cave, where she bore to Zeus a son called Aegipan.

This relief carved in the wall of a cave in Capo di Ponte, Italy, appears to be a prehistoric attempt to define space.

The five-tiered structure of this Buddhist temple in Cambodia architecturally symbolizes the world mountain, the mythic center of the universe.

Illustrated below are two models, one three-dimensional, one two-dimensional, of the same ideal universe. The text in the lower picture identifies the Holy Land of Sinai with the world mountain

Sion at its center, surrounded by the countries of the world; then come the seas, and from their farther shore springs the vault of heaven.

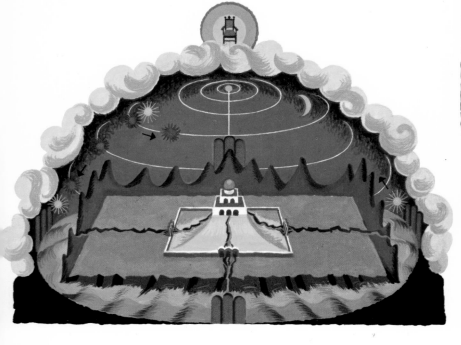

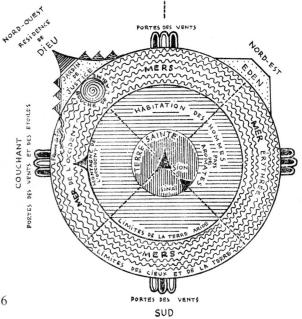

This modern model of the mythic world (right) combines all the features of an ideal universe in the form of a cosmic egg. Rooted in the dark depths of the underworld is the tree that unites earth and heaven. It grows through the plant and animal kingdoms into the heights of insect and bird life, and on through the realm of moon and stars toward the sun.

COSMOLOGY

One need only keep a camera trained on the polestar for the space of a night to obtain a striking image of a universe drawing life from its center *(above)*. Human cosmologies tend to serve as both model and likeness of the sacred and profane order of the universe. The

The world tree appears again in this drawing from a Shaman drum *(above left)*; with its roots in the underworld it rises through the inhabited earth to penetrate the realm of the gods. Five ancient-Chinese characters *(above right)* constitute a cosmic plan of the five world mountains of the universe, which is to be fashioned from the limbs of Pan-Ku (myth, page 66).

As late as the Middle Ages man believed in the possibility of penetrating the canopy of the stars at the world's edge and looking upon new worlds *(below left)*. Modern space travel *(below right)* is opening up a universe of revolving harmonies far surpassing any mythic conception.

In A.D. 712, by order of the Empress Gemmei, a *Record of Ancient Matters* was compiled and deposited in the Shinto temple at Nara, Japan. This document, the *Kojiki*, gives an exceedingly rich and fabulous account of the beginning of all things. The creators of our world, says the *Kojiki*, were twin deities, Izanagi and Izanami. Their names signify, respectively, "the male who invites" and "the female who invites." They first appeared upon the Floating Bridge of Heaven, which overlooked a misty sort of nothingness. Izanagi dipped a jeweled spear down into the mist. Gently he stirred the nothingness, which made a curdling sound: "Koworokoworo."

Izanagi lifted out his spear. From its point dripped curdled brine. The brine formed an island, onto which Izanagi and his twin sister stepped. There they erected a pillar and built a great hall. That done, they conversed in stilted fashion regarding the slight difference between their two bodies. It occurred to Izanagi that bodily union with his sister might bring interesting results, and she agreed. Accordingly, they stepped in opposite directions around the pillar which they had set up and met on the far side of it. Then Izanami said, "Ah, what a handsome young man!" Izanagi for his part replied, "Ah, what a lovely maiden!"

From the first union of the heavenly twins, a bloodsucking water leech was born, and from the second union, a small island of foam. These results were deemed unsuccessful, and so the couple retraced their steps around the pillar. This time, when they met on the far side, Izanagi spoke first. "Ah, what a lovely maiden!" and Izanami responded as expected. Their third union resulted right away in the eight islands of Japan. Then came the sea, the rest of the earth's surface, the seasons, winds, trees, mountains, and last of all the burning, swift, male Spirit of Fire.

But that impetuous child severely burned its mother in coming to birth. She lay down, vomited a host of subsidiary beings, and died.

Izanami's brother bent down over her feet, weeping, and from his tears was born the spirit who dwells on the slope of Mount Kagu. Then he buried her body at the boundary between Idumo and Papaki. That done, he drew his sword and cut off the head of the Fire Child. From its blood untamable creatures arose, and from its dismembered body thousands more came to be. Izanagi, meanwhile, slowly descended into the realm of Night. At the door of the Palace of Darkness, his lovely

basic features of that order are a center in the form of a mountain, tree, or axis linking earth and heaven, the four cosmic points on the circumference of the world, the harmony of the different parts, the inclusion in the cosmos of paradise and the world of the gods, and a layered structure representing the passage from darkness to light.

From outer space, our little Earth appears neat and self-contained – yet the secret of natural harmonies which maintain and sustain life is to a large extent still a mystery.

sister stood waiting. "Oh, Izanami," he said to her, "the lands which we have made are not yet finished. Therefore come back with me!"

"You should have come sooner," Izanami replied. "I do wish to return with you. Yet now I have eaten the food of this realm. I will step inside for a while and discuss this matter with the spirits here. Please do not follow."

Impatient love possessed Izanagi. He pulled from his hair one of two ornamental hair combs to use as a torch. Setting it

from her coffin, she pursued her brother toward the upper world. Izanagi cast his headband behind him as he ran. It turned into a bunch of black grapes, which his sister paused to devour. Then she came on again, running, with the Eight Spirit Thunders around her. Izanagi cast down his other hair comb. It turned into bamboo shoots, which his sister pulled from the ground and ate in her hunger. She sent ahead the sharp-tusked troops of Night, numbering fifteen hundred, but Izanagi beat them off with his sword.

Comparative mythology, applied to the different ways in which various peoples have pictured the world to themselves, reveals an underlying common structure as regards both spiritual conception and psychical expression. Circle and square form the basis of the cosmogonies of all higher civilizations.

The Aztec cosmogram from Mexico *(left)* consists of a cross, with the four past worlds (each of which ended with a catastrophe) in the arms and the present world in the center. The present world is occupied by the fire god Xiutecuhtli; the old gods occupy the elongated arches

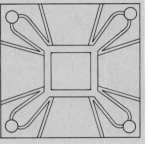

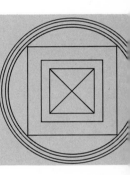

The great Vasudhara mandala from Nepal *(right)* shows the goddess in the center of the pure heavenly palace of the lord the universe. The colors the four parts of the worl symbolize the element and the spiritual attribut of the gods. Here a thre ringed circle and a squa

between the arms of the cross. Each of the four old worlds is cosmically ordered and features a central world tree; each tree has two branches forming three twigs, supports a bird of heaven, and is flanked by a primal couple. The signs and insignia of the gods are distributed with similar precision.

represent the univers The square has four gat and is divided into fo triangles (shown schema cally, *above right*), whi indicate the cosmic dire tion, the elements, and t visible and invisible qua ties of the deity comman ing the center.

ablaze, he entered the door. His sister lay rotting, and there were black maggots which fed upon her flesh from within.

Great-Thunder in her head,
Fire-Thunder in her breast,
Black-Thunder in her belly,
Crack-Thunder in her loins,
Young-Thunder in her left hand,
Earth-Thunder in her right hand,
Sounding-Thunder in her left foot,
Reclining-Thunder in her right foot.

Then Izanami screamed in fury, "You have put me to shame!" Arising, monstrous,

Near the level pass between the world whose dimensions we can guess and the world which is strange to us, a miraculous peach tree grows. Izanagi, out of breath, stopped underneath the tree. He flung three peaches at his pursuers. All, except Izanami herself, shrank back into darkness. Then, quickly, Izanagi rolled a great stone into place to block the pass. When his sister arrived, panting and wailing, at the far side of the stone, he spoke and formally divorced her forever.

"Oh, my handsome brother," she shrilled, "if you do this, I shall devour a thousand people of your country every day!" Izanagi

Pictured here, together with simplified layout diagrams, are two splendid examples from Mexico and Nepal. The large mandala *(opposite)* from Nepal is a sort of cosmogram representing the heavenly realm of the Buddhas and redeemer gods of Buddhism. Designed as aids to meditation, mandalas use geometric forms as vehicles of a particular religious and mystical message. Often designed to indicate the four directions as well as an immovable center, they convey both stillness and a sense of time passing.

replied resignedly, "Oh, my lovely sister, if you do that I shall cause fifteen hundred women to bear every night!"

With that, the human condition was set.

THE KILLING OF YMIR

Norse myth regarding nature's beginnings survives in an Icelandic poem called the *Völuspa,* or *Sibyl's Prophecy,* which dates from A.D. 1000 or thereabouts. It tells of an abyss, Ginnungagap, frothing with streams which twined in and out between twin whirlpools of fire and ice. From those streams, mist arose. The mist solidified into a cosmic cow called Audhumla. She licked the ice cliffs for nourishment.

Her warm tongue released three gods from the ice. Odin was the first of them; the others' names are in dispute. Meanwhile, a giant named Ymir arose out of the mist. He drank the cow's milk and grew very great. From between his toes crept hulking tribes of ugly giant children.

The gods agreed that Ymir would have to be done away with. He was too huge, too overshadowing. Therefore, Odin reached up and plunged an ashen spear into Ymir's heart. Salt blood gushed out. It washed the tribe of giants away to a concealed dimension of reality called Jotunheim, drowning most of them in the process.

Ymir's bones form the bedrock of continents. His flesh is earth. His hair is vegetation. His blood is the rivers and seas. His whole bulk lives on, in a sense, although it sprawls supine and blocks up bubbling Ginnungagap.

In order to illuminate nature, the three divine brothers who were born of the ice built a fire. From its sparks they made the stars. From its white and yellow flames they made the moon and sun. They set those beings of brilliance aloft, to circle Ymir's ice-blue cranium. The giants who had survived the deluge of blood were half-blinded and enraged by these developments.

The giants unleashed swift wolves in pursuit of the moon and sun. Each month one wolf takes bites out of the moon, which escapes him and grows whole again. The other wolf seldom gets the sun in his jaws, and when he does, he finds it too hot to swallow. He coughs the sun up again. But this will not always be so. Both wolves are tireless. Someday they will devour the lights by which we live.

We, that is to say humanity, are toys originally created by elvish beings who appeared spontaneously from the sockets of Ymir's bones. After we had been fashioned by those clever gnomes, Odin and his brothers breathed life, soul, and speech into us.

Shown here are but a few of mythic man's many attempts to portray the basic structure of the cosmos. They show that people everywhere approached

1 The three images of creation on this page illustrate the ideas of Tibetan Lamaism regarding the emergence of the cosmos. The circling of the five elements in a sea of flame gives rise initially to these overlaid spirals of light.

2 When the light spirals have expanded and filled space, the four continents and the subcontinents emerge from the primal ocean and the world mountain (Mount Meru) begins to rise toward heaven. We have here the basic structure of all cosmological symbolism, with the four parts of the half circle and the five stages of the world mountain, which widens toward the top. The attempt to represent the third dimension by using surfaces that open up is a typical feature of mythic cosmograms.

3 The third and final stage of the process can be seen in this complete cosmology as handed down by Tibetan tradition. The four continents rising out of the cosmic ocean are themselves crowned by the *axis mundi,* the world mountain, towering up into the realm of the gods.

2

3

this problem with a limited number of similar forms. The basic symbols that occur again and again are the circle, as defining both the earth and the universe; the square as ordering space; and the axis or center as key point of the created world. At that center stands the world mountain, the world tree, or man. It is man's task to give substance to the center of his world and from there eventually to rise to the heights of heaven.

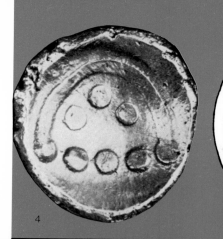

4

5

6

4–6 The three decorated bowls on the left may represent attempts to depict the cosmos. The first one, Germano-Celtic in origin, shows what looks like a rainbow above a series of circles. The other two are from the ancient-Middle Eastern culture of Elam, the middle one possibly suggesting a cosmic center between the oceans and the continents.

7

8

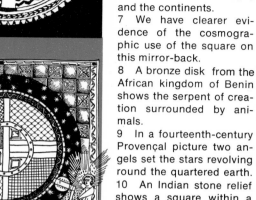

9

7 We have clearer evidence of the cosmographic use of the square on this mirror-back.

8 A bronze disk from the African kingdom of Benin shows the serpent of creation surrounded by animals.

9 In a fourteenth-century Provençal picture two angels set the stars revolving round the quartered earth.

10 An Indian stone relief shows a square within a circle. The couple in the center keep the wheel of the ages in motion.

11 The Egyptians depicted their cosmos enclosed within the cycle of the winged sun.

12 A Jain cosmogram from India shows a layered arrangement of worlds with the central *axis mundi*.

10

11

12

13–14 The two ancient-Spanish world maps are encircled by the phases of the moon and by oceans.

15 The Indian depiction shows the serpent and the tortoise supporting the earth, with the central world mountain, Mount Meru, in the center.

13

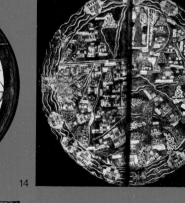

14

15

16

17

18

16 A cosmogram of the elements: beneath the sky the world is formed of water, earth, air, and fire.

17 One Greek idea of the world – as a disk surrounded by water, out of which Helios, the sun, rose in the east.

18 Even Hieronymus Bosch, in his *Garden of Earthly Delights,* set the earth like a disk in the sphere of the universe.

81

URANUS, CRONUS, AND ZEUS

The Greek myth of creation begins with deceptive gentleness. Chaos was first. From Chaos came Gaea, Mother Earth. She in turn gave birth to Uranus, Father Sky.

Uranus rose and fondly gazed upon his mother beneath him. He showered rain and sunshine down upon her hidden clefts, from which grass, flowers, trees, insects, birds, and animals of all kinds were born. Uranus filled the rivers and seas of Mother Earth with life also. His strength entered her caverns, from which gigantic Titans and one-eyed Cyclopes emerged.

Mother Earth loved the most fearsome sons of her stony wombs, but Uranus hated and feared them. Some he confined to Tartarus, an underworld. Gaea resented this. She found Uranus heavy now. She begged her seven remaining Titans to push him away from her. Cronus, youngest of the seven, took a lead in that struggle. Using a sickle chipped from a high peak of flint, he mercilessly castrated Uranus. From the blood which rained down, the relentless Furies sprang vengefully into being. Cronus cast his father's testicles into the sea. Aphrodite, the goddess of love, was born from the foam of them.

Uranus retreated to the outermost regions of the universe. There he remains. His eyes are stars, which view with regretful coldness the violence prevailing upon earth.

In his agony, Uranus had predicted that Cronus too would find himself overcome by his offspring. Cronus tried to keep that from happening. Deliberately, he swallowed his children just as soon as they were born. The Titaness Rhea, who was his bride, dutifully produced Hestia, Demeter, Hera, Hades, and Poseidon, only to see each one vanish down the gullet of Cronus. Her last child, Zeus, she saved by trickery. Wrapping up a boulder in swaddling clothes, Rhea told Cronus that it was the baby, and he swallowed the boulder.

Zeus grew up in hiding. Finally, when he was strong enough, he reappeared and somehow forced his father to disgorge the brothers and sisters previously gulped down. Between the old generation of Titans and the new generation of gods war was declared.

To increase his forces for the struggle ahead, Zeus fathered a number of divine children. His particular favorite among them was Dionysus-Zagreus. This golden-haired infant was not the Dionysus who would invent wine at a later point in the world's development. He was an older brother of that deity and a kind of father to ourselves.

By offering such toys as tops, jointed dolls, and Golden Apples of the Hesperides, the Titans lured Dionysus-Zagreus into the dark wood which at that time covered the island of Crete. There they tore him limb from limb and tossed the fragments into a caldron for boiling. When the torn god had been well cooked, the Titans devoured his meat and bones alike and drank the broth from the caldron's red-hot lip. They hoped that in this way they would come to share in the child's essential immortality.

Father Zeus searched everywhere for his lost son. Coming at last to Crete, he saw by the gleaming eyes of the Titans just what they had done. One of the Homeric Hymns (in Jack Lindsay's translation) describes what happened next:

Then Zeus no longer held back his power. On the height his heart was swarming with fury, and all his might he uttered forth. From Heaven and Olympus he swung, tossing his lightning-darts. The bolts he flung were fierce with thunder and lightning, and thickly they came out of his strong right hand with a sacred flame rolling: the life-giving earth with a shudder of sound took fire, and measureless forest crackled around. All land was seething and heaving, and Ocean-stream and the barren sea. Lapped round with a fiery steam stood the earthborn Titans. Numberless flames were blown to the brightening aether. Glare of the thunder-stone and lightning blinded the eyes of the strongest there.

The Titans were almost all burned up in that holocaust. From their ashes, humanity arose. The guilt, fear, greed, stupidity, and clumsiness of the Titans exist again in us. So, too, does some flickering godlike spark: heritage of Dionysus-Zagreus.

A more abstract and philosophical myth of creation begins with black-winged Night arising out of Chaos and dancing upon the seething depths. The dance of Night eventually stirred up a great wind in serpent form, called Ophion, which she embraced and warmed between her hands. Now the wind grew lustful, coiled about her, and joined in the dance.

Night assumed the form of a dove, brooding on the waves. She laid a silver egg upon the waters. The serpent-wind Ophion coiled seven times about the World Egg until it hatched and split open. The bottom half of the egg became the earth with its myriad inhabitants. The top half was the sky, sun, moon, and stars.

That myth shows signs of being extremely ancient and probably Middle Eastern in origin. In late classical times it was revived

A modern representation *(left)* of the ancient anthropogenic myth (page 85) of the Hopi Indians of North America leads us symbol by symbol through their way of interpreting and accounting for the world. Initially, there was the emergence of consciousness in the form of Tawa, the Sun Spirit *(top).* He created a cave world inhabited by insects *(bottom).* The insects failed to recognize the meaning of life, so he sent Spider Grandmother to lead his creatures by the difficult path of transformation to a higher level, where they became animals. When the animals in turn proved unsatisfactory some of them, again led by Spider Grandmother, attained by a further metamorphosis the third or human world. There the people founded the first civilization and set about looking for the meaning of life. But only after further emissaries had been dispatched – birds this time – did they find their way to the land of their destiny. In this new world, they were divided by language into Hopi, Navaho, and other tribes, and began to live the full life of man. The spider, the mythic leader and folk hero who shows man the way to each new step of his existence, ultimately teaches him to weave. The spider's connection with spinning and weaving makes it a symbol of eternity, which is the condition of man's metamorphosis and further development. In short, the myth reflects man's ascent through a continuing process of cultural individuation.

The picture on the right recounts an Australian myth of the origin of man and the beginnings of civilization. At the top we see two primal sisters at the source of life, and in the next compartment down we see them giving birth to the first men. The third compartment shows the first eight trees *(left)* planted by Djanggawul and the two sisters with their brother and the morning and evening sun *(right).* At the bottom we find a highly abstract résumé of the complete process.

There is an endless wealth and variety of creation myths dealing with the origin of man and the development of the tribes and peoples of the world. The author of human life on earth is often a first, divine couple, or the sky as deity, or some primeval demiurge of usually gi-

Then at last there was man;
and Prometheus, son of Iapetos, is said
to have taken earth, mixed it with running water,
and formed it in the image
of the gods that rule the universe.

OVID, METAMORPHOSES I, 80

gantic proportions. But it may also be the cosmic wind, the animals of the country concerned, the air, or the cosmogonic egg. There are a great many myths that have man being created on the moon or coming originally from the sun. Sun and moon, the two celestial objects most central to our existence, are also regarded as having originated various animals that myth counts among the authors of mankind. Certain tribes in India trace their origin to the *nagas* – semidivine beings who were half man, half snake. Other myths tell of godlike beings and Mother Goddesses, and of course there are the legendary heroes of ancient Greece. All these mythic precursors of the human race emerged in response to one basic question: where does life come from and what is it all about?

by Greek adherents to the cult of Orpheus and given a somewhat different conclusion. Orphic doctrine maintained that the first creature to leap out of the World Egg when it split in two was Phanes, or Eros (his names are interchangeable), a golden-winged, double-sexed god of love who contained within himself "the seed of all the gods."

A hostile commentator described Phanes as a serpent with a bull's and a lion's head flanking the human head in their midst. Other sources credited the god with a ram's

The rough approximation to a human figure pictured on the right evokes the myths attributing the origin of man to a primal being or giant of some kind. According to this tradition the gods first placed on earth a crude prototype creature from whose body sprang the different forms of terrestrial life. There

head as well. He roared, bellowed, bleated, hissed, and sang; calling nature forth by means of sound vibrations alone.

MAYAN ACCOUNT OF THE CREATION OF MANKIND

The Quiche Mayan myths of creation are related in the *Popol Vuh*. The name *Popol Vuh* has been translated as meaning the "Collection of the Council" or the "Collection of Written Leaves." This manuscript is one of the most important of the very few sources of pre-Columbian myth. It was discovered comparatively recently, having come to light only in 1830. The *Popol Vuh* asserts that in the beginning Hurakan, whose name means Heart of Heaven, passed over a universe of water which lay in darkness. When he called out the first land appeared.

Then Hurakan and the other high gods agreed that animals should be made. When animals had been created, the gods turned their attention to men.

are often a number of such prototypes, representing various attempts on the part of the gods to hit upon the true and proper form for their human creation. In the Indian myths it is Prajapati, "lord of creatures," or the primal man Purusha (literally: "person") who turn their bodies bit by bit into the various phenomena of the world, culminating in man and the animals. The Californian Indians tell of two primal beings, Murumda and Kuksu; another of their myths makes the coyote and the silver fox responsible in various emanations for the emergence of man and nature. We have already come across the primal being of ancient-Chinese mythology, Pan-Ku. He lived for a whole age in the primal cosmos before disintegrating to form the mountains, rivers, and living creatures of the world (myth, page 66).

The first men were carved from wood and life was given to them. But they proved to be irreverent to the gods and cruel to animals. So then Hurakan determined to destroy them. He caused a swelling of the waters of earth and a deluge. Thick rains fell upon the people. Their eyes were torn out by the bird Xecotcovach, their heads were torn off by the bird Camulatz, their bones and muscles were broken by the bird Tecumbalam, and they were ground into powder.

The god Hurakan tried once more. He took white and yellow maize and made a paste.

ter. And from these eight came all the Quiche, the Mayan people.

THE MAKING OF MEN

The Hopi Indians, a Pueblo tribe living in the southwestern desert of the United States, maintain that in the beginning there was only Tokpela, Endless Space. Somehow in this endless space a spark of consciousness was struck. The Hopi named this Tawa, the Sun Spirit. Tawa created the first world. It was a cavern of a kind, with noth-

"The Sun Spirit is displeased with what he has created. The *powaka* have made you forget what you should have remembered. Therefore, you ought to get away."

This time, however, Spider Grandmother made no offer to lead the faithful remnant into a new world. They had to find the way themselves, somehow or other. One old man said, "Have we not heard footsteps up in the sky?" Others agreed; they too had heard someone walking above. So they decided to send birds to see how things were up there, up through the Sipapuni, or Hole in the Sky.

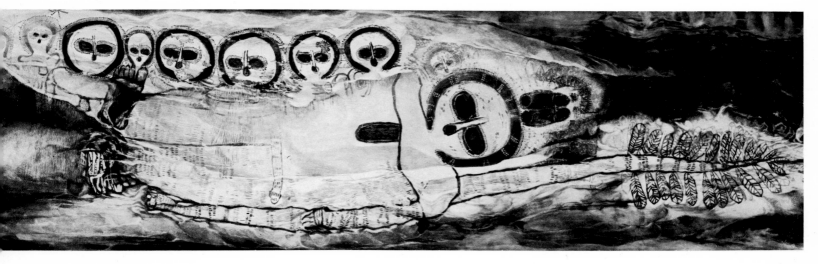

This reclining figure *(above)* is one of the primal beings of the Australian aborigines, the Wondjinas. He is lying on a world tree. Behind him and emerging from him we see the mythic first inhabitants of the Kimberley region of northeast Australia.

The Aztec picture *(far left)* shows the mythic birth of the gods from the womb of the Great Mother as the first phase of creation.

The Polynesian sea god Tangaroa *(left)* appears as a numinous creator spirit from the various parts of whose body gods, men, animals, and all the creatures of the world gradually emerge, take shape, and detach themselves.

From the paste he molded four men and named them: Iqi-Balam, or Tiger of the Moon; Mahacutah, or Distinguished Name; Balam-Agab, or Tiger of the Night; and Balam-Quitze, or Tiger Smiling Sweetly. Lest they become too much like gods, Hurakan breathed a cloud upon their eyes and thus reduced their vision so that they could no longer see too much. Then Hurakan placed them in sleep, and while they slept, he created wives for them: Cakixa, or Brilliant Water; Tzununiha, or House of the Water; Choima, or Beautiful Water; and Caha-Paluma, or Falling Wa-

ing but insects in it. The insects disappointed him. Tawa sent Spider Grandmother down to them as a messenger. She said, "Tawa, the Sun Spirit who made you, is unhappy because you do not understand the meaning of life. Therefore he has commanded me to lead you from this first world to a second one."

The journey upward to the second world proved very arduous and long. Before they reached it, many of the insects had metamorphosed into animals. But they still did not seem to understand the meaning of life. Therefore, Tawa sent Spider Grandmother to lead the animals upward until they reached a third world, which was somewhat lighter and less forbidding. On that new and extremely difficult journey, some of the animals became people.

Then Spider Grandmother taught the people how to weave cloth to keep their bodies warm and how to make pots for storing food and water. Men and women began to have some glimmering, after a time, of the meaning of life. But certain *powaka*, or sorcerers, distorted this intuitive knowledge. Gambling and promiscuity became the rule rather than the exception. Children ran about crying, unclean and uncared for. Worst of all, people began to feel that they had created themselves.

Once more, Spider Grandmother appeared. She spoke only to a few, saying,

The first bird they sent was a swallow. It reached the Sipapuni but lacked the strength to pass through into the further world. The next bird they sent was a dove. It mounted through the sky hole and at once descended again to report. There was, the dove informed the faithful, a new world up above.

Next they sent up a hawk, which explored further. The hawk reported that as far as it could see, the new world appeared uninhabited. Finally, the faithful sent up a catbird. The catbird flew through the new world until it came to a place much like the Arizona desert. There stood a stone hut beside an irrigated patch of earth where squash, melons, and maize were growing. A person sat between the house and the garden, sleeping, with his head on his knees. The catbird alighted nearby. After a while, the person awoke and lifted his head.

Two black lines were painted across his cheekbones and the bridge of his nose. His face was scarred and purplish with burns and was encrusted with dried blood. Around his neck hung a necklace of turquoise and a necklace of bones. His eyes were so deeply sunken under the ridge of his brow as to be almost invisible except for their glinting. The catbird recognized the person as Death. And Death asked gently, "Are you not afraid?"

"No," said the catbird. "I have come on

behalf of people in the world below this one. They would like to share this country with you. Would that be possible?" Death, whom the Hopi called Masuwu, thought for a while, gloomily. Then he said, "You see how it is in this place. If the people wish to come, then let them come."

Spider Grandmother commanded a chipmunk to plant a sunflower seed in a village square. She taught the people how to sing it up into the sky by the power of music alone. Each time that they stopped for breath, the sunflower stopped growing. Not only that, but before it had come near the Sipapuni it began to bend and droop under the weight of its blossom.

Violation of God's commandment, however, makes the first couple aware of their physical nature and they are forced to leave the innocent state of Paradise behind them. God appears and banishes them to mortal, terrestrial existence.

Having created the world in its original, serene state and called it Paradise, God created Adam, the first man. Eve followed, born from Adam's side – an ancient mythic concept that we also find in the Buddha legends.

The story of the Garden of Eden (told here in Lucas Cranach's great painting) is how the Christian religion illustrates the origin of man and his relegation to a probationary existence on earth.

"Pashumayni! Pashumayni!" which means "Be careful! Be careful!" Soon the entire bamboo was covered with figures struggling upward into the sky.

As the people emerged through the Sipapuni and set their feet upon the firm ground of the upper world, Yawpa the Mockingbird greeted each one: "You shall be a Hopi and speak the Hopi language," she would sing, or: "You shall be a Navaho and speak the Navaho language." In the same way she would assign the Apache tongue, and so on through the Indian tribes.

The tribes camped together around the Sipapuni. More people kept arriving. The latecomers were *powaka*. The man who had

So the chipmunk planted a spruce seed in place of the sunflower. The people sang a second song, and the spruce grew rapidly. Yet it too failed to reach the Sipapuni. Then the chipmunk planted a pine tree, but that did not grow quite tall enough either. Finally, the chipmunk planted a bamboo. The people sang well, and the bamboo grew up straight and tall. Between verses of the song, when the people were silent for a moment, a joint appeared in the stalk of the bamboo. Spider Grandmother was dancing silently back and forth to help the people sing the bamboo straight into the sky. Just at sunset, she cried out, "It is finished! The bamboo tip has passed through the Sipapuni!"

Now the people had a very long climb to make. Spider Grandmother warned them to take nothing on the journey. They were to leave all *powaka,* or sorcerers, below. As they began their ascent, Yawpa the Mockingbird fluttered about the bamboo crying,

been chief of the village below went and called down through the Sipapuni: "You who are still climbing must go on back down. It was to escape your influence that we came here. Do not follow us. You are not wanted."

Yet the people who were still struggling upward persisted. Therefore, Spider Grandmother's pilgrim charges grasped the tip of the bamboo and tore the entire stalk from the ground far below. They shook the bamboo and allowed it to fall back upon the third world, from which they had escaped. As the magical bamboo crumpled, thousands of doomed human beings toppled like seeds from its tottering and falling stalk, down into the darkness of the world below.

Darwinian Indians

Primitive Indians of southern California firmly believed that man is descended from

animals. That seems a curious idea but it is one which most people now share.

According to one nineteenth-century Indian source quoted by a contemporary missionary, the ancestors of mankind were coyotes who developed an odd habit of burying their dead. This custom brought about a gradual change in the coyotes themselves. They formed a strange habit of sitting up. Regrettably, this wore away their beautiful bushy tails. After many generations, they began standing upright. When that happened, their forepaws lengthened into human hands. Their sharp muzzles shortened, bit by bit, into human faces.

Two trees stand in the garden – the Tree of Knowledge and the Tree of Life. The couple, seduced by the serpent, chooses the fruit

of the former and is subsequently evicted from the state of ignorant grace.

The expulsion from the Garden ends the first stage of man's existence in the original unity of creation, and marks the beginning of his profane existence in a mortal world characterized by the existence of both good and evil.

CREATIVE SACRIFICE

The primitive headhunters of Borneo declare that mankind sprang from a living rock in the middle of the sea. The rock simply opened its mouth and out walked the first woman and the first man. Her name was Nunsumnundok. Kinharingan was her husband. "How can we walk?" Nunsumnundok asked. "There is no land."

Kinharingan thought perhaps they could walk on the water, and so they slid down the rock and tried. To their astonishment, they found that the water would support their steps. The couple scrambled back onto their mother rock and sat down to think. For a very long time they sat wondering in which direction they should walk out over the limitless sea.

Then they started. Their steps led to the house of Bisagit, a deity associated with disease and death. Bisagit presented the first man and the first woman with a handful of dust. Returning to their mother rock, they crumbled up a bit of it and mixed that with the dust from Bisagit. Earth grew from the mixture.

Kinharingan and Nunsumnundok had one son and one daughter. They killed their daughter and buried her. Sugarcane grew up from the bones of the daughter's arms, and banana trees from her fingers. The first coconut tree had its roots in the eye and nose holes of her skull. All sorts of animals, too, arose from this first human sacrifice.

The Aztec people of the high Mexican plateau traced the world's creation back to the heavenly lovemaking of a god and goddess: Citlaltonac and Citlalicue. The goddess gave birth to a flint knife, which she flung away. Its substance recalls the flint sickle with which the Titan Cronus castrated his Sky Father in Greek myth. Citlalicue's harsh offspring spontaneously produced no less than 1,600 gods and goddesses, like sparks struck from the flint surface. Those deities descended to the underworld and purloined a bone from that dark region's shadowy chief. Smearing it with their own blood, they immersed it in a blue bowl of light. Out of the bowl a human boy and girl were born, and also a pair of deities who deliberately set fire to themselves to serve as the sun and the moon.

LOVE AND DEATH

Leo Frobenius first recorded (in *African Genesis,* 1937) the following tale which was related to him by a Wahungwe Makoni witch doctor: God made man and called him Mwuetsi, which means moon. He gave

At the dawn of creation Vishnu reclines on the back of the *naga* Ananta in the middle of the primal ocean. Ananta, symbol of cosmic energy, protects Vishnu with his eleven heads. With the god in this painting from Rajasthan is Lakshmi, the goddess of beauty.

Mwuetsi a magical horn filled with *ngona* oil. Then he set him in the bottom of a lake. After some time Mwuetsi told God that he wanted to go up onto the earth to live. God said that would not be wise. Mwuetsi insisted, however, and God acquiesced. Mwuetsi went up onto the earth. It was cold and bleak. There were no animals, not even any trees. Mwuetsi wandered a long way. He prayed to God. "How shall I live here?" he asked. God said it was too late to turn back. "You have started on a path at the end of which death awaits you. Yet, for comfort on the way, I shall give you a person of your own kind."

At that moment a maiden, Massassi, the Morning Star, appeared. She went with Mwuetsi into a cave. They made a fire. They lay down, one on either side of the warm blaze.

In the night, Mwuetsi awakened. He wondered why God had given him the maiden as a friend. What was he to do with her? He unstoppered his *ngona* horn and moistened one finger with the oil it contained. Then he leaped over the fire. He touched Massassi's body with his oily finger. He leaped back over the fire. Then he slept again.

Toward dawn, after the fire had gone out, Mwuetsi awakened for the second time. He looked over toward Massassi. Her belly was much swollen. As the first rays of the sun entered the cave, Massassi woke up, groaning, and began to bear children. Her first children were grass, then bushes, then trees. The trees grew very high, and then the rains came. The earth was fruitful now. For two years, Mwuetsi and Massassi lived together joyfully. They gathered fruits to eat. They started a little farm. Then God took Massassi away. He set her down at the bottom of the lake, where Mwuetsi could not find her. Mwuetsi wept and cried out to God. He was terribly lonely. "I have warned you that you are going to your death," God said. "Yet now I will give you another friend." At that moment Morongo, the Evening Star, came to Mwuetsi and took his hand. They went together into the cave. Mwuetsi wanted to lie down in his usual place on the far side of the fire. "Don't be like that," Morongo said. "Lie over here with me."

Mwuetsi looked about for his *ngona* horn. "You won't need it," Morongo said. "I am different from Massassi." She showed him how to couple with her. Soon afterward, Mwuetsi went to sleep.

He woke up as the sun came in and found Morongo already in labor. That first morning she bore chickens, sheep, and goats. The second morning she bore eland and cattle. The third morning she bore girls and boys. By nightfall, all were fully grown.

The fourth night Mwuetsi again lay down beside Morongo. Lightning flashed at the cavern entrance. It shook the living rock of the ceiling. Heavy thunder echoed and re-echoed over the mountain above. Mwuetsi was afraid. He guessed God did not wish him to couple with Morongo any more. But she suggested that he roll a stone against the entrance to the cavern. Then God could not see what they were up to.

In the morning Morongo bore leopards, lions, scorpions, and snakes. Her last-born was a gigantic black mamba. Mwuetsi rolled away the stone from the mouth of the cave. Morongo's new brood scattered forth. God saw them. "I warned you," God said to Mwuetsi.

After that, Mwuetsi coupled with his grown daughters, while Morongo coupled with the great serpent which was her last-born. She had no more children. But Mwuetsi's daughters brought forth many boys and girls. It was not long before Mwuetsi found himself the king of a great people.

All his desires were satisfied, except the yearning that he still cherished in his heart for Morongo, the Evening Star. One night he went to see her. He entered her room. He pushed her down upon the bed. "Do not do this," Morongo said. But Mwuetsi persisted. The serpent who was Morongo's husband lay coiled underneath the bed. He lifted up his head. He bit Mwuetsi in the thigh. Mwuetsi, the first man, was very strong. He did not die immediately. However, he became very sick. Because he was sick, it did not rain. The streams dried up; animals died; the people too were perishing.

Mwuetsi's descendants made a circle. Within the circle they tossed magical dice and watched how the dice fell. They did this in order to learn what God wanted them to do.

"Mwuetsi, your king, is very sick, and you must send him back into the lake." That is what the dice told the people. So they strangled Mwuetsi and chose another man to be their king.

SEPARATION OF EARTH AND SKY

Polynesian creation begins with two beings in loving embrace. The first of these was Rangi, Father Sky; the second was Papa, Mother Earth. For more than a million years, unceasingly, these two made love. In the darkness between their bodies, all things were generated. Among the children of Rangi and Papa, certain divinities sprang up. These creatures could not abide the continuing darkness and turmoil. They came together in council and asked what ought to be done. The first to propose a solution to their difficulty was Tu-matauenga, the ferocious Father of Human Beings. He suggested killing both parents outright. Thus from the very beginning, mankind proclaimed its fierceness through the mouth of Tu-matauenga.

The Father of Forests, Tane-mahuta, had an alternative suggestion. "Let us push our parents apart," he said. "That way, Mother Earth will remain our support, and Father Sky will care for us on high."

After millennia of consultation, the gods elected to implement Tane-mahuta's proposal. Rongo-ma-tane, Father of Cultivated Foods, was first to stand up and strain with all his might against the rib cage of Rangi. But he could not push his father away. Tangaroa, Father of Fish and Reptiles, tried next. He met with no better success. Then Haumia-tikitiki, Father of Wild Foods, tried and failed. Tu-matauenga, Father of Human Beings, had no luck either. Finally, Tane-mahuta, Father of Forests, himself undertook the struggle. He planted his leafy head firmly down upon the navel of Mother Earth. Then he doubled up his legs and set the soles of his feet against Father Sky. His parents cried out, "What are you doing? How dare you show such disrespect to your parents?" Inexorably, Tane-mahuta straightened his back and kicked out with his enormous legs of teak. He pushed Father Sky far away.

Immediately there was light. But there was also bitterness. Tawhiri-ma-tea, Father of Winds and Storms, loudly berated his brothers for what they had done. In years to come Tawhiri-ma-tea was to take revenge for Father Sky by blowing pain and destruction down upon all creatures.

Bronislaw Malinowsky, the anthropologist, once defined myth as "the re-arising primordial reality in narrative form." Abundant justification exists for regarding ancient myth as the wellspring of modern literature in all its branches.

We recognize the fact that our own beginnings – the taproots of humanity – remain shrouded in mystery. So do the taproots of nature herself, although they may reside in what has been described as "the abyss of the nucleus." Yet, nonetheless, beginnings there must have been. Man keeps right on searching for evidence of them. We explore the past by means of observation and experiment, yes, and also along the frontiers of imagination itself.

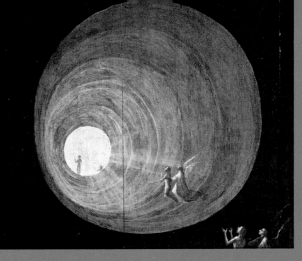

Arise, soul, arise. Ascend to your ancient home.

GINZA III, 511

A view by Hieronymus Bosch of the soul's ascent to the realm of everlasting light.

WORLDS ABOVE BELOW AND WITHIN

Sing a song
to the heaven-born light
that searches far,
to the sun god,
the Son of Heaven.

RIG VEDA X, 37

The ancient-Egyptian sky goddess Nut arches her body over the earth. Mother of the sun's course and wife of the sun god, she swallows the sun in the evening to bear it again in the east next morning. Shining down on the earth, she appears there as the goddess Hathor, the "eye of the sun." Nut represents the cycle of light, Hathor the sun's manifestation as day star.

Forces which we can neither observe directly nor explain satisfactorily play through everything and everyone, all the time. Even at the inorganic level, as electron microscopes reveal, mysteries abound. The mythmakers of all races and cultures have faced up to such mysteries in imagination. The kind of intelligence which creates mythologies is that which recognizes the presence of enormous and incomprehensible forces hidden away in the depths of nature – of worlds within worlds and beyond all the worlds that are directly known to us.

Physical extension and time-span are both relative matters, as Einstein showed mathematically. An earlier cosmologist, Sir Isaac Newton, knew how peripheral is all our knowledge to the shifting mysteries of the cosmos. "I seem to have been only like a boy playing on the seashore," Newton confessed, "and diverting myself now and then finding a smoother pebble or a prettier shell than ordinary, whilst the great ocean of truth lay all undiscovered before me."

Like "truth" in Newton's metaphor, myth too is oceanic in character: a limitless expanse of unknown depths, where the known and the unknown, fact and legend, the quick and the dead, swim forever. William Mariner's early-nineteenth-century *Account of the Natives of the Tonga Islands* speaks of that invisible ocean as "Bolotoo" or "Mbulotu" – a place to which all things without exception invariably flow. "If a stone or any other substance is broken," Mariner reported, "immortality is equally its reward; nay, artificial bodies have equal good luck with men, and hogs, and yams. If an axe or chisel is worn out or broken up, away flies its soul for the service of the gods. If a house is taken down, or any way destroyed, its immortal part will find a situation on the plains of Bolotoo; and, to confirm this doctrine, the Fiji people can show you a sort of natural well or deep hole in the ground, at one of their islands, across the bottom of which runs a stream of water, in which you may clearly perceive the souls of men and women, beasts and plants, of sticks and stones, and of all the broken utensils of this frail world, swimming or rather tumbling along one over the other pell-mell into the regions of immortality."

THE COMING OF THE SUN

Qat, the chief god of the Banks Islanders, created men, pigs, trees, and even the ancient rocks. His own mother had been a rock. Qat created things chiefly out of boredom and restlessness brought about by the fact that there was no nighttime. No one got any sleep when Qat was young.

A dark deity was said to live beyond the Torres Strait. In his eagerness to witness the dark one, Qat built a canoe. Taking a pig along for companionship, he paddled away through the strait to the foot of the sky. No one knows precisely what happened between the restless demigod and the Spirit of Darkness. Qat returned, bringing with him a cock and other birds in his canoe. Stepping ashore, he showed his brothers how to make sleeping mats. He told them not to be afraid when the sun began sinking down. When their own eyelids began to droop and darkness covered them, they were not going to die altogether.

Qat's brothers lay down and slept. He kept watch. The dawn was very long in coming. Impatiently, Qat seized a knife of obsidian. With it he sliced open the eastern sky. The birds began to sing, and his brothers awoke to see the sun rising through the wound in the sky.

Brazil Indians say that the Sun is pursued by dark Night. Once upon a time, Night lay coiled up in a gourd kept by a serpent. Someone uncorked the gourd at a wedding, whereupon Night escaped. The poor Sun has been running ever since.

Australian aborigines believed that in the dreamtime the Sun had no need of rest; so the day went on and on until men became very weary indeed. Then the god Norralie cast a spell over the Sun for the sake of the human race. By his incantations, he made the Sun descend and refresh its fires regularly, thus allowing mankind a time to rest.

BEASTS OF THE SKY

The Menik Kaien Negritos of Malaysia relate that once upon a time there were a man and wife called Ag-ag and Klang. These two had a child named Tnong, who took the shape of a dragonfly. The three lived together in a fine house built on pilings in a river. One day Tnong was flying about under the house, happily playing like the child he was, when the vibration of his wings lifted the dwelling right off its pilings. The house flew into the sky. Tnong kept flying about under it, not knowing what else he should do. His mother, Klang, came to the door. Looking out in astonishment, she became dizzy. She fell from the doorway. Falling through space, Klang developed wings and a hooked beak. She found herself transformed into a hawk. Soon afterward, Ag-ag went to the door of the flying house. He also fell and he became a crow.

But the house itself rose higher and higher,

In what loveliness do you appear,
O living sun,
in the light-mountain of heaven,
you who of all things first began to be.
Shining forth in the eastern light-mountain,
you fill the lands of the earth
with your beauty.
Your beams embrace all lands, extend
to the frontiers of your whole creation.
Far removed, you are yet
in your radiance present upon earth;
we behold you,
yet none can see your path.
When you go down
into the western light-mountain
the world is in darkness,
as if dead.
Men raise their arms in adoration
at your appearing.
Your rays give suck to all planted things;
you shine forth,
and for you they live and grow.

The Egyptian king Akhenaton, founder of a distinctive sun cult, lifts his arms toward the sun *(opposite)*, the rays of which bestow upon its worshipers light, strength, and life – represented by the ankh symbol in front of the foreheads of the two figures.

This Taoist crown from China *(above)* shows the flaming pearl of enlightenment and knowledge between two dragons. The doctrine of the inner light is common to many Asian religions.

The light of the sun is the *sine qua non* of all life and of the well-being of man and nature. So myth often equates the sun with the supreme divine power, describing its "rotation" in terms of the god's journey through the day world and the underworld. In the world of the mind, too, the dawn of light came to represent awareness, enlightenment, and knowledge, making light a universal symbol for the processes of the external and internal worlds.

The world lies cradled in your hand
as you created it.
In your shining forth,
men live;
In your going to your rest,
they die.
You are life's frame of time;
in you we have our being.

AKHENATON, HYMN TO ATON

Japanese myth tells how the sun goddess Amaterasu, angered by the impossible behavior of her brother, withdrew into a cave and left the world in darkness. At this thousands of cloud spirits persuaded the sky woman Ame-no-uzume to dance for them. Their noisy laughter at her performance eventually lured the inquisitive Amaterasu out of hiding *(above)*.

The symbol of the sun god Ra combines images of the sun and the eye *(left)*. The ancient Egyptians believed that Ra and Osiris, the rising sun and the liberated soul, were united in the realm of light. In the luster of the god's eye dwelt the brilliance, the power, and the very life of the kings of the Old Kingdom.

climbing westward, and Tnong kept with it. After some hours it gently descended into the mouth of a cavern. It tumbled through the cavern, eastward, to emerge again on the other side of the earth. Again it rose, to climb the sky. Tnong the Dragonfly made his home in the hurtling mansion, which became not only his residence but also the sun.

Tnong's affairs aloft are largely a mystery to human beings. It is known, though, that he is rather jealous of the moon. This is because the moon has so many stars for children. Occasionally, Tnong sends an enor-

in actual shape he resembles a lizard. All we see is the sun's belly, burning with concentrated light – the stars he has swallowed. The moon, his wife, sometimes sleeps with him at the center of the earth. More often, though, he is cross and drives her forth. Then she comes out in the night and plays with her children, who sing and dance as she passes among them. They are happy with

1 A minstrel sings to the Egyptian sun god Ra-Horus, depicted with a falcon's head supporting the red disk of the sun. Above are two solar eye symbols with the symbol of eternity between them.

2 This imposing stone relief shows the Aztec sun god Tonatiuh with a radiant crown of flame.

3 The Toltec god Nanahuatzin ignited the fifth sun, the one still giving light today, by his self-immolation.

4 An Aztec priest offers the heart of a sacrificial victim to the sun god. The flaming disk embodying the deity descends beneath the solar eagle, a key symbol in many sun mythologies.

5 The sun god of the tribes of Upper Volta holds the great disk of light aloft in his arms.

6 Very much in the image of the sun he represents is the great spirit Tawa of the Pueblo Indians. They regard him as the creator of mankind (myth, page 85).

mous butterfly to swallow up the moon. When that happens, the people make a great racket with instruments of bamboo. The noise frightens the butterfly away. The moon reappears from the shadow of the creature's wings.

According to a North American account, the sun and moon are a great chief and his wife; the stars are their children. The sun eats the children whenever he can catch them. That is why they run out of sight when they see the sun coming. At night he passes down into a tunnel and crawls along it to the middle of the earth, where he sleeps for a while. Toward morning he continues on through the narrow tunnel to its eastern exit. Emerging to the light of day, he chases his children through the sky because he badly needs their fires to keep himself alive. Not all the sun can be seen from the earth;

her and she with them. It hurts her feelings when the sun catches and eats some of their number, though he must. That is why each month she turns her face and blackens it down one side, mourning the little ones she has lost.

That myth accounts for celestial events with extraordinary neatness and elegance. It might be thought the product of a polished poet's fancy. But in fact the myth is drawn from a San Francisco newspaper of a century ago. Tooroop Eena, a Paiute Indian medicine man, dictated it.

In the Near East, in Hellenistic times, the full moon was invoked as Bearded Aphrodite – a bisexual deity. Its rays were the white beard, trailing to earth.

The Altai people of Siberia regard the moon as a sort of bird, with copper talons and a beak of ice. Their shamans, in a state

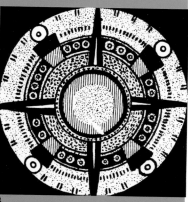

7 The solar wheel of the Vedic god Surya stands in the famous temple of the sun at Konarak, India.

8 This ancient-Mexican mural painting offers a strikingly graphic image of the sun as irradiating the universe.

In an enormous variety of shapes and manifestations, the sun (as the source of light in the world) has been celebrated by every civilization since the dawn of mankind. The circle, the earliest and most obvious symbol of the sun, dates back to prehistoric times. For living beings the sun is the essential light, giver of warmth and energy, nurturer of life. As fire it is

9 In this large stone relief, an Aztec calendar, the sun is shown governing the cycle of the months and the astrological signs.

10 The Assyrian sun god Shamash sits in his temple with the solar disk before him. He holds the symbol of eternity in his hand, and above him are the symbols of sun and moon.

the burner, the destroyer, withering and parching all it touches. Its light has always exerted a powerful fascination on man, appearing to him as all-seeing, a divine force from which none can hide. The sun commands the world and the rhythm of time; by day it is God's eye on the earth, at night it illuminates Osiris's realm of the dead. Each myth stresses a different aspect, personifying the sun under such names as Shamash, Helios, Apollo, Surya, and Savitri; it is also Atum, Osiris, Mithras, and *deus sol invictus,* the invincible sun god. Agents and bearers of the sun are the eagle, the phoenix, the horse, and the lion. The inner life, too, is governed by the same symbolism: sun and light represent mind and intellect, and when we attain knowledge we speak of "illumination" or "enlightenment." In the language of symbolism, the sun's energy is considered a male force, and its element is gold.

11 A Roman bas-relief from the third to fourth century A.D. depicts Sol, the sun god of the cult of Mithras.

95

of trance, call this bird down. It alights on a shaman's shoulder, invisibly, nearly bowling him over.

The Dusun people of North Borneo believe that the creator Kinharingan pounded rice into flour and called upon all the animals of the world to partake of it. When he saw their faces bent well down into the trough, the god suddenly demanded to know whether anyone present could cast off his

Terab came hissing among them. The enchantment compelled him to leave their rice alone and go and eat the moon.

Eclipses of the moon occur because the Terab has swallowed it. But the Dusun people have further enchantments which they employ at such times. They beat gongs and drums and recite certain verses until the Terab spits the moon out again. When he has done that, they put out baskets of rice

1 The Assyrian sun god Ashur appears on the horizon in the winged solar wheel of time.

2

own skin. Every creature but one had his mouth full at the time. Only the snake had been pretending to eat. He darted his glittering head up from the trough, flicked his forked tongue, and said, "I can."

The god bowed to the snake. "That being so," he said, "you will not die. That is to say, unless you fall into the hands of murderous mankind."

Kinharingan's human children imitated him in pounding rice to make flour. This they ate themselves, or tried to eat. But the Terab, a winged serpent, used to come and snatch the rice flour from them. The people were starving. The Terab was too big, and at the same time too elusive, for them to struggle against. It came and went through the air at its own pleasure. The people hoped that Kinharingan would see fit to restrict either its movements or its appetite. Kinharingan was gracious. He gave the people an enchantment to recite the next time the

flour for him as a reward. Like his quick-witted ancestor, the First Snake, the Terab is a dainty eater. Nobody sees him come to the baskets or go again.

THE PRURIENT MOON

The moon was once a man, a fat man. So say the aborigines of Australia. His weakness was women, and because of his obesity he experienced small luck with them. Every night he would wander abroad, seeking a mate. The girls could hear his heavy tread, he was so fat, and they saw his great pale belly gleaming in the dark. Before he could come near, they ran away, much to the moon's distress. His voice was high and rather sweet. He used to stumble along the riverbank, peering at the girls who liked to bathe in the cool stream when the nights were hot. He would sing to them from the

2 An Egyptian papyrus shows the hidden path of the sun through the realm of night. Four deities with serpent and scarab heads carry the sun god Ra toward the east. In the worship of the divine Khepri (at right, with a scarab on his head) the new sun of the coming day is born.

3 A Babylonian cylinder seal depicts the sun god Shamash, armed with bow and arrows, enthroned in a solar boat.

3

THE WAY OF THE GREAT LIGHT

The experience of the daily course of the sun is reflected in a variety of mythic symbols. The sun is a carriage drawn by fiery horses, or the bird-man Garuda bears Vishnu or other sun gods across the sky on its back; the winged sun symbol combines this "flight" of the day star and the path of its rays. Elsewhere the solar wheel is symbol of both the cycle of the seasons and the sun itself. The position of the sun at the winter and summer solstices was marked by altars and sacred stones in order to secure the sun god's goodwill and persuade him to return. Shrines dedicated to sun worship usually face the rising sun. The main temple at Abu Simbel was originally so oriented that at sunrise in mid-February and mid-October a ray of light, passing through the entrance,

penetrated more than fifty yards inside the building to fall on the statues of Ramses and Amon. And when the sun entered the western mountain on its way to the realm of death, it landed on a bark, hidden from mortal eyes, and was transported across the underworld Nile to bring light to the populace of Osiris's kingdom. In such ways has myth depicted the eternal cycle of the sun, the radiant god of life and death.

4 The Greek god Helios charges up the sky in his solar chariot drawn by a team of fiery horses.

5 The famous Trundholm chariot from Denmark bears the golden disk of the sun.

6 The great Hindu god Vishnu's mount is the bird-man Garuda.

7 But the chariot of the god Surya is drawn by the seven horses of the sun.

8 Ancient-Chinese myth also has the sun god driving a chariot pulled by a dragon-horse. Ten such chariots symbolized their day, which had ten hours instead of twelve.

9 An Egyptian funeral papyrus shows the young sun god as Horus, with the red sun on his head, making his nightly voyage over the mythic Nile toward the morning.

SUN WORSHIP AND SUN DANCE

As the sun came to be worshiped as a god in various civilizations, the celebration of its daily rebirth eventually gave rise to a ritual designed to ensure that the light- and life-giving planet never halted in its course. Its circular path, for example, determined the pattern of this cultic dance of the Dakota Indians round a symbolic world tree crowned by the solar

symbol (10). The Hopi, too, have a sun dance, while Nordic solstice rites center on the revolving wheel of the sun; the significance of both is the same. A number of well-known shrines – Heliopolis in Egypt; Cuzco, the Inca city in Peru with its sun temples; and Stonehenge in southern England (11) among them – bear witness to cults aimed at conjuring the source of light and energy into continued existence.

bushes and beg them to give him a ride in one of their canoes.

Purely for their own amusement, one midnight hour, a pair of maidens took it upon themselves to accommodate the prurient moon, at least in some degree. They let him sit amidships in their canoe. Swimming, and holding on to the canoe at either side, the two girls propelled the moon out upon the middle of the stream. They looked lovely, swimming. Overcome by desire, he would lean first to one side and then to the other, attempting to flirt with them. His pudgy hands poked and tickled them under the arms. The girls giggled merrily, laughed, and overturned the canoe. The moon sank, silent, with no remonstrance at all, into the flowing stream. Drowning, he turned away. His belly became smaller and smaller, crescent-shaped now.

The moon arose again, from another river, in the night sky. He beams down upon the women of this world, wistfully. And there too he drowns.

HIGH PARTINGS

Once upon a time a serpent deity named Wanojo arrived at Rossel, an island in the South Seas. He came from Sud-Est, which the Rossel people believe to be a much more ancient island than their own. With him, Wanojo brought a pig, a dog, a taro plant, the moon, and the sun. He made the pig a home on the north side of the island, and one for the dog on the south. The taro he planted in the middle. As for the sun and moon, he let them wander wherever fancy led.

The sun liked bathing in the warm salt tide best of all. Between dips he would laze about on the beach, growing rapidly. The moon, meanwhile, used to ascend to the hilltops and bathe in the coldest freshwater springs that she could find. She turned ever more icy, and she too was growing rapidly in size. It soon became apparent that neither the moon nor the sun could remain on Rossel for very much longer. Between them they would have burnt up the edges of the island and, at the same time, cracked its heart with cold. So, with Wanojo's consent, they climbed skyward, hand in hand.

Up aloft, the sun and moon separated. Their temperature differences were too great for comfort. Ever since then they have remained apart, going their separate ways through the warm days and coolness of night.

An Efik Ibibio legend from Nigeria holds that the sun and moon are man and wife. Once they lived upon earth. When they

1 A great pillar from the palace of Tula in Mexico depicts the priest-king Quetzalcoatl as god of the morning star.

2 This head of the Aztec night goddess Coyolxauhqui shows the phases of the moon on her forehead.

3 In the Minoan civilization of ancient Crete the sacred bull was widely worshiped as an incarnation of the moon deity. Visible on the flank of this clay figure is a crescent moon symbol.

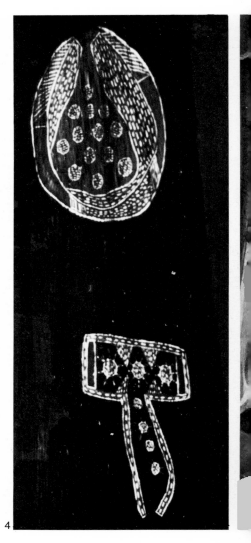

4 The Pleiades and Orion star groups, represented here in an Australian bark painting, figure in the myths of several peoples. To the Greeks the Pleiades were virgins who, pursued by the hunter Orion, were saved by being turned into stars (myths, page 104).

The distant world of the stars, the planets on their courses through the constellations, and the moon with its cyclical phases preoccupied mythic man from the earliest times as he sought to pin down the riddle of their existence in a "true" story. Pictured here are just a few of the forms to which his moon myths and star symbolism gave rise.

7 Within the circle of the full moon the Chinese goddess Heng O waits beneath the cassia tree, while the hare of the moon prepares the elixir that will turn her into the lunar toad.

8 A ritual ax depicting the moon spirit revered by the Quimbaya of South America.
9 This relief bust of the ancient-Persian moon goddess rests on a crescent moon.

5 The Greek moon goddess Selene, pictured here on one of her secret descents from heaven to visit the sleeping shepherd Endymion, had a total of fifty children by him.

6 The Greeks accounted for the origin of the Milky Way with the myth of the boy Herakles who once bit Hera in the breast. Some milk escaped and formed the distinctive band of stars.

10 A detail from an Indian mural shows the Milky Way and the constellations of the northern zodiac in the form of mythic heroes and animals.

11 The Hindu moon god Chandra is being pulled in the celestial chariot by an antelope, also a moon symbol.

12 The moon goddess Tlazolteotl, to whom the Huaxtecs of Mexico prayed for love and the gift of children.

13 Selene, here symbolizing the setting moon, rides her horse into the sea.

were here, they very often visited the flood, who was their best friend. They kept inviting the flood to visit their house in turn, but for a long while he demurred, regretfully explaining that he would not fit between the walls of their dwelling. The sun and moon therefore built a much larger house. Then the flood could no longer refuse, in courtesy, their invitation. The flood arrived at the door and called, "Shall I come in?" The sun replied, "Please do, my friend."

When the guest was knee-deep in the house, he asked, "Shall I keep on coming in?" Again, the sun replied, "Please do!"

The flood brought many relations along, including fish, reptiles, and sea beasts. Soon he rose to the rooftree of the house. The sun and moon perched on the roof. They felt less happy now, and their friend kept on rising. Eventually, the house was submerged altogether. The sun and moon circled away into the sky, to make a new home out of the reach of the friendly flood.

According to classical legend, the minerals common to our planet indicate the erstwhile presence of heavenly bodies here on earth. Iron is the cloak which Mars left behind when he deserted the earth; lead is Saturn's cloak; quicksilver is the cloak of Mercury and so on. Gold was the garment of the sun when that burning deity walked the earth, and silver was the nude moon's headdress.

Minhasser Islanders of the northern Celebes tell about a girl named Lingkambene, who lived with a large family in a house set upon tall poles. Lingkambene loved singing, dancing, and late parties, though her family disapproved. Once she arrived home not long before dawn and called up to her parents, asking them to let down the ladder for her.

Her parents thought they would teach her a lesson just for once, and so they refused to lower the ladder. Lingkambene therefore called out to her grandparents, but they too refused. Her uncle and aunt also decided against lowering the ladder for Lingkambene. So did her brothers and sisters. Lingkambene spread her arms and cried out bitterly to the sky god Rimassa, begging him to lower the ladder since none of her people would do it for her.

The ladder stayed where it was, up in her house. However, a chair suspended upon chains of gold swung from the sky. The night was just then beginning to fade. Lingkambene seated herself in the chair, clasped the chains in her hands, and prayed to Rimassa. She begged him, in the silence of her heart, to lift her up out of this untender world. Lingkambene's family gathered on the porch of their dwelling to see her

slowly rise into the sky. "Come back," they called. "If you do, we will sacrifice nine pigs for you!" Lingkambene shook her head. "Farewell!" she cried, and disappeared.

It was not long before Lingkambene arrived at a village in heaven which was very like her own village down below. The people were cruel, though. Her hands and feet were bound together, and a pole was passed through them. She was carried, dangling from the pole, to the river. There the people washed her thoroughly, and then they cut her throat. Her entrails were removed. Gay little Lingkambene was scraped clean, roasted, and treated in every way like a slaughtered pig.

The sun rose out of her forehead. The moon, bruised as it is, came from the back of her head. Her eyes, her heart, her liver, and her lungs became the chief constellations of the southern sky. Her minced flesh sparkled in the most distant heaven as numberless stars. The scraps that fell from the chopping block were glowworms.

OF EARTH, AND STARRY HEAVEN

"Let the windows of heaven be opened!" So Jehovah commanded, in the Old Testament story of the Flood. What windows? Stars are floodgates as well, it seems. Even today, the Yakut people of the Eurasian steppe regard the stars as crystals of a kind, well-sealed windows through which the gods peer down at us.

The Turko-Tatar people, living in tents, regard the sky as a greater tent. To them, the stars appear as holes in the tent, and the Milky Way is a seam across the top. There is a central tent pole, sticking straight up out of the north, which holds the sky aloft.

Many a myth refers to the constellation known variously in the West as the Big Dipper, the Plow, or the Bear. Chinese scholars used to gaze up into that majestically spinning assembly of distant suns and think about the ugliest man who ever was: sweet young Chung K'uei. His looks ought not, in kindness, to be described. His great achievement was to win first prize in the final exams for admission to mandarin rank in the ancient-Chinese civil service.

Custom required the emperor of China to personally present the winner with a golden rose. The emperor got through the first part of the ceremony well enough, but when the moment came for bending down and putting the token into K'uei's outstretched hand, his heart failed him. The face gazing up into his own – radiant with adoration and gratitude though it must have been – seemed a frightful offense to the exquisitely

The oldest-known mythologies began with the question of the origin of heaven and earth. In fact all myths are an attempt to interpret the still-unsolved riddle of the world and of human existence in terms of symbols and images. Not knowing the

Nut, the goddess of heaven depicted on this Egyptian sarcophagus *(below),* guides the soul of the departed. The sacred scarab at her feet indicates the nightly nadir of the sun and also of the soul. Above the goddess's head is the symbol of both the newly-rising sun and the soul in its resurrection.

true laws of nature and how they operated, man kept trying to picture to himself the way it all began. This reflection – or version – of reality, this account of the origin of things based on the real world as he saw it, became his myth. The fundamental separation of heaven and earth is often enacted in myth by gods and beings who emerge as a unity from the chaos of the primeval flood and divide into a male and a female being. All subsequent creation takes place through the medium of first couples, be they heaven and earth, light and darkness, or spirit and matter.

This Sumerian cylinder seal *(right)* represents the mythic marriage of heaven and earth in the primal state of the world before the great separation.

In Egyptian mythology (myth, page 65) the origins of procreation lie in the union of divine first couples, who are responsible for the unfolding of creation right up to the founding of the Old Kingdom. The first union was that of Shu and Tefnut, both created by the primal god Atum. Then came Geb and Nut *(below)*, whose separation led to the formation of earth and sky: the god Geb, reclining, became the hills and valleys of the earth; Nut, lifted forcibly from her lover's body, became the vault of heaven above the emergent world.

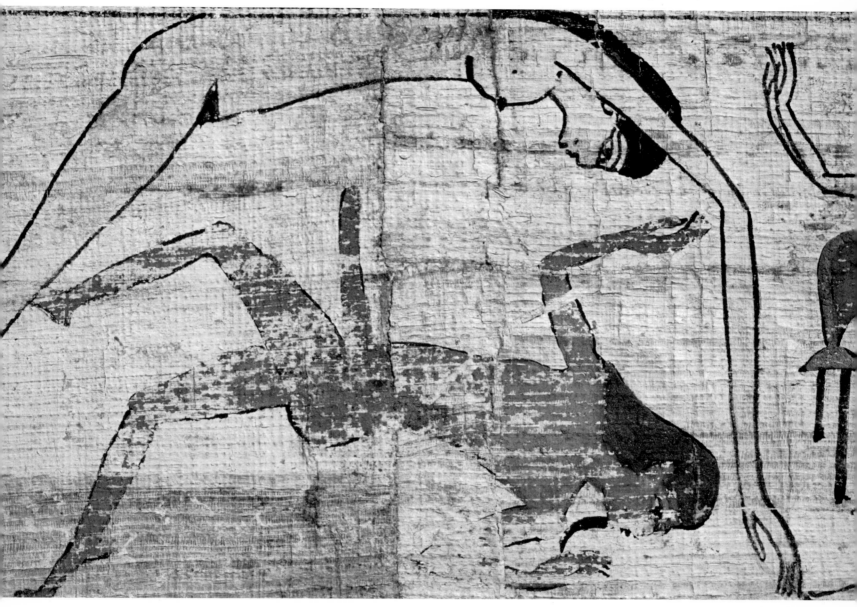

The Navaho Indians depict the lord of heaven with the stars as symbols of time and the spirit *(right)*; Mother Earth is shown with a maize plant to symbolize fertility.

Nordic rock carvings *(far right)* feature the pairing of the sky god – his body is the wheel of the sun – and the Great Earth Mother.

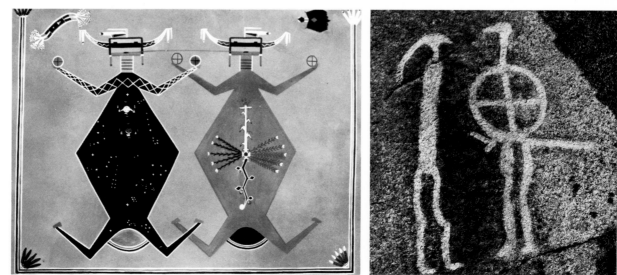

refined and carefully shielded vision of the emperor. So, at the last moment, the rose was withdrawn.

K'uei, despairing, cast himself from a high rock into the sea. He was about to drown when a dolphinlike spirit rose up beneath him and transported him to the deeper sea of stars. Since then, especially dedicated Chinese students are said to "stand on the sea monster's head." Ugly K'uei guides their destinies.

The aborigines of Australia possess star knowledge which is vast and explicit at the same time. Pointing to the stars which are called Capella, Castor, and Pollux in Western astronomy books, they tell the following story in which Purra the Kangaroo represents Capella, and the twin hunters Yurree and Wanjel represent Castor and Pollux. At the beginning of the hot season the twins set out in pursuit of Purra, and they kill him. The shimmering mirages of summer on the open plain come from the smoke of the fire over which they roast the starry beast.

Again, the aborigines say that Marpean-Kurrk and Neilloan (the star Arcturus and the constellation Lyra) are good friends to mankind. They are living beings who have long since found out that ant pupae and loan-bird eggs are good for people to eat. When those particular stars appear in certain quarters of the heavens, the season for gathering such foods is at hand.

An aboriginal myth from Roland Robinson's *Legend and Dreaming* (1952) describes the Milky Way as the drifting smoke of a celestial campfire. The fire was lit by Nagacork, the great transforming genius of this world, when he retired to rest among the stars. He sleeps now, Nagacork does, in the warmth of his fire. His woman lies nearby, and she is watchful still. She pillows her head on the palm of her left hand. In what constellations does the couple lie? Unfortunately the myth that has come down to us does not say.

The red-gold color of the planet we call Mars puts men in mind of passion, blood, and war. The Greek counterpart of Mars, Ares the god of war, had a "pigface," according to Sophocles. On the other side of the globe, the Melanesians maintain that Mars the planet is inhabited by a great red pig.

In China, the constellation Aquila and the star Vega are called the Herdsman and the Weaver Girl. The Weaver Girl used to be shy, concerned with close work in the house. This disturbed her father, the deity who stands outside time. To cheer and brighten her life, a marriage was arranged. Her father presented her to the Herdsman,

1 According to Tibetan tradition the great yogis dissolved at death into rainbow light in order to attain the Beyond.

2 On this Pueblo Indian crest the rainbow as bringer of rain surmounts two maize cobs.

3 The rainbow with its promise of blessing frames the fields and dwellings of men in this thirteenth-century miniature.

4 Certain Australian tribes honor the rainbow serpent Julunggul as their creator god and the bringer of civilization.

5 The victorious heroes of Nordic myth pass beneath the rainbow on their journey to Valhalla.

6 The Greek goddess Iris used the rainbow on her errands between men and the gods on Olympus.

7 Christian tradition on the other hand retained the idea of a ladder or ladders between earth and heaven (Jacob's dream).

8 When at the end of the fourth era of Aztec myth the sky fell in, Quetzalcoatl appeared as wind god and upholder of the vault of heaven to support the realm of the stars.

9 The rainmaker couple on this Australian bark painting execute magic rites to persuade the rainbow serpent to send the longed-for rain.

10 Some North American Indians draw a fourfold rainbow spiral in the sand to charm the rain.

11 In Peruvian myth the rainbow or arch of the sky is depicted in the form of a serpent held up by the jaguar god.

12 God appears in the rainbow to tell Noah that the Flood is over.

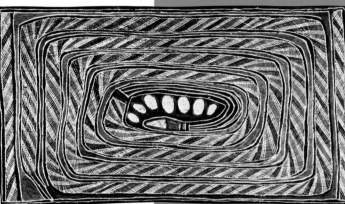

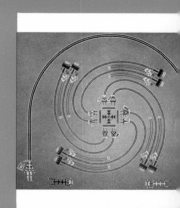

And God said, "This is the sign
of the covenant which I make between
me and you and every living creature
that is with you, for all future generations:
I set my bow in the cloud, and it shall be a sign
of the covenant between me and the earth.
When I bring clouds over the earth
and the bow is seen in the clouds,
I will remember my covenant."

GENESIS 9:12–15

who tended cattle on the far bank of the Milky Way. Their union was a happy one. Lost in admiration of her brilliant husband, the Weaver Girl neglected all the domestic arts that she had been wont to practice. Again her father was disturbed, and once again he intervened.

The god who stands outside time convened myriads of magpies for his new purpose. They shaped a winged bridge over the Milky Way. The Herdsman was ordered to step across it and go back to pasturing his cattle on the far side of the stream. Tearfully, he went. The moment he set foot upon the far bank, the magpies dispersed.

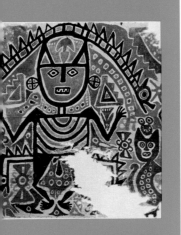

Mythically, the rainbow is the light of heaven, made up of sun and rain; it is the harbinger of rain, the hoped-for gift of the gods that will make the fields bear fruit. But the rainbow also figures as a bond between the human plane and the realm of the gods. It is the path taken by the messengers who ply between earth and heaven to communicate men's prayers and proclaim the will of the gods. In many myths, too, the rainbow is the bridge by which the souls of the departed reach the Other World (myths, pages 104 and 106).

The Weaver Girl has returned to her former habit of shy domestic industry. The Herdsman tends his cattle diligently in the meadows of darkness, which earthly eyes cannot see. One night a year, and for one night only, the lovers may be rejoined. On the seventh night of the seventh month of the year, people in the Orient pray that the weather will be clear. For legend holds that the magpies then flock together again, forming a winged bridge across the silver stream of heaven. If it were to storm, rain might wash away their trembling magpie bridge, across which the Weaver Girl runs to her husband.

Two myths from opposite sides of the world relate the origin of the Pleiades in much the same way. The ancient Greek account concerns the sea nymph Pleione, who once lay with Atlas the Titan. From their union sprang seven beautiful daughters. A giant huntsman, Orion, lusted after all seven. For five years Orion pursued the maidens over sea and land, but he could never corner a single one of them. Finally, Zeus himself was moved to pity by the fruitless pursuit. He set Orion in the heavens, as a constellation of stars, and he did the same with the sisters. But did the chase end there? Not altogether. Across the sky, for part of the year, Orion still pursues the Pleiades.

The Australian aboriginal parallel to that story was given to Roland Robinson by a Pitjandjara aborigine named Minyanderri, quoted in the *Feathered Serpent* (1956):

Old Man Yoola always wanting women. One day he saw seven sisters; he chased them. To get away, they flew into the sky. They came down again at the rock hole Karraloo. Old Man Yoola walked after them, slow, trailing his spear. That spear made valleys in this country. Old Man Yoola tracked the sisters all the way to the big waterhole Wankarreenga. When they saw him coming, they jumped in the water. He jumped in after them. Everybody drowned. Their spirits are Stars now, crossing the sky. Old Man Yoola still on the go. Sisters still saying no, no.

ORIGIN OF RAIN

Kintak Bong Negritos of the Malay jungle believe that a stone flower grows in the garden of the sky. When the blossom opens upward, the weather will be dry. When the plant droops, water runs from its gleaming petals to drip rain upon the earth. Is that stone flower the moon? No one can say for sure. The moon does seem to fill up, tilt, and droop in the course of each month. But maybe it is a reflection, and no more, of the true celestial stone flower.

THE STRIPED PATH

The Old Testament relates that after the sacrifice which Noah and his family performed on Mount Ararat, Jehovah set a rainbow in the sky as a covenant between himself and humanity. In Christian art of the Byzantine period and later, the Virgin Mary is often shown seated on a rainbow. So is the Buddha in Indian and Chinese painting.

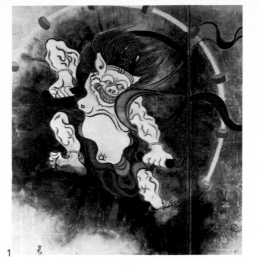

1 Japanese artists depicted the mythic god of thunder as a wild, drum-beating cloud demon.

2 A rare bronze figure of the Nordic thunder god Thor shows him with the hammer in his hands.

4 In West African myth the god of thunder and also of fertility – because he sends rain – is the ram Xevioso, pictured with the thunder ax in his mouth.

Thunder and lightning, two fascinating and (in their elemental power) menacing natural phenomena, have always been experienced by man as numinous; he has seen in them the work of the gods. Thunder was generally believed to be the threatening voice of the supreme deity or of a specific thunder god; in the Old Testament, for example, it is the voice of Jehovah. Both lightning and thunder were attributed to various instruments that the gods carried with them, the best known of these being the thunderbolt of Zeus. The

3 Like Zeus the Indian god Indra also used a thunderbolt, which in Tibet was depicted in this elegant form.

god Indra carried a similar weapon, and the Vedas tell of a mythic struggle in which he defeated the serpent demon Vrita with thunder and lightning, thus releasing the monsoon from the pent-up clouds to bless the land of India. The thunderbolt occurs chiefly in the myths of the Indo-Iranian peoples of antiquity. Another major thunder god symbol, which occurs in Nordic mythology as the instrument of the thunder god Thor, is the hammer. An allied concept are the magical smiths of northern-Asian myth, also described as gods of thunder because, of course, the forging of iron is all sparks and crashing blows. The eagle and the iron thunderbird also feature in myth as thunder gods.

5 The awesome thunder-
bird of the North American
Indians, which was be-
lieved to produce lightning
with its beak and thunder
by beating its wings.
6 The thunder god
Schango of the Yoruba
tribes of Nigeria bears on
his head a huge ax with six
eyes.
7 Clearly recognizable
on this relief of the Hittite
weather god Teshub are
the thunder hammer and
the sheaf of thunderbolts.
8 The Australian abori-
gines depict their lightning
and weather spirit as a demon framed by a double
arc springing from its
head.

6

7   8   9

9 The Assyrian storm god
Adad stands on the back
of a bull brandishing
sheaves of thunderbolts in
both hands.

10 In Greek statues of
Zeus the thunderbolt be-
came stylized to a heavy
dart pointed at both ends.   10

105

The Irish peasantry maintain that rainbows point to pots of gold which leprechauns have buried underground. This notion represents a degeneration, or rather a materialization, of ancient-Celtic lore, according to which rainbows bestowed treasure in the form of wisdom and awareness.

Siberian shamans adorn themselves with colored ribbons when they are about to enter a state of trance in order to embark on spirit journeys. They describe their ribbons as "rain bridges."

Rainbows conceived of as bridges are the means by which many mythic heroes of the South Pacific, such as Aukelenuiaiko of Hawaii, reached heaven.

In ancient Greece rainbows were identified with Iris, the messenger goddess. She was the indwelling spirit of the rainbow bridge between earth and sky. Messages which her fellow deities wished to convey gleamed down through her, as it were, prismatically.

OF LIGHTNING

Albert Einstein once leaned from the window of a speeding car to watch a thunderstorm pour lightning down over Princeton University. Drawing his head in again, the great scientist softly asked, "What is lightning?" The friend who was driving could not resist offering a reply. "Electricity?" he suggested. Einstein shook his head, smiling. "That's what you think!"

In Chinese myth, the Mother of Lightning, Tien Mu, was a divinity magnificently robed in blue, green, red, and white. She held a mirror in each hand. Where the reflections of the two mirrors crossed, lightning would crackle and flash.

Lightning once broke the arm of an old woman living in Kiangsi, according to legend. The old woman lay prostrate on the ground, trembling with shock. A voice cried from the clouds, "I have made a mistake!" At the same instant, a small bottle of ointment fell beside the old woman. Wonderingly, she applied the ointment to her broken arm. It became whole once again.

The people of the village ran to appropriate the little bottle of miraculous ointment. They could not lift it from the ground. Having defied their efforts for a time, the bottle finally rose up and flew away into the sky. To Mother of Lightning's sleeve it may have gone.

OF HEAT

Next to death and its light twin, birth, the most dramatically apparent transforming

1 The highly complex figure depicted here in bronze is the Tibetan tutelary deity Yamantaka, a bull-headed demon with nine heads and thirty-four arms. He emerges threat- eningly from a wreath of flame. He is lord of the underworld and, on account of his great power, vanquisher of Yama (the god of death) and consequently of death itself.

2 The temple walls of Angkor Wat in Cambodia are lined with friezes depicting all manner of Buddhist deities and spirits, including these celestial dancers.

3 This dragon-headed spirit boat, in which seven spirits are crossing to the Other Side, belonged to a shaman of the Tlingit Indians of Alaska.

DEMONS AND SPIRITS

The myths and religions of most peoples have an area set aside for demons, goblins, and other spirit beings. They form a pantheon as it were of their own with powers covering the whole range of man's dialogue with the supernatural. Man has tended to conceive of these spirits as animate beings exercising particular functions in the terrestrial or astral spheres – beings, incidentally, with whom his relationship may be a highly ambivalent one. They figure in myth as demonic enemies, as

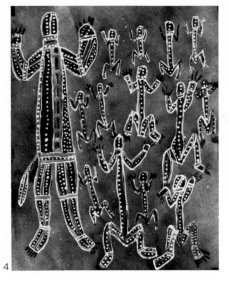

4 Certain aboriginal tribes of Australia still produce bark paintings representing the dances of local spirits known as *mimis*. The *mimi* is comparable with our Western fairy.

6 A temple frieze from Palmyra in Syria shows six genii armed with shield and staff who were worshiped as local tutelary spirits.

7 The good spirit Nomoi of Micronesian myth was believed to have the power to ward off the typhoon.

5 Large numbers of spirits, both protective and otherwise, have evolved in the context of Tibetan religion. This four-armed *dakini* is a tutelary goddess.

8–13 Demons and spirits may be benevolent, evil, or neutral. There are tutelary or protective deities such as this one from the Solomon Islands (8), or the cold-weather spirit of the Eskimos (9), or the *akuaku* spirits of Easter Island (10). The *yakshini* goddesses of India symbolize motherhood, fertility, and life itself (11). In Mali, figures depicting hermaphrodite ancestor spirits are handed down from generation to generation (12). A protective role is also ascribed to these Indian demons (13).

agents of the underworld that man is concerned to exorcize; or they may be celestial guides who help man on his way to the gods; or they may be the wandering souls of departed ancestors who intervene in the lives of their descendants. They may be benevolent; on the other hand they may take the form of dangerous demons who have to be ritually placated. All kinds of natural phenomena, including sickness and death, are attributed to them. In magical rites man invokes spirit powers against his enemies; the shaman summons up good spirits to drive out the demons of illness. Often spirits appear as aids and messengers of the gods, or as celestial fairies and guides of the souls of the departed. There is a wealth of local tutelary spirits, believed to act as guardians of house and land. Spirits of the dead may linger on in out-of-the-way places as spirit inhabitants of trees, stones, and the like.

14 This Khmer figurine from Cambodia depicts a dancing *asparas* or winged celestial nymph, a personage common to the mythologies of India, China, and Southeast Asia.

15 Modern Eskimo drawings of spirit beings resemble ghosts drawn by children or those used as illustrations in children's books.

107

powers are heat and cold. The Rig Veda relates that the divine Prajapati created all things by heating himself from within, and sweating out the world.

The Hindi word *tapas,* which at one time meant "heat," now signifies ascetic practices. Tibetan lamas have been reliably observed sitting out of doors wrapped in soaking-wet sheets on winter nights. The adventurous photojournalist James Burke (afterward killed in a fall from a Himalayan peak) photographed Indian ascetics living stark naked in a wilderness region of eternal snow. Such feats as theirs bring the world of myth down to earth, startlingly so.

The Algonquin Indian hero Glooscap (whose name means Deceiver-with-Words) used to befriend a tiny elf of summer and conceal it in the folds of his deerskin robe. Bare-handed and weaponless,

YGGDRASIL

The great ash Yggdrasil unites all aspects of Nordic life, from the underworld through the world of men to the realm of the gods and heroes. Of its three mighty roots, one dips into the triple fountain that is the source of all being; another is the seat of the three Norns or fates, spinning the thread of life; and the third root draws from the fount of wisdom, watched over by the giant Mimir. Snakes and deer feed on the roots, bark, and leaves of the ash. In the top of the tree the cock, eagle, and hawk keep watch and warn the gods of the approach of their enemies. The goat Heidrun browses in the lower branches and gives milk for Odin's warriors; and a squirrel, Ratatoskr, scurries ceaselessly up and down the trunk from the eagle (light) to the dragon (darkness), fanning the feud between them.

but for that one hidden ally, Glooscap would journey northward on the longest night of the year.

Glooscap would keep on walking and walking over the snow until he came to Winter's silently glittering lodge. He would enter, bow low to Winter, and sit down by the cold fire. Frozen in place there, as if sleeping, he would seem to be entirely in Winter's power. Even his frosty breath would appear motionless, clouding the blue of his face. Winter, however, would weep because of Glooscap's summer elf, which was working in secret. The eyes of Winter would soon turn into salt tears. His face would also dissolve, and his body. The wide, low lodge would collapse upon itself. The whole white scene would change to shimmering water, fields, and flowers. And Glooscap would be laughing.

Myths of Glooscap were first recorded by the pioneer American folklorist Charles

1

1 An Etruscan bowl depicts man between the tree of life and the tree of death. He holds a twig of each, symbolizing his position midway between paradise and the mortal, terrestrial world.

There is a quite remarkable consistency in the use and symbolic significance of the tree in almost all cultures and in the

the souls of the dead. And because it grows green again every year and produces the seeds of the future, it is also a major

2 From the tree in the Garden of Eden Adam and Eve ate the fruit of knowledge and mortality.

2

4

5 In this ancient-Chinese print, the tree of the universe fills the world, its luxuriant foliage embracing the animal, bird, and human spheres and extending right up to heaven.

most ancient myths. Its original mythic function is as the center of the world, a living axis topping the summit of the world mountain and reaching up to heaven. The tree itself usually incorporates three levels: its roots grow down through the earth to the underworld, while the trunk rises through the world of men and holds the crown up toward the unattainable heights of heaven. In mythic tradition, however, it is not only the *axis mundi* connecting the underworld with the realm of the gods; it is also the way by which the shaman ascends or descends on his ecstatic visits to the celestial spirits or

symbol of life, especially long life, of fertility, and of ripening and maturity. In its summer luxuriance and winter bareness it offers a symbol of life and death and of change generally. But the tree symbol is also tied up with the human soul and the mind, where it has to do with the unfolding of personality and the process of spiritual individuation. A further aspect, exemplified by the tree of the knowledge of good and evil in Genesis, also occurs in Indian and Nordic mythologies. This type of tree stands at the source of life and bears a fruit that grants enlightenment.

3 It is via the world tree that the Indonesian shaman makes his ecstatic journeys to the sky and to the underworld.

4 Only the righteous shall "flourish like the palm tree" (Ps. 92) and attain the fruits of life, as do the men in this medieval miniature.

6 A mid-seventeenth-century vision of the tree of the soul: drawing on the roots of will and spirit, it rises out of the world of darkness into the supreme, divine light.

The TREE *of the* SOUL.

SOLAR WORLD

7

8

9

10

7 Detail of a Siberian shaman costume showing the tree of life.

8 The decoration on this shaman drum from Lapland shows the world tree uniting the three levels of underworld, earth, and sky.

9 The Scythians of central Asia also worshiped sacred trees (detail of a scabbard).

10 The Jewish *menora*, or seven-branched candlestick, derives from an ancient-Mesopotamian tree of life symbol.

11

11 A Russian nomad tribesman painted this Great Mother holding the tree of life.

12 A woven cloth from Indonesia showing the shaman climbing the tree of life.

13 Beneath the winged disk of the Assyrian sun god Ashur the tree of life grows heavenward.

14 The sacred birch of the Tungus of Manchuria passes up through and supports the shaman's tent.

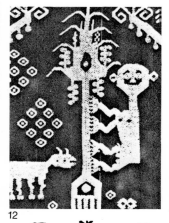

12

13

14

15

16

15 This Norwegian tree of knowledge with the first couple and the serpent is Christian in inspiration.

16 Animals, birds, fish, and representations of the cosmos surround the world tree of the Siberian Kets.

17 A pharaoh sits before the sacred tree of heaven with a lotus and various sacrificial offerings.

18 World mountain and tree of life are combined in this Javanese cosmogram.

17

18

Godfrey Leland. In *The Algonquin Legends of New England* (1884), he wrote, "It will be no small occasion of astonishment and chagrin a hundred years hence, when the last Algonquin Indian of the Wabano shall have passed away, that so few of our literary or cultured folk cared enough to collect this aboriginal literature." That prophecy proved all too accurate.

THE CENTER OF THE EARTH

The planet Earth has a most mysterious center which invisibly connects it with the rest of the cosmos. This unknown and perhaps unknowable something resides deep inside our spinning sphere. We call it "gravity" – a fantastically powerful and pervasive force.

Our ancestors in extreme northerly regions thought of earth's center in another way, as we have seen. They regarded it as an axis which extended out to the polestar and appeared to command the zodiac.

People living further south considered earth's center differently again. To them it was a mountain, a holy place. It might not seem the highest, people said, but it was so. This mountain was earth's "navel" – that is to say, the central point of earth as a living being. It was the one place where earth penetrated the celestial sphere.

To the Indians it was Mount Meru, or Sumeru, and stood directly under the polestar. To the Sumerians it was Mount Sumer, Mount of Lands. To the Palestinians it was the Holy Rock of Jerusalem, upon which Isaiah offered sacrifice and from which Muhammad leaped into Allah's garden. To the Egyptians it was the inaccessible Mountain of the Moon, from which the Nile flowed. And so on. Examples are legion, and they contradict one another from locality to locality.

People agreed only on the point that there is one and only one sacred mountain from which heaven may be gained. By building artificial replicas of it, they sought to put themselves in spiritual communication with the gods. The pyramids of Egypt, the Borobudur temple in Indonesia, the stepped pyramid temples of Central America, Maeve's Cairn in County Sligo, Ireland, and Silbury Hill in Wiltshire, England, are all such replicas.

To speak of the "North Pole" is to repeat a concept known to many primitive peoples. Lapps, Finns, Estonians, and Samoyed tribesmen have a different expression for it, though. What we call the North Pole they name the Sky Nail. Starry horses, tethered to the Sky Nail and galloping around it night

and day, make up the star clock of the north. So say the Buryat people. Kalmyk, Kirghiz, Bashkir, and Eskimo agree that some sort of pole or nail or pillar connects planet Earth to the polestar. The Teleut refer to it as the Sun Pillar.

The Koryak say that nowadays only a very few shamans know how to reach heaven. The way leads straight up, through the black, starless patch in the farthest north at night, beyond the polestar – that is to say, passing very near the Creator's all-seeing eye. A hundred years ago, according to Koryak belief, self-respecting shamans could make that climb on demand. A thou-

2

sand years ago, laymen could do it too.

In every family tent of the nomadic Soyot, at the foot of the main tent pole there is a small stone altar. From the top of the same tent pole, the Soyot fly blue, white, and yellow banners representing the colors of dawn. Such evidence as this has led Mircea Eliade to suspect that in primitive psychology "every human habitation is projected to the center of the world." Moreover, according to Eliade, "every altar, tent, or house makes possible a break-through in plane and hence ascent to the sky."

STRUCTURES OF HEAVEN AND HELL

It is often said that our ancestors regarded the earth as being essentially flat. It looked that way to their physical eyes, no doubt. Another common conception in myth is that of two mountains – pyramidal in shape – one of which points up and the other down. The bases of the two mountains meet and are joined at the earth's surface. The upper mountain is composed of air and other substances, largely invisible to mankind. The down-pointing mountain, on the other hand, is made of earth and mineral substances, again largely unknown to us.

Myths and religions have always regarded the center of their cultural and spiritual sphere of influence as the sacred midpoint of the universe, the navel of the earth, around which the lands of the profane world were gathered. These points were cosmologically oriented, marked whenever possible by a tower-shaped central temple signifying ascent to the higher realm of the gods. The best known are the ziggurats or stepped towers of

3

the Babylonians, the pyramids, and the temples of Mexico; the *stupas* and temples of India and Southeast Asia were also built as sacred centers of the universe.

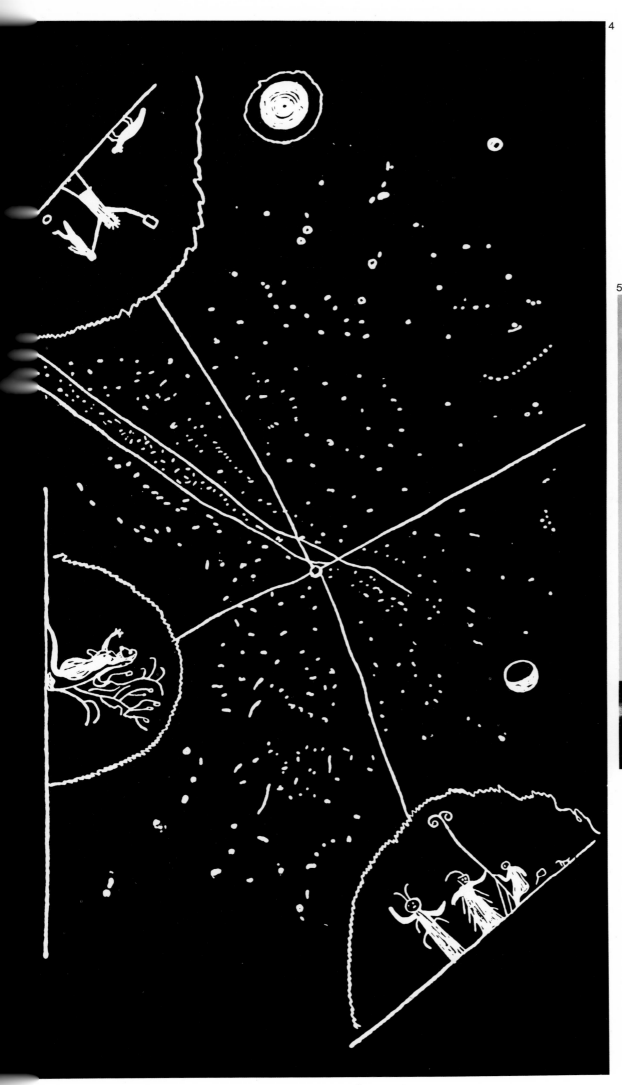

1 The geographical center of a sphere of cultural influence was often thought of in terms of the navel of the world. In this African relief the navel lies between countries and animals at the center of a quartered cosmogram.

2 The pyramids of Egypt are more than the tombs of pharaohs; they are world mountains oriented along precise cosmological lines.

3 This Mayan temple in Chichén Itzá was regarded as the sacred center of the world.

4 For the Chukchi of northeastern Siberia the polestar was the axis of the world between morning (top left), to which it is linked by the Milky Way, and evening (bottom right), where shamans make sacrifice to the sea god.

5 This minaret in Muslim Iraq takes the form of a round spiral tower above a square base, the ground plan of the ancient-Babylonian ziggurat.

The Biblical legend of the building of the Tower of Babel became a favorite theme with Christian artists, as in this fresco in St. Mark's, Venice *(above)*. The peoples of Babylon came together to erect a tower "with its top in the heavens" (Gen. 11:4).

The best-known tower or world mountain image in Western mythic tradition is of course the Tower of Babel. But we know that the construction of towers, pyramids, and other sacred centralized structures preoccupied many different peoples and cultures. The original concept seems to have been based on a special mountain as midpoint of the world connecting earth and heaven – Meru in India, Olympus, Sinai, Hermon, Zion – which men then attempted to reproduce in architectural terms. The pyramids of ancient Egypt, with their strict cosmological orientation and the finely calculated symbolism of their interior layout, also belong to the world mountain tradition, as do the stepped temples of various Mexican civilizations; the latter are quite clearly both sacred world centers and plat-

According to Genesis, however, the tower was a challenge on man's part to the omnipotence of God. Therefore God destroyed the tower *(above)* and "confused the language of all the earth" (Gen. 11: 9).

The Babel legend inspired Pieter Bruegel to a magnificent painting *(opposite)* in which the mighty tower as symbolic world mountain already rears seven stories heavenward – but the destruction of Babylon is at hand.

forms from which the gods can show themselves to men. Yet another idea is present in the numerous tower constructions to be found in the Near East and southern Asia. These were built for astrological purposes, on the one hand serving the worship of stellar divinities, and on the other making it possible to measure and calculate the planetary and stellar orbits from which the seasons and even individual fortunes could be read.

Such an image of the world's construction may appear rather too sophisticated, at first, to be the product of primitive and savage imagination. Yet there is enough documentation in myth to show that it was very widely accepted and believed.

Rabbinical tradition borrowed from the Babylonian the picture of heaven as a sort of seven-story mountain. King Solomon's throne, and the six steps leading up to it, was taken for a model in miniature of cosmic structure. Sheol, the underworld, was also thought to have seven tiers pointing downward like a series of cellars. "The seven abodes of Sheol are very spacious," says the *Jalkut Rubeni.* "In each abode are seven thousand caverns, and in each cavern seven thousand clefts, and in each cleft

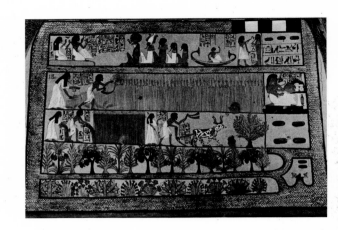

Through the Blessed Fields of the Egyptian paradise *(above)* flows the celestial Nile. There the initiate is fed the "bread of eternity" and drinks the "beer of everlasting life."

PARADISE

The myths and religions of mankind illustrate two concepts of paradise. The first relates to the undisturbed first state of the human race at the dawn of creation, when man was still a stranger to suffering and at one with his surroundings. This is the heaven on earth related in the "Golden Age" myths of Greece or India, the time of the "Golden Emperors" of China, the paradise of the Garden of Eden and of similar traditions in Persia and Babylonia. Eschatological myths and religions, those concerned with "last things," put the emphasis on a coming paradise of renewed union with the Almighty as the final redemption of man. Examples of this second type are the Valhalla of Nordic myth, the Happy Fields of Egypt, and the paradises of the Aztecs and the Muhammadans; in the Revelation to John this is the heavenly Jerusalem, and in Mahayana Buddhism it is the "western paradise" of Sukhavati, where the Buddha Amida reigns forever in imperishable splendor.

seven thousand scorpions. Each scorpion hath seven limbs, and on each limb are one thousand barrels of gall."

Apart from those gigantic mutant scorpions, "destroying angels" in Sheol judge and scourge the condemned soul "at every moment, half the year in the fire, and half the year in the hail and snow. And the cold is more intolerable than the fire."

The ancient Chinese spoke of an inner world, in the belly of the planet, where things were not necessarily pleasant. "China plowed under," as that realm has been described, was like a mirror image, an exact counterpart of the world above. Every province of China overlaid an under-

A twelfth-century Byzantine painting *(above)* shows a paradise inhabited by angels, planted with flowering trees, and watered by the four rivers of the Garden of Eden.

Their transgression of God's commandment cost Adam and Eve the privilege of continuing to live in Paradise *(right).*

One of the loveliest and richest descriptions of paradise is to be found in the literature of Mahayana Buddhism; its object is Sukhavati, the "western paradise" of the Buddha Amida *(opposite).*

Working outward from man and the earth as the center, myth and religion have evolved a multitude of detailed versions of how the heights of heaven and the depths of hell are structured. Myth in particular tends toward a layered arrangement: the seven heavens of Indian mythology, the seven, nine, or thrice-nine heavens of shamanism, and the twenty-one celestial spheres of Buddhist tradition. The Algonquin Indians say that Manitou lives in the twelfth heaven; Aztec myth numbered thirteen heavens; and Dante's great vision of paradise comprised seven planetary heavens. In the other direction, the underworld too was considered to be arranged in layers. The Aztecs had nine hells; Buddhism recognizes eighteen hells of cold and hot torment. Pictured here are a nineteenth-century miniature showing the seven heavens of the Indian cosmology, contrasted with a detail from the Dutch painter Jacob van Swanenburgh's vision of Charon's bark as a giant dragon devouring the dead.

Charon, his eyes red like a
    burning brand,
      Thumps with his oar the lingerers
        that delay,
      And rounds them up, and beckons
        with his hand.

And as, by one and one, leaves drift away
    In autumn, till the bough
      from which they fall
    Sees the earth strewn with all
      its brave array,

So, from the bank there, one by one,
    drop all
      Adam's ill seed, when signalled
      off the mark,
    As drops the falcon to
      the falconer's call.

Away they're borne across the waters dark,
    And ere they land that side
      the stream, anon
    Fresh troops this side come flocking
      to embark.

DANTE, HELL, CANTO III, 109–120
Translated by Dorothy L. Sayers (1949)

world province of the same dimensions. Moreover, every civil servant in the upper world had a double in the lower one. At Soochow, for example, governors, treasurers, and judges all maintained temples which were dedicated to their underworld counterparts. The military, too, possessed doubles. These were devils of a sort, which streamed like warrior ants to battle in eternal night.

Civil servants and men of war beneath the earth were just as venal, corrupt, callous, and occasionally cruel as their counterparts in the world of light. They required sacrifices which were equivalent to the taxes and bribes called for above ground. Struggles for power and position in the underworld were a matter of no small moment to mortal men. Chinese myth concerning underworld politics and war is enlivened by a certain wry wordliness. Then, too, it has a pervasive aura of anxiety.

The anthropologist Marcel Griaule conducted very extensive field research among the Dogon people of the Sudan. Griaule found that religion was just as much a part of their lives as the air they breathed. The floor plans of their houses, for example, represented the god Nommo lying on his right side. They plotted their fields in a spiral pattern to repeat the movement of earth's creation, as Nommo had commanded them. Every Dogon infant was regarded as a new incarnation of Nommo's cranium. On reaching puberty, one added the torso of the god to one's own development, but only in old age could one come to represent the whole body of the deity.

What did Nommo do to inspire such single-minded devotion? He taught the Dogon everything. How? By sending a solar boat sliding down a rainbow out of the sky. Its pilot was the first blacksmith, and its cargo consisted of metal models or symbols for everything under the sun. With them, each separate thing had many symbols, while each symbol, in turn, applied to many things.

There is a fourth dimension, according to the mathematics of science since Einstein, wherein space-time forms continuous curves, where parallel lines run together at last. Perhaps there is something similar – a "myth dimension," one might call it – in human thought. The myth dimension gently winds us back to the within of things again. Does it also point to the future? Will the evolution of human consciousness continue to require myth? In order to re-enter and, as it were, activate myth again, we must rediscover wonder; for as Aristotle noted long ago, out of wonder comes wisdom.

Power, magic, and intelligence are combined in this Aztec symbol of the double serpent.

You are born through flame,
O shining one.
You are the god Agni,
supreme force of life.
Great are you,
Great your works, O Agni,
who fulfilled the worlds
with your might.

RIG VEDA II, 2; III, 6

BRINGERS OF MAGIC AND THE ARTS

Out of the repeated use of primitive signs of magic, straight animal representations, and astrological symbols, there emerged the technique of adding and combining those signs and symbols in a meaningful way — and the elements of writing were born. The hieroglyphs of ancient Egypt are an intermediate stage in the process. Already highly abstract in some respects, they still retain the flavor of their natural and symbolic models. He who could read the writing knew the meaning of the message; he who possessed the meaning of the message had the power of knowledge over human and divine things.

The myth symbolism of ancient civilizations is often characterized by a high degree of identification between shape and meaning — e.g., the Indian god of fire, Agni, who is deity and fire at one and the same time. Another example is this Mochica Indian vessel depicting three maize gods. Modeled both as a whole and in detail on ears of maize, the vessel shows the cereal personified in divine form. Maize as fruit and deity as maize are one, both in form and significance.

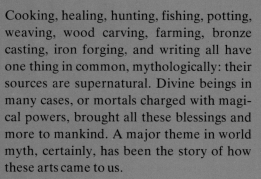

Cooking, healing, hunting, fishing, potting, weaving, wood carving, farming, bronze casting, iron forging, and writing all have one thing in common, mythologically: their sources are supernatural. Divine beings in many cases, or mortals charged with magical powers, brought all these blessings and more to mankind. A major theme in world myth, certainly, has been the story of how these arts came to us.

Energy in the form of fire is an essential tool in the development of numerous arts. It dwells in many things, quiescent, waiting. Myth often describes it as a spiritual being of a sort which was once difficult to evoke. The ancient Greeks credited a superhuman being, the Titan Prometheus, with having stolen the secret of fire from the home of the gods on Mount Olympus. He brought down a spark, hidden in a stalk of fennel, and distributed its fire to human friends. Greek peasants still use fennel stalks for transporting the Easter flame from churches to their homes after midnight Mass early on Easter Sunday.

According to the Jivaro Indians of northwestern Peru, the first man to figure out how to make fire by rubbing two sticks together was Takkea. Birds would attempt to steal his fire, but Takkea used to crush them as they flew between the door and the doorpost. Then he would roast his brave but foolish visitors and eat them at leisure. This went on until one day Takkea's wife happened upon Himbui the Hummingbird, who was fluttering helplessly along the path to the house. Thinking Himbui might be cold, she brought him in and let him warm himself beside the secret fire. The moment she turned her eyes away, Himbui dipped his tail into the flame. Then instantly he flew out of the house. Setting alight the dry bark of a tree with his tail, he called upon the people to come and share the blessing of fire.

A similar theme is related by the Djuan of northern Australia. They say that once in the dreamtime there was a sullen fellow named Koimul who had two fire sticks and knew how to use them. He never gave the secret of his sticks, or his fire either, to anyone. But Wirrit-wirrit the Hummingbird made a silent swoop and took the sticks from under Koimul's arm. Wirrit-wirrit it was who gave them to mankind. As a sign of this he still sports two especially long and flashing feathers in his tail.

The Aztec Indians of Mexico identified the hummingbird with their war god Huitzilopochtli (or Mexitli), who had given fire to the people and led them to their homeland on the Mexican plateau. Aztec art represented Huitzilopochtli in a green-feathered headdress and with the hummingbird perched on his right foot.

From the northeastern state of Assam in India comes a myth concerning a battle between Fire and Water. Fire lost and went to lick its wounds in stone and wood, particularly bamboo, where it hid. Nobody saw where it went except Grasshopper, whose big eyes noticed everything that went on. Grasshopper went and told Monkey, who taught himself how to use the fire that had hidden in the bamboo. Monkey in turn was observed by a man. The man thought he deserved the fire more than Monkey; so he stole it from him.

CHARACTERS FOUND AND LOST

How did man first learn to read and write? Is it possible that ibis tracks in the mud inspired the cuneiform clay printing of Babylonian scribes? Who knows?

The ancient Egyptians maintained that their god Thoth, who had the head of an ibis, taught them how to write. Thoth boasted to the other celestial deities of his gift, whereupon they giggled rudely. The sun god Ra asked what Thoth's purpose had been. "Why," croaked the ibis-headed one, "to help men remember things!" Ra roared with laughter. "You," he said, pointing at Thoth, "have given human beings the means to forget everything they know. They won't need to remember anymore. They'll simply note things down, like idiots without a thought or care."

The Ainu, primitive inhabitants of Japan's northernmost islands, believed that their own shamans had invented written characters a long time ago. A Japanese wizard came, they complained, and meanly made off with the whole lot.

The Sakhalin Gilyak of Siberia told a similar tale of woe to Charles W. Hawes. Their greatest shaman had long ago been prevailed upon to show his calligrams, or signs for words, to an importunate mandarin out of China. This occurred on the seashore. A storm arose; all but five calligrams were blown out to sea. The Chinese wickedly made off with the remaining five. The wind died down again. The Sakhalin shaman stood upon the cold sea strand, with nothing at all in his clenched fists.

THE SOLAR FORGE

Metalworking is regarded among many different peoples as being of divine origin, and the smith himself is held to be a magician. The Hebrews believed that it was the fallen angel Azazel who taught men the arts of metalcraft. The Buryat tribesmen of Mongolia say that Boshintoi is the blacksmith at the solar forge. He gave his nine sons, plumed with flames, to teach mankind. By word and example, the luminous children of Boshintoi showed people on earth all the working of metal. Men, however, were far too dull to grasp those lessons well. Therefore, in despair, the nine sons burningly entered human brides. From the white hiss of their extinguishment sprang nine earthly families of smiths.

Neighbors of the Buryat, the Yakut, say that blacksmithing is not a gift of heaven, but of the underworld. Heroes whose bones have been broken or crushed upon the battlefield must drag themselves down to an iron house, a mile beneath the surface of the earth. There lives a surly demon named K'daai Maqsin. Some suppliants K'daai burns in his fires, making them sweat metal. Others he carefully restores to life again, replacing their mangled limbs with new ones of bright iron. That same K'daai Maqsin, the Yakut maintain, invented blacksmithing.

Humanity must pay in blood for the privilege of smelting and casting metals from the bones of Mother Earth. This appears to have been believed by all our ancestors at one time or another, the world over. The following Chinese legend, for example, has many parallels.

The first great signal bell to ring out from Peking was created by Kuan Yu for the third Ming emperor, Yung Lo. Because of its great size, the bell proved exceedingly

1 Sho-Kwannon of Japanese Buddhism was the bringer of the wisdom of compassion for all.
2 The Babylonian god Nabu was worshiped as the Omniscient, personifying as he did all the wisdom of the gods.

3 The ancient Greeks believed that inspiration was the gift of the nine Muses, pictured here dancing with Apollo.
4 In Tantrism knowledge and wisdom were imparted by the god Cakrasamvara.

122

Various myths and religions have gods who bestow or in some way symbolize knowledge, intellectual abilities of one sort or another, or wisdom. They may originally have been historical persons who came to be deified (e.g., the Buddha); in many cases their symbolism seems to suggest that an early folk hero lies behind them. Such deities are basically attempts to represent the abstract phenomena of knowledge and wisdom in human form. The "wisdom" involved may be the philosophic dimension of knowledge or it may relate to particular skills or perceptions. Iconographically it

5

6

7

8

5 The Japanese deity Fudo Myo-o wields the sword of knowledge against hatred and the greed of the ignorant.

6 In ancient-Eyptian belief Maat was the goddess of knowledge, truth, and justice.

7 Athene, the patron deity of Athens, was the goddess of wisdom and of good counsel in war.

may be represented as a male or as a female figure. The Greek Muses, directed by Apollo, gave men inspiration in the nine fine arts. Gnostic teaching knew Sophia as the goddess of wisdom. In Indian Tantrism the higher spiritual wisdom is communicated by female divinities, or by the mystic union of divine couples whose male-female polarity may represent a coming-together of the opposites. The attributes of such divinities usually throw light on the particular quality they personify.

9

10

8 The Japanese Monju Bo-satsu is the bodhisattva of transcendental wisdom, as symbolized by the sword of knowledge and the book of wisdom in his hands.

9 Another personification of transcendental wisdom is the goddess Prajnaparamita. This statue of her is from the Angkor temple complex in Cambodia, but she is known throughout Mahayana Buddhism. Her meditative aspect symbolizes the "wisdom that has attained the other shore."

10 The *dakinis*, or celestial fairies, of Tibet impart secret knowledge through the medium of initiation.

difficult to cast. Kuan Yu's first two efforts failed miserably. The third time he tried, just as the molten metal was being poured, his daughter hurled herself headfirst into the hissing hot alloy. "For my father!" she cried as she fell. Such an ambitious work as his, she must have supposed, required a human sacrifice for its success.

Kuan Yu leaped to rescue his daughter. He caught hold of one of her feet, but even so he was too late. Her shoe came off in his hand.

The bell was hung in the tower over Peking's main gate. Emperor Yung Lo himself was present the first time it rang. The bell boomed marvelously loud and clear and musical. The booming faded to a sonorous roar, and that in turn was followed by a high thin aftertone which seemed to shrill the one word, "Hsieh," and "Hsieh," again. *Hsieh* means "shoe." Kuan Yu's daughter was calling for the shoe she had lost. But unfortunately there was no way to return it to her.

BEARERS OF KNOWLEDGE

Yakut shamans and blacksmiths of the Turukhansk region pray especially to Ai Toyon, Creator of Light. He takes the form of a huge, radiant two-headed eagle, perched at the very tip of the world tree. From Ai Toyon's wide-spreading, snow-white pinions, physical light and the light of knowledge alike descend to earth. When shamans dream, Ai Toyon descends upon them.

According to Norse myth, thought itself was represented by feathered spirits. Odin, the wise god of the Norsemen, made pets of two carrion crows, whose names were Hugin and Munin, or Thought and Memory — that is to say, the paired halves of consciousness. Odin used to send those shy, shadowy, strong-winged and straight-flying creatures out to the four corners of the world, from which they would return to his own shoulders instantaneously. Softly communicative, they imparted the secrets of the universe to Odin's ears alone.

At Delphi, in Greece, the god Apollo was believed to speak through a trancebound priestess and to answer every question truthfully. Delphi's prophecies were often of a riddling nature, however. When King Croesus inquired of the god whether or not he ought to defy and invade Persia, the oracle responded that such an action would destroy a great empire. Much encouraged, Croesus declared war. It was his own empire — not so extensive as the Persian, but nonetheless great in itself — which met with utter destruction.

His doctors could not diagnose it. One night, in sleep, the emperor came upon an imp in crimson trousers with one shoe on and the other shoe hanging from his belt. The imp had appropriated an embroidered box and a jade flute. It danced about the palace playing the flute and juggling the box in one hand, impertinently. The emper-

HEALING POWERS

Early in the eighth century, by Western reckoning, the Chinese emperor Ming Huang made an expedition to Mount Li in Shensi province. There he contracted an illness characterized by raging high fevers.

or accosted the creature and asked what it might be doing. "Your humble servant," said the imp, "is Hsu Hao — Emptiness and Devastation."

Irritated, the emperor clapped his hands for the palace guard. Immediately, a huge man in a blue robe appeared. He wore a wide

124

1 In ancient Peru the jaguar was elevated to divine status as a folk hero and fire bringer.

2 The Greeks' great hero was Prometheus, depicted here in an illustration for Ovid's *Metamorphoses.* He brought fire to earth, where he taught people how to use the new discovery. The two details on the right show him descending from heaven with the fire and being punished by Zeus.

2

FIRE –
A GIFT OF THE GODS

Without the transforming power of fire progress is virtually unthinkable. Various myths speak of fire as an element that the

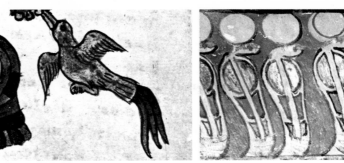

3

gods originally had in their charge; others very naturally trace its origin to the sun or to lightning. The figures associated with it in myth are either gods of fire, heroic descendants of the sun as mediators of the living light of heaven, lightning deities, or folk heroes. According to an Indian myth Matarishwan brought the fire of the god Agni to earth. When Izanami of the Japanese creation myth (page 77) gave birth to the fire god Hinokagutsuchi she was consumed by him, this event constituting the origin of the turn of the year. The Incas received fire from Viracocha, creator of the sun. The fire gods of the Assyrians were Gibil and Nusku, whose father was the moon, while Nordic myth tells of a fire demon called Loki. The angel Lucifer, as his name sug-

3 The hummingbird, bird of the south, was regarded in ancient Mexico as the bringer of the sun's warmth (myth, page 122).

4 The *uraeus* serpent, an Egyptian symbol of fire (as solar energy), of motion, and of power over life and death, bears the sun symbol on its head as well as the circular "long life" symbol.

5   6   7

5–7 The Aztecs' fire and hearth deity was called Xiuhtecuhtli (5), who also appears as the "old god" Huehueteotl (7). Agni, the Indian god of fire and personification of the fire of sacrifice (6), has a benevolent head and a malevolent one.

8   9   10

8–10 The Hawaiian fire goddess Pele (8) lives in the crater of Kilauea volcano. Here (9) the Aztec god Xiuhtecuhtli tends the fire at the world center. The Etruscan fire god Tinia (10) spoke in thunder and descended to earth in lightning.

2

11 In the creation myths of the Navaho, Coyote figures as the folk hero who climbed secretly up to heaven to steal fire from the gods. This sand painting tells the story of how after a long journey through the sky he brought the fire to men.

gests, once bore the light of heaven as fire down to hell, and Vesta, the Roman goddess of the hearth, was represented in her temple in Rome by an eternal fire guarded by virgin priestesses.

11

belt with a buckle of horn and heavy boots. The newcomer stretched forth his right hand and plucked out one of the imp's eyeballs. He crushed the round jelly in his fist, put the pulp in his mouth, and swallowed. Thereupon the imp vanished, and the emperor awakened with a start. He found that his fever had broken. He felt fine. The emperor called his personal staff to his bedside. Sitting up, he told what had happened in his dream. No one knew what to make of it. The court painter, however, undertook to commemorate the weird event by means of an ink and watercolor picture on silk. That painting, historians say, was handed down from generation to generation, well into the Sung dynasty. But now it has disappeared.

Tibetan legend tells how the holy man Vairocana came to the bedside of beautiful Queen Tshe-spon-bza as she lay dying. Passing one hand gently over her body, Vairocana drew forth a tiny black pin. The queen recovered instantly.

What is it like to grow up in a magic-haunted world, with a real medicine man for a teacher? A Hopi Indian chief named Don C. Talayesva, who had the dubious advantage of completing his education under white supervision, remembered well:

My earliest memories of my real grandfather, Homikniwa, he wrote, are full of kind feelings. I slept with him much of the time. In the morning before sunrise he sang to me and told me stories. He took me to his fields, where I helped him to work or slept under a peach tree. Whenever he saw me make a circle he stepped cautiously around it, saying that he had to watch me lest I block his path with my antelope power. He kept reminding me of this power. He also took me through the fields to collect healing herbs. I watched him sprinkle cornmeal and pray to the Sun God before picking up leaves or berries or digging medicine roots. Whenever mothers brought their sick children to our house, I watched him take their pinches of meal, step outside, pray, and sprinkle them to the Sun God, Moon, or the Stars, and to his special Medicine God. Then he would return to the patient, blow upon his hands, and begin his treatment. Even Mr. Voth, the missionary, came to him to learn about plants and herbs. He taught the white man many things. He taught me also all I ever learned about plants. He advised me to keep bad thoughts out of my mind . . . and learn to show a shining face even when unhappy.

By the age of six, little Talayesva "had almost stopped running after my mother for her milk." At that stage he "could ride a

The legendary vision of St. Eligius (*above*): Christ as blacksmith nails a shoe to the severed leg of the saint's horse. The wrought iron sculpture (*below*) represents the African Yoruba tribe's god of iron and war.

A remarkable number of myths tell of a figure who either is a blacksmith or has some kind of essential relationship to iron. Since the art of making and working metals is the key to all cultural progress, one of these figures invariably appears at the point where mankind enters a new phase of civilization. It is interesting to note that the

blacksmith himself is not necessarily a god; more usually he is a helper of the gods, an organizer, someone who gives form and order to the world of men. In India Brahmanaspati is the earliest mediator between gods and men. The divine Twashtri forged the weapons of Indra; in

Greek myth it was Hephaestus who made the armor of Achilles. The Book of Genesis gives Tubal-cain as the first ironmaster, and Nordic myth has Thor establish a new order among men with the iron hammer Mjollnir. The ancient-Egyptian creator god Ptah is a master craftsman who manufactures tools for Horus, while the

In the religion of Memphis in ancient Egypt the god Ptah (*left*), creator of the world, was also associated with crafts. He was in fact the patron deity of craftsmen.

The divine blacksmith Hephaestus (the Roman Vulcan) and his assistants, the Cyclopes, forge a new shield for Achilles to carry in battle against the Trojans (*below*). Standing on the left is Athene, the Greek goddess, in whom Hephaestus met his match (page 136).

tame burro, kill a kangaroo rat, and catch small birds, but I could not make fire with a drill and I was not a good runner like the other fellows. But I had made a name for myself by healing people."

In primitive as well as in some more sophisticated societies, women employ magical spells to heal the sick. Where did they learn the spells? Men often ask this. In general it is the women's own secret, which they jealously hide from men. For their part, men have invented endless legends to account for the women's predominance in the sickroom.

Buryat of eastern Siberia believe the celestial blacksmith Boshintoi was sent to men to teach them manual skills (page 122).

Then Hephaestus put a great anvil on the stand
and gripped a strong hammer in one hand
and a pair of tongs in the other.
He began by making a large and powerful shield,
adorned all over, finished with
a bright rim of gleaming metal . . .

HOMER, THE ILIAD, XVIII, 475–480
Translated by E.V. Rieu (1950)

In his book *Religion, Folklore, and Custom in North Borneo and the Malay* (1923), Ivor Evans relates a tale of the Kiau Dusun people of Borneo about some men who once went out hunting. They moved silently so as not to alert the birds in the trees overhead. As they went, they heard singing, much to their surprise. The singing was neither birdlike nor human; it seemed to come from a beast's throat. They crept along toward the sound, and as they went they could make out the words being sung:

The River Makadau was my first home.
Then I went to the River Serinsin.
From Serinsin to Wariu, from Wariu to
* Penataran,*
I came. From Penataran to the Kilambun,
And from the Kilambun to the Obang I
* journeyed,*
From the Obang have I come, to Tenokop.
Now I am old; I can no longer climb the
* trees.*

The men parted the branches which screened them from the sound of singing, and they peered through. They saw an orangutan sitting on the ground. He had finished his song. "What a clever animal," they said. "He is well traveled, too, but feeble now. Let's shoot him with our blow-pipes."
The orangutan looked up and saw the men aiming at him. "Do not destroy me," he cried. "Instead, go home and fetch the women of your village. Only let them come to me and I will instruct them in secret."
The men were much impressed. They felt that the beast must be some spirit in disguise – they built him a hut and brought their sisters to him for instruction. The orangutan taught the women spells for snakebites, for the sting of the centipede, and for fever. Then he taught them spells to recite over a wounded man so that his blood might clot and cease flowing.
After that, the orangutan expired in the arms of the women. A ghost arose from his lipless face, and the women reverenced it.

DRUMS, DECAPITATION, AND A PAPER MULE

When a shaman of the Ostyak Samoyed people requires a magical drum, he closes his eyes and stumbles off into the forest. He feels himself drawn blindly on until he bumps headlong into a tree. That is the one from which he must make his drum. Chance is not what brought him to it; he believes supernatural guidance did so. He will transform the tree into a drum, the music of which will transform him in turn.
Chinese mythology is particularly rich in stories of magic and sorcery. The Prince of Ch'i, Chiang Tzu-ya, once traveled a steep and dangerous path westward across icefalls and snowy wastes to reach at last the Palace of Abstraction. Just what happened there is not made clear in the ancient rec-

And behold, they brought him
a paralytic, lying on his bed;
and when Jesus saw their faith he said
to the paralytic, "Take heart, my son;
your sins are forgiven." And behold,
some of the scribes said to themselves,
"This man is blaspheming."
But Jesus, knowing their thoughts,
said, "Why do you think evil
in your hearts? For which is easier,
to say, 'Your sins are forgiven,'
or to say, 'Rise and walk'?
But that you may know
that the Son of man has authority

on earth to forgive sins"
– he then said to the paralytic –
"Rise, take up your bed and go home."
And he rose and went home.

MATTHEW 9: 2-7

In Phoenician myth Shadrafa, "the Healer," is conqueror of evil generally. He is pictured (*below left*) standing on the back of a lion beneath the symbol of the sun. A Roman statue of Aesculapius (*below right*), the Greco (Asclepius)-Roman god of healing, shows him with the staff and snake – to this day symbols of the art of medicine. Behind the old sage in the foreground of this Chinese painting (*opposite*) is a gourd full of medicine. Before the wise man stands a child, representing eternal youth, to whom he is handing a peach, the symbol of longevity. Advanced age and wisdom were the supreme goals of Taoism.

Health, relief from suffering, and long life are things man has always wished for and given graphic expression to in symbols, mythic figures, and benevolent gods. For not only spiritual well-being stems from the divine order; physical health too has always been regarded by man as a gift that either came direct from the gods or had its origin in the plant world, which also offered the means of healing. The most ancient myths tell of patron deities of the art of healing who instructed man in the secrets of medicine. Cases of recovery from apparently hopeless diseases exercised a numinous fascination that man could only explain in terms of the "will of the gods." Medical knowledge and skill were inevitably associated with divine power, and healers were considered to be in league with the gods. In ancient China the art of healing was attributed to the mythological emperors Fu Hsi, Shen Nung, and Huang Ti. Nordic myth attributed medicine – among other things – to the wise god Odin, though other Nordic gods and goddesses were also familiar with its secrets. Wisdom and the art of healing were often ascribed to the same god, as in the case of the Egyptian Imhotep and the Alexandrian god of healing, Sarapis. In Tibet the Medicine Buddha was believed to have brought to man the treatises of Indian medicine; he also brought the healing message of redemption in Nirvana as medicine for the suffering soul. Other Tibetan healing gods are the "Five Sisters of Longevity," who lived in the land of medicinal herbs. The gods of healing in ancient Greece were Priapus and above all Asclepius, at whose shrines the sick became well again through the healing sleep known as "incubation."

In Japan it is Jizo (*above left*), the compassionate bodhisattva, who is addressed as god of healing. He is the patron deity of travelers, pregnant women, and children. The Greek goddess Hera (*above center*), as Hera Eileithyia, announced the birth of children and was patroness of women in childbed. The Buddha Yakushi Nyorai (*above right*), the Japanese equivalent of the Indian Bhaisajyaguru, is depicted with a healing fruit in his hand. He cures both physical and mental suffering.

The divinity associated with medicine by the Melanau of Malaysia is Belam (*right*), who appears as a spirit to wash sick souls.

The Hopi Indians – like the shaman of northern Asia – regard the bear as a particularly sacred *kachina* or spirit (*below left*). His magical power and intelligence are such that he can heal the sick. The ancient Egyptians depicted Thoeris, the patron goddess of conception and pregnancy, from whom they besought the gift of children, as a pregnant hippopotamus (*below right*).

129

ords. It is understood, however, that he was presented to the Ancient Immortal of the South Pole. Like Moses on Mount Sinai, the Prince of Ch'i received a priceless document at the end of his visit. This was the list of promotions to the ranks of the Immortals.

Journeying homeward with his treasure, the Prince of Ch'i paused at the border country which Unicorn Precipice dominates. There he met a magician, Shen Kung-pao. "You," the magician said to him, "know how to drain marshes and change the course of rivers and the shapes of hills. You stand for civilization, which can toy with nature in such a way. But that is really child's play. Look at me. I can cut off this head of mine and toss it out beyond the moon and get it back again. I can also teach you the very nature of magic if you will only burn your list and cast your lot with me. There is nothing that you and I could not accomplish together."

Temptation overcame the Prince of Ch'i. "Do with your head what you said you could do," he demanded. "If I see that with my own eyes, then I will burn the list and follow you."

Shen Kung-pao carefully removed his Taoist cap and placed it on the ground. With his left hand he firmly grasped the hair of his own head and twisted it tight in a ribbon of blue silk. With his right hand he swung his sword decisively at his own neck, severing it. Then the sorcerer gently tossed his head skyward. The Prince of Ch'i, gazing up in wonderment, watched the head grow smaller and smaller and finally disappear in the blue infinity. The magician still stood, immobile, with the blood bubbling up from his truncated neck and returning again into his body like a quiet crimson fountain.

The Prince of Ch'i sat down in the shade under a tree. He had forgotten to ask how long the demonstration would take. It seemed to him now that he had made a rash promise. Yet he would carry out his word to cast his lot with this extraordinarily accomplished priest.

Suddenly the Immortal of the South Pole was with him under the tree. "You are a fool," said the Immortal. "You take mere tricks to be matters of consequence. I have observed this business from the Palace of Abstraction, and I know what you have promised our friend over there. But don't worry. My white crane has intercepted the sorcerer's head. The bird will dispose of the head somehow, whether by letting it drown in the ocean or by splitting it open upon a mountaintop. Meanwhile, the blood in that body over there will clot from long exposure to the air, causing the body to collapse and become a corpse."

The Prince of Ch'i pleaded, with a convincingness which only tender mortals can achieve, for the sorcerer's life. "After all," he argued, "no man who has developed such proficiency in the magical arts can be altogether worthless."

The Immortal smiled. Drawing back one sleeve, he stretched his right hand forth from the shade of the tree and flashed his yellow fingers in a brief imperious gesture. The white crane, flying high above with the intercepted head in its beak, observed the signal. It let the sorcerer's head drop. The Prince of Ch'i, gazing up, was much relieved to see the head sink and fall upon the neck of the magician. It settled on backward. At once, Shen Kung-pao raised his hands to his ears and yanked the head around into its normal position. His eyes opened. He saw the prince and the Immortal together under the tree. Without a word, he fled into the jungle.

The Prince of Ch'i took leave of the Immortal for a second time and recrossed the frontier of China.

Perhaps the most modest of the many Chinese sages who were said to posses transforming powers was Chang Kuo. The T'ang emperors T'ai Tsung and Kau T'sung both invited him to court, but he refused to go. He rode the distant mountains on a white mule of a spiritual sort. When evening came, he would fold the mule up like a thin slip of paper and tuck it away under his pillow. At sunrise Chang Kuo would gently lick the paper as if it were an envelope, in order to reanimate its nature.

In the year 723, Chang finally turned up at court for a brief visit. He entertained Emperor Ming Huang with a display of magical powers. Flowers would wilt and birds would fall when he pointed at them. He cheerfully downed a cup of poison and showed no ill effects from it. He rendered himself invisible and visible again at will. Impressed, the emperor offered to give Chang his own daughter in marriage. The sage gravely refused the offer. Chang also declined to pose for a portrait which the emperor had commissioned for the Imperial Hall of Fame. Before the sunset hour came, Chang drew his miraculous mule out of his sleeve. He licked it into life, mounted it, and hastened away.

After those events, the emperor asked the court necromancer, Yeh Fa-shan, to explain the real nature of Chang Kuo. "If I do so," the magician blurted, "I shall fall dead at your feet." The emperor, however, was most anxious to know the truth. He insisted, and finally Yeh Fa-shan told him: "Chang

One of the most important gods in the whole classical pantheon is Hermes, son of Zeus and the Pleiad Maia. It is said that at noon on the day he was born he invented the lyre, and that same evening he rustled the oxen of Apollo. The many myths about him add up to a unique picture of a bringer of culture and protective, patron deity. Originally Hermes was the guardian of flocks and of the fertility of the land. Subsequently his shrewdness and cunning make him the patron of merchants, and his eloquence associates him with orators and philosophers. As the messenger of the gods he communicates their will to men, and as guide of the soul he brings dreams and conducts the shades of the dead down to

A detail from a Greek vase found at Vulci in Etruria shows the god Hermes carrying the young Dionysus in his arms (*below*).

Hades. He is also bringer of the art of prophecy by omens. In fact his inexhaustible inventiveness makes him a kind of universal folk hero, divine adviser, and helper of mankind. Known to the later Romans as Mercurius, Hermes has affinities with the ancient-Egyptian ibis-headed god Thoth (myth, page 122).

Kuo is an albino bat which has flown to China from Primeval Chaos!" Having revealed that, Yeh Fa-shan fell dead on the spot. But some round off the myth by adding that Chang Kuo in his mercy reappeared for a moment and revived the man.

THE SPIDER'S WEB

Spiders are said to have imparted the weaving art. Spider Grandmother, Navaho Indians of the American Southwest insist, was

This early Greek statuette of Hermes (*left*) shows him in his role of protector of the flocks, carrying a symbolic ram on his left arm.

An Etruscan silver mirror (*below*) shows Hermes – with his winged helmet and serpent staff – in the company of Apollo and Jupiter.

The infant Hermes, back from stealing the oxen of Apollo, lies innocently in his bed while his divine parents deny that he had any part in the crime (*above*).

Hermes was still worshiped by the Gauls, who called him Mercurius (*top right*). This relief found near St. Rémy shows him with the usual emblems and the tortoise and goat of the earliest Hermes myths.

When Orpheus led his lover Eurydice back from Hades to the upper world Hermes, the messenger of the gods, lent the couple his services as guide (*above right*).

among the greatest benefactors of their race. Originally, the Greeks, too, may have credited a spider ancestor with having taught their people how to weave. But, as often occurs in myth, the Greek account familiar to us reverses things.

Once there lived a village maiden, Arachne, whose skill in weaving astonished everyone. Even the nymphs of the woodland used to gather at Arachne's door for the sheer pleasure of watching her work.

131

They felt she must have learned her skill at the knees of the goddess Athene. But Arachne denied any such suggestion. "I challenge Athene herself," the girl declared, "to surpass me in this activity." The goddess thereupon appeared in glory to accept the challenge at Arachne's door. The two set up their looms side by side.

SHAMANS: MAGICIANS AND PRIESTS

The chief home of shamanism was the northern regions of Europe, Asia, and America, where traces of shamanistic religions

various magical aids such as a drum, a costume that jingled and clattered, and certain disguises, the shaman performed dances to summon, adjure, or exorcize the spirits. His main job was to ward off the evil demons who preyed on men in the form of illnesses of all kinds. This involved calling up good

Athene worked swiftly; her flying shuttle pressed threads of purple and gold to create a tapestry wherein the immortals of Mount Olympus could be dimly discerned. Arachne meanwhile filled her tapestry with images of the girls whom Athene's father Zeus had seduced.

In craftmanship and aesthetic merit, the two creations appeared equally fine. Athene, however, was in no mood to settle for a

can still be found today (see map, pages 42 and 43). Until recently each tribe and community of these northern peoples had its own shaman, who was a great magician and connoisseur of the spirit world. He alone could accompany the souls of the dead to the Beyond, speak with the spirits, and make known their cryptic messages to men (myth, page 122). Using

spirits, with whose help the spirits of sickness were driven out. His magical contact with the realm of the dead also enabled the shaman to fathom the utterances of the wise old ancestors who told the fortunes of the living in oracular form. The shaman, in fact, was priest, doctor, and psychologist all in one.

3 A Samoyed shaman from the Urals is pictured in reindeer mask, with tamborine and drum, riding on the back of a bear to the land of dead souls.

4 This prehistoric Nordic rock drawing with antlered helmet is thought to represent a sorcerer or shaman.

5–6 Shamanism was common to the whole of northern Europe and Asia and parts of China, and its origins lie in prehistory. These two terracotta figures from third-century China represent sorcerers or shamans wearing typically Chinese headgear.

7 A carving found among the Koryak of eastern Siberia depicts a shaman holding his drum, an animal of Nordic myth at his feet.

8 The shaman costume of the Evenki Tungus of Lake Baykal is hung with pieces of iron and bells, whose clanking is supposed to drive off evil spirits.

1 The cavorting figures in this Turkish miniature are good and evil spirits measuring their strength against that of the shaman in a magical dance.

2 A Siberian shaman poses in front of his tent wearing a fringed and beribboned robe, holding an oval drum and a tamborine.

14 This drawing from Lake Onega of a shamanistic sorcerer shows him dancing in an animal mask, with a bow and arrow.

9–11 Through his ritual dance the shaman makes contact with the spirits of his tribe's ancestors in order to bring their message to men (9). The highly abstract shaman above (11) is taken from a Lapp drum design, while the engraving (10) shows a Tungus shaman in full dress including head ornament.

12 This wooden statue from British Columbia depicts a shaman transformed into a demon.

13 Among the Lapps the shaman lies down with his drum on top of him when he journeys in trance to the spirit world.

15 In Paleolithic cave drawings the shaman appears in the guise of a reindeer.

tied contest. Whether envy or pride compelled her to do it, she pronounced Arachne's subject matter outrageous and unacceptable. With that excuse, Athene declared herself the winner. Not stopping there, she clawed Arachne's creation to shreds. The anger of the goddess drove the simple girl frantic. Arachne retreated into her house.

Athene waited a few moments for her rival to return. Then, seething with anger, she pursued the girl indoors. She found Arachne swinging limp, an apparent suicide, with a broken neck. Arachne's eyes stared sightlessly. Her tongue protruded, swollen, from between her lips. Majestically, Athene approached. With her shuttle, she touched the nearly lifeless girl.

Arachne's hair, nose, and ears fell away. Her head rapidly withered and blackened. Her body shrank also; now it seemed nothing but belly, bristling with fur. Her limbs multiplied, but they were smaller than her fingers had been.

Reaching up, Arachne grasped the rope from which she swung. She hauled herself up to the rafter, swiftly and silently. With no delay, she pressed silvery filaments of thread from what had been her own navel. Using these, she set to work weaving once again. Diligent, clever Arachne had become an Arachnida, a spider.

THE RED-FOOTED GENIUS

Chinese musicians long revered a legendary person named Lan Ts'ai'ho. They spoke of her as the Red-footed Genius and hinted that she was really "a man who did not know how to be a man." The bisexual nature of this wild, birdlike, and distantly appealing creature reflects, perhaps, something ambiguous and harmonious at once in the very nature of art.

Lan Ts'ai'ho was a street singer, carrying a 3-foot wand with which she kept waving time to her own quavering verses.

Winter and summer, she wore one shoe only. Her garment was a cloak like a tattered patch of sky. She slept among the flowers or in snow. In cold weather, her breath went up like steam from a boiling caldron. In it, iridescent images of heaven were seen to drift. She did not know the meaning of money. When listeners tossed coins upon the ground at her feet, she would stoop to toss the same coins back again, thinking it a game. She drank a lot of rice wine; that and the perfumes of the air seemed to be her only nourishment. Her listeners could never know for sure whether Lan Ts'ai'ho was drunk or in a trance.

One time in the courtyard of the inn at Feng-yang Fu, she seemed to lose all discretion. She kicked off her one shoe; she stripped away her blue cloak. The wand with which she kept time fluttered to the ground; yet still she sang, rising up, effortlessly climbing the air. At rooftop level she paused to look briefly back over her shoulder, smiling, and then she disappeared.

1 Saul, in a crisis he had brought upon himself, resorted to magic and consulted the Witch of Endor. She called up the dead prophet Samuel, who foretold Saul's end "because you did not obey the voice of the Lord" (1 Sam. 28: 18).
2 The literally spellbinding beauty in this fifteenth-century Flemish painting is a young witch preparing a love potion.

MAGICAL JARS

Myths having to do with inexplicably beautiful jars, of unknown provenance, appear to have spread from Java all the way to the Philippines. A Tingguian tribesman of Luzon once showed the American anthropologist Fay-Cooper Cole a jar called Magsawi. "This was not made where the Chinese are," the native asserted. "My ancestors were hunting with a dog, one time, when this jar leaped out of a bush. The dog chased the jar for some distance, barking wildly. He was about to seize it in his teeth when the jar vanished, much to my ancestors' distress. They killed a sow and made a blood offering for success in the hunt. The jar again appeared, and the dog chased it to a hole in the rock. Thus Magsawi was brought to bay and captured. It talked to my ancestors, softly, many times. But now it only mumbles in a way that I cannot follow."

The Tingguian people also tell of a magician who used to herd jars like cattle. When he married, he took his young bride out to

WITCHES: DISCIPLES OF THE DEVIL

The realm of the secret and unknown on earth and in the underworld has always had a strong connection with the female and the maternal. Women's mediumistic and mantic gifts have further contributed to the association of these powers with those of spirits and de-

3–7 A priestess calls down power upon the coven (3) gathered within the magic circle. The winged Lilithu of this Sumerian relief (4) takes souls down into death. The threefold goddess Hecate (5) is mistress of the dead and of the spirit world. Pythia, the priestess of Delphi (6), was the mouthpiece of the famous oracle. The Chinese fairy Ma Kuh reclaimed land from the sea (7).

mons. The figure of the witch needs to be looked at in the wider context of the symbolism of death and secret knowledge, of divination and oracles. Examples of dark goddesses of the earth or underworld are the Hebrew Lilith and the Greek Hecate. A familiar figure in Germanic myth is the witch as black magician riding on a broomstick, fork, or goat to the Witches' Sabbath, held annually on Walpurgis Night in the Harz Mountains. Witches were known in Parseeism and in ancient Babylon, but they first began to achieve real importance in twelfth-century Christendom. It was an unenviable achievement, however, since they were believed to have whored themselves to the devil. Although in exchange for their services they received the power to harm their enemies by all kinds of magical means, this belief led to their persecution. Visionary and mediumistic gifts, however genuine, were regarded as machinations of the devil against Christ and the Church, and in an age when woman's image was in any case a negative one the witch was condemned as being utterly sinful – which of course in no way helped to clarify the problem of magic.

8–9 Witches rode broomsticks even in pre-Columbian times (8). Their dance in the Harz Mountains (9) is legendary.

11 The four witches of Dürer's engraving have met in secret to discuss deeds of sorcery and transformation.

10 In the Middle Ages men believed that witches had entered into a secret pact with the devil.

12 This eighteenth-century engraving shows a witch – rather a lovely one – at her pre-Sabbath toilet.

see his herd. The jars rolled around the couple and stuck out their tongues. The bride was terrified; she thought she and her husband were about to be devoured. As soon as he fed the jars, however, they became perfectly still.

Dayak tribesmen distinguish three sorts of magical jar. These are the Gusi, the Rusa, and the Naga. All three types look and feel exceedingly old. Their glazes, sometimes brown and sometimes green, display thousands of tiny cracks. The jars are the most treasured possessions of the Dayak, not to be parted with at any price. They say that each jar speaks in a low voice to those who have ears to hear.

THE BIRTH OF SCULPTURE

Hephaestus, the Greek god of smiths and artisans in general, found himself smitten with an unbearable passion for Athene, Goddess of Wisdom. He waylaid her on a snowy mountainside and attempted to plead his case. Athene, being virgin and glad of it, would not listen to him. Mad with frustration, Hephaestus hurled the goddess to the ground. With sooty hands, he stripped off her gleaming armor. Hephaestus was exceedingly strong in the arms and shoulders, as becomes a smith. But he was no warrior. Athene cooly and contemptuously bided her time with him. Not until his hairy arms were clasping her neck did she kick out. Hephaestus rolled heavily aside, severely hurt for the moment. His sperm spurted upon the snowy drifts.

Athene had proved impregnable; she was too much for Hephaestus. He had failed, in the heat of his lust, to scale the cold heights of wisdom. And yet his attempt resulted in something very valuable. From the spilled seed of agonized Hephaestus, said the Greeks, the first statues sprang up of their own accord out of the snow.

Contrast the highly philosophical and yet rather obscene Greek genesis of statuary with what the Tlingit of North America had to say concerning the origin of one particular statue and the life it generated. In this myth no hint of explanation or even of speculation occurs. The people who tell stories such as this do so in a heartfelt, believing way. They take part. So, for them, there appears to be no sharp distinction between nature and art.

A Tlingit Indian chief of the Queen Charlotte Islands was much in love with his wife. When she died, he asked all the best woodcarvers he could find to create an image of her which he might keep for remembrance' sake. Each and every one of them failed to

4 A Chinese patron saint of crafts and the art of invention sits among four assistants who carry various tools and treatises.

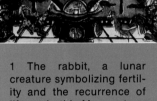

1 The rabbit, a lunar creature symbolizing fertility and the recurrence of life, as in this Mayan stone carving, is a well-known bringer of culture and civilization.

2 Even a hero of the stature of Achilles needed superhuman help and instruction, which he received from the centaur Chiron.

3 Chinese kitchen gods like this couple were believed to bestow blessing on the household and report favorably on its doings to the Jade Emperor in heaven (myth, page 140).

5 According to a very ancient Egyptian tradition the ram-headed god Knum created the art of pottery.

7 The jackal-headed god Anubis was revered throughout ancient Egypt as the patron of the care of the dead.

The origins of writing, architecture, music, and the working of metals are shrouded in myth, but always at the beginning stands a divine hero or goddess who embodies all future aspects of the new art. Minerva, for example, here illustrated by an Etruscan statue (6), brought the Romans art and wisdom and taught them weaving and other trades. Apollo was leader of the Muses (hence his surname *Musagetes*). Odin of Germanic myth and Thoth of ancient-Egyptian myth were bringers of writing (myths, page 122). The figure of Dionysus or Bacchus is associated with the introduction of viticulture and with the theatrical arts (9). Other teachers are partly historical, partly mythological figures who combine celestial and terrestrial attributes: Imhotep of ancient

Egypt for architecture, for example, or Hiram of Tyre, who helped Solomon build his great temple. Religious institutions, too, were brought to people in this way – by the Persian Mani, founder of Manicheism, or by Manu, who taught the laws of civilization to the people of India.

8 Fu Hsi and Nu Kua, the Chinese first couple, invented writing as well as founding the tribe and the social order (myth, page 66).

10 For the ancient Greeks Orpheus was the bringer of the art of music, prophecy, and knowledge of the mysteries.

11 Sarasvati of Indian myth, with her symbol the sitar, is the goddess of erudition and the arts.

12 Narada, a seer of Vedic myth, is the inventor of the lute and patron of music.

13 In the post-Homeric period the originally war-like Apollo became the divine musician.

13

14

14 Pegasus, the winged horse of Greek myth (page 160), was a symbol of the soaring spirit for Muse-inspired singers and poets.

15 A stylized version of his name-character becomes a depiction of the Chinese god K'uei Hsing, patron of scholars and poets.

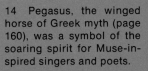

15

16

16 When Thoth, the ancient-Egyptian creator god with the head of an ibis, was called to be the scribe of the gods he invented the art of writing, of which he then became the patron deity.

137

carve anything resembling the woman whom he had loved. Now, there was a wood-carver in the chief's own village who had not been asked to make the attempt. His reputation was small, but this person had often seen the chief's wife passing by. He knew what she really looked like, as more renowned artists did not. So, on his own initiative, he carved her likeness in red cedar. When the image was finished, he invited the bereaved chief to his studio. The chief entered and saw his dead wife sitting in the dimness just as she used to look. The chief gave the wood-carver many slaves and blankets in exchange for the image. He brought it home and dressed it in his dead wife's clothes. Over its shoulders he laid her best marten-skin robe. He kept the image by him, at meals especially. Often he spoke to it. The image would appear to move slightly, and even to speak in return. He watched it closely every day, and he kept listening at its wooden breast. Once he distinctly heard a crackling sound, almost a groan, come from inside the image. To make it comfortable again, he shifted the carving's position. Where it had been he saw a baby cedar growing.

And ever since that time the best cedars are to be found on the Queen Charlotte Islands.

HARD-WON FOOD

Mangaia Islanders of the South Pacific have a strange tale to tell concerning a princess of their tribe who initiated a love affair with the Father of Eels. They used to meet in a rock pool near the shore. One day the Father of Eels informed the princess that his spirit would have to depart at last. When that occurred, she was to sever his head and bury it in the ground. She remembered and did as she had been bidden. From each half of the buried head grew a coconut tree. Husk a coconut, and one will find engraved upon it the eyes and mouth of the princess' lover.

In the sixteenth century the coastal Indians of Peru worshiped the god Pachacamac. It was Pachacamac who made the first man and first woman, but he neglected to provide them with food. The first man soon starved to death. The first woman found a few berries growing wild. On these alone she managed to exist. Pachacamac himself deigned to impregnate her. No sooner was her baby born than the god seized it for sacrifice. The infant's tender flesh, buried in the earth, gave rise to beans and gourds. Its little bones became roots of the manioc. Its teeth became life-sustaining maize.

Long ago, before white people came, the Blackfoot Indians of the North American Plains found themselves close to starvation. They were too weak even to look for game anymore. One brave, however, forced his squaw to venture out in search of firewood. As the woman was picking up fallen branches not far from the Blackfoot encampment, she noticed a small rock which the rains had washed down from a bank of earth. The rock seemed to stretch out crystal arms and speak to her. "Take me, I am powerful," said the rock. The woman put it inside her dress. Then she turned and went home to her husband. "I am going to make medicine," she told him.

The whole tribe gathered for the ceremony. They rubbed the rock with a bit of buffalo fat, and each person kissed it. Then they all danced in imitation of a herd of buffalo. "I am leading a hundred buffalo over the ridge," the woman sang. The others sang with her. But her husband, in his enthusiasm, changed the words. "I am leading more than a hundred buffalo!" he cried.

Later that night, a mangy old bull buffalo ambled into the Blackfoot encampment. "Don't kill him!" the woman warned. The Indians gently scratched the animal's back with pieces of firewood. It wandered off again. In the dawn, a great herd of bull buffalo appeared close by the camp. The Blackfoot braves went out and drove them all into a stockade. It seemed there would be plenty of meat now. But there were more than a hundred bulls in the stockade, too many, and too strong for it. The beasts broke down the palisade and escaped.

The next evening, only squaws danced. They called for buffalo cows to come, no more than a hundred of them. The magic rock which the woman had found was pleased at this; it tumbled down upon its face. In the morning, a hundred buffalo cows came down over the ridge. They were all killed. The Blackfoot tribe was prosperous and happy once again. Moreover, from then on the squaw who had found and recognized the rock was respected by her husband.

A NET OF RUSHES

There was a man named Kahukura, the Maori say, who much enjoyed travel and novelty. Not far from Rangiaowhia, one day, he came upon a beach where fishing had recently been done. There were some small fish lying about. The sand had been trampled, but not by human feet. There was no sign of a canoe. He thought that perhaps fairies had been at work there the night before, so he concealed himself, waiting by

The Greek forest god Pan (*left*), protector of flocks and inventor of the syrinx or panpipe, teaches the young Daphnis, son of Hermes, how to play it. Both are shepherd gods and patrons of light music.

A significant portion of the population of the Mediterranean re-

The good shepherd concept was common to other pastoral peoples of the Mediterranean region, as witness this Hittite stone relief (*below, center*) from Karatepe in Turkey.

Pan was also a popular figure in the Roman pantheon. This Etruscan statue (*above*) shows him playing the reed pipe that he invented in memory of the nymph Syrinx.

An ancient-Greek statue of Hermes Kriophoros (the "ram-bearer") shows that the later messenger of the gods was known to an earlier age as patron of shepherds and their flocks (*below*).

gion in classical times consisted of nomadic pastoral tribes, whose gods and mythic heroes exhibited qualities appropriate to that mode of existence. This is seen, for example, in the many myths and legends about gods of forest and field who intervene helpfully and instructively in the lives of men. The best-known of these is the goat-like Greek shepherd deity Pan, the god of mountain, wood, and meadow who was also honored as the inventor of musical instruments. When his lover, the nymph Syrinx, was turned into a reed he cut from it a pipe that he named after her; it became the typical instrument of pastoral music. On one occasion he even challenged Apollo to a musical contest (and won). In Italy the shepherd-god role was assumed by Faunus, a forest god who taught field and animal husbandry to the people of Latium. In India the many myths about Krishna, an incarnation of Vishnu, portray a divine shepherd figure playing on his flute and accompanying the cattle of the *gopis* or village herdgirls. It was Krishna who made the cow the sacred animal of the gods. He lived the life of a divine hero, battling with demons; the Krishna cult that grew up around him constituted a revolution in Indian religion.

India too was familiar with the mythological symbol of the divine shepherd and flute player in the form of the young god Krishna (*above*), protector of cattle and of the lovely *gopis* who tended them.

The good shepherd image came in turn to be applied to Jesus, who in his preaching tours of Israel gathered in the sheep of his spiritual flock, as this Roman statue symbolically represents (*below*).

139

the beach until nightfall in the hope that he would learn something to his advantage. He was a pale person, although not as white as the fairies themselves. He hoped that in the dark he would be mistaken for one of them. They might find out somehow that he was a human being and punish him for intruding, a risk he would have to take.

He waited patiently in his hiding place. The sun set; the twilight passed; the stars appeared in the transparent blackness of the sky. The sea played with the pebbles of the beach, rattling them gently about. Now the fairies came, out of nowhere it seemed. They brought with them a net made of rushes. They brought canoes made of the stems of flax. "Cast the net in the sea at Rangiaowhia," they cried, "and haul it in again at Mamaku."

The fairies cast the net in a wide semicircle. They hauled it in slowly, singing, some at either end. Kahukura had never seen a fishnet before. As brave as he was curious, he slipped out of his hiding place. He tugged away at the net with the best of them, and the fairies innocently accepted his help. The net was heavy, for the catch was large. Rhythmically, singing all the time, they hauled it in.

Toward dawn, the crescent of sea before the beach began seething and boiling with silver fish. The fairies hauled them right up onto the shore. They did not bother, as men do, to count the catch or to divide it evenly. Instead, each one knotted up a few twigs in a length of cord and thrust the twigs through the gills of the fish that pleased him. Thus each of the fairies made his own load of fish. As for Kahukura, he purposely knotted his string all wrong. His load slipped and fell away, strewing the sand. A few of the fairies ran to help him load up properly, but he was careful to make the same accident happen again, and yet a third time. The fairies were still trying to help him when the first rosy rays of the sun appeared on the horizon. At the sight of the light they turned and fled, leaving their net of rushes behind.

Kahukura carefully gathered up the fairy net and made off with it. By copying the way in which the net had been knotted, he created one of his own. Only fairies are able to use light things such as rushes for heavy purposes. Kahukura therefore made his own of flaxen threads. And that was the first fishnet used by human beings.

THE KITCHEN GOD OF CHINA

In China, as in France, the art of cooking commands particular respect. There is even a Chinese deity known as the Kitchen God

Particularly in torrid zones, rain is the dominant factor in human existence. Mythic man, very largely ignorant of the physical and meteorological laws governing the circulation of moisture, imagined gods whose mercy or ill will could account for the incalculable vagaries of the weather. A wide variety of cults and rites was evolved to put the gods in a good mood or otherwise invoke rain. Especially agricultural peoples – who often had no personified rain deity – tried through rainmakers to influence magically the onset or cessation of rain (by analogy rites, for example, such as sprinkling or burying water). Ameri-

Opposite: The Mexican rain god Tlaloc sits enthroned in a paradise of rain clouds above the paradise of blessed souls.

The Egyptian Nile god Hapi (*above*), in twofold form, brings the rain that causes the Nile to flood and water the fields.

This Navaho Indian statue (*above*) is one of their *uwanami* or rain gods.

An African rock painting (*above*) shows a rain ceremony that the goddess of heaven is rewarding with a downpour.

There is a thematic resemblance between the three rain gods of Mali (*above*) and the four rain spirits of the Navaho (*below*), whose arms stream rain.

can civilizations relied more on prayer and sacrifice to bring on the rain. Vedic India recognized the god Parjanya as lord of clouds, wind, and rain; Indra too, with his thunderbolt released rain over the parched land. In Peru it was also a thunder god – Illapa – who bestowed the blessing of rain. Taoism tells of four symbolic Dragon Kings who govern rain, storms, and scorching heat.

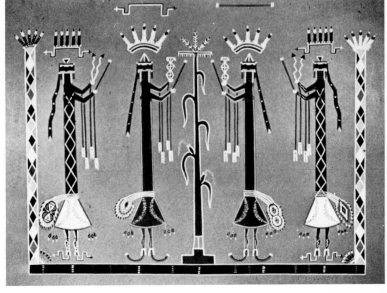

– or Stove King – Tsao Chün. The story of how he came to join China's divine pantheon is curious, to say the least.

Narrow, smoky, spiced with cooking odors, and ubiquitous – such is the temple of the Kitchen God. It is no more than a niche between the bricks in Chinese stoves. Once each year the Kitchen God goes away to heaven to make a report. The people smear his tiny image with honey at this time so that he may speak sweetly of them. He is a friend to the people, by and large.

The man responsible for introducing the Stove King's worship at an official level was a small-time magician and devotee named Shao-chün. He persuaded the emperor Hsiao Wu-ti (who reigned from 140 to 86 B.C., by Western reckoning) to offer the god a solemn sacrifice for the first time at the palace. In return, Shao-chün promised, the genial deity would give Hsiao Wu-ti a heap of gleaming gold bricks.

The bricks were only gold-plated. Shao-chün had imposed upon the emperor with alchemical tricks. It was too late to rescind the honors given to the Kitchen God but,

1–4 This well-known figure (1) from Honduras represents the Mayan god who, according to myth, discovered maize and taught men how to cultivate it. Quetzalcoatl (2), the "plumed serpent," was the mythic priest-king of Toltec Tula, creator of the world and founder of agriculture. In the Aztec myth of the maize plant the young growth was personified by the goddess Xilonen (4); Centeotl (3) was the god of maize.

Hsiao Wu-ti decreed, Shao-chün would have to die. The magician fell to his knees, begging for a reprieve of a few days. At the end of that brief period, Shao-chün suggested that a certain white ox be sacrificed. In the ox's belly would be found a useful message from the Stove King.

The sacrifice was duly performed. In the belly of the ox there was indeed a silken scroll bearing a written message for the emperor. Shao-chün should be spared, it read. Sadly, though, Hsiao recognized the handwriting. Shao-chün himself had written the message and given it to the ox to swallow. So he was hanged after all.

5 The Hittite king Shulumeli offers a libation to the god of the weather.
6 These four native spirits from Hatra in Persia hold various fruits of the earth.

OF STRONG DRINK

The Indians of the Western Hemisphere and natives of the South Pacific were still

7 From between two female spirits the great maize plant of the Navaho Indians rises toward heaven, a symbol of growth and maturity, the figure of a man.

8–9 The so-called White Lady, a rock painting at Tassali in the Sahara (8), represents the goddess of agriculture. This figure wearing a crown (9) is the Cretan goddess of poppy culture.

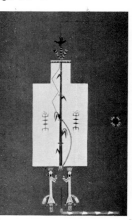

The Fertile Earth

The first successful cultivation of the land in the face of the powers of nature and heaven (rain and drought) was something mythic man attributed to the help and blessing of the gods. "All good things come from above," said Schiller, and the primeval desire he was expressing is supremely relevant to the relation between harvest and divine blessing. In the Mayan myth of the maize plant, the maize god himself lives through the whole vegetation

10–11 Both couples – the Roman Liber Pater and Libera (10) and the Greek Persephone and Pluto (11) – are symbols for corn and wine.

process to become the exemplar of maize cultivation. Weather gods provided for growth, and man came to see the life of his ears of corn as a symbol of the year and of life as such. Wine and corn are more than man's basic food; they stand in a complex relationship to the Earth Mother element of myth, to the soaring of the spirit, the recurrence of life, and man's ultimate ascent to the gods.

12 A Mexican picture strip shows the young maize god experiencing the four stages in the life of a maize plant as it is exposed to the different seasons (here personified as weather gods).

13 A Greek vase painting represents the goddess Ceres instructing Triptolemus in agriculture and charging him to carry the knowledge all over the world.

14 A cup by the Greek potter Exekias depicts the ship of Dionysus with its grape vines, a reference to the god's mythic role as the teacher of viticulture.

143

Stone Age peoples when Europeans invaded their lands, and yet they had already learned to utilize narcotics unknown in Europe. Such things constitute mixed blessings, as everybody knows. The magicians credited, in myth, with domesticating the plants are not always thought of as benefactors. Consider, for instance, the case of Pava and the bibulous Tangaloa-le-Mana. Pava lived on an islet called Saua, in the South Pacific, according to local legend. One day the god Tangaloa-le-Mana de-

Pava, clear away. But Pava held on to the discarded roots of the kava plant, which he had surreptitiously appropriated. He managed to survive the flood, and later on he introduced kava drinking to mankind.

Rarotonga Islanders have quite another story to tell regarding the kava plant. It never grew in heaven, they say. Its roots are eternal, resting in hell. Miru the Hag cares for the roots. She also plays hostess to unhappy ghosts. Miru has four beautiful daughters. These she permits to entertain

The strikingly animated figures of this rock painting (*above*) at Séfar in the Sahara are hunting maned sheep.

The spirit woman Nujalik, patroness of hunting for animals on land, is pictured in this Eskimo drawing (*below*).

scended there from out of the sky. The god thought himself unobserved, for Pava crept into the bushes at his approach. Tangaloa-le-Mana clapped his hands. Thereupon a bowl, strainer, cup, and kava plant (*Piper methysticum*) fell from the blue. The god chewed the stem of the plant and threw the rest of it away into the bushes. Then he spat the chewed kava into his strainer and prepared to make a kava brew, something which had been unknown upon earth until that moment. Heavy rain fell to help the god at his work. The rain washed the man,

the guests at her underworld home. The daughters ply all newcomers with powerful kava. One by one they fall asleep, stupefied by the drink. Then they are put into the ovens and cooked. The bodies of the dead make a feast for various household pets, while Miru and her daughters pluck out and eat their spirits like tidbits.

The lustful and quarrelsome family of the Greek god Zeus, upon Mount Olympus,

GODS OF THE HUNT

In all hunting cultures of antiquity, as well as in those that survive today, good-hunting gods are as important as the lords of the animal world. As heroes of weapons technology they often double incidentally as gods of war. But the hunted animals too have their protectors, forest

The moon goddess Artemis of ancient Greece, here adorning a piece of jewelry (*opposite, top*), was also goddess of fertility and of wild animals.

This picture (*left*) of the Mexican god of the hunt, Camaxtli, shows him with bow, arrow, and game bag.

A mythological hunting scene (*below*) by the School of Fontainebleau shows Orion hunting with Artemis, the goddess of the hunt, and Apollo.

gods or animal mothers who warn and hide them. The killing of animals, a necessity for the hunter, constitutes an intrusion into the world of animal souls and the territory of the gods. The hunter must therefore prepare himself with hunting magic, and after the hunt make sacrifice to the lord of animal life and fertility in order not to incur his wrath. In such societies indiscriminate killing is regarded as sacrilege against the tutelary deities of the animal world.

The aboriginal tribes of Arnhemland in northern Australia still make birch-bark paintings for hunting-magic purposes. This one (*below*) shows a figure hunting kangaroos with dart and throwing-stick.

The Egyptian war god Onouris (*right*), worshiped as "he who brings back the distant one," was also the divine huntsman. His right hand originally held a lance.

drank nectar both by day and by night. Kings of Greece in Homeric times were reported to "tipple like the gods." The Norse gods and heroes at Valhalla made much of intoxicating mead. Hindu gods of India regaled themselves with a mysterious life-giving liquor, long since lost to human knowledge, called soma. In heaven, according to Irish legend, "it rains brown ale."

MAUI-TIKI-TIKI-A-TARANGA

Surprisingly often in myth, mankind's greatest benefactors are portrayed as having been full of mischief. Trickster gods and friends to man, whose sometimes generous and sometimes cruel, but always arbitrary, deeds have served to advance human culture, occupy an important place in myth. Among them all, none was more marvelous than the Polynesian culture hero Maui. His story has long held the imagination of mankind over an immense maritime area stretching from Hawaii all the way southwestward across the scattered Polynesian islands to New Zealand. Maui shaped a weapon from his own grandmother's jawbone, crippled the sun with it, fished islands up, and made the gift of fire generally available. He tried, although he failed at last, to overcome death as well.

All this may have to do with human evolution, but on a cheerfully symbolic and even melodramatic level. Words (the grandmother's jawbone) are surely the most potent weapons in the arsenal of mankind. An acute sense of time (which makes the sun seem to move more slowly through the sky) is essential to human industry. Overseas exploration (especially in the South Pacific) does fish islands up. And, finally, when people light their own fires instead of having to rely on a communal hearth, they achieve liberty. But hear Maui's story.

Once upon a time the wisewoman Taranga went to fetch her children from the place where they sat watching older people dance. She had four sons, so she believed. Yet with them on this particular evening sat a fifth. Taranga told him to be off. She had never seen him before. "But," the infant insisted, "you are my mother. You gave birth to me prematurely, alone on a beach. You wrapped me up in a tuft of your hair and cast me away into the surf. The seaweed caught me and tangled about me. I rolled from side to side, enclosed in seaweed, far out at sea. The storm winds blew me in again. In the shallows, soft jellyfish clung about me. I was stranded in my net of seaweed and my envelope of jellyfish upon the shore. Seabirds flocked about, trying to

peck me to pieces. Black flies buzzed around my ears, seeking to lay their eggs in my body. But I was saved by the kindness of the Old Man of the Sea."

His mother rejoiced and publicly acknowledged her son. "It is true," she said, "that I cut off the topknot of my hair as a sort of swaddling band for you before casting you away into the sea. Therefore you shall be Maui-formed-in-the-topknot-of-Taranga, called Maui-tiki-tiki-a-Taranga."

Maui's mother took him to sleep with her. His elder brothers had been used to sharing her bed at night. They resented the little interloper. Night was the only time that Taranga's children could be with her. In the morning, before they were awake, she would depart. No one had any idea where Taranga went to spend the daytime hours. Baby Maui thought he would find out. He made a plan, which he kept to himself. One night, after his brothers and his mother had all fallen asleep, he rose and stopped up all the chinks of their little house with rags. The dawn light could not get in; it failed to awaken Taranga. She slept on until after sunrise. Then, suddenly awakening, she realized that something must be wrong. She rushed out of the house into the bright sunlight. Maui, on his hands and knees, peeped under the door to watch her go.

She pulled up a tuft of rushes, slipped into the ground where its roots had been, and disappeared. The rushes settled back into place. Maui ran out and pulled them up again. He saw a tunnel leading down and away into darkness. He put the rushes back in place and returned to the house. He removed the rags from the chinks. Sunlight streamed in. Maui's brothers awakened. He told them he was going on a journey to find his mother. They sneered at the idea.

"You," Maui said to his brothers, "have imbibed the milk of our mother's breasts. It is natural for you to love her. I love her more, however, and for one reason only: that I once lay in her womb. Because I love her, I must find where she dwells in the daytime. I believe that she goes to our father."

Maui transformed himself into a dove and flew away into the woods. His brothers were amazed. Circling secretly back toward the house, Maui slipped down into the tunnel which was hidden by the clump of rushes. He flew very swiftly in the tunnel, down through the darkness of the earth. It narrowed here and there, obliging him to dip one wing and then the other as he flew. At last the tunnel widened into a cavern, opening onto a pleasant countryside. Maui flew to a manapau tree and perched there. His mother and father sat underneath the

1

FISHER GODS

For all peoples living by the sea or beside lakes the fish is of particular importance – and not merely as their basic food. Its secret mode of existence, largely hidden from men's eyes, prompted a mythic identification with spirits or demons of

5

the sea. Sometimes such sea spirits were depicted as being half man, half fish. Fish also figure as the mythic mounts of water gods, for example of the Indian god Varuna. Even the supreme deity Vishnu once assumed the form of a fish, in order to save Manu. Before the ancient Greeks went out fishing they appealed to Poseidon, whose companion was the dolphin, for a good catch. As a symbol of intelligence the dolphin was sacred to Apollo.

5–6 The West African fish god Behanzin (5) is depicted with the head and body of a shark, while the Eskimos symbolize the spirit nature of the fish by giving it a woman's head (6).

6

2 An Australian aboriginal bark drawing depicts the tutelary spirit Dignuk, patron of night fishers.

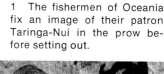

1 The fishermen of Oceania fix an image of their patron Taringa-Nui in the prow before setting out.

3 This Benin bronze from West Africa is of Olokun, a sea spirit depicted with fishtail legs.

4 The water nymph or mermaid is a common figure in Scandinavian myth. She is half fish, half maiden.

7–8 The Greek god of the sea was the mighty Poseidon (7), here armed with the trident of the dolphin fisher. An early Near Eastern fish goddess (8) also appears as half human, half fish.

tree. Some friends were with them. Maui fluttered down to a lower perch just over their heads. He plucked some berries from the tree and threw them down upon his parents. They looked up in surprise, but they could not see him at first. Then Maui cooed, to make his presence known. "It's a mischievous dove," the people said. They threw pebbles at him. Maui dodged every one. He waited for his father to throw a stone. Then, wounded by it, he tumbled down to the ground. The people ran to examine him, but as they bent over the broken-legged dove, Maui stood up. He was no longer a bird, nor was he a baby anymore. He was a godlike man.

Maui remained with his parents in their country. The queen of that land was his grandmother, Muri-ranga-whenua. She lived by herself in a wilderness. At certain seasons her descendants brought her food. Maui offered to do this. He took the food that was set aside for Muri-ranga-whenua and went off with it in the direction of the place where she lived.

But Maui did not bring the food directly to his grandmother. He concealed it, waiting until she became very hungry indeed. She kept expecting food to come. She sniffed the air; she smelled Maui. Her belly swelled up to enormous size. Someone was coming, and she meant to swallow him at a gulp. Slowly she turned round in her place; south, east, and north the air was clear. Westward, she smelled Maui again. "Someone is close to me!" she cried.

Maui spoke up hastily, "It is I, your descendant. I have food for you."

The old woman's stomach shrank down again. "If the west wind had not been in back of you and if you had not made yourself known," she told him, "I might have destroyed my own blood in my hunger. Such things are not right. Now present the sacrifice which you have brought."

"First," Maui said, "give me your jawbone. I require it for a weapon."

Strangely enough, a bargain was struck. The old woman gave her jawbone to Maui. Then he went away. He returned to his brothers on the surface of the earth. "Make a net," he ordered them. "You and I are going to pay a surprise visit to the sun." His brothers thought the sun was much too hot and too fierce a beast to meet at such close quarters. No mere humans could catch it, surely. "Make the net strong, very strong," was Maui's reply.

Maui and his brothers traveled far to the east. They moved only at night, hiding in the daytime so the sun would not see them. When they arrived at the place of the sun's rising, they covered it up with their net.

They staked the net down on either side. They stretched ropes in such a way as to be able to draw the net shut once the sun had climbed well into it. Two brothers hid themselves at one side of the sunrise place, and two at the other. Maui lay concealed behind a bush. He held the jawbone of his grandmother gripped in his right fist.

The sun came up fast and strong. It did not seem to feel the net at first. Its head rose, glowing, glaring, inside the net almost at once. Now its forepaws and shoulders were in the net. Now its whole red belly and its hind legs entered the net. Its bushy tail followed; it was off the ground in a moment, starting to climb the sky. Maui shouted to his brothers, and they pulled hard on the ropes. The sun fell to the ground, tightly netted. Maui rushed up to it. He beat the shining creature with his magical jawbone. The sun cried out in agony. It rolled about together with the net which entangled it. Maui kept on battering, bruising, and bloodying the sun.

The sun groaned, whimpered, and moaned. Maui's blows reduced the gleaming beast to subjection at last. Now it was silent. Maui stepped back, and his brothers let go the ropes. The noose slackened; the sun crept out of the net. Then, without looking back, it limped away up the path of the sky. From now on it would travel more slowly. Men would have longer days.

Maui's brothers used to go out fishing in order to support their families. Maui could not be bothered with that sort of thing. "Do you suppose such trifling work would be my style?" he asked. Meanwhile, he was making a hook in secret. He barbed the hook with a splinter from the jawbone of Muri-ranga-whenua and attached it to a magically strong line. The day came when he joined his brothers in a fishing expedition. Paddling out of sight of land, the brothers fished until the canoe was full. Maui, meanwhile, lazed in the bow. When they were about to start for home, he asked his brothers to wait for a bit while he made one cast of his hook.

Then Maui drew his hook from underneath his sash. The light flashed from its mother-of-pearl inlay. The hook was elaborately carved and ornamented with a tuft from a dog's tail. The brothers thought it rather fancy for fishing.

Maui requested a piece of bait to put on the hook. His brothers meanly refused to give him any, so Maui doubled up his fist and punched himself in the nose. He smeared the hook with the blood which dripped from his nostrils. Then he cast it down and let out his line. The hook sank slowly down and down, all the way to the bottom of the sea. It

Some of the wealth of myths about the life and works of the Polynesian god and culture hero Maui are told on these and the preceding pages. His scintillating yet ambivalent personality is typical of the mythic heroes who is also mischievous and ruthless. Yet it is only out of this ambivalence that his great gifts as a leader of men emerge. His tremendous and – from the rational point of view – apparently impossible deeds are symbolic in character; their actual meaning is to be found behind the mythic façade. With the magical jawbone of his grandmother he forms language, and uses it as well for all his other creative acts upon earth.

bring the culture of the gods to men. Maui was the fifth and principal son of the primal mother, who symbolized the maternal aspects of earth and night. All his major transformations took place in the realm of his mother (i.e., under the earth), from which Maui emerged each time strengthened for new cultural achievements. Maui is good and clever, but he He slows the course of the sun to make it shine longer on the land; he teaches men how to kindle fire; he fishes for islands – New Zealand, for example – and is creator and discoverer of the lands of the earth (*right*). But one thing no mortal can do, and neither can he: he cannot vanquish the goddess of death, Hine-nui-te-po, but is himself vanquished by her (*above*).

sank down past a carved figure on the roof-tree of a house. It sank down past the doorway and settled under the doorsill. Maui felt resistance at the end of his line. He pulled; the weight was very great. Maui pulled harder; the canoe tilted dangerously, shipping water. Maui's brothers cried out in terror.

The house of the Old Man of the Sea was slowly rising at the end of Maui's line. With it came all his estates, a vast island. The land rose underneath the boat, drawn up by Maui's hook. Now the canoe was aground, far inland. Maui had fished up the major part of New Zealand.

Maui got up one night and put out every hearth fire in the village. No one saw him do it. In the morning, no cooking could be done. Then Maui volunteered to go and fetch new fire from Mahu-ika, the Flaming One. Reluctantly, Maui's mother gave him directions for the journey.

Maui reached the abode of the fire goddess. He called out to Mahu-ika and begged some fire from her. Old as she was, she rose up in spiral form, swiftly, glaring round at him. "Where do you come from?" she demanded. Maui explained where he was from. Mahu-ika shook her smoky head. "I did not recognize you, but you must be my grandson. Welcome." When he again asked for fire, she gave it to him, plucking out a fingernail from which fire flowed.

Maui took the fingernail and went off. When he was out of sight, he threw it down and stamped on it until the fire was out. Then he returned to Mahu-ika. "Grandmother," he said, "the fire you gave me died. May I please have another one?"

She gave him another fingernail. He did as he had done before, and again went back to her. This continued until the old lady had plucked all the nails from her hands and from her feet as well, except from her big left toe. Maku-ika sensed that she was being tricked. Angrily, she wrenched out her one last toenail and flung it on the ground at his feet. "You have it *all* now!" she cried.

The earth caught fire. Maui fled, but fast as he could run, the flames could move still faster. Maui transformed himself into an eagle, but high as he could fly, the flames could leap still higher and they so burned the branches that he could land nowhere. Maui then transformed himself into a fish and dove into a pond of water; but the flames caused it to boil around him. So Maui transformed himself back into his man form and prayed to his ancestors Ta-whiri-ma-tea and Whatitiri-matakataka to send thunderstorms and a deluge of rain to save him. Driven by the wind, black clouds descended around Maui. Whirlwinds flat-tened the conflagration. Cold torrents of rain quenched it. Maui, fire-blackened and in pain, staggered home to his village. His grandmother, Mahu-ika, had spent herself but for a few sparks which she managed to hide away in the wood used for making fire sticks. His parents reproved him, but Maui said that he could not care less. From now on the villagers would be able to start their own fires by means of fire sticks, and fire would no longer be the exclusive property of Mahu-ika. As for him, he intended to go on doing great things.

Maui stayed with his parents for a time, more or less content; but one day Maui's father happened to mention yet another ancestress of his, Hine-nui-te-po, the goddess of death. He warned Maui against her, however, as someone to avoid. "For," he said, "Hine-nui-te-po's eyes are what makes the sunset red. The pupils of her eyes are jasper, hard, blind stone. Her hair is like seaweed. Her mouth resembles that of the barracuda. The teeth of her jaws are sharp as shards of volcanic glass. I do not think you can stand against this ancestress."

The robin, the thrush, the yellowhammer, and the water wagtail, which is called Ti-wakawaka, went with Maui. They journeyed westward together until they came to the abode of Death. She lay sleeping. Maui stripped himself. He gripped his magical weapon, the jawbone of Muri-rangi-whenua. "I am going to creep inside Death," he whispered. "Do not laugh at what you see. Each of you must keep utterly silent until I reappear between Hine-nui-te-po's jaws. Then you may laugh and sing to your heart's content."

Quietly, Maui entered his ancestress. He hacked his way up inside her with the weapon in his fist. Still she slept, oblivious. He reached her belly, and at last her throat. The birds could hardly contain themselves for glee. Little Tiwakawaka was the first to express what all of them felt. The water wagtail laughed out loud, a merry note. The other birds joined in; dawn was breaking. The old woman opened her eyes and looked about. One hand went to her throat. She clenched her teeth; she swallowed; and so Maui died.

Bold, and often enough mischievous as well, were those who brought the blessings of art and magic to mankind. Maui, for one, recapitulated in his infancy the whole slow evolution of life from the sea. In boyhood, he traced his mother home to a place not of this world. In youth, he acted out the appropriation of new prerogatives for mankind as a whole. And finally, as a man, he attempted to overcome death itself, and failed — as we all must.

A bird as bearer of deities is a mythic motif often encountered in India and the Far East. It symbolizes the fact that the gods come down from heaven. Here a Japanese Buddhist deity, Kujaku Myôô, rides on a peacock.

When from the egg of the sun bird
the sun was born,
Brahma, the eternally unborn,
in deep concentration took up
the two burning halves of the shell
beheld by the divine seers
and sang seven holy verses.
In this way the elephant Airavata
came into being, the mount
of Indra, king of the gods,
and after him emerged

ANIMALS MONSTERS AND MYTHIC BEASTS

seven elephants of great nobility.
The noble elephants became
the mounts of the god-king Indra
and of the fire god Agni
and fought in the battle
of the gods and titans.

THE MATANGALILA OF NILAKANTHA

The hare is a widely-used symbol in connection with the moon, Mother Earth, fertility, and the re-generation of natural things. This Mexican hare has the head of the sun god Tonatiuh emerging from its lap, representing the sun's rebirth in the morning from the womb of Mother Earth.

Opposite: For the last of his twelve heroic labors Herakles had to descend to Hades, bind Cerberus, the three-headed hound of hell, and bring him back to the upper world (myth, page 180).

What myths attach to the marvelous paintings of animals on the walls of the deep cavern at Lascaux in France? Those pictures date back some 30,000 years. So does the equally splendid depiction of charging bison across the vault of the great cave at Altamira in Spain. Prehistorians disagree about the connotations of these animal figures. Some say that they were painted as

An English woodcut of a centaur couple, from ca. 1520 (*above*).

At the level of the mythic consciousness animals occupied a quite different place and affected people in far more mysterious ways than is possible or even thinkable in our age.

one plants a seed, so that actual animals upon the surface of the earth might flourish and increase. Others suggest that the pictures were actually shot at with arrows to promote good hunting by contagious magic. Others again suppose that the paintings had something to do with initiation rites, in the course of which boys were prepared to become hunters. Yet others assume that the animals represented totems, of which more later.

Whatever the truth may be, it seems likely enough that stories of some sort were told regarding these wonderful images. The stories may well have been related by firelight, deep inside the caves. One can imagine the flickering fire, the shadows playing across the walls, and the paintings themselves seeming to drift like colored smoke through the shadows. In such an atmosphere as this, perhaps, mankind's first myths were bodied forth.

When one visits the caves in question and looks at the paintings, they themselves appear like shadows in a way. They are not naturalistic, and yet they carry more conviction than naturalism can. They seem to be fleeting impressions, extraordinarily vivid, but precise only in part. The bulges and hollows of the rockface itself do not distort the images, but support them. It is as if the painters of these miraculous works had seen animal shapes plunging from living rock and leaping up into darkness.

Everyone has watched flickering shadows on a wall create pictures, images of half-conscious fantasy. The effect can be startling indeed, like a dream experienced with open eyes. It is possible that the artists of Altamira and Lascaux visualized their subjects in just such a way, by firelight.

Above, left to right: The Egyptian soul-bird, a man in bird form, drinks from the fount of life. The centaur, originally Greek, appears here in a relief from Mathura, India. An Italian mosaic shows four lions sharing a single head. The griffin, half bird, half animal, became a popular heraldic device with rulers and city states. In India the mythic white bird Simurg, depicted carrying nine elephants, symbolizes the power of the soul.

The dragon (*below*) is the oldest symbol and heraldic animal in Chinese culture. The winged horse Pegasus (*below right*), tamed by the Greek hero Bellerophon (or some say by Athene), finally took his place with the immortals on Mount Olympus (myth, page 160).

An eighteenth-century Russian woodcut of the water-sprite Melusine (*below*) shows her as a composite of woman, fish, and dragon.

On the one hand mythic man was more involved with animals than we are today; on the other hand his attitude toward them was very much more detached. Certain animals were revered, others were dangerous and invested with demonic powers. Many animals appear in myth as helpers of man and of the gods. Birds, for example, function as celestial messengers, as molders of men's souls and bearers of dead souls to the Other Side. Other animals embody human

or heroic qualities or appear as centaurs, sirens, snake-men, or other hybrid creatures combining human and animal traits. Lesser-known animals – those living in the sea, for example – became in man's imagination fabulous creatures incorporating all that was strange, wonderful, and mysterious. Visions, prophecies, and esoteric speculations – as in alchemy – produced an autonomous pantheon of symbolic animals representing every celestial, terrestrial, and infernal power.

European treatises on myth or alchemy in the fourteenth to the seventeenth century imagined a variety of fabulous hybrids, including the basilisk (*far left*), the phoenix (*center*), and the griffin (*left*).

In China the birth of a great sage was said to be accompanied by the auspicious appearance of a mythic beast not unlike the unicorn (*above*).

This playing card illustration (*above*) uses the popular theme of the wild man or man of the woods riding on a unicorn.

This detail from the French *Lady and the Unicorn* tapestry (*above*) depicts a garden of animals with the Virgin and the Unicorn in the center. A popular medieval symbol, the unicorn was associated with power, purity, spiritual force, and divine creativity. It was also used to symbolize the presence of the word of God in the Virgin Mary.

The winged sphinx of this Assyrian relief (*left*) is a hybrid of various animals, bearing a certain resemblance to the Chimera of Greek mythology. Usually depicted as a lioness with the head of a woman, the sphinx is a strangler, a threatening monster, and custodian of the parting of the ways.

The unicorn was still popular in eighteenth-century American folk art (*above*).

153

THE ORIGIN OF THE ANIMALS

After the creation of the earth, the sun, and the moon, some living clay scraps were left over. A sky dweller named Ratu Champa thought he might be able to do something with these. For the purpose, according to Indonesian myth, he descended to Majapahit in Java. There he married a princess and sired a son. His main concern, however, was craftsmanship. This he practiced in secret. Ratu Champa made magical weapons, gongs, jars, all out of the living clay which he had brought from the sky. He concealed his creations in a mountain cavern. The cavern door he kept carefully shut, for everything inside it had independent life. Ratu Champa enjoyed making these things, but as time went on, he came to feel that they were useless.

Also, having chosen to take the shape and responsibilities of a human being, he found his life on earth frustrating and confining. Eventually he sealed up the cave and fled away into the sky.

Nothing hidden in the earth, whether it be gold, oil, or implements of magic, can remain hidden for all time. Ratu Champa's creations escaped. His gongs became tortoises and crawled away along the mountainside. His spears and arrows became snakes, both little and big, wriggling off into the underbrush. His daggers plunged into streams as fish. His jars turned into the shy deer of the forest.

ANIMAL WAR, ANIMAL POLITICS

Whatever happened to dinosaurs? Myth holds that some survived as dragons until just yesterday. Australian aborigines, however, possess a myth about a dinosaurlike creature which they say died before man came into being.

The Whowie was more than 20 feet long. He had six legs and a wide-jawed head like a lizard's. He was swift, but silent, for all his bulk; and he would swallow up quantities of animals as they slept. He lived in a cave on a riverbank in the Riverina district, all alone. Other creatures of the area hated and feared him. The water rats did so especially, because the Whowie subsisted largely upon them and their children. Eventually, the water rats called a general meeting of the animals, at which they suggested a broad alliance of forces and war to the death against the Whowie. Kangaroos, opossums, and platypuses responded bravely.

The animal allies crept up to the entrance of the cave where the Whowie slept during the day. They stacked bundles of reeds and

firewood around the cave mouth. They lit the fire. The Whowie awoke. They could hear him choking on the smoke inside the cavern, shaking the rock. For six days and nights they piled on more firewood. The Whowie, penned in by the constant flames, lashed about in agony. The sounds coming from inside the hill were those of mighty combat, but the Whowie had nothing to fight except the smoke and heat. On the seventh day the Whowie terminated his own torture by charging directly into the fire. He exploded out through it, stone-blind and scorched black. The animals pounced. In their hundreds, they sur-

A scene on the famous Gundestrup bowl (*above*) depicts the Celtic god Cernunnos surrounded by animals, his antlers possibly symbolizing the cycle of fertility.

The Greek goddess Athene, who may appear in a number of guises, is shown on this vase modeling a horse (*above*). According to one tradition, as Athene Hippia she taught the people of Cyrene how to breed and break in horses, herself inventing the bridle and taming the winged horse Pegasus.

The Incas of Peru worshiped Pachacamac as creator of the world (*above*). He had a secondary function as lord of animal oracles; he answered their questions through the movements of snakes and spiders.

A fresco in a Jutland church depicts a local legend in which God figures as the creator of fish and mermaids (*above right*).

Many cultures imagine an animal proctectress, a "Lady of the Beasts," as on this Greek bronze (*below*).

rounded him, biting and scratching. They forced him slowly into the river and then held his head under until he drowned.

Having destroyed the Whowie, the animals proposed to confirm and permanently establish their own newfound friendship by means of general intermarriage. It was suggested that the koala, for example, mate with the lyrebird, the dingo with the goanna, and the kangaroo with the emu. Only three species stood out against any such general mingling – the relatively austere frog, tortoise, and crow.

Those three were no match for the other animals. They could win their case only, if at all, by deceit, and so they proposed a feast to celebrate the coming intermar-

CREATORS AND PROTECTORS OF ANIMALS

Animals have been indispensable to man from the very earliest times, first as prey and subsequently as providers of milk, meat, and sources of energy for agricultural purposes. Certain animals (e.g., stag, bull, rabbit) also achieved great importance as fertility symols. Others, including the fish, serpent, owl, and lion, became divine symbols. The magical element attributed to the mysterious animal

soul resulted in animal sacrifices performed to obtain omens of human destiny. Thus, wherever we find accounts of the evolution of man and his world we find animals intimately involved in the whole process. A good example is this beautiful medieval illustration to the Genesis story (*right*), in which all the animals of God's creation are drawn up before Adam to be named. The other pictures on these two pages also concern the relationship between animals and their divine creators, who appear either as patron deities or, if it is a question of the domestication of particular species (e.g., the horse), as folk heroes.

riages. The feast got under way with three full days and nights of song-and-dance performances by the frog, tortoise, and crow. When the entertainment finally concluded, the assembled creatures felt half starved. Pelicans undertook the catering. They scooped a hearty supply of fish from the river. Heaped up on the bank, the fish lay ready to cook. At that point, the crow slyly raised an objection. He said it was not proper to fry fish so near the place where they had been caught.

The other animals would hear nothing of that; they were much too hungry to make a move elsewhere. To everyone's surprise, though, the kangaroo appeared to support the crow. Actually, it was the frog speaking, by ventriloquism. Insults were heaped upon the unoffending kangaroo, and tempers rose rapidly. The frog kept putting in a word here and there in the voice of one or another creature until they were all furious. Only the lyrebird kept cool; she made every effort to effect a reconciliation, but no one would listen. The moment came when the crow, cocking his bloodshot eye at the turmoil, sounded an imperious call to battle. That was heeded and outright war soon followed.

Then, gradually, a terrible thing happened. The animals lost the universal language with which they had begun, and each species perforce developed its own degenerate dialect. But the lyrebird, who remained aloof from the struggle, was able to imitate the dialect of each one.

War among the animals eventually settled into a more or less stable pattern in which the birds were joined together against the earth creatures. At first the bat sided with the birds. When, with his help, they began winning, he flitted over to the camp of the four-footed. Then, as they began to gain the upper hand, he rejoined the birds. Thus neither side could gain victory, and yet neither dared refuse temporary help from the treacherous bat. He commanded the field, in effect, a field which was increasingly blood-soaked and over which the sky gradually grew very dark.

Only darkness brought the beasts and birds to make peace. Few of them knew how to fight in the night. They longed for daylight to return, but it would not. The sun, disgusted by the continued carnage, had hidden its head.

At that point the bat hurled his boomerang northward, right around the earth. It returned, from the south, to the bat's hand. Again he hurled his boomerang, this time westward. It returned from the east, and with it came the dawn, shining once again. His first throw had separated night from

The name Heliopolis itself suggests the importance of the sun to this Egyptian city, famous for its cult centered on the god Ra. Ra soon became merged with Atum, depicted on this stone relief (*left*), and as Atum-Ra was identified completely with the light of the sun and its life-giving power. Atum, sole source of the seed that engendered the four divine couples of Heliopolis, was the supreme figure in the city's pantheon.

Depicted at left almost as a single entity is the first of the divine couples fathered by Atum – Shu, the god of air, and Tefnut, goddess of moisture.

From the first couple sprang Geb (the earth) and Nut (the sky, shown below in the form of a cow).

As cosmic power of darkness and destruction the god Set (*left*) was the antagonist and finally murderer of his brother Osiris. The legend of Osiris's death and rebirth (page 258) eventually became an essential component in Egyptian mythology.

Osiris, seen (*above left*) beside the *djed* pillar symbolizing eternal life, became lord of the world of the dead and of paradise.

The sisters Isis and Nephthys worshiped Osiris as the light of life in the form of the *djed* pillar, which supports the disk of the sun (*above middle*).

BUTO

BUBAST

HELIOPO

MEMPHIS

CROCODILOPOLIS

HERMOPOLIS

TALL AL-AMARNA

In the Memphis cosmogony the creator god was Ptah (*below left*), who fashioned the world with the understanding of his heart and the power of his word.

The sacred scarab god Khepri (*left*) in Buto was a symbol of the recurrence of the sun's light. Crocodilopolis worshiped Sebek (*below*), the sacred crocodile.

No other high culture of the age of myth had such a wealth and variety of zoomorphic gods and goddesses as did ancient Egypt. The map here shows the principal cities and temple sites of the Nile valley, each of which had its own supreme deity. These gods were fusions of often very ancient local animal deities with the supreme lord and creator god of the priest kingdom. Since there were several different cosmogonic traditions associated with local animal gods, the result was a number of complex deities represented with the heads of various animals. Among others the bull, the ram, the falcon, and the cow became – in the name of the creator, the Great Mother, or the sun – symbols of royal power. As can be seen on these two pages, the combinations of human and animal traits in the figures of the Egyptian pantheon are highly imaginative as well as artistically satisfying.

Ptah's consort was Sekmet, the lion-headed goddess (*above right*) supporting the solar disk of Ra.

The city of Bubastis took as its supreme deity the sacred cat Bastet.

Below, left to right: One function of the falcon-headed sun god Horus was to perform the coronation of the new pharaoh.
The god Knum of the island of Elephantine was also depicted with the head of a ram. He was creator of gods and of men.
The jackal-headed Anubis was revered as the tutelary deity of graves and the care of the dead.

Hermopolis became a center of the worship of Thoth (*below*). The ibis-headed god was creator of the world, hatched from the cosmogonic egg, as well as divine bringer of the art of writing and scholarship (myth, page 122).

This composite creator figure, Ptah-Sokaris (*right*) combines three elements: Amon as a ram, Ptah himself in human form, and the bird god Horus.

Amon, one of the old gods of Hermopolis, was made supreme deity of the city of Thebes. He is depicted here as Amon-Ra, king of the gods, enthroned with his consort Mut (*left*).

DANDARAH

THEBES

In the shrines of the temple of Dandarah the celestial cow and star mother Hathor was worshiped as the supreme goddess. This stone plaque (*right*) bears a very fine abstract image of the goddess with her horns enclosing the stars.

157

day. His second had made a path for the sun.

It was the bat – of swift unpredictable flight – who miraculously restored natural law and order to the world. But the animals had lost forever their common tongue.

THE EAGLE AND THE SNAKE

Cylinder seals – those miniature bas reliefs in semiprecious stone or ivory which were used for pressing signatures in wax upon important shipments and documents – are a prime source of documentation regarding ancient Mesapotamian myth. Seals dating to the old Akkadian period, for example, 5,000 years and more ago, often show a man upon a bird's back. What myth do they represent? The myth in question has been recovered in the form of printed clay tablets from King Ashurbanipal's library, together with Middle Assyrian fragments and some Babylonian, but it is still incomplete.

The sun god Shamash once bore witness to a solemn pact of peace between an eagle and a snake. The snake would live beneath the roots of a particular tree; the eagle would make her nest in its topmost branches. They would hunt together, and neither one would ever prey upon the young of the other. So much for their pact, but as soon as the eagle's fledglings could fly to safety from any attack by the snake, the eagle swooped upon the serpent's own relatively helpless brood and devoured them. The snake, returning to its empty nest at dusk, guessed what must have occurred. She prayed to Shamash for vengeance. Shamash replied by felling a wild ox in the snake's presence. The snake crept into the belly of the ox and quietly awaited her enemy. Sure enough, the eagle soon flew down out of the tree to tear with her hooked beak, hungrily, at the ox's belly. Thereupon the snake emerged to loop cold coils about the eagle's wings, bite away her plumage, and cast her into a pit.

This happened soon after the Deluge, during the reign of the first monarch of Sumer, King Etana. The king was childless. He prayed to Shamash for a son and heir. Shamash replied with advice. The sun god suggested that the king rescue the eagle from the pit and ride away on its back to the world where children are prepared for birth. The eagle's plumage had grown again by that time. Grateful to be rescued, she took King Etana upon her back. They flew to the gates of the sky, and it seemed that they were about to enter. Instead, they flew past the blue gates, higher, into the region of black emptiness and bright fire. Now Etana, gaz-

ing down, could not see any earth below. The eagle faltered, plunged . . . .
There the text is broken off.

SPIRIT WINGS

According to the Chinese, the birds actually instructed certain women in flying. Princess Nu Ying and Princess O Huang, the daughters of Emperor Yao, passed the secret to Emperor Shun, who reigned from 2258 to 2218 B.C. Taoist priests continued flying like birds, it is said, until more recent times. When and where a flying priest might happen to alight, he would be greeted as a "feather guest."

A Tlingit Indian woman who was past the age for bearing children walked out one day along the seashore, crying. A friendly dolphin swam inshore to ask what might be the matter with her. She confessed how things stood. She wished to bear a son, but she could not do it. The dolphin suggested that she swallow a pebble and wash it down with a bit of seawater. Gratefully, the woman did so, and instantly she conceived Yehl (or Yetl), the savior of the Tlingit people.

Yehl could appear as either bird or man. Once, in the form of a raven, he flew to heaven and stole fire for mankind. To bring back the waters in time of drought, he flew to the ends of the earth. Yehl's magical exploits, like his own conceiving, were ecstatic. They remind anthropologists of the spirit journeys undertaken by trancebound medicine men.

Ancient-Egyptian art represents the soul (the ba or khu) itself in bird form. So do archaic Greek tomb sculpture and vase painting. It may be that peoples of the eastern Mediterranean believed their souls to be actual birds. This conviction is still to be found among certain peoples today.

The Cheka Negritos of the Malay Peninsula call their own souls *biau*. The word refers also to a bee-eating bird with green plumage and a long beak. When a pregnant woman hears a *biau* cry from the forest, she knows that the soul of the child now in her womb has arrived. Similarly, when relatives of a dying person hear the bird, they recognize that his soul has already gone.

The *biau* brings messages, not only between the temporal world and worlds which exist out of time, but also here on earth. If a *biau* calls out persistently from the forest, the Cheka know they can expect a visitor. They answer the bird's cry with names of friends who might be on the way. As soon as they happen to name the right person, the bird will fall silent.

Among the earliest-known pictures of cattle are the Old Stone Age cave paintings of Lascaux (*above*) and other sites in southwest Europe.

In a well-known Greek myth Zeus seduced the lovely Europa by assuming the form of a bull (*below*). He got her to climb on his back as she was playing on the beach, and carried her off to Crete.

158

The horned, hammer-wielding figure in this Bronze Age rock carving from southern Sweden (*left*) is possibly the ox god Donar.

In the Mithras mystery cult of late Hellenistic and Roman times, the bull represented fire and life, transformed in death (*below*) into the self-regenerating power of the moon.

NOBLE STEEDS

Horses play an especially splendid role in myths around the world. The animal was first domesticated on the Asian steppes, and outstandingly strange stories such as the following are found in that region.

There was a woman of the Buryat tribe who possessed two husbands at one and the same time. Her first and favorite husband was the ghost of a great sorcerer who had died several generations before. Her second husband was a surly chieftain. To create a worthy and unusual gift for his bride on earth, the ghostly husband interfered with the chieftain's stables. He caused one of the mares to foal an eight-legged animal. The ghostly sorcerer intended the foal to become the woman's personal mount. The chieftain, however, was shocked at the sight of it, or he may have been jealous. In any case, he righteously amputated four of its eight legs. The woman saw him do so, and she wept. At the same moment, her ghostly husband snatched her up into the blue sky. She was to reign from that time forward as a guardian deity of the Buryat people.

No one who appreciates horses in the flesh would be likely to imagine that a second set of legs might actually improve the breed. Yet eight-legged horses abound in myth, over an area stretching from Iceland to Japan. Sleipnir, or Slipper – the tireless steed of the Norse god Odin – was eight-legged, for example. Why is this? Anthropologists theorize that the fact may derive from wooden ceremonial images of horses, with eight legs for the sake of sturdiness, upon which Mongolian shamans or medicine men once rode. Then again, a galloping horse may look and sound eight-legged at times. The horse as an actual creature "out there" and the horse as a mental projection or dream or onrushing idea may sometimes merge in myth.

Internal evidence suggests that the following legend is of great antiquity, dating back to perhaps 2600 B.C. In China there lived a warlord with a beautiful daughter of whom he was particularly fond. He happened to be overpowered and carried off by enemy raiders. For a long time, no more was heard of him. In her grief, his daughter made a public vow to give herself in marriage to anyone who could bring the warlord home safe and sound again. No sooner had her vow been announced than a magnificent stallion in the family stable broke its halter, jumped the barriers, and galloped away out of sight. After some weeks the horse turned up again, bearing the missing man on its back. However, instead of feeling gratitude

Many cultures, including some very early ones, have worshiped one or another representative of the bovine species – whether

bull, aurochs (a now extinct wild ox), or holy cow. It was among the first species to be exploited by man, serving him as both source of food and beast of burden. He also made use from the earliest times of the hide, bones, sinews, and horn. Moreover, the enormous strength and fertility of the bull and the life-giving milk of the cow were eminently suitable as symbols of the divine. The bull appears in myth as the sacred animal of Indra, as Vrishabha, the bearer of the world, or as bearer of the sun (the Egyptian Apis, page 15). He is an ambivalent figure, capable of embodying both fire and water, both solar and lunar forces.

Bull and cow also were important in the religion of the Kulli and Mohenjo-daro cultures of early India (*left*).

A fresco from Knossos, Crete (*below*), depicts young acrobats with a charging bull.

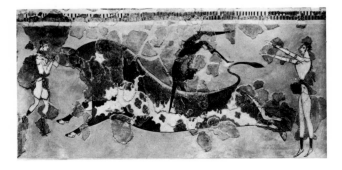

for his rescue, the warlord expressed disgust at the vow which his daughter had made. In order to free her from her promise, he promptly killed and flayed the animal to which he owed his life. He spread the stallion's hide out on the ground to dry. It rested there until a dewy morning when the warlord's daughter happened to pass close by. Then the horsehide arose, of its own accord, from the grass. Pulling up from the ground the pegs which had held it, the hide flung itself around the promised girl, enveloping her completely. Together, they flew off over the hills. The warlord gathered his cavalry and galloped in pursuit. At the end of ten days he found the stallion's hide lying lifeless and inert at the foot of a mulberry tree. Up among the mulberry leaves, weaving herself a wedding dress, was a silkworm, which had once been his daughter.

The most famous horse in myth is Pegasus, the winged steed whom the Greek hero Bellerophon captured and tamed. Bellerophon thereafter proved to be mighty in battle, raining rocks on his enemies from the back of his high-soaring friend. Emboldened by his success, he finally presumed to ride Pegasus up into the storm clouds which swirl over the peak of Mount Olympus, home of the gods. Zeus, who ruled on Mount Olympus at the time, looked down and saw a mere mortal ascending through the mists upon a winged horse. Regretfully, for he could hardly help admiring their courage, Zeus hurled a thunderbolt to stop horse and rider in their midair tracks. Bellerophon, blinded, scorched, and stunned, pitched out of the saddle and tumbled down the mountainside again. Pegasus, however, barely paused before wheeling up along the cold air currents to the immortals' home, where he really belonged.

Ever since then, poets in particular have claimed the winged steed for their companion. His second name, they say, is Inspiration. In thoughts, in dreams, sufficiently fearless minds may ride the wide-plumed animal to any heights.

But the most richly poetic celebration of the horse, perhaps, occurs in a chant which has a partly magical and partly medical purpose. Navaho medicine men sing this over sick patients to the present day, although only on rare occasions. Its purpose might crudely be described as an effort to draw a mythical animal down out of the sky and set him loose inside the minds of suffering people. To sit astride so wonderful a horse as this, even in imagination, could well constitute a healing experience. Here is the relevant passage from the chant, as translated by Dane and Mary Coolidge in *The Navajo Indians* (1930):

1–5 The Celtic goddess Epona, patroness of horses and grooms, was appropriately depicted on horseback (1); Odin (myth, page 159) rode an eight-legged horse named Sleipnir (2); and the archangel Gabriel sat upon the horse of heaven when he fought with Satan (3). The mythic mare Al-Burak carried Muhammad through the seven heavens (4), and Helios used horses to draw his sun chariot across the sky (5).

HOLY STEEDS

Many tasks are assigned to the horse in myth, but probably its primary significance has been as a symbol of swift movement. Thus it often serves the sun; it carries angels into battle with the dragon Satan; and many a

6–11 The swirling manes of Poseidon's horses vividly symbolize the foaming waves of the sea (6). Two winged horses whisk the prophet Elijah off to heaven (7). The falcon-headed sun god Horus rides his celestial horse (8). Kalki, the horse with which Vishnu will appear (9), at times personifies the god (11). Another celebrated horse in Indian myth is the Buddha's mount Kanthaka (10).

hero (e.g., Bellerophon myth, this page) has left the earth on a splendid charger to climb the heights of heaven. The concept of the horse as draft animal of the Greek sun god Helios arose directly out of the nature of the species. It is said that the Indian god Vishnu, in his tenth incarnation, will appear mounted on Kalki, brandishing his blazing sword to kindle the great conflagration that will end the present age.

In the teachings of Japanese Shinto Buddhism, an angry manifestation of the goddess Kwannon is as the protective deity of horses (*left*). Each of her three faces is surmounted by a horse's head.

The apocalyptic vision of John the Divine is full of mythic beasts, many of them winged horses of one kind or another (*right*).

Numerous tutelary deities of Tibetan religion are depicted on horseback. Here a scorpion god rides over a sea of flame (*above*).

A beautiful piece of sculpture from Tarquinia in Italy (*left*) shows two of the mythic winged horses that drew or bore such gods as Helios, Poseidon, and the goddess Athene.

A French heroic poem set in the time of Charlemagne tells of a wonder horse called Bayard that could carry all four sons of Duke Aymon in full armor – and was still faster than any other horse (*left*).

161

I am the Turquoise Woman's son.
On top of Belted Mountain
Beautiful horses – slim like a weasel!
My horse has a hoof like striped agate;
His fetlock is like a fine eagle plume;
His legs are like quick lightning.
My horse's body is like an eagle-plumed
    arrow;
My horse has a tail like a trailing black
    cloud.
I put flexible goods on my horse's back;
The Little Holy Wind blows through his
    hair.

His mane is made of short rainbows.
My horse's ears are made of round corn.
My horse's eyes are made of big stars.
My horse's head is made of mixed waters
(From the holy waters – he never knows
    thirst).
My horse's teeth are made of white shell.
The long rainbow is in his mouth for a
    bridle,
And with it I guide him.

CELESTIAL RAMS

The Berbers of North Africa are a nomadic group of tribes inhabiting the Atlas Mountains of southern Morocco and ranging eastward into the Sahara. Among them, the Kabyle people have a strange tale to tell about how their flocks came to be.

First Woman, say the Kabyles, once took a bit of flour and water in her hands and molded them in the form of a ewe. Her hands were sooty from the stove, and so the head of the ewe was blackened. She laid her damp and limp little creation in a stone trough of barley chaff.

Next day First Woman molded a ram. She made its horns curve downward so that it could not gore anyone. As she was laying it away in the trough, she heard the ewe which she had made the previous day begin bleating. The chaff had adhered to its downy flesh in the form of wool. First Woman gave the ewe some of her own couscous to eat. On the third morning First Woman made a second ewe out of dough. On the fourth she made another ram. These two animals were both altogether white. She made no more sheep after that. The neighbors heard strange bleating sounds from First Woman's house. They gathered in the street outside to ask what it was. "It's just my bread yelling," she told them.

Soon the sheep had grown sufficiently to go outside. They gently grazed here and there along the ditch beside the street. People had never seen such animals before. They asked First Woman about them. At first she would not admit that the animals were her own handiwork. She claimed that they had come to her in the night and asked to be taken in. Nobody believed this. Finally she said, "I made them out of dough and barley chaff. Try it yourselves if you like." Many people did try, but without success. Meanwhile, however, the first four sheep were mating and having offspring just as they do today.

The first ram which First Woman had made did not die in the ordinary way. It ran high into the mountains and tried to butt the red rising sun with its horns. The sun seized the ram and carried it on up out of sight.

A picture of that ram is to be found painted on the cliff above Haither, the wilderness sanctuary of the Kabyles. The painting is of great age. Parts of it have been obliterated by the recurrent frosts which flake away the rock surface. The figure of a human being can still be descried, however, below that of the ram. The figure's attitude is reverent and somehow questioning. Tribesmen say that he has gone to inquire of the beast regarding the path of the sun during the year. The first ram, having been seized by the sun, knows what the sun's diurnal and seasonal journeys are.

Along the Guinea coast of Africa, people tell of a stormy ram whose fleece is fiery gold. He can topple a coconut palm easily. He can overturn and burn up a house if he likes, and sometimes he does just that. His curving horns are white-hot to the touch. His breath is acrid, like the smell of dynamite.

The mother of this ram is a shy old ewe with a thunderous voice. In bygone times she did her best to keep her son at home, but he would always break away and rush to destroy men's dwellings. Therefore the people, who were powerful in those days, thrust the ram with its mother far away into the sky.

The ewe in the sky is sensible, not a lawbreaker, but very loud in her pleas to her son. The ram, on the other hand, has never grown up altogether. He keeps on plunging back to earth again, briefly, in the form of lightning.

AWESOME SWINE

The ancestors of the pig were as fierce as our own. From Ireland to Greece and back again, European legend tells of boar hunts in which great heroes were gored to death by swine. Pig tales of the South Pacific are, on occasion, equally horrific.

On Tana in the New Hebrides, once upon a time, a little girl was whirled to heaven by

A Canadian Indian painting of animals in the sky – a snake, thunderbird, and wolf atop a killer whale.

Far Eastern astrology uses exclusively animal symbols for the twelve months. These are the same in China and Japan (*right*).

The Aztecs depicted the sun as an eagle (*above*).

The constellation we call the Great Bear (*right*) has been called that for a very long time. Astrology was already sophisticated in ancient Babylon, with groups of stars being named after the animal shapes suggested by the position of the stars (*far right*).

Among the first animals mythologically located in the sky were incarnations of the sun and moon. Most animals were classified according to particular solar or lunar qualities. Rabbit, toad, and antelope appear in myth as moon animals. Birds of the eagle type, on the other hand, are

nearly always associated with the sun, for example the Horus falcon, the American Indian thunderbird, and Garuda of Indian myth. Similarly, the stars of the Northern and Southern Hemispheres grouped themselves in popular imagination into the shapes of animals, birds, and fabulous creatures of one sort or another.

The ceiling of the tomb of the Egyptian king Sethos I is painted with constellations in the form of gods and mythic beasts (*top, left*). The twelve animals of the ancient-Chinese calendar are gathered beneath the year tree (a pine), symbol of longevity (*top, right*). A Persian astrological miniature shows the conjunction of Mars (warrior and ram) with Jupiter of the radiant corona (*above, center*). The temple of Hathor at Dandarah contained this magnificent relief disk with the astrological animals and gods of the Egyptian zodiac (*above*).

163

the updraft of a bonfire. Like the heroine of *The Wizard of Oz,* she danced into a new and strange realm. A blind old woman befriended her, and she managed to show the woman how to overcome blindness by bathing in a pool. Thankfully, the woman lowered the little girl through a sky hole down to earth again. She also sent down, as gifts of gratitude to the earth people, the ancestors of the present-day pigs.

Pigs trotted erect in those days, whereas men walked exceedingly stooped. The birds, and in particular the water wagtails, felt especially friendly to pigs. The reptiles, led by the monitor lizard, sided with mankind. Once when the chief of pigs was holding forth at length under a tree regarding his own special qualities, a monitor lizard deliberately rolled off his perch and came down very hard on the pig's neck. The pig was forced onto all fours and has remained so ever since. Man, meanwhile, curious to see what had occurred, straightened himself up to his present erect posture.

Samoans tell of a cannibal chief who was accustomed to toss the chewed-over skulls of his enemies into an underground cavern. Those skulls grew to be swine. They trotted out one day, squealing with joy at the sunshine, much to the chief's surprise.

According to Hawaiian legend, the pig god Kamapuaa was so prepossessing as to win the volcano goddess Pele for his bride. They quarreled, separated, and made fierce war upon each other from age to age. Kamapuaa could change shape at will. Sometimes he was a small black pig, and at other times a gigantic white one. He could also turn himself into a man or into a little pigfish. To keep the lustful and jealous goddess Pele from boiling over, Hawaiians used to toss live pigs – or pigfish as the case might be – into her crater.

Solomon Islanders fear more than anything in the world a wild boar named Boongurunguru. He is curiously flatheaded. A tree wreathed in ferns grows upon his snout. A hornet's nest hangs underneath his chin, like a little beard. Boongurunguru leads a large herd of swine. No one must admit to having caught the sound of them, for such mention fills the air with flying reptiles. In the distance, the demon herd is huge. On close approach, however, they appear smaller than mice. When Boongurunguru enters a village, everyone dies.

Unworthy Messengers

The Nigerians say that the Chief of All Gods never approved of death. When people first began dying, he was horrified, they say. He sent a dog to tell them how to overcome their unexpected weakness. The dog was to explain that whenever anyone died, that person should be laid out in a compound and lightly dusted with ashes from a wood fire. After a day and a night the body would arise again, filled with life as before.

The dog is an intelligent animal, but easily distracted. At the outskirts of the habitations of men, the dog found a still-juicy bone upon a garbage dump. It turned aside to gnaw the thing and after fell asleep.

People were dying still, and their bodies were not being cared for as suggested. The Chief supposed some accident had befallen his canine messenger. Therefore, he sent a sheep with the same message once again and urgent orders to deliver it immediately. The sheep hastened. It was frightened. It trotted, panting, in among the habitations of men. "I have an urgent message," it bleated. The people gathered around. They were eager to obey the bidding of their Chief in heaven. The deaths among them had made them feel guilty in the extreme. They knew they must be doing something wrong. What was it?

When the tumult had died down a little, the sheep rolled its pale eyes and spoke. But fear had driven the Chief's message from the poor beast's mind. The people's eagerness to hear and obey only made things worse. "I think," the sheep said, "what you have to do is this. When anybody dies, be sure you bury him 6 feet down. Cover him well."

So that was done. Death confirmed its grip upon the human race. The celestial Chief, in his disappointment and disgust, made no further effort to right matters. No wonder our relations with the animals are no longer what they should be.

Manibozho and Chibiabos

William Strachey's *The Historie of Travaile into Virginia Britannia* (written about 1610) contains the following quotation from an Indian informant: "We have five Gods in all; our chief God appears often unto us in the likeness of a mighty great Hare; the other four have no visible shape but are indeed the four winds." The Indian added that the "Godlike Hare made the water, and the fish, and the great deer."

The Hare worshiped by Red Indians of Virginia possessed a very extensive cult stretching as far north as Hudson Bay and westward to the Pacific. He was sometimes identified with North America's greatest river. His names, in various Indian tongues,

Folklore abounds with tales of grotesque beasts and half-human, half-animal creatures believed to have inhabited the earth at one time. For some of them we even have a certain amount of paleontological evidence. Legend and fable illustrate the virtually limitless domains of dream, madness, and

1

individual fantasy. The forces of nature, personal visions, and the projection of animal qualities onto a world alive with magical possibilities have given rise to a wealth of fantastic images – prodigious monsters, demons, and complex mongrels – that may at bottom reflect man's fears and uncontrollable desires. Every kind of zoological aberration and mutation, as well as all the hidden power of the spirit world, is reflected in these terrible hybrid creatures of the imagination.

1 The fantastic creatures of the world of fable still retain their force today, capable of resurrection in such powerful images as Thomas Häfner's *Harpy* (1967).

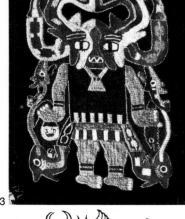

2 Schedel's book *World Chronicle* (1493) included various illustrations of fabulous beasts. This one evidently stems from the Greek centaur.

3 Peruvian folklore is full of such creatures as this vampire devil wearing a snake as a belt and brandishing a knife.

4 This medieval sea monster has a boar's head and the body of a fish with eyes all over it.

5 An appalling monster, from an epic cycle in a Bangkok temple, threatens to devour palaces and men.

were Manibozho, Nanibozhu, Michabo, Messou, and Missibizi. Brilliant white, that Hare leaped up out of the night. Did he begin as a tribal totem? Or did he represent the dawn itself, or possibly the sun? Or was he all things to the Indians, as "God" appears to us?

Père de Smet's account of his mission to the Indians of Oregon (first published in 1847) relates that the Great Hare, Manibozho, had a brother named Chibiabos. The hare loved his brother with the same intense protectiveness that Isis felt for Osiris and that the Greek corn goddess Demeter felt for her daughter Persephone.

Manibozho warned Chibiabos never to

6 This illustration from a sixteenth-century French work seems to be an attempt to depict something of the "hellishness" of Satan and his cohorts.

7 A medieval German saga tells of creatures that were half man and half crane, with a beak in the middle of a human face.

8 The Hai Riyo of Japanese fable was a bird with the head of the celestial dragon.

9 A North American Indian tradition tells of a human-headed sea monster that drives the salmon to the shore in spring.

leave his sight, but once he did anyway. Lured out onto the thin ice of a frozen lake, he was drowned. The Manitos, spiritual ancestors of the Pawnee Indians, destroyed Chibiabos. Along the shore of the lake hopped the Great White Hare, Manibozho, shrieking with grief and rage. He waged war upon the Manitos, but their spilled blood was not enough to drown his sorrow.

Manibozho turned away. He blackened his face with ashes. He wept and would not shine upon the world with his former glory. For six long years, Manibozho sat solitary in his dark lodge, calling his brother's name. The world was cold, dark, frostbitten, belly-shriveled. The Manitos who still survived were not the same as those who had drowned Chibiabos.

Better the Great Hare's fury, they thought, than his present melancholy. They built a lodge not far from Manibozho's own dwelling place. Between their lodge and his, a banquet was prepared. Each of the Manitos

165

filled a magical medicine bag with healing preparations. They presented all the medicine bags to Manibozho at his door. Gravely, with due ceremony, they invited him to the feast. It appeared that the silent, long-eared figure in the shadowy lodge lifted up his head a little at their word. It seemed that he signaled for them to leave the medicines in the doorway. They did so and discreetly withdrew. Soon they could hear Manibozho washing his face. He came out of the lodge and approached them. They gave the Great White Hare a sacred liquor. As he drank, sorrow left him. He danced with the Manitos. He sang their holy songs. He feasted with them. Then, together, they smoked the pipe of peace.

By magic, Manibozho and the Manitos proceeded to invoke Chibiabos. They built a lodge for him, and he came to life inside the lodge. But it was forbidden to enter there or to set eyes on him. Through a chink in the logs, blindly, they presented Chibiabos with a glowing ember of wood. He accepted the offering. Then, invisibly, Chibiabos went away again. He rules over Spiritland.

GREAT ESCAPES

African-born slaves brought a rich store of legend to the American South. Joel Chandler Harris preserved some of this material in his classic *Nights with Uncle Remus*, a story collection which has delighted people ever since its original publication in 1883. The "Uncle Remus" tales center upon a running battle of wits between two animal characters: "Br'er Rabbit" and "Br'er Fox." For instance, one of them tells how Br'er Fox made a sticky black baby doll of tar and set it in Br'er Rabbit's path. The silently smiling and motionless image seemed insolent to Br'er Rabbit. Angrily, the rabbit kicked, cuffed, and finally butted the insensate tar baby. He was hopelessly stuck to it when Br'er Fox gloatingly appeared. "You've got me at your mercy," Br'er Rabbit confessed. "So chop off my head, boil me if you must, but please, oh please don't toss me in the briar patch – for that is the one thing I most dread!"

Thereupon Br'er Fox, with an evil grin, did just what Br'er Rabbit had begged him not to do. But, of course, since briar patches are like home to rabbits, his enemy thus escaped.

Folklorist Aurelio Espinosa collected no less than 152 versions of this tale, largely from Africa. Among the more degenerate is a story told by Nuer tribesmen in which the image is made of sticky red resin and passed off as Fox's bride – with obscene

results. But all these tales derive, Espinosa believed, from an Indian one which truly deserves the name of myth. This may be found in a Buddhist collection known as the *Jataka*. It runs as follows.

The bull Apis was sacred to Ptah, creator god of the Memphis pantheon. Apis combined the symbol of the sun god Ra (the solar disk supported between its horns) with the wings of Horus, which sprouted from its back.

Alone in the depths of a forest, once upon a time, Prince Five Weapons was set upon by the shaggy, tree-size ogre known as Hairy-Grip. Instantly, the prince let fly with his arrows, fifty of them in quick succession. But they merely stuck fast in the tangle of the ogre's pelt. He hurled his spear and swung his sword against the ogre, with just the same result. Undaunted, the prince used his fists and his feet and even tried butting with his head. So he became fully caught; he hung suspended, like a fly in a spider web, from the ogre's chest and belly. Yet helpless though he now was, the prince still breathed defiance. "Inside my body," he coldly told the gloating ogre, "there is another weapon still, which you don't understand at all. It is a kind of sword, hidden away in me, called Knowledge. Devour me, I dare you; for that concealed weapon which you must also swallow will make mincemeat of your gullet!"

After a long, thoughtful pause, the ogre carefully and respectfully released his prey.

At the magico-mythical stage of farming or hunting, many cults have featured animal sacrifice in recognition of the close connection between man's fate and that of both animals and gods. Many of the major civilizations of antiquity have left evidence of the enormous importance of animals to man and also of the divine qualities with which man invested certain beasts. Among the best-known examples are the sacred bulls of Ur, Crete *(opposite)*, and Egypt, the white fox Inari of Japan, the sacred bear of northern Asia, and the Indian holy cow. For hunting peoples, animals were an essential source of food. Killing an animal, however, represented an intrusion into the animal world, and the sight of the dying animal revealed to man the numinous power of that world and of its ruler, the lord of the animals. Consequently a significant portion of the slain animal must be sacrificed to the lord of the animals; firstly as a thank-offering to obtain his blessing on the next hunting expedition, and secondly to appease the tutelary aspect of the god in order to discourage him from avenging the invasion of his kingdom. The early Cretan frieze on pages 168 and 169 shows such a liquid and animal offering in procession. Animal sacrifice was also used by certain Indian and Southeast Asian peoples to propitiate their ancestor spirits, and even today the Mexican descendants of the Mayas slaughter a pair of turkeys as a rain and fertility sacrifice. The ritual slaying of animals has always played an important part in fertility cults generally. In Babylon horses were sacrificed to the sun god, and in India a horse sacrifice, the *asvamehda*, was performed after lengthy preparation in order to celebrate a great victory and the consecration of a new king. The Nepalese sacrifice rabbits and doves and sheep to the dreadful goddess Kali. The originally Persian Mithras cult centered on the sacrifice of a bull, and even Socrates, when he died, asked his friends to sacrifice a cock to the gods.

FABULOUS FOXES

There was a time when our ancestors used to change places with animals, according to their own accounts. Arcadian Greece was haunted by werewolves – men who actually ran with the wolves – Pausanians tells us. African legend, again, is filled with crocodile men, and so on. More civilized societies, such as the ancient Chinese, as a rule ascribed the mingling of animal and human shapes to sorcery. The Chinese felt that foxes, for instance, were apt to be sorcerers in disguise, and vice versa. Fox magicians had human weaknesses. Their perspectives on life were apt to be a little odd, as certain tales attest.

Once a peasant in the province of Shantung looked up from his hoe to see a cultivated lady stumbling toward him over the furrows. At first he thought she might have lost her way. There was a redness in her eyes, however, which alerted him to her fox nature. It seemed that she had come to make a midnight appointment with him. They were to meet, she said, at the door of his bachelor hut between the fields.

That night in bed, the peasant found the girl delightful but curiously downy; her whole body was fuzzed with light brown hair. He gave her all the satisfaction he could. As she was leaving, he said, "Wonderful creature that you are, you can surely relieve the terrible poverty under which I suffer!" With that they parted, and he stumbled bleary-eyed into the fields to work.

Next night, the fox lady returned. The peasant again asked her for money. She said she had forgotten it. This went on for some weeks. The peasant was losing his health, owing to the well-known propensity of fox ladies to feed on the energy of their human lovers. He had almost resolved to turn the fox lady away when she finally came with a couple of coins. The coins looked like silver but were only pewter. The peasant complained of this. "Everyone has a destiny," his lover explained, "and yours is definitely inferior. Did you expect gold?"

"I had always heard that fox ladies were surpassingly beautiful," the peasant responded. "You yourself are not. To tell the truth, you are very plain and ordinary looking. Why is that?" The lady replied, smiling, that her kind always did their best to adapt themselves to present company. This mild quarrel signified the end of their affair.

A seventeenth-century man of letters named P'u Sung-Ling collected many such legends of the fox people from all parts of China. The world is in his debt, for stories of the sort which he retold tend to be related by the hearth or around the campfire,

This Celtic god (*left*) has the boar as his symbol. Artemis, the Greek goddess of the hunt, has the stag (*above*).

The many emblems and attributes of gods, heroes, and religious figures are direct references to their function and relationship to man. The emblem may be an animal or an object. Animals figure in this role as mounts or messengers of the gods or as embodying a particular quality or characteristic. For example, the eagle appears as mount of the sun god, but also sometimes as the sun itself. Indeed, when a pantheon contains a number of similar deities – as in India, Tibet, and Mexico – the attributes of a particular figure are often our only clue to their identity.

Attributes of the Nordic god Odin *(above)* were the two ravens Hugin (thought) and Munin (memory), who went with him everywhere (myth, page 124).

This Greek coin shows Athene on one side and on the other her symbol of intelligence and wisdom, the owl *(below)*.

An Akkadian seal *(above)* shows, on the left, the goddess Ishtar with her lion.

Attributes are particularly important when distinguishing the many Tantric deities of India and Tibet. The demon goddess Durga *(opposite)* is identifiable by her panther.

A sow suckling her young *(below)* identifies Isis, the Great Mother of Egyptian myth.

orally. All too seldom are they written down. Among P'u Sung-Ling's strangest legends was one concerning a farmer who owned a stack of straw the size of a small barn. A fox made its home in the straw. The fox used to show itself to the farmer in the form of an old man. In that guise it would draw the farmer in among the straw, where they had many a long gossip together.

One evening, as they were talking, the farmer asked the old fox where he vanished at night. "I go to drink in a tavern," the creature replied. "Come along and you will see." With that, it laid a trembling paw upon the farmer's arm. A wind arose, which whirled them both away to a strange town. They entered a tavern arm in arm. A feast was in progress. The pair ensconced themselves on a kind of balcony overlooking the banquet table. At that remove, they took part in the happy uproar. The fox man would occasionally nip down the stairs to fetch a pot of wine or a raw fish dish from the great table. No one seemed to notice him at all. After an hour or so of this, the farmer happened to look down and saw a dignified person in crimson costume setting a platter of kumquats on the table below. "Those look good," he said to his companion. "Won't you ask him for some?" The fox shook his head. "I am not permitted to approach a person of such integrity."

At that moment the scales fell, as it were, from the farmer's eyes. "In seeking the companionship of a fox," he thought, "I have lost my own integrity long since." The farmer felt terribly dizzy. Toppling from his chair, he fell onto the banquet table below. The revelers were much astonished. They asked where he had come from. For answer, the farmer pointed up toward the balcony. But there was no balcony. It seemed he must have fallen from one of the large roof beams above. His former friend was nowhere to be seen.

As best he could, the farmer explained what had happened. The people at the party were delighted by his story, which soon spread far and wide. They took up a collection to pay his traveling expenses home again. This was very necessary because home proved to be a thousand miles away.

The Binding of Fenrir

Among the uncanny beasts of our fear are some which cannot be called monsters – they appear normal enough – and yet terrify most of all. They are like the carnivores that one occasionally encounters in a bad dream, huge animals with slavering jaws and blood-dark eyes, who nonetheless ap-

pear peaceful for the time being. Such dream beings, psychologists explain, embody powerful, destructive passions which we ourselves project. They are shadowy images of that which appears most threatening in ourselves, anxieties and dangerous desires concealed in bestial guise.

Of all the beasts known to myth, Fenrir, the wolf, howls most eerily perhaps. The Icelandic *Eddas* (epic poems) relate that when Fenrir first appeared in Asgard – the heavenly city of the Norse gods – he was only a cub. Yet even at that time he sent shudders of fear throughout the heavenly host. Warlike though they were themselves, the shining inhabitants of Asgard fell back before the gray wolf cub. He trotted at large in the streets of Asgard, sniffing about curiously and even wagging his tail, as a friendly dog might do. Only the god Tyr dared to stretch out his hand to stroke the creature's bristling neck. He used to feed the cub with chunks of beef impaled on the point of his sword. Rapidly, Fenrir grew. The wolf soon stood waist-high to the gods themselves.

Though he had done no harm to anyone as yet, the gods decided on chaining him up. They made a chain of heavy iron, each link as thick as a man's wrist. This they put upon Fenrir. He submitted willingly. But the wolf kept growing. Before long he snapped the iron collar and chain.

The gods forged a second chain, twice as heavy as the first. This also they put upon Fenrir. He stood shoulder-high to them now. Yet still he was obedient after his fashion. His eyes appeared more red than before, however, and he was sometimes moved to growl in a low voice. Increasing still in size, he snapped the second collar and chain.

No merely metal bonds could hold him anymore. Therefore, the gods consulted with the dwarfs under the earth. The dwarfs understood the danger loping through the streets of Asgard. They willingly agreed to weave a thread which not even Fenrir could break.

The wolf was sportive. He enjoyed leaping and bounding, with gaping jaws, amid the warriors. His feelings appeared to be hurt when the gods shrank back from such sport. But now they explained to Fenrir that all such games require elbowroom. They offered to bring the wolf to a distant island, where he would be free to run and bound to his heart's content among them.

Fenrir went along gladly. He was the first to leap ashore out of the ship. He asked what games they were to play together. Then the gods showed him the dwarf-spun thread. Ostentatiously they played tug-of-war with it. The thread held firm, slender though it appeared. Then they tied one end of the thread to the bedrock of the island. The other end they offered to Fenrir. He sniffed it suspiciously. They told him the new game they had in mind, namely, to knot the thread about Fenrir's neck and then see him break it, as they themselves could not.

His great bulk trembled uncertainly; the hairs of his neck bristled up. Fenrir stood gazing out over the lifted faces of the gods. He smelled deceit. In the uncertain silence he growled for Tyr. The one god who had dared to pet and feed him when he was a cub stepped forward soothingly, sword hand outstretched. Gently, not breaking the skin, Fenrir clamped his great jaws upon the wrist of Tyr. "Now," he growled between his teeth, "bind me."

With trembling fingers the gods knotted the thread about the neck of Fenrir. Then all except Tyr stood back from him. The great wolf swelled himself. He rose up on his hindquarters and lunged. The thread held, snapping his head back with a jerk. Three times Fenrir lunged. He did not once let go of the sword hand of Tyr, however, but kept it firmly and gently clamped between his jaws. Now his fiery eyes looked down upon the face of Tyr, who had been his friend. Fenrir knew that he was helpless. He was helpless, and Tyr also. The great jaws of the wolf ground shut. He swallowed Tyr's sword hand.

Tyr could not die. His companions cauterized the wrist with boiling pitch. Then they took the sword of Tyr and jammed it up through the underjaw of Fenrir. The wolf coughed horribly, spewing blood and foam upon the ground. But Fenrir, too, was unable to die. No one cared to cure the wolf's wound or to ease his pain. In their fear the gods departed. They left Fenrir alone.

His howls are heard over the water still, sometimes, when the wind blows up a gale. A poisonous river gushes from his torn jaw. The treachery of the gods, their cowardice, keeps him coughing and spewing forth poison froth, year after year.

He will escape, someday. The gossamer thread will fray through, finally, and part. Then Fenrir will leap loose to run among the stars of heaven, biting their silver thighs. The skies will rain blood on that night called Ragnarok, the Twilight of the Gods. It is then that the gods, and men also, will die.

THE SEAL MOTHER

When hunting is poor, the Eskimos send a shaman to intercede with Takánakapsâluk, the Mother of Sea Beasts (also called Sedna). According to legend, she was once a pretty Eskimo girl. Her lover was a bird spirit. When Sedna tried to escape from him in a boat with her father, the spirit caused the waves to rise up in anger. Terrified, the girl's father threw her overboard to appease the sea. When she tried to climb back in, he chopped off her fingers. They became seals, walruses, and whales.

To reach her house is no easy matter. The shaman begins by diving invisibly through the bottom of his igloo. Swimming first through snow and afterward through icy salt water, he approaches the depths of the ocean. Clashing rocks bar his way. By a supreme effort, he spurts safely through them. Then he comes to the open roof of the Mother's cavern. A guardian dog howls and growls at him. As the shaman floats down, the dog cowers into silence.

The Mother, by the liquid fire, welcomes her visitor. She tells him that, sitting as it were in the eye of the sea, she knows all things which take place on dry land. Sadly waving her flippers before his eyes, she says she means to keep her seals at home until people demonstrate more reverence for life.

The Mother, Takánakapsâluk, bows her head. Since her hands are flippers, she cannot comb out the vast floating tangle of shadows and seaweed, alive with tiny creatures of the ocean bed, which is her hair. Gently crooning, the shaman combs it for her. Perhaps he can persuade her to release a few seals after all. The people on dry land above are starving, he explains. That is why they are thoughtless at times.

THE GREEDY BROTHER

There was a man who lost his way in the jungle and came upon a lodging which he had never seen before. Darkness was falling, and so he entered the house. Si Ungin, a Bajau of Kotabelud in Borneo, told the anthropologist Ivor Evans what happened next.

Soon what appeared to be people came in. They brought food and drink to the stranger. But instead of water they offered him blood, and instead of rice they gave him maggots to eat. The young man was discreet beyond his years. He managed to choke down a little of the blood and the maggots also.

Then they brought the guest something to sleep on, but it was not a sleeping mat, only a banana leaf. He lay down on it anyhow and composed himself for sleep. In the darkness, swarms of mosquitoes descended upon his flesh. He held himself still, rigid with distress, wondering what to do. The

The animals of myth, in contrast to fanciful creatures of legend and fable, are usually taken from nature or depart only minimally from natural forms. These animals are a link between gods and people and can only be understood in this context. They thus possess the character of true symbols. Apis actually stands for Ptah, the Horus falcon stands for the sun. The tortoise and the boar *are* Vishnu, just as the horse Kalki will be his last manifestation. This close magico-mythical relationship between people, animals, and gods comes out particularly in mystery cults such as the funerary rites of ancient Egypt. But animals also play an important part in the heroic struggles in the domain midway between the divine and the human – for example in the labors of Herakles (myth, page 180). Serpent, scarab, and the celestial cow Hathor incorporate several layers of meaning. Typical riding animals are lion, horse, bull, ea-

gle, and again the serpent. Animals as divine attributes relate to particular characteristics and hidden powers of the deity concerned.

The gate of Hades was guarded by the terrible three-headed hound Cerberus (*left*).

The Celtic bear goddess Artio (*far left*) sits before the animal sacred to her. The bronze was found near Bern, Switzerland.

others in the house were all perfectly quiet now. Nobody seemed to be slapping at the swarms or to be in any way disturbed by them. Very gently, the young man brushed the mosquitoes away from his body. He was careful not to injure any. They went away and did not return.

In the morning, his hosts presented him with a large hollow section of bamboo, stoppered and sealed. "Do not open this," they warned, "until you are safely home again and in the midst of your family. We

This Zapotec funerary urn (Mexico) combines a bat's face and other animal traits in an attempt to ward off demons (*above*).

An Aztec shield made of gold and feathers (*above*) depicts the coyote that served Quetzalcoatl.

In ancient Mexico the jaguar god (*far left*) was worshiped as creator of the fourth sun of the last cosmic era.

According to Roman tradition the orphan children Romulus and Remus were suckled by a she-wolf (*left*).

The city of Bubastis in ancient Egypt worshiped the cat goddess Bastet (*right*).

will set your feet on the right path and then leave you."

When he reached home and opened the box, the man found gold ornaments and silk cloths of many colors. It was a sumptuous gift, which he distributed among his family. His elder brother looked on and was envious.

Secretly, that afternoon, the elder brother slipped away to find the mysterious longhouse. He too was welcomed there just as he had hoped. But when they brought him blood and maggots for dinner, he grimaced with disgust. He would not eat or drink. When they brought him a banana leaf to sleep on, he complained bitterly of the indignity. When mosquitoes descended upon him in the night, he slapped at them, cursing, and killed several hundred.

By morning, his body was half-drained of blood. He rose very pale, weak, and shaken. His hosts said he would have to find his own way home. But the elder brother, too, received a bamboo box as a going-away present. He also was told not to open it until he reached home.

The elder brother soon paused to open his present in private. He thought he would keep the whole treasure for himself. As he unstoppered the bamboo, scorpions ran from it up over his hands, arms, chest, and neck. He fell back on the path, writhing and beating at them. They stung him to death.

DANCING INSECT

Lucian, the late classical Greek scholar, noted that it was not possible to discover a single ancient mystery from which dancing was absent. According to him, the way to reveal the mysteries was customarily to dance them out.

Kalahari Bushmen of the South African desert speak of their own religious mysteries in just that way. What we call myths they describe as dances. "I do not dance that dance," they may say, by way of claiming ignorance of some particular myth.

Dancing practiced in celebration of myth ought to offer the dancer, as Mircea Eliade has suggested, "a new dimension of life: spontaneity, freedom, sympathy with all the cosmic rhythms and, hence, bliss and immortality."

Bushmen especially revere that long-legged dancer from the insect realm, the praying mantis, whom they call Cagn. He created them, they explain.

Cagn also made the eland to hunt, and made the moon from the shoe of his foot. He was unfailingly generous, once upon a time. Constant quarrels embittered him. He had been eaten by ants and his bones scattered abroad. Cagn survived even that; yet now he appears forgetful, even cruel. The Bushmen gently remind him, whenever they see Cagn, that they are his children and that he really ought to care for them. Their present state is not prosperous because of Cagn's carelessness.

TIME OUT OF MIND

At Tung-P'ing there lived a drunkard named Ch'un Yu Fen. One day during the ninth moon of the seventh year of Cheng Yuan (A.D. 791 according to Western calculations), Ch'un lay down in the shade of a locust tree on his front lawn. The two companions who were with him withdrew to

wash their feet at the door of the house. The heat of wine in his head combined with the cool shade to cast Ch'un into a profound slumber. He dreamed that a pair of courtiers dressed in purple approached him and asked him to mount a carriage drawn by a white horse.

1 An ancient-Indian myth (page 62) tells how the world was created by the churning of the ocean of milk, with the serpent Vasuki serving as the churning-rope.

Wonderingly, Ch'un did so. The carriage seemed to whisk through a hole in the locust tree under which his body lay. Ch'un was too frightened to speak. The carriage sped through a landscape strange to him. It came to a city and a great palace. Ch'un was greeted by the king himself. "Your father," the king informed him, "did not disdain my promise to give you my daughter in marriage."

Ch'un had reason to believe that his father had been either slain or captured on the northern frontier. Perhaps, he thought now, he himself had been transported there. In any case he was a stranger in a place unknown. He had no choice, he felt, but to accept whatever came.

That evening, as preparations for the wedding got under way, dozens of beautiful girls surrounded Ch'un and playfully reminded him of moments when he had flirted with them. He could not recall the face of a

This Cretan goddess with a snake in each hand was the prototype of several similar deities of Gnostic traditions.

3

4 5

A Khmer bronze from Cambodia shows the threefold head of the *naga* or snake king Mucalinda, who once sheltered the meditating Buddha from the rain.

Egyptian gods are often depicted with the *uraeus* serpent as symbol of energy and power.

The once beautiful Medusa's hair was turned by Athene into a writhing mass of snakes.

The "subtlety" of the serpent of the Garden of Eden was Adam and Eve's undoing.

The headpiece of this Mexican "goddess of the thirteen serpents" consists of tightly woven snakes.

In his campaign against idolatry the Hebrew prophet Ezekiel smashed the serpent images of the idolaters.

8

An eighth-century Viking relief shows the Nordic god Thor fishing the snake of Midgard or Middle Earth."

7

0 This Benin bronze of spirit being has snakes – symbolizing its magical power – emerging from the eyes and nostrils to devour frogs.

10

THE SERPENT

Of all the animals in myth and religion none has so varied and ambivalent a significance as the serpent. One of the most ancient and widespread concepts is the great world serpent that lives in the primal ocean or at

6

the roots of the central world tree. The snake appears as the guardian of treasure or the keeper of the cosmic energy of creation, or alternatively as the great destroyer of the created world. Its dangerous character, embodying secretive carnal deceit, comes out perfectly in the Garden of Eden story. In Indian yoga and among the American Hopis, on the other hand, the snake is recognized as a symbol of creative energy and the yearning spirit. Another Indian concept is that of the *nagas* or serpent protectors of the gods and the Buddha. In the Greek mysteries of Asclepius the snake and its poison embodied the principle of healing and of life.

single one, and yet they did seem familiar somehow. They fell back as the princess herself approached Ch'un. Her beauty surpassed anything that he could have imagined.

The marriage was a happy one. Ch'un served the king, his father-in-law, diligently and well. Soon he had three children of his own. He undertook to lead the king's forces in battle, sometimes sucessfully and sometimes not. After twelve years his wife died. At the funeral, a priest prophesied catastrophe for everyone. A deluge was coming, and Ch'un would be responsible.

"I think," the king told Ch'un, "that you had best return to your own home." Ch'un was astonished. "Isn't this my home? My children are here." Suddenly the king laughed. "In three years," he said, as if from a great distance, "you will see them again." Ch'un awakened under the locust tree. The years had been only moments. His companions had not even finished washing their feet. Ch'un called for an ax. He chopped open the tree. Inside it was an ant city. He saw the king and queen, winged, with crimson heads.

He even saw his wife's grave in the coil of a root shaped like a dragon's tongue. A wind was rising, and the sky darkened swiftly. The wind filled the gleaming leaves of the tree with an urgent whispering sound. Big drops of rain spattered down. Ch'un and his companions ran for the house. As they reached the door, lightning flashed behind them, and the rain became a torrential downpour.

Next day, Ch'un discovered that the ant city had been swept away. That sobered him.

Following pages:

The Indian miniature (page 176), showing a goddess riding on a lion with the sun in her right hand, is a symbolic portrayal of the cosmos. The lion, which is made up entirely of men, women, and various animals, represents the animate world on which the sun bestows its light.

This Tantric picture (page 177) is an intricate blend of mythic, psychological, and religious elements. The bird Garuda, an attribute of both Shiva and Vishnu, is pictured standing on the demon Hiranjakasipu and displaying pictures of the three incarnations of Shakti – Durga, Kali, and Devi – on its wings and body; they symbolize life, death, and rebirth. In the center sits Brahma, the creator god.

The gold plaque (*right*) from Rhodes depicts a Greek bee goddess. In antiquity the bee was symbolic of cleverness and orderliness. Sacred to Demeter, it featured in the mysteries celebrated at her temples in Eleusis and Ephesus.

The sacred scarab Khepri *(above)* was worshiped by the people of Buto in ancient Egypt as embodiment of the rising sun and hence of the supreme creator god Atum. Called both "The Living One" and "The One To Be," Khepri symbolized the self-regenerating life force. The sacred scarab was also the god of transformation and, particularly in Heliopolis, symbol of the birth of the new sun from the womb of the earth.

Ch'un changed his habit of life entirely. The king had said that he would see his children again in three years' time. That did not give him very long to live, he guessed, before going back down between the roots of the world.

THE KEEN KEENG

Some Australian aborigines still speak with trembling awe of a lost race of demiurges whom they name the Keen Keeng. The creatures were winged like bats, but otherwise humanoid. Apart from seemingly effortless flight, their physical powers did not appear great. Yet every member of the Keen Keeng was a magician, and their powers of conception far exceeded human consciousness.

The brave Winjarning brothers, heroes of the aborigines, were captured long ago by the Keen Keeng people. The Winjarnings were brought into a cave and made to sit, tightly bound, with their backs to a fire which leaped up from a pit. They witnessed three days and nights of ritual dancing around the fire pit, but could see only the shadows which were cast by the dancers on the wall in front of them. They heard the singing clearly and memorized it.

At last the moment came when the brothers were unbound and permitted to turn around. Their captors pushed them gently forward, right to the edge of the pit. Below, the flames twisted and licked. The brothers were expected to leap down willingly. However, they were able to resist the allure of the fire. Their captors, meanwhile, moved as in a reverential dream, exhausted by their own rituals. For three days and nights the Keen Keeng had been dancing in the guise of various animals around the fiery pit, and this had completely sapped their strength. The constant chanting had reduced their voices to whispers.

The Winjarnings stretched, easing the stiffness of their joints and feeling the blood pulse back into their unbound limbs. Both twins were exceedingly strong. They plucked up the Keen Keengs nearest to hand and hurled them down into the fire. The rest ran away, howling with fear. The Winjarnings left the cave, free men.

They remembered the chants and dances which they had learned while in captivity. These they transmitted to their own race. The initiation rites which some aborigines have practiced ever since are based on things which the Winjarnings learned in the Keen Keengs' cavern. But their own initiations do not end in ritual burning or in human sacrifice. Far from it. They conclude with a deliberate turning around to greet with fresh eyes the light of the sun.

Plato, the philosopher, long ago compared mankind as a whole to prisoners sitting fast-bound in a cavern. We have our backs to the entrance, and we see shadows – only shadows – of the real world. Those shadows are cast over the shoulders of mankind, onto the cavern wall which all of us are facing.

BIRDS OF OMEN

Throughout the skies of myth, birds serve as messengers. In England, country people count the magpies they happen to meet. "One for sorrow, two for joy, three for a marriage, four for a boy." In classical Greece and Rome the flight of birds was anxiously observed as a means of foretelling the future. Chinese, Japanese, Indian, and Arabian myths also make birds the emissaries of uncanny forces.

A single-legged bird was once observed hopping up and down the terrace of the palace of the Chinese Prince of Ch'i. The prince himself caught a glimpse of it. The bird belonged to no species he had ever seen. Much puzzled, the prince sent a messenger to the province of Lu, where Confucius was residing in exile. He asked the great philosopher what to do.

The reply which Confucius sent back read as follows: "It appears that you have seen a Shang Yang, that is to say, a bird of rain. It may not look like much to you, but it is able to change its size at will, and it can flood whole countrysides or dry up rivers entirely. In former times, children used to amuse themselves by hopping about on one foot while frowning intently, pretending to be a Shang Yang. They pretended that the game would bring on rain. Think about this; all customs have significance. The bird has come at last to Ch'i, your messenger tells me. Heavy rain will fall soon, now. Have your people make every preparation against floods."

Not only Ch'i but also various adjacent provinces were inundated. Because necessary precautions had been taken, Ch'i itself escaped almost unscathed. Commenting on what had occurred, an ancient-Chinese historian wrote in the margin of his text: "Alas! How few listen to the words of the sages!"

The Hindu *Mahabharata* refers to creatures of ill omen called Vartikas, who possess only one wing, one eye, and one leg. When they are seen facing the sun and vomiting blood, trouble is surely on the way.

In Japan there lived a monstrous firebird, called the Tengu. Once it pounced upon a

In Far Eastern mythologies animals appear primarily as symbols of the seasons, of the polarity of *yin* and *yang,* and of the twelve months of the zodiac. What was known of their nature and habits played an important part. The picture here relates to winter. In terms of *yin* and *yang,* winter is extreme *yin* – moist, dark, and female. As

such it bears the sign of the "Dark Warrior," which unites the snake and the tortoise, two animals that came to symbolize the *yin* force through their association with dampness and with the earth in which they hibernate. The dots and lines on the tortoise's carapace represent the constellations of the winter sky.

young water dragon which dwelt in the garden of a Buddhist monastery. The dragon was too small to fight the Tengu. Like a grass snake carried off by an eagle, it hung helpless in the firebird's talons. The Tengu flew to a desert country and dropped the dragon into a dry cleft of rock to die. Then it flew back to the Buddhist garden again.

A monk who had been drawing water from the well was there, pitcher in hand, searching the garden for the little dragon. When the Tengu's shadow fell across the monk, he looked up, and realizing what must have occurred, shook his fist at the bird.

The Tengu was irresistibly attracted by rage in any form. Therefore, it swooped and carried off the angry monk. It dropped him over the same dry cleft of rock in which the dragon lay broken and half destroyed. Spreading his wide sleeves as he fell, the monk floated down gently into the cleft. Most of the water in his pitcher had spilled out, and yet there was a little left. This he poured, with blessings, upon the poor dragon's wilting head. One touch of pure water caused the creature to swell and grow like a storm cloud. Lashing its rainbow tail, the water dragon broke the rocks apart. The monk climbed upon his back and together they flew home to the garden.

The Arabian phoenix, or cinnamon bird, never really died, according to myth. It would escape old age by casting itself into a flame, from which the glistening creature always arose newborn again. Cinnamon sticks were twigs from nests built by the phoenix, Greeks and Romans supposed.

FEAR OVERCOME

Fear, not to mention bone-quivering awe, never seems to retreat entirely from human consciousness. Greek myth related that a great dragon out of Anatolia once routed the gods from Mount Olympus and harried them southward into Egypt. There Zeus concealed himself under a ram's head and woolly cloak. The sun god Apollo scampered along the wall; he was a mouse now. Hermes, trembling, grew the head of a hound with ears pricked up. Liquid-eyed Hera assumed cow form, and so on. The immortals, it seems, were terrified out of their normal selves.

That episode, the Greeks believed, explained the peculiar nature of Egyptian religious statuary. Nile temples were crowded with carved figures which possessed human bodies and animal heads. Obviously, Greek travelers told themselves, Egyptians had received certain misapprehensions during

the time that the frightened Olympians sojourned among them. They had been half taken in by the disguises of the gods.

Zeus's half-human son, mighty Herakles, was the hero of the common man in Greece. He cut away the hundred heads of the water-monster Hydra in a swamp near Lerna. He used a flaming torch to cauterize each one of the dragon's twisting necks so that they would not sprout new heads. He also fought hand-to-hand with the Nemean lion, whose hide appeared impervious to all weapons. Herakles throttled the beast and then turned its own claws upon itself to flay the body. He used the lion's hide, thereafter, as his own armor.

Laborious, indefatigable, Herakles showed himself to be. He it was who wrestled and threw the mad, gigantic Cretan bull. He spent a full year chasing down the supernaturally swift Ceryneian hind. He contended with man-eating mares and plague-bringing Stymphalian birds. He even collared Cerberus, the triple-headed guardian dog of the underworld. "He rid us," wrote the Athenian playwright Euripides, "of the beasts of our fear."

The famous *Gerona Codex* from Spain contains this vision of John the Divine's "dragon with seven heads and ten horns" (*above*).

A fourteenth-century French tapestry (*top*) illustrates an incident from the Revelation to John: a dragon with seven heads surrenders the scepter of his authority to a lion-headed beast rising out of the sea.

The dragon has assumed a wide variety of forms in people's imaginations through the ages. The European dragon usually takes the form of an enormous winged fire-breathing crocodile, though winged snakes with several heads also occur frequently. Apart from the original dragon of Greek mythology – the nine-headed Lernaean hydra eventually killed by Herakles – the most fierce dragon depictions

In China the dragon is the earliest mythological beast, symbolizing the fertility of the earth and the power of the emperor (*above*).

The Ouroboros dragon of alchemy (*above*) devours itself and so symbolizes the endless cycle of destruction and renewal.

This seven-headed dragon battling with the gods (*above*) is taken from an Akkadian seal.

This Chinese tapestry (*above*) shows the dragon as symbol of fertility from heaven (i. e., rain) and long life. An ancient-Chinese clay tile (*right*) combines the mythic idea of the phoenix with the body and horned head of the celestial dragon.

occur in Far Eastern cultures and in medieval paintings of St. Michael and St. George. In Eastern traditions, however, the dragon is a benevolent symbol of fertility, power, and creativity or it figures as the custodian of hidden treasure. In China it is the bringer of rain and patron of water.

The dragon theme – here a detail from a Korean tomb mural (*right, above*) – occurs throughout the East, where it is of great importance in astrology as well. Dragon dances, originally performed as fertility rites, are still held in China every year; harvest time is the occasion for this traditional procession with an enormous dragon (*right*).

Winged Eros visits a young bride to waken her desire.

LOVERS AND BEARERS OF DIVINE SEED

This early-Italic statue of a Mother Goddess holding five babies in her arms was intended as a symbol of fertile motherhood.

Six warriors and noblemen known as great lovers in a paradise of sensuality look up at a radiant and seductive vision of a love goddess. The beauty in the halo, however, is Venus not in her ideal state but in her earthly, eroticized association with the female sex. The vision ultimately bears the taint of human weakness and the perils of desire and passion. The two cupid figures, with their clawed feet and bows and arrows, symbolize the negative, animal side of erotic love. Although the apparition takes place in a paradise of ripening fruit trees offering all the delights of the beautiful, the mere presence of these only seemingly angelic spirits is sufficient to bring out the demonic aspect.

Myth offers a neat explanation of the human condition. Again and again, myth insists that we are double-natured, children of both earth and heaven – the reason being that gods or other supernatural creatures long ago intruded their own seed into the chain of human generation. Hence that disturbing spark of the divine in each person. There is a hint of this in the Old Testament, for example. The sons of God are said to have consorted – early on – with the daughters of men. Were such connections physical in the sense that we know, or does this have only symbolic meaning?

Virgin births are frequently met with in myth. They signal the coming to earth of a savior, more often than not, and this is notably true among the Indians of the Western Hemisphere. In South America, for example, the Uaupe people of Brazil say that their savior Jurupari was virgin-born. The Incas of Peru used to maintain the same regarding Viracocha. Far to the north, in Canada, the Huron tribe revered Joske-ha, born of a virgin. The following legend was collected from the Zuñi Indians of the southwestern United States and published by the *Journal of American Folklore* in 1918. According to the Zuñi, there once lived a maiden whose virginity was sacrosanct. Soldiers guarded her at all times, and she was not permitted to leave her house. Yet every precaution proved fruitless because the sun itself was her secret lover. She used to receive the sun god through a chink in the roof.

When her guards noticed that she had become pregnant, they were frightened. They decided to kill the maiden. But the sun lifted her up out of her prison as a mist and set her feet upon a new path. She came to a man planting a field. "What are you putting in the ground?" she asked him. "Pebbles!" he lied. In response she cursed his seed and nothing grew from it. She came to a second farmer and asked him the same question. "Wheat and corn," he truthfully answered. She made sure that his crop would flourish. Then she went across a deep river. The soldiers who were pursuing her could not cross it and went no farther. Alone on the far bank, she labored and gave birth to twin girls. The pigs and dogs which were there kissed her, but the mule disdained to do so. Therefore, mules have no children.

That Zuñi legend carries haunting Christian echoes, and somehow a few pagan ones as well. More haunting still, however, is the following myth.

A strange thing was seen flying from the waters of a South Pacific lagoon, once upon a time. In itself it would not have appeared strange, however, as it was only a child's

kite merrily dipping and flapping over the waves and up into the air. What did seem odd was that no one, apparently, was holding on to the string of the kite. From the kite itself, soaring over the water, the taut string led down directly to and through the waves. The people gathered on the shore, watching, and yet disbelieving what they saw. The kite approached them with its string still taut. A chubby hand rose from the water, clutching the string in its fist. Then came the arm, the dripping locks, and the glistening body of a little boy. He had been running underwater, flying his kite. Now he dashed up into the shallows to give the string more slack. The kite danced in the sky. The little boy saw only his kite and did not see the people closing in to catch him. At the last moment, though, the thudding of their bare feet upon the sand alerted him. Turning, he ran straight back underwater, reeling his kite in after himself. The people went out in canoes to look for him; but though their best swimmers and divers searched along the coral reef neither he nor his kite could be found.

Next day, the kite again appeared over the water. The people ranged themselves along the beach, hoping this time to catch the little boy. He splashed up into the shallows, but again he proved too quick for everyone. His kite tugged him along as he played, making his movements both erratic and swift. He ran dancingly, like a butterfly, leaping and hovering. When he paused, still out of reach, the people were panting and sweating. The suspicion had begun to dawn on them that this little fellow was exceedingly special. Though they felt at home on or above the surface of their familiar lagoon, he seemed to be equally at ease above and below the water. "Only one of you can catch me," he called out laughing. "Fetch Apakura. I shall not run from her."

The little boy stood still, winding in his kite. Apakura came down from the village to the shore. She waded straight across to the sandbar on which the little boy stood, kite in hand. Kneeling down on the sand, Apakura gazed questioningly into his eyes. Some god had been his father, she supposed. And no doubt people were beginning to think that she herself was the child's mother; but she knew better. Apakura was a virgin.

"Do you remember," the little boy asked her, "the loincloth which you lost in the tide last year? It was a fine one, tufted with red hair from a dog's tail. Perhaps you were sorry to lose it? Well, it was not lost. My ancestor and yours, the sea god Rongota-kawiu, carried it down beyond the reefs. He treasured your loincloth, mother. He shaped me from it, by slow degrees, in your

The Great Mother of myth combines in her usually formidable person all the essential qualities of the female. Fertility was attributed in all primitive cultures to the power of the moon, and the early Mother Goddesses were usually moon goddesses as well. The curious horn in the hand of the figure from Laussel (6) is believed to symbolize this dual function. The majority of the idols illustrated here, with their exaggerated womanly contours, are about twenty thousand years old. It was very much later that the Great Mother assumed personal form and was given various names. This seems to have happened during periods when an originally matriarchal social order was giving way to a patriarchy. And just as these Great Mother images enjoyed the spiritual allegiance of prehistoric man for thousands of years, modern man still feels the fascination of such figures as Inanna, Ishtar, Artemis, Isis, Gaea, and the Indian Shakti – those splendid, numinous figures who grace the great mythologies of conception, birth, and death.

8 A Turkish female idol dating from the sixth millenium B.C.

1-6 Most of the earliest Mother Goddess idols stem from the Paleolithic civilizations of France. The famous "Venuses" of Lespugue (1), Brassempouy (2), and Menton (3) stress the fertility aspect. Similar figures are the Austrian "Venus of Willendorf" (5), a somewhat slimmer version from the Greek island of Naxos (4), and this Mother Goddess with a horn from Laussel, France (6).

7 This Neolithic sculpture from Turkey is believed to represent a "holy family": on the left the sacred marriage of Father God and Mother Goddess, and the mother with her divine child on the right.

honor. Now he has bidden me to come up on to dry land as your obedient son. May I still fly my kite? I know that after I grow up there will be violent work for me to do. The sea god says that I shall bring vengeance upon the enemies of your family and mine, out of the ocean."

The depths of ocean have given rise to many seeming miracles. Aphrodite, the love goddess of the ancient Greeks, was herself ocean-born. The severed genitals of the sky god Uranus gave rise to her divine form, and then soft breezes wafted her ashore at Paphos, on the island of Cyprus. She appeared riding a scallop shell into the shallows. Nude and smiling, she might have seemed defenseless. But on the contrary, Aphrodite proved one of the mightiest of deities.

TRISTRAM AND ISEULT

The legendary lovers best known in western European tradition were childless and they suffered a tragic fate. Their story is Celtic in origin and derives from Welsh legend. It was Gottfried von Strassburg who gave it literary permanence in the thirteenth century, but his version is less familiar today than Richard Wagner's opera on this same theme.

Tristram and Iseult (or Tristan and Isolde in Wagner's opera) were the lovers' names. Sir Tristram was the nephew and protégé of Cornwall's King Mark, and Iseult was Mark's queen. The lovers' affair therefore violated sacred bonds. They were forced into it, however, by the magical action of a love potion. The king tried and failed to turn a blind eye to what was happening. At last he called upon Iseult to prove her faithfulness to himself through a public "trial by fire."

Iseult shrewdly arranged for Tristram to meet her at a riverbank on the way to her ordeal. He was to come disguised as a pilgrim and offer to take her across the stream on his back. Iseult publicly accepted the offer. On the far side, Tristram deliberately stumbled and fell with Iseult in his arms. King Mark's entourage abused him for being so careless with their queen. The unhappy procession passed on to the place of trial. And there Iseult swore a solemn oath in the presence of her husband, King Mark. It was "that no man in the world had carnal knowledge of me nor have I lain in the arms of anyone but you, always excepting the poor pilgrim, for with your own eyes you saw me lying in his arms."

Having sworn the oath, Iseult took red-hot iron in her hands and carried it. She was not

"To refuse a request from you that sleep in the arms of the King of Heaven, would be both wrong and impossible," replied laughter-loving Aphrodite, and took from her bosom the curiously embroidered girdle in which all her magic resides, Love and Desire and the sweet bewitching words that turn a wise

man into a fool. "There," she said, handing it to Hera; "take this girdle and keep it in your bosom." And as she pointed out the curious stitches, she added: "All my power resides in this, and I have no fear that you will come back from your mission unsuccessful."

HOMER, THE ILIAD, BOOK XIV, 211-221 Translated by E. V. Rieu (1950)

THE GODDESS OF LOVE, APHRODITE/VENUS

Botticelli's painting *(above)* illustrates the mythic birth of the Roman love goddess Venus, who in Greek myth (this page), as Aphrodite, was born of the foam *(aphros)*. She is goddess of love in the broadest sense: her original function was to ensure conception and consequently procreation; then she became the goddess of air, earth, and ocean, born of heaven through the medium of water; and eventually she came to patronize the whole spectrum of ethical and physical love. She was the wife of Hephaestus and the lover of, among others, Ares, Adonis, Poseidon, and Anchises. The spring festivals of Adonis and

The Louvre's famous *Venus de Milo (left)* in fact depicts the Greek goddess Aphrodite, wife of the divine blacksmith Hephaestus *(above).*

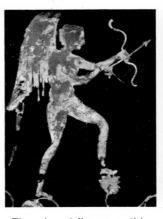

The winged figure on this Greek vase *(above)* is Eros, son of Aphrodite and god of sensual desire, armed with his traditional bow and arrow. When Venus is shown with the god Priapus *(above right)*, the emphasis is on procreative power, fertility, and passion.

the Roman *pervigilia Veneris* were dedicated to her. As symbols of love, beauty, and sensual desire, Aphrodite/Venus, Adonis, and Eros/Cupid have had a profound influence on the art and civilization of the whole Western world.

The birth of Cupid is depicted in this French painting *(above)* with an almost baroque extravagance of form. Venus, whom the Romans identified with Aphrodite, is the mother. An earlier, Renaissance work by Lucas Cranach *(opposite)* shows Cupid with a virginal Venus.

The Greek clay relief *(right)* shows Hermes climbing into Aphrodite's chariot, which is being drawn by Eros and Psyche.

In this Pompeian fresco *(below)* we see Mars, the Roman god of war (the Greek Ares), keeping a secret assignment with the goddess of love.

Poseidon *(below right)* enjoyed numerous fruitful affairs, including one with Aphrodite, both before and after he married the beautiful Amphitrite and became lord of the sea.

Aphrodite's liaison with Adonis *(above)* gave rise to the Greek nature festivals celebrated in his name.

Virgil traced the descent of the Romans to Aeneas, shown here *(above right)* with his parents Aphrodite and the Trojan prince Anchises.

This Greek sculpture *(right)* shows Aphrodite and her child Eros with Pan, the forest god.

187

burned at all. Thus, miraculously enough, the truth of her oath was verified.

As Gottfried von Strassburg put the case: "Christ in his great virtue is pliant as a windblown sleeve. He falls into place and clings, whichever way you try Him, closely and smoothly, as He is bound to do. He is at the beck of every heart for honest deeds or fraud. Be it deadly earnest or a game, He is just as you would have Him. This was amply revealed in the facile queen."

The lovers' final parting, and their last reconciliation in death, make up the sorrowful burden of the tale. Yet all the same Sir Gottfried's account insists upon the sweetness of love, as something greater than death itself.

Tristram and Iseult, so often parted in life, were buried together. According to the legend a tree sprouted from their common grave; whenever it was cut back, it sprouted miraculously again on the following morning, keeping in its branches and its shade their memory, forever green.

LOVE'S ARROWS

The Chinese tell of a lying lady who had worse luck than Iseult at the beginning, but better luck at the end. In the year 965, by Western reckoning, the last Prince of Shu fell before the conquering Sung. The prince's favorite concubine, Lady Fei, thereupon found herself reduced to a mere item of war booty. Inwardly unwilling, outwardly compliant, she joined the new emperor's retinue. With her she brought the portrait of a man. It was apparent that she treasured, even worshiped, this portrait. The emperor found himself growing jealous of it. Whom, he demanded, did the picture represent?

Lady Fei would not say at first. In point of fact it was the slain Prince of Shu, standing with bow in hand, whom she loved still. The emperor persisted in questioning her about it, finally forcing Lady Fei to find refuge in an untruth.

"It is a picture of the Purveyor of Children, Chang Hsien, who shoots at the Dog Star with his bow. In my country, all women who desire children worship this god. He makes us fruitful, you see. And, since I am especially desirous of bearing a prince of the imperial House of Sung in my womb, I presume to keep this picture ever by me, even in your august presence."

The emperor was much impressed. That night he dreamed that the man in the picture came to him and spoke: "The Dog Star devours many children before they are born. Only I, with my arrows, can keep him

at bay. Therefore, have copies made of the portrait in Lady Fei's possession. Let those copies be put on permanent display in temples throughout China!"

The emperor obeyed the dream command. Thus it was that Chang Hsien, the Prince of Shu, achieved high honor in Chinese religion.

MAMADI SEFE DEKOTE

The Soninke tribe of the Sudan has a legend about a serpent who served a city. The monster, whose name was Bida, caused a rain of gold to fall in the streets of the Soninke capital three times each year. In return, the people periodically fed a lovely virgin to Bida.

Mamadi Sefe Dekote, He Who Speaks Little, once lay with an excessively beautiful virgin named Sia Jatta Bari. The hero had given her a quantity of gold to induce her to come to him. However, she would not make love. She explained that she was destined for Bida. In the morning, Bida would take her. "You and I have been friends," she added consolingly, "but no friendship lasts forever."

Mamadi Sefe Dekote was furious. He sent Sia away. At dawn he sharpened his sword. He tested the sharpness of the blade by splitting a single grain of barley in midair. Mamadi Sefe Dekote went to the deep well on the east side of the city. Sia was there in her wedding dress, patiently waiting.

Bida's enormous head slowly rose over the rim of the well. The serpent eyed Sia. Then he withdrew his head. The people cried to Sia and to Mamadi Sefe Dekote: "Make your farewells. Part quickly. It is time!"

Again Bida reared his head up out of the well. His great jaws gaped redly. He looked at Mamadi Sefe Dekote and again withdrew into the bowels of the earth. Again the people cried out that Sia and her friend must part.

A third and final time, Bida's head emerged. He kept coming, rising, swaying over the crowd. Now he looped his glistening neck and swooped his great head down toward Sia. Mamadi Sefe Dekote was ready, however. He swung his sword upward, once, and sliced off Bida's head. The head fell with a crash, to roll bounding down the street. It stood upon its stump at the corner and opened its jaws. Its fiery forked tongue was vibrating.

"For seven years, seven months, and seven days, may you be without golden rain." Bida's head pronounced that curse. Then it toppled over and lay still in the dust of the street. Bida's body, meanwhile, slipped

Daphne, shy and beautiful daughter of the river god Peneius, fled before Apollo's advances. When she cried out for help, she was turned into a laurel tree (Greek: *daphne*).

In a key incident from the Indian *Ramayana* epic the beautiful Sita is abducted by the evil Ravana *(left)*. A thirteenth-century English tile *(right)* shows King Mark with his young nephew Tristram, whose tragic love for Queen Iseult has inspired many an artist (myth, page 186).

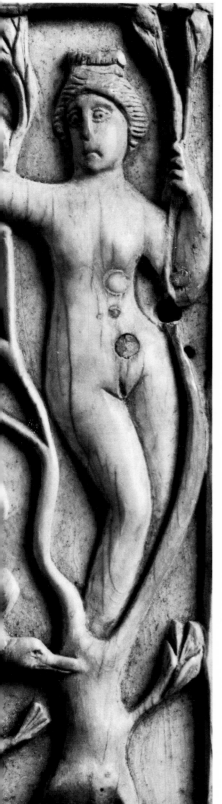

TRAGIC LOVE

The whole gamut of emotions experienced in the context of earthly love is reflected at the level of myth in the many legends and sàgas in which love figures as the driving force. It is especially the theme of tragic, unrequited love that lies at the core of some of the most beautiful myths, a classic example from ancient Greece being the story of Phaedra. In her anger at being rejected by the unyielding Hippolytus she accused him before her husband Theseus of having tried to seduce her. Theseus had Hippolytus killed through the agency of his mighty father, Poseidon, and Phaedra hanged herself. The same motif appears in the earlier myth of Bellerophon and Antaia, and in the Old Testament story of Joseph and Potiphar's wife. Often virtue's only refuge is transformation, as when Daphne was turned into a laurel tree to escape the advances of Apollo, or the nymphs Pitys and Syrinx into a pine tree and a reed, respectively, to protect them from the lustful Pan. Some of the most moving stories are those of the "Romeo and Juliet" pattern, in which the lovers find each other but are prevented by adverse circumstances from coming together. The best-known medieval example of forbidden love is the originally Celtic saga of Tristram and Iseult (or Tristan and Isolde) immortalized in Thomas Malory's famous collection, *Le Morte d'Arthur* (myth, page 186). Another popular theme is the kidnapping of the loved one and her eventual rescue and liberation, as exemplified by the Indian epic of Rama and his beautiful wife Sita, who was abducted by the demon Ravana (page 234).

The suspicious King Mark eavesdrops on Tristram and Iseult, but the lovers, having spotted his reflection in the pond, confine themselves to innocent subjects – no difficult matter for them since according to one version Tristram occupied the position of tutor at King Mark's court.

189

away backwards down the well. The people were terribly distressed. They wished to kill Mamadi Sefe Dekote.

Mamadi was too quick for them. Already he had leaped astride his horse and pulled Sia up with him. His steed was the fastest in the city. Mamadi and Sia got clean away to another town. The hero knew, however, that he was in disgrace. He had destroyed the chief blessing of his people. He had interfered with a holy sacrifice, bloodily indeed. Now he was poor. He had no more gold for Sia. Moreover, she still remained aloof. No longer would she come to him, under any conditions. "I have a headache," she explained one day. "Perhaps if you were to cut off one of your toes with that sharp sword of yours, I might rub my brow with the toe and thus relieve my pain."

Mamadi, without a word, cut off one of his toes and presented it to her. The next day, though, she seemed no better. She thought that perhaps one of his fingers might contain the proper medicine. So he cut off a finger and gave that to her.

The third morning it appeared that Sia's headache was gone. But still she had no wish even to meet with Mamadi. She sent him a message to explain the new situation. "I do not love people with nine fingers and nine toes," the message said. "Why should I give myself to such as you?"

Mamadi gave a witch the last of his money. In return the witch prepared a love potion and mixed it with a hair oil. This she brought to Sia's house. Pretending to be a hairdresser, she offered to demonstrate her work. Sia agreed. But no sooner had one side of her head been rubbed than Sia jumped up and said, "Mamadi is calling me!" She ran away to Mamadi.

"I did not call you," said Mamadi. "I understand that you cannot love any man who has only nine fingers and nine toes." Sia therefore went back to the hairdresser witch, who rubbed in a little more oil. Again Sia felt she had been called by Mamadi. Again she ran to see him, and again he rebuffed her. She returned to the witch and sat trembling under the old woman's fingers until her coiffure was complete. Then she jumped up and went to Mamadi a third time. "Haven't you been calling me?" she pleaded. "I hear your voice and nothing but your voice inside my head."

"Yes, I called you," Mamadi said. "I wanted to tell you to come to me tonight." Sia looked at him, her eyes wet. "Tonight," she promised, "I shall come to our marriage."

Mamadi went to his house to get things ready. When the bed was prepared, he called in a slave named Blali. The slave understood that he would have to obey orders precisely or else die.

After dark, Sia came to Mamadi's house. She crept into his bedroom. She saw his shoes beside the bed. She got in under the blankets. "Friend," she whispered, "I know that you are not called Mamadi Sefe Dekote for nothing. You are truly a man of few words. Yet speak to me now, I beg of you." Her lover made no reply, except to take Sia in his arms. They embraced passionately, in every way, hour after hour, until dawn began to lighten the room. Then Mamadi strode in at the door.

"Blali," he shouted angrily, throwing open the shutters, "why have you not yet groomed my horse today?"

"Master," Blali replied from the bed, "please forgive me for being late. I have been busy with this woman here."

Sia sat up. She looked at Blali. She looked at Mamadi. In the gray light, her bruised breasts shook. She stood up. Her knees were trembling. She walked slowly to the door. Turning, she said to Mamadi, "You pay back well." Then she went home, and it was not long before Sia died of her shame.

NO RESCUE

Orpheus was the sweetest singer and most accomplished musician the world had ever seen. His lyre, said the ancient Greeks, was presented to Orpheus by Apollo himself. When he played and sang, wild animals gathered around and even the trees swayed in harmony.

When his bride, Eurydice, was bitten by an adder and went down to the land of the dead, Orpheus could not be consoled. Taking his lyre, he followed her spirit.

He came before the king and queen of the Shadowy Realm, Hades and Persephone. Orpheus begged them to restore his wife to him and to the sweet sunshine. Charmed by his music, they agreed, but on one condition. They commanded Orpheus to lead the way back to the world and never once turn round to see whether his wife was following him.

He succeeded in that until the very last moment. As Orpheus was about to step up onto earth again, he did glance anxiously back over his shoulder. Yes, his wife was still behind him, but only for a moment longer. Pale with horror, he watched her fade back into eternal darkness.

There was a North American Indian Orpheus, a brave of the Californian Tokumni Yokuts tribe. When his wife died and was buried, the brave appeared utterly stunned.

Through the mute silence they made their way
        till they had almost
    reached the surface of the earth.
Here, anxious in case his wife's strength be fa[...]
        and eager to see her,
the lover looked behind him, and straightwa[...]
    Eurydice slipped back into the depths.

OVID METAMORPHOSES, BOOK X, 53-57
Translated by Mary M. Innes (1955)

Her face half hidden by a veil *(above)*, the beautiful Eurydice sets out with Orpheus on the journey back from the underworld. The underworld was ruled by Persephone and Hades, depicted inside this Greek cup *(above opposite)*.

The divine Orpheus charmed the animals and even the trees, with the magic of his lyre playing *(above)*. Titian's painting *(opposite)* captures the moment when Orpheus looks back at his beloved, who fades before his eyes.

190

Orpheus has become immortal through his divine music and his love of the beautiful nymph Eurydice. Eurydice dies of a snakebite and is taken down to the underworld. Singing so movingly that even the animals share his grief, Orpheus too comes to the underworld. Here Persephone, the goddess of death, gives Eurydice back to him on condition that he not look round at her until they reach the day. But Orpheus, unable to resist the temptation, does look back and so loses her forever.

ORPHEUS AND EURYDICE

Flinging his body down upon the grave, he refused to stir from that spot. On the second night his wife arose in spirit from the grave. She drifted slowly west; he followed.

They reached a dark gorge filled with the thunder of a river in flood. A narrow rope bridge was the only way across. A gigantic raven perched on the middle of the bridge, croaking with bloody beak. The brave made sure to go carefully in the footprints of his wife's spirit; thus he safely crossed the bridge. He entered Spiritland. The chief of that place was astonished and rather pleased to see a living person. A feast was placed before the brave. The cups and dishes filled up of their own accord. The brave's spirit wife was summoned.

The chief said, "You two go and lie together in one bed. But do not sleep!" The flesh was weak. Toward dawn, the brave fell asleep. He woke up clasping a maggoty green log. The following night the chief said, "Try once more!" Again, however, the brave fell asleep. Again he awakened embracing a rotten log.

Sorrowfully, the chief handed a few sunflower seeds to the brave. "Chew these!" he commanded. The brave did so and found himself at home again, by his wife's grave. The brave called his tribe to a feast. He told where he had been and what he had done. Next day, the brave died of snakebite.

THE BEE BRIDE

Human passions are often not so different from those of animals. For that matter animal sympathies may have something human about them, at least in the mythic realm. Myth, in fact, records many passionate although uneasy partnerships between lovers of different species.

In Borneo there was a man named Rakian. He belonged to the Dusun people. Rakian used to gather the nests of wild bees. At the top of a tall tree one day, he found a nest of a sort that he had never seen before. The bees which buzzed around it were pure white. He took his knife out of his sash and began hacking roughly at the branch from which the nest was suspended. A cry of pain came from inside the nest. Rakian, much surprised, put his knife away again and very gently set to work detaching the nest from the branch. He put it carefully in his basket and brought it home. There he put the nest, still in the basket, above his bed. The bees made no objection.

In the morning Rakian went out to work in his rice field. He returned at dusk to find that rice and fish had been cooked for him. He could not imagine who had prepared the

191

dinner, since he lived alone. Gratefully, he ate and then went to bed. The next day, and the next, the same thing happened. On the fourth day Rakian only pretended to go to work. He circled back and hid behind a tree, watching the house. After a while a beautiful woman appeared from his door, carrying a jug. She went off in the direction of the river to get water for cooking. Rakian rushed into the house and looked at the nest over his bed. The nest was intact, but there were no bees in it.

Quickly, he concealed the nest in the rafters. Then he hid himself under some clothes. The woman returned. She saw that the nest was gone. "Someone," she cried out in consternation, "has taken my sarong! It cannot be Rakian, for he is away in the fields. I am afraid that he will return soon and find me."

Rakian came out of his hiding place. "Why are you here?" he asked the woman. "Perhaps you want to steal my bees." The woman would not speak to him. "Well," Rakian told her, "since you are here, perhaps you will be good enough to cook my dinner." The woman refused to do any such thing. After a strained silence, she burst out at him. "Where is my sarong? All my clothes and goods are in it. I believe you have hidden it on purpose." Rakian admitted that was true. "I am afraid to give it back to you," he said, "because if I do, you will get into it again." The woman shook her head. Shyly, for the first time, she smiled at him. "No, I will not," she said. "My mother has given me to you because I have no husband among my own people and because you have no wife here where you are."

Without a word, Rakian got up and brought the bees' nest down from its hiding place in the rafters. He gave it to the woman. She held it in her lap. Looking over the top of the nest into his eyes, she pledged herself to him. "But never tell your friends," she warned, "that your wife is a bee woman." Rakian promised that he never would.

He kept the secret for more than a year. Meanwhile, the bee woman bore a beautiful child. At the celebrations following the child's birth, however, Rakian got drunk and gave away the bee woman's secret. His friends were shocked to learn the truth. The bee woman herself was terribly ashamed. Taking the shape of a white bee, she flew away. Rakian, with their child in his arms, stumbled off after her.

At the end of a week he came to a longhouse on a riverbank. He entered the house. Bees clustered thick about the roof beams. Rakian was terrified that they might swarm down upon him and the child in his arms. Still he stepped forward, from room to room. There were twelve rooms in the house. Before they reached the middle of it Rakian's child began to cry. "Have you no pity on our child?" Rakian called out. A sound was heard from somewhere above, and his wife appeared. The bees dropped from the rafters in the form of people. Rakian became a member of the bee tribe. His own tribe never saw him again.

FORBIDDEN MARRIAGES

Otherworldly wives do not always work out well, as this gently ironic tale from Nigeria attests. King Effion of Duke Town, Calabar, amassed an enormous amount of wealth from the slave trade. Thus he was able to buy as many wives as he wished, and he had dozens. But, as so often happens, the surfeit of wives in King Effion's life conspicuously failed to satisfy the restlessness of his heart. In old age he fell desperately in love with a girl of a sort he had not known before. She was the daughter of a poor rooster.

The king, who by now had become used to having everything his own way, summoned the cock to court and offered the bird six puncheons of palm oil as a bride price, and the bargain was struck. The virgin daughter – light of foot, laughter-loving, and quick – went to live with the king. His other wives were cast into the shade by her.

To celebrate his good fortune and introduce his young favorite to the people, King Effion held a feast of foo-foo, palm-oil chop, and *tombo* wine. The feast began early in the morning, when the king's throne was brought out from his audience hall and set in the open space of the royal compound. The king sat down, with the cock's daughter close by at his right hand. The people squatted in a circle before them. There were hundreds present; it was a solemn and happy moment. Everyone felt hungry, but in the best way, knowing that they would be wining and dining all day long. The good things were about to be brought on. But first, a maidservant came with a small dish of corn and scattered that upon the bare ground at the king's feet. She had been instructed to perform this odd action by the king's jealous wives.

The rooster's daughter, seeing the corn spread out before her, immediately got down on her hands and knees and began pecking it up. Of course, the other wives had hoped that she would behave so, but the guests present at the feast did not take kindly to it; and King Effion was mortified. The feast was canceled; so was the marriage. The cock's daughter was sent to her father's house in disgrace.

Broken-hearted, King Effion ordained that men should never again take bird or animal brides. He expired soon afterwards.

The Calabar people also tell of a beautiful but vain girl named Afiong Edem. Against the wishes of her parents she married a stranger simply because she thought him handsome enough to match her own good looks.

After the wedding they set off for the stranger's country. No sooner had they crossed the frontier than friends of the groom greeted and rapidly dismantled him. It seemed that he had borrowed the feet and legs of one man, the hands and arms of another, the torso and face of a third, and so on, in order to go a-wooing into the girl's country. Now he was reduced to nothing but a skull, and yet Afiong Edem had to honor and obey him. She would never have escaped at all but for the kindness of the old crone who was the skull's mother. The mother called upon a beneficent spider to dress Afiong's hair in a particular way, and then upon a soft breeze to waft her home again to the land of the living.

The Calabar people were surprised and pleased to find Afiong in their midst again. But when he had heard her story, the chief of the tribe decreed that in future no one should marry a stranger.

If certain myths cast a cold and bitter light upon the mysteries of the heart, others touch the same shadowy realm with glory. The following Maori legend concerns a true, gentle heroine.

Hine-Moa was the most beautiful of all Maori princesses. She had good reason to be proud, yet she was not. In secret she loved a commoner named Tutanekai. She loved him for his music, his ease, his youth, his modesty. Tutanekai had built a small pavilion on a hill across a wide lake from the residence of Hine-Moa's family. On full-moon nights he used to sit there, playing a kind of horn with a low, slow carrying sound. A youth named Tiki, who was his closest friend, sat with him. Tiki played a flute, the high lilting music of which harmonized well with the deep, urgent horn. Their music used to drift softly across the lake, sweetly confused and dimmed on the south wind. Hine-Moa strained to hear it. Her whole body would listen.

Tutanekai sent her a message begging her to come to him. She replied that she would, and gladly too. Tutanekai, filled with joy, told his father of this. "Impossible," his father said, laughing. Tutanekai's brothers mocked him for supposing that a princess would ever consent to come to him. The

THE WHITE COW

This Pompeian mural shows Daedalus (in the foreground) with the white cow he made out of wood for Pasiphae, daughter of Helios and wife of King Minos of Crete. Pasiphae and her daughters Ariadne and Phaedra in Greek mythology are figures of tragic love, embodying all the confusion, despair, and madness of that emotion. Pasiphae was originally a moon goddess, represented standing beneath a white cow. The story of her un-natural passion for the white bull of King Minos was a later development. Driven by that passion, she is said to have asked the inventor Daedalus to make her a white cow in which she could crouch and receive the deluded animal. The ruse was successful, but its fruit was the Minotaur, a monster with a human body and the head of a bull who henceforth demanded a yearly quota of sacrificial victims. The Minotaur was kept in the labyrinth beneath Minos's palace at Knossos – until Theseus arrived from Athens and with the help of Ariadne, who had fallen in love with him, managed to kill the monster and escape from the labyrinth.

youth blushed with shame. Yet still, in the cool of the night, he would mount his pavilion with Tiki and send yearning music out over the lake.

Meanwhile, the princess' friends began to suspect that she loved Tutanekai. They were glad that the lake separated the two. They kept a close watch on the canoes to prevent Hine-Moa from paddling across to her lover.

One calm night, Hine-Moa felt the music drawing her unbearably from afar. She resolved to go to Tutanekai. Since there was no canoe for her, she strung together six dry hollow gourds of the sort used for floating nets. She swam with these to buoy her up, three on each side. Yet even with their help Hine-Moa was risking her life. The lake, dappled with moonlight, appeared an endless path in the darkness. When exhausted, she would cling to the few rocks or stumps of trees which rose above the rippling surface. When there were no such things as these to cling to, she would turn upon her back and drift for a while, floating, half asleep.

The music drew her still. Gathering what was left of her strength, she would turn over once again and swim on, pulling herself along with her cupped hands. She felt as if she were trying to climb a tower of black glass. Now the moonlight's reflections were dazzling her eyes. She was in tears, thinking that she might die and never reach Tutanekai. It seemed that she could do no more. She sank; her feet touched bottom; she was very nearly there. Struggling on, she came to a narrow shore of rock. Just beyond it lay the hot spring which is called Waikimihia. She slipped over the ledge into the spring. Slowly, the bubbling waters of the spring warmed her again and calmed the thumping of her heart. Not far from where she lay in the soothing warmth of the spring, Tutanekai and Tiki were still playing their music.

The two young men became thirsty. Tutanekai sent a slave down to the lake to fill a calabash with cold water. The slave dipped his calabash from the ledge between the lake and the spring. He did not see Hine-Moa, who concealed herself in the shadows of the rock. Disguising her voice to sound like that of a man, she gruffly called out to the slave. She asked for whom he was getting water. Startled, the slave replied, "For Tutanekai." Hine-Moa ordered him to bring it to her instead. Wonderingly, the slave did so. Hine-Moa drank her fill and then deliberately shattered the calabash against a rock.

The slave, much distressed, went back to report this occurrence to his master. The slave was sent with another calabash back to the lake to fetch water. But that also Hine-Moa broke. The same thing happened a third time.

Tutanekai told the poor slave to go home to bed. Then he set down his instrument and picked up his war club. Angrily, and yet filled with foreboding too, he strode down to the water's edge. Who was the rude person in the spring? Raising his club, he peered down into the steaming water. He could see no one there. Hine-Moa, overcome by modesty, had hidden herself under an overhanging rock.

Tutanekai felt slowly along the edge of the spring with his free hand. He held his war club in readiness to strike. His hand touched the hand of another. The hand was small, smooth, soft, and wet. A startled cry arose from underneath. "Come out!" Tutanekai shouted.

The legend says that Hine-Moa rose up out of the water as bare and beautiful as a wild white hawk, that she stood upon the rock as poised as the shy white crane, and that Tutanekai took her then and there up to his house, in secret.

In the morning, when the villagers came out to cook there breakfasts, it was noticed that Tutanekai stayed inside. His foster-father, Whakaue, sent someone to awaken Tutanekai. At the foot of the bed he saw four feet where he had expected to find two; so back he went to Whakaue, to report. "Tutanekai has someone with him." "Go back and find out who it is," Whakaue replied. So back to the house the messenger went and this time recognized Hine-Moa. "It's Hine-Moa, it's Hine-Moa!" he cried. The villagers found this hard to believe. Tutanekai's half-brothers, who were very jealous indeed, scoffed and scowled.

But everyone felt awed, soon afterward, when the young couple themselves stepped into the level light of the rising sun. They were shining with happiness and grace.

FATHER OF GODS AND MEN

When the Greek god Zeus was a child, the infant lay hidden in a willow tree and received nourishment from wild things of the forest. Bees brought him honey, and a Pan-like goat girl gave him suck. The waving green foliage of the willow so shielded him that, as it was said, he scholiast Hyginus remarked, "he could not be found on land, or sea, or in the air either.

"Ancient mythologems of child-gods are surrounded by, and evoke, an aura of fairy-tale." So stated the mythologist Karl Kerényi in *Essays on a Science of Mythol-*

The frequent motif of miraculous conception and birth may represent an attempt to answer the question of how the first egg came to be fertilized. In some myths miraculous circumstances are attributed to the conception of the original Creator. But quite as often it is the spiritual leaders of mankind who are imagined to have been conceived and born in a supernatural way (myths, page 184). The large pillar medallion on the left, from Bharhut, India, shows Queen Maya's miraculous con-

ception of the Buddha. Queen Maya had a dream about a white elephant that descended on her like a cloud of fertility and wisdom. It walked round her three times before touching her between the legs and entering her womb. In this myth the coming of the Buddha, who was to redeem men from ignorance, is seen as a miraculous event accompanied by a whole panoply of supernatural phenomena. Above we see the angel Gabriel as he appears before the Virgin Mary in Roger van der Weyden's painting *The Annunciation*. "The Holy Ghost shall come upon thee, and . . . that holy thing which shall be born of thee shall be called the Son of God." (Luke 1:35)

ogy (1949). "The nursing of the child by divinities or wild things in the myth of Zeus," he continued, "shows us two things: the *solitariness* of the child-god, and the fact that he is nevertheless *at home* in the primeval world."

But solitude was hardly the way of Zeus. He grew up to beget a pantheon in heaven and a heroic hall of fame on earth. Early saints of the Christian church were scandalized by Zeus's lusty behaviour. Not only did he seduce his own sister, his mother, and his daughter, but Zeus also pursued, they calculated, no less than seventeen consecutive generations of mortal women. He conducted his amours, often enough, in disguise. Zeus had been a thrush at Hera's breast, a swimming bull between Europa's knees, a shower of gold falling slantwise across Danaë, a swan beating Leda down, and even a golden serpent which coiled around Alexander the Great's mother.

Zeus married twice, and his affairs made Hera – his second wife – insanely jealous. The first wife of Zeus is seldom mentioned. She was his sister Metis, the original Greek goddess of wisdom. Her child was destined to be greater than Zeus himself, providing it appeared in the usual way. Zeus had reason to believe and fear that prophecy. He had exiled his own father Cronus to Tartarus. Cronus as well had castrated his father Uranus. Zeus had no wish to be treated so. He watched Metis slowly swelling, growing bigger every day, and the sight appalled him. In the darkness of the belly of Metis lay curled a mystery, male or female, destined to overcome him.

So Zeus suggested a contest to see which of them could take the tiniest shape. Metis agreed to make the first try; she turned herself into a fly. Immediately, Zeus snatched her out of the air, popped her into his mouth, and swallowed her. That was the end of Metis as a personage with a will of her own. Her immortal wisdom, however, continued to live. Zeus had that inside his own belly now, thanks to trickery and speed of hand. Contemplatively, at leisure, the god proceeded to digest his erstwhile wife and sister.

Later, Zeus paid for his trick. He developed a frightful headache. Clashing sounds inside his cranium drove him to the point of madness. At last he called upon his son, the blacksmith Hephaestus, to perform an emergency operation. Obediently, Hephaestus drove a flint wedge into the skull of Zeus. Out sprang the daughter of Metis, fully armed and spear in hand. But the new goddess of wisdom had not come to birth in the usual way, and so Zeus had nothing to fear from her. Athene was destined to support her father in all things, never to betray him. Her birth from the cranium of Zeus may be said to signify a whole new spiral of human consciousness. Conception – no longer in the generative sense of the word but as an intellectual activity in its own right – was to become the dominant aspect of Greek culture.

PARVATI'S CHILDREN

Hindu mythology mingles romantic with ascetic elements in astonishing ways. Sometimes erotic, sometimes comic, it is always highly serious as well. An example concerns the god Shiva, who used to practice austerities in the high Himalayas. Once when he was meditating, his wife, the mountain goddess Parvati, crept up behind him. She put her hands over his eyes and challenged him to guess who she was. Would the god recognize his own true bride or not under such circumstances?

The sun went pale, the mountains shook the snow from their shoulders, and the animals concealed themselves. All nature was terrified. This unexpected darkness and fear upon the earth prevailed for only a moment. A third eye opened in the brow of Shiva, just above Parvati's coolly enfolding hands. Its light restored all the former glory of the world.

The Shiva Purana relates that once when Parvati was in her bath, her divine husband entered unexpectedly. This offended Parvati's modesty. When he had gone again, the goddess rubbed a bit of scurf from her skin. It was the baby Ganapati, her firstborn son. She set the child to guard her door against further intrusions. Shiva thought that unfair. The god unleashed various forces of destruction which blasted the boy's head. Parvati wept; her son was slain, she thought. Her sorrow quenched the flames of Shiva's rage. He slashed off the head of an elephant and set that on the child's shoulders. Ganapati lived again. The boy now possessed an elephant's head on top of his rotund, babyish body, an incongruous sight.

That is one story of what happened. A cooler account, given in the Brahma-Vaivarta Purana, maintains it was the gaze of the planet Saturn which destroyed the head Ganapati had a birth. Saturn represents negative aspects of destiny, not only in Western astrology, but also in that of the Hindus. The planet had not offered to shine upon the newborn, for fear of hurting him. Parvati herself, according to this myth, had insisted upon Saturn's doing so. She did not wish her boy to miss adversity.

The Ganapati Upanishad describes the child-god in the following way:

He has one tusk and four arms. . .
A mouse is seen on his flag.
Red, obese, he has ears like winnowing
*   baskets.*
He is dressed in red; his limbs are painted
*   with red sandal paste.*
He is worshipped with red flowers. . .

Why one tusk? The story goes that Ganapati had a sweet tooth; he just loved honey cakes. One day when he had consumed far too many of these temple offerings, Ganapati went out riding on his favorite mount, a gigantic mouse. Frightened by a serpent in the path, the mouse reared. Ganapati fell heavily to the ground. His distended belly split; the cakes spilled out. Crossly, he gathered them up again, replaced them in his

The Christ child appears as a blaze of light inside his mother's womb *(below)*. Mary, the bearer of this miracle, is pictured sitting at her distaff, winding thread for the purple cloth of the temple – an occupation attributed to her by the Apocryphal Gospels.

When Queen Maya *(right)* gave birth to the Buddha in a grove of sal trees near Kapilavastu, she was in a standing position. Her arms grasped the branches of a tree as the Buddha miraculously emerged out of her side. The appearance of supernatural signs confirmed that this was no ordinary birth.

196

The pictures on these two pages all depict the arrival of a god – and consequently the start of a new era – in the form of a birth, but a wondrous one clearly distinguished from the ordinary human process. The extraordinary character of the birth of a divinity may be reflected in miracles for example, or in signs that appear in the sky (e.g., the star over Bethlehem). Two of the pictures here show gods being born from the World Egg, a familiar concept in the great cosmogonic and theogonic myths. The egg-shaped cosmos is particularly clear in a Persian sculpture of the birth of Mithras, where the motif is repeated in the two halves of the burst

Surrounded by the signs of the zodiac, the Greek god Phanes emerges from the cosmic egg.

shell from which the god is emerging *(right)*. But what chiefly preoccupied mythic man was the phenomenon of conception, which for a long time he believed was brought about by the moon, by dew, or by clouds. Not only gods but also the great teachers and saviors of mankind enjoyed or will enjoy mysterious nativities. Saoshyans, the last redeemer heralded by Zoroaster, will be born of a virgin. The Buddha's birth was marked by the appearance of the thirty-two tokens of the Perfect One, and another Indian legend tells how the Tantric Padmasambhava came into being as a radiant child floating on a lotus flower in the lake.

The infant Krishna, like the Buddha, emerged from his mother's side *(above)*.

Another birth from the World Egg was that of Mithras, the ancient-Persian god of sunlight and fertility.
Here too the egg is framed by the signs of the zodiac.

This Greek relief *(above)* depicts the birth of Dionysus. His mother was Semele but he was born from the thigh of Zeus. The third figure is Hermes, to whom Zeus entrusted the child.

The subject of this Greek vase painting *(above right)* is the birth of Athene, the goddess of wisdom and of war, from the head of Zeus (myth, page 195). After swallowing his first wife Metis in the early months of her pregnancy, Zeus began to suffer from violent headaches. Hephaestus split the god's skull open with his ax and out sprang Athene, "fully armed, with a mighty shout."

Extraordinary births or supernatural circumstances accompanying births are a feature of the myths of all peoples. In Greek mythology Dionysus emerged from Zeus's thigh, Athene from his head (myth, page 195). Births of gods from the heads of other gods also occur in India. They symbolize projections of mental and spiritual qualities; Athene, for instance, was born after Zeus had eaten her mother Metis, goddess of prudence. In many cases it is the accompanying symbolism that is important. Certain Australian aborigines believe that the first man sprang from a mimosa, and other plants too figure in myth as "mothers." But the most common procrea-

tion symbol, particularly in Indian myth, is the tree. The Buddha's birth was associated with a tree and had its prototype in the *yakshinis,* tree nymphs who were traditionally associated with fertility. Buddhist myth is also rich in symbols of spiritual procreation and birth, with the Bodhisattva Avalokitesvara being created from a ray of light and his consort Tara from one of this tears. Related to the miraculous birth is the theme of the abandoned infant who evinces exceptional qualities. Romulus and Remus and also Zeus, Poseidon, Dionysus, and Moses, all abandoned at birth, went on to do great things.

Another Greek myth describes the miraculous birth of the beautiful Adonis, god of vegetation. He was the son of King Kinyras and his daughter Smyrna who, a prey to incestuous passion, contrived by a ruse to share her father's bed. When the king discov-ered the crime and went after her the gods, hearing her prayers, turned her into a myrrh tree, from the trunk of which Adonis was born nine months later. The tree is one of the most powerful symbols of ever-recurring fertility.

The same concept occurs in Mixtec myth, where the first couple emerged from a split tree trunk *(above right).*

The Persian hermaphrodite god Zervan *(above)* bore Ormazd, the god of light, and the demon Ariman.

The gentle redeemer goddess Tara *(above middle)* is an emanation of the compassionate Avalokitesvara, from whose tears she is believed to have sprung.

Tezcatlipoca *(above)* one of the Aztecs' most feared deities, was born of the sun.

Depicted on this frieze *(left)* in four scenes is the myth of Romulus and Remus, the traditional founders of the city of Rome. They were the twin sons of Mars, god of war, and Sylvia, the daughter of ex-king Numitor, who had been ousted from the throne by his brother Amulius. Amulius, as part of his policy of wiping out his brother's line, had the boys thrown into the Tiber. This was in flood at the time and they were washed up on land. A she-wolf found the boys and took them to her den to suckle them. There they were discovered by Faustulus, one of the king's shepherds; he took them home to his wife, who gave them the names Romulus and Remus and brought them up. Eventually the boys managed to kill the usurper Amulius and to restore Numitor to the throne. It was from him that they received the privilege of founding a city on the spot where they had been found.

belly, and closed the wound. To keep things in place properly, he employed the luckless serpent as a belt. As he was knotting the serpent about himself, the moon and stars giggled. Ganapati, furious, pulled out one of his own tusks and hurled it up at the moon.

Why did the god ride a mouse? The Sanskrit word *musa,* for "mouse," comes from the root *mus,* which means "to steal." The mouse steals what people enjoy, not caring whether its loot be good or evil. In this way it resembles the inexplicable and unknowable element in each of us which inhabits the hole called "intellect." A secret mental force creeps out unnoticed from ourselves to ingest the essence of our own experience. That mouselike thing, according to learned commentators, is really none other than the divine aspect of each human being.

Again, why do Ganapati's ears resemble winnowing baskets? This is because the god winnows the words which devotees address to him. He throws away the dust of their vice and the chaff of their virtue. Only the true grain of experience will he accept.

Ganapati obviously stands for a reconciliation of opposites. His elephant head, for example, is said to represent the macrocosm or cosmos as a whole, while his baby body stands for the microcosm as represented by humankind. He has a great many names, for example, Ganesha, Vighnesvara, Gajanana, and Gajadhipa. In Japan he is called Binayaka and is worshiped in a highly esoteric way. There, he is represented coupling with a goddess.

Japanese sculptures of this subject must not be more than seven inches high. They are carefully hidden away from public scrutiny. Together, Binayaka and his paramour are called by a single name – Shoten – and are taken to represent the realization of enlightenment. Actors, gamblers, geishas, pimps, and prostitutes pay special reverence to Shoten, it appears. This may seem a strange final development for a god who was conceived from an impulse of modesty and whose first mission was to protect his mother from intrusions by her own husband. It demonstrates the extremes of metamorphoses which gods may undergo as they pass from culture to culture.

Shiva and Parvati had a second son, and his conception too was most unusual. Shiva was in the mountains, practicing austerities. His consort understood that the world was endangered. Demons were getting the upper hand. Only a warrior son of Shiva's own could turn the tide of battle in favor of the divine family. Parvati therefore presented herself to her husband. She tried desperately to attract his attention and arouse his lust. But he was so deep in meditation that for a very long time he failed to notice her. Then something happened; at this point in the story the texts are perhaps deliberately obscure. All we can say for sure is that the seed of Shiva never entered Parvati's womb.

It fell first into the mouth of Agni, the fire god. From there the seed descended somehow to the Ganges, sacred river of India. The Ganges nurtured it for a while and then swept it into a place called the Forest of Arrows. In that forest the seed became a divine youth. Like Athene, the virgin warrior goddess of the Greeks, this second offspring of Parvati and Shiva was both chaste and fierce. To prove his power, he thrust a lance into the ground and challenged the strongest of the gods to pull it out again.

When they tried, the forests and the distant mountains shook. But only he could remove it.

The divine youth was called Skanda (or Karttikeya). He has seven heads and twelve arms, and he is said to have been nourished by the Pleiades, whose seven stars gave milk to his seven mouths. His twelve hands hold a bow and arrows, a sword, an ax, and a thunderbolt, among other things. His mount is the peacock, Paravani, the serpent's enemy. Learned commentators on his legend say that just as Skanda's peacock destroys serpents, so he himself breaks the serpentine wheel of time. He represents eternal force which cuts right through and across human experience.

So the greatest lovers in Hindu mythology surprisingly produced only two children, and both of them unnaturally. Of relations between the divine brothers very little is said, but Shiva once teased them into competing with each other. He challenged them to circumscribe the earth and find which one possessed the greatest speed of limb. Skanda dashed off at once. While the young warrior was away, Ganapati ambled cheerily around his own parents. To walk around your parents, he explained, is the same thing as circling the earth itself. Skanda soon arrived home, panting and sweating. By that time, however, plump Ganapati had been proclaimed the victor.

Skanda led a long and arduous campaign against the demons of the earth and vanquished them. He used to be widely worshiped in the north of India, but now his cult is confined to the southern tip of the subcontinent (where he is worshiped as Subrahamanya).

The name Skanda has piqued the curiosity of some scholars. Is it an abbreviated form, perhaps, of Iskander? That is how the name

This seal from northern Syria *(above)* shows a fertility goddess standing on a bull beneath a rainbow.

Fertility goddess images occurred everywhere during the second and first millennia B.C. The three clay figures pictured below *(left to right)* are from Israel, Syria, and India.

The Canaanite fertility goddess Qodshu *(above)* offers a lotus to her male, Egyptian counterpart Min, and serpents to Resheph, the Canaanite god of plenty.

This small figure *(below)* of a female divinity offering her breast is from Bronze Age Denmark. It is thought to represent Freyja, the Norse goddess of fertility and love.

Below *(middle and right)* are two Mother Goddesses exhibiting archaic forms. The first is from Mycenae with a child on her arm and the other, a Neolithic figure from Thrace.

One of the finest and best known classical images of the great, all-nourishing Divine Mother of the animate world is the Roman statue of Artemis of Ephesus *(opposite)*.

The Chinese Mother Earth is shown *(below)* on a lion with a stag's head and a bull's hoofs.

We return on these two pages to the theme of the Great Mother, the giver of life and nurturer

The Mother Goddess Asherah *(below)* of Mycenae feeds two goats with ears of corn.

These three Celtic Mother Goddesses *(top)* carry horns of plenty to symbolize the fertility and generosity of nature.

One of the silver plaques *(above)* on the famous Gundestrup caldron from Denmark depicts bird and animal motifs around a female form that is believed to represent a fertility and nature goddess.

and protector of the young. Her function is clarified by symbols of fertility, of ripening nature, and of her relationship to the animate world; in other words these goddesses embody the procreative aspect of Mother Earth, the fruits of the earth, and the care of young life. All these qualities are combined in the magnificent statue of Artemis of Ephesus *(left)*. She offers her many breasts to suckle the animal world, representatives of which are grouped symbolically in various places on her body, and holds out her arms in the gesture of a mother providing nourishment for all created beings. The Great Mother always occupied first place in the pantheons of the ancient matriarchal societies.

A sixth-century B.C. sculpture *(below left)* from southern Italy shows a Mother Goddess suckling twins. The Bagas of Guinea used this portrayal *(below right)* of their fertility goddess Nimba as a cultic mask.

of Alexander the Great was spelled in Asiatic lands. Did Skanda's wars upon the demons actually reflect the Macedonian prince's campaign of conquest in the East?

A HEAVENLY MESSENGER

The Buryat peoples of Siberia say that long ago the gods sent an eagle to teach heaven's secrets to mankind. Unfortunately, human beings failed to grasp what the fierce bird, with his swooping gestures and paralyzing screams, was trying to tell them. Despairing, the great eagle flew away over the earth. Far below him, under a tree, slept a Buryat woman. The eagle saw her. He wheeled about in the middle of the air. He swooped down from the sky, like a whistling wind, and stuck his yellow talons into the woman's thighs. She awakened in the furiously beating embrace of his great wings, there on the ground. It was as if a blizzard of

Three divine couples from very different cultures are the Roman Jupiter and Juno *(above)*, the god and goddess with child in this early Turkish relief *(below far left)*, and the Tantric Adi-Buddha with his *dakini (below left)*.

A variety of functions – but usually that of exemplar – is fulfilled in religion and myth by the gods and humans who appear as couples, very often complementing each other in some way. Divine couples (e.g., Shiva and Shakti) initiate the process of creation. But they may also, as in the case of Osiris and Isis, provide a model for a particular earthly couple; thus the king and queen of ancient Egypt saw themselves as deputizing for this divine couple. In Western alchemy the king and queen were important as figures

icicles and fire possessed her. That woman gave birth, later on, to the first human intermediary between earth and heaven: the first shaman.

THE SEMINAL STORY OF BITIOU

The following Egyptian myth offers a spectacularly deep perspective on the working of human imagination. Parts of it apparently date back 4,000 years or more. However, the first written version which has come down to us is the so-called *D'Orbiney Papyrus* at the British Museum in London. The version retold here dates from the reign of Pharaoh Ramses the Great in the thirteenth century B.C.

One sunset hour, an Egyptian youth named Bitiou was driving his cattle home to the family barn. Just outside the barn door the lead cow stopped dead. Lowing, in a language which only Bitiou understood, she

An Australian bark painting *(above)* shows rainmaker Wuluwai with his wife Bunbulama. The Lapp divine couple Mader-Atcha (left) and Mader-Akka were the mythic creators of mankind *(above right)*. A well-known Indian divine couple is Krishna and his lover Radha *(below)*.

in the mystic marriage and metamorphosis of the elements. All new creations of the alchemical process involved the union of opposites. Similarly, Indian Tantrism set up the ideal of the divine couple as a mystic union designed to achieve symbolically the reconciliation of spiritual opposites. As an ideal for earthly alliances we have the many heroic couples recorded in myth and legend, such immortal exemplars of unconditional love as Orpheus and Eurydice in the divine sphere (myth, page 190) and Romeo and Juliet in the literary.

In this painting *(left)* by a Tantric artist the Indian creator god Shiva sits with his wife Parvati on the lotus throne (myth, page 196). The earthly couple Joseph and Mary are pictured on their flight into Egypt *(above)*.

The trinity *(above)* of Osiris, Isis, and their son Horus was the principal group in the Egyptian pantheon (myth, page 258).
An ancient-Egyptian relief *(below)* shows King Akhenaton (Amenhotep IV) and Queen Nefertiti basking with three of their children in the radiance of the divine sun Ra.

warned him: "Your brother Anapou is standing there behind the door with a knife in his fist." Bitiou stooped and glimpsed the shadow of Anapou's feet under the door. He wheeled about and ran for his life, with Anapou close behind him. Ra, the sun god, who notices everything, interrupted the pursuit. Mercifully, he caused a deep river to flow between the brothers. Then Anapou stopped and called out over the water, "I would have killed you if I could, oh my brother, for my wife says you tried to rape her."

Upon hearing this, Bitiou cut off his own testicles and hurled them into the river for the fishes to eat. "Your wife lied," he shouted. "Now I must go far away. But if ever you see the beer in your cup cloud over, you must search for me." Then Anapou, weeping bitterly, went home and with the same knife he had sharpened for his brother, killed his wife. Bitiou, meanwhile, made his sad way to a distant valley. There he shut his heart up, for safekeeping, in an acacia tree.

Knum, the potter god, was moved to create a bride for Bitiou out of living clay. She was fragrant, and when she washed her hair, it perfumed the river. Bitiou trusted that beautiful but artificial girl. He showed her the secret of his heart's safety: the acacia tree.

Egypt's pharaoh found himself drawn upriver by the fragrance of Bitiou's bride. Greatly did he desire her. "I shall be your queen," she said, "if you cut down that tree." She pointed to the acacia. The moment it was felled, Bitiou also died. At the same instant, far away, Anapou's beer clouded over. Anapou rose up. For seven long years he searched Egypt for his brother's heart. At last he found it, in an acacia berry.

Anapou placed the berry in a cup of fresh water. Immediately the cup, the water, and the berry transformed themselves into a huge, majestic white bull without stain. The bull, who was Bitiou, bellowed and ambled into the palace where his former bride now reigned as the pharaoh's queen. She recognized him. In fear and trembling, she ran to the pharaoh. "Will you grant my heart's desire?" she begged. He swore to do so.

At the queen's request and in consideration of his oath, the pharaoh regretfully slit the white bull's throat. The blood ran out upon the ground. From it, in good time, there grew two flourishing persea trees. The people worshiped the trees and made sacrifice to them as if they were divinities. Hearing of this, the queen brought foresters and ordered them to chop both trees down.

As her orders were being fulfilled, a little

The ancient-Egyptian Hathor, originally a sky goddess who became the patroness of lovers, was first depicted as a woman with the head of a cow and later, as here *(above)*, giving suck to kings, in this case Amenophis II.

Every occurrence of love in the Greek world was attributed to Eros *(below)*, the winged son of Aphrodite.

Bes *(below)* originally a Sudanese deity, reached Egypt during the twelfth dynasty. He was the patron of love and birth.

For the Greeks the great goddess of love was Aphrodite *(right)*, called Venus by the Romans (myth, page 186). In the art and literature of the West she has come to epitomize not only love but all womanly qualities. Her name has been used for the earliest-known depictions of the female in such prehistoric figures as the "Venus of Willendorf" and the "Venus of Laussel" (page 185).

The Germanic Freyja, pictured in this Christian mural as a witch riding on a broomstick *(above)*, was primarily a goddess of love, though she had other functions as well, including those of bringer of the harvest (in which case she is shown carrying a horn of plenty) and leader of the Valkyries.

For the people of the Mesopotamian region the goddess of love and fertility was Ishtar *(left)*.

The Aztecs worshiped Xochipilli *(below far left)* as patron of flowers, beauty, and love.

Astarte *(below middle)* was the Phoenician goddess of fertility and love.

Harvest goddess Tlazolteotl *(below)* of ancient Mexico was also the goddess of sensual delight.

THE GOD OF LOVE

To Aphrodite
"What grief is gnawing at your heart,
Sappho, that you invoke me?
What turbulence of yearning lies
So heavy on your breast?
Whom shall I coax into your net,
Which of your darlings' senses melt?
Who is it dares defy you?
He flees? Good, he shall pursue you.
He spurns this gift? Then let him go.

As varied as the experience of love itself are the manifestations of the gods and goddesses of love, fertility, procreation, and birth. Many of them incorporate all these aspects at once; in others a particular aspect is stressed and we get a god or goddess of love, beauty, or erotic desire. For example, eroticism comes out very clearly in the Indian Kama and the Greek Eros. Certain manifestations of the Great Mother and her erotic and procreative power – Ishtar of Mesopotamia, Astarte of Phoenicia – were the object of religiously motivated fertility cults, with ritual acts of love being performed in the shrines

and temples dedicated to them. Sacred prostitution was common throughout the Mediterranean region in classical and, in the context of Gnosticism, late classical times. Ritualized sexual relations also formed part of the Tantric Shakti cult in India.

Top and above: Kama is the Indian god of love. The top relief shows him with his wife Rati riding a peacock, symbol of desire. Next he is pictured astride an elephant composed of nine goddesses.
Above left: Psyche and Eros are the divine epitome of romantic love.

And if he loves you not,
Soon he shall burn for you, knowing
Himself rejected."
Oh come, come to me now, ease my pain,
And what my bosom hotly craves
Yourself bestow, my sweet, yourself
Be my confederate.

SAPPHO

chip of wood flew straight from the ax edge to lodge between the queen's smiling lips. Then and there, she conceived a son. Her firstborn was none other than Bitiou again. The queen gave suck to the same person whom she herself had murdered in manhood, had murdered again when reincarnated as a bull, and had murdered yet a third time when reincarnated as a tree.

Years passed; the pharaoh died, and the new Bitiou became pharaoh. Sending for his faithful elder brother, Bitiou made him Prince of the Nile. As for his wicked mother, Bitiou accused her before his people and told of all her efforts to destroy him. Then he had her executed.

LOVING SACRIFICE

The body's life force resides largely in the blood. Perhaps its miraculous power has never been more dramatically portrayed than in a Dusun myth told to Ivor Evans by Limbong of Tambahilik, in the Temasuk district of North Borneo. The story mingles apparent foolishness with richly rewarded sacrifice, both for the sake of a father's love. There was a poor man named Kaduan, who had a wife and seven daughters. Except for himself, the entire family fell ill with an ulcerating condition of the legs. They were so helpless and hungry that they ate the ashes of the household fire around which they lay. In this extremity, Kaduan conceived a seemingly impossible plan. "Since I am still well and can walk," he promised his daughters, "I shall go and fetch husbands for you." So saying, he set out from their tumbledown hut and went into the jungle. After a while he came to a river with sands of beaded gold, shaded by trees whose blossoms were bells merrily tinkling on the cool breeze. Kaduan bathed himself in the river and then waded across. On the far bank he found a well-carved mansion seven doors wide.

On the railings of the mansion's porch dozens of fat fowl roosted in the sunshine. Well back in the shade sat the corpulent man of the house, sweating and smiling. Boldly, Kaduan mounted the steps and greeted the man. "I am journeying to seek husbands for my seven daughters," he announced. "My home is as wealthy as yours. When I left it, I wore cloth of gold as you do now. During my travels my fine clothes rotted from my back; and I was forced to replace them with the rags of tree bark in which you see me now."

The man of the house, whose name was Gerlunghan, made Kaduan welcome. He caused his seven sons to set seven trays of

KRISHNA AND THE MARRIAGE OF HEAVEN AND EARTH

Opposite: The young Krishna, having stolen the *gopis'* saris, hides in a tree while they frantically search for something with which to cover themselves.

The beautiful shepherd girl Radha comes to Krishna in a grove. Krishna's love for Radha and the other *gopis* is a key theme in Indian love mysticism.

The eighth incarnation of the Indian supreme deity Vishnu is the young god and hero Krishna. His cult grew around the first century A.D. and formed the basis of Tantrism. Even as a boy Krishna was invested with miraculous powers and performed many

A lotus flower in his hand, Krishna approaches the house of Radha *(below left)*. Their love affair was the subject of countless songs and miniature paintings *(below)*.

Three classic scenes *(below)* depict the union of Krishna and Radha. The object of paintings like this was to inspire earthly lovers with divine love.

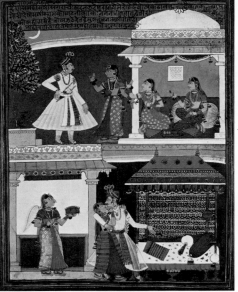

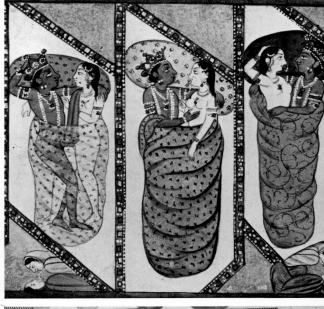

heroic deeds to free mankind from various predicaments. But more important that these, in terms of the development of the Indian religion of divine love *(bhakti)* and of Tantric yoga, was the young god's love life. A handsome youth and an expert player on the shepherd's flute, he was happiest in the company of the *gopis* or shepherd girls, who were all in love with him. Transforming himself into various guises, he bestowed his favors on them all. His first choice, however, was beautiful Radha. Krishna's love life provides the symbolic background to the religious concept of a heavenly or ideal love between God and man and the free play of divine power. The worship of Krishna and Radha inspired a deeply religious surrender to the beloved god. It became one of the chief aims of Tantrism to realize Krishna's supernatural love as a way of ennobling the profane love of men.

When the *gopis* wanted to dance, Krishna miraculously multiplied his physical presence so that each girl believed she was dancing with the god in person *(above)*. He did the same when he went bathing with them in the River Jumna *(above right)*.

One of the heroic deeds of the young god Krishna was to subdue a dangerous serpent demon called Kaliya by dancing on its head. Here *(below)* we see him holding the serpent's tail with his left hand.

rice and seven jars of rice wine before the guest. Kaduan consumed all that. Afterward, Kaduan courteously belched, picked his teeth for a time, and at last confessed, "I am tired of searching for sons-in-law worthy of my seven daughters' great wealth and beauty. Your seven sons, Gerlunghan, appear stalwart enough. I will present my daughters to them, I think." Kaduan proceeded to describe his own house as a magnificent structure having seven gables open to the winds of heaven. Cordially, Kaduan invited Gerlunghan and his sons to see it for themselves.

Accordingly, they all set off together across the river and into the jungle. As they neared Kaduan's home, however, he raced ahead. Rushing into his half-ruined hut, Kaduan ordered his wife and daughters to flee for their lives. Unable to walk because of their ulcerated legs and dressed only in shreds of dusty bark, his dear ones crept away as best they could into the underbrush. Kaduan also hid. Then Gerlunghan and his seven sons came up to the deserted place of misery. Bewildered, they stood looking about. "Kaduan has made fools of us," Derlunghan decided. At that moment, Kaduan stood up from his hiding place. He approached Gerlunghan and his seven stalwart sons, weeping and crying out, "Kill me!"

Gerlunghan's youngest son drew from the silken sash around his waist a keen-edged knife. He raised the weapon to strike at Kaduan. Kneeling down upon the broken threshold of his home, Kaduan feebly raised his arm in an instinctive last-minute effort to defend himself. The blade descended. It cut Kaduan's left forearm to the bone. Blood flowed abundantly. From the blood came buffalo, cattle, and all sorts of edible fowl. Where the hut had been, a mansion of seven gables stood. From inside the mansion sounded the music of gongs. Kaduan's blood, streaming down over his body, crystallized into gems and cloth of gold, a splendid costume. His wife and children appeared out of the underbrush. They were well and whole again, and beautiful. They, too, were magnificently attired. "This man," Gerlunghan said to his sons, "is even wealthier than I. Not only that, but his daughters are at least as smooth and strong as each one of you." And he bowed down to Kaduan to show his respect.

Kaduan killed seven of his new buffalo for a great marriage feast. After seven days and nights, it was finished. Then Gerlunghan, the rich man, journeyed homeward. But his seven strong sons remained behind with the daughters of Kaduan.

Zeus is the head, Zeus the middle,
in Zeus all things have their end.
Zeus is the fundament of earth
and of the starry heavens.
Zeus is manly,
Zeus is an immortal woman.
Zeus is the breath of all things,
Zeus the inexhaustible movement of fire.
Zeus is the root of the sea,
Zeus sun and moon,
Zeus is king.

ORPHIC

Hera *(above)*, queen of heaven and wife and sister of Zeus, sits on her throne.

As the beautiful but unhappy virgin Danaë languished in prison, Zeus came to her in the form of a shower of golden rain *(below)*.

Zeus visited Leda in the form of a swan *(below)*, after which she is said to have given birth to the Dioscuri from an egg. This beautiful image of the swan as a bird of Aphrodite has inspired countless artists and poets.

The fruit of Zeus's brief affair with Alcmene was the mighty warrior Herakles. When Alcmene *(below)* later met her death on a pyre in Thebes Zeus had her taken up to Elysium.

Standing beside her daughter Calliope in this Greek vase painting is the goddess Mnemosyne, who through union with Zeus became the mother of all nine Muses.

The Greek goddess Demeter *(left)*, a sister of Zeus, conceived by him a daughter called Persephone. The alliance of Zeus as god of heaven with the earth goddess Demeter accounted in mythological terms for the fertility of the earth.

Hera, daughter of Cronus, was both sister and wife to Zeus. Queen of heaven and earth, she was also the patroness of marriage. Hera was famed for her jealousy and for her rigorous persecution of Zeus's lovers.

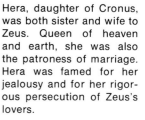

Ganymede, son of Tros, the founder of Troy, was so beautiful that Zeus assumed the form of an eagle to carry him off to Olympus, where he became the god's lover and cup-bearer. Ganymede lives on in the night sky as the constellation Aquarius.

By turning himself into a bull Zeus succeeded in abducting the beautiful Europa *(right)* and carrying her off to Crete.

Stories of open or secret love affairs are part and parcel of the mythical career of the Greek god Zeus (page 195). In fact he owed his dominant position in the hierarchy of the Greek pantheon not so much to his victory over the Titans – a gift from his mother Gaea – as to his many love matches. A striking feature of these often short-lived liaisons is that they were confined to the god's closest female relations; sisters and daughters, he seems to have seduced them all.

When Io, a virgin priestess of Hera, attracted the attention of Zeus, she was turned into a heifer by Hera and placed in the custody of the hundred-eyed Argus. Zeus sent Hermes to pipe Argus to sleep *(below)*.

And if straightforward courtship did not get him his way he resorted to deception and transformation. On closer examination, however, his "lechery" may be interpreted more positively as an active intervention in the evolution of a new world; that is, his amours were responsible for a well-stocked pantheon of gods and goddesses, each with a particular function.

Hermes *(below on the left)*, the messenger of the gods and helper of mankind, was Zeus's son by the nymph Maia *(right)*, another of the divine lovers.

MERCIFUL HEALING

Of all the Chinese myths which celebrate the transforming powers of love, none is dearer to pious Taoists than the story of Miao.

In ancient times, during the Golden Heavenly Dynasty, there lived a headstrong monarch who had three daughters but no sons. It was important to the king's own security that his daughters marry well; and the first two chose rich noblemen for their husbands. However, the youngest of the three, Miao, announced her intention of marrying a poor doctor and devoting her life to healing the sick. Her father felt that such a course of action would be entirely wrong for someone of Miao's breeding. He refused permission.

Miao thereupon begged to be allowed to retire to the Nunnery of the White Bird in Lung-shu Hsien. Reluctantly, the king agreed. In secret, he sent instructions to the mother superior of the nunnery. His daughter must be made miserable, he ordered. Obediently, the mother superior set Miao to work in the kitchen all alone.

The Spirit of the North Star swept the kitchen for her. A dragon dug a well conveniently near the kitchen door. A tiger brought her fuel for the ovens. Hundreds of birds flew in and out carrying fruit, nuts, and vegetables in their beaks for the delicious salads which Miao made. When all was prepared for a meal, the dinner bell sounded without being struck.

In despair, the mother superior sent a letter to the king informing him of what had taken place. Supernatural forces seemed to will that Miao remain. If the king still wished her home again, the letter concluded, he would have to take her away by force. This message infuriated the king. He sent troops to burn down the nunnery. As the flames mounted and converged, the nuns accused Miao of bringing disaster upon them. "It is true," she said, and prayed aloud: "Sovereign of the Universe, there was a time when you left your palace and climbed the snowy mountains to attain perfection. I came here with the same object in mind. Will you not save me and my sisters in devotion?"

Taking a bamboo pin from her hair, Miao plunged the point of it into the roof of her mouth. She spat out blood to the four winds, copiously. Clouds of black and silver piled thick over the nunnery. The clouds dissolved in torrential rain, which immediately put out the fire.

Then Miao surrendered to her father's troops and was fetched home. Once more the king asked if she would consent to marry a nobleman; once more she refused.

Beside himself with rage, the king ordered her immediate execution. The sky darkened. The headsman's sword descended upon Miao's neck. The sword shattered. Spears were then thrust at her defenseless body; they splintered on contact. At last the king ordered that his daughter be strangled with a silken cord, and it was done. Thereupon a tiger rushed onto the execution ground. Seizing Miao's lifeless body between its teeth, the tiger hurtled away again.

Miao's soul awakened in the shadowy depths of hell. A young man, dressed in gleaming blue, appeared before her. "The Ten Judges of the Lower Regions," he told her, "are most impressed by what they have heard concerning your life in the upper world. They would enjoy hearing and seeing you pray here below."

Miao agreed, on one condition. She asked that the prisoners of all the hells be freed from their chains and brought to witness her prayer. Accordingly, the two chief constables of hell, Ox-Face and Horse-Head, struck the chains from the captives and led them into her presence. Miao thereupon began her devotions. Before she had finished, the instruments of torture in the demons' fists became lotus flowers.

Yama, the keeper of the Register of the Dead, was disturbed. Consultations were held, and the fates rearranged. Miao awakened in her own revivified body, on earth again.

Mounting the tiger which had saved her corpse from burial, she traveled to the Monastery of the Immortals. There she remained for nine years, gradually attaining perfection. Meanwhile her father, the king, had fallen ill. His sickness was repulsive and agonizing, but worst of all, he appeared unable to die. Hearing of this, Miao went to her father's palace disguised as a mendicant priest. "I see the precise nature of your illness," the seeming priest informed the king. "It is easily curable, and yet the cure will not be found in any pharmacy, nor would anyone agree to sell it."

Groaning, the king asked what the remedy might be. "The hand and eye of a living person," she told him. "The person who will give these things to you resides at the Monastery of the Immortals."

When the king's ministers reached the monastery to obtain the remedy, Miao was there in her proper form to greet them. She offered her own left hand and eye. "Be quick," she requested, "cut these things from me. Why do you hesitate as if you were young girls?" Regretfully, the ministers did as they were bidden. The blood flowing from her wounds, dripping to the ground,

Compassionate love finds symbolic expression in the figure of the Bodhisattva Avalokitesvara, the deity known in China as Kuan-yin and in Japan as Kwannon. This Buddhist redeemer is surrounded by myths and legends seeking to explain how he is able to appear with so many

hands – often, as in the Japanese figure here *(far right),* holding something in each one. Avalokitesvara, the "lord who looks down in kindness and compassion," depicted so movingly in this statue from China *(right),* is the embodiment of heaven's mercy and love for man. He was sent by the Buddha Amitabha to help people in their search for enlightenment. He hears the cries of suffering humanity and responds with a generous sympathy. Avalokitesvara figures frequently in the religious art of Tibet *(above),* always representing some emanation of divine compassion.

had an odor of incense. Placing Miao's hand and eye upon a golden plate, they took their leave.

The eye and hand were carefully ground down and mixed with honey. The ointment was rubbed into the king's body. Immediately, his whole left side healed up. His right side, however, remained as horribly and agonizingly diseased as before. Once again, therefore, he despatched his ministers to the holy place. Miao met them as before. This time she commanded them to cut off her right hand and pluck out her right eye for the king. So that was done. The resulting ointment worked as expected; the ulcers which had bloated and lacerated the king's

right side vanished as darkness before the rising sun. Sitting up in bed, he asked his ministers to describe the saint who had given her hands and eyes to him. After some hesitation they confessed that she resembled his late daughter, Miao.

Healed, finally, the king began to sense something of his true relation to his saintly daughter. Together with his queen, the weeping monarch set out on a pilgrimage to the Monastery of the Immortals. After many adventures the old couple found themselves face to face with Miao. The sockets of her eyes, the mutilated stumps of her wrists, dripped blood upon the altar where she stood; and yet her voice was comforting. As soon as he heard her speak, the king abased himself in the dust, saying, "I have committed a great crime."

At that moment, Miao regained her normal form, complete in every limb, surrounded with the radiance of heaven. She descended from the altar and embraced her parents. "Must I still marry a nobleman?" she asked, smiling. "No," the king replied, "let me rather beg permission to give up my kingdom, remain with you here, and begin practicing virtue."

There is one force for transformation which plays through all others, although it remains hidden and has never yet been pictured satisfactorily. Princess Miao, for one, possessed it in abundance. This force has many names. The Greek playwright Sophocles equated it with Aphrodite, Goddess of Love. In a famous passage (translated here by Sir Richard Livingstone), Sophocles argued that love is not love alone:

The word *tantra* refers to the union of opposites in the form of a divine or human couple *(above)*.

This Tantric mandala *(below left)* depicts the five "powerful enjoyments": fish, meat, cereal, wine, and sex.

Many Indian temples are adorned with sculptures representing the heavenly delights of erotic love *(below)*.

Tantrism is a meditational system that aims at the experience of the highest bliss in physical and spiritual relations by cultivating the totality of one's erotic potential. Ancient scriptures containing the mystical teachings and ritual instructions of Tantrism are called *tantras.*

But in her name lie many names concealed:
for she is Death, imperishable Force.
Desire unmixed, wild Frenzy, Lamentation:
in her are summed all impulses that drive
to Violence, Energy, Tranquillity.
Deep in each living breast the Goddess
*   sinks,*
and all become her prey; the tribes that
*   swim,*
the fourfoot tribes that pace upon the earth,
harbour her; and in birds her wing is
*   sovereign.*
In beasts, in mortal men, in gods above.
What god but wrestles with her and is
*   thrown?*
If I may tell – and truth is right to tell –
she rules the heart of Zeus without a spear,
without a sword. Truly the Cyprian
shatters all purposes of men and gods.

Yoga positions calculated to provide the maximum sexual enjoyment are the subject matter of whole series of Tantric drawings *(above right)*.

The Buddhas of Tibetan Tantrism are depicted in mystic union with their female partners *(right)*. God and goddess symbolize the union of awareness and wisdom in the Tantric gnosis.

In this most important of all Tantric yantras *(below)*, the outer triangles are occupied by divinities.

Briefly, they teach that earthly delights stem from the union of opposites achieved with an ideal partner. Such a union is said to exemplify the harmony of creation and be a step toward perfection (i. e., union with God). The power of love thus becomes central to the whole of existence. *Kama,* or "desire," is a creative principle aiming at the perfection of life on earth, just as the divine love that Krishna bore the shepherd girl Radha represented the cosmic energies of creation in action on earth (page 207). Among the Tantric aids to meditation are mantras, sacred sounds that may be visualized as yantras, and mandalas, symbols of psychic wholeness.

A wood carving *(opposite)* from southern India celebrates the heavenly joys of the *tantra* adept, who is able to satisfy several women simultaneously.

The Revelation to John describes with mounting drama the great battle between God and his angels and the infidel world, culminating in the Day of Judgment when the kingdom of God arises with the souls of the redeemed (after the *Luther Bible,* 1534).

There is unrest
among the giants;
the ancient horn of Gjallar
sounds the end.
Surt comes up from the south
with scorching embers;
the sun flashes
from the sword of the gods.
Giantesses fall, rocks split,
Men go down to Hel,
the sky bursts.

SIBYL'S PROPHECY

COMBAT IN HEAVEN AND ON EARTH

This Greek vase painting shows Zeus appearing with thunder and lightning to wage war on the Titans.

In this detail from the *Last Judgment* by Hieronymus Bosch, angels as divine powers of light come floating down from heaven to vanquish the demons of darkness.

People have been fighting since earliest time – either against the elements, the animals, or among themselves. Eventually human combat grew to be the expected thing. As Edward Gibbon put the case (in his *Decline and Fall of the Roman Empire*), history itself "is a river of blood." So naturally combat has been a recurrent theme in world myth. Some of the earliest stories that we possess concern wars of the elements, of gods, of animals, of men and women, and of all these mixed together in various ways. There are myths fraught with appalling violence and others which turn upon rules of fair play and the sporting chance.

Certain myths of combat cater to the sedentary spectator-sportsman's delight. Others, however, have been shaped to inspire feelings of awe, pity, and terror. Combat is "to the death," often enough, and myth naturally reflects the fact. Then, too, forces which are mysterious and frightening in themselves may decide which way the battle goes. The greatest heroes are those whose human intuition or superhuman wisdom enables them to sense and to manipulate such irresistible hidden powers.

Herakles of Greece wrestled with various mysteries. There was, to take a famous example, the time when he challenged the Titan named Antaeus, son of Mother Earth. They began wrestling bare-handed, in the dust. Again and again Herakles felled the Titan, only to see Antaeus bound up again, refreshed, seemingly stronger than before. There was obviously no use in trying to pin Antaeus in this manner.

Herakles gripped the Titan about the waist and heaved him up one last time off the ground. He was about to hurl his enemy down once more when a dim thought, born of despair, came into his mind. Perhaps Antaeus was receiving new strength from his mother, from Earth herself. Thinking this, Herakles stood like a pillar holding Antaeus aloft. He would not let him touch the ground; and Antaeus, cut off from his mother, withered like an uprooted flower. He died in Herakles's inexorable grip, unable to touch the earth that was the secret source of his strength.

THE TALE OF THE HEAVY FEATHER

The folk hero of the Mande people of Africa is named Kassa Kena Gananina. He could kill twenty antelope with a single blow of his iron staff. One day a monstrous dragon-bird of the kind called Konoba swooped down upon Kassa Kena Gananina and hovered in such a way as to shade him completely. The Konoba opened its yellow

An Achaemenian seal from Mesopotamia bears this impression *(above)* of a warrior, armed with bow and arrow, in combat with a winged lion. The portrait in the center beneath the sun symbol may represent the moon god Nanna-Sin.

One of the celebrated metopes *(below right)* from the Greek city of Selinus shows the hero Perseus decapitating the Gorgon Medusa. Behind him, ready with help and wise counsel, stands the war goddess Athene.

The scene on this Swedish helmet plate *(above)*, a man fighting a wolf, is thought to represent the mythic capture of the wolf Fenrir by the Nordic god Tyr. The myth (page 171) further prophesies that Fenrir will one day devour the sun.

A South Indian relief *(below)* shows the goddess Durga fighting the buffalo demon Mahisasura, whom she defeated after a heroic struggle.

The main themes of classical and oriental myth come down again and again to the same basic situation: a confrontation between two mutually exclusive yet interdependent opposites. The great cosmogonic myths tell of a division of chaos into light and darkness, two "powers" incompatible but complementary. This primal polarity gradually gave way to symbolic, animate creatures whose struggles illustrated a concept of the emergence of the world through a perpetual clash of opposites. The pictures on these two pages show something of the variety of mythic accounts of the battles of gods and heroes against the demonic agents of the principle opposed to evolution. Myths describing the liberation of man from monsters of one kind or another, while often relating to ideas about the origin of time and the changes affecting sun and moon, also symbolize this struggle of the powers of light against the demons of darkness and ignorance, as in the Indian myths of the incarnations of Vishnu. Other phenomena too, such as the supercession of ancient deities, cultural changes, the concept of a cyclical succession of ages, or the advent of new civilizations, often find mythic expression in the form of a combat, with the adversary branded as a demon being defeated.

This Mesopotamian clay relief *(left)* shows the mythic struggle of a hero or god against a female demon with three eyes and a sunlike headpiece.

Vishnu is seen in a relief from South India *(right)* in his fourth incarnation, as the "man-lion" Narasimha, killing the demon Hiranyakasipu who had dared to blaspheme against the supreme deity.

The Cretan bronze plaque *(above)* apparently illustrates the young Zeus's fight with the wild goats. Zeus is assisted by the Curetes, shown banging their shields with their spears. Zeus was the son of Rhea, who hid him in a cave to protect him from his father Cronus (myths, pages 82 and 194).

The subject of this Greek terracotta *(right)* from Aegina is the young hero Bellerophon on his winged horse Pegasus (myth, page 159). Bellerophon's mythic antagonist was the Chimera, a three-headed, fire-breathing monster composed of a lion, a goat, and a snake.

beak and asked in a croaking voice, "Which shall I take, you or the antelope which you have killed this morning?" For answer, Kassa Kena Gananina hurled his iron staff at the monster. It wheeled and fluttered to the ground, stone-dead.

In its fall, unfortunately, the Konoba loosed a lone feather which happened to descend across the shoulders of Kassa Kena Gananina. Strong though he was, the weight of that one feather struck him down and half buried him in the ground. He called for his friends to come and remove the feather from his back, but though many of them attempted together to lift the weight from him, they could not do it.

After a while, an old woman came along the path carrying a child on her back. Kassa Kena Gananina begged her to help him. Stooping down, the old woman softly blew upon the feather and softly, softly she blew it away so that Kassa Kena Gananina could rise again. The old woman, meanwhile, went over to the slain Konoba and picked it up, giving it to the little child to carry. Then the old woman stepped away down the path with the little child on her back playing happily with the dead monster.

THE DEEDS OF GOROBA-DIKE

The black hero of the following tale of combat was a formidable fighter and was gifted with a keen sense of mystery and romance. Like numerous heroes in myth, he possessed rather dangerous magnetism. Events arranged themselves around him, as it were, in shock-wave patterns. His name was Goroba-Dike, and he belonged to the Fulbe tribe.

It so happened that the Fulbe people suffered a long period of subjection to the Fasa of North Africa. Eventually they drifted southward across the Sahara Desert, out of their conquerors' reach. They were a pastoral tribe, wandering herders, and yet were just as fiercely contemptuous of strangers as their former masters had been of themselves. Fanatic Moslems and increasingly men of the sword, they spread fear wherever they went. Fulbe lords prided themselves on skill in hand-to-hand fighting. Each employed a personal bard, or "mabo," as a war correspondent committed to singing his praises. Now, Goroba-Dike's mabo was a man named Ulal.

Goroba-Dike himself was a younger son in a household which had long dominated the Massina district. Though his family was wealthy, he received no inheritance as a younger son and therefore went to live with Mabo Ulal in Bammama country. Goroba-

THE LABORS OF HERAKLES

Herakles, or Hercules, the hero who became a god, was fathered by Zeus on the mortal Alcmene. Indirectly he spent the whole of his long and eventful life in the service of Zeus's wife Hera,

Herakles doing battle with the evil Triton Acheloos *(above).*

First Labor – Herakles's first labor was to drive the monstrous Nemean lion back into its cave and strangle it with his bare hands.

Second Labor – His second commission was to dispose of the Lernaean Hydra, a nine-headed monster whose heads grew again as fast as Herakles lopped them off. In the end he burned out the necks with a glowing tree-trunk.

Third Labor – Here Herakles had to capture alive the Arcadian stag with golden antlers and feet of iron. He chased the animal on Mount Ceryneia for a year before he finally managed to hit it in the foot with an arrow.

FIRST LABOR

SECOND LABOR

THIRD LABOR

SEVENTH LABOR

EIGHTH LABOR

NINTH LABOR

Seventh Labor – The Thracian king Diomedes used to feed his wild mares on human flesh. In his seventh labor Herakles stole the horses, threw the body of Diomedes to them, and then brought them to Eurystheus in Mycenae.

Eighth Labor – The eighth labor was to capture the white bull of Minos that Poseidon had brought out of the sea.

Ninth Labor – In obedience to his ninth commission Herakles secured the belt of the Amazon queen Hippolyte for Eurystheus's daughter. Hippolyte was killed in the struggle.

Hera, determined to get rid of Herakles, sent two enormous snakes to destroy him in his cradle, but the infant strangled them with his bare hands *(right).*

The large relief *(right)* shows Herakles, armed with club and bow, going out hunting in his traditional lionskin.

paying for his father's infidelity. Even before his birth, Hera had swindled him out of his birthright, the kingdom of Argos. Herakles's whole life (myths, pages 180 and 216), from the heroic deeds of his youth – including the twelve major labors performed for his master Eurystheus – to his crimes, purification, and elevation to Olympus, is a metaphor of victory over death, man's dream of achieving the immortality of the gods. The powers against which he struggles in his twelve labors, for example, mostly represent death. Following his victory over Cerberus, the hound of hell, Herakles was surnamed Kallinikos ("He of the splendid victory"), and a common superscription over doors in the late classical period was "The son of Zeus, Kallinikos Herakles, lives here; let no evil enter!"

Fourth Labor – Herakles's fourth task was to hunt the Erymanthian boar. He drove the animal through deep snow until it was so worn out he was able to catch it and bring it alive to Eurystheus, who was so frightened that he hid in a stone pitcher.

Fifth Labor – The fifth labor was to drive off the Stymphalian birds, which had brass beaks and claws, and feathers used as arrows.

Sixth Labor – The sixth task was to clean out the vast stables of Augeas. Herakles succeeded by diverting a river through them.

FOURTH LABOR   FIFTH LABOR   SIXTH LABOR

TENTH LABOR   ELEVENTH LABOR   TWELFTH LABOR

Tenth Labor – Herakles traveled to the island of Erytheia for his tenth commission: fetching back to Greece the oxen of Geryon.

Eleventh Labor – The eleventh labor took Herakles to the Atlas Mountains, in search of Hera's golden apples, which were guarded by the Hesperides and the dragon Ladon. He managed to get three apples by outwitting Atlas.

An amphora scene (right) shows Herakles killing the centaur Nessos in the River Evenos. This episode later cost him his own life when the hero's unsuspecting wife sent him a garment steeped in the centaur's poisonous blood.

Twelfth Labor – For his twelfth and final labor Herakles descended to the underworld, bound Cerberus, the monster who guarded the gate, and brought him up to the light of day.

Dike's blood, he himself passionately contended, was the bluest of the blue; yet his life was little better than that of a wandering brigand; this made him bitter and, it must be confessed, cruel. For example, Goroba-Dike used to have Bammama babies ground up small and fed in mash to his warhorse. That sort of thing distressed the Bammama so they bribed Mabo Ulal to lure Goroba-Dike as far away from their country as possible.

The mabo bided his time. Then one night by the campfire he quietly remarked, "Sariam is a long way off. But did you know that Hamadi Ardo, the king there, is a Fulbe? I am told that the youngest of his three daughters is still unmarried. The princess has a ring, a very narrow one. She says that she will marry no man but the one whom that ring fits."

Goroba-Dike stretched out his hand and admired his long and narrow fingers. More than anything else about him, they clearly demonstrated his Fulbe blood. "Come," he said, "let us ride."

Not far from Sariam, Goroba-Dike and Mabo Ulal stopped at the house of a peasant who belonged to the subservient Pulu tribe. Goroba-Dike put off his sword and his silken clothes and dressed himself in a few of the peasant's rags. Leaving Mabo Ulal and their horses at the peasant's house, he walked into Sariam. There he pretended to be a poor Pulu in search of work. He found a job operating the bellows in a blacksmith's shop.

Not long after that, King Hamadi Ardo lost his temper with his youngest daughter. "It seems," he complained, "that you will never in your life discover a man whose finger your marriage ring fits. You certainly won't do it at the present rate. Therefore, I have decided to order a convocation of every Fulbe bachelor in my kingdom. All must try the ring. You are to marry the one whom it fits, with no questions asked."

The gathering took place accordingly. Hundreds of bachelors turned up, but not one of them managed to squeeze the silver ring belonging to the princess past the second knuckle of his forefinger. The king despaired. It seemed that his daughter would remain forever without a husband. He was about to adjourn the assembly when Goroba-Dike stepped forth from the crowd. "I am no warrior," Goroba-Dike said, "yet I too am a Fulbe."

"Stretch out your right forefinger," the king commanded. The king's daughter slipped her silver ring over his finger; it was a perfect fit. The princess wept. She had no wish to marry such a dirty, poor, common person; but there was nothing for it. The wedding took place at once, and that night she slept with her husband.

Next morning, Burdama tribesmen made a raid on the outskirts of Sariam and stole many of the king's cattle. The warriors of Sariam mounted their horses and galloped in pursuit of the raiders. Goroba-Dike refused to join in the pursuit. He mounted a donkey and rode slowly off in another direction. Secretly, he was on his way to the farmhouse where he had left Mabo Ulal and the horses, together with his weapons. When he arrived there, he explained the case to the mabo. Quickly he armed himself to ride off again, on horseback.

Cutting cross-country at a gallop, he approached the war party who were pursuing the cattle raiders. Armed, swathed in silk, and splendidly mounted, he looked like a champion. The Fulbe failed to recognize him. They asked whether he would help them fight the raiders and recover King Hamadi Ardo's cattle. "What?" he replied. "Hasn't the king got sons-in-law who will fight for him?"

The warriors nodded. "Yes, three of them. But one has run away, and the other two are not much use in a fight. That is the problem."

"Well," said Goroba-Dike, "if the king's two sons-in-law who are here will each give me an ear, then I will take part and win the victory for them. They can pretend to have lost their ears honorably in battle."

Goroba-Dike's brothers-in-law were both such cowards that they tremblingly agreed to do what the stranger required of them. Each cut off an ear for him. Goroba-Dike put the ears into his wallet. Then he led the charge against the Burdama raiders, scattering them and winning back the cattle they had stolen.

After the battle he rode off by himself cross-country to the peasant's house. He gave his weapons to Mabo Ulal, who wiped them clean. Changing his rich apparel for the same rags he had worn before, he mounted his dusty donkey and rode slowly back into Sariam. He arrived in time for the victory celebration. His brothers-in-law were boasting before the king of how they had each lost an ear in the heat of battle. No one paid the slightest attention to Goroba-Dike. He sat in the corner, silent, fingering the ears which were concealed in his wallet. Later that night, his bride absolutely refused to make love to him. She made him sleep on the far side of the room.

In the morning the Burdama returned, seeking revenge. They made ready to attack the town from the north. All the Fulbe warriors, except Goroba-Dike, massed together to defend the north gate. Goroba-Dike mounted his donkey and rode out from the south gate. The people heaped abuse on him as he went. He reached the farmhouse and told Mabo Ulal what had happened. Then, fully armed, he rode back again toward town.

He was barely in time. The Burdama had fought their way through to the courtyard of the king's palace. Two of them had seized Goroba-Dike's bride and were about to carry her off. Goroba-Dike struck down one of the abductors with a mighty thrust of his spear. The other sliced at his thigh as he rode by, making a bad wound there. Goroba-Dike wheeled his horse and killed the second man. The grateful princess did not recognize him. She tore off a piece of her gown to bind Goroba-Dike's wound. Then he rode on, fighting hard, pursuing the Burdama through the streets. Once they had been dispersed and victory was assured, he rode back to the farmhouse and changed into his rags again.

There were many dead to be mourned that night, but also a great victory to celebrate. It looked as if the Burdama would not dare to come back for a long time. The warriors bragged of their own heroism as the women teased Goroba-Dike's wife. "We wonder where your husband was during the fight, don't you?" they asked. "I have married a coward, a dirty ape," was her reply.

After the celebration the princess could not sleep. She gazed across the room in the semidarkness. Her despised husband lay there in disarray, snoring loudly. The rags had slipped from his body. She could see his thigh, oozing blood from underneath a bandage. Then she noticed that the bandage was the strip she had torn from her own gown. She crept across to him. Gently she awakened him and asked, "Where did you get that wound?" Goroba-Dike got up on one elbow. "That is something for you to consider," he said. "Who bandaged you?" the princess asked. Goroba-Dike smiled slightly. "That also is for you to think about." She asked who he might really be. "A king's son," Goroba-Dike said. "I thank you," said his wife to him, and they were friends. Still, for the time being, he swore her to secrecy.

Next morning, Goroba-Dike rode out to the farmhouse and changed into his own clothes once more. He returned to town, followed at a respectful distance by Mabo Ulal. In the great square he dismounted. Mabo Ulal did likewise, then drove a pair of silver pegs into the ground. To these they tied their horses. The people gathered round, and soon the king himself appeared with his family.

The princess stepped smiling up to Goroba-

Dike and clasped his hand. "This is the man who is my husband," she announced. "He it was who saved us from the Burdama."

The king could not believe what he heard. The warriors assured him, however, that it was true indeed. Only Goroba-Dike's brothers-in-law seemed less than sure. "It is not really certain," they protested, "that this man has done anything to be proud about." Thereupon, Goroba-Dike dipped his fine long fingers into his wallet and pulled out the ears taken from his brothers-in-law. Quietly, in the sudden stillness which filled the square, he presented the gruesome proof.

THOR

Another myth of combat involves the Norse god of thunder, Thor, who was the strongest and most generous of the northern gods. He would try anything once. Thor even dared to wrestle with old age and death for mankind's benefit, although he was defeated in the contest. His hammer, Mjollnir, was the thunderbolt. Short in the handle, it resembled a heavy iron cross; and when he hurled it at his foes, the hammer whirled through the air like a fiery swastika. It would hit very hard indeed and immediately return to his right hand again.

Thor once journeyed to a place called Gjottun, or Grittown, in order to reclaim a hostage from the giant Hrungnir. The giant was sharpening his weapons on a huge whetstone when Thor appeared. Hrungnir laid his battle-ax aside, picked up the whetstone, and hurled it with all his might against the god.

There was no time to dodge the missile, and so Thor hurled Mjollnir. The hammer shattered the stone and returned to Thor's right hand. After that, it was but the work of a moment for Thor to hammer Hrungnir down. Yet the god himself had suffered severe wounds. Fragments of the whetstone sank deep into his brow.

Thor released Hrungnir's prisoner, a hero named Orwandill, and put him in a basket. Swinging the basket in one hand, the god returned along the way he had come. One of Orwandill's toes stuck out of the basket, through the wickerwork. In the course of the journey, it froze solid and broke off. Thor, noticing this, stopped and tossed the frozen toe into the sky. It glitters there still. Orwandill's toe became the morning star, which is dear to farmers everywhere.

By sorcery, Orwandill's grateful bride removed most of the stone fragments from Thor's brow. Yet in her happiness at finding her husband safe and well, she totally forgot

SHEN I, THE COSMIC ARCHER

According to an ancient-Chinese tradition there were once ten suns, though only one crossed the sky in each day. It happened, however, that in a time of great confusion all ten suns appeared simultaneously, which threatened to dry up the earth. At this the hero Shen I, the "cosmic archer," took up his wondrous bow and shot the nine superfluous suns out of the sky (myth, page 256). The illustration shows three of them already lying dead on the ground in the form of sun ravens. This myth of a struggle against suns may be evidence of a collective memory of a time when the earth was lit by a number of moons or bright stars. On the other hand, in China, as in India and Egypt, the power of kings and emperors was equated with that of the sun, and the myth may simply reflect the succession of such rulers.

the final spell of all. One last triangular chip of Hrungnir's whetstone therefore remained in the forehead of Thor, to torment him until the end.

BUDAK YOID INTOIE

The following epic comes from Malaysia's seemingly primitive Berang Senoi people. The repetitions with which this myth abounds are like the glittering facets of a cut and polished crystal. They all seem to illuminate, albeit in a dreamlike way, the sensitive thrust of the hero's destiny.

Budak Yoid Intoie was the youngest of seven brothers in a family of ironworkers. His brothers would not permit him to learn their craft, explaining that he was too little. So Budak collected every scrap of iron that dropped from their anvils until he had a great heap of glittering bits. These he melted down and beat out again to make the biggest chopping knife ever seen. Only he was strong enough to lift it. He told his parents and his brothers that he was going to seek his fortune in the world at large. He planted a flowering shrub just in front of the

A famous Viking stone relief on the Isle of Man illustrates a scene from the Nordic epic poem *Ragnarok,* "Doomsday of the Gods," which reaches its dramatic climax in a fight to the death between Odin and the wolf Fenrir. Clearly recognizable are Odin with his ravens, and the wolf who eventually eats him.

family dwelling. "When the blossoms of this shrub close, I shall be in great danger," he said. "When they wither away, I shall be dead."

Then Budak Yoid Intoie set off through the jungle, carving a track through the trees with his chopping knife. The sound of the trees falling was "prung punggau, prung punggau, prung punggau!"

He had not gone far before he met a man called Pull-the-Canes. They stopped to chew betel nut together. Budak Yoid Intoie asked the man, "Do you possess a knife?"

"If I did, I would not be Pull-the-Canes," was his reply. So Budak Yoid Intoie proposed a wager. "My knife is in that tree stump. If you can lift it out, I shall be your servant. If not, you shall be mine."

Pull-the-Canes was unable to lift the knife. Budak Yoid Intoie plucked it out of the stump and cut his way forward, with Pull-the-Canes following him.

Budak Yoid Intoie and Pull-the-Canes met another man, whose name was Thump-the-

Banks. The three sat down to chew betel nut; Budak Yoid Intoie made the same wager with Thump-the-Banks that he had made with Pull-the-Canes. Once again he won the bet. Followed by two servants now, he proceeded on his way. Then Budak Yoid Intoie met yet another man, called Shove-the-Country-Around, who in the same way became Budak Yoid Intoie's servant.

Budak Yoid Intoie and his three followers traveled on until they came to the sea. They wished to cross, but there was no boat available. Budak Yoid Intoie took his knife and said a strong charm over it, a charm not in any common tongue. Before he had finished, the knife was long enough to bridge the sea. Budak Yoid Intoie and his friends crossed it, but not without danger. A dragon reared up out of the sea and tried to snatch the travelers; this annoyed Budak Yoid Intoie. Upon reaching the far shore, he quickly shrank the knife and used it to chop off the dragon's head. The dragon's body sank down into the reddened tide, and its head drifted away.

The head lodged at the mouth of a river, near the bathing place of a rajah. It was so big that the rajah's men were unable to shift it out to sea again. It became a severe problem when it began rotting and polluting the water. The rajah promised his only daughter in marriage to the man who could devise a way to get rid of the head, and Budak Yoid Intoie, traveling down the coast with his companions, came to hear of this. He went to the rajah's bathing place and took a look at the dragon's head. It was no great matter, he decided; he would not require his knife. Then, with one finger, he pushed it away. It floated out to sea.

Budak Yoid Intoie had no particular desire to marry the rajah's daughter, and so his servant Pull-the-Canes took her. She had previously been engaged to a hero named Bonsu, who boarded his warship and sailed directly to the rajah's palace as soon as he heard of her marriage. He meant to get revenge. Budak Yoid Intoie tried to reason with the jilted man, but Bonsu would not listen. To make matters worse, Budak Yoid Intoie's knife was far away above him in the sky. He burned incense, and its fragrance rose to where his knife waited invisibly. Then he chanted a magic spell. The knife descended once again into his hand, but now it was no larger than a rice leaf.

Budak Yoid Intoie slowly descended the steps of the rajah's palace. He paused, waiting for Bonsu to do something. Bonsu lashed out with his sword, but Budak Yoid Intoie jumped easily aside. Bonsu's sword hacked the lowest step of the palace in two. Again, and yet again, Bonsu struck out.

Budak Yoid Intoie avoided every cut, without once lashing back. He leaned against a tree, casually. Bonsu thrust hard, but Budak Yoid Intoie had slipped aside. Bonsu's sword entered the tree, and he could not pull it out again. Then Bonsu called for spears, daggers, and a gun; none had any effect on Budak Yoid Intoie. Bonsu returned to his ship, aimed a cannon, lit the fuse, and fired. Budak Yoid Intoie easily evaded every cannonball, but the village around him was destroyed.

Now Budak Yoi Intoie began to be angry. He danced a war dance, there on the beach, and challenged Bonsu to come down out of his ship to fight, sword against sword. Budak Yoid Intoie's blade was still only the size of a rice leaf. Bonsu sneered and taunted the hero. Budak Yoid Intoie made a chopping gesture with his miniature sword. Bonsu bowed mockingly, and his head fell off.

Budak Yoid Intoie collected all Bonsu's weapons and made them whole again. He restored Bonsu to life, set his head back on his neck, and sent him off to his home. Then, taking his servants Thump-the-Banks and Shove-the-Country-Around with him, he journeyed on along the shore of the sea. Soon he came to the palace and bathing place of another rajah. The dragon's head had preceded him and lodged there as well. The same adventures took place there as at the first rajah's palace. This time it was Thump-the-Banks who married the rajah's daughter. Budak Yoid Intoie traveled onward, and still the dragon's head preceded him. At the third rajah's palace, Shove-the-Country-Around found a bride. Now that his three followers were well cared for, Budak Yoid Intoie felt free to go on further adventures. First, however, he planted flowering shrubs in the palace gardens of each of his three former servants. "If the flowers close while I am gone," he told them, "I shall be in great danger. If they wither away, I shall be dead."

Then he traveled on until he came to a city called Bandar Benua, which was without life. There were no people, not even any animals in the streets. The silence was appalling. Budak Yoid Intoie mounted the citadel, entering the palace at the top. He came to the innermost room and found nothing but a large drum. He began to beat the drum with his fingers and the palms of his hands in order to break the oppressive silence around him. No sooner had he begun than a girl's voice called out from inside the drum. He lifted it and found a lovely princess crouched before him.

The city, she said, had been plucked bare of life by a seven-headed roc. The monstrous

223

bird came every evening to perch on the palace roof. It was nearly as big as the palace itself. No sword was big enough to sever its seven heads. When he heard this, Budak Yoid Intoie returned to the terrace; the princess crept back into her drum. The sun was setting now. Budak Yoid Intoie burned incense, and the fragrance drifted from the blue bowl of dusk into the sky. It summoned his knife down to him, this time full size.

The roc rose like a cloud in the south, black with seven searching heads. It swooped down, silently, to perch upon the palace roof. The blazing eyes in one of its heads lighted upon Budak Yoid Intoie. He swung his big knife in a circle; the head fell. It rolled down from the citadel and lodged at an intersection of the streets below.

Now the remaining heads began croaking in unison. "Laur! Laur! Laur!" cried each one. Budak Yoid Intoie climbed up onto the roof of the palace and chopped at the feathered necks, severing every head. The blood of the roc poured out and down, clogging the gutters of the city streets. The great bird toppled from its perch. With outstretched wings it fell, slowly, to the terrace; then all was still. The princess came out from the inner room and saw the bird's huge corpse, broken, glittering, and running blood. Budak Yoid Intoie was nowhere to be seen. He lay trapped under one of the creature's scaly wings.

The parents and six brothers of Budak Yoid Intoie noticed that the flowers he had planted in front of their house were closing. They set out to find and rescue him. Pull-the-Canes, Thump-the-Banks, and Shove-the-Country-Around noticed the same thing about the shrubs in their palace gardens and also went looking for him. They all arrived at the city of Bandar Benua at about the same time after some weeks of searching. They found the princess. She had been trying desparately every day to lift the roc's wing and release her hero.

The princess, together with Budak Yoid Intoie's family and followers, now succeeded in lifting the wing and freeing him. He was weak from his ordeal, but very happy. He decided to stay in Bandar Benua, marry the princess, and make himself the rajah. Together they would repeople the city.

POLYDEUCES AND AMYCUS

From *The Voyage of Argo* by Apollonius of Rhodes comes the account of a famous fight between two powerful men, the Greek Polydeuces and the Bebrycan king Amycus.

Amycus was an ogre for strength, a natural-born fighter who had never been defeated in his life and whose vanquished rivals were thrown over a handy cliff. Polydeuces, by contrast, was a still downy-cheeked Greek nobleman, relatively slight of build, whose power lay in sheer boxing skill and swiftness of hand. Their gloves were made of heavy oxhide thongs without any padding.

Amycus attacked first, like a great wave crashing down upon a narrow sailing vessel. But just as a skilled helmsman avoids the full onrush of wave after wave in a storm, riding across them as they come, so Polydeuces slipped aside, unscathed, again and again. Finally, when he felt he had learned all he needed to know about Amycus's relatively crude fighting style, he began returning blow for blow. The mingled din that came from cheek and jaw resounding to their fists was like that of the hammering in a shipyard. At last, having punished each other to the point of exhaustion, the men stood back a while, gasping for breath and wiping the sweat and blood from their bodies.

Again they closed in, and now the ogre Amycus's superior strength began to tell. Gaining confidence, he rose on tiptoe like a man felling an ox, stretched to his full height, and brought his heavy fist down at Polydeuces' left ear. Coolly, and not until the last possible moment, Polydeuces stepped inside the swing. Amycus's wrist smacked stingingly down on the slighter man's shoulder. At the same instant, Polydeuces counterpunched: a right cross to the temple. The king fell to his knees in agony and, within seconds, rolled over dead.

NO-CHA

The serenity of Confucian philosophy and Buddhist religion stands in contrast to the extravagance and wild violence of much Asiatic myth. Consider for example the legend of Li-Ching – heaven's prime minister – and his unruly son. He can be recognized by his implacably warlike bearing and by the miniature pagoda which he balances on the palm of one hand. In Western churches, saints are sometimes depicted carrying models of cathedrals to show that these places are under their special protection. Li-Ching's pagoda, however, is a weapon which he employed against his own unruly son. Their conflict came about in the following way.

Li-Ching's wife once dreamed that a Taoist priest slipped into her bedroom. Sitting up, she protested indignantly at the intrusion. "Woman," said the priest, "receive the

The Swedish tapestry *(above)* from the Viking period shows the supreme trinity of the Nordic pantheon: Odin with his ax, Thor with his hammer, and Freyr, the god of fertility, holding an ear of corn.

Two famous Viking picture stones *(above)* from the Swedish island of Gotland show the procession of the fallen to Odin's Valhalla.

The Valkyries, mistresses of the warrior's fate, appeared on the battlefield *(below)* to pick out the dead and dying heroes destined for Valhalla.

NORDIC WARRIOR GODS

Heroic struggles between giants and gods occur in great numbers in the collections of Germanic myths known as the *Eddas*. Some of them are illustrated on these two pages. Odin, mounted on his eight-legged warhorse Sleipnir, rides with the Valkyries to gather up those who have fallen in battle and carry them off with him to Valhalla, the dead warriors' hall of honor. From there they will ride out to fight the last great battle at the end of the world. This doomsday or twilight of the gods is called Ragnarok, the day when men join battle with one another before the whole world goes up in flames. It is then that

In this medieval reconstruction *(above)* we see the one-eyed god Odin armed with his lightning scepter, mounted on his warhorse Sleipnir. A Swedish stele *(right)* shows Thor, hammer in hand, fishing for the Midguard serpent.

A medieval mural in Schleswig Cathedral depicts the goddess Freyja with her drinking horn, riding a kind of wild cat *(above)*. She was the goddess of love and of the summer as well as being the cupbearer of the gods.

the gods arm themselves for the final engagement against the forces of evil – the giants under Ymir, the sons of Muspell under Loki, and Surt with his fire. The wolf Fenrir devours Odin and is slain by Odin's son Vidar. Thor defeats the serpent of Midgard but dies from having inhaled its poisonous breath. Freyr is vanquished by Surt, who then sets fire to the world. "The sun will turn black, the earth sink into the sea, and the bright stars fall out of the sky." These Germanic myths embody a theology according to which the cosmos exists in and through combat and will one day be destroyed by it.

According to the Nordic creation myth (page 80) the cow Audhumla licked the first man or men out of the ice while the primal giant Ymir was drinking from her udder *(above)*.

The figure on this Swedish picture stone *(left)* is Loki, father of evil and the wiliest antagonist of the good gods of the Nordic pantheon. He is shown riding on the wolf Fenrir, one of his creations. Some sources refer to Loki, rather than Surt, as the god of fire.

225

child of the Unicorn!" Swiftly, he thrust something at her. She awakened, not knowing what it had been. The pangs of childbirth began at once; and as best she could in between sighs and groans, she told Li-Ching what had occurred. The prime minister, distressed, retired to an adjoining room. He had not been there long when servants rushed in to fetch him back to his wife's bedside, for she had given birth to something incredible: a sort of ball which rolled and bounced about the room, glowing with a reddish light. Li-Ching slashed at the object with his sword and it fell apart. From the two halves a very white-faced baby emerged, scowling.

They named the boy No-cha. At the age of seven, when he had already grown to a height of 6 feet, he asked permission to take a walk with his tutor outside the town. His mother agreed, but told the child not to stay away too long. His father might become anxious.

Beyond the town gate, No-cha came upon a clear stream, and with his tutor's permission, he entered the water, still wearing his red silk trousers. The water reddened and began to boil. Far away in the Eastern Sea, the crystal palace of the Dragon King, Lung Wang, was disturbed on its foundations by the boiling of the water; so Lung Wang sent an officer to investigate. Following the trail of the incarnadined current, the officer bounded up along the Nine Bends River and came to where the boy was bathing. He rushed to seize the boy. No-cha leaped aside and drew a golden bracelet from his wrist. He hurled it wordlessly at the draconic officer, who fell dead. No-cha went on enjoying his swim.

Lung Wang waited for a time and then sent his son Ao Ping at the head of an armed guard to see what had happened. When Ao Ping arrived and saw his father's emissary lying dead, he angrily hurled his trident at No-cha. The boy evaded the weapon and returned the salvo with fireballs, which enveloped the Dragon Prince. No-cha hauled the blackened corpse of Ao Ping away from the stream and cut it open. He pulled out the sinews one by one and wove them together to make a belt as a present for his father. Meanwhile, Ao Ping's militia fled back downriver to report.

Lung Wang, the Dragon King, now roused himself. Weeping, he went from his crystal palace to the fortress home of No-cha's family. He bitterly complained to Prime Minister Li-Ching. "You have a monstrous son," Lung Wang rumbled. "I mean to lay a formal charge against him at the Gate of Heaven."

Being forewarned, No-cha waited in ambush outside the Gate of Heaven the next day. When Lung Wang came along, No-cha leaped on the Dragon King's back and ripped off with his fingers forty or more scales. Lung Wang was constrained to transform himself into a tiny blue fly. Humming with anger, the monarch whirled up and away.

No-cha swaggered home again, whistling. In the tower of his father's fortress he came upon what looked to be an ordinary bow and arrow. Just for something to do, he shot the arrow off in a southerly direction. It hissed as it flew, leaving a crimson trail upon the faint blue of the atmosphere. The

In West Bengal people fix pictures of the tiger god Bayhut-Bonga *(above)* to the doorframes of their houses to guard against tigers.

Gate guards are particularly common in China and Japan. This *lokapala (above right)* guarded a Buddhist temple, while the Men Shen *(above far right)*, a deified general of the T'ang dynasty, looked after a private house.

The tutelary deity Vajrapani *(right)* was set up as a temple guardian. Chung K'uei *(far right)* was a notorious subduer of demons (myth, page 100).

arrow proceeded mile upon mile until it reached K'u-Lou Shan, Skeleton Hill. There it entered the throat of a demon, the lover of a formidable goddess named Shih-Chi Niang-Niang.

Emerging from her cavern to find her lover slain, the goddess pulled out the arrow and examined it. She saw that it came from the

Protective deities of temples, monasteries, shrines, houses, and people occur throughout southern Asia from India to Japan. They are variously described as world kings, world guardians, tutelary gods, temple guards, or celestial guardian spirits. In postures either threatening or defensive they stand at the entrances to every sacred building. The greatest variety of forms is to be found in Tibet, which also has female tutelary deities. The function of these figures is to defend the place in question against evil spirits, infidels, and others who for one reason or another are barred

from entering. Even today pressed leaves bearing depictions of tutelary gods and demons are often pinned up over the door at New Year celebrations and for the blessing of new houses. They are believed to have the power to ward off snakes and sickness.

Standing twenty-three feet high outside a temple in Thailand, this giant figure is supposed to keep out demons and infidel spirits.

The Japanese Bishamonten *(below left),* one of the four guardians of the cardinal points of the universe, was the protector of human life against illness and demons.

A statue *(below)* from Tokyo depicts another "divine guardian" in the act of drawing his sword.

A common type of Indonesian temple guard is represented by this *rakshasa (below)* from Java.

At the beginning of the New Year the Chinese fix above the doors of their houses pictures of the god Yü-lei *(above)* riding on a lion.

fortress of the prime minister. Mounting her blue phoenix, she rode furiously through the air to Li-Ching's tower. Not even No-cha dared to face the vengeful goddess. He fled to the dwelling of T'ai-i Chên-jên, who had originally been responsible for No-cha's conception and was now his teacher. Protectively, the Taoist priest tossed up a sphere containing nine fire spirits. These enveloped Shih-Chi Niang-Niang and her blue phoenix in a whirlwind of flame. They crashed to earth, transformed into insensate stone.

The priest advised No-cha to hurry home again. Lung Wang together with the three other Dragon Kings was on the point of carrying off the boy's parents. No-cha returned to the fortress just in time. "I am the one who killed Ao Ping!" he cried. "Therefore, I should be the one to pay the penalty!" With that he cut off his own arm and then sliced open his stomach. "I am returning to my parents that which I received from them," he murmured, and died.

However, the story of No-cha was not ended. After burying his mutilated body, his mother secretly caused a temple to be built in No-cha's honor on a distant mountain. The temple contained a statue which portrayed No-cha and which the people of the mountain worshiped. One day Prime Minister Li-Ching happened upon the temple while making a journey. He stopped in as a courtesy to the local deity. When he saw the statue of his miscreant son, Li-Ching fell into a fury. He whipped the statue with chains until it crumbled. Then he burned the temple down.

No-cha's ghost thereupon fled, wailing, to the cavern of his former mentor, the Taoist priest T'ai-i Chên-jên. In pity, the priest spread three lotus leaves and two lotus stalks upon the ground. The ghost of No-cha stretched out on them. T'ai-i Chên-jên performed various rites, at the conclusion of which No-cha stood up tall and fierce, reborn in the flesh. On wheels of fire, No-cha immediately whirled off to destroy the prime minister. He would have succeeded in adding patricide to the list of his sins, but for the magical pagoda which Li-Ching hurled like a grenade. It enveloped the impetuous boy in pangs of conscience, whereupon a reconciliation between father and son took place.

Prime Minister Li-Ching and No-cha were to wage further war, but in alliance now. They both fought for the rising house of Chou, against the fading Yin dynasty.

The last Yin emperor had a warlike son and a heroic daughter. Those two dared oppose the Chou forces led by No-cha and his father. At the first encounter, No-cha hurled his magic bracelet and shattered the right arm of the young man, whose sister sprang to avenge the injury. She flung a five-fire stone into the ranks of Chou, where it did great damage. No-cha's father, however, released a rainbow-bristled hound of heaven which jumped at her and bit her throat open.

Both brother and sister were healed by sorcery, but they had learned their lesson. Not even the bravest and noblest children of a house that is doomed can stand against the onrush of destiny.

As for No-cha, in the heat of battle he had heard his name called out, three times over. For the first time in his life, he was frightened. That disembodied voice threatened to call forth the soul from his body. Swiftly, No-cha transformed himself. As a blossoming lotus, cool but with fiery leaves, he survived the sound of his own name – which might well have destroyed him. In a flower, soul and body are one and the same. No magical incantation can separate the two. Yet No-cha had suffered a wound all the same. After that, the boy was notably less brash.

With the slow fading away of Prime Minister Li-Ching and his impetuous son, four Diamond Kings of heaven undertook to defend the Chou empire. The first of these warriors wielded a lightning-swift sword called Blue Cloud. The second champion was less portentously armed; he carried a pearl-embroidered parasol alone. But when he turned the parasol upside down, there were earthquakes, and when he turned it right side up, impenetrable darkness covered the land. The third member of the team was musical; he possessed a guitar, the eerie twanging of which would set enemy encampments and even whole cities on fire. The fourth and youngest Diamond King kept a white rat in a panther-skin purse. When released, that rat became a winged, impervious, man-eating white elephant.

One might suppose that those four would be the winners in any war, and yet they met their match in the person of a demon named Huang T'ien Hua. He sported nothing but a $7^{1}/_{2}$-inch spike, sheathed in silk. That modest-seeming implement projected from its point a beam of light which could burn through almost anything, in laser fashion. The first three Diamond Kings were vanquished by it, but the fourth was not. So Huang transformed himself into a double of the youngest Diamond King's pet, the monstrous white rat. Creeping into the panther-skin purse, Huang waited patiently. The last of the Diamond Kings reached in. Huang bit his hand off at the wrist, and after that it was no contest.

PARSIFAL JOUSTING

Christianity is very rich in legends of armed combat. The so-called Dark Ages of Europe stand like some shadowy arras behind the luminous figures associated with King Arthur's court. Sir Lancelot du Lac, King Ban's son, of Benwick, and knight of the Round Table, was one such glorious warrior. Sir Galahad was another, and Sir Parsifal a third. The most complete story of Parsifal's career was put together by a German knight named Wolfram von Eschenbach early in the thirteenth century. He portrayed that paragon of Christian chivalry as being both pure in heart and very passionate – a highly volatile mixture.

In a forest meadow, on a snowy morning, Parsifal watched as a falcon captured a goose. Three drops of blood fell from the goose's neck upon the snow. The hero's eyes fixed upon them; and he reined in his horse and sat staring down, remembering his wife, whom he had not seen for years. "Who created colors so pure?" he thought. "Condwiramurs, this really resembles you. God is good to me, to have set this reminder here. Honor be to the hand of God and to everything that He has made! Condwira-

Early-Greek myth tells of a battle between the Titans and the gods of Olympus – a mythic symbol for the replacement of the old religious order by the Hellenic religion. When Zeus, son of Cronus, seized power in heaven the Titans, sons and daughters of the old god Uranus, rose up against the new gods (myth, page 82). The mighty ten-year war between the Uranides and the Cronides, referred to by Greek writers as the Titanomachia, is depicted in full on a frieze nearly eight feet high and four hundred feet long adorning the Pergamum altar. The Titans' base was Mount Othrys, while Zeus and his tribe fought from Mount Olympus. Zeus fetched the Hecatoncheires ("hundred-handed") and the Cyclops up from Tartarus, and with their thunder and

lightning it proved possible to subdue the Titans and dispatch them to Tartarus in their turn. Gaea, the Earth Goddess and mother of the Titans, made a last attempt to win power for her children by sending Typhon, the monster of Tartarus, to kill Zeus. Zeus, however, subdued him too and was able to consolidate the rule of the Hellenic gods.

One of the most famous works of Greek art is the altar of Zeus from Pergamum, a Greek city in Asia Minor. A frieze round the altar depicts the Olympian gods' struggle against the Titans. In this detail *(above)* Athene subdues the Giant Enceladus (some accounts have the Giants fighting alongside the Titans). On the left is Nike, winged goddess of victory.

This triple bust *(right)* in the Acropolis Museum, Athens, is believed to represent Typhon, the monster Zeus defeated in a last, decisive battle to secure his throne.

Up on high the Father
of men and gods thundered ominously,
and down below,
Poseidon caused the wide world
and the lofty mountain-tops to quake . . .
Such was the turmoil
as the battle of the gods began.

HOMER, THE ILIAD, BOOK XX, 56-67
Translated by E.V. Rieu (1950)

The sixteenth-century Italian painting *(above)* shows Odysseus blinding the one-eyed Cyclops Polyphemus, who had imprisoned the Greeks in a cave and was eating Odysseus' companions at the rate of one a day. The heroes made their getaway by clinging to the bellies of Polyphemus's sheep when he let them out of the cave.

The detail *(left)* from Giulio Romano's famous *Fall of the Giants* illustrates a crucial phase of the Titanomachia: the Giants are crushed beneath the hail of boulders hurled by the "hundred-handed" Gyes, Cottys, and Briareos, who fought on the side of Zeus.

Here *(above)* the battle of the Giants and the Titans against the gods of Olympus is depicted in a Roman bas-relief. The Giants with their serpent tails are shown armed with rocks to meet the onslaught of the gods.

229

The wild hunt of Odin (or Wo-
tan) takes place at Yuletide –
Yule being the feast of the winter solstice – during the nightly
storms. Odin, god of the dead
(and also god of the winds and
of battle), summons the dead
souls to ride with him across the
sky. This magnificent apocalyptic painting by the Norwegian P.
N. Arbo is a vision of one such
hunt, with the Valkyries and the
warriors of Valhalla charging
along the cloud path between
setting sun and rising moon, accompanied by black dogs and

the birds of night. On this occasion they are urged on by Thor
brandishing his hammer, in his
goat-drawn chariot. Thor was
the god of thunderstorms and
physical strength; his hammer,
called Mjollnir, would fly back
into his hand like a boomerang
after administering its blows
(myths, pages 221 and 296).
The splendid silver and gold image of Mjollnir *(above)* is from
eastern Gotland.

murs, I see your image here. The snow surrounds the crimson blood with its whiteness; the blood lies crimson on the snow. These are the colors of your face and your lovely body, Condwiramurs; that you must confess." In spirit, Parsifal was home once again and with Queen Condwiramurs in her bedchamber.

As Parsifal was brooding on the image before him, a squire from King Arthur's court rode up. When he saw a stranger sitting armed on horseback with spear erect, he assumed that a deliberate challenge was meant and swiftly informed King Arthur's knights of this. Sir Sagramour thereupon rode out to attack the silent champion; but Parsifal, intent upon his dream of love, did not even see Sagramour's approach. His horse did, however, and automatically wheeled to meet the charge. The motion removed the sight of the drops of blood from before Parsifal's eyes, and he came to himself just long enough to unhorse Sagramours. Then, without a word of triumph or reproach, he returned to gazing on the drops of blood again.

Sir Kay was the next to ride against Parsifal. Finding the knight motionless in the saddle, he struck him with his spear shaft so that Parsifal's helmet rang. "Wake up!" shouted surly Sir Kay. "You shall sleep soon again, but never between sheets. The snow shall be your bed soon!" With that, Sir Kay backed off his steed, leveled his spear, and charged full tilt. Again, Parsifal's mount wheeled to meet the attack; and again Parsifal came out of his trance long enough to fight back. Parsifal unhorsed Kay so violently as to break an arm and a leg.

Sir Gawain was the third knight to ride against the bemused lover. Parsifal sat holding upright in his mailed fist the stump of the lance which he had shattered in unhorsing Sir Kay; and his glance was still fixed on the three drops of blood. Now, Sir Gawain happened to be the greatest ladies' man in Arthurian legend. One glance told him what Parsifal's trouble was. Riding up close, in a gentle manner, Sir Gawain drew from his sleeve a yellow silk headband. This he let fall, to cover the blood drops on the snow.

Parsifal lifted his head. "Alas my lover and my wife," he cried, "who has removed you from my sight? Here in bright sunlight, a mist before my eyes has taken you away. And what has happened to my spear?" Sir Gawain then spoke to him and explained what had occurred. He offered to bring Parsifal to King Arthur's encampment. And in this manner did Parsifal, who was to find the Holy Grail, join the company of King Arthur's knights.

HARMONY THROUGH COMBAT

The Dusun people of North Borneo say that once a half-boy was born possessing only a right arm, right leg, right half torso, and right half head. In spite of all this, he lived. The half-boy felt very sorry for himself, as well he might; and, in his misery, he grew up mean and nasty to his parents, much to their distress. When he reached puberty, the half-boy went away, hoping to find his other half somewhere in the wide world. Crawling as best he could, he reached a clear stream and bathed himself, then hopped up the bank into a strange village. There was another half-boy there, a pathetic fellow possessing only a left arm, left leg, left half torso, and left half head. The two half-boys locked limbs and wrestled hotly, rolling in the dust; but the combat turned out to be of a healing sort. For, when the dust had settled after a time, a whole youth stood up where the two half-boys had been. "Which way to my village?" he asked. The people said, "Here it is, you never left home." Now his parents were happy, and the village rejoiced as did the youth himself.

MAGICAL COMBAT

Not all combat in myth is overtly violent. Consider for example the following Maori tale of subtle warfare which took place in a South Pacific paradise of fruitfulness and ease.

Once upon a time there was an island chieftain named Tinirau who invited a magician from a nearby island for a feast. When the magician, Kei, arrived, Tinirau stepped down to the shore and called, "Tutunui!" A whale which was disporting itself far out in the ocean heard the call and immediately swam in to greet its friend, then lay unprotestingly in the shallows while Tinirau cut a generous slice of flesh from its side. When Tinirau had finished, the whale swam away again while the old chieftain roasted the flesh and served it up to his guest. Later on, Kei begged Tinirau to call the whale once more, explaining that he would like to ride home to his own island on the creature's back.

Rather reluctantly, Tinirau agreed. The whale performed its mission in a docile mood. It brought Kei to the shore of home; then it shook itself gently as a signal for the magician to dismount from its back. But Kei held on. He pushed Tutunui's head down hard and stuffed the whale's blowhole with sand, strangling the creature there in the shallows. Then he called his people to come and drag the whale up onto the beach.

They soon sliced it up and indulged themselves in a whale-meat banquet.

The fragrance of Tutunui's barbecued flesh drifted far out across the sea. At last it came to Tinirau's nostrils; and the old chieftain wept for his friend the whale. He vowed vengeance upon Kei; but lacking warriors, he sent forty women to apprehend the magician.

Singing as they went, the women paddled across to Kei's island. They pretended to have come in a festive mood and danced and sang in the presence of Tinirau's enemy. After the fun was over, as the fires burned low, sleep filled Kei's spacious house. The old magician slept with the rest, but he appeared to be awake, for he had put mother-of-pearl over his eyelids and they glinted in the dark. Tinirau's forty women, who were only pretending to be asleep, were not fooled by Kei's trick; and when they were sure that he was sound asleep, they gently lifted him and passed his somnolent form from hand to hand, down to their canoe on shore. He was light as a bundle of sticks and still dead to the world as they put him into their canoe and paddled home with him. At Tinirau's island they formed another line and passed the still sleeping magician from hand to hand, until they could lay him down beside the main pillar of the house, just as if he were in his own home. Kei slept on, alone, knowing nothing of this.

In the morning the magician woke up to see Tinirau sitting outside his door. Kei rubbed his eyes, yawning, and sat up. "How came you here?" he wondered aloud. Tinirau smiled, "I ought to ask you that," he said. "But," Kei objected, "this is my house, not yours." "Is it?" Tinirau asked. Then Kei looked about and saw where he was. He bowed his head in silence, knowing that for the death of Tinirau's pet whale, Tutunui, he would have to die. He could only wish that his death would not be slow.

There is another Maori legend which says that what is now the northernmost island of New Zealand was once dominated by a fortress which very few people dared even to approach. At the center of the fortress was a tower, and in the tower rested a carved wooden head. Its grinning teeth were those of a crocodile and its power was this: when strangers approached, the sorcerers who served the head would warn it and the head would shout out something unintelligible. The vibrations of that shout seemed slight at first and were harmless to anyone who stood in the head's presence. Yet, as the vibrations spread beyond the walls of the fortress, they increased, and all living things within a mile or so of the citadel invariably died, shaken apart by the sound of the hidden head.

A good magician, Hakawau, eventually undertook to destroy the head. He and his apprentice hid themselves near the fortress and by means of spells called out the forces of the head within the walls. A great battle took place in midair between those evil forces and the spirits which Hakawau himself summoned. Though the wind whistled and howled, the sky remained perfectly clear; and it is doubtful whether the sorcerers inside the fortress even knew that a battle was taking place, for the conflict was invisible and lasted but a few minutes. When it was over, Hakawau and his apprentice rose from their hiding place and calmly approached the fortress.

The sorcerers on the walls immediately informed those within that two strangers were coming, the message was passed to the tower, and the sorcerers who were inside hastened to warn the magical head. But to their astonishment they discovered that the polished wood of the head had become rotten and the mother-of-pearl eyes had fallen from their round sockets, where termites were now at work. When the head tried to shout, it could only moan in a barely audible voice. The head was dying.

Hakawau and his apprentice entered the fortress where the evil magicians, knowing themselves to be without power, made a show of welcoming the strangers. They offered food and drink, which Hakawau and his apprentice were wary enough to refuse, saying that they had only just eaten, when in fact they had taken no food on the journey at all. Then they departed; but as they left, Hakawau turned and struck the threshold once with the palm of his hand. As he did so, all the evil sorcerers died.

Welsh legend from the Dark Ages also tells of battles in which not a blow was struck and yet great damage was done. One of these concerns gentle Saint Collen, the great-great-grandson of King Bran. He lived as a hermit at the foot of Glastonbury Tor, in Somerset. The few human inhabitants of the region did homage to Gwyn ap Nudd, a fairy monarch, as they explained to Saint Collen. He scoffed at them, saying that Gwyn and the fairies were mere demons in actuality and not worth thinking of.

It was not long before a pair of footmen, arrayed in blue and crimson livery, appeared in Saint Collen's hermitage. "We are servants of Gwyn ap Nudd," they said. "He bids you come and speak with him at noon on the top of Glastonbury Tor."

The saint refused the invitation, but the messengers came back a second and yet a third time; then Saint Collen deemed it

SIGURD, THE NORDIC HERO

The most famous son of the tribe of the Völsunga was the invincible hero Sigurd. His life and victorious deeds form the basis of the Sigurd Saga and the thirteenth-century German epic poem, the *Nibelungenlied* (in which he is referred to as Siegfried). Sigurd's principal "labor" is to secure the Nibelungs' hoard of gold, which is guarded by the dragon Fafnir. Sigurd does an apprenticeship with a smith, who forges him a sword called Gram. At the same time Odin acquires for him the mighty stallion Grane. After a lengthy heroic fight, Sigurd defeats the dragon and secures the treasure. The Nibelungs' gold is his undoing, however, despite the fact that he succeeds in freeing Queen Brünnhilde.

A detail *(left)* from the portal of a stave church in Hyllestad, Norway, shows Sigurd with the blacksmith Regin who forges for him the razor-sharp sword called Gram.

The splendid Swedish rock drawing *(above)* depicts Sigurd's fight with Fafnir, the dragon who guards the hoard of the Nibelungs on GnitaHeath.

Another well-known figure of Celtic myth, the god Ogmios *(below),* is comparable in many respects to the earlier Greek hero Herakles, though he also has something of the Roman Mercury.

would be prudent to attend. Arming himself with only a bottle of holy water, Saint Collen ascended the hill. Though Glastonbury Tor was bare of buildings at that time, he found a wondrous castle when he went up. Pages and trumpeters led him into the presence of Gwyn, who was seated upon a golden throne. The fairy king ordered various delicacies to be brought and invited the saint to eat. "I do not nourish myself upon twigs and leaves," was Collen's chilly response.

King Gwyn remained smiling and hospita-

THE RAMAYANA

The *Ramayana,* a celebrated Indian epic written by the poet Valmiki and comprising some 24,000 couplets, describes Rama's long and perilous struggle against the *asuras* – a kind of Indian Titan – under their lord Ravana. The myth belongs in the same tradition of battles between gods and giants, or be-

tween the powers of light and the demons of darkness. Briefly it tells that Rama's wife Sita was captured by the demon king Ravana and carried off to Lanka, the city of the "Titans." At the hand of the gods Ravana was invulnerable – he could only be vanquished by a human being. It cost Rama much suffering and many furious battles to recover his bride. But with the help of the monkey king Sugriva, who built a living bridge across to Lanka with h

ble. "And what do you think of the livery which my house servants are wearing?" he asked the saint. "Crimson on one side and dark blue on the other makes a handsome display, don't you agree?"

Saint Collen did indeed agree. He found the servants' motley wholly appropriate. "It shows which side of each demon is being frozen in hell at this moment and which side is being seared red-hot!" With that remark,

the saint made the sign of the cross and poured out his bottle of holy water upon the tile floor. The castle, the serving men, and Gwyn ap Nudd himself vanished abruptly. Saint Collen returned to his hermitage.

monkey hordes, Rama and his heroic companions were able to cross to the city, defeat Ravana, and set the beautiful Sita free. Since Rama is an avatar or incarnation of the supreme deity Vishnu, the story offers a link between myth and the origins of religion.

Opposite, top: Lakshmana, Rama's loyal half brother, in combat with Surpanakha, the jealous demoness who started the feud between Rama and Ravana.

Here *(left)* the monkey general Hanuman, Rama's comrade in arms, is fighting the abductor Ravanna.

This detail *(right)* shows the rival armies – gods and monkeys against the *asuras* – in combat.

Valmiki's *Ramayana* epic is also sacred in Thailand. This painting *(above)* from a Bangkok temple shows the monkey king Sugriva, with his general Hanuman, forming a living bridge between the mainland and Lanka, where the demon Ravana was king. Rama, who had concluded an alliance with Sugriva, crossed the bridge with the monkey army and defeated his wife's seducer in a heroic battle.

The *Ramayana* material keeps on cropping up in Indian painting in one form or another. Here *(above)* the hero Rama appears as the ten-armed Parashurama, to join battle with the even more generously endowed demon king Ravana.

A Mighty Sword

Hatupatu is said to be the most resourceful human hero of the Maori. Hatupatu's father had been humiliatingly beaten by a chief named Raumati. His war canoes having been burned, the old man could do nothing further against his enemy. His three eldest sons, moreover, seemed to have no stomach for war. Their pleasure was to go on hunting expeditions, for weeks at a time, in the high mountains. They speared succulent birds and roasted them over the campfire. This was their great joy in life.

The youngest in the family, Hatupatu, went along on these expeditions. However, he was considered too little to take part in the hunting. He only gathered firewood and did the washing up. His brothers never allowed him to eat the best parts of the birds they caught. They would give him only the dried-out scraggly bits to munch upon. This exasperated Hatupatu. He used to weep even as he chewed and his brothers mocked and ridiculed him. He would pretend that the smoke from the campfire made him weep.

The brothers cured some of the birds in the smoke of the fire and laid them away in pots. These they meant to take home at the end of their expedition. Hatupatu, left alone at the camp all day, guarded the potted birds which his brothers had set aside. His little belly was pinched and sore from hunger, and his heart was bitter. So, one morning, Hatupatu pried into the pots and gobbled up everything there was in them. That done, he thought of a plan. He broke branches from bushes around the campsite and trampled the grass. Then he bruised himself with a stick and deliberately bloodied his own face. When he heard his brothers returning through the forest, he lay down on the ground as if wounded and left for dead. His brothers naturally thought that a war party had made an attack upon the camp and carried off the meat.

It took the brothers some weeks to collect another supply of potted birds. When they had done so, Hatupatu played the same trick a second time. The brothers began to suspect something. They continued as before and laid in a third supply. When it was ready, they prepared a trap for Hatupatu. They hid themselves in a place which overlooked the campsite. They watched him open the pots and begin eating. Then his brothers rushed down upon Hatupatu. They kicked him and beat him severely. Leaving him unconscious by the campfire, they set off for home. They told their parents that Hatupatu was lost. They said they had looked everywhere for him.

By means of enchantments, Hatupatu's parents sent a sacred cloth to fly through the air, find Hatupatu, and wrap him in its healing power. The cloth did as it was bidden. Hatupatu rose in the morning, taller and stronger than before. He made a spear for himself and went hunting. Now he was free; he could do as he liked, or so he thought.

Hatupatu's very first spear throw missed its aim and passed through the lips of a monster whom he had failed to see. Kurangaituku was her name. She had been creeping up, invisible, to spear the same bird at which Hatupatu aimed. Her lips, elongated like a beak, were Kurangaituku's spear. She tore Hatupatu's weapon from her lips. Angrily, she spat blood. Hatupatu could see her now; he turned and ran away through the forest as fast as he could. Kurangaituku followed him.

"Step out, stretch along, step out, stretch along," Kurangaituku called to her feet. "There you are, Hatupatu, not far from me," she cried, catching him in her outstretched hands.

Gently, she seized the boy. She carried him back over the mountains, far away to her cavern. In it were many lizards and snakes, tame creatures. Many birds lived in the cavern too. They flashed their feathers in the dim light, beautifully, and sang sweet songs. The monster had a cloak of thick dog's fur, red in color, there within the cave, and also a flaxen cloak and one of red feathers. She also had a two-handed sword which was magnificently carved. She gave Hatupatu raw birds to eat. He put them to his lips and let them fall inside his cloak, slyly, so that Kurangaituku might suppose that he was swallowing what she offered. Afterward, the monster took Hatupatu into her bed.

Next day, she went hunting. Hatupatu stayed behind in the cavern. He roasted the birds which he had pretended to eat raw. Now he made a leisurely picnic of them. He was pleased with the place where he was. Kurangaituku did not seem, after all, to be so very terrible. She was a rich monster, indeed. Hatupatu, gazing about and wiping his lips with the backs of his hands, wondered how best to rob her blind.

After some weeks, he found sufficient courage to make the attempt. "Kurangaituku," he said to her as the sun rose, "this morning you had better go a long distance away. Go to the first mountain range, to the second, to the tenth, to the hundredth, to the thousandth mountain range. When you have got there, begin hunting birds for us two."

Kurangaituku agreed. She strode off happily, flapping her great wings. In a moment

Christian tradition describes the end of the world in terms of a final separation of good from evil. At this Last Judgment the heavenly angel hosts (right) will arrive to take the souls of the faithful to paradise and drive the damned down into hell and the arms of Satan.

The ordeal of the holy man at the hands of the demons of darkness – a well-known theme in all the great religions of the world – finds expression in classical Christianity in the story of the temptation of St. Anthony (above). The saint is visited by hideous and frightful demons who, epitomizing all that is sinful and infernal, seek to shake his faith.

This bronze figurine of the Mesopotamian demon Pazuzu (right), a winged creature with the feet of an eagle and the claws and head of a lion, was probably worn as an amulet to guard against evil.

GOOD AND EVIL

As if in obedience to some natural order of things, the cardinal themes of myth and religion – and consequently of human life and ethics – center on the question of good and evil, or, put another way, knowledge and ignorance. And again and again the mythic expression of that question uses the antitheses of heaven and chaos, light and darkness. Ranged on one side are the gods of light and the redeemers of mankind. Opposing

them are the demons, Titans, and inhabitants of hell who wage perpetual war on the gods and incessantly thwart man's strivings toward the light of knowledge. The many myths concerning temptation by the forces of evil and battles between gods and demons symbolize man's never-ending yearning for emanicipation from darkness and ignorance.

When the wicked demon Mahisasura assumed the form of a buffalo, in an attempt to dispossess the Hindu gods, he was destroyed by the powerful goddess Durga *(above)*.

An Islamic miniature *(far left)* from the fourteenth century shows a demon king with the head of a bull riding a black lion.

In a dramatic piece of demonic symbolism the Tibetan goddess of the magic dagger *(middle)* destroys evil in the form of hatred and lust.

The Christian painting *(left)* emphasizes the terrible, demonic aspect of the Prince of Hell and his assistants, to whom the souls of the damned will be delivered at the Last Judgment.

she had passed the first range and was out of sight. Hatupatu picked up her two-handed sword. He cut about with it at the friendly lizards and serpents. They were too trusting; none escaped. Then Hatupatu swung at the birds, the little pet birds who made the cavern bright with music. All but one of these he managed to kill. That one flew out of the cavern and darted away after Kurangaituku.

"Oh Kurangaituku," the bird sang as it flew, "ruin and death have been in our home." It took the bird a long time to reach the place where Kurangaituku was hunting, but for the monster to return was a matter of moments only. "Step out, stretch along, step out, stretch along!" Kurangaituku called to her feet as she came on. "There you are, oh Hatupatu, not far from me!" she cried.

Truly, Hatupatu had not yet run very far from the cavern mouth. He was heavily burdened with the sword, the cloak of dog's fur, the flaxen cloak, and the cloak of red feathers belonging to the monster. When he heard her voice, he stopped dead at the foot of a rock. "Oh, rock," he implored, "open for me. Open!" To his astonishment, the rock opened. Hatupatu slipped inside it. Kurangaituku rushed by overhead.

Her shadow passed across the rock as she flew. Then Hatupatu came out again and made off in another direction. Kurangaituku, wheeling, saw him go. Again she pursued him. Again he hid himself within a rock. Thus they went on, hiding, wheeling, and running, until they came to the sulfur springs of Te Whaka-rewa-rewa. The warm crust of the rock held firm under Hatupatu's feet. Kurangaituku crashed through to the hot springs of sulfur underneath the crust and was scalded to death.

Hatupatu's adventure vastly increased his faith in himself. The very rocks had opened for him; perhaps the sea would be equally kind. He dived into the water and swam underneath its surface for a very long time. He came up at the island of Mokoia, which was his family home. His parents saw him rise, dripping, in the dawn. They loudly welcomed him. Hatupatu warned them to be quiet. If his brothers were to hear of his return just now, they might succeed in killing him. Hatupatu went and hid himself in the underground storehouse where sweet potatoes were kept. He stayed there for some weeks, gaining in strength with every sweet potato that he ate.

When he felt strong enough, Hatupatu told his parents to announce his presence. His brothers were outraged at the news. Standing before the cellar door of the storehouse, they challenged Hatupatu to come up. Each

The art of antiquity, such as these two statues, has had much influence on our ideas of a god of war. The Romans worshiped the mighty god Mars (above) as their leader in battle, while the contentious Greeks sacrificed to two war gods simultaneously: Ares, the Roman Mars, and Athene (opposite), the wise counsellor who could yet be terrible in her anger.

Pallas Athene now inspired
Diomedes son of Tydeus with
audacity and resolution, so
that he might eclipse all his
comrades-in-arms and cover himself
with glory.

HOMER, THE ILIAD, BOOK V, 1–4
Translated by E.V. Rieu (1950)

Far Eastern mythology features a whole series of gods of military leadership ("general" gods, one might call them). They were also, like the figure in this Chinese fresco *(above)*, appealed to as protectors of warriors.

In the Semitic Middle East it was the supreme deity Baal *(below right)* who led warriors in the field.

Below, left to right:
Karttikeya (or Skanda), son of Shiva and Parvati, was believed to have sprung from a flame in the River Ganges (myth, page 196). This motherless birth took place under the sign of the planet Mars, and the fact that it involved the incompatible elements fire and water made Karttikeya an ideal god of war.

The Egyptians worshiped the falcon-headed Mont as their god of war. A local deity of the city of Hermonthis, he was regarded as an incarnation of the sun god Ra. Both sun and falcon are symbols of the battle of light and darkness.

This powerful looking, primitive figure is Ku or Kukailimoku, the war god of the Hawaiian Islanders.

The writings of Julius Caesar contain references to a Celtic war god whom he calls Mars and who was probably either Cernunnos *(above right)* or Teutates.

of them was armed. Feelings of guilt for what they had already done to Hatupatu made each man murderous.

Hatupatu, standing below in the cool dimness, gripped in both his hands the sword which he had stolen from the monster's cavern. A death's head was on the hilt of the sword. Its eyes, inlaid with mother-of-pearl, glinted. Hatupatu climbed up out of the storehouse. When his brothers had last seen him, he was just a boy. Now he had become a man. He rose slowly up, glaring. Now he stood before them. He let the point of his sword rest lightly upon the grass at his feet. He was waiting. He guessed his brothers could not long abide the tension of this meeting. At any moment they might spring at him, all three together, and try to hack him down.

Barely had they begun to move when Hatupatu's sword whirled round like lightning, shattering their weapons in their hands. "Oh my sons," their father cried aloud, "it is a sad thing for me that you are so fierce in peace when you ought to be fierce in war. My enemy, Raumati, boasts of his dominance over me. You do not dare, obviously, to try to restore our family's honor by making war upon him. This tribe of mine is once again sufficiently numerous to defeat Raumati's people. But I am too old to lead the warriors, and you are too cowardly!"

Shamed by this reproach, Hatupatu's brothers prepared canoes and marshaled a war party to go against Raumati. Hatupatu was not invited along. After the war canoes had gone, Hatupatu folded together thirty cloaks of red feathers. Diving underwater with them, he swam beneath the canoes, all the way to Raumati's country. When the war party pulled up on the enemy shore, Hatupatu was already there, spreading his red feather cloaks on the beach to dry.

The brothers each commanded a division of 340 men. Hatupatu had none to command. But, as if playing a game, he set up thirty figures of straw along the beach. He dressed each in a red cloak. His brothers marched their divisions inland, one after the other. They were going to attack Raumati's stockade.

Raumati, the tough old warrior, stood in his watchtower overlooking his palisades. The blue tattoo marks on his brow seemed to darken stormily as he eyed the approach of his enemies. He could sense from the way the brothers led their troops that they would not be much good in a fight. Cowardice shows itself in a footstep, or a mere turn of the head, to those who have knowledge of such things. Raumati decided not to passively await attack. He ordered his own troops out of the stockade. He led them down the hill against the brothers' army, at a rush.

The battle was confused at first, but soon Raumati's troops forced the brothers' men into retreat. As they approached the beach again, the brothers themselves broke and ran. Raumati, at the head of his own forces, pressed forward eagerly. Then, through the swirl of battle, he saw what seemed to be reinforcements drawn up on the beach. They stood as still as death itself, in glittering red feather cloaks. There were thirty terrifyingly impassive figures guarding the shore.

Their leader, Hatupatu, stood swinging his two-handed sword, daring Raumati to approach. There was no fear in him, nor in that thin red line of officers at his back. For a moment Raumati hesitated, and in that moment the whole battle swayed the other way. Hatupatu sprang forward. With one stroke he cut off Raumati's head. This he hid under his cloak.

Hera, Athene, and Aphrodite *(above)* each promised Paris fabulous gifts for the golden apple inscribed "for the most beautiful." Paris gave it to Aphrodite, and was rewarded with the beautiful Helen.

Here we see Helen *(opposite top)* after her abduction by Paris, living at the court of King Priam of Troy.

This detail *(below)* from a Chalcidian vase shows the dead Achilles lying on the ground, Paris's arrow in his heel. Glaucus has tied a rope round one ankle but is himself run through by the hero Ajax.

In triumph, the war party paddled home. As they approached Mokoia, boastful chants arose from each canoe. The brothers stood in the prows, with folded arms, smiling. From the shore their father called out gleefully. "Show me," he cried, "the head of my old enemy!" The three older brothers, each in turn, lifted a severed enemy head. Each claimed his own trophy to come from the shoulders of Raumati. Their father wept, however, at the display. "No," he said, "Raumati has escaped all three of you."

Then Hatupatu took from its place of concealment in his feather cloak the head of Raumati. He held it up in the sunshine for all to see. The blue tattoo on the brow glimmered like an unspoken thought. Joy came to Hatupatu's father's heart.

The divine blacksmith Hephaestus hands Thetis the armor he has forged for her hero son Achilles *(below)*.

Above: Achilles (second from left) and Hector were attended at their final duel by Athene (left) and Apollo.

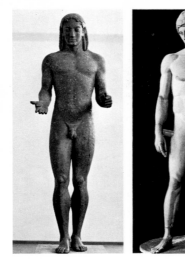

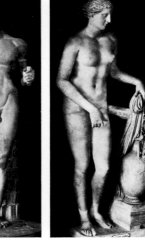

Apollo *(above)* and the war god Ares *(middle)* both supported the Trojan cause. Apollo helped Paris to his victory over Achilles; Ares assisted Penthesilea, the queen of the Amazons and an ally of Priam.

To thank him for judging her the fairest of the goddesses, Aphrodite *(above)* helped Paris bring Helen from Greece to Troy. But that reward brought on a war that lasted ten years, ending in the destruction of Troy.

The subject of Homer's *Iliad* is the momentous ten-year struggle over Troy. The cause of the war was trivial enough: a fit of womanly pique. At the marriage of the goddess Thetis and the mortal Peleus (the parents of Achilles), Eris, the goddess of strife, furious at not having been invited, threw a golden apple into the midst of the assembled gods. The apple was inscribed "for the most beautiful." The goddess Athene promptly claimed it for her own – and so did Hera and Aphrodite. At this Zeus singled out the handsome young Paris, son of Priam, king of Troy, to decide which of the three should have it. Paris chose Aphrodite, (the famous Judgment of Paris) and as a reward

Achilles binds the wounds of his comrade-in-arms Patroclus *(below)*.

Three gods who backed the Greeks in the Trojan war were Athene *(below left)*, Hera *(middle)*, and Poseidon *(right)*. The war goddess Athene was the protectress of Achilles, and Hera sent a storm to

try and prevent the abduction of Helen. Poseidon guided the Greeks' ships on their crossings to Asia Minor, though he later turned against Odysseus and prevented him from returning home (page 249).

the grateful goddess promised him the most beautiful woman in all Greece – namely Helen, the wife of the Spartan king Menelaus – on condition that he abduct her by a ruse. He succeeded in doing so and Menelaus, swearing vengeance, secured the services of the mightiest warriors and rulers of Achaea for a campaign against Troy. The gods themselves also took sides and played an active part in the hostilities. Led by their hero Hector, the Trojans were successful in a number of major engagements. But one of the opponents (Odysseus) had the clever idea of the wooden horse and managed by this means to smuggle a picked force into the city. Thus Troy fell.

241

Superficially, Hatupatu's story appears the opposite of edifying. Deprived in the first place by his cowardly brothers, he turned to thievery while still a boy. Befriended by a female monster, he robbed her also. He won the great battle against Raumati, his father's enemy, by using scarecrows of a sort: straw figures of steadfast officers in red feather cloaks. His entire myth exhibits a fairy tale quality. It might seem to be the daydream of an imaginative weakling, but not so. Like most important myths, Hatupatu's also deals with an expansion of consciousness. It was a childish thing, natural and not wicked after all, for him to try to trick his brothers. By responding so violently, and then abandoning him, they awakened Hatupatu to a keen appreciation of the world's edginess. Then when the monster Kurangaituku took him, as it were, under her wing, he learned that nature herself can be both caressing and murderous. After that, he was ready to break the swords of his own brothers, if need be. To destroy wily old Raumati was no problem for him because by that time Hatupatu's magical experiences had made him a new person. Power in awareness he now possessed.

FLAMING DARTS

The Great Mother, Coatlicue, gave birth to thousands upon thousands of stars. Then she swelled enormously, pregnant yet again. Her previous children felt certain that Coatlicue had committed some evil, and that she would soon give birth to a monster, so they rushed to murder their own mother while the child was still in her womb. But Golden Bells, Coyolxauhqui, the loveliest of all the stars, was only pretending to take part in the attack. She rushed ahead of the rest to warn her mother. Just then, however, the last and greatest of Coatlicue's children sprang brilliantly to life. This was Huitzilopochtli, the blazing sun, whose darts destroyed in a moment the whole advancing host of his elder brothers and sisters.

Ancient Aztec Indian legend gives that account of primordial sunrise, making it a family fight which was to reecho in nature every day. The legend adds that when Huitzilopochtli realized that Golden Bells' intentions had been peaceful, he cut the head from her shoulders and gave it new life, or half-life, aloft as the waxing and waning moon.

Love, and war, make the world go round. So myth attests. Combat is necessary on the supernatural plane, and is reflected throughout nature, including human na-

The literature of India contains important myths dealing with two major themes: the cyclical ages of the world between the dawn and decline of successive creations, and interventions on the part of the gods to preserve the divine order whenever it is threatened with destruction. These crises are invariably associated with the appearance of a demon who seeks to plunge the world into chaos. The two pictures reproduced here belong to the body of myths dealing with the avatars or earthly incarnations of Vishnu, a tradition in which creation themes are bound up with the idea of the bestowal of a divine order. The Indian miniature *(right)* shows Vishnu's first incarnation, as Matsya (Sanskrit: "fish"). While Brahma rested through the night preceding the new creation, the waters rose to cover the earth. In his sleep the god dropped the Vedas, the sacred

scriptures and repository of all wisdom, and the demon Hayagriva carried them off to the bottom of the ocean. Vishnu appeared in the form of a fish god with a club in his hand and fought the demon for a thousand years before finally defeating him and recovering the Vedas. The smaller picture shows Vishnu in his third incarnation; this time he assumed the form of a boar to destroy the demon Hiranyaksha, who had dragged the whole earth down to the seabed.

ture. Harmony we may achieve at times, but conflict will almost always have some part in it, whether overt or not.

The Aztecs, as everyone knows, were a terribly fierce race which fell before the yet more hardbitten conquistadores of Spain. Moctezuma, the Aztec emperor, divined his people's fate long before conquering Cortes appeared on the scene. The facts of his extraordinary premonition are set down in C. A. Burland's authoritative account, *The Gods of Mexico* (1967):

Because Moctezuma was so intimately associated with the rituals of religious worship, he was much more sensitive than most of the leaders of his age. This led to his projection of visions in which the gods appeared to him. The most famous one is when a grey bird appeared in the palace and stood in front of the king. On its forehead he observed the magical, black mirror of Tezcatlipoca. In the mirror he saw all the stars of the sky. This was immediately clear to him because of his long experience in observing the heavens. As he gazed, he saw the heavens change, and there was a vision of strangely armed men approaching to destroy Mexico and himself and the gods.

The most famous of all Hindu philosophical dialogues, the Bhagavad-Gita, hinges upon the hero Arjuna's reluctance to fight a battle in which he may be forced to slay his own relatives. Krishna, a personification of the supreme deity, demonstrates to Arjuna that he must fight. Killing and dying are not so terrible, Krishna explains, because:

As the Dweller in the Body endures childhood, youth, and age, he also passes on to other bodies altogether. Steadfast people do not grieve over this. They understand that That is indestructible by which all This is interpenetrated. It is but the bodies of the Body Dweller, undying, everlasting, infinite, that have an end. . . . For this Body Dweller may never in any body be wounded, O son of Bharatra; therefore you should not grieve for any creature. Look instead upon your own appointed destiny, and do not fear it. Nothing is more to be welcomed by a warrior than righteous war.

Moreover, Krishna makes clear, combat is unavoidable. It exists in celestial regions as well, not only on the earth.

"Let there be light!" the God of the Hebrews commanded, "and there was light." From that moment until the present, nonetheless, Jehovah has been contending with the Prince of Darkness. Every god of light has the same struggle on his hands, needless to say. It will not go away.

243

One of the heroic deeds of Herakles was to capture the two Cercopes of Ephesus, who had stolen his weapons. On this sixth-century metope he is seen carrying them tied to a staff, though he later set them free.

Fate has laid on each man as law
the unalterable efficacy
of his horoscope,
safeguarded by a causally
determined train of good and evil
in consequence
of which two deities,
fate's servants,
born of themselves,
govern man's existence.
They are Hope and Chance
and through deceit
and coercion they make man
abide by the law.

DISTANT QUESTS AND MORTAL TESTS

At the end of their epic search Parsifal and Galahad achieve the mystic vision of the Holy Grail, the quintessence of Christian redemption.

The one is clear for all to see in the
predetermined outcome,
being now good and happy,
now dark and cruel.
Some she raises up
in order to cast them down;
others she casts down in order
to raise them
to more brilliant heights.
Most she governs by such deception;
hoping, they believe
what they desire
and experience what they
least expect.

VETTIUS VALENS (SECOND CENTURY B.C.)

A great many fairy tales begin with an untried youth in humble circumstances – often a youngest son – going out into the world to seek his fortune. He may eventually win the hand of a princess in marriage and "rule over half a kingdom."

First, though, the youth must undergo a succession of quests and tests (set, as a rule, by his prospective father-in-law) which prove terribly difficult to accomplish as well as perilous. That standard pattern of fairy tale is to be found in myth as well, but there the stakes for which the hero contends may be extremely high. It is tempting to suppose

that their conclusion is always one and the same. Whether the hero happens to gain a princess, a kingdom, a healing medicine, a talisman, or some other reward appears immaterial. He actually earns self-integration, balance, wisdom, and spiritual health. In every case, according to Campbell, the phantasmagorical adventures of the hero symbolize inner development. Final success spells the conclusion of an initiation into eternal mysteries. Doctors and patients who practice therapies based on the work of the Swiss psychologist Carl Jung take a similar view. Jungian analysis amounts, in

Constellations in their astrological interpretations fill both the northern and southern skies in Einhart's great map. Star deities, of course, go back much earlier than these sophisticated mythological configurations. In Babylon, for example, where there was a well-developed religion of astral deities, the stars were called upon like gods to tell the future.

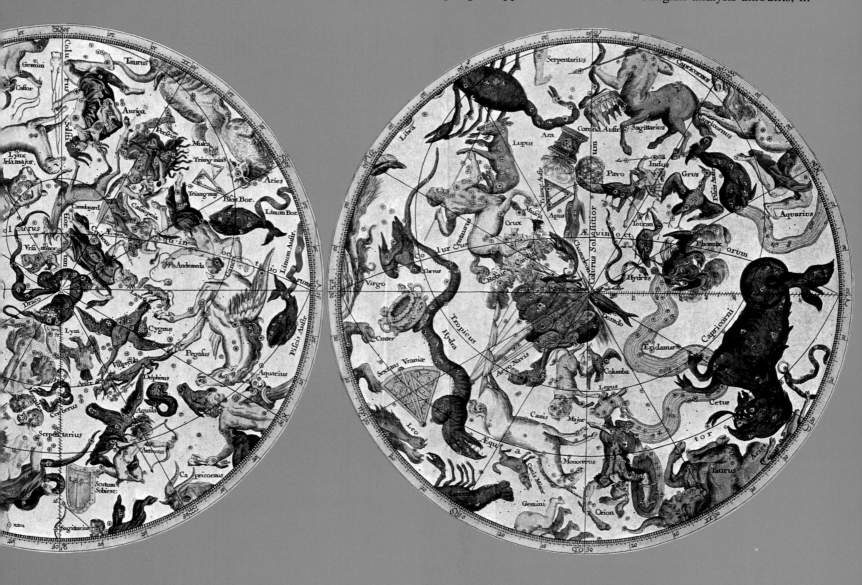

As planetary fates they at times achieved such importance that no course of action was undertaken without the stars having been consulted first. Many of the star deities of myth, linked together in pictures of heroes and animals, still form the basis of present-day astrology, providing a continuing oracle to man's hopes and fears.

that stories of distant quests and mortal tests, whether in fairy tale or myth, reflect some universal fact of human existence. By means of stories, possibly, we give a certain glamour and resonance to our own necessarily constricted quests and to the seemingly mild tests of everyday life.

But stories can do more than that for us. They may even serve to point the way that we ourselves ought to travel. Such has been the interesting contention of Joseph Campbell. *The Hero with a Thousand Faces,* Campbell's most influential book, gathers together various questing myths to show

part at least, to a startling personal journey through the world of myth.

Among the most distant and difficult journeys anyone can undertake is that which leads to the realm of the dead. Since everyone is destined to set foot upon that path, it is not too surprising to find that hundreds of myths from all parts of the world deal with it. Consider, for instance, the following adventure of China's legendary King Mu.

The king was restless, and fearless as well. He stepped from his throne to travel west and west again, all the way to Mount Kunlun. When he arrived there, he kept on journeying, toward the setting sun. But in the valley west of Mount Kunlun he found his way barred by a river of melted snow. Hissing and foaming, the river rushed mile-wide between its slippery banks. The fish and the turtles in that river took pity on King Mu. Swimming against the current, side by side, they formed a footbridge of their own backs, precarious in the extreme, for him to cross.

On the far bank the dark Queen Mother of the West greeted Mu with a gentle smile. In her palace of snow and crocuses she comforted the weary king, and she taught him a special song to carry home again, all the way back to the country of dawn.

According to that ancient-Chinese myth, Death's empire lies west of the world itself, on the far bank of the rushing river of life. The queen of that wintry empire deals kindly with courageous pilgrims. She even lets the best of them remember her somewhat, whether in dreams or in a song such as King Mu brought back, when they journey eastward again to be reborn.

JASON AND THE ARGONAUTS

One of the most famous of all quests is that of Jason and the Argonauts in Greek legend. In the account given by Apollonius of Rhodes and others, King Pelias was warned by an oracle to beware of a visitor wearing only one sandal, who would usurp his kingdom. When he saw Jason, the king was paralyzed with fear, for Jason had only one sandal. He had lost the other while helping an old woman across a raging stream. Pelias thereupon dispatched Jason to distant Colchis (on the Black Sea) in the hope that he would be killed on the long and dangerous journey.

Jason was commissioned to procure the magical hide of the ram Chrysomallus which had carried Phrixus and his sister Helle from Boeotia to Colchis. During the flight, Helle fell into the straits which bear her name to this day, the Hellespont. But Phrixus held on and managed to arrive safely at Colchis, where he sacrificed the ram to Zeus and hung its Golden Fleece in a grove sacred to Ares, the god of war.

Jason undertook the expedition to Colchis in the company of fifty or more heroes. Among them were Castor and Polydeuces, Herakles, Calais and Zetes (twin sons of the North Wind), the prophetic Orpheus, and Mopsus the magician.

With the help of the goddess Athene, their ship, the *Argo,* was quickly built and launched. A unanimous vote among them all secured for Herakles the captaincy of the expedition; but with unaccustomed modesty he resigned the honor to Jason.

Sailing through the Dardanelles, passing the Bosphorus, and journeying on across uncharted reaches of the Black Sea, the *Argo* confronted a weird hazard in the shape of rocks which kept clashing together with a mighty roar. The Argonauts thereupon let loose a dove, emblem of Aphrodite. As the dove flew between the clashing rocks, they snapped shut, clipping a feather from its tail. Fast behind came the *Argo,* assisted by the goddess Athene, who was pushing from the stern. Again the rocks closed in and just snipped a small bit off the *Argo's* stern ornament.

Upon reaching Colchis at last, the Argonauts made their way upriver to the grove of Ares, where Phrixus had sacrificed the ram. A giant serpent had been posted to guard the Golden Fleece. No one could approach the place where the fleece hung on a tree, for the serpent never slept. As the *Argo* came to rest near the grove, the serpent hissed in warning, and its hissing echoed through the dank and dripping wood. But Medea, the beautiful and witchlike princess of that place, sang the serpent to sleep for Jason's sake.

Jason almost slept as well, so potent was the spell the sorceress made. But now he pulled the Golden Fleece down from its tree. Even in that black wood, the ram's fleece shone to light their path back to the riverbank where the ship was waiting.

THE QUEST FOR IMMORTALITY

Rites of passage to and from realms unknown are likely to be rough indeed, not to say fatal for the unprepared. This is made very clear in the oldest epic preserved in writing; the story of the Sumerian hero Gilgamesh.

Immortality, nothing less, was what Gilgamesh sought for himself. His way led through the bowels of a vast mountain called Masha.

On the far side of the mountain, Gilgamesh knew, the garden of the gods was to be found. Shamash, the sun god, reigned there in eternal glory. Gilgamesh hoped that Shamash would listen to his plea; but first, he had to thread his way through a sharp-edged and soaking-wet, crystalline world of crushing darkness. His claustrophobic ordeal has been rendered (in N. K. Sandar's prose translation of *The Epic of Gilgamesh,* 1960) as follows:

When he had gone seven leagues the darkness was thick and there was no light, he

The marvelous Christ figure of Chartres Cathedral with the book of life in his hand *(left)* is a symbol of redemption.

Faust standing inside the magic circle of the zodiac *(above)* – a paradigm of man's search for the all-embracing wisdom of the philosophers' stone.

An aura of heroism surrounded the figure of the medieval knight *(above left)* in his quest for foreign dominions and love.

In the branch of alchemy known as melothesia medieval scholars sought to tell the future through the relationship between constellations and parts of the human body *(above right).*

The search for knowledge and meaning is illustrated in this Renaissance painting of the seven liberal arts on the mountain of knowledge (right). The personification of each branch of learning is attended by a figure who has made a notable contribution in that field. With Theology at the top of the mountain, immediately below the deity, sits St. Augustine, signifying that supreme wisdom was equated with knowledge of God.

An early-Spanish painting (below left) shows St. Martin sharing his cloak with a half-naked beggar. After Joan of Arc had led the French troops to victory she fell into the hands of the English (below).

QUESTS AND QUESTERS

Human beings have always had a goal of some kind, have always sought a state of completion or redemption, either here on earth or in union with the gods after death. They have pursued earthly goals as discoverers of distant lands or as warriors or conquerors; they have striven for technical progress in the form of improved tools and greater control over nature; and they have looked for long life and happiness on earth. Numerous myths reflect man's sometimes meandering efforts to reach these targets, culminating in the achievement of a new level of being. Obstacles and ordeals mark the mythic path to any kind of accomplishment.

In their search for new lands (below left) the Vikings reached Newfoundland, Nova Scotia, and the Mediterranean.

Charles Lindbergh (above) made the first solo air crossing of the Atlantic. His fame as the lone adventurer achieved mythic proportions.

The mythic phoenix was an Egyptian symbol of the rejuvenation and return of the sun. Grown old, it set fire to its nest and emerged from the flames reborn (near right). In the Indian Mahabharata, at the moment of Drona's death his soul soars triumphantly heavenward in the form of a lotus flower (right center). Medieval alchemists sought an allegory for their ideal of the philosophers' stone in the figure of the hermaphrodite (far right).

The North American Hopi and Pueblo Indians give their children little spirit dolls or kachinas (right). The purpose of these symbols of supernatural forces is to help the children to acknowledge their own tribal gods and bow to their authority.

Even today science and society pursue objectives that they themselves constantly set higher. Religions and philosophies are directed toward such goals as redemption, freedom, knowledge, and wisdom, broadening the quest to include such questions as the right way to live, man's relationship with God, and the possibility of life after death.

In Taoist mysticism and ancient-Chinese myth the horned dragon of heaven with the pearl of everlasting life (above left) symbolized the search for wisdom, happiness, and immortality.

The people of Haiti seek through Voodoo ceremonies and trance states to obtain the spirits' answer to future events (above).

247

could see nothing ahead and nothing behind him. When he had gone eight leagues Gilgamesh gave a great cry, for the darkness was thick and he could see nothing ahead and nothing behind him. After nine leagues he felt the north wind on his face, but the darkness was thick and there was no light, he could see nothing ahead and nothing behind him. After ten leagues the end was near. After eleven leagues the dawn light appeared. At the end of twelve leagues the sun streamed out. . . . Shamash saw him, and he saw that he was dressed in the skins of animals and ate their flesh. He was distressed, and he . . . said, "No mortal man has gone this way before, nor will, as long as the winds drive over the sea." And to Gilgamesh he said, "You will never find the life for which you are searching." Gilgamesh said to glorious Shamash, "Now that I have toiled and strayed so far in the wilderness, am I to sleep, and let the earth cover my head for ever? Let my eyes see the sun until they are dazzled with looking. Although I am no better than a dead man, still let me see the light of the sun!"*

The Greek saga of the Argonauts, a myth cycle of searches and wanderings, centers on the quest for the Golden Fleece that hung in the grove of Ares in Colchis on the Black Sea coast, guarded day and night by a dragon (myth, page 246). On the way there Polydeuces defeated King Amycus of the Bebryces in a boxing match, afterwards tying him to a tree (myth, page 224). In Colchis Jason, the leader of the Argonauts, managed with the aid of the king's daughter Medea to put the dragon to sleep and seize the object of his quest.

The romantic spirit which breathes from that long quotation appears indigenous to the heart of man. The story of Gilgamesh, hopelessly high-hearted hero that he was, dates back some four thousand years.

TASKS OF LOVE

The people of the Sudan have a tradition of legend as romantic as any in the world. Witness the following Soninke tale of a quest which – like that of Gilgamesh – proved impossible to fulfill.

Annallja Tu Bari was the daughter of a king who ruled a small town and the few surrounding villages. He lost the villages in war; then he died without a male heir. In her grief, Annallja declared that she would marry no one but a conqueror. He would have to add eighty villages to the little kingdom that she had inherited. Her court was the most melancholy in the world. No suitor dared attempt such a vast conquest. The princess herself entirely forgot how to laugh, and yet every year she grew more lovely.

A prince of Faraka, whose name was Samba Gana, left his distant home to find his own way in the world. At every village where he stopped, Samba Gana would challenge the ruling prince to single combat. He always won. But Samba Gana did not feel like settling down just yet. He freely gave each village back to the prince from whom he had won it.

One evening, when Samba Gana lay encamped on the bank of the Niger River, his bard sang to him the story of Annallja Tu Bari. Samba Gana heard the song through. Then he sprang to his feet: "We ride at once to the princess!" he cried.

It was a long journey, but Samba Gana did not pause on the way. He soon strode into the melancholy presence of Annallja. "Show me the territory which I am to conquer for you," he said, bowing low. Without a smile, Annallja directed him to circle out a hundred miles or so and conquer every village he came to. "I go," Samba Gana told her. "I shall leave my bard to cheer you with his songs, if possible, while I am making war."

Samba Gana fought with and overcame eighty princes in turn. Each one he sent to Annallja's court as a suppliant. All their villages became hers, and they themselves remained in the presence of Annallja Tu Bari. Her retinue was soon the most brilliant in Africa. Samba Gana himself returned in triumph to Annallja. "I have revenged your father upon every neighbor," he boasted. "Still, you do not smile. Why?"

"Because," she replied, "your bard has been singing about the serpent Issa Beer. It lives near the source of the Niger. If you were to conquer that serpent, then I would smile and laugh as you do."

Samba Gana rode high into the mountains. He came to a place of snow. There lived Issa Beer, more than a mile in length, steaming, with coppery scales. Its fangs were as long as elephant tusks. Under the flat ridge of its forehead, its eyes glowed like campfires. It was a slow creature, yet capable of swallowing down an ordinary man on horseback at a single gulp. Samba Gana fought for eight long years against Issa Beer. He splintered eight hundred lances and eighty iron swords upon the serpent's scales. Now he had only one sword and one lance left; both were stained with the serpent's blood. Issa Beer did not wish to fight any more. Samba Gana gave the lance to his bard. "Take this to the princess," he ordered. "Tell her I have subdued the serpent. See whether she smiles at last."

Weeks later the bard returned. He brought a message from Annallja Tu Bari. The princess desired Samba Gana to conduct Issa Beer to her capital. She needed the monster to dig out a river for her. Samba Gana laughed. "She asks too much," he said. Taking up his one remaining sword, he plunged its point into his own heart.

Drawing out the sword, the bard rode back again with it. "This sword," he said, laying it at the feet of the princess, "is stained with two kinds of blood. My master laughed, as he died. Yet you still seem melancholy."

Annallja Tu Bari mounted her horse. She rode, with all her people, into the country of snow. They found Samba Gana's body covered with ice. Eight thousand people dug the shaft of his tomb. They hollowed out the burial chamber underground. They built the sacrificial chamber at ground level. They piled the pyramid higher and higher, until it loomed above the peaks of the surrounding mountains.

After eight years, at sunrise, Annallja Tu Bari climbed to the top of the pyramid. "It is finished," she said. "Samba Gana's tomb

Odysseus, king of Ithaca, can be said to represent the Greek ideal of prudence, cunning, daring, and wisdom. He was married to the beautiful Penelope when war summoned him, together with the Achaeans, to Troy (pages 240–243). It was Odysseus' ruse – the wooden horse – that finally brought about the fall of Troy after a ten-year siege. Odysseus then embarked for home, a voyage that turned into an unprecedented ordeal because of the obstacles the angry Poseidon placed in the hero's way. What put the sea god in such a rage was the fact that Odysseus, blown off course to the land of the man-eating Cyclopes, there blinded his captor Polyphemus, Poseidon's son. After a visit to the kindly Aeolos, god of the winds (and also a son of Poseidon), Odysseus was within sight

the edge of Hades to ask his fate of the sage Tiresias. He then sailed safely past the dangerous singing Sirens and be-

tween the terrible rocks, Scylla and Charybdis. When they reached Thrinacia, his companions did exactly what they had been told not to do, namely slaughter the oxen of Helios. They were punished by Zeus with shipwreck and death. Only Odysseus survived – he drifted on a piece of flotsam to the island of Ogygia, where he spent seven years with the nymph Calypso. Released eventually at

Helped by four of his companions, Odysseus blinds the one-eyed Cyclops Polyphemus (below),

while in the Roman bronze relief (left) he is seen in combat with Scylla, here depicted as a water demon. In order to resist the temptation of the Sirens' song Odysseus had himself bound to the mast, having first plugged his companions' ears with wax (below left and below).

of his island home when his curious companions accidently let the unfavorable winds escape from Aeolos's sack. The party, already much reduced, was driven to the land of the cannibal Laestrygones and then on to the sorceress Circe. After a year Circe let Odysseus go, but not without first sending him to

the gods' command, he just made it to the island of the Phaeacians, who escorted him on the last leg of the journey to Ithaca. He entered his house disguised as a beggar and with the help of his son Telemachus killed the suitors who had been importuning the faithful Penelope.

One of Odysseus' stopovers was on the island of Ogygia, where the lovely Calypso (left) promised him eternal youth if he would stay with her. He stayed for seven years before she released him to continue his journey home to Ithaca.

is as great as his name." She laughed, then, for the first time. Immediately afterward, she died. Her body was placed in the burial chamber beside that of Samba Gana.

A Transforming Quest

A Polynesian hero named Rupe was transformed by the requirement of his quest. His younger sister had been cast away. She had vanished across the sea. Rupe missed his sister terribly, but he had no idea where to search for her. One direction seemed as good or bad as another. The wide world, with all its seas and oceans, appeared limitless. As Rupe brooded on this, he found himself transformed into a dove. Sorrow had given him wings, as it were. He rose pure white, plumed with despair, into the upper air. He circled up until he could no longer see the earth. High overhead he found himself among people rather like those whom he had known below. They could tell him nothing concerning his sister, but they did say that in the heavens above theirs, he might hear news of her.

Flying and resting, now as a bird and again as a person, Rupe ascended from one celestial sphere to another until he reached the tenth heaven. There the God of the Birds, Rehua, greeted him. Rehua called for calabash halves to be laid out as dishes. He ordered a fire lit. Slowly he loosened the bands of his thick hair. Birds flew from their hiding places in Rehua's tresses. His slaves caught some, killed them, and roasted them over the fire. They set the roasted birds in the calabash dishes before Rupe.

Rupe did not wish to be discourteous. "Yet how could I," he asked Rehua, "dare to eat the flesh of birds which have been nourished upon the insects nestling in your sacred hair?" Rehua made no answer. The food slowly cooled in the calabashes, untouched. At last Rupe broke the silence. Quaveringly, he asked, "Rehua, do you know something about which I care very much?"

Rehua replied with a calming gesture. He pointed to the island of Motu-tapu, in the tenth world below.

Transformed into a dove once again, Rupe spiraled downward from heaven to heaven until he reached Motu-tapu. There he perched on the windowsill of a chief's house. People hurled spears at the dove, for sport, but he turned their weapons aside with his bill. They tried to snare him, and yet he easily avoided the nooses which they tossed.

Then his younger sister came. She was the wife of the chief. She had recently given

Enkidu barred the gate
with his foot,
denying Gilgamesh entry.
Seizing each other,
they sank to their knees
like bulls,
smashed the gateposts,
set the walls a-trembling!

Gilgamesh and Enkidu,
seizing each other,
sank to their knees like bulls,
smashed the gateposts,
set the walls a-trembling!
As Gilgamesh went down on one knee,
his foot to the floor,
lo! he threw Enkidu and
his anger cooled.

Epic of Gilgamesh

HEROES AND ANIMALS

There are numerous variations on the mythic theme of the hero required to do battle with monsters or particular types of animal. They represent attempts to grasp the complex nature of man's relationship to members of the animal world; some are his enemies, some his prey, and some – the domesticated species – his allies. This motif occurs in the myths of all cultures independent of cultural ties or geographical propinquity. We know of such images from Ur, Babylon, Greece, the Germanic North, America, and even the Eurasian cultural sphere. As far as one can tell from written sources, which usually represent late and sophisticated developments, such myths relate to vital

A silver plaque of the famous Gundestrup Caldron shows the head of a Celtic god holding a stag in each hand (opposite, top).

An Assyrian relief (right) shows Gilgamesh holding a lion cub. His right hand grasps the tail of a larger lion.

A helmet plate from Torslunda in Sweden (far right) shows a hero evidently in combat with two bears that have attacked him.

struggles between culture bringers, heroes, and animals of various kinds. Nor is it only incidents with animals that are described; not infrequently such symbolism conceals a struggle with cosmic forces or with the political and religious structures of older cultural systems in the process of disappearing. Even when patron deities of animals – e. g., an aspect of Ishtar – are shown flanked by animals, the idea of a threat successfully subdued is often being symbolized.

A Persian talisman in the Teheran Museum (above left) uses the same motif of a hero beset by two wild beasts.

A Persian relief (opposite, center) shows the Sumerian hero Gilgamesh (myth, page 246) with two lions he has subdued.

A Mesopotamian seal impression (opposite, bottom) depicts a mythic battle between a bull god and two lions.

A very fine piece of decorative inlay work found in one of the royal tombs at Ur shows a hero flanked by a pair of bulls with human faces (above). The scene probably illustrates a mythic combat.

The so-called Gilgamesh motif – a hero between two winged lions – originated in the Sumerian culture. It recurs in modified form in this bronze banner plaque (left) from Luristan, Persia.

251

birth to a baby boy. Her thoughts were filled with gentleness. "Let me look at the dove," she said. It hopped onto her wrist. She stroked it soothingly. She looked into its eyes and saw that it was really her brother. After a moment's thought, she called for her child to be brought to her. When he saw the infant, the dove who was Rupe grew very large. His sister, with the baby in her arms, climbed onto Rupe's back. They flew away together, never to return.

HIKU AND KEWELU

In Hawaii, the House of Kalakaua traced its ancestry back to Princess Kewelu, a maiden of the white sea strand. She loved Hiku of the forest; and he left his mountain fastness to live with the maiden in her coastal home. Garlanded with flowers, they played up and down the beach; but Hiku grew weary of such a soft life and wandered away, back into the rugged mountain region which was his home.

His bride, in tears, tried hard to follow him; but the vines clung round Kewelu as the forest thickened, and soon she could neither go on nor return. Imprisoned among the vines, she began to struggle, turning and twisting desperately. Her efforts only served to wind her ever more tightly in the sinuous embrace of the creepers of the forest. Bound tight and strangled, she died. Her soul descended out of sight.

Hiku's father told him what had occurred. Filled with remorse, Hiku searched far and wide until he found a hole leading deep underground. He descended the hole along a ladder of hanging vines, taking nothing with him into the bowels of the underworld except an empty coconut shell.

In the darkness Hiku tracked Kewelu's gleaming soul, stalking it just as carefully as he would the shiest forest creature. And the moment that Kewelu's soul paused to look around, he snapped his shell shut on it, catching the soul inside like a butterfly. Then swiftly he swarmed back up the vine into the air again.

Kneeling beside the beautiful corpse, Hiku opened his coconut shell a crack and clamped it over Kewelu's big toe. Her soul, startled, blundered into the toe. Hiku gently massaged her foot, her soul spread there, like a new warmth. He rubbed her ankle, her calf, her knee, and so on. Her soul spread further and deeper into her body. At last it reached home in her heart. Kewelu breathed again. She opened her eyes and looked at him. Her soul looked out of her eyes.

THE ROUND TABLE

The Saga cycle of King Arthur and his knights originated in Celtic England, where it was first mentioned in the sixth century. The material was considerably expanded on its way through Spain, France, Germany, eastern Europe, Scandinavia, and Iceland. As early as the twelfth century the French writer Chrétien de Troyes linked the sagas with the Grail legend, and in Wolfram von Eschenbach's *Parzival* (written ca. 1200) the life-style of King Arthur and his knights became the pattern of courtly knighthood. The historical Arthur must have been a Celtic military leader who defended his people against the advancing Saxons around 500 A.D. The Arthur of literature and myth was a factor in European culture for nearly a thousand years after that date. King Arthur and his wife Guinevere held court at Camelot in Cornwall, where they entertained the noblest knights in the land. His helper, the wizard Merlin, advised the king to install a round table at which he and his queen could sit with twelve chosen knights. At the Round Table everyone was equal, and there was no greater honor for a knight than to be admitted to its sessions. Here the king held merry feasts but also conferences at which the knights resolved to perform noble deeds to protect the oppressed. Following their association with the Grail legend the Arthurian knights became noble questers after the secret of the Holy Grail, symbol of the search for the true Christendom. From the late eleventh century onward, numerous Arthurian brotherhoods or "courts of King Arthur" were founded to uphold the ideal of the noble knight and champion of the good. The picture on the right shows the admission of Sir Galahad to the Round Table, where as a newcomer he will occupy the vacant throne.

252

The cup, the cup itself, from which our Lord
Drank at the last sad supper with his own.
This from the blessed land of Aromat –
After the day of darkness, when the dead

To determine the rightful king the candidates attempt to draw a sword from a stone *(left)*. Young Arthur alone succeeds and duly mounts the throne.

This medieval manuscript initial *(below)* illustrates an unpleasant story according to which King Arthur was responsible for a kind of "Massacre of the Innocents."

Went wandering o'er Moriah – the good saint,
Arimathean Joseph, journeying brought
To Glastonbury, where the winter thorn
Blossoms at Christmas, mindful of our Lord.
And there awhile it bode; and if a man
Could touch or see it, he was heal'd at once,
By faith, of all his ills . . .

ALFRED TENNYSON, THE HOLY GRAIL

THE HOLY GRAIL

The Arthurian legend provides a very early image of a sophisticated concept of knighthood and the courtly life. The Round Table became a pattern of medieval princely splendor and openness of heart and mind, with Arthurian brotherhoods building special halls like those in Danzig and Thorn (Toruń) in memory of the great Celtic king and his knights. It was an entirely natural development that the Grail legends emerging in twelfth-century France and Spain soon came to permeate the Arthurian saga. For the idea of a candidacy for the search for the Holy Grail (reportedly preserved by Joseph of Arimathea), expressing the gothic yearning for the mystic penetration of Christendom, dominated the world of medieval legend. Today the Arthurian cycle must be looked at in the wider context of the work of the French and German writers – principally Chrétien de Troyes and Wolfram von Eschenbach – who handed down the Grail legends and the unrealizable ideal of courtly love in such romances as *Parzival* and *Tristan and Isolde*. Further additions came from the story of the knight Titurel and the sagas of Hartmann von Aue, which also took the Arthurian material as their starting point. According to one version of the legend Arthur never died, and certainly his story at least never has.

The later legends of the Arthurian cycle tell of the great love of Lancelot and Guinevere, King Arthur's wife. Lancelot became so obsessed that he demanded a kiss as proof that his love was requited *(right)*.

Soon afterwards, however, Guivenere was abducted by another suitor. Lancelot used his sword to cross a river, fought two lions, defeated his rival, and set the queen free *(left)*. This was only one of the ordeals he was required to undergo for his love.

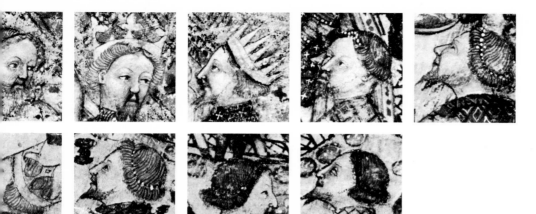

The stone head *(above left)* is a fifteenth-century idealization of King Arthur, the figure around whom so many sagas were woven. The smaller pictures, details of the painting on the preceding page, show the eleven noble knights summoned by Arthur to his first Round Table. The best-known names were Gawain, Galahad, Parsifal, Tristram, Gareth, Bors, and Bedivere. A whole series of other names can only be proven historically very much later. Lancelot was a symbol of worldly knighthood and love. The Galahad of the English version of the Grail saga corresponds to the Parzival of the German romance.

SPIRIT JOURNEY

A Chinese hermit of the Western Mountains named Yuan-shih T'ien-wang had a favorite disciple, Chin. One day Chin begged his master to inform him of things deep in the past.

To this request Yuan-shih T'ien-wang agreed without saying anything at all; he simply pointed upward, causing a rainbow shimmer to emanate from himself. Chin fell into a sort of faint; and then two spirit beings appeared and offered to take him on a trip into and through "the plain of luminous shadows."

Chin could never afterward remember the journey, nor could he recall arriving at any particular place at the end of it. Yet, wherever it may have been, he saw Yuan-shih T'ien-wang conversing quietly with the two supernatural guides who had stepped from the rainbow. The sage spoke to them as follows: "When our Creator, Pan-Ku, had completed his work, he died into the world. His physical body, which had grown truly immense, was now the entire universe. Some spark of him, however, drifted beyond space; and that spark was restless, unfixed, adventurous. It entered space once again and came to the peak of a mountain. There, every day, it watched the comings and goings of the woman T'ai Yuan."

"Every day she climbed the mountain to receive her only nourishment from the sun, the moon, and the colors of clouds. She was middle-aged, solitary, and absolutely without desire. Her qualities were such that the spark of the Creator, Pan-Ku, felt drawn to her; and she breathed in that spark. It was myself, of course. T'ai Yuan was my virgin mother."

This magnificent chalice is supposed to be modeled after the Holy Grail, the cup used by Christ at the Last Supper. The Holy Grail, as a symbol of Christian redemption, came to represent the supreme goal of noble knighthood. According to one tradition its first defender was Titurel, the son of the French king. He is said to have received it from the angels on Montsalvat.

Below: At the end of his great quest Galahad is rewarded with a vision of the Holy Grail on an altar guarded by angels. The kneeling knight has here achieved the supreme goal of his existence, whereas Bors and above all the too-worldly Lancelot are allowed to worship the Grail only from a distance.

The purest of the Grail questers was Galahad, seen here *(above)* on a white horse and with a guardian angel on his helmet, fighting the Seven Deadly Sins in order to attain the Seven Virtues.

DOCTOR'S ORDEAL

The best-loved man of medicine in Chinese myth was called Li Hollow-Eyes. The ordeal which he had to undergo to get that name is described as follows.

Originally, Dr. Li was a stately fellow, benign and plump in appearance. He used to leave his body now and then for the sake of the medical profession. At such times, Dr. Li would traverse in spirit form the Mountains of the West. He walked on high slopes, which few mortals could reach. By sunny pools of melted snow he would stoop down and gather wild flowers for their healing essences. He sealed the nectar of each flower up in his spirit bottle, which resembled an ordinary leather flask.

Dr. Li's physical body was too delicate and slow for long journeys and arduous ascents.

He would therefore leave it sleeping under the care of a disciple. It was important to watch over Dr. Li's sleeping body, lest some evil creature slip inside it, like a hand into a glove, and make off. If the doctor's own spirit failed to return within a week, the body was to be cremated, for safety.

Once, while Dr. Li's spirit was away on a mission, his disciple received a very unsettling piece of news. The disciple's own mother, it seemed, was gravely ill and at the point of death. The disciple had already learned a good deal of medicine from his master. There was a chance that he could save his mother's life. Yet honor bound him to remain beside the sleeping body in his care. He did so until six days had passed. On the sixth day he received a message saying that his mother could not possibly survive the night. Her one wish was to see her son again before dying. What was the disciple to do? Dr. Li's spirit had never been gone so long. The doctor's body, now that he examined it, seemed rigid, cold, and utterly lifeless. The disciple decided to cremate it, twelve hours before the proper deadline. He did so, with due ceremony. Then he hurried away to his mother's bedside.

The next morning the doctor's spirit returned. The ashes of what had been his body were still warm and smoking slightly. There was no time to lose; he had to find another body right away. Otherwise, his spirit would expire on the wind. Dr. Li rushed into the forest to seek a body, fast. Any very recently expired creature would do. Yet, in the few moments of choice which were left to him, Dr. Li gambled with life and rejected the bodies of a dead ant, bee, and parakeet. In those forms he would not have been able to continue practicing medicine. His spirit was growing weaker by the minute. His time was almost up when, to his delight, he saw stretched out upon the ground and half hidden by leaves the exceedingly emaciated figure of a human being. Whoever it was had been a begger in all probability and had died of starvation only recently. There was no time for more detailed investigation of the corpse. Dr. Li slipped inside it at once, and breathed a sigh of relief.

The doctor lay still for a long moment while his spirit filled and revitalized every molecule of his new fleshly garment. Then, rising with some difficulty, he staggered off through the forest. There was an urgent matter to be attended to, he guessed. His disciple must have had good reason for disobeying his instructions. Dr. Li's new body was twisted and bowed. His eyes gleamed like belt buckles in their cavernous sockets, yet with as kindly a light as ever.

SHEN I, THE COSMIC ARCHER

As Chinese myth goes, the story of Li Hollow-Eyes is remarkably straightforward. The legends told about Shen I are more typically exuberant. To analyze Shen I's career, on earth and in heaven as well, would be profitless. One can say, however, that his trials and triumphs led well beyond the realm of death – a region through which he appeared to pass more than once. In the end, Shen I's one love affair led him to assume cosmic responsibilities. But there was prodigious power and speed in him right from the start, as Emperor Yao witnessed:

In the twelfth year of the Emperor Yao's reign – that is to say about 2346 B.C. – he met a young archer in the street. The emperor demanded to know why the youth presumed to carry a bow and arrow in the heart of the city. The archer replied that he had come to display his skill, and that without his tools he would not be able to do so. "In that case," replied the emperor coldly, "transfix the pine tree on the hilltop over there."

The youth notched his arrow and let fly. The arrow flew off in the direction of its target. "How do I know that you have hit the mark?" the emperor asked. Instead of replying, the youth mounted a passing breeze and himself sped off through the air after the arrow. A moment later he returned with it in his hand. A piece of the pine's bark still clung to the arrowhead. Yao was impressed, as well he might be. "I name you Shen I, Divine Archer," he pronounced. "You will lead my armies against the many enemies of our people."

Shen I destroyed many monsters, including wild boars of enormous size. He killed the thousand-footed serpent of Tung-T'ing Lake and even forced the wind god, who pressed thunders from a terrible black sack, to recall them and shut them up.

Following his victory over the wind god, Shen I contended with nine fierce phoenixes in the far west of China. Posted on the snowy crest of a triple peak, they issued forth tongues of fire from their beaks, forming nine false suns whose rays threatened to destroy the land. Eastward the false suns mounted, spitting black and orange as they rose; but Shen I wisely ignored the phantom suns. Instead he saved his arrows for the throats of the nine birds themselves. As the throat of each bird was laid open by an arrow, the false sun above it dissolved into a mushroom cloud. Shen I's troops then climbed the peaks to recover the phoenixes. They found nothing but nine red stones, each pierced by an arrow.

The quest for eternal youth, the secret of everlasting life, is not only a recurrent subject of myth, sagas, and fairy tales (myth, page 246). It also preoccupied the alchemists as well as those religions that posited the possibility of a transcendental life after death. Man's continuing fear of old age and death is reflected today in the success of the innumerable "fountains of youth" offered by the pharmaceutical industry and the advocates of naturopathy. Myths on this subject usually center on the water of rejuvenation, of life, of physical or mental rebirth – a secret essence that the gods themselves fight over. The spring is the Biblical symbol of never-ending, never-ebbing life and lies at the origin of the whole Holy Water ritual.

Hebe, the Greek goddess of eternal youth, is seen (far left) carrying the nectar and ambrosia which she fed to the gods to keep them immortal.

Water as a symbol of purification and everlasting life plays an important part not only in many Western myths and religious traditions (e. g., baptism) but also in Taoism. On this ritual vessel from Tibet left) the heavenly dragon guards a symbolic container for the water of eternal youth.

This French tapestry (above) is an allegorical representation of the fountain of eternal youth with various symbolic deities gathered round it.

Bhima, one of the heroes of the Mahabharata, is here seen performing his famous exploit of defeating five enemies simultaneously (left). His adversary Durjodhana tried to drown him in the Ganges, but he emerged rejuvenated and stronger than before.

After the adventure of the phoenixes, Shen I traveled northward on a current of luminous air. He was moving in the same direction that he had seen taken by a streak of light across the stars. That streak of light, he guessed, must have been caused by one of the dragons belonging to the goddess Chin Mu. The current of luminous air brought Shen I to the door of a mountain guarded by monsters; but when he brandished his bow, the monsters fled. The door opened, and Chin Mu appeared. With no preamble whatsoever, Shen I said, "I have heard that you possess a pill of immortality." The goddess at once agreed to give it to him, provided that he would build a new palace for her. Its walls were to be of jade, its trimming of aromatic woods, its roof of glass, and its steps of agate. Shen I built the palace in two weeks. The goddess rewarded him as promised with the magic pill, but she warned him to wait a year before swallowing it. Shen I was not quite ready yet, she explained, to receive the medicine's full benefit.

On the way home again, Shen I found himself overtaken by a raging flood. Undaunted, he shot an arrow into the water, which immediately reared backward, hissing and dispersing as if in pain. Through the mist of it, Shen I descerned a man clothed in white, riding a white horse, and accompanied by a whole troop of cavalry. In the midst of the troop, rode a young lady whose black hair streamed out behind her in flight. Shen I could see his arrow dangling from the right eye socket of the first rider. He shot a second arrow into the streaming coils of the lady's hair, pinning her, as it seemed, to the visible world. The others vanished with the receding flood, but the lady remained behind. "I am Heng O," she told him, "the younger sister of the water spirit. You have spared my life. According to divine law I must now submit to you as your wife."

Emperor Yao was duly informed, and the marriage feast was held at the palace. As a wedding gift the emperor presented the couple with a mansion to live in. Shen I kept to himself the secret of the pill of immortality which he possessed. For the time being he concealed the pill inside a crack in the highest roofbeam of his new home.

Soon after, an ogre named Tso Ch-ih, or Chiseltooth, began threatening Emperor Yao's realm. The ogre, whose round eyes could stare down the strongest of men, had a tooth 10 inches long and so strong that it could crack the toughest flint. Shen I journeyed south to deal with him. The archer's taunts brought the ogre raging up out of a cavern. Swinging a padlock on a chain, the ogre rushed at him. Shen I shot an arrow straight into his gaping mouth. The tooth broke off. The ogre, shriveling visibly, turned to flee. Shen I shot a second arrow directly between the ogre's shoulder blades. Chiseltooth was no more.

Heng O, meanwhile, had noticed a soft light and sweet odor filling her new home; it seemed to come from the ceiling. Setting a ladder against the highest beam, she climbed up to investigate and soon found Shen I's pill of immortality. Wonderingly, she put it on her tongue. As it dissolved, she found herself weightless, unencumbered, and happy as never before. At that moment Shen I returned from his adventure.

When he ordered her to descend the ladder, she refused. Seizing the ladder, he drew it out from under her. From her position in the middle of the air, she gazed down at him, uncertainly. Angrily he brandished his bow, but Heng O simply drifted away through the high window. Shen I dashed out of the door in pursuit. In the full-moon night he could see his wife drifting rapidly higher and higher, diminishing in size.

In his anger, Shen I would have shot her if he could, but just at that moment a hurricane snatched him up. He found himself kneeling before the throne of Tung-Hua Ti-Chum, a god who sits outside the wheel of time. The god ordered a sarsaparilla cake with red icing to be brought and commanded Shen I to eat it. The archer obeyed. "Go," the god commanded him, "and find the three-footed celestial cock which was caged up on T'ao-Hua Shan, Peach Blossom Hill."

Heng O meanwhile continued her flight until she reached a very cold and glassy world whose only vegetation was cinnamon trees. She was alone there and was feeling sick. She vomited the coating of the pill of immortality, which immediately assumed the form of a white snowshoe hare and hopped away. To overcome the bitter taste in her mouth, Heng O drank some dew and ate a little cinnamon. Then she made herself as comfortable as she could in that bleak situation.

Shen I soon fulfilled the mission laid upon him in heaven. He found the celestial cock with three feet – the spiritual father of every rooster on earth. He mounted the glorious and glistening creature, which at once flew straight up to the red disk of the sun. There Shen I made his new home.

After a little time, the thought of his vanished bride returned to him. Riding a sunbeam, he went to visit her. When Heng O saw him coming, she tried to run away. Quietly he took her hand. "I am not annoyed any longer," he said. "Nor must you be. I shall build you a palace of cinnamon wood and precious stones. This will be called the Palace of Great Cold. Once every month, in the dark of the moon, I shall visit you here."

THE WAY AND ITS MYSTERY

Ts'ao Kuo-chiu was a prince of the Sung family; he was a goatish youth, wildly lustful. Complaints of rape which were brought against him at court forced him to flee for his life. He climbed high into the wilderness Mountains of the West; as he did so, the embroidered silken garments which he had on rotted away, falling from his back. He pressed ahead, naked and hungry. Fruits, roots, and nuts were now the prince's only food. He had left all his former desires behind him as he climbed. Women, meat, and wine were now far from his mind. Simple and wild, he lived like a wind sprite among the crags. One might have taken him for an insane person. The Immortals, who once were ordinary men and women, knew better than to make that mistake, and one day they paid him a visit. Solitary young Ts'ao Kuo-chiu did not appear surprised to see the Immortals.

"What are you doing?" they asked him. "Following the Way," he replied. "And where might the Way be?" He pointed to the sky. "Where is the sky, then?" He pointed to his heart, and at that moment Ts'ao Kuo-chiu also became an Immortal.

ISIS AND OSIRIS

Even the pyramids of Egypt are destined to wear away. The life that is saved today must inevitably be lost at last. Just one art may be called ultimate, the one which stands outside time. Resurrection is its name. The earliest incidence of this in myth concerns the Egyptian deity Osiris.

Osiris brought agriculture to the Nile valley, and also induced the Egyptians to cease being cannibals. Once he had set them on the paths of peace and righteousness, Osiris traveled abroad. He carried the blessings of civilization to the Middle East and beyond. Meanwhile, at home, his wicked brother Set plotted against Osiris. The god returned to find that Set had built a coffin for his body. Osiris was entirely without guile. He lay down inside the coffin to show that it was the right size for him. Set thereupon slammed the coffin lid and nailed it down. He tipped the coffin, with its precious burden, into the Nile.

Isis, who was sister, lover, and wife to Osiris, searched everywhere for him, weeping. The land of Egypt dried up.

Osiris's coffin had floated out to sea, northeastward, all the way to the port of Byblus on the Palestinian coast. On the beach where it lay stranded, a tree grew up. The tree enclosed the coffin and what it contained. Over the course of years the tree flourished exceedingly. It grew straight and tall at the water's edge, providing a welcome shade for the king of that country. Eventually it was cut down and set up again as the central pillar of the king's own palace. No one knew or guessed what was inside the pillar. The palace prospered, however.

The wide wanderings of Isis brought her at last to Byblus. She sat by the well of the city. The people were impressed by her stillness and austerity. The queen herself came to look upon Isis, who sat veiled. The queen invited the stranger into the palace. As soon as Isis reached the central pillar of the hall and smelled the fragrance of the wood, she knew that Osiris must be nearby, and so she agreed to stay as nurse to the queen's own little boy. The child sucked milk from the fingertips of the goddess. When no one was about, Isis used to dip him in the fire. One night the queen came in unexpectedly and witnessed her child's immolation. Screaming, terrified, she rushed to snatch the baby from the flames. Only then did she notice that he was unharmed. "I would have given him eternal life," Isis explained. "I can do nothing more for him now, but there is something you can do for me. Have this column cut open. Its heart is mine."

The coffin was duly discovered inside the column. The king provided a ship to carry it and Isis back to Egypt. There Isis opened the coffin. Gently she breathed into the nostrils of her brother, lover, and husband. Isis was winged now, like a swallow, and she enfolded him in the fanning of her wings. The rhythm of her breathing and her wingbeats filled the cold corpse with life again. Osiris lived.

At that moment, the drought which had long held Egypt in its grip was loosened. The Nile rose to flood the fields with nourishing waters. Green shoots sprang up everywhere, and the people rejoiced. The god Set, however, did not. Although Osiris bore him no grudge, Set kept murder in his own heart. Next time, he decided, he would tear and rend his brother into little pieces which could never be rejoined.

Set accomplished his end. He hacked up the living flesh of his brother into fourteen pieces, which he then scattered to the four winds. Isis, however, laboriously located every separate fragment of flesh. Reverently, tenderly, she planted each and every one in the earth. Since then, Osiris has reigned in the underworld.

Theseus, son of King Aegeus, was the founder hero of the Athenian state and an incarnation of Poseidon. The life of Theseus is a mythic reflection of the overthrow of Cretan rule by the mainland Greeks. At sixteen Theseus managed to topple the gigantic rocks beneath which Aegeus had left him sword and sandals, and with them he set out for Athens. On the way he ran into the first of his adventures, killing a whole series of dangerous monsters and brigands that were infesting the country. Theseus's greatest

Best-known of the heroic deeds of Theseus was his killing of the bull-headed Minotaur *(above)*.

A Greek red-figured bowl *(right)* shows Theseus subduing a centaur. Theseus assisted his friend Peirithous, king of the Lapithae, in his war against these monsters.

SIMPANG IMPANG

The Sea-Dyaks of Sarawak relate that certain ancestors of theirs once long ago went into the jungle to look for game but found nothing. At last they sat down to rest upon what appeared to be the trunk of an enormous fallen tree. One of their number drove the point of his knife into the bark of it, and blood issued forth. They were sitting upon the king of all pythons. It lashed about to try to enclose them in its grip and swallow them, but the men were too much for it. They hacked the creature up and fried a

This painting *(below)* depicts in concentrated form – and transposed into the context of Renaissance Italy – Theseus's killing of the Minotaur in the labyrinth that Daedalus had built for King Minos.

achievement, however, was to kill the Minotaur in the labyrinth of Minos, king of Crete. Following the murder of his son in Athens, Minos had demanded a blood tribute every nine years in the form of seven youths and seven virgins who were thrown to the Minotaur. Theseus volunteered as one of the youths. He managed to kill the Minotaur and to find his way out of the labyrinth again. Athens was freed of the shameful tribute and Theseus became its king, reuniting the townships under the capital and founding the feast of the Panathenaea.

During the battle against the Amazons, which he fought with Herakles and Peirithous, Theseus carried off the Amazon queen Antiope *(below)*.

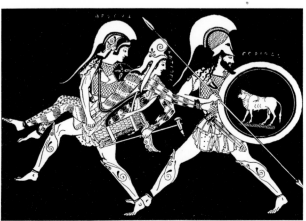

little of its flesh over a campfire. As the grease of the python's flesh danced in the hot pan, so raindrops danced upon the leaves round about. The men, huddling under the shelter of a tree, finished their feast.

The rain continued and became a downpour; it washed away the men and washed away what remained of the python. It filled the valleys and eradicated all human habitation. Just one woman escaped to the top of a high mountain with a dog. The animal crept in under the shelter of a hanging creeper which the wind caused to scrape across a crack in the cliff. The woman followed the dog into the crack. They huddled there as the creeper scraped and scraped upon the rock. Sparks were generated by the friction. The woman caught them and made fire from them to warm herself and the dog. Then she took the creeper for her husband. In time, she was given a child by it; but it was only half a child. The little thing,

paused to ask the way to the wind's house. The birds made no reply. The tree, however, twisted round on its roots to point out the right direction. "Tell the wind," it moaned, "to come and blow me down soon, for I am weary of these voracious birds which torture me."

Not long after that, Simpang Impang came to a stagnant lake. The green scum on its

The search for a meaning to life finds expression in many myths, sagas, and cultural traditions as

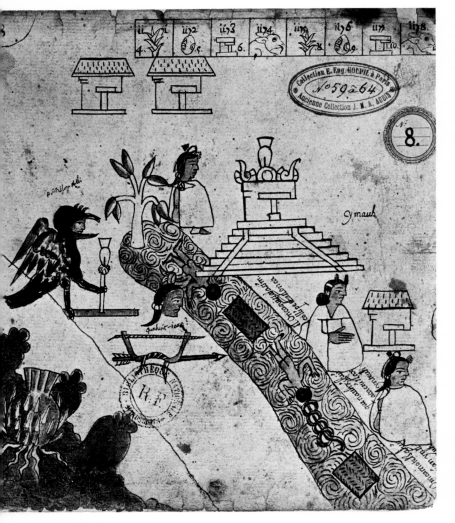

A late-Aztec drawing of the way of the dead *(left)* shows dead souls floating down a river which rises to the tree of life, with a sun temple on one side and a soul-bird on the other.

Their quest for the promised new king of the world brought three "wise men" from the East *(right)* in search of the infant Christ, led by the star of Bethlehem.

According to Biblical tradition the object of Moses' quest was a place for his people to live. God appeared to him in person *(opposite, top)* and directed him to Israel, which was known from then on as the Promised Land.

This picture stone from Sweden *(opposite, bottom)* shows various scenes from Nordic myth concerning the heroes whose goal was Valhalla, the "life after death" reserved to those who fell in battle.

which she named Simpang Impang, could only hop about on one leg and feed itself one-handed.

Simpang Impang found a few grains of rice which a rat had concealed for its own use. The boy put the precious food out on a leaf to dry. The rat came home and angrily disputed with Simpang Impang for possession of the few grains. "As you have robbed me," squealed the rat, "so my children will rob your children forever." The wind came by just then, snatched the rice up from the leaf, and scattered it miles away. Simpang Impang got up on his one foot and hopped off after the malicious wind, with little hope of ever catching it. A great hunger drove him on.

After a time he came to a very ancient tree. Birds sat about on its withered branches, pecking and eating the tree's few green buds as they emerged. Simpang Impang

surface wrinkled up and opened like a pair of lips. Words bubbled up from the depths. "Tell the wind," the lake implored, "to come and clear my outlet, which is blocked up by a lump of gold." Simpang Impang promised to deliver the message and hopped on along the shore of the lake. His path led between a sugarcane and a banana plant which also spoke to Simpang Impang. "Ask the wind," they begged, "to give us branches like other beings of our kind. We are now without arms to embrace the wind."

Soon after his encounter with the plants, Simpang Impang reached the bare place where the wind lived. "What have you come for?" whistled the wind in his ears. Simpang Impang replied that he had come to demand the rice grains which the wind had stolen. "Then follow me," hissed the wind, dashing off across the surface of a

well as in the great religions. The rich testimony of the fine arts is an eloquent illustration of this search on man's part for the true purpose of his being, for the higher spheres of the gods, or for an answer to the problem of life and death. The world of myth contains some splendid cycles dealing with man's probation through life, combat, and his aspiration to perfection. The perfection aspired to may be that of love, political organization, individual existence, or the commonwealth of mankind; it may also find expression in the creation of the world, in the course and direction of cosmic events, in preparation for the Beyond, and in union with the divine order of things.

This Egyptian statue *(below)* represents Iris. When her consort Osiris was murdered, Isis set out in search of his dismembered body (myth, page 258).

Izanagi's search for his wife Izanami led the Japanese creator hero to the underworld (myth, page 77).

deep river. Simpang Impang could not hop on the water as the wind did, but a friendly fish followed after the wind and back again. Such was the blind haste of the wind that it did not seem to notice the substitution. "You have chased me across the water," the wind confessed, "Now follow me up in the air!" And it whirled away over the tallest trees. This test was answered for Simpang Impang by a swallow, who flew after the wind as it circled and then returned. Again the wind accepted the substitution. "You are more agile than one would have thought," whispered the wind. "Now let me see you squeeze yourself through a blowpipe, as I know how to do." A friendly ant crawled through the blowpipe in Simpang Impang's place.

"You have passed my three tests," the wind hummed to Simpang Impang, "and I congratulate you for it. Yet those grains of rice I scattered will never be restored."

Simpang Impang was furious and called to his father the creeper. From his father's bones he made fire sticks, kindled a fire, and set alight the wind's long tail. Now the wind howled in pain, whirling round and round Simpang Impang. "Put out the sparks in my plumage," cried the wind, "and I shall make you a whole man!" Simpang Impang lifted his one hand. There was a clapping sound and the fire went out. Simpang Impang now had a whole body: two hands, two feet, everything that he needed to be complete.

Feeling harmonious in his heart, Simpang Impang made friends with the wind and gave it the messages which he had received from the ancient tree, from the stagnant lake, from the sugarcane and the banana. "Well," the wind whispered, "I shall do what you wish for the tree and the lake. The sugarcane and banana plant I cannot help."

THE SINGING LUTE

The Fasa people of the southern Sahara used to be often at war with the Burdama and the Borloma. They fought heroically under the leadership of their crown prince, Gassire. Gassire himself was gray-haired, already a grandfather, and he longed to inherit the shield of his father the king. He longed for his father's death as a lover waits and longs for the appearance of the evening star. But the old king would not die.

One day Gassire rode out alone against the enemy and scattered them in his fury. He fought more like a demon than a man. Frustration drove him to do this. Afterward the women bathed him and clothed him in a fresh garment. He walked alone into a field.

He heard a partridge singing, and he felt he understood what the song meant. The partridge had been in combat with a snake. It sang a victory song.

"All creatures must die and rot away to dust," the partridge exulted. "I too; and yet the song of my deeds will not die. It will be sung again and again from generation to generation, outliving every king who ever was."

Gassire turned and went to talk with a wise old man. He told him just what he had heard the partridge singing in the field. The old man moaned and said, "Gassire, you are rushing to your doom. There was a time when the Fasa lived on the shore of the sea. In those days there were bards who sang of their deeds. The bards were not good fighters themselves. They shone best in the banquet halls, after the battle was over. But you shall be a bard and a hero too. The king your father is not ready to die and leave you his shield. So you must carry a lute into battle. Your lute will ring with sword strokes. Down-dripping blood it must absorb."

Next day, Gassire and the eldest of his eight sons went out to fight against a host of the Burdama. Gassire's eldest son died in that struggle. Gassire rescued his body and carried it home on his back. His son's blood oozed down over the lute which Gassire carried in place of a shield. Each day for the following week, Gassire took one of his sons with him into battle. Each evening he rode home again with another corpse upon his back. In this way all his eight sons were slain, and the blood of each one stained Gassire's lute.

The people thought Gassire must be insane, throwing away his own sons' lives like that. No member of the Fasa tribe would have anything to do with Gassire now. Cursing the crown prince's name, they drove him forth into the desert.

Gassire camped alone on the flinty waste, under the stars. He could not sleep. He sat by his campfire with nodding head. The bloodstained lute lay beside him. He touched it not, and yet now the instrument began to sing exultant battle songs. Gassire wept to hear it. Back home, in the same hour, his father the old king expired.

THE BARD BROUGHT BACK

Efateze Islanders, in the New Hebrides, tell a tale of a quest which led down and down, from hell to hell, in a long descending spiral. The legend's entertainment value for them resides largely in the rather hypnotic reiteration of place-names given.

The chief of the Bau Tribe called for his bard, Nabuma Ekbu, to come and sing at a feast, but the bard had perished, been buried, and gone down to Bokas, the first underworld. When he heard this, the chief himself descended to Bokas. He learned there that the bard had died again, had been buried, and had gone down to Magapopo, the second underworld. Descending further, the chief learned in Magapopo that the bard had died again, had been buried there, and had gone to Magaferafera, the third underworld. Descending once again, he learned in Magaferafera that the bard had died a fourth time, had been buried again, and had gone down to Maganaponapo, the fourth underworld. He descended to Maganaponapo, and was told that the bard had died there, had been buried, and had gone to Mateika, the lowest underworld. The chief descended to Mateika, and asked after Nabuma Ekbu. "Behold his bones!" the people cried.

So the chief gathered up the bones of Nabuma Ekbu in a basket and carried them back. Through Maganaponapo, through Magaferafera, through Magapopo, through Bokas, and back to the surface of the earth, to a sacred place of his tribe. The drums were sounded and people danced to them. From the basket, the bones of Nabuma Ekbu sang and kept the feast.

TO HELL AND BACK

A folktale of the Tatars of the Sayan Steppe concerns Kubaiko, a heroine well inured to hardship and danger. Demons had carried away her brother's head, and concealed it deep in the underworld. Undaunted, Kubaiko went after it, neither ceasing nor faltering until she stood, in the depths, before Death, the Erl King or Irle Khan, as the Tatars call him. Irle Khan was touched, in his heart of lead, by Kubaiko's courage.

"Mortal," he said, "regard the seven horns which thrust up through the floor of my throne room. These are the horns of a red ram which is buried below. Lay hold of the horns, pull as hard as you can . . . if you can raise him, your brother lives again."

Now, the ram of which Irle Khan spoke was the sun, horned with the seven planets. And the sun rises anew each and every day, whether pulled from the earth or not. But, when he set Kubaiko the task, the boiling basalt brain of Irle Khan was too dull to comprehend this truth.

Kubaiko, struggling hard, freed the red ram. As it came up out of the floor of night, she saw her brother whole and well again and they were home.

As the plumed serpent Kukulkan (right), Quetzalcoatl was the Mayas' best-known symbol for fertility and the blessing of the maize fields.

This mask set with turquoises represents the god and culture hero Quetzalcoatl, the focal point of worship in the Toltec civilization that had its capital at Tula.

In the Borgia Codex Quetzalcoatl is depicted with his two chief attributes: the serpent round his head and the sun bird at his belt (above).

In his aspect as earth serpent Quetzalcoatl appears as the herald of day, swallowing the morning star Venus, here represented in human form (below).

The bewilderingly complex cultures of the Toltecs, Mayas, and Aztecs yet evince a broad unity of interpretation, as we see from the meaningful arrangement of religious and secular symbolism centering on the great god and culture hero Quetzalcoatl. His form and presence are not only confined to the heavenly sphere; they also manifest themselves in various deities incorporating the changing function and significance of the supreme deity. The mere fact that the two common mythological

Maya warriors wore on their helmets feathers from the Quetzal or sun bird, though this head *(above)* from the temple of Palenque may in fact represent a priest of Kukulkan or Quetzalcoatl.

A frieze on the Aztec temple at Xochicalco *(below)* depicts Quetzalcoatl as a serpent with a coat of feathers, the commonest symbol of this god of heaven and earth.

symbols of the bird of heaven and the serpent (sun and earth) are both present in the mythic figure of the plumed serpent Quetzalcoatl is an indication of his universality. But between heaven and earth is man with his questions concerning life and death, light and darkness, eternal life or unconditional annihilation. With complete mythological consequentiality the universal Quetzalcoatl therefore also figures as the god of life and death. All the rituals and achievements of the Aztecs are to be looked at with this in mind.

As supreme deity Quetzalcoatl was also lord of life and death. The front of one stone stele depicts the god of death *(above, far left)* and the back, the god of life *(second from left)*.

Another incarnation of Quetzalcoatl was Ehecatl, the god of the wind *(above, second from right)*, whose function was to blow rain clouds away.

Quetzalcoatl was also a great culture hero and bringer of the arts, smithery, and weaving *(above right)*.

263

THE NGONA HORN

Sometimes a quest may occur in one's own backyard, as it were. The doors of revelation are not always on the far horizon. A stone, a leaf, or a sheet of water may be the gateway to other-world adventure. The Wahungwe people of Southern Rhodesia have a myth which bears out this idea. Nine young ladies swore eternal friendship once upon a time. They were all unmarried, but they all took lovers, as the custom was. The day came when the first of their number was blessed with a baby boy. The

This early relief of the archangel Michael in combat with a dragon *(above)* was the prototype of similar but more warlike medieval representations *(above right)*.

The dragon-slaying motif reappears in the St. George legend *(below)*, and in an early-Persian illustration *(bottom)* from the time of the Mongol occupation.

baby's father was unwilling to acknowledge it, however. He cherished his own freedom, and although he loved the mother in his way, he did not wish to marry her.

The girls discussed this matter together one morning after washing their laundry at the riverbank. It seemed that having children at all was a burden for women in general; it was an imposition. If fathers refused to acknowledge their own sons, then those sons ought to be thrown into the water. This suggestion was made maliciously. The one girl of the nine who was blessed with a son had made her friends jealous.

Fights with dragons are a common theme of myth, providing from the very earliest times a suitably dualistic mode of expression for the battle of good against evil. Indeed, encounters with dragons came to symbolize both historical and mythic truths. The dragon, a monstrous

This Japanese painting *(above)* shows the storm god Susano battling with the dragon of the sea. Susano is a son of the sun goddess Amaterasu. As lord of the seas and of storms he is comparable with the Greek Poseidon.

Needing water to sacrifice his cow, Cadmus had first to kill the dragon that guarded the well *(above)*. He sowed the dragon's teeth, and from them sprang the warlike ancestors of the inhabitants of Thebes in Greece.

chthonic creature combining the destructive powers of lion, snake, and fire, is the embodiment of evil, the demonic, and the underworld. The subduing of this monster, necessary in order to attain the precious, the pure, or the true, is in myth also one of the ordeals to be faced on the path to perfection. In the religious sphere a fight with a dragon may symbolize the struggle of the gods of light (and knowledge) against darkness (ignorance), or it may give mythic expression to the subjugation of primitive cultures by superior forms of society.

St. George figures again in this Gothic wood carving *(above)* as a knight slaying a dragon that symbolizes the powers of evil.

Another fight with a dragon is illustrated in the famous Persian "Book of the Kings," the *Shâh-nâme,* where the figure of the warrior hero Rustam symbolizes the Iranians' struggles against the Turanians, the wild tribes that lived to the east.

Persuaded by their arguments, she picked up her own baby boy by the heels. She swung him around and flung him out into the middle of the stream. The little creature fell with a small howl of bewilderment and made a little splash. He did not rise again. The young mother went home and told her parents what she had done. They scolded her severely. She ran away, back to the riverbank. There was no one about. She flung herself into the water and disappeared under the surface.

Nude, but for his magical *ngona* horn, the young man who had fathered the girl's child went to look for her. He strode straight into the river. The waters covered him, but still he walked along, unconcerned. He caught up with the girl, who was there too. Hand in hand they traversed the deep bed of the river, looking for their son everywhere.

After a time, they came upon the house of the water lions. Those blue-backed beasts are seldom seen. Their hands and feet are human. The water lions' house had many jars in it. They asked the young man which jar his son might be in. The young man

The famous four outings of the young Prince Gautama taught him the reality of old age, illness, death, and asceticism *(above)*.

Even the strictest and most exhausting ascetic practices failed to bring the Buddha knowledge of salvation *(right)*.

The famous cave paintings of Ajanta show scenes from the Buddha's life and row upon row of other Buddhas still seeking Enlightenment *(below left)*.

In Gautama, the Buddha, the mythic quest for the supreme goal and all its attendant ordeals becomes historically recognizable reality. The Buddha, born about 560 B.C. with every prospect of leading the comfortable life of a prosperous Indian prince, realized instead the necessity for seeking the truth. His search produced a body of knowledge that laid the basis for one of the world's great religions. The Buddha chose solitude in order to explore through his own experience the universal law of birth, suffering, and death. The stages on his path to Enlightenment are clearly symbolic in character: on his four outings the young prince met

asked his *ngona* horn. Then he pointed to the right one. The child emerged, unharmed.

"We are going hunting," the water lions said. "We will devour you in the morning." After the water lions had gone, the young man pointed his *ngona* horn at the child. He made the child very small in this way. Then he put the child down inside the *ngona* horn. That done, he pointed the *ngona* horn at the young woman. He made her very small also. He put her too inside the horn.

Seated beneath the *bodhi* tree, the Tree of Enlightenment *(above)*, the Buddha is relentlessly assailed by the demons of Mara, the evil one, who seek to sway him from his firm decision.

four deities in the forms of an old man, a sick man, a dead man, and an ascetic. He too first sought the way of salvation through asceticism, without success. It was only while meditating under the Tree of Enlightenment that he attained knowledge, saw how to overcome the world, and found the path to eternal salvation. He then took five disciples and taught them the Four Noble Truths.

Not many centuries after the Buddha's stay on earth there emerged from the old body of teaching a very much extended system known as the Mahayana. Mahayana Buddhism soon spread throughout the Far East, where it today forms the dominant religion. The chief feature of the Mahayana is the appearance of a bodhisattva and after him of many other bodhisattvas who vow to stay in the world of rebirth until all living creatures are redeemed. The original Buddhist goal of individual salvation is thus deliberately subordinated to the good of the community; one's own salvation is less important than the deliverance of others. The concept of the bodhisattva or "being destined for Enlightenment" had the effect of reviving older mythic prototypes, and the emergence of such beings was celebrated and exalted in myths and legends. This happened, for example, with the Bodhisattva Avalokitesvara ("he who looks down in compassion"), who is pictured here *(right)*. Avalokitesvara embodies the central idea of the Mahayana, symbolized by his many heads and the circle of arms extended in help and sympathy. Moreover, this visionary painting shows him with an eye in each hand with which to show the sufferer the way to salvation, for as well as being the great healer the bodhisattva is man's helper in the never-ending quest for Enlightenment.

The colossal statue of Amida Buddha at Kamakura in Japan *(opposite, bottom)* is thought to be the largest work in bronze of its kind (height: 11.36 meters, or 37 feet). Amida Buddhism was a particular form of Buddhism that spread in Japan. Amida himself was called the Buddha of Infinite Light, and the mere mention of his name by the reverent worshiper was supposed to bring deliverance. It was Amida who appeared to the dying as a shining light to guide them to the paradise of the Western Heaven.

Finally, he pointed the horn at himself. He too became tiny. He climbed into the horn and pulled the stopper into place behind himself.

At dawn the water lions returned. Their prisoners appeared to have escaped. They could not understand this. Angrily, they searched and searched. One of their number came upon the *ngona* horn. He put it in his mouth. The *ngona* horn bruised his teeth. The water lion spat the *ngona* horn out into his hand. He threw it far away, out of the water. It landed on the bank of the river.

There, in the pure air, the young man, the young woman, and their child came out from the *ngona* horn. They were happy. In a moment or two they had regained their proper size. The young woman took the *ngona* horn on her back. The young man picked up the baby. Then, hand in hand, the couple walked home to the village. They were married soon afterward.

THE TRIALS OF LANGOAN

As all married people soon learn, marriage itself is a severely testing situation. To fail in a marriage is to undergo mutilation of a sort. To succeed, on the other hand, means doubling one's powers and – more to the point – one's sensitivities. The few married couples who succeed in remaining lovers throughout their lives together merge in such a manner as to confront the world foursquare. They have no "blind side," as it were. But such marriages are not made in heaven, nor do they result from dumb luck alone. Usually, the lovers will be found to have passed through quarrels of a searingly painful, fierce, and finally tempering kind. This holds good for sophisticates and savages alike, it seems. Every culture has legends to relate regarding the test of character which marriage must involve. Take, for instance, the following myth told by a Dusun tribesman. It concerns a seemingly unfortunate farmer named Langoan.

He moved two or three times, clearing new fields in the thick Borneo jungle. It was no use; some disaster always overtook his crop. The breaking point came when he went out one day and found swarms of proboscis monkeys busily engaged in pilfering the newly ripened rice from his field. Langoan, outraged at such unnatural behavior, seized his spear and ran into the monkeys' midst. He succeeded in wounding one of their number. All the rest swung away, chattering, into the trees. The one which he had wounded, however, stood transformed into a beautiful woman.

"The rice which you thought you had lost over the past few seasons," the woman informed Langoan, "was reaped for you and me by my people! Come, and I'll show you."

Langoan followed the woman to a village which lay nearby but which he had never before noticed. He was honored there and became prosperous. He married the woman; they had a child. Life with his new family was blissful in every way. Yet Langoan became restless before very long and wandered off to another village to join in a festival.

He stayed away for one week. For most of that time he was drunk. Moreover, on the final night of his visit he slept with a woman of the other village. When he got home again, his wife greeted him coldly. "You have been unfaithful," she said. Langoan roundly denied it. Thereupon his wife showed him a looking glass which contained an image of himself and the woman of the other village making love. Langoan found the image very distressing. To prevent his wife from abandoning him, he bound her wrists and ankles tightly to his own. They went to bed that way. Yet when he woke up in the morning, the bonds were loosened. His wife and child were nowhere to be found.

Langoan searched far and wide through the jungle. He longed to get his wife and child back again. One day a herd of deer attacked him. To be charged upon by such normally shy creatures was a terribly upsetting experience. He escaped them, however, by hiding in a hole beneath the roots of some trees.

Next morning, a herd of little pigs attacked Langoan. Normally, pigs are passive vegetarians who provide food for men. Langoan fled from them and found his way back to the hole under the roots. He spent a second night there, in great fear. Toward dawn he slept and had a dream. In the dream a wise man came to him and said, "Langoan, you are a coward. If I were looking for my wife, I would not run away from animals. If necessary I would fight them!"

At sunrise, Langoan crawled out of his hiding place. Warily, he walked through the jungle. The day was hot and exceedingly still. The leaves hardly trembled. Langoan stopped walking and looked around. Out of the green silence, squealing arose. A pure white rhinoceros came crashing through the bushes, straight at Langoan. There was no time at all in which to dodge the beast. He seized its lifted horn and swung himself up onto its shoulders.

Langoan rode the plunging rhinoceros in the direction of his own house. The animal halted at his doorstep, shook its great bulk, and reared. It seemed about to crush him against the doorpost. Langoan let go. Falling backward, he slid from the beast's flank. He struck his head against the step. The animal thundered off into the jungle. Langoan lay panting and bruised. He heard a child crying inside the house. He thought he should take care of it, but for the moment he was too shaken to move. The crying stopped almost at once.

Langoan got up and entered the house. The child who had cried was his own. His wife was there comforting the little one. Langoan embraced them both. The quarrel was over now.

SKY BIRD

The testing aspect of marriage appears in Polynesian myth also – for example, in the story of Tawhaki and Tango-tango. Tawhaki was mortal at first, but this did not prevent the angelic princess Tango-tango from falling in love with him. Invisibly, at night, she would fly down to Tawhaki's sleeping place. Before dawn she would steal away again into the sky. Tawhaki used to wake up in a strange mood, uncertain of what had occurred. The bed would still hold something of the fragrance of his dream, and yet he would be alone.

The illustrations made for Ferdausi's famous *Shâhnâme* or "Book of Kings" (written ca. 982–1014) in the seventeenth century show various scenes from the life of the Persian hero Rustam, whose labors invite comparison with the Greek hero Herakles. Rustam's miraculous birth took place at the entreaty of the mythic bird of heaven and with the aid of his feathers coupled with the chanting of a wizard. His life was a series of victorious encounters with dragons, demons, and enemy warriors, his chief function being to defend his kings against capture by their enemies.

1 Rustam in battle with the White Demon.

2 In search of a powerful mount, Rustam came across the stallion Rakush, whom he caught with a lasso.

3 Rustam fought a dragon to save his king Quabus from defeat and death.

4 Here is another scene from Rustam's fight with the White Demon.

5 Here Rustam defeats the Turanian warrior Puladvand.

6 Following one battle the Iranian warrior Bizhan was captured by the Turanian Afrâsjâb and held prisoner in a swamp. Rustam appeared, defeated Afrâsjâb, and released the prisoner to fight again.

7 To get the better of so powerful an antagonist as Rustam called for a superhuman feat: the demon Akwan picked up the piece of ground on which the hero was sleeping and threw it bodily into the sea.

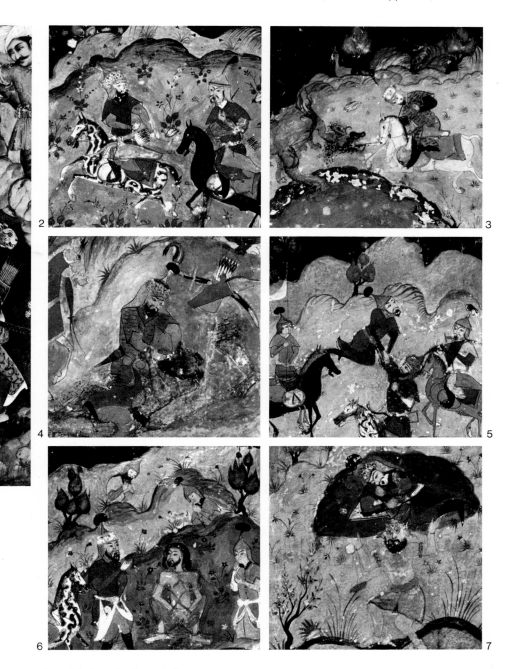

The time came when Tango-tango conceived a baby by Tawhaki. Then she made a brave choice; she decided to bear the baby upon earth. She explained herself to Tawhaki and thereafter lived with him as his wife.

Their child was a little girl. Tawhaki took it, whereupon the baby urinated in his arms. Holding his daughter out at arm's length, Tawhaki made a grimace of disgust and exclaimed, "How badly this little thing smells!" Hearing these words, Tango-tango burst into bitter tears. She snatched the child away and mounted the sky with her. Tawhaki leaped to catch hold of his heavenly bride's foot, but he was too late.

A month passed. Tawhaki was consumed with grief. He told his younger brother that he was going to reach heaven if he could. His brother offered to accompany him. First they traveled to the distant home of their grandmother, Matakerepo. They found her sorting taro roots with her old hands. She was quite blind. She had ten taro roots to begin with. As she counted them, Tawhaki quietly filched one. Very carefully she counted them again, and meanwhile Tawhaki filched another one. This went on until the old woman realized that she was being tricked. Someone was within reach, stealing her taro roots. She rose up, seized her sword, and blindly swung it in a wide arc. Tawhaki and his brother shrank down upon the ground. The sword sheared the air over their heads. The old woman sighed with frustration. Then she put down her weapon and sat on it. Tawhaki, rising to his knees, punched her in the nose. Immediately, the scales fell from her eyes. She could see again. She recognized her grandchildren, and she wept over them.

Tawhaki explained their mission. Matakerepo informed him that it was not impossible, but dangerous. They would have to climb the tendrils of a vine which hung down from heaven. Tawhaki's brother went first. He caught hold of a loose tendril and began climbing. The tendril swung out to the horizon and back again, buffeted by circling winds.

It seemed certain that Tawhaki's brother would be cast away, either in a distant ocean or else on some lonely mountaintop, and die. Tawhaki watched him gyrate in the sky, appearing and disappearing amid the scudding clouds. At just the right moment, Tawhaki called to his brother to loosen his grip and fall. His brother was not badly hurt. "Go home, please," Tawhaki told him. "You must take care of our inheritance in case I myself do not come back." His brother obeyed.

Then, very carefully, Tawhaki chose a

strong tendril to climb. The one he selected was rooted up above in heaven, but it had struck new roots into the earth as well. He climbed all day, not daring to look down. At evening, he hauled himself up over heaven's rim. There he transformed himself into an ugly old man. He let himself be captured and taken as a slave into the town. He was made to bear axes and firewood. He was the slave of the slaves of his true bride, Tango-tango, who sat with their little girl.

Tawhaki amused himself for a day or two by performing miraculous labors, things no slave could do. For instance, he shaped a whole canoe from the trunk of a tree in a few moments' time. Tango-tango began to suspect the truth about him. When that happened, he threw off his disguise. He caught up their daughter in his arms and hugged her.

Then he embraced his bride. "I have come," he said, "in order that I may complete the proper ceremonies for our daughter." Tango-tango consented to this. She was falling in love with her lover all over again, and she persuaded him to stay on with her in heaven. Tawhaki became the spirit of thunder and lightning. One can hear him in heaven now and then, playing with his family.

Like Tawhaki, thought too can climb the skies and win unfamiliar heavens. Thought seems to have a luminosity of its own, between moments of darkness; sometimes it hovers motionless, while at other times it exhibits bursts of unbelievable speed. Thought changes course in a moment. It appears far off, or very near, only to vanish again in the twinkling of an eye.

There are such things as adventures of the mind alone – dangerous quests undertaken along the borders of myth and ordeals of the imagination which sometimes result in madness if not death itself. Sir Philip Sidney put all this with Elizabethan exuberance when he wrote that the poet "lifted with the vigour of his own invention, doth grow in effect another nature, in making things either better than Nature bringeth forth or, quite anew, forms such as never were in Nature, as the Heroes, Demigods, Cyclops, Chimeras, Furies, and such like: so as he goeth hand in hand with Nature, not enclosed within the narrow warrant of her gifts, but freely ranging only within the Zodiac of his own wit."

THE NINE HEROINES AND THE NINE HEROES

These two early-fifteenth-century paintings by the French artist Jacques d'Yverni in La Manta, a château near Saluzzo in northern Italy, show groups of nine male *(below)* and nine female figures *(right),* representing kings and queens. The

number nine had been regarded as possessing magical properties long before d'Yverni's time and had always been heavily invested with symbolism. A group of nine lent itself to an arrangement of three times three figures or a triple trinity, an ideal of three raised to its own power that recurs in these representations of the eighteen principle figures of medieval French tradition. The larger illustration shows nine rulers, emperors, or kings with all the insignia of their office standing in conversation with one another like a group of noble knights. Reading from left to right we have three non-Christian, three Jewish, and three Christian rulers who had all proved their knightly worth. Symbolically, the group unites the three cultures that went to form the West, namely the Roman Empire, the Jewish religion, and Roman Christendom, each represented by its three noblest figures. The most outstanding of these are Caesar for Rome (second from left), David for Jewry (center), and King Arthur (third from right) as a champion of Christendom; the figure next to him is Charlemagne, with the imperial orb in his hand. The companion group of nine noble women comprises (from left to right) Deyphille, Synoppe, Yppolitte, Menalippe, Semiramis, Lampheto, Thamaris, Theukra, and Penthesilea.

An interesting parallel to the phoenix of Egyptian and later of Greco-Roman myth is this Far Eastern symbol of resurrection from chaos. The bird is widely used in myth to symbolize the soul and its reincarnation; it also stands for mind and light.

DEATH AND REBIRTH

The posture of this mummy from Peru is reminiscent of the way the ancient Egyptians too used to preserve their dead. The idea was to enable the deceased to continue to partake of food in the Beyond. The Egyptian books of the dead contain whole rituals for the magical resuscitation of mummies as a symbolic preparation for the afterlife.

Man's existence is subject to the indissoluble polarity of life and death – a mythic insight illustrated by this two-sided statue of the Aztec god Quetzalcoatl as god of life *(left)* and as god of death.

Those chosen by the gods live,
and so you too.
You rise with Orion in the eastern sky
and descend with him in the west,
together with Sothis,
who leads you on heavenly paths
through the pastures of Taru.

PYRAMID APHORISM 442

"I was in a dense, gloomy forest. Fantastic, gigantic boulders lay about among huge

autobiography *Memories, Dreams, Reflections* (1961), described a nightmare which he experienced in middle age. "Then there were crashings in the underbrush," he continued, "and a gigantic wolfhound with a fearful gaping jaw burst forth. At the sight of it, the blood froze in my veins. It tore past me, and I suddenly knew: the Wild Huntsman had commanded it to carry away a human soul. I awoke in deadly terror, and the next morning I received the news of my mother's passing."

A ship that ferries the souls of the departed to the Beyond appears in the myths of ancient Egypt, in Greece (as Charon's boat), in Celtic myth, and on this Sumatran tapestry.

jungle-like trees. It was a heroic, primeval landscape. Suddenly I heard a piercing whistle that seemed to resound through the whole universe. My knees shook."
Thus the psychologist C. G. Jung, in his

Forces of destruction range the real world all the time and they do cast their frightening reflections into the pool of dreams. A high proportion of world myth concerns itself with such images. Animal, human,

273

and superhuman, by turns, they haunt us all. We know, as Jung knew, that each of us must die. Yet destruction is only the dark side of a re-creative process: life itself.

BITTER REVENGE

He who sows passive ingratitude may reap a whirlwind in the course of time. Such is the lesson of a chilling myth from the Borneo jungle. It concerns a seemingly harmless and indeed helpless old man whom no one loved.

An endless variety of images illustrates mythic man's ideas and fantasies concerning the sufferings he might be destined to endure after death. The underworld was either a place where

bounds. The underworld was divided into different districts or levels corresponding to different grades of damnation and torment. Ancient-Chinese and shamanistic myth contain detailed accounts of seven or nine underworlds, and Dante conceived a magnificent vision of a multi-storied hell. Underworlds as a temporary state that the soul is required to pass through in order to be purged occur in the Christian idea of the refining fire (purgatory) as well as in Hindu myths about the realm of Yama. The Buddhist hell is de-

The ancient chief of the Tengkurus, in Tempassuk, was Aki Gahuk. He had seven sons and four daughters, all of whom married and moved away from home. The time came when Aki Gahuk grew so old and feeble that he could no longer walk. His children were embarrassed by the old man's continuing hold on life. They fed him, grudgingly, but they refused to provide him with any clothes at all. In his embarrassment, being naked, Aki Gahuk used to sit in the river with his elbows resting upon a flat stone. There he would brood, sunning his reverend head while the waters swirled over his body. His children would come and fling

A relief on a Late Neolithic menhir from France *(top)* is believed to represent a Celtic goddess of death or Mother of the Underworld.

An Italian woodcut *(above)* illustrates the appalling vision of a Lucifer with three mouths. He has the wings of a dragon and is seen standing in the middle of hell, devouring Judas and two other sinners.

pallid souls led an endless shadow existence (Hades), or more often a realm of agony and terror in contrast with a more optimistic vision of a paradise of some kind. In any case, the underworld was usually seen as a hell in which earthly deeds must be atoned for in terms of an eternity of anguish. Far from confining it to the souls of the dead, myth peopled the underworld with a variety of appalling images of torture and destruction in the form of lords of the underworld, demons, devils, and dreadful beasts. Here mythic man's imagination knew no

In the Tibetian hell the judge of the dead is Dharmaraya, shown here with the sword and mirror of justice in his hands.

scribed in even greater detail, being divided into eighteen realms of torment either hot or cold. Religions use hells and underworlds in conjunction with a whole apparatus of demons as a threat with which to instill obedience to ethical principles in this life.

In ancient-Mesopotamian religion it was Nergal, god of death *(far left)*, who dragged people through plague or war down to his underworld realm.

Tibetan religion recognizes various manifestations of the god of death. This one of Indian extraction *(left)*, is Yama, depicted with a bull's head and riding on the back of a bull. He was believed to have conquered death and was worshiped as a tutelary deity.

The Indians of Central America believed that the world of the dead was ruled by Mictlantecuhtli and his consort Mictecacihuatl or Coatlicue, pictured here *(left)*.

A splendid example of Mixtec goldsmith work *(below)* shows Mictlantecuhtli, the prince of hell, with his elaborate headdress.

The Japanese king of the underworld *(above)*, is one of a group of ten rulers of the nether kingdom.

This Chinese scroll painting *(left)* represents the king of the seventh hell, a personification of the judge of the dead, Yama, who determines the torments of the dead in accordance with their earthly deeds.

Coatlicue with her skirt of many snakes was the Aztec goddess of the earth. But as the earth not only gives life but eventually takes it back again, the logic of myth made Coatlicue also the goddess of death and consort of Mictlantecuhtli.

275

him something by way of sustenance every now and then, but they really wished that he would die.

Instead, however, Aki Gahuk appeared to grow stronger and his body changed in appearance. His wrinkles formed an increasingly regular pattern of scales. His skin hardened; it glittered now in the water. His arms and legs grew ever stumpier. His head flattened out upon the rock. His eyes, always on the lookout for sight of his children, bulged upward. His jaws kept widening because of the constant hunger with which he was afflicted. His buttocks grew together and became pointed; he developed a tail.

All this was most embarrassing to Aki Gahuk's progeny. "Father," his children called out from the riverbank, "it seems that you have no intention of dying now. Therefore, climb up out of the water. Come home with us. We will provide you with clothes, after all, to cover yourself."

Aki Gahuk yawned at them from his rock, showing the long rows of his teeth, and then he spoke. "It is too late for that," he said. "Previously you had no pity for me. Now I am another creature. I cannot come home with you. Instead, I shall swim downstream and take a wife."

Aki Gahuk's children could not help laughing at that idea. "No one will marry you, Father," they shouted. "You are too poor, and too ugly by far!"

"I shall call upon Pang, the monitor lizard," Aki Gahuk replied with dignity. "At the mouth of the river she will come and lie with me. Our descendants will be creatures of the water and the land, equally. Baskers in the sunshine, ravenous, powerful swimmers with armored tails and with jaws that can crush bone, cold-blooded, so shall they be. And I shall give them permission to prey upon you and your children, from generation to generation."

The Polynesians, too, composed unforgettable legends on the theme of mean ingratitude. Consider, for instance, the story of the king who found fault with his wife's cooking. Manaia was his name, and Kuiwai was his bride. He invited his tribe to a feast and put Kuiwai in charge of the whole thing. But when the ovens were opened and she brought the baskets of baked meats before the people, laughter arose: nothing had been cooked right. The meat was all underdone. Manaia felt his heart harden with chagrin. Rising from his place, he beat his wife with his fists in front of everyone. Then he cursed her in a loud voice. "Are the logs which you used to heat the ovens as sacred as your brother Ngatoro's bones?" he demanded. "Is that why you did not use enough to make the stones hot? Will you

Myth tells of both descents and ascents of the souls of the departed. Just as the gods descend to earth from the distant heights of heaven, so from earth does man proceed after death to an underworld or alternatively to a redeeming paradise that appears to be identical with the gods'

A relief on a Greek tombstone *(top)* shows a personified soul wandering through the world of the Beyond. The head is surrounded by a halo.

The sun god Ra, with the head of a ram, sails down the underworld Nile toward the east in the bark of the sun *(above)*. His nightly voyage figures in the Egyptian books of the dead as a symbol of the soul's journey through the underworld toward rebirth.

Persephone, the daughter of Zeus and Demeter, was ab-

ducted to the underworld by Hades to be his wife and rule as queen *(above)*. In her anger Demeter arrested the growth of nature, with the result that Persephone was allowed to return for part of each year.

heaven. According to some traditions the soul passes through the narrows of death down into a somber world of shades; other traditions picture it soaring heavenward to a kingdom situated in the clouds or on the moon. Both traditions involve a journey to a completely unknown world, a journey beset with similarly unknown and consequently appalling obstacles and dangers. Rites and ceremonies are therefore performed in the hope of seeing the soul safely across to the Other Side. In Celtic Ireland the dead were taken on a last sea voyage to the land of the dead. Ships also occur in the burial rituals of the ancient Egyptians and various Southeast Asian peoples, but they are found above all among the Vikings, who buried their dead kings in the magnificent vessels they had sailed to their conquests. The notion of accompanying the dead also plays an important part in shamanism and in Tibetan burial ritual. But the people who went to the greatest lengths to secure the souls of their kings and noblemen a comfortable existence in the world to come were the ancient Egyptians, as the pyramids and the burial chambers in the Valley of Kings testify.

Visits by the gods to the earthly sphere are another aspect of travel between the worlds. Here the Buddha, escorted by gods, descends a ladder from the Trayamstrimsha heaven to proclaim his gospel upon earth *(left)*.

On this Etruscan tomb relief *(above)* a winged guide of the dead, who may be Charun, is seen conducting a departed soul to the underworld. Charun, derived from the greek Charon, took on decidedly demonic traits in the Etruscan culture.

A rock drawing from New Guinea *(above)* shows a stylized ship of the kind that many Southeast Asian peoples believe ferries departed souls to the land of the dead in the west. Often they even launch corpses on boats down rivers.

This Stone Age rock engraving from Italy depicts a warrior fighting a labyrinthine figure with eyes in its center. It symbolizes the victory of rebirth over the moment of death.

The soul's journey to the Beyond is here depicted in an Australian aboriginal bark painting. It illustrates not only the paths leading to the land of the dead but also possible obstacles to be overcome on the way.

dare to humiliate me ever again in this way? If you do so, I promise you I shall serve Ngatoro's flesh up to my guests personally. His flesh shall fry upon the red-hot stones of my ovens!"

Kuiwai crept away, crying. She hid herself until nightfall. When darkness came, she cast off her garments of the day and clothed herself instead in a ritual sash of young rushes. She called her sister to her, and her daughter. She took the household gods out of their wrappings and stood them up under the stars. The three women prayed to the gods for guidance, and for vengeance as well. Graciously, the gods offered to transport Kuiwai's daughter to the distant home of Ngatoro. He was the man King Manaia had threatened to cook and serve.

The daughter's journey was not long, being magical. The gods themselves were her canoe. Swiftly, safely, they bore her along between the tops of the high waves and the stars. She came to New Zealand, to the shores of Lake Roto-rua. There stood the fortress of Ngatoro's people. Alone, carrying the gods in their wrappings, Kuiwai's daughter approached the main gate. Instead of passing through the gate like a common person, she climbed over the top of it. She walked straight to the sacred enclosure where Ngatoro was accustomed to sit and give judgment. He recognized his niece at once. He asked for news of his sister, Manaia's wife. Then the girl told how Kuiwai had been cursed and beaten and how Manaia had threatened to fry Ngatoro's flesh on the stones of his ovens.

The people, hearing this, rushed down to the river and bathed themselves to wash away the contamination of Manaia's curse. Then, under the direction of their priests, they dug a long pit and ceremonially cast into it the spirits of Manaia's people. With sharp clamshells they scraped the spirits of their enemies out of the air. They trampled each and every spirit down, deep in the pit. They filled the pit with earth again and beat the earth down with the palms of their hands. They laid enchanted cloths and baskets where the pit had been in order to keep down the spirits of their foes.

The proper rites having been observed, Ngatoro prepared for war. He caused a totoro tree to be felled, and a huge canoe hollowed from its trunk. One hundred and forty warriors embarked in the canoe. Helped by the favorable Pungawere wind, they sailed steadily for seven days and nights to Manaia's island.

They concealed the canoe in a sea cave. Then Ngatoro disguised himself and slipped into Manaia's village. He soon managed to contact his sister. She recognized

him, as no one else did. Kuiwai let him know that Manaia's priests were using sorcery to draw Ngatoro and his followers nearer and nearer over the sea. One hundred and forty earth ovens had been dug along the crest of the hill behind the village. It was there that Ngatoro and his band were to be cooked and eaten.

"Well," said Kuiwai's brother with a smile, "and when is this to be?" Kuiwai replied that the priests had promised a feast for the very next day.

"In the morning," Ngatoro said to his sister, "climb up onto the roof of your house. Look toward the hill."

Ngatoro brought his warriors by night up the far side of the hill. At dawn they reached the earth ovens which the priests had built to receive their bodies. Mounds of green leaves lay by the ovens, ready for wrapping each victim. The firewood was there as well, and the stones ready to heat. Ngatoro's warriors stripped themselves. They hid their garments under some bushes. Then

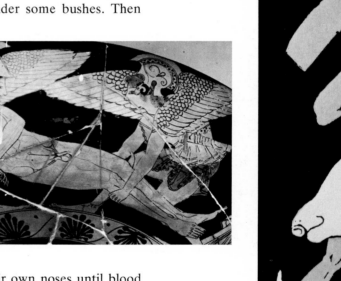

they punched their own noses until blood ran. Each one smeared himself with his own blood. They rolled in the dust until they resembled corpses. Then each one went and lay down in an earth oven. But each warrior kept a war club concealed under his body.

The sun rose. Manaia's priests came, singing, in solemn procession up the hill. They examined the earth ovens. Each oven contained what appeared to be the body of an enemy, drawn by enchantment from across the sea. The priests shouted triumphantly. The people streamed up from the town. They looked at the bodies joyfully. They made ready the fires.

"I'll have that plump shoulder there," one hungry woman cried. "I'll dig the cheeks out of this head, tender and hot," another said. Soon the whole tribe had gathered, laughing and joking in this happy way and crowding around the ovens, weaponless. Ngatoro stood up. His hundred and forty warriors also arose, all at once. They swung

The Greek vase painting *(below left)* shows the death of Sarpedon, who was killed by Patroclus during the Trojan War (page 240). Two winged deities, Hypnos (Sleep) and Thanatos (Death) are seen bearing the body away.

This Mayan idol *(below left)* represents a canine guide of the dead on their journey to the underworld.

A bird with a human head occurs in many Egyptian paintings as a symbol of the soul of the departed and its ability to soar freely through the air to the realm of the gods *(above left* and *above).*

A Dayak drawing from Borneo *(above left)* shows a dead man with a bee hovering above his head to symbolize his soul. The Benin of West Africa acknowledge a demon of death with an outsize head *(above right).*

In a variation of the relief at the top of page 277 Charun is seen wielding his typical attribute, the hammer of death *(below right).* A servant follows the horse bearing the departed.

The myths of many peoples contain the idea of the soul being transformed at death into a bird. Or, if the departed himself does not become a bird, winged creatures of all kinds from angels to insects play an important part. The bird symbol is bound up with the idea of the soul as a non-corporeal being presumed to be capable of flying through the air without let or hindrance. Associated symbols here are such "birds of death" as the raven, the owl, and the vulture, Ancient-Egyptian religion divided the soul into ba, the part that soared heavenward in the form of a bird, and ka, the part that lived on in the mummified body.

An Etruscan vase painting *(above)* shows Alcestis taking leave of her husband Admetus, in whose stead she is dying. Two demons of death have come to fetch her: Charun with his hammer and Tuchulcha with his snakes. Herakles would not let her die, however, and brought her back from the lower world.

A Greek tomb relief *(left)* shows a birdlike harpy or demon of death carrying off a female soul.

The bull of Amenti, the ancient-Egyptian underworld in the west, is pictured here bearing a mummy on his back, possibly that of Osiris. Above him flies a bird, tracing the path of the liberated soul.

Persephone *(above)* carries a dead soul down to the kingdom she rules with her husband Hades.

Harpies and other birdlike creatures figure in myth as bearing the dead to the Beyond; in the Manichaean and Christian traditions, angels escort the souls of the departed to heaven and the divine light. The Mayas of Central America and the shamanistic peoples of central Asia widely believed that the soul turned into a bird at the moment of death and emerged from the mouth of the corpse to fly off to the Beyond. Guides of the dead such as the Greek Hermes Psychopompos also assume the forms of dog or wolf; the jackal-headed Anubis of Egyptian myth performed a similar function. Another mythic tradition tells of guides who determine man's fate, of a good and an evil demon who accompany man through life and on into the Beyond, where they act as his counsel before the judge of the dead.

279

their war clubs; the blood ran in streams and trickled down the hill. When the massacre was completed, Ngatoro ordered the fires to be lit. A feast followed, lasting until sunset. The best of Manaia's people were devoured.

Here is yet another story of vengeful war. This concerns one of the briefest battles ever to take place in myth.

Hotunui was a Maori chieftain of no great power, but he was blessed with a clever son. Once upon a time he noticed a canoe come in from the sea heavy-laden with fish. He sent a slave down to the shore to ask for something nice out of the catch. The fisherman would not give him any. "Is Hotunui's head the flax that grows in the swamp at Otoi?" the fisherman rather obscurely demanded. "Or is his topknot flax, that the old fool cannot go there to get some flax to make his own nets with instead of troubling me for fish?"

Not long after that, Hotunui's son Maru-tuahu returned from a journey. The old chief haltingly repeated what had been said. "It is a bad people," he said, "trying to lower the authority of their betters."

Maru-tuahu thought the problem over glumly, in silence. Then he set himself to catch and dry great quantities of mackerel. He also began making an enormous net, the largest ever seen in that country, and the strongest. These preparations required a full year. When they had been completed, he sent messengers to the tribe of the fisherman who had insulted his father. He invited the whole tribe to a banquet and a net-stretching ceremony.

The feast which Maru-tuahu prepared was actually composed of rotten wood set out in heaps and rows. Maru-tuahu had covered the wood with a thin layer of dried fish. It looked like a sumptuous feast in the sunlight. But before the banquet could start, the net had to be stretched.

A thousand guests together undertook the work. They sweated over it, chanting in unison, fighting off their tiredness, and thinking of the wonderful banquet in store for them. When they had the lower end of the net properly stretched out and held fast with pegs, Maru-tuahu came with his warriors to lift the upper end from the ground. It was not quite clear at first just what Maru-tuahu's men were going to do. They walked slowly sideways, lifting the net at arm's length over their heads. They were doubling it back over the guests. Now they ran, letting it drop. The thousand guests of Maru-tuahu sat trapped in the net. His warriors trampled and clubbed them down through the strings of it. The guests were as helpless as caught fish; all perished.

THE BEYOND

These two pages show just a few of mythic man's repeated attempts to make the fate that awaited him after death less

awesome and less incomprehensible. They range from the fantastic illustrations to Dante's poetic vision of hell, to magnificent images of the soul's elevation to paradise or the city of God, scene of heavenly delights. On the one hand we have the total horror of suffering in various kinds of hell offering every conceivable torment; on the other hand we find the liberated soul achieving the highest dimension of purity and spirituality. There is also the ancient-Egyptian idea of the dead living on forever in a paradise in which they enjoy in another form the unalloyed pleasures of an ideal earthly existence.

An Egyptian papyrus painting (right) shows the inhabitants of Amenti, the land of the dead situated between the rivers of life. They are seen enjoying an idealized version of the life they led on earth.

One of the grandest visions of hell to come out of the West was the "Inferno" of Dante's Divine Comedy. Botticelli illustrated it with this inverted pyramid (below) comprising the different circles or levels of torment to which sinners were assigned. At the vertex stands the all-devouring prince of hell, Satan himself.

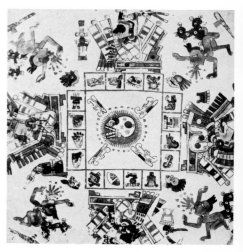

The Aztecs pictured the world of the dead in the form of a square.

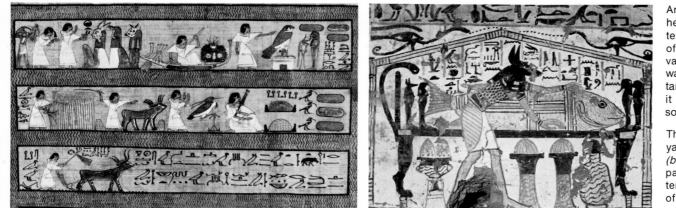

Anubis, the early jackal-headed god of death, tends the mummified body of a fish god *(left)*. Preservation of the physical body was of the utmost importance to the Egyptians, for it was there that the ka soul lived on.

This illustration to Bunyan's *Pilgrim's Progress (below)* traces Christian's path from earthly existence to the Celestial City of God.

In Dante's vision, the alternative to hell is the seven-tiered mountain of purgatory, with paradise at the top *(far left)*.

Charun, the Etruscan demon of death, here seen holding up the vaults of the underworld *(left)*, also had the function of accompanying the dead to the infernal court.

FIRE, FLOOD, AND DROUGHT

Between the deliberate cruelties of mankind and the indifferent force which natural
catastrophes express, there seems not much
to choose.

The divine, too, are unpredictable. On that
point, the myths of all peoples agree. Jehovah, for example, chose the Jews to be his
earthly emissaries, bent them to his laws,
and brought them up out of Egypt. Yet, as
they were crossing the desert by way of
Mount Hor under the guidance of Moses, in
hunger and thirst, Jehovah suddenly sent
down fiery serpents among them. "And
they bit the people; and many of Israel
died."

Monan, the Creator of the Brazil Indians,
also lost his temper with his own people. He
sent 100-mile serpents of flame swarming
along the Amazon valley. The wizard Irin
Mage was moved, fortunately, to extinguish
that threat. He drowned the fiery serpents
in a torrential thunderstorm. By then, however, most Brazilians had already been reduced to cinders and wisps of smoke.

The Tinguians of Luzon relate that their
gods sent a flood to cover all the earth. In its
efforts to escape the deluge, fire hid itself,
creeping deep inside wood, stones, and
iron. The most terrible disaster that the
world had ever known brought unexpected
blessings to a new race of men. They found

This Greek vase painting *(right)*
offers a positively festive vision
of the underworld. The figure
on the throne is Hades, lord of
the realm of the dead. Beside
him stands his wife Persephone
with a flaming scepter in her
hands. At top right the hero
Theseus and his friend Peirithous appear before Dike, the
goddess of justice. Below them
we see three judges of the dead,
presumed to be Aiacus, Triptolemus, and Rhadamanthus. At
top left Megara sits mourning
the dead sons of Herakles, and
beneath her Orpheus with his
lyre leads a group of blessed
ones to the temple. Below the
temple Herakles, holding Cerberus on a chain, and Hermes,
the messenger of the gods and
guide of the dead, both enter
Hades unscathed. Hecate advances to meet them with her
torch, and on either side Sis-
yphus and Tantalus pay for their
misdeeds in endless, senseless
suffering.

out how to release fire from its hiding places
and make it bake their bread.

Natives of British New Guinea say that the
whole world except the summit of Mount
Tauga was once submerged in a single vast
deluge. It looked as though even Tauga's
snowy peaks would soon sink from sight in
the flood. But when the gray waves, rising
hungrily around the shoulders of the mountain, approached its topmost cliffs, the
rockface cracked and a great diamond-
studded serpent head emerged. Radaulo,
king of snakes, slowly uncoiled, mile upon
mile, from the groaning rock. His tongue
licked out, fiery, forked, to taste the cold

Charon, usually depicted
as a rough sort of fellow,
ferried the dead from the
shores of life across the
Acheron to the gates of
Hades *(above)*. Only four
mortals ever stepped into
Charon's bark alive: The-
seus and Peirithous, who
outwitted him; Herakles,
who was too strong for
him, and Orpheus, who
charmed him with song.

282

waves. They foamed backward, hissing, tumbling, flowing away down the mountainside. Urging the waters on with his tongue, Radaulo pursued them all the way home to their ocean bed.

Throughout myth, stories of fire and flood are matched by fears for the future. In Mexico, for example, the highly civilized Aztecs anxiously computed fifty-two-year cycles of star time. At the end of one such cycle, they calculated, the whole world would fall prey to devouring flames. However, nobody could say for certain which cycle might prove final.

"Natural disasters" never seem quite natural, after all, to the people who must undergo them. Numberless myths explain such happenings as being chastisements for

The fate of the unrepentant sinner is portrayed with horrible realism in a miniature (right) from the Très Riches Heures du Duc de Berry.

The flames of hell in this Japanese painting (below) show that the idea of a refining fire is not an exclusively Christian invention.

Not only before God are all men equal but also before the devil. A detail from Stefan Lochner's Last Judgment (below right) shows a king, a bishop, and even a cardinal in the hands of Satan's servants.

There is an almost comical quality about Hieronymous Bosch's vision of hell (above) in his Garden of Delights triptych.

human impiety or disobedience. Consider, for example, the ancient–Egyptian myth according to which Ra, the sun god, once lived upon the earth. The people were not so impressed by him as they should have been. They thought he seemed old and

The vault mosaics in the Florence Baptistery include this vision of hell in which a voracious Satan is assisted by giant snakes, lizards, and toads (above).

These visions of hell convey a vivid impression of the endless torment mythic man saw awaiting those who fell into this abyss. To most of us nowadays hell is little more than a synonym for minor exertions that really have nothing "hellish" about them at all, but for thousands of years hell was a very real and ever-present factor in human existence. Hells are places where the demons of evil and destruction live, and various religions have exploited them to bring home to people the consequences of allegedly wrongful thoughts and actions. It was this "educative" purpose that gave rise to the lurid images produced above all in the Christian Middle Ages, images that abound in the most appalling tortures and torments, described with positive relish. Many of the torments of hell represent symbolic counterparts of earthly crimes and vices, with fire and water as elemental opposites playing the principal role. Of all visions of hell, those of the Buddhist religion are perhaps most clearly tailored to psychologically combating individual misdeeds. In a series of nine hot and nine cold hells sinners must either freeze or burn in atonement for their crimes. The judge of the dead weighs their good deeds against the bad, and hands over the guilty to the devil's lieutenants for execution.

This Chinese scroll painting (left) shows the sufferings awaiting the sinner who is cast into the Buddhist hell. Enthroned at the top is the judge of the dead, who hands the condemned over to the demons of the nine hot hells.

285

feeble and so they ignored the god's commands.

Thereupon Ra sent the goddess Sekmet against them. Sharp in the tooth, Sekmet pursued the Egyptians up and down the Nile valley, devouring as she went, wading in blood. Even Sekmet could not eat all the Egyptians at one time, however. She slept, swollen, under a tree, and while she slept Ra had a change of heart. He decided to save the remnant of the people. To do so, he prepared beer, 7,000 jars of it, and colored the beer to resemble blood.

Sekmet, upon awakening, lapped up the beer. She thought it was blood that she was drinking. Her thirst assuaged, the goddess staggered up and away from the haunts of men. She ate no more people.

Sekmet seems to have been a goddess of plague, and of drought also. This paradox is resolved when one recalls that she remained at all times an emissary of the sun. Egyptians feared the mists of sunrise, especially in the delta region, as being noxious – rife with insect life and invisible vapors of disease. They feared even more, however, the scorching fierceness of the sun's rays at noon. On certain ancient Egyptian papyruses of an astrological nature, Sekmet is identified as the burning "eye of Ra."

Next to fire and flood comes drought as a universal destroyer. Drought appears relatively passive and slow, but no less devastating. Some of the strangest legends on record are those dealing with drought and with irrepressibly piercing and positive forces ranged against the menace.

The savior god of the Huron Indians once slew a monstrous frog, and with good reason. The frog had swallowed all the sweet waters of the world. The god, Ioskeha, saved our planet from drying up. He pierced the frog through and through. He led each stream and river, which the frog's round belly released, home to its proper channel again.

That myth was told to a Jesuit father, Paul le Jeune, in the course of his mission to the Great Lakes region of North America early in the seventeenth century. It seemed at the time to be an exceedingly strange story. And yet, astonishingly enough, more recent research shows that it exists worldwide.

The most exalted version of the myth is to be found in the Hindu Aitareya Brahmana. There a monstrous dragon, Vittra, swallows the sacred waters. The god Indra goes against the dragon, although in fear and trembling. Finally, Indra slashes Vittra open, and the waters rush free again.

In a recognizably similar vein, the Andaman Islanders have told the following story. Once upon a time a woodpecker played a mean trick on a toad, with disastrous results for the whole world. The woodpecker was eating honey from a bees' nest high up in a tree. A toad, resting at the foot of the tree, called croakingly up to ask for a share in the feast. The woodpecker suggested that the toad grasp hold of a creeper hanging from the tree. He promised to haul the toad up so that they could share the feast together. The toad agreed. The woodpecker pulled him up almost all the way and then deliberately let him drop. The toad, being severely bumped, and bruised in his feelings also, hopped off to plot revenge. It occurred to him that if he were to drink up all the pools, ponds, lakes, and streams of fresh water, the woodpeckers and their kind would die of thirst.

But could he do it? The toad resolved to try his best, in any case. He started small, and as he drank he grew. The time came when the fresh waters of the world were all inside the toad. He was a smooth blue-green mountain of water. His skin had stretched to the breaking point, and water dripped from the corners of his mouth to streak his wide, pale belly.

The other animals were dying of thirst. The plants, also, were wrinkled and sere. This delighted the toad. He danced for joy in the presence of his enemies. He whirled, he leaped, and suddenly he vomited. The waters rushed out from his mouth across the world again.

Australian aborigines of the Lake Eyers district have a like tale to tell. They say it was a frog who swallowed up the waters. The frog, however, did no dancing. It sat, complacent, dignified, and full to brimming. The animals made a circle around the frog. They dared not attack so immense and majestic a being as that which it had now become. With eyes like moons, it blinked sleepily around at them. Perhaps it heard their dry rasping coughs, but if so the frog gave no sign. It simply sat.

The animals staged mock battles among themselves, played tricks on one another, and cracked dusty jokes. They were hoping against hope that if only they could induce the frog to laugh, he might give up some drops of water. Like Louis XV, however, he sat tight. "I do not like buffoons who fail to make me laugh," that French monarch was once heard to remark. Queen Victoria, in her day, was known to pronounce the dreadful words, "We are not amused." The frog, for his part, said nothing at all.

At last a long, limbless clown of a kind most closely related to water stood on the tip of its tail before the frog's calm gaze. It was an eel, wriggling upright and somehow dancing now, an absurd sight. The frog chuckled.

An exact parallel to the nightmarish visions of hell on the previous pages is provided by the many images – again occuring mainly in the Christian world – of a beautiful, otherworldly paradise to which the souls of the faithful will one day be admitted. The religions of antiquity all had their picture of heaven, just as do the great living religions of today. Common to them all is the purged soul's

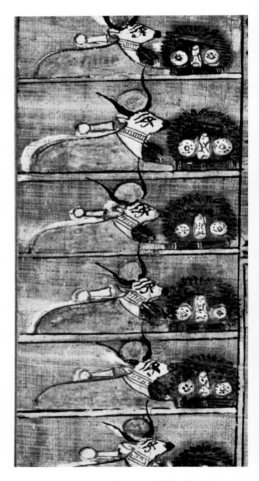

hope of eternal life in the presence of the immortal gods. In Egypt heavenly herds of cattle roamed the blessed fields of plenty (above). The Christian heaven of the saints is the longed-for realm of everlasting oneness with the angels before the throne of God. A common feature of heavens is a division into different levels, culminating in the supreme blessedness of purest light. Among the most splendid examples are the depictions of the "Western Paradise" of Buddhism, in which the liberated faithful enjoy eternal life in endless, shadowless light.

Ancient-Chinese myth told of a group of wise men who reached the heavenly court of the goddess Hsi Wang Mu *(right).*

Up above the stars the young Quetzalcoatl squats naked between two old gods preparatory to his descent to earth *(below).*

On completion of their earthly pilgrimage the resurrected saints assemble in heaven to worship the Lord *(above).*

Taoism's eight Immortals enjoy eternal life in the green gold "Paradise of the West" *(below),* which they have reached by means of alchemy and yoga.

At the center of the Tibetan "Paradise of the West" lives Amitabha, the Buddha of Infinite Light *(right).*

This drawing *(below)* represents the heaven of the Koryaks of Siberia, where the souls of the departed live in union with the gods.

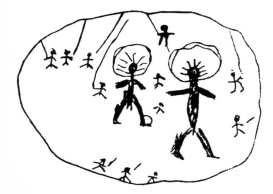

And the world
that is called "Sukhavati"
and that belongs
to the Buddha Amitabha
is rich, prosperous, good
to live in, fertile, lovely,
and full of gods and men.
And in that world
are neither hells nor
animal creation, neither
a realm of
departed spirits nor Titans nor
premature birth.

SUKHAVATI-VYUHA

The eel danced higher, spiraling, with slow, bobbing gestures. Now the frog rocked with laughter, choking and chortling, until its sides split open and the waters of the world gushed out.

DANCING MONKEY

The Senoi people of the Malay Peninsula fear thunderstorms more than anything else. Lightning destroys numbers of them each year. Moreover, the storms uproot trees and fling these down upon the Senoi and their huts. Finally, the sort of thunderstorm which occurs suddenly and barely obscures the sun brings raging fevers to the Senoi. Therefore, they respect a number of taboos for fear of inviting foul weather. One such taboo concerns monkeys. It is forbid-

den to dress up a monkey or to laugh at it. The reason for this particular prohibition is contained in the following myth.

There was a shaman, or "halak," once who shot a pig-tailed macaque with his blowpipe. He was about to roast the animal for dinner when his father-in-law turned up at the house. "If you are really a halak," said his father-in-law, "you should be able to bring that monkey to life again!" The halak demurred; such an action would not be proper, he said. Finally, however, pride got the better of him. He pulled his poison dart from the monkey and squeezed the venom out with his fingers. The monkey came to life again. They dressed the little creature in coat and trousers and gave it a sword to carry. The monkey was delighted; it danced on the ground outside the house.

After a time, the halak said that the demonstration was finished. His father-in-law insisted that it continue anyhow. By now the villagers had gathered round to watch the monkey's antics. Everyone was much amused. Two of the halak's three wives (all of whom were sisters) came out of the house to watch the monkey dance. Meanwhile,

The dead march out of the charnel house with drums and trumpets *(above)* to proclaim the temporality of earthly existence.

In a fantastic vision of destruction Leonardo da Vinci drew this vortex of toppling cliffs and floods pouring in from all sides *(left).*

The Great Flood destroyed all except the inmates of Noah's ark, the nucleus of a new people that had made a convenant with God *(above).*

When the second angel of St. John's vision on Patmos blew his trumpet, a mountain of fire fell into the sea, turning it to blood *(above).*

Inscription on the Gate of Hell:
Through me
the road to the city of desolation,
through me
the road to sorrows diuturnal,
through me
the road among the lost creation.

DANTE, L'INFERNO, III, 1–3
Translated by Dorothy L. Sayers (1949)

Mythic visions of a coming catastrophe that will mark the end of the world usually incorporate the most powerful destructive forces in nature: earthquake, fire, and flood. In the Revelation to John fire fell from heaven mixed with blood, "and a third of the earth was burned up." In Genesis God sent weeks of torrential rain to sweep away the old order in a mighty flood. Flood myths are universal except in Africa, where they are hardly known. According to Indian myth, at the end of each Brahma age the world sinks beneath the waves, from which Vishnu creates it anew. A related end-of-the-world saga occurs in the Nordic *Edda,* when Fenrir, the hound of hell, and the Midgard serpent are let loose and the gods and Titans wipe each other out (page 222). Brueghel's famous painting *(below)* combines the horrors of a great conflagration with those of battle and plague in a terrible vision of a world sinking back into chaos.

A nadir of despair is represented by Brueghel's apocalyptic landscape *The Triumph of Death (below).* Its whole horrifying expanse reflects nothing but panic, death, and destruction. The army of the dead advances in serried ranks with wagons to collect the dying. And the last bell to be heard on earth tolls from a withered tree the knell of the triumph of death.

289

the halak, much distressed, stepped back into the house and put his hands upon the shoulders of his youngest wife. She was the one he liked best. Modestly, she had stayed within. He turned her into a small stone. This he put into a carrying basket. With the basket on his arm, he stepped out of the house again and walked away into the jungle. The people turned to watch him go.

At that moment they ceased to laugh. The monkey ceased to dance. A storm arose over the trees, swift as a flight of birds. The lightning flashed; the villagers were all burned up. The halak, meanwhile, had taken shelter under a tree deep in the jungle. The lightning failed to find him or his favorite wife. He changed her from a pebble into a girl again. Then he stopped the storm by means of a brief spell:

Brou gek-gek-gek!
S'lak bejut!
S'lak n'rik!
Srek asut!

LONG WAYS

The Sakai Negritos stand rather in awe of the neighboring Malays, whose culture is far more advanced than theirs; and the myths of the Sakai perhaps owe something to Malay influence. Be that as it may, the Sakai say that when they die, their souls spiral out through the whorl of hair at the back of the head and go to the gate through which Malay souls enter heaven. There the Sakai are roughly turned away to wander until they find further progress barred by a gulf of boiling water. There is a bridge across the gulf, a slippery one, made of a single immensely long tree trunk which has been stripped of its bark.

Sakai children trip lightly across this bridge; but adults are not so fortunate. Almost invariably, they slip off and tumble into the boiling water below, where a demon named Yenang fishes them out again and thrusts them into a fire to dry. Their torments do not end until they have been reduced to a fine powder.

Fiji Islanders say that death is a reef upon which squats the demon Nanggananangga. Nanggananangga seizes the souls of all bachelors and beats them to a pulp, like captured squid. Then he tenderly devours them.

Married men may fare farther, across the sea and into the mountain country of Kauvrandra, where the soul comes to a precipice overlooking a bottomless lake. There, a serpent deity, which is coiled up at the edge of the precipice, will softly ask the soul what it accomplished in life. The trembling soul does well to boast of having had

great wealth and many wives. If the serpent be sufficiently impressed it will invite the soul to sit upon a steering oar which projects out from the side of the cliff.

As soon as the soul has straddled the oar and begun to enjoy the cool breezes which waft up from the lake below, he falls; he tumbles down into the lake. There he may drown, or else he may discover Murimuria, the paradise at the core of existence.

For the Semang Pygmies of Malaysia, death is an intermediate stage between life and life again. First, they say, you must leave your body. Then, after seven days, you must go down to the shore of the sea and walk out over a long switchback bridge called Balan Bacham. At the far end of that bridge there sits a kindly Chinoi woman dressed in ferns; let her disguise you in the same manner. Then, jumping off the bridge, you must rush past a Negrito ogre before he can think to reach out and devour you.

You have now reached the island of Belot. The spirits who have gone before you gather round you now. They will break every single bone in your body. They will

At the Last Judgment the worlds divide beneath the angels' trumpets, tombs burst open, the damned go to hell, and the saints are assured of bliss *(above)*.

Anubis, god of death, sets up the scales of justice before the throne of the lord of the Egyptian underworld, Osiris *(above)*. In them man's deeds are weighed to determine his fate: death or rebirth?

turn your eyes backward in your skull so that only the whites show. All this will prepare you to enter the shadow of the tree of life, the Mapic Tree.

Smooth, heavy breasts blossom upon the Mapic Tree. Climb the warm boughs and drink your fill, feeling yourself grow young again. Someday you will be reborn.

Eskimo and Mongol cosmologists agree that the land of the dead is a real place far to the south. Winter in their country, they say, is summer down below; and daytime with them is nighttime in the Southland of the Dead. The tides, again, are opposite to theirs. When fish and game prove hard to come by, northern hunters console themselves as best they can with the thought that the dead, at least, must be enjoying excellent hunting. In short, experience is reversed in the land of the dead. There, rivers run backward, sweeping in from the sea,

At the Last Judgment an angel will appear, blowing a mighty trumpet to wake the dead *(above)*.

A mosaic in the cathedral of Torcello, near Venice, shows the archangel Michael with the scales of justice *(below)*. Two winged demons attempt to disturb him.

In this medieval sculpture *(below center)* two devils seek to tip the scales in their favor and win another soul for hell.

The Tibetan Book of the Dead tells of weighing the good or bad *karma* of the deceased, on scales filled with white and black stones *(below right)*.

The end of the world, like the death of the individual, is only the beginning of a new life in the world to come, according to myth and religion. At the threshold of the Beyond sits the court of the Last Judgment or some similar concept – a great reckoning up of the deeds of a man's life to determine whether in the life to come he shall suffer torment and destruction or enjoy eternal bliss. According to Biblical tradition the dead will be summoned from the grave at the Last Trump, the just to join

The ancient Persians too believed that the dead must undergo a final ordeal: the just were able to cross the knife-edged Cinvat bridge unharmed, while sinners plunged into the abyss *(left)*.

Japanese myth describes the court of the dead with analogous symbolism *(below)*. The judge on the left is noting down the charge on a long tablet; the other one is opening a scroll that relates the dead man's deeds.

God in endless light and the damned to be cast down into hell. Here, as in so many other mythic accounts, we find the symbol of the scales of justice determining man's fate in the afterlife. The scales are set up by the lord of the underworld, by God, or by the judge of the dead. The trial of the dead opens with the reading of the charge, after which counsel for the defense lays his weight of good in the scales. The scales motif occurs in the West, in Egypt, in India, in Tibet, and throughout the Far East. Another motif, occurring in ancient Persia and Ireland, for example, represents a kind of final ordeal: the dead are required to cross over the abyss of death, whereby the just survive unscathed but the damned stumble and fall to their doom.

291

steadily narrowing and climbing, each to its mountain goal. In Death's realm even the aging process is reversed, with souls wending backward day by day toward babyhood again.

In Mongol tombs, weapons are left broken. The purpose of that, the shamans explain, is to ensure that those same weapons will be whole again in the realm of the dead. Cups and pitchers are set upside down beside the corpse to make sure they will not spill. And examples of this sort can be almost indefinitely multiplied. Beltir tribesmen reverently leave a full flask of liquor in the left hand of the corpse – provided he was right-handed in life.

TALKING BONE

When jealous women destroyed the body of Orpheus, the sweet singer, his head floated away down the River Hebrus, into the Aegean Sea, and across to the island of Lesbos. There it rested, and for generations the hollow of bone still spoke, prophetically, to all who came there and had ears to hear its faint harmonious hissings. But when Apollo discovered that attendance at his own oracular shrines was being neglected, he forever silenced Orpheus's skull.

The Nupe people of Nigeria relate that a hunter once came upon a human skull and enquired of it, facetiously, "What brought you here?" Clackingly, the skull replied, "Talking brought me here."

At once the hunter ran to inform the king that he had located a talking skull. "I don't believe it," said the king, "and unless you can prove your case, I shall have you executed for attempting to make a fool of me." Then the king, with his bodyguard, accompanied the hunter to where the skull lay waiting.

"Skull, speak again!" the hunter implored. But the skull would not. The hunter was decapitated on the spot. After the king and his bodyguard had departed, the skull opened its white jaws and sardonically enquired of the hunter's head, "What brought you here?" The head lay thinking and then replied, "Talking brought me here!"

THE VENGEFUL GODS

Once long ago Tawhiri-ma-tea, the Maori god of winds, swooped upon his brother Tane-mahuta, the forest god. He snatched out handfuls of Tane-mahuta's leafy hair, he lashed him with lightning and heavy rain and destroyed his children. Tane-mahuta's domain was laid low.

A Scythian gold plaque found in Hungary illustrates the mythic motif of the soul's journey to paradise (left). An eagle as sky and sun bird soars with a liberated soul toward the light.

The idea of a ladder reaching up to heaven is one of the oldest concepts in myth. This eleventh-century manuscript illumination (right) shows a "ladder of the virtues" between the dragon of hell and the light of heaven. Virtuous monks are seen climbing the rungs representing the different virtues, while the sinners plunge headlong into the dragon's mouth.

Biblical tradition tells of the prophet Elijah's ascent to heaven in a chariot of fire drawn by sun horses (above left).

A fifteenth-century German woodcut (above) shows Alexander, dressed as a knight, attempting to reach heaven in an improvised aircraft. Two griffins, chained to a basket, lift it into the air as they strain to reach a piece of meat impaled on Alexander's lance.

Christ disappeared into the clouds before the eyes of his disciples when he ascended into heaven (left).

THE JOURNEY TO PARADISE

For the Altai of Siberia the shaman's ascent to the heaven of the god Bay Ulgen begins with the sacrifice of a horse *(left)*. Passing through the shaman's cultic tent the path continues up the nine-branched sacred birch to reach, after a series of incidents en route, the radiant presence of the god.

Birth, death, and rebirth or re-surrection constitute the cycle of existence both on earth and in the hypothetical worlds to come that feature in myth. Opposed to the descent into hell is the ascent to heaven, the realm of the gods. The liberated soul's journey to that blessed place is usually described with simple

This Italian mural *(below)* shows a ladder set up at the center of the earth between hell and heaven. An angel decides with the scales of justice whether the dead shall ascend or descend.

Joan Miró's hare, symbol of life, crouches before an expanding spiral that after circling between earth and sky

plausibility in terms of age-old mythic motifs: a heavenly chariot drawn by a team of winged horses, or the great bird of heaven, usually the messenger of the sun, who carries the soul to the world above. Other messengers of the gods as guides of the dead occur in Greek myth and in the ancient-Persian religion of Manichaeism. The ladder of heaven is another common symbol, as is the central world tree connecting underworld, earth, and heaven. Ladder and tree both have a purifying function: shamans, wise men, and powerful souls are able to climb them, but they pitch the unjust into hell.

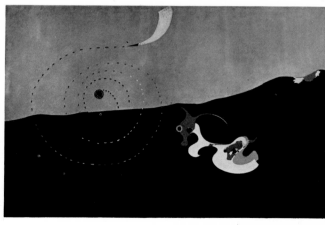

finally plunges into the light. It represents the movement of energy between spirit and matter.

Then Tawhiri-ma-tea whirled out over the ocean to attack the sea god, Tangaroa, and his children. He whipped the waters up into mountains, exposing the seabed. Tangaroa fled, weeping salt tears. His seaweed hair streamed out behind him, foaming on the darkness of the tormented deep. His children, the lizard and the fish, separated into two groups, some fleeing inland for shelter among what was left of the trees, while the others dived to the deepest parts of the sea which Tawhiri-ma-tea could not reach.

Next Tawhiri-ma-tea whirled off to find his brothers Rongo-ma-tane and Haumia-tiki-tiki, the gods of cultivated and uncultivated food. Their mother, the Earth, hid them away where Tawhiri-ma-tea could not find them. Finally Tawhiri-ma-tea went after his brother Tu-matauenga, the god of men. Against him Tawhiri-ma-tea threw every hurricane and wind at his command, Terrible-Rain, Long-Continued-Rain, Merciless-Hailstorm, and their howling progeny. Tu-matauenga, however, took shelter and remained unharmed.

There was little that the god of men could do against Tawhiri-ma-tea, for having attacked him. But he resolved to revenge himself on his four brothers for having failed to support him in the fight against Tawhiri-ma-tea.

Fierce Tu-matauenga snared the birds of the forest who were the children of Tane-mahuta. He netted the fish of the ocean who were the children of Tangaroa; and he dug up edible roots which were the children of Rongo-ma-tane and Haumia-tiki-tiki. The children of his four brothers formed the food of Tu-matauenga's revenge. We descendants of Tu-matauenga still continue the punishment.

The Wahungwe people of Southern Rhodesia say that there was once a time when not a drop of rain fell for a full year. Throughout that period, all girls of marriageable age piously disported themselves with the young men in an effort to bring on the rain. But it would not fall. Finally, the witch doctors ordered that a nubile virgin be sacrificed. By then, however, not a single one was to be found in all the land.

The solution which was hit upon was to imprison a young girl who had not reached puberty, shutting her up in a stone tower for safekeeping. She would be sacrificed later, when she was ready. Food was brought to her by women only, she was allowed to see no man. She matured very slowly, while the drought continued. The grasslands were barren and brown, the cattle died, and people were starving; but it was not time.

For three years not a drop of rain fell. Then at last the maiden was ready. She was

brought out from the tower and taken to a tree which grew over an ant heap. A pit was dug for her in the side of the ant heap. She was buried alive there as the tribe danced around the tree singing.

The tree grew steadily for three days and nights, while the people danced around it to encourage it. The crown of the tree spread wide, casting a welcome shade; and by the third night the massive tree had grown so large that its leaves obscured the moon and stars. On the morning of the fourth day, a wind arose in its leaves, rustling through them. Slowly clouds formed. Then a few raindrops spattered in the dust. The rain

turned to a thunder shower, and finally into a downpour which continued for thirty days and nights without stopping.

HAPPY RETURNS

The Norse god Thor was a good friend to the common people. One night, just for something to do, he stopped in to visit a

The idea of the resurrection and return of the hero beyond compare or the longed-for savior is one of the most powerful themes associated with man's hope of a life to come. The savior or redeemer, being not of this world, is subject to no one-time earthly death but instead ascends to heaven in order to show man the way. In the Far East it is Amitabha, as the Buddha of Redemption, who points the way to Nirvana. The resurrection of the one heralds the rebirth of the many to everlasting life in a state of primal union with the origin of all things.

1–4 The Buddhist wise men (the *arhats*) combine the symbols of longevity and otherworldly beatitude as the guardians of the Buddha's teaching.

5 The Greek god of healing, Asclepius, raises a dead man to life.

6 In this Byzantine painting of the resurrection of Christ the guardians of the tomb, blinded by the divine light, stagger back as Christ the conqueror of death ascends into the clouds.

7 In the blazing aura of a thousand radiant Buddhas, the Buddha appears as redeemer and symbol of life to the throng of monks and worshipers calling his name.

8 Lazarus, who has been four days in the tomb, is raised to life again by Jesus' command.

9 Christ is pictured here on his descent into hell to bring back Adam and Eve.

295

poor peasant family. They wished to offer him dinner, but the house held not one bite to eat. Thor said not to worry about that, for he would provide meat for the table. Thor slaughtered his two goats, Tanngnjost and Tanngrisnir, flayed them, then spread the two skins out beside the fire. After the meat had been cooked and eaten, he gathered up the bones and laid them on the hides. One of the thighbones had a crack in it. Unthinkingly, the youngest son of the house had pried that bone open with a knife in order to get at the succulent marrow.

After dinner, Thor spent the night comfortably in the family's one bed, while his hosts slept on the floor. At dawn, the god arose and lifted his hammer Mjollnir. Immediately, his two goats got up whole again and full of life, ready to pull his chariot. But one of the animals limped slightly.

The walls of the tomb of Ramses VI are richly decorated with scenes from the Egyptian books of the dead. In this detail *(opposite)* we see, in the lower triangle, Osiris with the constellation Scorpio. Above is a line of ram-headed gods, between whose legs we see the souls of the dead, represented as birds, making their way through the underworlds toward the new light of the life to come.

Related to the cycle of life between birth and death is the symbolic notion of a coming back to life, represented as a resurrection from the land of the dead and a return to the light. Wherever myths and religions enshrine a belief in an afterlife of the soul, the mind, or the body they also tell of underworlds or of intermediate realms from which gods or chosen ones emerge to partake of salvation. In Greek myth it is Herakles and Orpheus whose outstanding abilities enable

An Armenian legend relates that a troop of fairies once borrowed a farmer's ox and slaughtered it for a wedding guest in the forest. A human hunter happened upon their festivities and pocketed an ox rib as a souvenir of the occasion. The fairies looked everywhere for it, except in the huntsman's pocket. Finally, they made a wooden model of the missing rib and added it to the heap of ox bones which had been carefully saved. Then they charmed the ox back to life and drove it home to the farmer's barn, almost as good as new.

The Gauzi people of southern Bessarabia say that, with God's help, Adam also brought bones to life. The Hebrew prophet Ezekiel did the same thing. "I prophesied," Ezekiel proclaimed, "as I was commanded; and as I prophesied, there was a noise, and behold a shaking, and the bones came to-

When Orpheus was leading Eurydice out of Hades *(above)*, one forbidden look back at his lover was enough to lose her forever (page 191).

Nordic myth too knew the concept of a return from the underworld. In this illustration from the *Edda (above right)* we see the god Hermod, in full armor and mounted on an eight-legged horse, riding to deliver Odin's son Balder from the torments of hell.

them to visit Hades and return unscathed. The switch from underworld to earthly existence may also be important as regards the mythic understanding of the changing seasons, as reflected in the stories about the Greek queen of the underworld, Persephone, or the Babylonian goddess Ishtar. A well-known theme in Egyptian religion was the soul's passage through the underworld in the west, from which it emerged to new freedom in a pleasanter, divine existence. The concept centers on the myth of Isis and Osiris (page 258) and the nightly journey and daily reappearance of the sun god Ra. In the New Testament Christ's descent into hell and subsequent resurrection reveal the true nature of his victory over death.

This Greek vase painting shows the lovely goddess Persephone returning from the underworld. She is accompanied by Hermes, the messenger of the gods,

without whose help the long journey back from the depths of Hades would have been impossible.

Herakles *(above)* is one of the few figures of myth who was able to enter the realm of the dead unscathed and subsequently leave it again.

Christ emerging from the tomb with the cross in his hand *(below)* – the Christian symbol of deliverance from death.

gether, bone to bone. And when I beheld, lo, the sinews and the flesh came up upon them."

Moso tribesmen of Yunnan province in China say that their savior, Dto-Mbha Shi-lo, was pounced upon by cannibal devils (360 of them, one for almost every day of the year) as soon as he was born. Where a thousand roads cross, the devils stuffed the child headfirst into a bronze caldron of boiling oil. They clamped the lid down on his pink, small, feebly kicking feet. No sound escaped their victim, but the caldron itself hissed, thumped, and bubbled merrily enough. For three full days and nights, patiently, the 360 devils boiled their tender prey. Then, as the fire died away, they clustered greedily, each bearing a long spoon. They lifted off the lid; and the Moso savior, Dto-Mbha Shi-lo, sprang forth unharmed.

When a good Moso dies, Dto-Mbha Shi-lo is sure to lead him safely down through the nine infernal regions of the earth and up again along the seven golden terraces to the Tree of Heaven.

LAST MYSTERIES

In the year 627, King Edwin of Northumbria held a council to decide whether he should accept the teaching of a Christian missionary. According to the Venerable Bede's *A History of the English Church and People*, which was written only a century later, one of pagan King Edwin's more thoughtful advisers clinched the case:

Your Majesty, when we compare the present life of man with that time of which we have no knowledge, it seems to me like the swift flight of a lone sparrow through a banqueting-hall where you sit in the winter months to dine with your thanes and counsellors. Inside, there is a comforting fire to warm the room; outside, the wintry storms of snow and rain are raging. This sparrow flies swiftly in through one door of the hall, and out through another. While he is inside, he is safe from the winter storms; but after a few moments of comfort, he vanishes from sight into the darkness from whence he came. Similarly, man appears on earth for a little while, but we know nothing of what went before this life, or what follows. Therefore, if this new teaching can reveal any more certain knowledge, it seems only right that we should follow it.

Not long before the Spanish conquest of Peru, an Inca ruler of that region of the world began doubting the faith in which he had been raised. The sun, he had been taught, was the single omnipotent being. Yet, the king observed, the sun obeyed exceedingly strict laws in each and every motion. Who legislated for the sun? Some higher power, apparently. But what, or who, was it? The king ordered a temple to be erected and kept empty, dedicating it humbly to "the Unknown God."

The Taoist philosopher Chang Tao-ling once led his three hundred disciples to the highest peak of Yun-T'ai. They saw before them on the far side of the mountain a fathomless blue abyss. Some 30 feet down the precipice, a slippery spur of rock jutted out into space; and at the point of the rock, a peach tree grew, its ripe fruits glowing against the backdrop of nothingness. "Which one of you," Chang asked his disciples, "dares to gather that tree's fruit?"

One of them, a young man named Chao, dropped down to the spur of rock and ran out along it to reach the tree. Beneath it he stood plucking the peaches and placing them in the fold of his cloak, gathering one for each person present. Then he ran lightly back with his burden to the place where the rock spur joined the precipice, and tossed his peaches one by one up to the disciples and to Master Chang.

The Master, leaning out over the precipice, stretched his right arm 30 feet down to help Chao climb up again, saying, "Chao showed courage. Now I will make a similar attempt. If I succeed, I shall have a big peach for my reward." With that he leaped from the precipice, alighting in the branches of the peach tree. He was closely followed by Chao, who stood in the branches at his right side, and by another disciple, Wang, who leaped and alighted at the Master's left. Chang spoke to the two in tones too low for the others at the top to hear what was being said. Suddenly, all three people, and the peach tree as well, vanished into space.

Myth often resembles religious experience. There is art in it, art galore, and even magic. In myth we meet friends and foes from the animal kingdom, from the elements themselves, and from wholly nonphysical realms. We find profound knowledge of nature, and of human nature also, reflected in it. There everything appears transformed and yet dimly recognizable even so. This is because myth continually intercedes, as it were, between the little that we know and what we do not know as yet. Although it cannot be defined, myth may be pictured in a way. It is the glistening interface between consciousness and creative chaos.

These two pictures illustrate high points in the earthly existence of Gautama, the Buddha. The statue below records the moment when the Buddha proclaimed the Four Noble Truths in his first address at Sarnath, near Benares; the scroll painting opposite shows the consummation of the Buddha's life when he entered Nirvana, the state of perfect redemption. Each stage of the Buddha's life on earth became a struggle for the attainment of knowledge. Having attained Enlightenment, the Buddha began his career as a teacher and redeemer of mankind. He thus fulfilled in his own person the age-old mythic pattern, recognizable in his miraculous birth, in the extraordinary abilities of which he showed evidence even as a child, and in the supernatural powers revealed by the miracles he performed before his monks.

The Buddha, also described as the spiritual head of mankind, made all his major decisions with the whole of humanity in mind. The Tree of Enlightenment accordingly became the center of the Buddhist universe, while the "wheel" of Buddhist teaching was the old wheel of the law set in motion by the rulers of India. The whole of nature is said to have gone into mourning when the Buddha entered Nirvana. Monks, laymen, and all the animals of creation assembled to lament the passing of the conqueror of suffering.

Similar in form but far removed in terms of time and place of origin, these two images both show the way of light and life, which are ultimately identical. The Egyptian scarab god *(below)* rolls the ball of the sun nightly through the underworld toward the east, where Horus rises to bear it across the day. In the Egyptian books of the dead the sun's journey through the underworld is analogous to the soul's journey – the rebirth of light and life. The Tibetan-Buddhist wheel of life *(opposite)* sums up the essence of Buddhist teaching concerning reincarnation and the soul's ultimate liberation from the cycle of rebirth. The three animals in the center symbolize the vices that are the reason for the black semicircle of damnation. The white semicircle represents the conquest of evil and leads to Nirvana. The six worlds are places of reincarnation among gods, Titans, men, animals, hunger spirits, and hell creatures. Every man determines by his own actions in which sphere he will be reborn.

The fabulous treasure of the Egyptian king Tutankhamen includes this golden falcon with the sun disk poised on his head. The disk shows the scarab god Khepri rolling the ball of the sun before him. Khepri here has the wings of Horus. The five looped crosses around his head are symbols of eternal life.

The Buddhist wheel of life *(opposite),* a pedagogic instrument dealing with the cycle of rebirth and ultimate liberation from it, contains the six spheres of existence symbolizing the reincarnations that await man according to the state of his individual *karma.*

300

Recommended Reading

SELECTED BY MIRCEA ELIADE

I. COLLECTIONS Of MYTHS

Campbell, Joseph, *The Masks of God,* 4 vols. (New York: Viking Press, 1959–1968). A rich and encyclopedic collection with valuable commentary. Volumes include *Primitive Mythology, Oriental Mythology, Occidental Mythology,* and *Creative Mythology.*

Eliade, Mircea, *From Primitives to Zen* (New York: Harper & Row, 1967). A thematic source book containing thousands of mythic texts arranged in content-oriented categories. Now available as a set of four paperbacks: *Gods, Goddesses and Myths of Creation; Death, Afterlife and Eschatology; Man and the Sacred;* and *From Medicine Men to Muhammad.*

Eliot, Alexander, *Creatures of Arcadia* (New York: Bobbs-Merrill, 1968). Classical animal myths of importance to literature and art.

Frazer, Sir James George, *Folklore in the Old Testament,* 3 vols. (London: Macmillan & Co., 1919). Biblical stories provide the starting point for rich excursions into the myths and legends of other peoples.

Frobenius, Leo, *African Genesis* (New York: Stackpole Sons, 1937). Cosmogonic myths, all gathered from the African continent.

Gray, Louis H. (ed.), *The Mythology of All Races,* 13 vols. (Boston: Marshall Jones Co., 1916–1933). Somewhat dated, but still the most complete collection in the English language. Volumes are organized geographically: South American, North American, Indian, Iranian, Chinese, Japanese, Germanic, Slavic, etc.

Kramer, Samuel Noah (ed.), *Mythologies of the Ancient World* (Garden City, N.Y.: Doubleday, 1961). A convenient handbook with chapters on various world mythologies contributed by leading contemporary scholars in their own areas.

Long, Charles H., *Alpha: The Myths of Creation* (New York: George Braziller, 1963). An excellent collection of cosmogonic myths from all over the world, conveniently arranged in thematic categories.

Middleton, John (ed.), *Myth and Cosmos: Readings in Mythology and Symbolism* (Garden City, N.Y.: Doubleday, 1967). A collection of anthropological essays on the theme of myth, with many authors presenting materials collected in their own field work.

Oakes, Maud, and Joseph Henderson, *The Wisdom of the Serpent* (New York: George Braziller, 1963). A collection of myths devoted to the themes of immortality, resurrection, and the origin of death.

Pettazzoni, Raffaele (ed.), *Miti e leggende,* 4 vols. (Turin: Unione Tipografica, 1948–1963). Probably the finest collection of myths ever assembled, under the direction of the greatest of Italian historians of religions.

Pritchard, James B., *Ancient Near Eastern Texts,* 3d ed. (Princeton, N.J.: Princeton University Press, 1969). A massive collection of Egyptian, Babylonian, Assyrian, Phoenician, Hittite, and Canaanite myths, rituals, omens, and spells which cast light on much of the material in the Old Testament.

Thompson, Stith (ed.) *Tales of the North American Indians* (Bloomington: Indiana University Press, reprinted 1966). An extremely rich set of myths and folktales including trickster stories, journeys to the other world, etc.

II. THEORIES OF MYTH AND OF MYTHIC INTERPRETATION

Bachofen, J. J., *Myth, Religion and Mother Right* (Princeton, N.J.: Princeton University Press, 1967). Puts forth theories of the development of culture through distinct matrilineal and patrilineal stages, each of which has its own characteristic myths.

Baumann, H., "Mythos in ethnologischer Sicht," *Studium Generale,* 12 (1959): 1–17 and 583–597. Perhaps the best summary of the various anthropological approaches to myth.

Bolle, Kees W., *The Freedom of Man in Myth* (Nashville, Tenn.: Vanderbilt University Press, 1968). Takes up the problem of the relation between myth and literature.

Cassirer, Ernst, *The Philosophy of Symbolic Forms: Vol. II: Mythical Thought* (New Haven, Conn.: Yale University Press, 1955). A philosophical and phenomenological analysis of myth as a specific form of thought and of language.

Dorsin, Richard M., "Current Folklore Theories," *Current Anthropology,* 4 (1963): 93–112. A very convenient summary of the different schools of folklore analysis.

Eliade, Mircea, *The Myth of the Eternal Return* (also published as *Cosmos and History: The Myth of the Eternal Return)* (New York: Harper & Row, new ed., 1965). A discussion of the importance of the cosmogonic myth and its repetition in rituals of renewal.

——, *Patterns in Comparative Religion* (New York: Meridian Books, 1958). A morphological study of the important themes in myth: the sky, sun and moon, vegetation, sacred space, and sacred time.

——, "Myth, Nineteenth and Twentieth Centuries," *Dictionary of the History of Ideas* (New York: Scribners, 1973), Vol. 3, 307–318. A brief discussion of the major trends in the recent study of myth.

Feldman, Burton, *The Rise of Modern Mythology: 1680–1860* (Bloomington: Indiana University Press, 1972). An invaluable source book on earlier theories of myth.

Frankfort, H., H. A. Frankfort, et al., *Before Philosophy: The Intellectual Adventure of Ancient Man* (Baltimore: Penguin Books, 1951). An extremely stimulating, though perhaps overromanticized, view of the mythmaking mind. Largely dependent on materials from the ancient Near East.

Freud, Sigmund, *Totem and Taboo* (New York: Vintage Books, 1946). The most important work on the psychoanalytic study of myth, containing Freud's view on the primordial parricide, the totemic feast, and so forth.

Hooke, S. H. (ed.), *Myth and Ritual* (London: Oxford University Press, 1933). The opening manifesto of the British "Myth and Ritual" school.

——, *Myth, Ritual and Kingship* (Oxford: Clarendon Press, 1958). A reassessment of the "Myth and Ritual" position, twenty-five years after the appearance of the book cited above. These essays center on the theme of kingship in the ancient Near East.

Jensen, Adolf E., *Myth and Cult among Primitive Peoples* (Chicago: University of Chicago Press, 1963). An extremely exciting book, with much valuable information on *dema* deities and a theory of the relation of myths to culture levels: myths of hunters, of tuber planters, of cereal planters, etc.

Jung, C. G., and K. Kerényi, *Essays on a Science of Mythology* (Princeton, N.J.: Princeton University Press, 1949). The best introduction to the Jungian view of myths as the manifestation of the collective unconscious through its various archetypal forms.

Lang, Andrew, *Myth, Ritual and Religion,* 3d ed. (London: Longmans, Green & Co., 1901). One of the many books Lang devoted to his struggle with Max Müller, and to his theory of the priority of high gods.

Lévi-Strauss, Claude, *The Savage Mind* (Chicago: University of Chicago Press, 1966). An extremely stimulating book, devoted to the problem of the nature of the workings of primitive thought and paying special attention to the process of category formation.

——, *Mythologiques,* 4 vols. (Paris: Librairie Plon, 1964–1972). An exhaustive and extremely detailed structural analysis of certain myths of North and South America. Two volumes have now appeared in English translation: *The Raw and the Cooked* (New York: Harper & Row, 1969) and *From Ashes to Honey* (New York: Harper & Row, 1973). The other two, *L'origine des manières de table* (Paris: 1968) and *L'homme nu* (Paris: 1972) are scheduled for translation.

Lévy-Bruhl, Lucien, *Primitive Mentality* (Boston: Beacon Press, 1966). In large measure, Lévy-Strauss's *Savage Mind* is a response to Lévy-Bruhl, who argued that primitive thought was radically different from our own, being what he called "pre-logical" in nature.

Littleton, C. Scott, *The New Comparative Mythology: An Anthropological Assessment of the Theories of George Dumézil* (Los Angeles and Berkeley: University of California Press, 1965). A convenient summary and critique of the views of Dumézil, who has worked to show the social basis of Indo-European myths.

Malinowski, Bronislaw, *Myth, Science and Religion and Other Essays* (Garden City, N.Y.: Doubleday, 1948). Contains Malinowski's statement of his highly influential theory of myth as a "charter" for the organization of society.

Max Müller, Friedrich, *Contributions to the Science of Mythology* (London: Longmans, Green & Co., 1897). One of the best statements of Müller's theory of the importance of solar mythology and myth as a "disease of language."

Pettazzoni, Raffaele, *Essays on the History of Religions* (Leiden: Brill, 1954). Several very important essays on such topics as the "truth of myth," the high god, and so forth.

Propp, Vladimir, *Morphology of the Folktale* (Bloomington: Indiana University Press, 1958). A major contribution to the study of thematic elements in myths, legends, folk stories, etc.

Ricoeur, Paul, *The Symbolism of Evil* (Boston: Beacon Press, 1967). A philosophical exploration of differing notions of evil and sin drawing largely from mythic materials and phenomenological in its orientation.

Schmidt, Wilhelm, *The Origin and Growth of Religion* (London: Methuen & Co., 1931). This is a convenient summary of Schmidt's theories on the origin and development of religion from a period of "primordial monotheism" through all the following stages. It is derived from his twelve volume *Der Ursprung der Gottesidee*.

Sebeok, Thomas A. (ed.), *Myth: A Symposium* (Bloomington: Indiana University Press, 1958). A collection of nine essays on the problem of myth, all of them widely different in their orientation.

Tylor, Edward B., *Primitive Culture,* 2d ed. (New York: H. Holt, 1889). Presents Tylor's theory of "animism" – the belief in spiritual beings – as the origin of religion. A very important book that was highly influential on early studies of myth, such as Andrew Lang's.

Vries, Jan de, *The Study of Religion: A Historical Approach* (New York: Harcourt, Brace & World, 1967). An informative survey of studies devoted to myth and religion.

III. SPECIFIC STUDIES OF MYTH WITHIN A GIVEN CULTURE AREA

Beckwith, Martha Warren (ed.), *The Kumulipo: A Hawaiian Creation Chant,* 2d ed. (Honolulu: University of Hawaii Press, 1972). An excellent introduction to the nature and function of the Polynesian cosmogonic and genealogical chants.

Danielou, Alain, *Hindu Polytheism* (Princeton, N.J.: Princeton University Press, 1964). A rich and sympathetic treatment of the Indian pantheon and the many myths attached to the various deities.

Dorson, R. M., *Folk Legends of Japan* (Tokyo: Tuttle, 1962). An interesting collection of legends, many of which seem to have mythic backgrounds.

Duchesne-Guillemin, Jacques, *Zoroastrianism: Symbols and Values* (New York: Harper & Row, 1966). An easily accessible treatment of some of the more important themes in Iranian myth and religion.

Dumézil, Georges, *Mythe et épopée,* 3 vols. (Paris: Gallimard, 1968–1973). An extremely detailed, controversial, and brilliant analysis of Indo-European myths ranging from India to Ireland.

——, *The Destiny of the Warrior* (Chicago: University of Chicago Press, 1970). The most exciting of Dumézil's works to be translated into English. Deals with sins of the warrior, initiatory ordeals, transformation into animal form, and other important themes.

Eliade, Mircea, *Australian Religions: An Introduction* (Ithaca, N. Y.: Cornell University Press, 1972). An attempt to interpret the most important mythic themes of Australian aborigines: traveling myths and so on.

Engnell, Ivan, *Studies in Divine Kingship in the Ancient Near East,* 2d ed. (Oxford: B. Blackwell, 1967). A "Myth and Ritual" interpretation of kingship. Extremely informative, but perhaps too doctrinaire in its approach.

Frankfort, Henri, *The Problem of Similarity in Ancient Near Eastern Religions* (Oxford: Clarendon Press, 1951). A direct attack upon the foundations of the "Myth and Ritual" position.

Gaster, Theodor H., *Thespis: Ritual, Myth and Drama in the Ancient Near East* (New York: Harper & Row, 1961). An extremely stimulating presentation and argument for the origins of theater in myth and rite.

Grant, Michael, *Roman Myths* (New York: Scribner, 1972). A meticulous presentation of Roman myth, with special attention to the political overtones present in the telling of the myths.

Guthrie, W. K. C., *The Greeks and Their Gods* (Boston: Beacon Press, 1954). Perhaps the best and most sensitive presentation of the Greek myths.

Herskovitz, J. Mellville, and Frances S. Herskovitz, *Dahomean Narrative: A Cross-Cultural Analysis* (Evanston, Ill.: Northwestern University Press, 1958). Rich mythic material from West Africa, and an extremely well done introductory chapter on "A Crosscultural Approach to Myth."

Kramer, Samuel Noah, *Sumerian Mythology* (New York: Harper & Row, 1961). The best edition of some of the most ancient myths.

Krickeberg, Walter, et al., *Pre-Columbian American Religions* (New York: Holt, Rinehart and Winston, 1968). A convenient collection of essays on ancient North and South American religions, with much attention given to mythic materials.

Morenz, Siegfried, *Egyptian Religion* (Ithaca, N. Y.: Cornell University Press, 1973). The best work to appear on Egyptian religious forms to date.

Otto, Walter, *The Homeric Gods* (New York: Pantheon Books, 1954). An extremely warm and sensitive study of the Greek myths.

Philippi, Donald L. (trans.), *Kojiki* (Tokyo: University of Tokyo Press, 1968). The most important source for Japanese mythic material.

Radin, Paul, *The Trickster: A Study in American Indian Mythology* (New York: Schocken Books, rev. ed., 1972). A fascinating mythic cycle concerning the trickster figure of the Winnebago Indians, with commentaries by Radin, Jung, and Kerényi.

Reichel-Dolmatoff, Gerardo, *Amazonian Cosmos* (Chicago: University of Chicago Press, 1971). A superb book, perhaps the finest study of South American myth, religion, and symbolism ever written. Much valuable material on the shaman, the Lord of the Animals, and so on.

Ringgren, Helmer, *Religions of the Ancient Near East* (Philadelphia: Westminster Press, 1973). A very thorough and readable introduction to Egyptian, Semitic, and Akkadian myths and religions.

Schaerer, H., *Ngaju Religion: The Conception of God among a South Borneo People* (The Hague: Martinius Nijhoff, 1963). A marvelous study of the religion of this Oceanic people, drawing mainly from their complex and fascinating cosmogonic myth.

Smith, W. Robertson, *Lectures of the Religion of the Semites* (London: A. & C. Black, 1894). Now somewhat dated, but extremely influential for the theories presented as well as for the rich materials.

Turville-Petre, Gabriel, *Myth and Religion of the North* (London: Weidenfeld and Nicolson, 1964). Probably the best book in English on Norse and Germanic mythology.

Werner, Edward Theodore Chalmers, *Myths and Legends of China* (New York: Blom, 1922). Contains many fascinating traditions of mythic origin. Little in the way of analysis, but the materials are well worth while.

——, *A Dictionary of Chinese Mythology* (New York: Julian Press, 1961). An invaluable source book, with well-organized indexes. A reference book to consult, rather than to read for pleasure.

Widengren, Geo., *King and Savior,* 6 vols. (Uppsala: Lundquist Bokhandeln, 1945–1955). Brilliant studies on such themes as ascension, revelation, and the tree of life.

Zimmer, Heinrich, *Myths and Symbols in Indian Art and Civilization* (New York: Harper & Row, 1946). A very rewarding study of some of the most important Indian mythic themes, with special attention given to their expression in art.

Acknowledgments

The publisher wishes to express special gratitude to the following individuals who gave so generously of their time and efforts in the graphic research for this book:

Dr. Arthur Bachmayer, Lucerne
Miss Brigitte Baumbusch, Scala, Florence
Professor Joseph Campbell, New York
Miss Clarke, Thames & Hudson, London
Miss Faithfull,
    Hamlyn Picture Library, London
The staff of Giraudon Photographie, Paris
Mrs. Heller, Werner Forman Archive,
    London
Mr. Michael Holford, London
Dr. Detlef-I. Lauf, Hüntwangen
The staff of the Mansell Collection,
    London
Mr. Leonard von Matt, Buochs
Dr. Rudolf Michel, C.G. Jung Institute,
    Zurich
Miss Mostyn, Hamlyn Picture Library,
    London
The staff of Photothèque Robert Laffont,
    Paris
Miss Tyres,
    Indian Section at the Victoria and
    Albert Museum, London
Miss Weiske, Hirmer Fotoarchiv, München

SOURCE MATERIAL

In addition to the list of recommended readings (pages 302/303), the following titles were consulted during the research for this book:

Alexander, H. B., *World's Rim: Great Mysteries of the North American Indians* (1967).
Alleau, R., *Histoire des Sciences occultes.*
Apollonius, *The Voyage of Argo,* tr. by Emil v. Rieu (1959).
Ariosto, *Orlando Furioso,* ed. by A. Bartlett Giamatti and Stewart A. Baker (1968).
Bachofens, J. J., *Gesammelte Werke,* Vol. VII (1958).
Bailey, J., *The God-Kings and the Titans* (1973).
Barthell, Edward E., Jr., *Gods and Goddesses of Ancient Greece* (1971).
Bataille, George, *La Peinture Préhistorique Lascaux ou la Naissance de l'Art* (1955).
Batterbury, Michael, *Chinese and Oriental Art* (1961).
Bazin, Germain, *The History of World Sculpture* (1968).
Bede, *A History of the English Church and People.*
Bennett, J. G., *The Dramatic Universe,* Vol. 1 (1956).
Berlitz, Charles, *The Mystery of Atlantis* (1971).
Biblia, tr. by Martin Luther (1534).
Biedermann, Hans, *Altmexikos Heilige Bücher* (1971).
Bihalji-Merin, Otto, *Masken der Welt* (1970).
Boas, Franz, *Primitive Art* (1927).
Boisselier, Jean, and Jean-Michel Beurdeley, *Plastik in Thailand* (1974).
Brandon, S. G. F., *Man and God in Art and Ritual* (1975).
Burland, C. A., *Myths of Life and Death* (1974).
——, *The Gods of Mexico* (1964).
Campbell, Joseph, *The Flight of the Wild Gander* (1951).
——, *The Hero with a Thousand Faces* (1968).
——, *The Mythic Image* (1975).
Ceram, C. W., *Der erste Amerikaner* (1972).
Champeaux, Gérard de, and Dom Sébastien Sterckx, *Le Monde des Symboles* (1966).
Charleston, Robert G., *World Ceramics* (1968).
Cohane, John P., *The Key* (1969).
Conze, Edward (tr.), *Buddhist Scriptures.*
Cook, Arthur B., *Zeus: A Study of Ancient Religion,* 5 vols. (1914).
Cook, Roger, *The Tree of Life* (1974).
Coolidge, Dane, and Mary Coolidge, *The Navajo Indians* (1930).
Coomaraswamy, Ananda K., and Sr. Nivedita, *Myths of the Hindus and Buddhists.*
Cumont, Franz, *Mysteries of Mithra,* 2d ed. (1911).
Daniken, Erich von, *Chariots of the Gods* (1970).
Davy, M. M., *Encyclopédie des Mystiques* (1972).
Dayrell, E., *Folk Stories from Southern Nigeria, West Africa* (1910).
Dodds, Eric R., *The Greeks and the Irrational* (1951).
Doresse, Jean, *Secret Books of the Egyptian Gnostics* (1960).
Eliade, Mircea, *Shamanism: Archaic Techniques of Ecstasy* (1972).
Eliot, Alexander, *The Horizon Concise History of Greece* (1972).
Elisofon, E., *The Sculpture of Africa* (1953).
Encyclopedia Britannica, 24 vols. (1973).
Eschenbach, Wolfram von, *Parzival.*
Evans, Ivor, *Religion, Folklore, and Custom in North Borneo and the Malay* (1923).
Finegan, Jack, *Archeology of World Religions,* 3 vols. (1952).
Frankfort, Henri, *The Problem of Similarity in Ancient Near Eastern Religions* (1951).
Frazer, James G., *The Golden Bough: Study in Magic and Religion,* 13 vols.
Freud, Sigmund, *Moses and Monotheism,* ed. by Katherine Jones (1955).
Friedlander, Gerald (ed.), *Pirke de Rabbi Eliezer* (1971).
Galanopoulos, George A., and Edward Bacon, *Atlantis: The Truth Behind the Legend* (1969).

Gaster, Theodor H., *The Dead Sea Scriptures,* rev. ed. (1956).
——, *The Oldest Stories in the World* (1958).
Gibbon, Edward, *Decline and Fall of the Roman Empire,* 3 vols.
Goethe, Johann von, *Faust,* tr. by Bayard Taylor.
Goodspeed, Edgar J. (ed.), *Apocrypha.*
Grant, Michael, and John Hazel, *Who's Who in Classical Mythology* (1973).
Graves, Robert, *The Greek Myths,* 2 vols. (1955).
——, *The White Goddess* (1961).
Gray, John, *Near Eastern Mythology* (1969).
Green, Roger L., *Myths of the Norsemen* (1970).
Greenway, John, *Literature Among the Primitives* (1964).
Grey, George, *Polynesian Mythology* (1969).
Guerber, Helene A., *Myths of Greece and Rome* (1764).
——, *Myths and Legends of the Middle Ages* (1909).
Haile, Bernard, and Maud Oakes, *Beautyway, A Navajo Ceremonial* (1957).
Harris, Joel Chandler, *Nights with Uncle Remus* (1883).
Hinnells, John, *Persian Mythology* (1973).
Holy Bible, Revised Standard Version, (1952).
The Horizon Book of the Arts of China (1969).
The Horizon Book of Lost Worlds (1962).
The Horizon History of Africa (1971).
Howells, William, *The Pacific Islanders* (1973).
Ions, Veronica, *Indian Mythology* (1967).
Jenkins, Elizabeth, *The Mystery of King Arthur* (1975).
Jobes, Gertrude, *Dictionary of Mythology, Folklore, and Symbols,* 2 vols. (1962).
John, Ivor B., *The Mabinogion* (1901).
Jones, Gwyn, *Welsh Legends and Folk-Tales* (1955).
Journal of American Folklore (1918).
Joyce, P. W., *Old Celtic Romances* (1962).
Jung, Carl G., *Symbols of Transformation,* ed. by G. Adler et al., tr. by R. F. C. Hull (1967).
——, *Man and His Symbols* (1964).
——, *Memories, Dreams, Reflections* (1961).
Kellett, Ernst E., *The Story of Myths* (1927).
Kenton, Warren, *Astrology* (1974).
Kerényi, Karl, *The Gods of the Greeks.*
——, *Essays on a Science of Mythology* (1949).
King, Francis, *The Western Tradition of Magic* (1975).
Klossowski de Rola, Stanislas, *Alchemy* (1973).
König, Marie E., *Am Anfang der Kultur* (1973).
Laffont, *Dictionnaire des Symboles* (1969).
Larousse, *World Mythology* (1963).
Laszlo, G., *Steppenvölker und Germanen* (1970).
Lauf, D.-I., *Das Bild als Symbol im Tantrismus* (1973).
——, *The Heritage of Tibet* (1976).
Leland, Charles Godfrey, *The Algonquin Legends of New England* (1884).
Lévèque, Jean-Jacques, and Nicole Menant, *Islamic and Indian Painting* (1970).
Livy, *The Early History of Rome,* tr. by Aubrey de Selincourt (1960).
Lommel, Andreas, *Masks* (1970).
——, *Prehistoric and Primitive Man* (1966).
Luce, J. V., *Lost Atlantis* (1969).
Lucretius, *Of the Nature of Things,* tr. by Wm. E. Leonard.
McAlpine, Helen, and William McAlpine, *Japanese Tales and Legends* (1959).
McGraw-Hill, *Encyclopedia of World Art,* 15 vols. (1960).
Mackenzie, Donald A., *Myths of Babylonia and Assyria* (1763).
Mariner, William, *Account of the Natives of the Tongo Islands.*
Matt, Leonard von, and Mario Moretti et al., *Kunst und Land der Etrusker* (1969).
Mellaart, James Çatal Hüyük (1967).
Menzel, Donald H., *Astronomy* (1971).
Mode, H., *Fabulous Beasts and Demons* (1975).

Muhammad, *The Koran.*
Müller, Karl O., *Prolegomena zu einer wissenschaftlichen Mythologie* (1825).
Müller, Max F., *Upanishads,* 2 vols. (1963).
Neumann, Erich, *The Great Mother* (1972).
Newall, V., *The Encyclopedia of Witchcraft and Magic* (1974).
New Larousse Encyclopedia of Mythology (1959).
Nicholson, Marjorie H., *Voyages to the Moon* (1960).
Nigg, Walter, *The Heretics* (1962).
Nilsson, Martin P., *Greek Folk Religion* (1972).
Opie, Iona and Peter Opie (eds.), *Oxford Dictionary of Nursery Rhymes* (1951).
Ovid, *Metamorphoses,* tr. by Mary Innes.
Parke, H. W., and D. E. Wormell, *The Delphic Oracle,* 2 vols. (1956).
Patrick, R., *Egyptian Mythology* (1972).
Pausanias, *Description of Greece,* 6 vols, tr. by J. G. Frazer (1897).
Pecker, Jean-Claude, *Le Ciel* (1960).
Picard, Barbara L., *Celtic Tales* (1965).
Poignant, Rosalyn, *Oceanic Mythology* (1967).
Purce, Jill, *The Mystic Spiral* (1974).
Rawson, Philip, *Tantra* (1973).
——, and Laszlo Legeza, *Tao* (1973).
Readers Digest, *Folklore, Myths, and Legends of Britain* (1973).
Reed, Philip, *The Seven Voyages of Sindbad the Sailor* (1962).
Ricci, F. M., *Beato di Liebana* (1973).
——, *Apocalisse* (1969).
Robinson, Roland, *Feathered Serpent* (1956).
——, *Legend and Dreaming* (1952).
Rose, Herbert J., *Handbook of Greek Mythology* (1959).
Sandars, N. K., *The Epic of Gilgamesh* (1960).
Schmidt, Wilhelm, *Der Ursprung der Gottesidee,* 12 vols. (1912–1955).
Seyffert Oskar, *Dictionary of Classical Antiquities* (1956).
Smith, Bradley, *Mexico: A History in Art* (1968).
Smith, Robin, and Keith Willey, *New Guinea* (1969).
Spence, L., *Myths of Mexico and Peru.*
——, *North American Indians* (1745).
Squire, Charles, *Myths of the Celts and Britons* (1748).
Stanford, W. B., and J. V. Luce, *The Quest for Ulysses* (1974).
Steiner, Rudolf, *Egyptian Myths and Mysteries,* tr. by Norman Macbeth (1971).
Strachey, William, *The Historie of Travaile into Virginia Britannia.*
Strassburg, Gottfried von, *Tristan,* tr. by Arthur T. Hatto.
Taylor, Paul and W. H. Auden, *The Elder Edda* (1969).
Terry, Charles S., *Masterworks of Japanese Art* (1956).
Tylor, E. B., *Primitive Culture* (1871).
Van Duyn, Janet, *The Egyptians.*
Vermes, G., *The Dead Sea Scrolls in English* (1962).
Von Franz, Marie-Louise, *Creation Myths* (1972).
Weston, Jesse L., *From Ritual to Romance* (1957).
White, Terence H., *The Bestiary: A Book of Beasts* (1960).
Willett, Frank, *Ife* (1967).
Willetts, William, *Foundations of Chinese Art* (1965).
Wright, David (tr.), *Beowulf* (1957).
Wu Ch'eng-En, *Monkey,* tr. by Arthur Waley (1958).
Wyl, J. von, *Der Luzerner Totentanz* (1941).
Yeats, William B., *Irish Folk Stories and Fairy Tales* (1957).

List of Illustrations and Photo Credits

42 *Top to bottom, left to right:*
Stonehenge, England. P: Aerofilms Ltd.
Bear. Sculpture, Resen Mose, Denmark. Publisher's Archives.
Esus. From Jupiter altar (detail). Musée de Cluny, Paris.
The Uffington White Horse. England. P: Aerofilms Ltd.
Stone slab. From Huminge, Gotland. Museum of Visby, Gotland. P: Axel Poignant.
Shaman's drum. See page 111.
Horned god. From Holzgerlingen, Württemberg. Museum of Antiquities, The University, Newcastle.

43 *Top to bottom, left to right:*
Mercury. See page 131.
Epona. Museum of Alesia. P: Hétier.
Sleipnir. See page 160.
Gravestone (detail). From Niederdollendorf, ca. 700–800. Publisher's Archives.
Freyr. Norse. Statens Historiska Museum, Stockholm. P: Werner Forman Archives.
Loki. From Kirkby Stephen, Weltmoreland. P: Axel Poignant.
Yggdrasil. See page 109.
Shaman's drum. Publisher's Archives.
Shaman's journey. Siberia. Publisher's Archives.
The *axis mundi*. Siberia. Publisher's Archives.
Shaman's drum. Publisher's Archives.
Shaman. Chalk drawing, Finno-Ugric.
Shaman. See page 133.

44 *Top to bottom, left to right:*
War god. Relief (detail) from King's Gate, Hattusa, Hittite, 14th c. B.C. Ankara Museum.
The four rivers of Paradise (detail). See page 116.
Christ. Mosaic (detail), Hagia Sophia, Byzantine, 13th c. P: Erich Lessing.
Zoroastrian fire altar. Coin of King Shahpur I (d. A.D. 272), Persia. Hermitage, Leningrad.
Muhammad's ascension (detail). See page 160.
The Tower of Babel. Oil on copper, by Johann Rottenhammer (?). Musée d'Art et d'Histoire, Genève.
The crossing of the Red Sea. Publisher's Archives.
Moses receiving the Law from the hand of God. Relief (detail), Byzantine. Staatliche Museen, Berlin.
Lilithu. See page 135.
Nergal. See page 275.

45 *Top to bottom, left to right:*
Zervan. See page 199.
Armati. Amlash, Persia, ca. 900 B.C. Teheran Museum.
Anahita. Achaemenian. P: Giraudon.
Equestrian investiture of Ardashir I by god Ormazd. Relief (detail), Naqs-i-Rustem, 3rd c. Publisher's Archives.
Bull. Pottery, Tepe Gawra, North Iran, 3rd. mill. B.C. British Museum, London.
Baal. See page 24.
Ishtar. Terracotta, Sumerian. Louvre, Paris.
Adad. Babylon, ca. 8th c. B.C. Directorate General of Antiquities, Baghdad.
Winged human-headed genius. See page 236.
Winged deities. Cylinder seal, Assyrian, 990–600 B.C. P: Mansell Collection.

Cuneiform writing. Publisher's Archives.

46 *Top to bottom, left to right:*
Four-headed Brahma. See page 61.
Shiva Candrasekhara. South India. Musée Guimet, Paris.
Birth of Buddha. See page 197.
Mandala. See page 79.
Vishnu and Lakshmi. See page 88.
Shiva. Bronze sculpture, India, 11th–12th c. Musée Guimet, Paris. P: Leonard von Matt.
Krishna and the serpent Kaliya. Scene from the *Krishnalila*, New Delhi, India. P: Bulloz.
Brihadisvara Temple, Tanjore, India. Publisher's Archives.
Angkor Thom. Khmer, Cambodia, late 12th–early 13th c. Publisher's Archives.

47 *Top to bottom, left to right:*
Yin-yang symbol. See page 64.
The Buddha Amida. See page 266.
Dragon. China. Publisher's Archives.
Izanami and Izanagi. See page 64.
Amaterasu. See page 93.
Guardian. See page 226.
Buddha of wisdom. See page 123.
Stone pagoda of Kumsan-Sa. Southwest Korea. Publisher's Archives.
Pagoda of T'ien-ning-sse. Peking, China. Publisher's Archives.
Horyu-ji Temple. Nara, Japan. Publisher's Archives.

48 *Top to bottom, left to right:*
Ship of the dead. See page 273.
Ship of the dead. Stone carving, western New Guinea. P: Claus Hansmann.
Witch doctor. Sumatra. P: Radio Times Hulton Picture Library.
Dayak. Borneo. See page 278.
Banaitja. See page 60.
Kanguruh woman. Aboriginal bark painting, Australia. State Library of South Australia, Adelaide.
Aboriginal creation myth. See page 83.
Mimi spirit people. Aboriginal bark painting, Australia. State Library of South Australia, Adelaide.
Men dancing at ceremony. Aboriginal bark painting, Australia. State Library of South Australia, Adelaide.
Timara, the Fisher. Aboriginal bark painting, Australia. State Library of South Australia.

49 *Top to bottom, left to right:*
Nomoi mask. See page 107.
Ritual statuette. New Caledonia. Museum für Völkerkunde, Basel.
Fetish. Carving, New Ireland. British Museum, London.
Divinity. Wooden statuette, Nukuoro, central Carolines. Hamburgisches Museum für Völkerkunde und Vorgeschichte.
Maui. See page 149.
Ku. See page 60.
Belam. See page 129.
Tangaroa. See page 84.
Tiki. See page 60.
Giant statues. See pages 10–11.

50 *Top to bottom, left to right:*
Spirit canoe. See page 106.
Kachina bear. See page 129.

Thunderbird. See page 105.
The Great Hare. See page 63.
Thunderbird. See page 162.
Totem Pole. South Alaska. National Museum of Canada, Ottawa. P: Richard Inglis.
The myth of Mother Spider (detail). See page 82.
Sand paintings. From the Navaho myth of "Beautyway." Publisher's Archives.

51 *Top to bottom, left to right:*
Fish amulet. See page 147.
Cliff Palace, Mesa Verde, Colorado. Publisher's Archives.
Sun dance. Dakota Sioux. The American Museum of Natural History, New York.
Bee *kachinas*. See page 16.
Tawa. See page 95.

52 *Top to bottom, left to right:*
Gigantic head. Olmec culture, Mexico. Museo de Antropologia de la Universidad Veracruzana, Jalapa.
Two-faced sculpture, with common eye. Mexico. Museo Nacional de Antropologia e Historia, Mexico City.
Sun god on sun disk. From *Codex Laud*, Mexico. Bodleian Library, Oxford.
War goddess. Mexico. P: Jean Bottin.
Feathered serpent. See page 263.
Quetzalcoatl. See page 142.
Toltec pillar. See page 98.
Aztec calendar. See page 95.
Plumed coyote. Aztec culture, Mexico. P: Gisèle Freund.
Sun pyramid. Teotihuacán, Mexico. Publisher's Archives.
Kukulkan pyramid. (Correction: not Huracan, as stated in caption.) See page 112.

53 *Top to bottom, left to right:*
Christopher Columbus (1451–1506). Publisher's Archives.
Hernando Cortez (1485–1547). Publisher's Archives.
Francisco Pizarro (1470–1541). Publisher's Archives.
Maize goddess. See page 120.
Machu Picchu. Amazona. P: Emil Schulthess.
Inca wall. Peru. Publisher's Archives.
Fish with symbolic plants and stars. Pachacamac, ca. 1000. Museum für Völkerkunde, München.
Mythical bird or butterfly. Tiahuanaco, ca. 1000. Museum für Völkerkunde, Berlin.

55 The moon king with his people. Rock painting, Southern Rhodesia. Frobenius Institute, Frankfurt/M.

56 Buddhist mandala. Bhutan, ca. 18th c. P: Dr. D.-I. Lauf.

57 "People of the Myth." Navaho sand painting, North America. Publisher's Archives.

CREATORS OF NATURE AND MANKIND

58 *Top:* Rock engraving. Valcamonica. Italy. Publisher's Archives.
Bottom: Creation of the stars. Mosaic, Dome of Monreale Cathedral, Sicily, 12th c. P: Scala.

59 Starry sky. P: California Institute of Technology and Carnegie Institute of Washington.

60 *Top:* Tiki. Carved wood, Maori, Polynesia. British Museum.

Middle left: Sea volcano. P: Ackermann.
Middle center: God creating sun and moon. Fresco by Michelangelo (1475–1564), Sistine Chapel, Rome. P: Anderson-Giraudon.
Middle right: Mother Goddess. Ton figurine, Cyprus, ca. 2500 B.C. British Museum.
Bottom left: Ku. Hawaii. British Museum.
Bottom right: Banaitja. Arnhemland, Australia. National Gallery of South Australia, Adelaide. P: Charles P. Mountford.

61 *Left:* Ptah. Egypt. Louvre, Paris. P: Giraudon.
Top right: Brahma. Sandstone, Khmer, Cambodia, 10th c. Musée Guimet, Paris. P: Leonard von Matt.
Bottom right: Pan-Ku. Lithograph, China, 19th c. British Museum.

62 Serpent and World Egg. Publisher's Archives.

63 *Top to bottom, left to right:*
Tobacco pipe in the shape of a frog. Mound builders, Kentucky, U.S.A. British Museum. P: Axel Poignant; Hamlyn Picture Library.
The Great Hare. Rock painting, Lake Mazinaw, Canada. Royal Ontario Museum, Toronto. P: Selwyn Dewdney.
Amon-Ra. Egypt, 1413–1337 B.C. Staatliche Museen, Berlin.
Bird-men. Stone from Easter Island. P: Axel Poignant.
Head of dog. Stirrup vessel, Mochica culture, Peru. Rietberg Museum, Zurich.
The snake Kurrichaelpongo. Aborigine painting, Australia. Publisher's Archives.
Ibis representing Thoth. Egypt. P: Roger Wood Studio.

64 *Top left:* Izanagi and Izanami. Silk painting, Japan, 19th c. Museum of Fine Arts, Boston. Hamlyn Picture Library.
Bottom left: Fu Hsi and Nu Kua. Stone rubbing, China, Han period, 2nd c. P: Claus Hansmann.
Yin and *Yang*. Red lacquer panel. China. Wellcome Institute, London. P: Michael Holford Library.

65 *Top:* Double-headed figure. Hittite, 3rd mill. B.C. P: Giraudon.
Middle left: Shu and Tefnut. Aegis, Egypt. P: Mansell Collection.
Middle right: Twin idol figure. From Alaca Hüyük, Ankara, Turkey. P: Hirmer.
Bottom: Male-female deity. From *Codex Zouche-Nuttall*, Mixtec culture, Mexico. British Museum. P: Hamlyn Picture Library.

66 Gaea. Terracotta statuette, Tanagra. Bosély Museum, Marseille. P: Mansell Collection.
Top: Tlazolteotl giving birth to Centeotl. Collection Robert Wood Bliss, Washington. P: W. Bruggmann.
Middle row, from left to right:
Mother Goddess with child. Khond tribe, India. Victoria and Albert Museum, London. P: Hamlyn Picture Library.
Mother Goddess. Knossos, Crete. P: Rudolf Hoegler.
Mother Goddess. Indus culture, India, 2700–1800 B.C. Karachi Museum. P: Laffont.
Mother Goddess. Amlach,

Iran, 9th–8th c. B.C. Private collection. P: Istvan Racz.
Earth Mother. Pottery lamp, Ashanti tribe, Ghana. British Museum.
Bottom: Coatlicue. Aztec culture, Mexico. Nacional Museo de Antropologia, Mexico City. P: Schwitter.

68–75 Greek pantheon. Genealogy according to Barthell, Edward E., Jr., *Gods and Goddesses of Ancient Greece* (1971). Drawings by Franz Coray.

76 *Top left:* Ancient cosmogram. Capo di Ponte, Valcamonica, Italy. Palaeolithic. Publisher's Archives.
Top right: Bakong Temple. Built 881 in Hariharalaya, Angkor, Cambodia. Publisher's Archives.
Middle: Picture of the universe. Franz Coray drawing.
Bottom: Mythic map. From the Henoch book. Publisher's Archives.
Right: Cosmic World Egg. Drawing by Franz Coray.
Top left: Star circles around the polestar. P: M. Steiger.
Top middle: The *axis mundi.* Shaman's drum. Iceland. P: Courtesy Thames and Hudson.
Top right: The five world mountains. Scroll, China. British Museum, London. P: Hamlyn Picture Library.
Middle left: Man breaking through the heavens. Engraving, ca. 1130. Publisher's Archives.
Middle right: Rocket. P: Keystone.
Bottom: The planet Earth from 22,300 miles in space. P: NASA.

78 The five regions of the world. From *Codex Fejervary-Mayer,* Aztec culture, Mexico. Merseyside County Museums.

79 Mandala of the goddess Vasudhara. Nepal, 1504. British Museum, London.
Top: Cosmic mandala. Lamaism, Tibet. P: Dr. D.-I. Lauf.
Middle: Creation of the four continents. Tibet. P: Dr. D.-I. Lauf.
Bottom: Mandala. Tibet. P: Dr. D.-I. Lauf.

81 *Top to bottom, left to right:*
Golden rainbow cup. Celtic, ca. 100 B.C. Publisher's Archives.
Painted cup. From Elam. Publisher's Archives.
Picture of universe. Painted plate. Publisher's Archives.
Image of the cosmos. Mirror, China, 403–249 B.C. Publisher's Archives.
Ouroboros. Bronze disk, Benin. P: Laffont.
Angels setting in motion the first heaven. Manuscrit provençal, France, 14th c. Publisher's Archives.
Wheel of life. Northwest India, 1st–2nd c. British Museum.
Nut forming the sky. Interior painting of sarcophagus, Egypt, 5th c. B.C. The Metropolitan Museum of Art, New York; Gift of Edward S. Harkness, 1914.
Yantra of the southern continent. India, 18th c. Gal. Krugie. P: Nicolas Bouvier.
World map. From "Lambertus floridus," 18th c. manuscript. Bibliothèque Nationale, Paris. P: Nicolas Bouvier.

World map. From Beatus NAL 2290, "Commentary on the Apocalypse." Bibliothèque Nationale, Paris.
Turtle carrying the twenty-one worlds. Designed by Brahmin, Hindu. P: The Bettmann Archives, New York.
The world. From "Universal Cosmography," 1559. Publisher's Archives.
The universe. Greek, 1559. P: Ronan Picture Library.
The creation of the world. Retable of the *Garden of Earthly Delights,* shutters closed. Painting by Hieronymus Bosch (ca. 1450–1516). Prado, Madrid. P: Oronoz.

82 Navaho creation myth. Drawing by Franz Coray.

83 *Left:* Scene from the Djanggawul myth. Aboriginal bark painting by Mawalan and Wandjuk Marika. Australia, 20th c. New South Wales Art Gallery, Gift of Dr. Stuart Scougall.
Right: Prometheus. Greek, 2nd c. B.C. British Museum.

84 *Left:* Great Mother giving birth to the gods. From *Codex Borgia,* Cholula-Tlaxcala culture, Mexico, 15th c. Br. Museum.
Right: Tangaroa. Rurutu Islands, Central Polynesia. British Museum, London.

85 Wandjina. Kimberley Mountains, Australia. Museum für Völkerkunde, Munich.

86–87 Paradise. Painting by Lucas Cranach the Elder (1472–1553). Kunsthistorisches Museum, Wien.

88 Vishnu reclining on the serpent Ananta. Miniature, Rajasthan, India, 17th c. National Gallery, Prague. P: Werner Forman Archive.

WORLDS ABOVE, BELOW, AND WITHIN

90 Paradise (detail). Painting by Hieronymus Bosch (ca. 1450–1516). Doge Palace, Venice. P: Scala.
Nut. Relief ceiling painting, Temple of Hathor, Dandarah, Egypt, 1st–4th c. A.D. P: Hirmer.

91 The sun. P: Emil Schulthess.

92 Akhenaton and Nefertiti. Egypt. Museum of Cairo. P: Werner Forman Archives.

93 *Top:* The secret of the golden flower. Crown, silver gilt, Liao dyn. China 907–1125. Museum of Fine Arts, Boston.
Middle: Amaterasu. P: Hamlyn Picture Library.
Bottom: The eye of Ra. Egypt, 21st dyn. British Museum, London. P: Michael Holford Library.

94 *Left:* Tonatiuh. Aztec culture, Mexico. Mexico Museum. P: Henri Stierlin.
Top: Sun god Ra and harpist Djed. Stele, Egypt, 21st–22nd dyn. Louvre, Paris. P: Cliché Musées Nationaux.
Middle: Nanahuatzin. Toltec culture, Mexico. Museum für Völkerkunde, Wien. P: Hamlyn Picture Library.
Bottom left: Heart-offering to sun god. Pre-Columbian, Mexico. Museum für Völkerkunde, Berlin.
Bottom right: Sun god. Upper Volta. P: Publisher's Archives.

95 *Top row, from left to right:*
Sun wheel. Konarak, India, 13th c. P: Claus Hansmann.
Sun symbol. Fresco in Cempoallan, Veracruz, Mexico. P: Courtesy Akademische Drucks- und Verlagsanstalt, Graz.
Calendar. Sun stone, Aztec culture, Museo Nacional de Antropologia, Mexico City. P: Hamlyn Picture Library.
Middle right: Shamash. Abu Habbah, Assyrian, 9th c. British Museum, London.
Bottom left: Tawa, the Sun Spirit. Pueblo Indians, North America. Smithsonian Institution, National Anthropological Archives.
Bottom right: Sol. Relief, Mitraem Piazza Dante, Rome, Italy, 3rd–4th c. P: Leonard von Matt.

96 *Top:* Ashur. Relief, palace of Ashurnasirpal, Assyria, 885–860 B.C. University of Chicago Press.
Middle: The course of the sun. Papyrus, New Kingdom, Egypt, A.D. 150–1090. Bibliothèque Nationale, Paris. P: Giraudon.
Bottom: Shamash. Babylonian seal, ca. 2360–2180 B.C. Baghdad Museum. P: Hamlyn Picture Library.

97 *Top to bottom, left to right:*
Helios with quadriga. Mosaic, Greece. Rheinisches Landesmuseum, Bonn.
Trundholm sun chariot. Denmark, 14th c. B.C. National Museum, Copenhagen.
Vishnu and Lakshmi on the bird Garuda. India. Victoria and Albert Museum, London.
Surya. India. P: Dr. D.-I. Lauf.
Sun dance. Painting by Short-Bull, Chief of the Oglala, Dakota, and Sioux Indians, North America, ca. 1930. The American Museum of Natural History, New York.
Sun chariot. China. Publisher's Archives.
Horus in sun bark. Funeral papyrus, Egypt. Palais de la Découverte, Paris.
Stonehenge. England. P: Georg Gerster.

98 *Top left:* Quetzalcoatl. Toltec pillar, Tula, Mexico. P: Vautier-Decool.
Bottom left: The moon. Aztec culture, Mexico. National Museum of Anthropology, Mexico. P: Vautier-Decool.
Top right: Bull figure. Clay, Late Minoic III, Crete. Palace of Phaistos. Publisher's Archives.
Middle right: Orion and the Pleiades. Bark painting by mini-mini people of Groote Eylandt, Australia. National Gallery of South Australia, Adelaide. P: Charles P. Mountford.
Bottom right: Selene and Endymion. Painting, Casa dell' Ara Pompeii. P: Leonard von Matt.

99 *Top left:* Heng O. Bronze mirror, T'ang dyn., China, ca. A.D. 618–907. Victoria and Albert Museum, London.
Top middle: Moon creature. Ceremonial ax, gold, Quimbaya culture, South America. British Museum, London.
Top right: Moon goddess. Persia. Publisher's Archives.
Middle left: Creation of the

Milky Way. Painting by Tintoretto (1518–1594). National Gallery, London.
Middle right: The signs of the zodiac. India. British Museum, London. P: Hamlyn.
Bottom right: Chandra. Water color, Calcutta, India, ca. 1885. Victoria and Albert Museum, London.
Bottom middle: Goddess of the moon, Ceramic statuette, Juaxtecan, Mexico, 1300–1600. Museo de Antropologia de la Universidad Veracruzana, Jaopa, Veracruz.
Bottom right: Selene. Greece. British Museum, London. P: Michael Holford Library.

100 Nut. Wooden sarcophagus, Thebes, Egypt, 2nd c. British Museum, London.

101 *Top:* Marriage of heaven and earth. Cylinder seal, Sumer, early 3rd mill. B.C. Oriental Institute, Univ. of Chicago.
Middle: Geb and Nut. Egyptian papyrus. British Museum. P: Michael Holford Library.
Bottom left: Father Sky and Mother Earth. From the "Hail Chant," Navaho drawing, North America. Museum of Navaho and Ceremonial Art, Inc., Santa Fe. P: Hamlyn Picture Library.
Bottom right: Earth Goddess and god of heaven. From Slänge, Bohuslän, Denmark. National Museum, Copenhagen. P: P. V. Glob.

102 *Top to bottom, left to right:*
Yogi. Tibet. P: Dr. D.-I. Lauf.
Pueblo Indian crest. North America. P: Charles Miles.

103 *Top:* Rainbow. Detail of a miniature from the *Livre des Propriétés des Choses,* 13th c. Bibliothèque Nationale, Paris.
Julunggul. Bark painting by Dowdi of Millingimbi, Arnhemland, Australia. P: Kerry Dundas; Hamlyn Picture Library.
Bridge to Valhalla. Stone. Historical Museum, Stockholm. P: Claus Hansmann.
Iris. Vase painting, Greece. P: Michael Holford Library.
Jacob's Dream. Miniature from *The Bible of Charles V, King of France,* 1371. Publisher's Archives.
The arch of the sky. From *Codex Vindobonensis Mexicanus,* Mixtec culture, Mexico. Publisher's Archives.
Wuluwaid and Bunbulama. Bark painting from Yirrkalla, Australia. The State Library of South Australia, Adelaide. Collection of Charles P. Mountford.
Whirling rainbows. From the "Night Chant," Navaho drawing, North America. Museum of Navaho Ceremonial Art, Inc., Santa Fe.
Middle: God's pact with Noah. From "Wiener Genesis," *Codex Theologicus graecus 31.* National Library, Vienna.
Bottom: The arch of the sky. Chimu textile, Peru. Museum für Völkerkunde, München.

104 *Top:* God of thunder. Painting by Ogata Korin (1658–1716). National Museum, Kyoto. P: The Zauho Press.
Middle left: Thor. Bronze statuette, Iceland, ca. 1000. P: Werner Forman Archive.

Middle right: Indra's thunderbolt Vajra. Tibet. P: Dr. D.-I. Lauf.
Bottom: Xevioso. Bas-relief, Fon Palace of Glèle, Abomey, Dahomey. Musée de l'Homme, Paris. P: Giraudon.

105 *Left:* Thunderbird. Wooden carving, North America. British Museum, London.
Top: Schango. Wooden club, Yoruba tribe, Africa. Publisher's Archives.
Middle left: Adad. Relief, Assyrian. Louvre, Paris. P: Giraudon.
Middle: Lightning spirit. Bark painting, Australia. P: Axel Poignant.
Middle right: Teshub. Relief, Hittite, Sinjerli, Turkey. P: Mansell Collection.
Bottom: Zeus. Bronze figure, Dodona, Greece, ca. 470 B.C. Staatliche Museen, Berlin.

106 *Top:* Yamantaka and his shakti. Bronze figure, Tibet, 17th c. Collection Philip Goldman, London. P: Werner Forman Archive.
Middle: Asparas. Angkor Wat, Khmer art, Cambodia. P: Vautier-Decool.
Bottom: Shaman's charm. Tlingit, Alaska. Museum of the American Indian, Heye Foundation, New York.

107 *Top to bottom, left to right:*
Dance of the spirits. Bark painting, Mimi people, Arnhemland, Australia. State Library of South Australia, Adelaide.
Dakini. Tibet. P: Dr. D.-I. Lauf.
The six genii of Bet-Phasiel. Relief, Palmyra. Damascus Museum.
Wooden mask of Nomoi. Micronesia. Publisher's Archives.
Squatting figure. Bougainville, Solomon Islands. P: Axel Poignant.
Negakfok. Mask, Eskimo, Alaska. Museum of the American Indian, New York.
"Moai paepae" statue representing an *aku-aku.* Easter Island. Musée de l'Homme, Paris.
Yakshini. Pillar of the railings of a *stupa* from Mathura, India, 2nd c. P: Michael Holford Library.
Hermaphrodite figure. Dogon, Mali. P: Eliot Elisofon.
Two *rakshasas.* Bali. Bernisches Historisches Museum, Abteilung für Völkerkunde.
Asparas. Khmer art, Cambodia. Musée Guimet, Paris. P: Scala.
Caribou spirit. Modern lithograph, Eskimo. Publisher's Archives.

109 The myth of Yggdrasil. Norse. Drawing by Franz Coray.

110 *Top:* Two trees. Cup, Etruscan, 6th c. B.C. Louvre, Paris. P: Musées Nationaux.
Middle left: The original sin. From *Codex Vigilianus.* El Escorial, Madrid. P: Oronoz.
Middle: The tree of life. Detail of ceremonial cloth, Sumatra, Indonesia. Publisher's Archives.
Middle right: Tree of life. From *Commentarios al Apocalipsis del Beato de Liebana.* Gerona Cathedral, Spain. P: Oronoz.

Bottom: Tree of the universe. Relief, China, A.D. 168. Publisher's Archives.

111 *Left:* The tree of the soul. British Museum, London. P: Courtesy Thames & Hudson.
Top to bottom, left to right:
Shaman's descent to the underworld. Detail of shaman's costume, Siberian, late 19th c. American Museum of Natural History, New York.
The world center. Shaman's drum, Lapland. Danish National Museum, Copenhagen.
The sacred tree. Scythian scabbard (detail), from the Melgunov Treasure, Lower Dnieper, 6th c. B.C. Hermitage Museum, Leningrad.
The golden *menora.* Arch of Titus, Rome, after A.D. 81. Publisher's Archives.
The great goddess. Siberia, 5th c. B.C. Hermitage Museum, Leningrad. P: APN, Novosti.
The world tree. Ceremonial textile (detail), Soemba, Indonesia. Publisher's Archives.
Tree of life under winged disk of god Ashur. Assyrian. British Museum, London. P: Michael Holford Library.
Shaman's tent. Drawing, Tungus tribe, Manchuria. Publisher's Archives.
The tree of knowledge. Detail of cupboard, Norwegian popular art, 1715. Historisk Museum, Bergen.
Tree of life. Drawing, Siberian-Celtic, 19th c. Publisher's Archives.
Tree of life. Tomb of Sennufer, Thebes, Egypt. P: Hassia.
Winged mountain tree. Shadow theatre. Leather, Gunungan, Java. Publisher's Archives.

112 *Top:* The world navel. Africa. Collection Müller, Solothurn. P: Walter Dräyer.
Middle: The pyramids of Kings Cheops, Khepri, and Mycerinus. Egypt. P: Hirmer.
Bottom: Kukulkan pyramid. Mayan culture, Chichén Itzá, Mexico. P: A. G. Formenti.

113 *Left:* The polestar, axis of the world. Drawing, Chukchi, Siberia. Publisher's Archives.
Right: Minaret. Samarra, Iraq. P: Picturepoint.

114 *Top:* The building of the Tower of Babel. San Marco, Venice, A.D. 120–30. P: Scala.
Bottom: The demolition of the Tower of Babel. Engraving by Cornelius Anthonisz (Tennissen) (1499–1533). Publisher's Archives.

115 Tower of Babel. Painting by Peter Brueghel, the Elder (ca. 1530–1569). Kunsthistorisches Museum, Wien.

116 *Top:* Paradise. Tomb of Senedjem, Deir-el-Medinah, Egypt, 20th dyn. P: Hassia.
Middle: The four rivers of Paradise. Jacob of Kokinobaphos, ms. Gr. 22210. Bibliothèque Nationale, Paris.
Bottom: Adam and Eve chased from Paradise. From the *Bible of San Pedro de Roda.* Bibliothèque Nationale, Paris.

117 The paradise of Amida. Taima Mandara, Japan. Musée Guimet, Paris.

118 The seven floors of heaven. Indian miniature, 19th c. Bibliothèque Nationale, Paris.

119 The boat of Charon. Painting

by Jakob van Swanenburgh (1571–1636). P: Courtesy of Verlag F. Bruckmann, Munich.

BRINGERS OF MAGIC AND THE ARTS

120 *Top:* Symbolic serpent. Aztec culture, Mexico. British Museum, London.
Middle: Tomb of Chamoas (detail). Thebes, Egypt. P: Fpg.
Bottom: Maize gods. Mochican Indians, Peru, 1st c. B.C.-9th c. A.D. British Museum, London.

121 P: Rolf Theiler.

122 *Top left:* Sho-Kwannon. Buddhist, Japan. Museum of Dazaifu near Fukuoka, Kynshu. P: Vautier-Decool.
Top right: Nabu. Babylonian, 9th c. B.C. British Museum.
Middle: The nine Muses and Apollo. Painting by Baldassare Peruzzi (1481–1536), Siena. P: Scala.
Cakrasamvara. Painting on cloth, Tibet, 18th c. Collection Joseph Campbell, New York. P: Nikki Ekstrom.

123 *Top, left to right:*
Fudo Myo-o and his servants. Wooden sculpture, Nara, Japan, Epoch Kamakura. P: Vautier-Decool.
Maat. Egyptian, 19th dyn. Archaeological Museum, Florence. P: Alinari.
Athene. Temple of Ceres, Paestum. P: Leonard von Matt.
Monju Bosatsu. Gold on silk, Edo period, Japan, 18th c. Seattle Art Museum, Gift of Mr. Sheffield Phelps. P: Hamlyn Picture Library.
Left: Prajnaparamita, also goddess Tara. Sandstone, Prah Khan, Angkor, Cambodia, 12–13th c. Musée Guimet, Paris. P: Leonard von Matt.
Right: Dakini. Bronze sculpture, Tibet, 17th c. Philip Goldman Collection, London. P: Werner Forman Archive.

124 *Top:* Jaguar. Mochican culture, Peru, 1st c. Museum für Natur und Völkerkunde, Basel. P: Hans Hinz.
Prometheus. From ms. Holkham 324. Collection of the Earl of Leicester, Norfolk.

125 *Top to bottom, left to right:*
Hummingbird. From *Codex Magliobechiano,* Mexico. Biblioteca Nazionale Centrale, Florence.
Uraeus serpent. Tomb of Senourtem (detail), Deir el Medina, Egypt. P: Fpg.
Xiuhtecuhtli. Aztec culture, Mexico. P: Werner Forman Archive.
Agni. Wooden relief, India. Musée Guimet, Paris. P: Giraudon.
Huehueteotl. Pottery figure from Cerro de las Mesas, Veracruz. P: Vautier-Decool.
Pele. Wooden sculpture, Hawaii. Musée de l'Homme, Paris.
Xiutecuhtli. From *Codex Fejervary-Mayer,* Aztec culture, Mexico. City of Liverpool Museums.
Tinia. Bronze sculpture, Etruscan. Fitzwilliam Museum, Cambridge.

The myth of the Coyote. Sand painting, Navaho, North America. Museum of Navaho Ceremonial Art, Inc. Santa Fe, New Mexico.

126 *Top:* The legend of St. Eligius. Fresco, Jütland, Denmark, ca. 1300. National Museum, Copenhagen.
Bottom: The god Gu. Wrought iron sculpture, Yoruba, Africa. Musée de l'Homme, Paris.

127 *Top:* Ptah. Egypt. Louvre, Paris. P: Giraudon.
Hephaestus and the Cyclopes. Museo nuovo nel Palazzo dei Conservatori, Rome. P: Alinari-Giraudon.

128 *Top:* Healing the sick of the palsy. From Martin Luther Bible, Mark 2: 1–12. Private Collection.
Bottom left: Shadrafa, "the Healer." Bas-relief, Amrith, Phoenicia, 5th c. B.C. Louvre, Paris. P: Giraudon.
Bottom right: Aesculapius. Roman statue. P: Sonia Halliday.

129 *Left:* Gods of longevity, wealth, and happiness. China. Bibliothèque Nationale, Paris. P: Courtesy Thames & Hudson.
Top, left to right:
Jizo. Camphor wood, Japan, Fujiwara epoch. Museum Dazaifu, near Fukuoka, Island of Kyu-shu. P: Vautier-Decool.
Hera Eileithyia. Terracotta statuette, Paestum, Italy. Museum of Paestum. P: Leonard von Matt.
Yakushi Nyorai. Japan. P: Hamlyn Picture Library.
Middle: Tribal figure. Sculpture, Melanau tribe, Sarawak, Malaysia. British Museum.
Bottom left: Kachina bear. Painted cottonwood, Hopi Indian, North America. Museum für Völkerkunde, Berlin.
Bottom right: Thoeris. Karnak Temple, Egypt. 26th dyn. (663–525 B.C.). Cairo Museum. P: Marburg.

130 Hermes and the child Dionysus. Mixing bowl (detail), Vulci, Etruria, 5th c. B.C. Museo Etrusco Gregoriano, Vaticano. P: Hinz.

131 *Left:* Hermes. Greek statuette. Museum of Fine Arts, Boston; Pierce Fund.
Top left: Apollo, Jupiter, and Hermes. Silver mirror, Etruscan. Museo Archaeologico Nazionale, Florence. P: Leonard von Matt.
Top right: The Gallic Mercurius. Musée de St-Remi-de-Provence. P: Jean Roubier.
Bottom left: The infant Hermes. Black-figured jar, 6th c. B.C. Louvre Paris. P: Réunion des Musées Nationaux.
Hermes, Orpheus, and Eurydice. Bas-relief, Greek, 5th c. B.C. P: Mansell Collection.

132 Shaman dancing with spirits. Turkey, 16th c. Topkapi Museum, Istanbul. P: Courtesy Thames and Hudson.

133 *Top to bottom, left to right:*
Shaman. Siberia. Staatliches Museum für Völkerkunde, Munich.
Shaman with magic drum. Siberia. Publisher's Archives.
The dancer. Järrestad par.

Skåne, Sweden, early 1st mill. B.C. Lunds Universitets.

Exorcist. China, 3rd c. Musée Cornuschi, Paris. P: Giraudon.

Two-headed sorcerer. Funerary pottery, Han dyn. China. Musée Cornuschi, Paris. P: Giraudon.

Shaman beating a drum. Walrus tusk with black paint, Koryak statuette, eastern Siberia. Ethnographical Museum of the Peoples of the U.S.S.R., Leningrad. P: Novosti.

Shaman costume. Tungus, Lake Baykal, Siberia. National Museum, Copenhagen.

Shaman dancing with drum. Engraving by Nicholas Witsen. Publisher's Archives.

Shaman. Tungus tribe, Siberia. Publisher's Archives.

Shaman with drum. Finno-Ugric, Lapland. P: W. Stalder.

Shaman. Tsimshian statue, British Columbia, Canada. Musée de l'Homme, Paris.

Shaman in trance. Lapland. P: Radio Times Hulton Picture Library.

Hunting sorcerer. Lake Onega, U.S.S.R. Publisher's Archives.

Sorcerer. Paleolithic, Grottes des Trois Frères, France. P: Courtesy Trianon Press.

134 *Left:* Cave at Endor. Etching by Salvator Rosa. P: Radio Times Hulton Picture Library.
Right: Witch preparing a philter. Painting from the Flemish School, mid. 15th c. Museum der bildenden Künste, Leipzig. P: Gerhard Reinhold.

135 *Top to bottom, left to right:*
Witches' coven. P: John Moss, Colorific Photo Library Ltd.
Lilithu. Terracotta relief, Sumer, ca. 2000 B.C. Collection Colonel Norman Colville. P: Giraudon.
Hecate. Museo Capitolino, Rome. P: Mansell Collection.
Pythia in Delphi. Black painted plate. Antikenabteilung Berlin. P: Claus Hansmann.
Ma Kuh. Painting by Hsiang Kun, Chinese. British Museum, London. P: Michael Holford Library.
Witch on broom. Pre-Columbian, Mexico. Publisher's Archives.
Witches on broomsticks. Leipzig, 1668. P: Radio Times Hulton Picture Library.
The devil and a witch. Woodcut, 1493. P: Mansell Collection.
Four sorcerers. Engraving by Albrecht Dürer (1471–1528). British Museum, London.
Witch getting ready for the Sabbath. Engraving 18th c. Bibliothèque Nationale, Paris.

136 *Top to bottom, left to right:*
Rabbit. Mayan culture, Guatemala, 3rd–5th c. Publisher's Archives.
Achilles and the centaur Chiron. Wall painting, Basilica of Herculaneum, ca. A.D. 75. P: Leonard von Matt.
Kitchen gods. China. British Museum, London.
Patron saint of all artisans and engineers. Woodcut icon,

China. P: Courtesy Thames and Hudson.
Knum. Egyptian papyrus, 18th dyn. P: Michael Holford Library.
Anubis. Egypt. P: Fpg., D. Edwards.
Minerva. Bronze sculpture, Etruscan, 6th c. B.C. British Museum, London.
Fu Hsi and Nu Kua. Stone rubbing, China. Publisher's Archives.

137 *Left:* Bacchus and Vesuv. Painting, Casa del Centenario. Museum, Naples. P: Leonard von Matt.
Top to bottom, left to right:
Orpheus. Roman mosaic, Solunto near Palermo. Museo Archeologico Nazionale, Palermo. P: Leonard von Matt.
Sarasvati. Ivory statuette, India. National Library, Vienna. P: Hamlyn Picture Library.
Narada. Archaeological Garden, Lahitpur, Nepal. P: Courtesy Verlag A. Bongers.
Mount Parnassus. Fresco by Raphael (1483–1520), Vatican. P: Scala.
Pegasus. Greek coin, 330 B.C. P: Leonard von Matt.
K'uei Hsing. Chinese. Private Collection.
Thoth. Egypt. P: Roger Wood.

138–139 Pan and Daphnis. Sculpture by Eliodoro. Museum Naples. P: Anderson.

139 *Top left:* Pan. Bronze statue, Etruscan, 4th c. B.C. British Museum, London. P: Michael Holford Library.
Top middle: Shepherd. From the gate of Prince Asitavad, Karatepe. Hittite, Turkey, 8th c. B.C. P: J. Powell.
Vishnu as Krishna. Carved wood panel from processional chariot. India, 17th c. Musée Guimet, Paris. P: Michael Holford Library.
Hermes Kriophoros. Greek, ca. 6th c. B.C. Br. Museum.
Jesus, the Good Shepherd. Louvre, Paris. P: Chuzeville.

140 Tlaloc. Fresco, Teotihuacan culture, Mexico, 1st–6th c. Institute Nacional de Antropologia e Historia, Mexico City. P: Hamlyn Picture Library.

141 *Top:* Hapi. Carving, Abu Simbel, Egypt, 19th dyn. P: Roger Wood Studio.
Middle left: Rain god. Navaho Indian, North America. Musée d'Ethnographie, Genève.
Middle: Rain ceremony. Rock painting, Southern Rhodesia. Frobenius Institute, Frankfurt.
Middle right: Carved Door. Dogon tribe, Mali. Musée de l'Homme, Paris.
Bottom: Four rain spirits. From the "Shooting Chant," Navaho sand painting, North America. Museum of Navaho Ceremonial Art, Santa Fe, New Mexico.

142 *Top to bottom, left to right:*
Yum Caax. Mayan culture, Mexico. British Museum.
Quetzalcoatl. Mayan culture, Mexico. P: Giraudon; Hamlyn Picture Library.
Centeotl. Aztec culture, Mexico, 11th-13th c. Instituto Nacional de Antropologia e Historia, Mexico. P: Giraudon.
Xilonen. Aztec culture, Mex-

ico. P: Hamlyn Picture Library; Henri Stierlin.
King Shulumeli. Bas-relief, Hittite. Museum of Archaeology, Ankara. P: Hirmer.
Four deities. Hatra, Iraq. Publisher's Archives.
Giant corn plant. Sand painting, Navaho Indian, North America. Museum of Navaho Ceremonial Art, Santa Fe, New Mexico.
The "White Lady." Fresco, Ananrhet, Tassili. P: Mission Henry Lhote.
Goddess of the poppies. Terracotta statue, Gazi near Heraklion, Crete. 1400–1200 B.C. P: Leonard von Matt.

143 *Top to bottom, left to right:*
Liber Pater with Libera. Roman sculpture from Djemila, Algeria, 2nd or 3rd c. Loyola University of Chicago, Jesuit Community. P: R. Schoder.
Persephone and Pluto. Relief. P: Scala.
The growth of maize. From *Codex Fejervary-Mayer.* Mexico. Merseyside County Museums, Liverpool.
Ceres and the secret of agriculture. Skyphos of Hieron, Greece. P: Mansell Collection.
Dionysus. Red-figured cup by Exekias, Greece, mid. 6th c. B.C. P: Hamlyn Picture Library; Deutsche Phototek, Dresden.

144 *Top:* Artemis. Gold pectoral ornament, Karneiros, Rhodes, Greece, 7th c. B.C. British Museum, London.
Middle: Hunting scene. Rock painting, Séfar, Sahara. P: Maximilian Bruggmann.
Bottom: Nujalik. Eskimo drawing. Publisher's Archives.

145 *Top:* Camaxtli. By Fray Diego Duran. Mexico. Biblioteca Nacional, Madrid.
Middle: Orion hunting with Artemis and Apollo. Drawing, School of Fontainebleau. Musée des Beaux-Arts, Rennes.
Bottom: Wili-Wilia. Aboriginal bark painting, Arnhemland, Australia. State Library of South Australia, Adelaide. P: Charles Mountford.
Right: Onouris. Egypt, ca. 700 B.C. British Museum.

146 Taringa-Nui. Polynesia. British Museum, London.
Middle: Behanzin. Wooden statue, Dahomey. Musée de l'Homme, Paris.
Bottom: Fish with a woman's head. Soapstone carving, Eskimo, Cape Dorset. Gimpel Collection. Scott Polar Research Institute, Cambridge.

147 *Top left:* Dignuk. Bark painting, Arnhemland, Australia. State Library of South Australia, Adelaide.
Top middle: Olokun. Bronze statuette, Benin, Africa, 16th c. Rijksmuseum voor Volkenkunde, Leiden. P: Hamlyn Picture Library.
Mermaid. Wall painting, Vigersted Church, Sealand, Denmark, ca. 1450. National Museum, Copenhagen.
Middle: Poseidon. Silver stater (coin), Poseidonia, Paestum, 540 B.C. P: L. von Matt.
Fish goddess. Near East, 18th or 17th c. B.C. British Museum, London.

148 Maui destroyed by Hina. Carved door (detail), Maori, Polynesian. Wanganui Museum New Zealand. P: Axel Poignant.

149 Maui. Panel from Maori meeting house, Polynesia. Museum für Völkerkunde, Hamburg. P: Hamlyn Picture Library.

ANIMALS, MONSTERS, AND MYTHIC BEASTS

150 *Top:* Kujaku Myôô riding on peacock. Ink and colors on silk, Ninnaji Temple, Kyoto, Japan, 11th or 12th c. P: Courtesy Editions Skira.
Bottom: Seated rabbit. Jade, Aztec culture, Mexico. Dumbarton Oaks, Harvard University, Washington.

151 Herakles and Cerberus. Greek vase. Louvre, Paris. P: Hamlyn Group Library.

152 *Top to bottom, left to right:*
Centaur couple. Woodcut, England, 1520. Publisher's Archives.
Soul-bird. Relief from the Tomb of Amen-em-inet, Memphis, Egypt. Egyptian Museum, Munich.
Indian centaurs. Relief from Mathura, ca. 2nd c. Museum Lucknow, India.
Many-bodied lion. Mosaic, Otranto, Italy, 12th c. Publisher's Archives.
Griffin. Madonna della Luce, Perugia, Italy. Publisher's Archives.
Mythical bird Simurg. Gouache on paper, Kangra School, Persia, 18th c. P: Ajit Mookerjee, Courtesy Thames and Hudson.
Dragon. China. National Palace Museum, Taipei.
Bellerophon and Pegasus. Sculpture by Bertoldo (ca. 1420–1491). Kunsthistorisches Museum, Wien.
Melusine. Woodcut, Russia, 18th c. Publisher's Archives.

153 *Top to bottom, left to right:*
Basilisk. Woodcut, Nuremberg, Germany, 1510. Publisher's Archives.
Phoenix. Woodcut, Germany. Publisher's Archives.
Horse-griffin. Woodcut, Italy, 17th c. Publisher's Archives.
The Lady and the Unicorn. French Tapestry, ca. 1480. Musée de Cluny, Paris. P: Réunion des Musées Nationaux.
Unicorn. Drawing, China. Publisher's Archives.
Wild man and unicorn. Playing card by the Master E.S. Publisher's Archives.
Winged sphinx. Archaeological Museum, Ankara, Turkey. P: Rolf Ammon.
Unicorns. Drawing, watercolor and ink on paper, Eastern Pennsylvania, North America, ca. 1795–1830. The Henry Francis du Pont Winterthur Museum.

154 *Top:* Cernunnos. Celtic, caldron from Gundestrup, West Himmerland, Denmark. National Museum, Copenhagen. P: Werner Forman Archive.
Middle left: Athene. Capua, Italy, ca. 460 B.C. Antikenmuseum, Staatliche Museen Preussischer Kulturbesitz, Berlin. P: Jutta Tletz-Glagow.

Middle right: Pachacamac. Fragment of textile, Inca culture, Peru. British Museum.
Bottom: Lady of the beasts. Bronze vessel. Greek or pre-Roman, 600 B.C. Historical Museum, Bern.

155 *Left:* God creating fish and mermaids. Vault decoration, Gjerrild Church, Jutland, ca. 1500. Danish National Museum, Copenhagen.
Right: Adam naming the animals. Aberdeen University Library.

156 *Top:* Atum. Bas-relief on stone stele, Karnak, Egypt, ca. 1400 B.C. P: Werner Forman Archive.
Middle left: Shu and Tefnut. Egypt. P: Mansell Collection.
Middle right: Nut. Tomb of Sethi I (detail), Valley of the Kings, Egypt. P: Hassia.
Osiris. Tomb of Horemheb (detail), Valley of the Kings, Egypt. P: Hassia.
Isis and Nephthys. Any Papyrus, Egypt, ca. 1300 B.C. British Museum, London.
Set. Detail of throne of Sesostris I, limestone, Egypt, 12th dyn. Cairo Museum. P: Hirmer.

157 *Top to bottom, left to right:*
Scarab god. Tomb of Nefertari (detail), Valley of the Queens, Luxor, Egypt. P: A. Martin, Courtesy Editions Arthaud.
Ptah. Cairo Museum.
Sekmet with sun disk. Granite statue, Egypt, ca. 1400 B.C. Staatliche Museen, Berlin. P: Marburg.
Bastet. Limestone, Egypt, 13th–10th c. B.C. Fitzwilliam Museum, Cambridge.
Crocodile, emblem of Sebek. Magical papyrus, Egypt. British Museum, London.
Thoth. Relief, temple of King Sethos I. Abidos, Egypt, 19th dyn. P.J. Mazenod.
Composite deity. Egypt, ca. 6th–4th c. Fitzwilliam Museum, Cambridge.
Horus. Egypt, 1587-1375 B.C. Louvre, Paris. P: Giraudon.
Knum. Egypt. British Museum, London. P: Michael Holford Library.
Anubis. Egypt, ca. 1000 B.C. Museum Hildesheim. P: Rolf Ammon.
Amon and Mut. Egypt, 19th dyn. Louvre, Paris. P: Giraudon.
Hathor. Palette from Gerze, Egypt, 4th mill. B.C. Publisher's Archives.

158 *Top:* Bull. Rock painting, Lascaux, France, Palaeolithic. P: Hans Hinz.
Bottom: Zeus in the shape of a bull. Red-figured krater, National Museum Tarquinia. P: Hirmer.

159 *Top:* Ox god. Rock carving, Scandinavia. Danish National Museum, Copenhagen. P: P.V. Glob.
Middle: Mithras. Fresco, Italy. P: Scala.
Bottom top: Horn-twisted bull. Kulli culture, India. Publisher's Archives.
Bottom: Bull game. Fresco, Palace in Knossos, Crete, 1700–1400 B.C. Museum Iraklion, Crete. P: Leonard von Matt.

160 *Top to bottom, left to right:*
Epona. State Museum, Lux-embourg. Publisher's Archives.
Sleipnir. Stone carving of Tjangvida in Alskogs, Gotland, Sweden, ca. 700. P: Claus Hansmann.
The archangel Gabriel. Palech painting, Russia, ca. 1700. P: Claus Hansmann.
Muhammad. Persian miniature, A.D. 1502. Seattle Art Museum; Eugene Fuller Memorial Collection.
Helios with quadriga. Metope from Athene Temple, Ilion, Greece. Staatliche Museen, Berlin. P: Rolf Ammon.
Neptune. Painting by Niccolò dell'Abate, ca. 1512–1571. Galleria Estense, Modena. P: Scala.
Elijah rising to heaven. Folklore painting, Sweden. Nordiska Museum, Stockholm.
Horus. Bas-relief, Egypt, 5th–6th c. Louvre, Paris. P: Réunion des Musées Nationaux.
Kalki. From the *Mahabharata*, Indian manuscript. Bayerische Staatsbibliothek, Munich.
Buddha riding on Kanthaka. Bronze statuette, Burma. Publisher's Archives.
Vishnu. Polished sandstone, Khmer culture, Cambodia, 10th c. Musée Guimet, Paris. P: Leonard von Matt.

161 *Top left:* Bato Kwannon. Color and ink on silk, Heian period, Japan. Museum of Fine Arts, Boston; Fenollosa-Weld Collection.
Top right: Winged horses. From *Apocalisse*, Franco Maria Ricci, Editore, Parma, 1969.
Middle: Than-ka. Tibet, beginning 19th c. P: Claus Hansmann.
Bottom left: Winged horses, Etruscan, Tarquinia, 3rd c. B.C. P: Mansell Collection.
Bottom right: The horse Bayard and the four sons of Duke Aymon. From "L'épisode ardennais de Renaud de Montauban," French Chanson de Geste, 12th c. Bibliothèque Nationale, Paris.

162 *Top:* Thunderbird and killer whale. Painting on wood, Nootka Indian, North America, ca. 1850. The American Museum of Natural History, New York.
Middle: Sign of the zodiac. Japan. P: Michael Dixon.
Bottom: Sky map. Publisher's Archives.

163 *Top to bottom, left to right:*
The circumpolar stars. Ceiling, Tomb of Sethos I (detail). Valley of the Kings, Thebes, Egypt. P: Hassia.
Year tree with the twelve animals of the zodiac. Teak and porcelain, China. Museum für Völkerkunde, Wien. P: Fritz Mandl.
Signs of the zodiac. Japan. P: Michael Dixon.
The eagle drawing life from the serpent. *Codex Vaticanus*, Aztec culture, Mexico. British Museum, London. P: Hamlyn Picture Library.
Conjunction of Mars and Jupiter. From Albumasur's treatise, 13th c. Publisher's Archives.
Zodiac of Dandarah. Egypt. Louvre, Paris. P: Giraudon.

The Great Bear. Publisher's Archives.

164 Harpy. By Thomas Häfner, 1967.

165 *From top to bottom, left to right:*
Vampire devil. Textile, Peru. Museo Nacional de Antropologia y Arqueologia, Lima.
Man-headed monster. From Schedel's *World Chronicle* (1493).
Sea dragon. From *Monstrum in Oceano Germanica,* by Claus Magnus, 1573.
Monster from the *Ramayana* cycle. Wat Phra Keo Temple, Bangkok, Thailand, early 19th c. P: Claus Hansmann.
Demon. From *Le cabinet du Roi de France,* 1581. Bibliothèque Nationale, Paris.
Agrippine. From Schedel's *World Chronicle* (1493).
The Hai Riyo. Chi-on-in Monastery, Kyoto.
Sea monster. Wooden mask. Kwakiutl, British Columbia, Canada. Museum of the American Indian, New York. P: Hamlyn Picture Library.

166 Apis bull. Bronze sculpture, Egypt. Museum of Alexandria. P: Rolf Ammon.

167 Bull head. Rhyton, steatite, Kato Zakros, East Crete, 1450 B.C. Museum Iraklion, Crete. P: Leonard von Matt.

168–169 Animal sacrifice. Painted stone sarcophagus, Hagia Triada, Crete, ca. 1400 B.C. Museum Iraklion, Crete. P: Leonard von Matt.

170 *Top left:* God with boar on torso. Celtic, Euffignex, France. Musée d'Antiquités Nationales, St. Germain-en-Laye. P: Giraudon.
Top right: Artemis. Greek terracotta statuette. Smyrna. Louvre, Paris. P: Claus Hansmann.
Bottom: Durga. Stone sculpture, Bhaktapur, Nepal. P: Dr. D.-I. Lauf.

171 *From top to bottom:*
Odin. Sculpture by Thorvaldsen (ca. 1768–1844). NY Carlsberg Glyptotek, Copenhagen.
Head of Athene, and on the reverse, Athene's owl. Coin, Greece, 5th c. B.C. Bibliothèque Nationale, Paris. P: Giraudon.
Ishtar, Shamash, and Ea. Akkadian seal impression, 2360–2180 B.C. British Museum, London. P: Michael Holford Library.
Sow. Green glazed pottery, Egypt. British Museum, London. P: Michael Holford Library.

172 *Top:* Artio. Pre-Roman sculpture of Celtic bear goddess. P: Archives photographiques, Paris.
Bottom: Jaguar. Carved frieze, Teotihuacán, Tula, Mexico. P: Vautier-Decool.

173 *Top:* Cerberus. Watercolor illustration for *Dante's Inferno* by William Blake (1757–1827). The Tate Gallery, London.
Middle left: Feathered coyote. Shield, Aztec culture, Mexico. P: Hamlyn Picture Library.
Middle right: Bat god. Funeral urn, Zapotec culture, Mexico. Collection Kurt Stavenhagen, Mexico. P: Gisèle Freund.

Bottom left: Romulus and Remus. Musei Capitolini, Rome. P: Scala.
Bottom right: Bastet. Bronze sculpture, Egypt, 600 B.C. Cairo Museum. P: Hassia.

174 *Left:* The churning of the sea. Hindu miniature, 18th c. Musée Guimet, Paris.
Right top: Snake goddess. Palace in Juonos, Crete, 1700–1400 B.C. Museum Heraklion, Crete. P: Leonard von Matt.
Right bottom: Thor fishing the Midgard serpent. Bronze plaque, Viking, 8th c. Historiska Museum, Stockholm. P: Werner Forman Archive.

175 *Top to bottom, left to right:*
The *naga* Mucalinda. Khmer art, Cambodia. Musée Guimet, Paris. P: Scala.
The *uraeus* serpent. Tomb painting (detail), Egypt, 20th dyn. P: Hassia.
Head of Medusa. Sculpture by Gian Lorenzo Bernini (1598–1680). Palazzo dei Conservatori, Rome. P: Anderson.
The tree of life and death. Painting by Berthold Furtmeyer, ca. 1481. Bayerische Staatsbibliothek, Munich.
Goddess of the thirteen serpents. National Museum Mexico. P: Gisèle Freund.
Ezekiel. Engraving, 17th c. Publisher's Archives.
Spirit. Bronze head, Benin, West Africa. British Museum.

176 Cosmic lion. Miniature, 17th or 18th c. The Pierpont Morgan Library, New York.

177 The bird Garuda symbolizing the universe. India, 19th c. P: Nicolas Bouvier.

178 *Top:* Bee goddess. Gold plaque, Caninos, Rhodes. Museum of Fine Arts, Boston. P: Marija Gimbutas.
Bottom: Scarab. Tomb of Seti I (detail), Valley of the Kings, Egypt. Publisher's Archives.

179 Tortoise and snake. Rubbing from a relief, China. British Museum, London.

180 *Top:* Fantastic beings. Tapestry of the Book of Revelation (detail), Angers, France, 1377. P: Michael Holford Library.

180–181 Scene from the Apocalypse. From *Beato di Liebana,* published by Franco Maria Ricci.

181 *Top to bottom, left to right:*
Dragon. Tempera painting on *stupa*, Bäzäklik, Eastern Turkestan. Museum für indische Kunst, Berlin.
Ouroboros. Greek manuscript, Bibliothèque Nationale, Paris.
Seven-headed dragon. Akkadian seal impression (2360–2180 B.C). Iraq Museum. Directorate General of Antiquities, Baghdad. P: Hamlyn Picture Library.
Dragon. Tapestry, Sung dyn. Collection of the National Palace Museum, Taipei.
Dragon. Grey earthenware, China, Han dyn. Victoria and Albert Museum, London.
Dragon. Wall painting, tomb near P'yongyang (detail), Korea. Publisher's Archives.
The great king of all the dragons. Hand scroll (detail), China, 11th c. British Museum, London.

LOVERS AND BEARERS
OF DIVINE SEED

182 *Top:* Eros visiting a bride. Terracotta relief (fragment), Tarentum, Italy, 5th c. B.C. Ashmolean Museum, Oxford. *Bottom:* Fertility goddess. Tufa, Italic, 4th–3rd c. B.C. Museo Provinciale Campano, Capua. P: Scala.

183 The Triumph of Venus. Painting on plate, School of Verona, Italy, 15th c. Louvre, Paris. P: Réunion des Musées Nationaux.

184 *Top:* Venus of Lespugue. Ivory, France, Palaeolithic. Musée de l'Homme, Paris. *Bottom:* Venus of Haçilar. Turkey, 6th mill. B.C. Museum of Ankara. P: Boudot-Lamotte.

185 *Top row, left to right:* Venus of Brassempouy. France, Aurignacian. Musée de l'Homme, Paris. Venus of Menton. France, Aurignacian. Musée de St Germain-en-Laye. P: Jean Vertut. Idol. Marble, Naxos, Greece. Ashmolean Museum, Oxford. Venus of Willendorf. Krems, Austria, Palaeolithic. Naturhistorisches Museum, Wien. Venus of Laussel. France, Palaeolithic. Musée de l'Homme, Paris. *Bottom:* The sacred marriage. Çatal Hüyük, Anatolia, Neolithic. P: James Mellaert.

186 *Top:* The Birth of Venus. Painting by Sandro Botticelli (ca. 1444–1510). P: Scala. *Middle left:* The Venus of Milo. Hellenistic, 2nd or 1st c. B.C. Louvre, Paris. P: Réunion des Musées Nationaux. *Middle right:* Hephaestus. Greek, 400–350 B.C. British Museum, London. *Bottom, left to right:* Eros. Greece. P: Michael Holford Library. Venus and Priapus-Hermes. Pompeii, Italy, ca. 200 B.C. National Museum Naples. P: Leonard von Matt. The Birth of Cupid. School of Fontainebleau, ca. 1540–1560. Metropolitan Museum of Art, New York.

187 *Left:* Venus and Cupidon. Painting by Lucas Cranach (1472-1553). P: Scala. *Top to bottom, left to right:* Hermes. Earthen relief, Locri, Italy, 5th c. B.C. Museo Reggio Calabria. P: Leonard von Matt. Ares and Aphrodite. Painting, ca. A.D. 70. Museum Naples. P: Leonard von Matt. Neptune/Poseidon. Museo Laterano, Rome. P: Mansell Collection. Venus and Adonis. Painting by Titian (1477–1576). The National Gallery of Art, Washington. Venus and Anchises. Ceiling (detail) by Annibale Carracci (1560–1609). Palazzo Farnese, Rome. P: Scala. Aphrodite and Pan. National Archaeological Museum, Athens. P: TAP Service.

188 Apollo and Daphne. Ivory relief, 13th c. Museum of Ravenna. P: Mansell Collection.

189 *Top left:* Phaedra. Greek relief. British Museum, London. *Top middle:* Abduction of

Sita by Ravana. Gold and tempera, Jaipur, India, 19th c. A.D. Victoria and Albert Museum, London. *Top right:* King Mark and Tristram. Tile, Chertsey, England, 13th c. British Museum. *Bottom:* Tristram and Iseult. Cornwall, 6th c. Publisher's Archives.

190 *Top:* Eurydice. Stone relief. National Museum, Naples. P: Mansell Collection. *Bottom:* Orpheus. Marble sculpture, Byzantine, 4th c. Byzantine Museum, Athens. P: Claus Hansmann.

191 *Top:* Persephone and Hades. Interior of red-figured cup, Greece. British Museum. *Bottom:* Orpheus and Eurydice. Painting by Titian (1477–1576). Galleria dell' Accademia, Bergamo.

193 Daedalus and Pasiphae. Painting, Casa dei Vettii, Pompeii, A.D. 70–79. P: Leonard von Matt.

194 The dream of Queen Maya. Pillar medallion from the railing of the *stupa*, Bharhut, India, ca. 100 B.C. P: Courtesy Joseph Campbell.

195 The Annunciation. Painting by Rogier van der Weyden (1400–1464). Louvre, Paris. P: Réunion des Musées Nationaux.

196 Christ in the Virgin's Womb. Painted wood panel by Walchmayr, ca. 1400. Germany. Staatliche Gemäldegalerie, Berlin.

197 *Left:* Birth of Buddha. Indian Museum, Calcutta. P: Giraudon. *Right top:* Birth of Phanes. A.D. 117–138. Galleria Estense di Modena. *Right middle:* Birth of Krishna. India, 11th c. P: Scala. *Right bottom:* Birth of Mithras, Persia. Museum of Antiquities, University of Newcastle.

198 *Top left:* Birth of Dionysus. Bas-relief, Rome. Vatican Museum. P: Mansell Collection. *Top right:* Birth of Athene. Greece. British Museum, London. P: Sonia Halliday. *Left:* Birth of Adonis. Painted bowl, Urbino, Italy, 16th c. Victoria and Albert Museum. *Right:* Birth of the first human couple. From *Codex Vidobonensis Mexicanus 1*, Mixtec culture, Mexico. P: Courtesy Akademische Druck- und Verlagsanstalt, Graz.

199 *Top left:* Zervan giving birth to Ormazd and Ariman. Silver plaque, Luristan, Persia. Art Museum, Cincinnati. *Top middle:* Tara. India. British Museum, London. *Top right:* Birth of Tezcatlipoca. Stone relief, Aztec culture, Mexico. P: Vautier-Decool. *Bottom:* The tale of Romulus and Remus. Italy. Museo Pio Clementino, Vaticano. P: Scala.

200 *Top to bottom, left to right:* Fertility goddess. Seal impression, North Syria. British Museum, London. Qodshu. Canaanite fertility goddess, Egyptian sculpture, ca. 1300 B.C. British Museum.

Fertility goddess. Canaanite, 930–620 B.C. Phototèque Laffont. Fertility goddess. Syria, ca. 1000 B.C. P: Charles Lénars. Mother Goddess. Bengal, 2000–1000 B.C. Victoria and Albert Museum, London. Goddess of fertility, possibly Freyja. Late Bronze Age, Jutland, Denmark. National Museum, Copenhagen. P: Werner Forman Archive. Mother Goddess with child. Mycenae, 1400–1200 B.C. Louvre, Paris. P: Claus Hansmann. Fertility goddess. Clay, Thrace, Neolithic. Naturhistorisches Museum, Wien.

201 *Left:* Diana of Ephesus. Alabaster and bronze. Roman, 2nd c. National Museum, Naples. P: Anderson. *Top left:* Three Mother Goddesses. Bas-relief, Celtic. P: Larousse. Earth Mother. White jade carving, China. The American Museum of Natural History, New York. *Middle:* Fertility goddess. Silver caldron of Gundestrup, North Jutland, Denmark. National Museum, Copenhagen. *Middle right:* Asherah. Mycenae. Louvre, Paris. P: Giraudon. *Bottom left:* Goddess with twins. Syracuse, Sicily. 6th c. B.C. P: Leonard von Matt. *Bottom right:* Nimba. Mask of the Baga, Guinea. Staatliche Museen für Völkerkunde, Munich.

202 *Top:* Jupiter and Juno. Roman relief. National Museum, Palermo. P: Hirmer. *Middle row, left to right:* Pair of divinities. 18th c. B.C. Museum of Archaeology, Ankara. P: Hirmer. The Adi-Buddha with his *dakini*. Bronze sculpture. Tibet, 18th c. A.D. P: Eliot Elisofon. Wuluwai and Bunbulama. Aboriginal bark painting, Yirrkalla, Australia. State Library of South Australia. P: Charles P. Mountford. Mader-Atcha and Mader-Akka. Lapp drum design. P: W. Stalder. *Bottom:* Krishna and Radha. South India, ca. 18th c. P: Dr. D.-I. Lauf.

203 *Left:* Shiva. Gouache on paper, Basohli style, India, 17th c. P: Sven Gahlin; Courtesy Thames and Hudson. *Top:* The Flight to Egypt. Painting by Fra Angelico (1400–1455). Museo di San Marco, Florence. P: Scala. *Middle:* Osiris with Isis and Horus. Egypt, 22nd dyn. Louvre, Paris. P: Giraudon. *Bottom:* Amenhotep IV with his family. Egypt. Staatliche Museen, Berlin. P: Marburg.

204 *Top to bottom, left to right:* Amenophis II suckled by Hathor. Egypt. P: Roger Wood. Bes. Egypt. The University Museum, University of Pennsylvania, Philadelphia. Freyja. Wall painting, Germanic, 12th c. P: Toni Schneiders. Eros. Terracotta statuette, Myrina, Greece. P: Bruckmann; Courtesy Hamlyn Picture Library.

Ishtar. Phoenician. P: Hirmer. Aphrodite. Greece. Rhodos Museum. P: Hirmer. Xochipilli. Carving, Aztec culture, Tlalmanalco Mexico. P: Irmgard Groth Kimball; Courtesy Hamlyn Picture Library. Astarte. Bronze statuette, Phoenician, 1400–1200 B.C. Louvre, Paris. P: Réunion des Musées Nationaux. Tlazolteotl. Stele from the region of Tulantzingo. Mexico. Publisher's Archives.

205 *Top:* Kama. India. Victoria and Albert Museum, London. *Left:* Amor and Psyche. Roman statuette. Museo Capitolino, Rome. P: Mansell Collection. *Right:* Kama riding symbolic elephant. Trichinopoly painting, India. Victoria and Albert Museum, London.

206 Krishna and the *gopis*. Relief, Koubakonam, India. P: Hamlyn Picture Library.

207 *Top to bottom, left to right:* Radha and Krishna in the grove. Nurpur painting, India, 18th c. Victoria and Albert Museum, London. Krishna and the lotus flower. Miniature, Basohli, Jammu-Kashmir, ca. 1680. Victoria and Albert Museum, London. Krishna and Radha. School of Mewar, India. P: Michael Holford Library. The loves of Krishna. Gouache on paper, Rajasthan, India, 19th c. P: Sven Gahlin. Krishna dancing with the shepherdesses. Painted cotton, India. P: Marburg. Krishna bathing in the river with the *gopis*. Gouache on paper, Kangra, India, ca. 1820. P: Ajit Mookerjee. Krishna. Chola bronze, India, 16th c. Victoria and Albert Museum, London.

208 *Top to bottom, left to right:* Hera. Greek, 5th c. B.C. Museo di Spina, Ferrara. P: Hirmer. Danaë. Painting by Jan Gossaert (Mabuse) (ca. 1478–1533). Alte Pinakothek, Munich. P: Scala. Leda and the swan. Museo Archaeologico, Palazzo Ducale, Venice. P: Mansell Collection. Alcmene. Greek vase, 350–325 B.C. British Museum. P: Michael Holford Library. Mnemosyne and Calliope. Greek vase. National Museum, Syracuse. P: Hirmer. Demeter. Greek bas-relief, 5th c. B.C. National Museum, Athens. P: Hirmer. Hera. Marble statue, Greek, 4th c. Paestum Museum. P: Leonard von Matt.

209 *Left:* Zeus and Ganymede. Sculpture by Benvenuto Cellini (1500–1571). Galleria Nazionale del Bargello, Florence. P: Scala. *Top:* The rape of Europe. National Museum, Palermo. P: Scala. *Middle:* Io, Argos, and Mercury. Wall painting by Pinturicchio (ca. 1454–1513). Vatican Museum. P: Scala. *Bottom:* Hermes and a nymph. Marble relief, Prykaneionio, Thasos, Greece. Louvre, Paris. P: Hirmer.

210 Avalokitesvara. Tibet. P: Dr. D.-I. Lauf.

211 *Left:* Kuan-yin. Wood with polychrome, China, Sung dyn. Art Institute Chicago.
Right: Kwannon. Kochi (Shikoku), Japan, Kamakura period. P: Vautier-Decool.

212 *From top to bottom:*
Kundalini yoga (detail). Nepal, ca. 18th c. P: Dr. D.-I. Lauf.
The five "powerful enjoyments." Rajasthan, India, 19th c. Collection Ajit Mookerjee. P: Courtesy Thames and Hudson.
The erotic joys of heaven. Temple sculpture, India, 1000 A.D. P: Courtesy Thames and Hudson.
Yoga posture. Nepal, 18th c. Collection: Ajit Mookerjee. P: Courtesy Thames and Hudson.
Shri yantra. Nepal, ca. 1700. P: Courtesy Thames and Hudson.
The union of Buddha. Tibet. P: Dr. D.-I. Lauf.

213 Heroic delight in the heavens. Wood carving, South India, 18th c. Collection: Ajit Mookerjee. P: Courtesy Thames and Hudson.

COMBAT IN HEAVEN AND ON EARTH

214 *Top:* The Revelation. From *Luther Bible,* 1534. Publisher's Archives.
Bottom: War of the Titans. Amphora, Greek, 4th c. B.C. Louvre, Paris. P: Mansell Collection.

215 *The Last Judgment* (detail). Painting by Hieronymus Bosch (ca. 1450–1516). Akademie der bildenden Künste, Vienna. P: E. Mandl.

216 *Top:* King shooting monster. Achaemenian cylinder seal, Babylonian, 590–330 B.C. P: Werner Forman Archive.
Middle left: Monster on chain. Bronze mold. Viking. Statens Historiska Museum, Stockholm. P: Werner Forman Archive.
Middle right: Perseus cutting off the head of Medusa. Metope, Temple C, Selinus, Sicily. National Museum, Palermo. P: Scala.
Bottom: Durga killing the demon Mahisasura. Rock sculpture, India, 7th c. Mahabalipurum Temple, Madras, India. P: Werner Forman Archive.

217 *Top left:* God and female demon. Mesopotamia, 2nd mill. B.C. P: Goldner.
Top right: Vishnu as Narasimha. Wood relief, South India, 17th c. Musée Guimet, Paris.
Middle: Zeus fighting with beasts. Bronze plaque, Museum Iraklion, Crete. P: Leonard von Matt.
Bottom: Bellerophon and Pegasus. Terracotta relief, Aegina, Greece, 460–450 B.C. P: Leonard von Matt.

218 *Top to bottom, left to right:*
Herakles fighting with Acheloos. Greek. Museum of Tarquinia. P: Scala.
Herakles fighting with the lion of Nemea. Silver didrachmon, Heraclea, South Italy, 370–330 B.C. P: Leonard von Matt.
Herakles slaying Hydra. Fresco, catacomb Via Latina, Rome. P: André Held.
Herakles captures the hind. Attic black-figured jar, Vulci, Italy, ca. 540 B.C. British Museum, London.
Herakles and the horses of Diomedes. Etruscan bronze group, Palestrina. British Museum, London.
Herakles fighting the bull. Attic lekythos with white ground, Gela Museum, Sicily. P: Leonard von Matt.
Herakles and the Amazons. Attic black-figured jar (detail) Vulci, Italy, 510–500 B.C. British Museum, London.
Herakles strangling two snakes. Vettier House, Pompeii. P: Leonard von Matt.

219 *Left:* The hunting Herakles. Naples Museum. P: Leonard von Matt.
Top to bottom, left to right:
Herakles and the boar. Attic black-figured jar, Vulci, Italy, ca. 550 B.C. British Museum.
Herakles and the Stymphalian birds. Attic black-figured jar, Vulci, Italy, ca. 550 B.C. British Museum, London.
Herakles cleaning the stables of Augeas. Marble, Roman relief. Vatican Museum. P: Leonard von Matt.
Herakles and Geryon. Attic black-figured jar, ca. 540 B.C. British Museum, London.
Herakles with the Hesperides. Attic red-figured water jar, ca. 410 B.C. British Museum.
Herakles with Cerberus. Water pitcher, Cerveteri, created by Greek master in Etruria, 530–520 B.C. Villa Giulia, Rome. P: Leonard von Matt.
Herakles killing Nessos. Attic amphora, 7th c. B.C. National Museum, Athens. P: André Held.

221 Shen I, the cosmic archer. China. Publisher's Archives.

222–223 The Thorwald Cross. Carved stone slab, Viking, Isle of Man. P: Werner Forman Archive.

224 *Top:* Odin, Thor, and Freyr. Tapestry, Viking, Skogs Church, Hälsingland, Sweden, 12th c. Statens Historiska Museum, Stockholm. P: Werner Forman Archive.
Middle: Representation of Valhalla, and Viking ship. Carved stone slab, Viking, Gotland, Sweden. Statens Historiska Museum, Stockholm. P: Werner Forman Archive.
Valkyrie in battle. Sculpture by Stephan Sinding (1856–1922). P: Mansell Collection.

225 *Top left:* Odin. From the 1760 *Edda.* Det Kongelige Bibliotek, Copenhagen.
Top middle: Thor. Memorial stone (detail), Altuna, Sweden-Antikvarisk-Topografiska Arkivet, Stockholm. P: ATA.
Top right: Freyja. Wall painting, Dome of Schleswig. P: T. Schneiders, Bavaria Verlag.
Left: Procession. Carved stone slab, Gotland, Sweden, ca. 700. P: Claus Hansmann.
Middle: Loki. Carved stone slab, Uppsala, Sweden, ca. 700. P: Claus Hansmann.

The giant Ymir and the cow Audhumla. Painting by N.A. Abilgaard (1743–1809). National Museum of Art, Copenhagen.

226 *Top to bottom, left to right:*
Tiger god. Water color on paper, protective door-poster, Santal, West Bengal. Archer Collection, London. P: Claus Hansmann.
Lokapala guardian. Painted carved statue, China, 9th–10th c. Musée Guimet, Paris.
Door guardian. Color on paper, China, Shang dyn. British Museum, London.
Vajrapani. Guardian statue, Todaiji Temple, Nara, Japan. Publisher's Archives.
Chung K'uei. Stone rubbing, China. P: Claus Hansmann.

227 *Left:* Guardian giant. Wat Phra Keo, Cambodia. P: J.M. Scialom.
Top left: Bishamon-ten. Woodcut, Kongo-in Shrine, Mount Koya, China. P: Publisher's Archives.
Top middle: Divine guardians. Japan, 13th c. National Museum, Tokyo. P: Zauho Press.
Top right: Yü-lei. New Year's picture, woodcut, China, 19th–20th c. P: Claus Hansmann.
Bottom: Temple guardian. Java, 14th c. P: Vautier-Decool.

229 *Top left:* War of the Titans. Greek frieze, Great Altar of Zeus (detail). Pergamum Museum, Berlin. P: Bruckmann.
Top middle: Three-bodied monster. Akropolis Museum, Athens. P: Boudot-Lamotte.
Top right: Odysseus and Polyphemus. Painting by Pellegrino Tibaldi (1527–1596). Palazzo Poggi, Bologna. P: Villani.
Middle: Battle between gods and Giants. Roman bas-relief. Vatican Museums, Rome.
Bottom: Fall of the Giants. Painting by Giulio Romano (1499–1546). P: Radio Times Hulton Picture Library.

230 Thor's hammer. Silver with gold filigree, Erikstorp, Gotland, Sweden, 11th c. Historiska Museum, Stockholm. P: Claus Hansmann.

231 *The Wild Hunt.* Painting by P.N. Arbo. P: O. Vaering.

233 *Top:* Sigurd and Regin. Wood carving of church portal, Hyllestad, Setesdal, Norway. P: Werner Forman Archive.
Middle: Sigurd and Fafnir. Stone carving, Södermanland, Sweden. Antikvarisk-Topografiska Arkivet, Stockholm. P: ATA.
Bottom: Ogmios. Stone relief, Celtic. Archaeological Museum of Aix-en-Provence. P: Jean Roubier.

234 *Top:* Lakshmana's vengeance. Relief, Gupta style, India, 5th c. P: Boudot-Lamotte.
Scene from the *Ramayana.* Wat Phra Keo Temple, Bangkok, Thailand, 19th c. P: Claus Hansmann.

235 *Top left:* Ravana struggling with Hanuman. Indian bazaar painting, Kalighat, Calcutta, India, 1880. Archer Collection, London. P: Claus Hansmann.
Top right: The battle beneath the walls of Lanka. Scene from the *Ramayana.* Moghul school, New Dehli, India, ca. 1600. P: Bulloz.
Rama and Ravana. Painting on pergament, India, 18th c. Collection Lobue-Authier, Geneva. P: Nicolas Bouvier.

236 *Top:* Angels from the Last Judgment. Fresco by Pietro Cavallini, late 13th c. Sta. Caecilia in Trastevere, Rome. P: Alinari.
Bottom: Pazuzu. Bronze sculpture, Mesopotamia, 9th–7th c. B.C. Louvre, Paris. P: Lauros-Giraudon.

236–237 The temptation of St. Anthony. Painting by B. Parentino (1434–1531). Galleria Doria Pamphili, Rome. P: Anderson.

237 *Top right:* Durga. Charuba painting, India, 18th c. Victoria and Albert Museum.
Bottom left: The king of the demons. Islamic miniature, 14th c. Bibliothèque Nationale, Paris. P: Giraudon.
Bottom middle: Mahishasoura-mardini. Andhra, India, 9th c. P: Boudot-Lamotte.
Bottom right: Lucifer. From a French treatise on Antichrist, Judgment, Heaven, and Hell, 15th c. Bodleian Library, Oxford.

238 Mars. Marble statue, Roman, A.D. 81–96. Capitole Museum, Rome. P: Leonard von Matt.

239 *Left:* Athene. Greek statue, Aphaia Temple, Aegina. P: Leonard von Matt.
Top: Genius of war. Buddhist fresco. South China, Ming period. Musée Guimet, Paris. P: Giraudon.
Middle: Baal. Stele from Ras Shamra, Phoenician, 14th c. B.C. Louvre. P: Giraudon.
Bottom row, left to right:
Karttikeya. Matoura, India, 1st, c. P: Boudot-Lamotte.
Mont-Ra. Egypt. P: Mansell Collection.
War god. Three-dimensional wooden sculpture. Polynesia. British Museum, London.
Horned god. Stone relief. Celtic. Publisher's Archives.

240 *Top:* Paris with Hera, Athene, and Aphrodite. Painted panel (detail), Florence, Italy, 15th c. The Metropolitan Museum of Art, New York; The Collection of Giovanni P. Morosini, presented by his daughter Giulia, 1932.
Bottom: Hephaestus presenting the armor he made for Achilles. Painted bowl, Greece, ca. 450 B.C. King's Museum, Berlin. P: Mansell Collection.

241 *Top to bottom, left to right:*
Priam and Helen. Painted bowl, Tarquinia, Italy. P: Mansell Collection.
Apollo. Greek sculpture, ca. 540–545 B.C. National Museum, Athens. P: Scala.
Mars Borghese. Roman sculpture. Louvre, Paris. P: Giraudon.
Aphrodite of Knidos. Marble statue, Roman copy of a Greek work, ca. 350 B.C. Vatican Museums, Rome.
Achilles and Hector. Red-figured Attic vase, ca. 490 B.C. British Museum. P: Mansell Collection.
The sack of Troy. Chalcidian vase (detail), ca. 540–530 B.C. P: Mansell Collection.

Achilles binding the wounds of Patroclus. Attic red-figured vase, ca. 450 B.C. P: Mansell Collection.
Minerva. Stone relief. Acrople Museum, Athens. P: Mansell Collection.
Juno. Stone relief. National Museum, Palermo. P: Mansell Collection.
Poseidon. Greek amphora. P: Giraudon.

242 The third avatar of Vishnu. Miniature, India. P: Dr. D.-I. Lauf.

243 The first avatar of Vishnu. Miniature, India. P: Dr. D.-I. Lauf.

DISTANT QUESTS AND MORTAL TESTS

244 *Top:* Herakles carrying the two thieves. Metope from Heraion, near Paestum, end of 6th c. P: Leonard von Matt.
Bottom: Parsifal and Galahad. Miniature from French ms. ca. 1470. Bibliothèque Nationale, Paris.

245 Planisphaerium. By G. C. Eimmart. Publisher's Archives.

246 *Top left:* Christ. Gothic statue, Chartres Cathedral. P: Caisse Nationale des Monuments historiques.
Top right: Faustus. Title page of the *Tragical History of D. Faustus* by Christopher Marlowe, 1604. P: Mary Evans Picture Library.
Middle: St. Martin of Tours. Catalan painting. Museo Episcopal Vich, Barcelona.
Bottom: Mounted knight. Chess piece. National Museum of Antiquities of Scotland.

247 *Top to bottom, left to right:* The mountain of knowledge. Miniature, Florence, Italy, 15th c. Musée de Condé, Chantilly. P: Giraudon.
Viking ship resting on sea monster. From ms. Ashm. 154, 12th c. Bodleian Library, Oxford.
Charles Lindbergh. P: Swiss Museum of Transport and Communications.
Joan of Arc. P: Radio Times Hulton Picture Library.
Phoenix. From ms. Ashm. 1511. Bodleian Library, Oxford.
Drona. Scene from the *Mahabharata*. India. British Museum, London. P: Michael Holford Library.
Hermaphrodite figure. Miniature from a German ms. Nuremberg, ca. 1530. Berliner Kupferstichkabinett. P: Jörg P. Andres.
Zodiac man. From ms. Augsburg, "Der Teusche Kalender Meister Almansor spricht," ca. 1483. P: Hamlyn Picture Library.
Kachina doll. Hopi Indians, North America. P: Bührer.
Celestial dragon. Detail of mandarin robe, China, Ch'ing dyn. Publisher's Archives.
Voodoo ceremony. Haiti. P: Guido Mangold, Camera Press.

248 Scene from the voyage of the Argo. Engraved bronze container, Palestrina, 4th–3rd c. B.C. P: Leonard von Matt.

249 *Top to bottom, left to right:* Odysseus blinds the Cyclops Polyphemus. British Museum.
Scylla. Relief, Roman bronze cup, ca. 1st c.
Odysseus. Alabaster urn, Etruscan, Volterra, 2nd c. B.C. P: Leonard von Matt.
Odysseus and the Sirens. Attic red-figured jar, Vulci, Italy, ca. 480 B.C. British Museum. P: Mansell Collection.
Calypso. Terracotta statuette (detail), Tanagra. P: Giraudon.

250 *Top:* Lord of the beasts. Gundestrup Caldron (detail), Celtic. National Museum, Copenhagen.
Middle: Gilgamesh lifting lions. Circular plaque, Iran, 9th c. B.C. W. R. Nelson Gallery of Art, Kansas City.
Bottom: Bull-man fighting lions. Cylinder seal, Mesopotamia. P: Werner Forman Archive.

251 *Top left:* Hero with lion. From the palace of King Sargon II, Assyrian, 721–705 B.C.
Top right: Hero fighting bears. Bronze mold, Viking, Sweden. P: ATA.
Middle left: Hero between beasts. Talisman, Luristan. Teheran Museum. P: J. Powell.
Middle right: The hero's conquest of two human-headed bulls. Inlaid soundbox of harp (detail), Ur. Louvre, Paris. P: Réunion des Musées Nationaux.
Bottom: Hero fighting two griffons. Bronze sculpture, Luristan, 8–7th c. B.C. Deutsches Jagdmuseum, Munich.

253 King Arthur's Round Table. From a French ms. Bibliothèque Nationale, Paris.

254 *Top to bottom, left to right:* King Arthur proves his right to the throne. From a French ms., ca. 1290. Bibliothèque Nationale, Paris.
Two knights from King Arthur's Round Table (detail of page 253).
King Arthur. Stone head, unknown sculptor, 15th c. Germanisches National Museum, Nuremberg.
King Arthur with boatload of babies. British Museum.
Lancelot and Guinevere. The Pierpont Morgan Library, New York.
Guinevere and Lancelot. From a French ms., 14th c. Bibliothèque Nationale, Paris.

255 *Top row:* Knights of King Arthur's Round Table (details).
Middle left: Chalice made for the Duke of Berry. France. British Museum, London.
Middle right: Galahad fighting the Seven Deadly Sins. From a French ms. Bibliothèque Nationale, Paris.
The quest for the Grail. Victorian tapestry, woven by William Morris's factory, design by Edward Burne-Jones. Birmingham City Museum.

257 *Top left:* Hebe. Greek vase (detail). P: Giraudon.
Top right: Chalice for the water of eternal life and youth. Cult vessel, Tibet. P: Dr. D.-I. Lauf.
Middle: The fountain of youth. French tapestry after a

cartoon by Il Rosso (1495–1540). Kunsthistorisches Museum, Vienna.
Bottom: Bhima. Stele of red clay, Nepal, 18th c. P: Courtesy Verlag A. Bongers.

259 *From top to bottom:* Theseus slaying the Minotaur. Red-figured vase, Greece, 5th c. B.C. British Museum.
Theseus killing a centaur. Red-figured bowl, Greece, 5th c. B.C. Staatliche Glyptothek und Antikensammlung, Munich.
Theseus's adventures. Painting by Piero di Cosimo (1462–1521). Louvre, Paris. P: Giraudon.
Theseus abducting Antiope. Red-figured vase, Greece, ca. 5th c. B.C. British Museum.

260 *Left:* The search for a new world. Aztec culture, Mexico. Bibliothèque Nationale, Paris.
Right: The three wise men. Painting by Stefano di Giovanni Sassetta (ca. 1400–1450). The Metropolitan Museum of Art, New York.

261 *Top:* The Lord shows Moses the Promised Land. From a German Bible. Publisher's Archives.
Middle right: Isis. Green glazed porcelain statue, Egypt. British Museum, London. P: Michael Holford Library.
Bottom left: Episodes from a hero's life. Carved stone slab, Gotland, Sweden, ca. 700. Antikvarisk-Topografiska Arkivet, Stockholm.
Izanami and Izanagi. Japan. P: Larousse.

262 *Top:* Mask of Quetzalcoatl. Turquoise mosaic inlaid on wood, Mixtec culture, Mexico, ca. 1300–1450. British Museum, London.
Middle: Quetzalcoatl. From *Codex Borgia,* Aztec culture, Mexico. P: Courtesy Akademische Druck- und Verlagsanstalt, Graz.
Bottom: Quetzalcoatl. From *Codex Vaticanus,* Mexico. P: Hamlyn Picture Library.

263 *Left:* Kukulkan. Stone carving, Mayan culture, Chichén Itzá, Mexico, 3rd c. British Museum, London.
Top right: Warrior. Mayan culture, Mexico, 7th c. P: Gisèle Freund.
Middle: Pyramid of Xochicalco (detail of side wall). Aztec culture, Mexico. P: Hamlyn Picture Library.
Bottom, left to right: Quetzalcoatl, lord of death. Huastec culture, Mexico, ca. 1000. The Brooklyn Museum, New York; Henry L. Batterman and Frank Sherma Benson Funds.
Quetzalcoatl, lord of life. As above.
Quetzalcoatl, in the shape of Ehecatl. Rijksmuseum voor Volkenkunde, Leiden.
Quetzalcoatl. Toltec culture, Mexico. Musée de l'Homme, Paris.

264 *Top left:* St. Michael and the dragon. Stone relief, St. Nicholas's Church, Ipswich, England, ca. 1000. P: Courtauld Institute of Art.
Top right: The slaying of the dragon. From the *Apocalisse,* published by Franco Maria Ricci, 1969.

Middle: St. George and the dragon. Painting by Paolo Uccello (1397–1475). Musée Jacquemart-André, Paris.
St. George and the dragon. From a Persian manuscript, Mongol school, ca. 1295. The Pierpont Morgan Library, New York.

265 *Left:* St. George and the dragon. Limewood sculpture, Germany, ca. 1390. Bayerisches Nationalmuseum, Munich.
Top: Susano fighting the sea dragon. Japan. P: Aldus Books.
Middle: Cadmus fighting the dragon. Ancient Laconian cup. P: Giraudon.
Bottom: Scene from the *Shâhnâmeh.* Persian miniature, 1486. British Museum, London. P: Hamlyn Picture Library.

266 *Top to bottom, left to right:* Prince Siddhartha. Stone relief, India. Victoria and Albert Museum, London.
The fasting Buddha. Gandhara, India, ca. 2nd–3rd c. P: Scala.
Meditating Buddha. Ajanta, South India. P: Scala.
The Enlightenment of Gautama. Stone relief, India, 2nd c. P: Freer Gallery of Art, Washington.
Buddha. Bronze statue, Japan, Kamakura period. P: Vautier-Decool.

267 Avalokitesvara. China, 19th c. P: Courtesy Prof. Alex Wayman.

268 Rustam fighting the White Demon. From the *Book of the Kings* by Firdusi, Indo-Persian, ca. 1620. Bibliothèque Nationale, Paris.

269 Rustam's heroic deeds. From Bukhara ms., Persia, 17th c. Courtesy Sir Harold Bailey. P: Hamlyn Picture Library.

270–271 *Top:* The nine heroines. Miniature from "Le Chevalier errant," French ms., ca. 1394. Bibliothèque Nationale, Paris.
Bottom: The nine worthies of the world. From a French ms., 14th c. Bibliothèque Nationale, Paris.

DEATH AND REBIRTH

272 *Top left:* Phoenix. Flag (detail), Japan early 14th c. Publisher's Archives.
Top right: Quetzalcoatl. Aztec culture, Mexico, ca. 1000. The Brooklyn Museum, New York.
Bottom: Mummy. Peru. Musée de l'Homme, Paris.

273 *Top:* Quetzalcoatl. Aztec culture, Mexico, ca. 1000. The Brooklyn Museum, New York.
Bottom: Ship of the dead. Weaving, South Sumatra. Koninglijk Instituut van de Tropen, Amsterdam.

274 *Top:* Female figure. Relief on menhir, Saint-Sernin, Aveyron, France, late Neolithic. Publisher's Archives.
Middle left: Lucifer devouring Judas. From *Opere del poeta Danthe,* printed by Bernardino Stagnino, Venice, 1512. Publisher's Archives.
Middle right: Dharmaraya. Tibet. P: Dr. D.-I. Lauf.

275 *Top to bottom, left to right:*
Nergal. Terracotta relief, Kish, Mesopotamia, ca. 2100–1500 B.C. Ashmolean Museum, Oxford.
Yama. Tibet. Ashmolean Museum, Oxford.
Mictecacihuatl. Totonac culture, Mexico. National Museum, Mexico. P: Vautier-Decool.
Shokō-ō. Wooden statue, Kamakura epoque. Kamakura Museum. P: Vautier-Decool.
Mictlantecuhtli. Gold mask, Mixtec culture, Mexico, 8th–11th c. National Museum, Mexico. P: Vautier-Decool.
Yama, king of the seventh hell. Scroll painting, China. Horniman Museum, London. P: Michael Holford Library.
Coatlicue. Stone sculpture, Aztec culture, Mexico. National Museum of Anthropology, Mexico. P: Werner Forman Archives.

276 *Top:* The soul on its journey. Tombstone, Greek. National Archaeological Museum, Athens. P: TAP.
Middle: The navigation of Ra. Tomb of Horemheb. Valley of the Kings, Thebes, Egypt. P: Hassia.
Bottom: Persephone traveling to the underworld. Bas-relief. Greek. P: Leonard von Matt.

277 *Left:* The Buddha's descent from the heavens. Grey stone relief, Northwest India, 2nd–4th c. Victoria and Albert Museum, London. P: Boudot-Lamotte.
Top: The journey of the dead. Funerary stele (detail), Etruscan, Certosa near Bologna. P: Leonard von Matt.
Middle left: Soul ship. Rock engraving, New Guinea. Publisher's Archives.
Middle right: Center of the labyrinth. Rock engraving. Valcamonica, Italy, 3rd–2nd mill. B.C. P: E. Anati.
Bottom: The soul on the pathway to the land of the dead. Aboriginal drawing, Australia. P: Axel Poignant.

278 *Top:* Soul-bird. Coffin of Nebudjat (detail). Ptolemaic or Roman period, from Akhmin, after 200 B.C. P: Michael Holford Library.
Middle: Scene from the Trojan War. Vase painting, Greek. British Museum.
Bottom left: Dog with death symbols. Stone idol, Mayan culture, Mexico. Publisher's Archives.
Bottom right: Harpy. Relief from the so-called Harpy tomb, Greece, 6th c. B.C. British Museum, London.

279 *Top left:* Soul-birds. Wall painting, tomb of Iri-Nufer, Deir-el-Medineh, Egypt, 13th c. B.C. P: Hassia.
Top middle: Spirit. Dayak, Borneo. Publisher's Archives.
Top right: Messenger of death. Bronze plaque, Benin, Africa. P: Werner Forman Archive.
Middle left: The parting of Alcestis. Vase painting, Etruscan, 4th c. B.C. Publisher's Archives.
Middle right: Journey of the magistrate to the Beyond. Alabaster urn, Roman relief. Volterra Museum. P: Leonard von Matt.

Bottom left: Bull of Amenti. Egypt, 26th dyn. British Museum, London.
Bottom right: Persephone carrying a soul to the Beyond. Terracotta sculpture, Boetia, ca. 460 B.C. Staatliche Antikensammlung, Berlin. P: Claus Hansmann.

280 *Top:* The negative vortex. By Sandro Botticelli (1445–1510). Illustration for Dante's *Inferno.* Biblioteca Apostolica Vaticana, Rome.
Bottom: The land of the dead. From *Codex Borgia,* Aztec culture, Mexico. Museo Borgiano, Vaticano.

281 *Top left:* The deceased in the afterworld. Scene from the "Papyrus of Ani," Egypt. British Museum, London.
Top right: Anubis. Tomb of Khabekhnet (detail), Deir-el-Medineh, Egypt, 19th dyn. ca. 1250 B.C. P: Hassia.
Middle: The pilgrim's progress to the Celestial City. From an English ms., 19th c. P: Mansell Collection.
Bottom left: Dante at the gate of hell and foot of purgatory. Illustration for Dante's *Divine Comedy* (detail), 15th c. P: Mansell Collection.
Bottom right: Winged Charun. Wall painting (detail), Etruscan, tomb of Orkus, Tarquinia, 1st c. B.C.

282 The River Styx. Painting by Joachim Patinir (ca. 1485–1524). P: Hans Hinz.

283 The Greek underworld with Hades and Persephone. Vase painting, Greece. P: Mansell Collection.

284 *Left:* Hell. Detail from the *Garden of Earthly Delights,* triptych by Hieronymus Bosch (ca. 1450–1516). P: Mansell Collection.
Top: Hell. Miniature from *Les Très Riches Heures du Duc de Berry* (1340–1416). Musée Condé, Chantilly. P: Giraudon.
Middle left: Jigoku Soshi. Detail from hell scroll, Japan, early Kamakura period, ca. 1200. National Museum, Tokyo.
Middle right: The Last Judgment (detail). Painting by Stefan Lochner. Wallraff-Richartz-Museum, Cologne. P: Rheinisches Bildarchiv.
Bottom: The underworld. Mosaic vault (detail), Florence Baptistery, 13th c. P: Alinari.

285 Buddhist hell scene. Scroll painting, Japan. Horniman Museum, London. P: Michael Holford Library.

286 The herd of heaven. Scene from the "Papyrus of Ani," Egypt. British Museum, London. P: Michael Holford Library.

287 *Top left:* Christ glorified in the court of heaven. Painting (detail) by Fra Angelico (ca. 1400–1455). National Gallery, London.
Top middle: The Immortals at the court of Hsi Wang-Mu. Scroll painting, Chinese, 19th c. British Museum, London.
Top right: Quetzalcoatl. From *Codex Vindobonensis Mexicanus 1,* Mixtec culture, Mexico. P: Courtesy Akademische Druck- und Verlagsanstalt, Graz.

Middle: The eight Immortals. Colored woodcut, Taoist, Chinese. P: Claus Hansmann.
Bottom left: The three worlds. Siberia. Publisher's Archives.
Bottom right: Amitabha. Tibet. P: Dr.-I. Lauf.

288 *Top:* The house of death. By Jakob von Wyl, early 17th c. From *Der Luzerner Totentanz.* Publisher's Archives.
Left: The Flood. Black chalk drawing by Leonardo da Vinci (1452–1519). Windsor 12378. Reproduced by Gracious Permission of Queen Elizabeth II.
Middle: The price of life. Detail of anonymous drawing for *De arca Noe,* early 17th c. Bibliothèque de Genève. P: Nicolas Bouvier.
Bottom: Scene of the Apocalypse. Detail of the Apocalypse Tapestry by Nicolas Bataille, Angers, end 14th c. P: Publisher's Archives.

289 *The Triumph of Death.* Painting by Pieter Brueghel the Elder (ca. 1525–1569). Prado, Madrid. P: Mas.

290 *Middle:* The weighing of the souls (detail). Scene from the *Book of the Dead,* Egypt, ca. 1350 B.C. P: Mansell Collection.
Bottom: Angel blowing a trumpet. Painting by Luca Signorelli (1441–1523). Fresco (detail), Cathedral from Orvieto, Italy. P: Mansell Collection.

291 *Top: The Last Judgment.* Painting by Fra Angelico (1400–1455). Museo di San Marco, Florence. P: Scala.
Middle left: Michael weighing the souls. Mosaic (detail), dome of Torcello Cathedral, Italy, 12th c. P: Alinari.
Middle: Weighing of souls. Tympan of west door (detail). St. Lazare, Autun. P: Mansell Collection.
Middle right: Weighing of souls. From the Tibetan Book of the Dead (detail). P: Dr. D.-I. Lauf.
Bottom left: The souls of the dead crossing the bridge of judgment. Persian miniature. Bibliothèque Nationale, Paris.
Bottom right: Two judges of the Beyond. Painted wooden statues, Kamakura epoque, Japan, 13th c. Kyoto Museum. P: Vautier-Decool.

292 *Top:* Ascension. Golden jar, Nagyszentmiklos, Hungary. Kunsthistorisches Museum, Vienna.
Middle left: Elijah's ascension to heaven. Fresco (detail), St. Nicolas Orphanos, Salonika, Greece, 14th c. P: Hassia.
Middle right: Alexander's ascension. Woodcut, German, early 16th c. Publisher's Archives.
Bottom: Christ's resurrection. Victoria and Albert Museum, London. P: Aldus Books.

293 *Left:* The heavenly ladder. From ms. dated 1081. Princeton University Library; Robert Garret Collection of Medieval and Renaissance Manuscripts.
Top: A shaman's ascent to heaven. Altai, Siberia. Publisher's Archives.
Middle: The ladder of salvation. Mural painting (detail).

St. Peter and Paul, Rome. Publisher's Archives.
Bottom: The Hare. Painting by Joan Miró, 1927. The Salomon R. Guggenheim Museum, New York.

294 The resurrection. Panel by Elias Moschos, 1687. Byzantine Museum, Athens.

295 *Top to bottom, left to right:*
The 11th Lohan, Tsu-tschaba-na-ta-ka. The 2nd Lohan, A-dsi-ta. The 13th Lohan, Ba-ha-ka-la. The 7th Lohan, Ka-na-ka-ba-sa. All stone rubbings, China. P: Claus Hansmann.
Asclepius. Fresco (detail), late 3rd c. Musée National des Antiquités, Alger.
The resurrection of the Buddha. Color painting on silk, Japan, Heian period, ca. 1086. Kyoto Museum.
Bottom left: Christ raising Lazarus. Wooden relief, 4th c. Museo Civico, Brescia. P: Anderson.
Bottom right: Christ descending into hell. Wall painting (detail), Kariye Jami, Constantinople, ca. 1310. Dumbarton Oaks Center for Byzantine Studies, Washington.

296 *Left:* Orpheus and Eurydice. Fresco by Baldassare Peruzzi. Palazzo della Farnesina, Rome. P: Alinari.
Hermod. Scene from the *Edda,* dated 1760. Norse. National Library, Copenhagen.

297 *Left:* Osiris. Scene from the Book of the Dead, tomb of Ramses VI, Egypt. P: Hassia.
Top: Persephone returning from the underworld. Vase painting, Greece. The Metropolitan Museum of Art, New York; Fletscher Fund, 1928.
Middle: Herakles. Farnese School, Italy. National Museum, Naples. P: Scala.
Bottom: Christ's resurrection. Fresco by Piero della Francesca (ca. 1420–1492). Museo San Sepolcro, Borgo San Sepolcro, Italy. P: Scala.

298 Buddha's first speech in Benares. India. P: Dr. D.I. Lauf.

299 Buddha's ascension to Nirvana. Hanging scroll (detail), Japan. Museum für Ostasiatische Kunst, Cologne.

300 Falcon with sun disk. From the treasure of Tutankhamen, Egypt. Cairo Museaum. P: Hassia.

301 The wheel of life. Buddhist, Tibet. British Museum.

Index

318